S.A. Schoff

John Adams

BOSTON

PUBLISHED BY CHARLES C. LITTLE, & JAMES BROWN.

THE

WORKS

OF

JOHN ADAMS,

SECOND PRESIDENT OF THE UNITED STATES:

WITH

A LIFE OF THE AUTHOR,

NOTES AND ILLUSTRATIONS,

BY

HIS GRANDSON

CHARLES FRANCIS ADAMS.

VOL. II.

BOSTON:
CHARLES C. LITTLE AND JAMES BROWN.
1850.

PREFACE.

A Diary is the record in youth of a man's sentiments, in middle life, of his action, and of his recollections in age. To others, it can be interesting only if it have impressed upon it the stamp of strong individual character. But with this as a substratum, notices of striking scenes, of extraordinary events and noted contemporaries, may be superadded to form a memorial worth transmitting to posterity.

The fragments now published can scarcely be said to fill up this idea; yet, beginning as they do with the writer's entrance into responsible life, and extending through a large part of a great career, they may be considered as in a measure superseding the necessity of an elaborate biography. Perhaps the propriety of the insertion of so large a portion of the early entries may be questioned. The answer is, that they go far to effect the main object of showing character. The moral and meditative cast of the author's mind is thus laid open at an age when that of most men is yet slowly gaining maturity. The leading principle of his life may thus be easily traced by those fond of psychological investigations, from his first theological investigations, through his legal studies, and still more strikingly, his early practice, into the mental habits which formed the politician and the statesman. Incidental to this, and accessary to it, are the pictures of domestic life in New England during a period which has been somewhat overshadowed by the superior interest attaching to earlier and to later times. Puritan Massachusetts, whilst dropping much of her early religious bigotry, was yet nursing in the French wars the stern qualities that carried her successfully through the fiery trial of the Revolution. She contained one, whilst Virginia furnished the other, of the two germs of public sentiment which have since spread extensively over this continent, and which bid fair yet to develop themselves indefinitely. To these two types of mind all classes of American opinion may be ultimately reduced. The state of society through which the first of these was evolved, until from a religious it took a political direction, and the influences through which the change was shaped, gain much illustration from the following pages.

The broken and partial nature of this Diary is the circumstance most to be regretted about it. As the time advances towards the most interesting events in the Revolution, the record becomes less and less satisfactory. It is a great disadvantage attending even the most regularly kept of such works, that just in proportion to the engrossing interest of the action in which the writer finds himself engaged, is the physical inability to command the leisure necessary to describe it. Thus it happens in the present case, that the sketches sometimes stop just when the reader would have them begin, and at other times no notice whatever is taken of events which are the most prominent in the life of the writer. Yet, after making all suitable deductions from the value of these papers on this account, it is believed that much is left richly to reward perusal, particularly since some of the most marked instances of deficiency are compensated for by resorting to the reminiscences of a later period. The passages from an autobiography are not indeed entitled to claim quite so high ground on the score of authority in matters of fact as the contemporaneous record, but they merit attention as well on account of the superior animation of the style as of the circumstance that they do supply some of the details that are wanting in the other. Even on the score of accuracy, the papers of other persons treating of the same events, which have since found their way to the light, go a great way to establish the substantial truth of the narrative from memory. A good degree of credit may therefore be confidently assigned to it, even though we admit that it belongs to a different class of evidence. Whilst the editor has endeavored, so far as it may be done, to unite in the present volume, the substance of the Autobiography with the Diary, he has carefully tried to keep the two so distinct as to furnish to the critical reader every opportunity to distinguish the nature of the testimony. Twenty-five or thirty years can pass over the head of no man without affecting the exactness of his recollection of events. If we consider how small a share of the public documents now at the command of every one, was readily accessible, or was actually consulted in the year when the Autobiography was written, the wonder is rather at the tenacity than the failure of the writer's memory.

The editor has sought to avoid burdening the text with annotation. Yet so rapidly does time obliterate the traces of local names and history, and particularly after periods of civil convulsion, that occasional explanation seems required to smooth the way for the general reader. In performing this duty, it is always difficult to reach the golden mean, and particularly in American annals, where the extent to which an acquaintance with details can be presumed is so unsettled. Of late, the greatly increased attention paid to this subject tends to justify the inference that much may be taken for granted as now well understood. Yet the smallest examination of many of the popular works of the day will suffice to show that almost as much still remains to be elucidated. The omission to note the change wrought by the revolution in the classification of the social system has already done something to obscure the history of political opinion during the first stage of free government. Neither is the relative advance of the respective Colonies in the course of the struggle, or the nature of the difficulties peculiar to each, generally comprehended. To acquire right notions on these matters, it is necessary to ascend some distance for a starting point. Every thing that can illustrate the state of opinion, of manners, and of habits, prior to the year 1776, is of some value to the right conception of what has happened since. Guided by this idea, the editor has taken the liberty, either to supply such explanatory matter as he deemed likely to be of use to the curious, or, where he did not, to indicate as briefly as possible the sources in which fuller information may be readily obtained.

It is proper, in cases of publication like this, to define the extent to which it has been carried. The editor has suppressed or altered nothing in the Diary, which might be considered as bearing either against the author himself, or against any other person, for that reason alone. Wherever any omission has been made, it has been from other motives than those of fear or favor. The main purpose has been to present to the public a fair and unbiased picture of the mind and heart of an individual, so far as this may be supposed to command any interest. To do this, it is as necessary to retain the favorable or unfavorable opinions expressed of men, including himself, as those of things or of events. No true, honestly written Diary can be regarded as in itself a correct general history. It is good always as biography, often as furnishing materials for history, and that just in proportion as it appears on its face never to have been written or prepared for publication. But if this be true, it is obviously perverting its character to attempt to make patchwork of it, by selecting to be seen only such passages as show a single side. Rather than this, it were wise not to publish at all. The effect is to make an opinion for the reader instead of allowing him to form one for himself, to control rather than to develop his judgment. In the present instance at least, the fact may be relied on, that no experiment of the kind has been tried. The reader is more likely to feel disposed to find fault with being supplied beyond his wants than with having less than he might get.

This volume embraces all of the Diary written prior to February, 1778, the period of the writer's first departure for Europe;

but that portion of the Autobiography covering his Congressional life is barely commenced. It likewise includes all the notes taken of debates in the Continental Congress which the editor has been able to find. The meagre and unsatisfactory nature of these would forbid their publication, if it were not for the circumstance that they constitute almost the sole remaining memorial of the kind that has come down to us. Imperfect as they are, it is believed that they will serve to throw some light upon the civil history, or that portion which is least understood, of the great contest.

For the purpose of clearly distinguishing the passages of the Autobiography from the Diary, they are, in all cases, marked with brackets at each end of the extract; and, when so brief as to be placed among the foot notes under the text, they are indicated by an asterisk, instead of the small numerals prefixed to the editor's explanations.

CONTENTS OF VOLUME II.

DIARY:

WITH PASSAGES FROM AN

AUTOBIOGRAPHY.

DIARY.

THESE are loose fragments of journal in the hand-writing of JOHN ADAMS upon scraps of paper scarcely legible, from 18 November, 1755, to 20 November, 1761. They were effusions of mind, committed from time to time to paper, probably without the design of preserving them; self-examinations at once severe and stimulative; reflections upon others, sometimes, not less severe upon his friends; thoughts such as occur to all, some of which no other than an unsullied soul would commit to writing, mingled with conceptions at once comprehensive and profound.

J. Q. A.

1755. NOVEMBER 18. We had a very severe shock of an earthquake. It continued near four minutes. I then was at my father's in Braintree, and awoke out of my sleep in the midst of it. The house seemed to rock and reel and crack, as if it would fall in ruins about us. Chimneys were shattered by it within one mile of my father's house.[1] *

1 This is the first entry, and is printed because it seems to have originated the plan of a Diary. It refers to one of the most memorable events of the kind which ever took place. The destruction of the city of Lisbon occurred on the first day of this month. Although less severe in its effects on this side of the Atlantic, it is yet remembered as the worst ever known in English America. "It seems to have been greater in Massachusetts than any other colony. In Boston, many chimneys and walls of houses were much shattered, but no house thrown down." The government noticed it by appointing a day of fasting and prayer.

* [In the public exercises at Commencement I was somewhat remarked as a respondent, and Mr. Maccarty, of Worcester, who was empowered by the selectmen of that town to procure them a Latin master for the grammar school, engaged me to undertake it. About three weeks after Commencement in 1755, when I was not yet twenty years of age, a horse was sent me from Worcester, and a man to attend me. We made the journey, about sixty miles, in one day, and I entered on my office.

For three months I boarded with one Greene, at the expense of the town, and by the arrangement of the selectmen. Here I found Morgan's Moral Philosopher, which I was informed had circulated with some freedom in that town, and that the principles of Deism had made considerable progress among persons in that and other towns in the county.]

1756. January 16. Reading Hutcheson's Introduction to Moral Philosophy. Dined with Major Chandler.*

18. Sunday. Heard Mr. Maccarty.[1]

February 11. I am constantly forming, but never executing good resolutions. I take great pleasure in viewing and examining the magnificent prospects of Nature that lie before us in this town. If I cast my eyes one way, I am entertained with the savage, unsightly appearance of naked woods, and leafless forests. In another place a chain of broken and irregular mountains throws my mind into a pleasing kind of astonishment. But if I turn myself round, I perceive a wide, extensive tract before me made up of woods and meadows, wandering streams and barren plains, covered in various places by herds of grazing cattle and terminated by the distant view of the town.[2]

12. Thursday. Heard Mr. Welman preach the lecture, and drank tea with him at home; where he made this observation, namely, that "Dr. Mayhew was a smart man, but he embraced some doctrines not generally approved."[3]

13. Friday. Supped at Major Gardiner's, and engaged to keep school at Bristol, provided Worcester people at their ensuing March meeting should change this into a moving school,[4] not otherwise. Major Greene this evening fell into some conversation with me about the Divinity and satisfaction of Jesus Christ. All the argument he advanced was, "that a mere crea-

1 The Rev. Thaddeus Maccarty, pastor of the first parish of Worcester for thirty-seven years, and the person who engaged the writer to come to Worcester. In the Autobiography he is mentioned with respect and esteem. He had been driven from the town of Kingston a few years before this because he was suspected of liberality to Whitefield. *Coll. Mass. Hist. Society*, vol. xiii., p. 209.

2 Worcester at this time contained a population certainly not exceeding 1500.

3 Rev. Jonathan Mayhew, afterwards the well known pastor of the West Church in Boston. Religious opinions had been for a long time the principal subject of difference among the people of Worcester, as indeed they were everywhere in Massachusetts. A few years before this, Mr. Maccarty and Mr. Mayhew had been brought into direct competition as candidates for settlement in the parish, and the former carried the day with only two votes dissenting.

4 "The instructor of those days was migratory, revolving in his circuit round a centre not then fixed to a particular location." *Lincoln's Worcester*, 297.

* [The family of the Chandlers were well-bred and agreeable people, and I as often visited them as my school and my studies in the lawyer's office would admit, especially Colonel Gardner Chandler, with whom I was the most intimate.]

The Chandlers exercised great influence in the county of Worcester until they took the side of government in the revolution, and lost their position.

ture or finite being could not make satisfaction to infinite justice for any crimes," and that "these things are very mysterious." Thus mystery is made a convenient cover for absurdity.

15. Sunday. Staid at home reading the Independent Whig.[1] Very often shepherds that are hired to take care of their masters' sheep go about their own concerns and leave the flock to the care of their dog. So bishops, who are appointed to oversee the flock of Christ, take the fees themselves but leave the drudgery to their dogs, that is, curates and understrappers.

16. Monday. We have the most moderate winter that ever was known in this country. For a long time together we have had serene and temperate weather, and all the roads perfectly settled and smooth like summer.

The Church of Rome has made it an article of faith that no man can be saved out of their church, and all other religious sects approach to this dreadful opinion in proportion to their ignorance, and the influence of ignorant or wicked priests.

Still reading the Independent Whig.

Oh! that I could wear out of my mind every mean and base affectation; conquer my natural pride and self-conceit; expect no more deference from my fellows than I deserve; acquire that meekness and humility which are the sure mark and characters of a great and generous soul; subdue every unworthy passion, and treat all men as I wish to be treated by all. How happy should I then be in the favor and good will of all honest men and the sure prospect of a happy immortality!

18. Wednesday. Spent an hour in the beginning of the evening at Major Gardiner's, where it was thought that the design of Christianity was not to make men good riddle-solvers, or good mystery-mongers, but good men, good magistrates, and good subjects, good husbands and good wives, good parents and good children, good masters and good servants. The following questions may be answered some time or other, namely, — Where do we find a precept in the Gospel requiring Ecclesiastical Synods? Convocations? Councils? Decrees? Creeds? Confessions?

[1] By Thomas Gordon, the Translator of Tacitus and author of Cato's Letters. His works have passed into oblivion, but at this period they were much read on account of their free and independent spirit. The Tacitus and Cato's Letters are placed by the side of Sidney and Locke and Bacon, in a special bequest of Josiah Quincy, Jun., to his son in his last will. "*Memoir*," &c., p. 350.

Oaths? Subscriptions? and whole cart-loads of other trumpery that we find religion encumbered with in these days?

19. Thursday. No man is entirely free from weakness and imperfection in this life. Men of the most exalted genius and active minds are generally most perfect slaves to the love of fame. They sometimes descend to as mean tricks and artifices in pursuit of honor or reputation as the miser descends to in pursuit of gold. The greatest men have been the most envious, malicious, and revengeful. The miser toils by night and day, fasts and watches, till he emaciates his body to fatten his purse and increase his coffers. The ambitious man rolls and tumbles in his bed, a stranger to refreshing sleep and repose, through anxiety about a preferment he has in view. The philosopher sweats and labors at his book, and ruminates in his closet, till his bearded and grim countenance exhibits the effigies of pale want and care and death, in quest of hard words, solemn nonsense, and ridiculous grimace. The gay gentleman rambles over half the globe, buys one thing and steals another, murders one man and disables another, and gets his own limbs and head broke for a few transitory flashes of happiness. Is this perfection, or downright madness and distraction?

20. Friday. Symptoms of snow. Writing Tillotson.[1]

21. Saturday. Snow about ankle deep. I find, by repeated experiment and observation in my school, that human nature is more easily wrought upon and governed by promises, and encouragement, and praise, than by punishment, and threatening, and blame. But we must be cautious and sparing of our praise, lest it become too familiar and cheap, and so, contemptible; corporal as well as disgraceful punishments depress the spirits, but commendation enlivens and stimulates them to a noble ardor and emulation.

22. Sunday. Suppose a nation in some distant region should take the Bible for their only law-book, and every member should regulate his conduct by the precepts there exhibited! Every member would be obliged, in conscience, to temperance and frugality and industry; to justice and kindness and charity

[1] This means that the writer, who was at this time inclining to the ministry, was engaged in copying large extracts from the works of Tillotson. A volume still remains, written in a very minute hand, and filled with passages from the works of various authors.

towards his fellow men; and to piety, love, and reverence, towards Almighty God. In this commonwealth, no man would impair his health by gluttony, drunkenness, or lust; no man would sacrifice his most precious time to cards or any other trifling and mean amusement; no man would steal, or lie, or in any way defraud his neighbor, but would live in peace and good will with all men; no man would blaspheme his Maker or profane his worship; but a rational and manly, a sincere and unaffected piety and devotion would reign in all hearts. What a Utopia; what a Paradise would this region be! Heard Thayer all day. He preached well. Spent the evening at Colonel Chandler's, with Putnam, Gardiner, Thayer, the Doctor[1] and his lady, in conversation upon the present situation of public affairs, with a few observations concerning heroes and great commanders,— Alexander, Charles XII., Cromwell.

24. Tuesday. We are told that Demosthenes transcribed the history of Thucydides eight times, in order to imbibe and familiarize himself with the elegance and strength of his style. Will it not be worth while for a candidate for the ministry to transcribe Dr. Tillotson's works?

27. Friday. All day in high health and spirits. Writing Tillotson. That comet which appeared in 1682 is expected again this year; and we have intelligence that it has been seen about ten days since, near midnight, in the east. I find myself very much inclined to an unreasonable absence of mind, and to a morose and unsociable disposition; let it therefore be my constant endeavor to reform these great faults.

28. Saturday. Attended Mrs. Brown's funeral. Let this and every other instance of human frailty and mortality prompt me to endeavor after a temper of mind fit to undergo this great change.

1756. March 1. Monday. Wrote out Bolingbroke's Reflections on Exile.

2. Tuesday. Began this afternoon my third quarter.* The great and Almighty author of nature, who at first established

1 Probably Dr. Willard, with whom he soon afterwards took up his abode.

* [Three months after this, (during the second quarter,) the Selectmen procured lodgings for me at Dr. Nahum Willard's. This physician had a large practice, a good reputation for skill, and a pretty library. Here were Dr. Cheyne's works, Sydenham, and others, and Van Swieten's Commentaries on Boerhaave. I read a good deal in these books and entertained many thoughts of becoming a physician and a surgeon.]

those rules which regulate the world, can as easily suspend those laws whenever his providence sees sufficient reason for such suspension. This can be no objection, then, to the miracles of Jesus Christ. Although some very thoughtful and contemplative men among the heathen attained a strong persuasion of the great principles of religion, yet the far greater number, having little time for speculation, gradually sunk into the grossest opinions and the grossest practices. These, therefore, could not be made to embrace the true religion till their attention was roused by some astonishing and miraculous appearances. The reasoning of philosophers, having nothing surprising in them, could not overcome the force of prejudice, custom, passion, and bigotry. But when wise and virtuous men, commissioned from heaven, by miracles awakened men's attention to their reasonings, the force of truth made its way with ease to their minds.

3. Wednesday. Natural philosophy is the art of deducing the general laws and properties of material substances from a series of analogous observations. The manner of reasoning in this art is not strictly demonstrative, and, by consequence, the knowledge hence acquired is not absolutely scientific, because the facts that we reason upon are perceived by sense, and not by the internal action of the mind contemplating its ideas. But these facts being presumed true in the form of axioms, subsequent reasonings about them may be in the strictest sense scientific. This art informs us in what manner bodies will influence us and each other in given circumstances, and so teaches us to avoid the noxious, and embrace the beneficial qualities of matter. By this art, too, many curious engines have been constructed to facilitate business, to avert impending calamities, and to procure desired advantages.

6. Saturday. Rose at half after four. Wrote Bolingbroke's letter on retirement and study.

7. Sunday. Heard Mr. Maccarty all day. Spent the evening and supped at Mr. Greene's with Thayer. Honesty, sincerity, and openness I esteem essential marks of a good mind. I am, therefore, of opinion that men ought, (after they have examined with unbiased judgments every system of religion, and chosen one system, on their own authority, for themselves,) to avow their opinions and defend them with boldness.

12. Friday. Laid a pair of gloves with Mrs. Willard * that she would not see me chew tobacco this month.

14. Sunday. Heard Mr. Maccarty, all day, upon Abraham's faith in offering up Isaac. Spent the evening very sociably at Mr. Putnam's. Several observations concerning Mr. Franklin,[1] of Philadelphia, a prodigious genius, cultivated with prodigious industry.

15. Monday. I sometimes in my sprightly moments consider myself, in my great chair at school, as some dictator at the head of a commonwealth. In this little state I can discover all the great geniuses, all the surprising actions and revolutions of the great world, in miniature. I have several renowned generals but three feet high, and several deep projecting politicians in petticoats. I have others catching and dissecting flies, accumulating remarkable pebbles, cockle shells, &c, with as ardent curiosity as any virtuoso in the Royal Society. Some rattle and thunder out A, B, C, with as much fire and impetuosity as Alexander fought, and very often sit down and cry as heartily upon being outspelt, as Cæsar did, when at Alexander's sepulchre he recollected that the Macedonian hero had conquered the world before his age. At one table sits Mr. Insipid, foppling[2] and fluttering, spinning his whirligig, or playing with his fingers, as gaily and wittily as any Frenchified coxcomb brandishes his cane or rattles his snuff-box. At another, sits the polemical divine, plodding and wrangling in his mind about "Adam's fall, in which we sinned all," as his Primer has it. In short, my little school, like the great world, is made up of kings, politicians, divines, L. D.'s, fops, buffoons, fiddlers, sycophants, fools, coxcombs, chimney sweepers, and every other character drawn in history, or seen in the world. Is it not, then, the highest pleasure, my friend, to preside in this little world, to bestow the proper applause upon virtuous and generous actions, to blame and punish every vicious and contracted trick, to wear out of the tender mind every thing that is mean and little, and fire the

1 Benjamin Franklin, whose growing reputation in Europe, on account of his experiments in electricity, was coming back to increase his reputation at home.

2 There is no such English word, but its meaning is clear enough.

* [The family of the Willards of Lancaster were often at Worcester, and I formed an acquaintance with them, especially Abel Willard, who had been one year with me at College, and had studied the law under Mr. Pratt in Boston. With him I lived in friendship.]

new-born soul with a noble ardor and emulation? The world affords no greater pleasure. Let others waste their bloom of life at the card or billiard table among rakes and fools, and when their minds are sufficiently fretted with losses, and inflamed by wine, ramble through the streets assaulting innocent people, breaking windows, or debauching young girls. I envy not their exalted happiness. I had rather sit in school and consider which of my pupils will turn out in his future life a hero, and which a rake, which a philosopher, and which a parasite, than change breasts with them, though possessed of twenty laced waistcoats and a thousand pounds a year. Methinks I hear you say, This is odd talk for John Adams! I'll tell you, then, the occasion of it. About four months since, a poor girl in this neighborhood, walking by the meeting-house upon some occasion in the evening, met a fine gentleman with laced hat and waistcoat, and a sword, who solicited her to turn aside with him into the horse stable. The girl reluctated a little, upon which he gave her three guineas, and wished he might be damned if he did not have her in three months. Into the horse stable they went. The three guineas proved three farthings, and the girl proved with child, without a friend upon earth that will own her, or knowing the father of her three-farthing bastard.

17. Wednesday. A fine morning. Proceeded on my journey towards Braintree. Stopped to see Mr. Haven,[1] of Dedham, who told me, very civilly, he supposed I took my faith on trust from Dr. Mayhew, and added, that he believed the doctrine of the satisfaction of Jesus Christ to be essential to Christianity, and that he would not believe this satisfaction unless he believed the Divinity of Christ. Mr. Balch was there too, and observed, that he would not be a Christian if he did not believe the mysteries of the gospel; that he could bear with an Arminian, but when, with Dr. Mayhew, they denied the Divinity and satisfaction of Jesus Christ, he had no more to do with them; that he knew not what to make of Dr. Mayhew's two discourses upon the expected dissolution of all things. They gave him an idea of a cart whose wheels wanted greasing; it rumbled on in a hoarse, rough manner; there was a good deal of ingenious talk in them, but it

[1] The Reverend Jason Haven, then just ordained as pastor of the first parish in Dedham.

was thrown together in a jumbled, confused order. He believed the Doctor wrote them in a great panic. He added further that Arminians, however stiffly they maintain their opinions in health, always, he takes notice, retract when they come to die, and choose to die Calvinists. Set out for Braintree, and arrived about sunset.

21. Sunday. Vernal equinox. Spent the evening at Mr. Wibird's[1] with Messrs. Quincy,[2] Cranch,[3] Savil, in conversation upon the present situation of public affairs. Mr. Quincy exerted his talents in a most eloquent harangue. Mr. Cranch quoted the Bishop of Quebec's letter[4] concerning the French Missionaries among the Indians. Some, he says, are very good men.

24. Wednesday. Set out for Worcester; dined at Dedham, and rode from thence in the rain to Mendon. Supped and lodged at Josiah Adams's.

25. Thursday. Rode to Uxbridge; tarried at my uncle Webb's, and lodged with Mr. Nathan.[5]

26. Friday. Rode to Grafton; dined at Josiah Rawson's. He

1 The Rev. Anthony Wibird, for forty-five years pastor of the first church in Braintree, had been settled the year before, February 5, 1755.

2 Josiah Quincy, the elder, often mentioned in this Diary. In this year he retired from active business, and resided in Braintree from this time until his death in 1784. He was the friend and correspondent of many distinguished men of his times, several interesting letters from whom, addressed to him, are published in the Memoir of Josiah Quincy, Jun., by his son.

3 The late Judge Richard Cranch, had emigrated from Devonshire, in England, ten years before, in company with General Palmer, who had married his sister. He was now living in Braintree.

4 This letter was printed in the Boston Evening Post, of September 8, 1755. It seems to have been considered so important in its manifestation of the hostile spirit of the French Catholics, "the turbulent Gallicks" spoken of in the letter to Nathan Webb, as to have been issued in a separate sheet, and sold at a low price. The note appended to the advertisement in the Post reads as follows: —

"N. B. It ought to be read (for more reasons than one) by every intelligent man in North America."

The war between Great Britain and France was not formally declared until May of this year, 1756. But it had already been carried on in America for many months. The forcible removal of the French neutrals of Acadia, took place in 1755, a measure of grievous wrong, the true character of which haply might have been forgotten but for the immortality lately given to it by the verse of Longfellow.

5 This is the Nathan Webb to whom had been addressed, in the preceding month of October, that remarkable letter which will be found fully commented upon in the preceding volume. The journey on horseback to Worcester, spending three days on the way, is in some contrast with the habits of the present generation.

exerted his Rawsonian talents concerning the felicity of Heaven. I sat and heard, for it is in vain to resist so impetuous a torrent. Proceeded to Worcester; drank tea at Mr. Maccarty's, and spent the evening at Major Gardiner's.

27. Saturday. The stream of life sometimes glides smoothly on through the flowery meadows and enamelled plains; at other times it drags a winding, reluctant course, through offensive bogs and dismal, gloomy swamps. The same road now leads us through a spacious country, fraught with every delightful object; then plunges us at once into miry sloughs, or stops our passage with craggy and inaccessible mountains. The free roving songster of the forest now rambles unconfined, and hops from spray to spray, but the next hour, perhaps, he alights to pick the scattered grain, and is entangled in the snare. The ship which, wafted by a favorable gale, sails prosperously upon the peaceful surface, by a sudden change of weather may be tossed by the tempest, and driven by furious opposite winds upon rocks or quicksands.[1] In short, nothing in this world enjoys a constant series of joy and prosperity.

29. Monday. We find ourselves capable of comprehending many things, of acquiring considerable degrees of knowledge by our slender and contracted faculties. Now may we not suppose our minds strengthened and capacities dilated, so as fully to comprehend this globe of earth with its numerous appendages? May we not suppose them further enlarged to take in the solar system in all its relations? Nay, why may we not go further, and suppose them increased to comprehend the whole created universe, with all its inhabitants, their various relations, dependencies, duties, and necessities? If this is supposable, then a being of such great capacity, endowed with sufficient power, would be an accomplished judge of all rational beings — would be fit to dispense rewards to virtue and punishments to vice.

1 At this very time one of Britain's most finished poets was engaged in depicting the fate of one of her monarchs, through the use of this figure. The lines, applied to the unfortunate Richard the Second, will recur to every cultivated mind.

"Fair laughs the morn, and soft the zephyr blows,
  While proudly riding o'er the azure realm,
In gallant trim the gilded vessel goes,
  Youth on the prow, and pleasure at the helm;
Regardless of the sweeping whirlwind's sway,
  That, hush'd in grim repose, expects his evening prey."

April 10. Saturday. The man to whom nature has given a great and surprising genius, will perform great and surprising achievements. But a soul originally narrow and confined will never be enlarged to a distinguishing capacity. Such a one must be content to grovel amidst pebbles and butterflies through the whole of his life. By diligence and attention indeed, he may possibly get the character of a man of sense; but never that of a great man.

15. Thursday. Drank tea and spent the evening at Mr. Putnam's, in conversation concerning Christianity. He is of opinion that the apostles were a company of enthusiasts. He says that we have only their word to prove that they spoke with different tongues, raised the dead, and healed the sick, &c.*

23. Friday. I can as easily still the fierce tempest or stop the rapid thunderbolt, as command the motions and operations of my own mind. I am dull and inactive, and all my resolutions, all the spirits I can muster are insufficient to rouse me from this senseless torpitude. My brains seem constantly in as great confusion and wild disorder as Milton's chaos; they are numb, dead. I have never any bright, refulgent ideas. Every thing appears in my mind dim and obscure, like objects seen through a dirty glass or roiled water.

24. Saturday. All my time seems to roll away unnoticed. I long to study sometimes, but have no opportunity. I long to be a master of Greek and Latin. I long to prosecute the mathematical and philosophical sciences. I long to know a little of ethics and moral philosophy. But I have no books, no time, no friends. I must therefore be contented to live and die an ignorant, obscure fellow.

25. Sunday. Astronomers tell us with good reason, that not only all the planets and satellites in our solar system, but all the unnumbered worlds that revolve round the fixed stars are inhab-

* [At breakfast, dinner, and tea, Mr. Putnam was commonly disputing with me upon some question of religion. He had been intimate with one Peasley Collins, the son of a Quaker in Boston, who had been to Europe, and came back a disbeliever of every thing; fully satisfied that religion was a cheat, a cunning invention of priests and politicians; that there would be no future state, any more than there is at present any moral government. Putnam could not go these whole lengths with him. Although he would argue to the extent of his learning and ingenuity to destroy or invalidate the evidences of a future state, and the principles of natural and revealed religion, yet I could plainly perceive that he could not convince himself that death was an endless sleep.]

ited, as well as this globe of earth. If this is the case, all mankind are no more in comparison of the whole rational creation of God, than a point to the orbit of Saturn. Perhaps all these different ranks of rational beings have in a greater or less degree committed moral wickedness. If so, I ask a Calvinist whether he will subscribe to this alternative, "Either God Almighty must assume the respective shapes of all these different species and suffer the penalties of their crimes in their stead, or else all these beings must be consigned to everlasting perdition?"

26. Monday. The reflection that I penned yesterday appears upon the revision to be weak enough. For first, we know not that the inhabitants of other globes have sinned. Nothing can be argued in this manner till it is proved at least probable that all these species of rational beings have revolted from their rightful Sovereign. When I examine the little prospect that lies before me, and find an infinite variety of bodies in one horizon of, perhaps, two miles diameter, how many millions of such prospects there are upon the surface of this earth, how many millions of globes there are within our view, each of which has as many of these prospects upon its own surface as our planet; great and marvellous are thy works! &c.

28. Wednesday. Drank tea at Mr. Putnam's, walked with him to his farm, talked about all nature.

29. Thursday. Fast day; heard Mr. Maccarty, spent the evening at Mr. Putnam's. Our proper business in this life is not to accumulate large fortunes, not to gain high honors and important offices in the state, not to waste our health and spirits in pursuit of the sciences, but constantly to improve ourselves in habits of piety and virtue. Consequently the meanest mechanic who endeavors, in proportion to his ability, to promote the happiness of his fellow men, deserves better of society, and should be held in higher esteem than the greatest magistrate who uses his power for his own pleasures, or avarice, or ambition.

30. Friday. Reading Milton. That man's soul, it seems to me, was distended as wide as creation. His power over the human mind was absolute and unlimited. His genius was great beyond conception, and his learning without bounds. I can only gaze at him with astonishment, without comprehending the vast compass of his capacity.

May 1. Saturday. If we consider a little of this our globe, we find an endless variety of substances mutually connected with and dependent on each other. In the wilderness we see an amazing profusion of vegetables, which afford sustenance and covering to the wild beasts. The cultivated plains and meadows produce grass for the cattle, and herbs for the service of man. The milk and the flesh of other animals afford a delicious provision for mankind. A great part of the human species are obliged to provide food and nourishment for other helpless and improvident animals. Vegetables sustain some animals; these animals are devoured by others, and these others are continually cultivating and improving the vegetable species. Thus, nature upon our earth is in a continual rotation. If we rise higher, we find the sun and moon, to a very great degree, influencing us. Tides are produced in the ocean; clouds in the atmosphere; all nature is made to flourish and look gay by these enlivening and invigorating luminaries. Yea, life and cheerfulness is diffused to all the other planets, as well as ours, upon the sprightly sunbeams. No doubt there is as great a multitude and variety of bodies upon each planet, in proportion to its magnitude, as there is upon ours. These bodies are connected with, and influenced by each other. Thus, we see the amazing harmony of our solar system. The minutest particle, in one of Saturn's satellites, may have some influence upon the most distant regions of the system. The stupendous plan of operation was projected by Him who rules the universe, and a part assigned to every particle of matter, to act in this great and complicated drama. The Creator looked into the remotest futurity, and saw his great designs accomplished by this inextricable, this mysterious complication of causes. But to rise still higher, this solar system is but one very small wheel in the great, the astonishing machine of the world. Those stars, that twinkle in the heavens, have each of them a choir of planets, comets, and satellites, dancing round them, playing mutually on each other, and all, together, playing on the other systems that lie around them. Our system, considered as one body hanging on its centre of gravity, may affect and be affected by all the other systems within the compass of creation. Thus, it is highly probable every particle of matter influences and is influenced by every other particle in the whole collected universe.

2. Sunday. I think it necessary to call myself to a strict account how I spend my time, once a week, at least. Since the 14th of April, I have been studying the first part of Butler's Analogy.

3. Monday. Spent the evening and supped at Mr. Maccarty's. The love of fame naturally betrays a man into several weaknesses and fopperies that tend very much to diminish his reputation, and so defeat itself. Vanity, I am sensible, is my cardinal vice and cardinal folly; and I am in continual danger, when in company, of being led an *ignis fatuus* chase by it, without the strictest caution and watchfulness over myself.

4. Tuesday. Let any man, suppose of the most improved understanding, look upon a watch when the parts are separated. Let him examine every wheel and spring separately by itself. Yet, if the use and application of these springs and wheels is not explained to him, he will not be able to judge of the use and advantage of particular parts; much less will he be able if he has only one wheel. In like manner we, who see but a few cogs in one wheel of the great machine of the universe, can make no right judgment of particular phenomena in nature.

7. Friday. Spent the evening and supped at Mr. Maccarty's. A man's observing the flux of the tide to-day, renders it credible that the same phenomenon may be observed to-morrow. In the same manner, our experience that the Author of nature has annexed pain to vice, and pleasure to virtue, in general, I mean, renders it credible that the same, or a like disposition of things, may take place hereafter. Our observing that the state of minority was designed to be an education for mature life, and that our good or ill success, in a mature life, depends upon our good or ill improvement of our advantages in minority, renders it credible that this life was designed to be an education for a future one; and that our happiness or misery, in a future life, will be allotted us according as our characters shall be virtuous or vicious. For God governs his great kingdom, the world, by very general laws. We cannot, indeed, observe many instances of these laws, but wherever we see any particular disposition of things, we may strongly presume that there are other dispositions of things, in other systems of nature, analogous and of a piece with this.

8. Saturday. Went a shooting with Mr. Putnam; drank tea with him and his lady.

9. Sunday. Since last Sunday I have wrote a few pages of the Spectator; read the last part of Butler's Analogy; wrote out the tract upon Personal Identity, and that upon the Nature of Virtue. A poor week's work!

11. Tuesday. The first day of Court. Nature and truth, or rather truth and right are invariably the same in all times and in all places; and reason, pure unbiased reason, perceives them alike in all times and in all places. But passion, prejudice, interest, custom, and fancy, are infinitely precarious; if, therefore, we suffer our understandings to be blinded or perverted by any of these, the chance is that of millions to one, that we shall embrace errors. And hence arises that endless variety of opinions entertained by mankind. The weather and the season are, beyond expression, delightful; the fields are covered with a bright and lively verdure; the trees are all in bloom, and the atmosphere is filled with a ravishing fragrance; the air is soft and yielding; and the setting sun sprinkled his departing rays over the face of nature, and enlivened all the landscapes around me; the trees put forth their leaves, and the birds fill the spray.

12. Wednesday. Rambled about all day, gaping and gazing.

14. Friday. Drank tea at the Colonel's. Not one new idea this week.

15. Saturday. A lovely day; soft vernal showers. Exercise invigorates and enlivens all the faculties of body and of mind; it arouses our animal spirits, it disperses melancholy; it spreads a gladness and satisfaction over our minds, and qualifies us for every sort of business, and every sort of pleasure.

16. Sunday. The week past was court week. I was interrupted by company, and the noisy bustle of the public occasion, so that I have neither read nor wrote any thing worth mentioning. Heard Mr. Thayer, and spent the evening at Mr. Putnam's very sociably.

17. Monday. The elephant and the lion, when their strength is directed and applied by man, can exert a prodigious force. But their strength, great and surprising as it is, can produce no great effects when applied by no higher ingenuity than their own. But man, although the powers of his body are but small and contemptible, by the exercise of his reason can invent engines and instruments, to take advantage of the powers in nature, and accomplish the most astonishing designs. He can

rear the valley into a lofty mountain, and reduce the mountain to a humble vale. He can rend the rocks and level the proudest trees; at his pleasure the forest is cleared, and palaces rise; when he pleases the soaring eagle is precipitated to earth, and the light-footed roe is stopped in his career. He can cultivate and assist nature in her own productions, by pruning the trees and manuring the land. He makes the former produce larger and fairer fruit; and the latter to bring forth better and greater plenty of grain. He can form a communication between remotest regions for the benefit of trade and commerce, over the yielding and fluctuating element of water. The telescope has settled the regions of heaven, and the microscope has brought up to view innumerable millions of animals that escape the observation of our naked sight.

23. Sunday. Heard Mr. Maccarty. He is particularly fond of the following expressions: carnal, ungodly persons; sensuality and voluptuousness; walking with God, unregeneracy, rebellion against God; believers; all things come alike to all; there is one event to the righteous and to the wicked; shut out of the presence of God; solid, substantial, and permanent joys; joys springing up in the soul; the shines of God's countenance.

When we consider the vast and incomprehensible extent of the material universe, those myriads of fixed stars that emerge out of the remote regions of space to our view by glasses, — and the finer our glasses the more of these systems we discover; — when we consider that space is absolutely infinite and boundless, that the power of the Deity is strictly omnipotent, and his goodness without limitation, who can come to a stop in his thoughts and say, hither does the universe extend and no further?

"Nothing can proceed from nothing." But something can proceed from something, and thus the Deity produced this vast and beautiful frame of the universe out of nothing; that is, He had no preëxistent matter to work upon, or to change from a chaos into a world. But He produced a world into being by his Almighty fiat, perhaps, in a manner analogous to the production of resolutions in our minds. This week I have read one volume of Duncan Forbes's works, and one half of Bentley's Sermons at the Boilean Lectures.

24. Monday. Had the projectile force in the planets been greater than it is, they would not describe circles, but very

eccentrical ellipses round the sun; and then the inhabitants would be tormented, yea, destroyed, and the planets left barren and uninhabitable wastes, by extreme vicissitudes of heat and cold. It was many million times as likely that some other degree of velocity would have been lighted on, as that the present would, if chance had the disposal of it; and any other degree would have absolutely destroyed all animal and sensitive, if not vegetable, inhabitants. *Ergo*, an intelligent and benevolent mind had the disposal and determination of these things.

28. Friday. If we examine critically the little prospect that lies around us, at one view we behold an almost infinite variety of substances over our heads. The sun blazes in divine effulgence; the clouds, tinged with various colors by the refracted sunbeams, exhibit most beautiful appearances in the atmosphere. The cultivated plains and meadows are attired in a delightful verdure, and variegated with the gay enamel of flowers and roses; on one hand we see an extensive forest, a whole kingdom of vegetables of the noblest kind; upon the hills we discern flocks of grazing cattle; and on the other hand a city rises up to view, with its spires among the clouds. All these, and many more objects encounter our eyes in the prospect of our horizon, perhaps two or three miles in diameter. Now every animal that we see in this prospect, men and beasts, is endued with a most curiously organized body. They consist of bones, and blood, and muscles, and nerves, and ligaments, and tendons, and chyle, and a million other things, all exactly fitted for the purposes of life, and motion, and action. Every plant has almost as complex and curious a structure as animals; and the minutest twig is supported and supplied with juices and life, by organs and filaments proper to draw this nutrition of the earth. It would be endless to consider, minutely, every substance or species of substances that falls under our eyes in this one prospect. Now let us for a minute consider how many million such prospects there are upon this single planet, all of which contain as great, and some a much greater variety of animals and vegetables. When we have been sufficiently astonished at this incomprehensible multitude of substances, let us rise in our thoughts, and consider how many planets, and satellites, and comets, there are in this one solar system, each of which has as many such prospects upon its surface as our earth. Such a view as this may

suffice to show us our ignorance; but if we rise still higher in our thoughts, and consider that stupendous army of fixed stars that is hung up in the immense space, as so many suns, each placed in the centre of his respective system, and diffusing his enlivening and invigorating influences to his whole choir of planets, comets, and satellites; and that each of this unnumbered multitude has as much superficies, and as many prospects, as our earth, we find ourselves lost and swallowed up in this incomprehensible, (I had almost said) infinite magnificence of nature. Our imaginations, after a few faint efforts, sink down into a profound admiration of what they cannot comprehend. God, whose almighty fiat first produced this amazing universe, had the whole plan in view from all eternity; intimately and perfectly knew the nature and all the properties of all these his creatures. He looked forward through all duration, and perfectly knew all the effects, all the events and revolutions that could possibly and would actually take place throughout eternity.

29. Saturday. Drank tea at Mr. Putnam's.

What is the proper business of mankind in this life? We come into the world naked, and destitute of all the conveniences and necessaries of life; and if we were not provided for and nourished by our parents, or others, should inevitably perish as soon as born; we increase in strength of body and mind, by slow and insensible degrees; one third of our time is consumed in sleep, and three sevenths of the remainder is spent in procuring a mere animal sustenance; and if we live to the age of threescore and ten, and then sit down to make an estimate in our minds of the happiness we have enjoyed, and the misery we have suffered, we shall find, I am apt to think, that the overbalance of happiness is quite inconsiderable. We shall find that we have been, through the greatest part of our lives, pursuing shadows, and empty but glittering phantoms, rather than substances. We shall find that we have applied our whole vigor, all our faculties, in the pursuit of honor, or wealth, or learning, or some other such delusive trifle, instead of the real and everlasting excellencies of piety and virtue. Habits of contemplating the Deity and his transcendent excellencies, and correspondent habits of complacency in, and dependence upon him; habits of reverence and gratitude to God, and habits of love and compassion to our fellow men; and habits of temperance, recollection, and self-government, will afford us a real and substantial pleasure. We may then exult in a consciousness of the favor of God, and the prospect of everlasting felicity.

30. Sunday. Heard Mr. Maccarty. "You, who are sinners, are in continual danger of being swallowed up quick, and borne away by the mighty torrent of God's wrath and justice. It is now, as it were, restrained and banked up by his goodness. But he will, by and by, unless repentance prevent, let it out in full fury upon you." This week I have wrote the eighth Sermon of Bentley's Boilean Lectures. Read part of the first volume of Voltaire's Age of Louis XIV. I make poor weeks' works.

31. Monday. When we see or feel any body, we discern nothing but bulk and extension. We can change this extension into a great variety of shapes and figures, and, by applying our senses to it, can get ideas of those different figures; but can do nothing more than change the figure. If we pulverize glass or salt, the original constituent matter remains the same, only we have altered the contexture of its parts. Large loads and heaps of matter, as mountains and rocks, lie obstinate, inactive, and motionless, and eternally will remain so, unless moved by some force extrinsic to themselves. Dissolve the cohesion, and reduce these mountains to their primogenial atoms; these atoms are as dull and senseless as they were when combined into the shape of a mountain. In short, matter has no consciousness of its own existence, has no power of its own, no active power I mean, but is wholly passive; nor can thought be ever produced by any modification of it. To say that God can superadd to matter a capacity of thought, is palpable nonsense and contradiction. Such a capacity is inconsistent with the most essential properties of matter.

June 1. Tuesday. The reasoning of mathematicians is founded on certain and infallible principles. Every word they use conveys a determinate idea, and by accurate definitions they excite the same ideas in the mind of the reader that were in the mind of the writer. When they have defined the terms they intend to make use of, they premise a few axioms, or self-evident principles, that every man must assent to as soon as proposed. They then take for granted certain postulates, that no one can deny them, such as, that a right line may be drawn from one given point to another; and from these plain simple principles they have raised most astonishing speculations, and proved the extent of the human mind to be more spacious and capable than any other science.

2. Wednesday. When we come into the world, our minds are destitute of all sorts of ideas. Our senses inform us of various qualities in the substances around us; as we grow up our acquaintance with things enlarges and spreads; colors are painted in our minds through our eyes; all the various modulations of sounds enter by our ears; fragrance and fœtor are perceived by the smell; extension and bulk by the touch. These ideas that enter, simple and uncompounded, through our senses, are called *simple ideas*, because they are absolutely one and indivisible. Thus, the whiteness of snow cannot be divided or separated into two or more whitenesses. The same may be said of all other colors. It is, indeed, in our power to mix or compound colors into new and more beautiful appearances than any that are to be found in nature; so we can combine various sounds into one melodious tune; in short, we can modify and dispose the simple ideas of sensation into whatever shape we please. But these ideas can enter our minds no other way but through the senses. A man born blind will never gain one idea of light or color. One born deaf will never get an idea of sound.

5. Saturday. Dreamed away the afternoon.

14. Monday. He is not a wise man, and is unfit to fill any important station in society, that has left one passion in his soul unsubdued. The love of glory will make a General sacrifice the interest of his nation to his own fame. Avarice exposes some to corruption, and all to a thousand meannesses and villanies destructive to society. Love has deposed lawful kings, and aggrandized unlawful, ill deserving courtiers. Envy is more studious of eclipsing the lustre of other men by indirect stratagems, than of brightening its own lustre by great and meritorious actions. These passions should be bound fast, and brought under the yoke. Untamed, they are lawless bulls; they roar and bluster, defy all control, and sometimes murder their proper owner. But, properly inured to obedience, they take their places under the yoke without noise, and labor vigorously in their master's service. From a sense of the government of God, and a regard to the laws established by his providence, should all

our actions for ourselves or for other men primarily originate; and this master passion in a good man's soul, like the larger fishes of prey, will swallow up and destroy all the rest.

15. Tuesday. Consider for one minute the changes produced in this country within the space of two hundred years. Then the whole continent was one continued dismal wilderness, the haunt of wolves and bears and more savage men. Now the forests are removed, the land covered with fields of corn, orchards bending with fruit, and the magnificent habitations of rational and civilized people. Then, our rivers flowed through gloomy deserts and offensive swamps. Now, the same rivers glide smoothly on, through rich countries fraught with every delightful object, and through meadows painted with the most beautiful scenery of nature and of art. The narrow huts of the Indians have been removed, and in their room have arisen fair and lofty edifices, large and well compacted cities.

July 21. Wednesday. Kept school. I am now entering on another year, and I am resolved not to neglect my time as I did last year. I am resolved to rise with the sun, and to study the Scriptures on Thursday, Friday, Saturday, and Sunday mornings, and to study some Latin author the other three mornings. Noons and nights I intend to read English authors. This is my fixed determination; and I will set down every neglect and every compliance with this resolution. May I blush whenever I suffer one hour to pass unimproved. I will rouse up my mind and fix my attention; I will stand collected within myself, and think upon what I read and what I see; I will strive, with all my soul, to be something more than persons who have had less advantages than myself.

22. Thursday. Fast day. Rose not till seven o'clock. This is the usual fate of my resolutions. Wrote the first three chapters of St. James. Wrote in Bolingbroke pretty industriously. Spent the evening at Mr. Paine's. The years of my youth are marked by divine Providence with various and with great events. The last year is rendered conspicuous, in the memorials of past ages, by a series of very remarkable events, of various kinds. The year opened with the projection of three expeditions,[1] to prevent the further, and remove the present, depredations and

[1] The events referred to are fully narrated in all the histories of the time. *Hutchinson*, iii. 31 – 42. *Grahame*, iii. 382, et seq. *Hildreth*, ii. 455, et seq.

encroachments of our turbulent French neighbors. I shall not minute the gradual steps advanced by each army, but only the issue of each. Braddock, the commander of the forces destined against Du Quesne, and six or seven hundred of his men, were butchered in a manner unexampled in history; all routed and destroyed without doing the least injury, that we know of, to the enemy. Johnson, with his army, was attacked by the Baron Dieskau, but happily maintained his ground and routed the enemy, taking Dieskau prisoner. Monckton and Winslow, at Nova Scotia, gained their point, took the fortresses, and sent off the inhabitants into these provinces. Boscawen bravely defended our coast with his fleet, and made great havoc among the French merchant-ships. All these actions were performed in a time of peace. *Sed paulo majora canamus.* God Almighty has exerted the strength of his tremendous arm, and shook one of the finest, richest, and most populous cities in Europe, into ruin and desolation, by an earthquake.[1] The greatest part of Europe and the greatest part of America, have been in violent convulsions, and admonished the inhabitants of both that neither riches, nor honors, nor the solid globe itself, is a proper basis on which to build our hopes of security. The British nation has been making very expensive and very formidable preparations to secure its territories against an invasion by the French, and to humble the insolent tempers and aspiring prospects of that ambitious and faithless nation.[2] The gathering of the clouds seems to forebode very tempestuous weather, and none can tell but the storm will break heavy upon himself in particular. Is it not then the highest frenzy and distraction to neglect these expostulations of Providence, and continue a rebellion against the Potentate who alone has wisdom enough to perceive, and power enough to procure for us the only certain means of happiness, and goodness enough to prompt him to both?

23. Friday. Rose at seven; wrote the two last chapters of St. James.

24. Saturday. Rose at seven; wrote a little in Greek; afternoon wrote Bolingbroke.

[1] The earthquake of the first of November, 1755, which destroyed Lisbon, and was followed in America by that mentioned in the first page of the Diary.

[2] It was part of Governor Shirley's plan for 1756, to remove the French from the Lakes; to this end he proposed to raise three thousand men in Massachusetts Bay, as the proportion of the Province to an army of nine thousand, to be completed by the rest of New England and New York. *Hutchinson*, iii. 44-46

25. Sunday. Rose at half after six. Good sense, some say, is enough to regulate our conduct, and to dictate thoughts and actions which are proper upon certain occasions. This, they say, will soften and refine the motions of our limbs into an easy and agreeable air, although the dancing master was never applied to; and this will suggest good answers, good observations, and good expressions to us, better than refined breeding. Good sense will make us remember that others have as good a right to think for themselves, and to speak their own opinions, as we have; that another man's making a silly speech does not warrant my ill nature and pride in grasping the opportunity to ridicule him and show my wit; a puffy, vain, conceited conversation, never fails to bring a man into contempt, although his natural endowments be ever so great, and his application and industry ever so intense; no accomplishments, no virtues, are a sufficient atonement for vanity and a haughty overbearing temper in conversation; and such is the humor of the world, the greater a man's parts, and the nobler his virtues in other respects, the more derision and ridicule does this one vice and folly throw him into. Good sense is generally attended with a very lively sense and delight in applause; the love of fame in such men is generally much stronger than in other people, and this passion, it must be confessed, is apt to betray men into impertinent exertions of their talents, sometimes into censorious remarks upon others, often into little meannesses to sound the opinions of others, and, oftenest of all, into a childish affectation of wit and gayety. I must own myself to have been, to a very heinous degree, guilty in this respect; when in company with persons much superior to myself in years and place, I have talked to show my learning; I have been too bold with great men, which boldness will, no doubt, be called self-conceit; I have made ill natured remarks upon the intellectuals, manners, practice, &c., of other people; I have foolishly aimed at wit and spirit, at making a shining figure in gay company; but, instead of shining brighter, I only clouded the few rays that before rendered me visible. Such has been my unhappy fate. I now resolve, for the future, never to say an illnatured thing concerning ministers or the ministerial profession; never to say an envious thing concerning governors, judges, ministers, clerks, sheriffs, lawyers, or any other honorable or lucrative offices or officers; never to affect wit upon laced waistcoats, or large

estates, or their possessors; never to show my own importance or superiority by remarking the foibles, vices, or inferiority of others. But I now resolve, as far as lies in me, to take notice chiefly of the amiable qualities of other people; to put the most favorable construction upon the weaknesses, bigotry, and errors of others, &c.; and to labor more for an inoffensive and amiable, than for a shining and invidious character.

26. Monday. Rose at seven; read carefully thirty lines in Virgil.

27. Tuesday. Read carefully thirty lines in Virgil. Wrote a little in Bolingbroke at noon, and a little at night. Spent the evening at Mr. Putnam's.

28. Wednesday. Read about forty lines in Virgil, and wrote a little at noon. Nothing more.

29. Thursday. Rose at half after six; read a little Greek

30. Friday. Dreamed away the time.

31. Saturday. The nature and essence of the material world is not less concealed from our knowledge than the nature and essence of God. We see ourselves surrounded on all sides with a vast expanse of heavens, and we feel ourselves astonished at the grandeur, the blazing pomp of those stars with which it is adorned. The birds fly over our heads and our fellow animals labor and sport around us; the trees wave and murmur in the winds; the clouds float and shine on high; the surging billows rise in the sea, and ships break through the tempest; here rises a spacious city, and yonder is spread out an extensive plain. These objects are so common and familiar that we think ourselves fully acquainted with them; but these are only effects and properties; the substance from whence they flow is hid from us in impenetrable obscurity.

God is said to be self-existent, and that therefore he must have existed from eternity, and throughout immensity. God exists by an absolute necessity in his own nature; that is, it implies a contradiction to suppose him not to exist. To ask what this necessity is, is as if you should ask what the necessity of the equality between twice two and four is; twice two are necessarily in their own nature equal to four, not only here, but in every point of space; not only now, but in every point of duration. In the same manner God necessarily exists, not only here, but throughout unlimited space; not only now, but throughout all duration, past and future. We observe in the animate and in the inanimate creation a surprising diversity and a surprising uniformity. Of inanimate substances there is a great variety, from the pebble in the streets quite up to the vegetables in the forest; of animals there is no less a variety of species, from the animalcula, that escape our naked sight, quite through the intermediate kinds up to elephants, horses, men. Yet, notwithstanding this variety, there is, from the highest species of animals upon this globe, which is generally thought to be man, a regular and uniform subordination of one tribe to another, down to the apparently insignificant animalcules in pepper water; and the same subordination continues quite through the vegetable kingdom. And it is worth observing that each species regularly and uniformly preserve all their essential and peculiar properties without partaking of the peculiar properties of others. We do not see chickens hatched with fins to swim; nor fishes spawned with wings to fly; we do not see a colt foaled with claws like a bird, nor man with the clothing or armor which his reason renders him capable of procuring for himself. Every species has its distinguishing properties, and every individual that is born has all those properties without any of the distinguishing properties of another species. What now can preserve this prodigious variety of species and this inflexible uniformity among the individuals but the continual and vigilant providence of God?

August 1. Sunday. Heard Mr. Maccarty all day. Spent the evening at the Colonel's. The event shows that my resolutions are of a very thin and vapory consistency. Almost a fortnight has passed since I came to Worcester the last time; some part of the time I have spent as frugally and industriously as I possibly could; but the greatest part I have dreamed away as usual. I am now entering upon a new month and a new week; and I should think that one month would carry me forward considerably, if I could keep up a continual presence of mind and a close application at all proper times; this I will labor after.

2. Monday. Agreeably to the design laid last night, I arose this morning before the sun.

7. Saturday. All this past week my designs have been interrupted by the troubles and confusion of the house. I shall be able to resume the thread of my studies, I hope, now. Wrote

pretty industriously in Bolingbroke. I have never looked attentively into my own breast; I have never considered (as I ought) the surprising faculties and operations of the mind. Our minds are capable of receiving an infinite variety of ideas from those numerous material objects with which we are surrounded; and the vigorous impressions which we receive from these, our minds are capable of retaining, compounding, and arranging into all the varieties of picture and of figure; our minds are able to retain distinct comprehensions of an infinite multitude of things, without the least labor or fatigue. By curiously inquiring into the situation, fruits, produce, manufactures, &c., of our own, and by travelling into or reading about other countries, we can gain distinct ideas of almost every thing upon this earth, at present; and by looking into history we can settle in our minds a clear and a comprehensive view of this earth at its creation; of its various changes and revolutions; of its various catastrophes; of its progressive cultivation, sudden depopulation, and gradual repeopling; of the growth of several kingdoms and empires; of their wealth and commerce, wars and politics; of the characters of their principal leading men; of their grandeur and power; of their virtues and vices; and of their insensible decays at first, and of their swift destruction at last. In fine, we can attend the earth from its nativity through all the various turns of fortune; through all its successive changes; through all the events that happen on its surface; and through all the successive generations of mankind to the final conflagration, when the whole earth, with all its appendages, shall be consumed and dissolved by the furious element of fire. And after our minds are furnished with this ample store of ideas, far from feeling burdened or overloaded, our thoughts are more free, and active, and clear than before, and we are capable of diffusing our acquaintance with things much further; we are not satiated with knowledge; our curiosity is only improved and increased; our thoughts rove beyond the visible diurnal sphere; they range through the heavens and lose themselves amidst a labyrinth of worlds; and, not contented with what is, they run forward into futurity, and search for new employment there. Here, they can never stop; the wide, the boundless prospect lies before them; here alone they find objects adequate to their desires.

I know not by what fatality it happens, but I seem to have a necessity upon me of trifling away my time. Have not read fifty lines in Virgil this week; have wrote very little.

12. Thursday. Friday. I know not what became of these days.

14. Saturday. I seem to have lost sight of the object that I resolved to pursue. Dreams and slumbers, sloth and negligence, will be the ruin of my schemes. However, I seem to be awake now; why can't I keep awake? I have wrote Scripture pretty industriously this morning. Why am I so unreasonable as to expect happiness, and a solid, undisturbed contentment, amidst all the disorders and the continual rotations of worldly affairs? Stability is nowhere to be found in that part of the universe that lies within our observation; the natural and the moral world are continually changing; the planets, with all their appendages, strike out their amazing circles round the sun; upon the earth one day is serene and clear, no cloud intercepts the kind influences of the sun, and all nature seems to flourish and look gay; but these delightful scenes soon vanish, and are succeeded by the gloom and darkness of the night; and, before the morning appears, the clouds gather, the winds rise, lightnings glare, and thunders bellow through the vast of heaven. Man is sometimes flushed with joy, and transported with the full fury of sensual pleasure, and the next hour lies groaning under the bitter pangs of disappointment and adverse fortune. Thus, God has told us by the general constitution of the world, by the nature of all terrestrial enjoyments, and by the constitution of our own bodies, that this world was not designed for a lasting and a happy state, but rather for a state of moral discipline; that we might have a fair opportunity and continual incitement to labor after a cheerful resignation to all the events of Providence, after habits of virtue, self-government, and piety; and this temper of mind is in our power to acquire, and this alone can secure us against all the adversities of fortune, against all the malice of men, against all the operations of nature. A world in flames, and a whole system tumbling in ruins to the centre, have nothing terrifying in them to a man whose security is builded on the adamantine basis of good conscience and confirmed piety. If I could but conform my life and conversation to my speculations, I should be happy. Have I hardiness enough to contend with Omnipotence? or have I cunning enough to elude Infinite Wis-

dom? or ingratitude enough to spurn at Infinite Goodness? The situation that I am in, and the advantages that I enjoy, are thought to be the best for me by Him who alone is competent to judge of fitness and propriety. Shall I then complain? Oh! madness, pride, impiety!

15. Sunday. If one man or being, out of pure generosity and without any expectation of returns, is about to confer any favor or emolument upon another, he has a right and is at liberty to choose in what manner and by what means to confer it. He may convey the favor by his own hand or by the hand of his servant, and the obligation to gratitude is equally strong upon the benefited being. The mode of bestowing does not diminish the kindness, provided the commodity or good is brought to us equally perfect, and without our expense. But, on the other hand, if one being is the original cause of pain, sorrow, or suffering to another, voluntarily and without provocation, it is injurious to that other, whatever means he might employ, and whatever circumstances the conveyance of the injury might be attended with. Thus, we are equally obliged to the Supreme Being for the information he has given us of our duty, whether by the constitution of our minds and bodies, or by a supernatural revelation. For an instance of the latter let us take original sin. Some say that Adam's sin was enough to damn the whole human race, without any actual crimes committed by any of them. Now this guilt is brought upon them not by their own rashness and indiscretion, not by their own wickedness and vice, but by the Supreme Being. This guilt brought upon us is a real injury and misfortune, because it renders us worse than not to be; and, therefore, making us guilty upon account of Adam's delegation or representing all of us, is not in the least diminishing the injury and injustice, but only changing the mode of conveyance.

22. Sunday. Yesterday I completed a contract with Mr. Putnam to study law, under his inspection, for two years.* I

* [But the Law attracted my attention more and more, and, attending the courts of justice, where I heard Worthington, Hawley, Trowbridge, Putnam, and others, I felt myself irresistibly impelled to make some effort to accomplish my wishes. I made a visit to Mr. Putnam and offered myself to him; he received me with politeness and even kindness; took a few days to consider of it, and then informed me that Mrs. Putnam had consented that I should board in his house; that I should pay no more than the sum allowed for my lodgings, and that I should pay him a hundred dollars when I should find it convenient. I agreed to his proposals, without hesitation, and immediately took possession of his office.]

ought to begin with a resolution to oblige and please him and his lady in a particular manner; I ought to endeavor to oblige and please everybody, but them in particular. Necessity drove me to this determination, but my inclination, I think, was to preach; however, that would not do. But I set out with firm resolutions, I think, never to commit any meanness or injustice in the practice of law. The study and practice of law, I am sure, does not dissolve the obligations of morality or of religion; and, although the reason of my quitting divinity was my opinion concerning some disputed points, I hope I shall not give reason of offence, to any in that profession, by imprudent warmth.

Heard Crawford upon the love of God. The obligation that is upon us to love God, he says, arises from the instances of his love and goodness to us. He has given us an existence and a nature which render us capable of enjoying happiness and of suffering misery. He has given us several senses, and has furnished the world around us with a variety of objects proper to delight and entertain them. He has hung up in the heavens over our heads, and has spread in the fields of nature around about us, those glorious shows and appearances by which our eyes and our imaginations are so extremely delighted. We are pleased with the beautiful appearance of the flowers; we are agreeably entertained with the prospect of forests and meadows, of verdant fields and mountains covered with flocks. We are thrown into a kind of transport and amazement when we behold the amazing concave of heaven sprinkled and glittering with stars. He has also bestowed upon the vegetable species a fragrance that can almost as agreeably entertain our sense of smell. He has so wonderfully constituted the air, that by giving it a particular kind of vibration, it produces in us as intense sensations of pleasure as the organs of our bodies can bear, in all the varieties of harmony and concord. But all the provision that He has made for the gratification of our senses, though very engaging and unmerited instances of goodness, is much inferior to the provision, the wonderful provision that He has made for the gratification of our nobler powers of intelligence and reason. He has given us reason to find out the truth, and the real design and true end of our existence, and has made all endeavors to promote them agreeable to our minds, and attended with a conscious pleasure and complacency. On the contrary, He has made a different course of life — a course of impiety and injustice, of malevolence and intemperance — appear shocking and deformed to our first reflections; and since it was necessary to make us liable to some infirmities and distempers of body, He has plentifully stored the bowels and the surface of the earth with minerals and vegetables that are proper to defend us from some diseases and to restore us to health from others.

Besides, the powers of our reason and invention have enabled us to devise engines and instruments to take advantage of the powers that we find in nature, to avert many calamities that would otherwise befall us, and to procure many enjoyments and pleasures that we could not otherwise attain. He has connected the greatest pleasure with the discovery of truth, and made it our interest to pursue with eagerness these intense pleasures. Have we not the greatest reason, then, yea, is it not our indispensable duty, to return our sincere love and gratitude to this greatest, kindest, and most profuse Benefactor? Would it not show the deepest baseness and most infamous ingratitude to despise or to disregard a being to whose inexhausted beneficence we are so deeply indebted?

23. Monday. Came to Mr. Putnam's and began law, and studied not very closely this week.

THE choice of a profession having been finally determined, an interval of more than two years occurs in the Diary, embracing the remainder of his term of residence at Worcester. The following extracts, from the Autobiography, find their place here.

1757. [While I was at Worcester, three great personages from England passed through that town. Lord Loudon was one; he travelled in the winter from New York to Boston, and lodged at Worcester in his way. The relations we had of his manners and conduct on the road, gave us no great esteem of his lordship's qualifications[1] to conduct the war, and excited gloomy apprehensions. The young Lord Howe, who passed from Boston to New York, was the very reverse, and spread everywhere the most sanguine hopes, which, however, were too soon disappointed by his melancholy but heroic death.[2] The third was Sir Geoffrey Amherst, afterward Lord Amherst, and commander in chief of the English army. Amherst, who had arrived at Boston from the conquest of Louisburg, marched with his army of four thousand men across the country, and halted a few days at Worcester, having encamped his army on the hill behind the present court house. Here we had an opportunity of seeing him, his officers and army. The officers were very social, spent their evenings and took their suppers with such of the inhabitants as were able to invite them, and entertained us with their music and their dances. Many of them were Scotchmen in their plaids, and their music was delightful; even the bagpipe was not disagreeable. The General lodged with Colonel Chandler the elder, and was very inquisitive concerning his farm, insisting on rambling over the whole of it. The excellent order and discipline observed by these troops, revived the hopes of the country, which were ultimately fully satisfied by the entire con-

1 "Yes," said Innis, "but he is like St George on the signs, always on horseback, and never rides on." *Franklin's Works*, i. p. 219. *Grahame*, iv. p. 3.

2 The Assembly of Massachusetts voted him a monument, which was placed in Westminster Abbey. *Hutchinson*, iii. p. 71.

quest of Canada, with the help of the militia of the country, which were sent on to their assistance[1] with great confidence.

At the time when Fort William Henry was besieged, there came down almost every day despatches from the General to the New England Colonies, urging for troops and assistance. Colonel Chandler the younger had sent so many expresses that he found it difficult to get persons to undertake the journeys. Complaining of this embarrassment one evening, in company, I told him I had so long led a sedentary life that my health began to fail me, and that I had an inclination to take a journey on horseback. The next morning, by daybreak, he was at my chamber door with despatches for the Governor of Rhode Island; he said a horse was ready. Without hesitation I arose and was soon mounted. Too much despatch was necessary for my comfort, and, I believe, for my health; for a journey so fatiguing, to a man who was not on horseback more than once a year on a short visit to his parents, I cannot think calculated to relieve a valetudinarian. Arrived at Providence I was informed that Mr. Greene was at Newport, with the General Assembly. I had then to ride through the Narraganset country, and to cross over Conanicut to Rhode Island. In the woods of Narraganset I met two gentlemen on horseback, of whom I took the liberty to inquire whether the Governor was still at Newport? One of them answered he was not; but the gentleman with him was the Governor. My despatches were delivered to him, and he broke the seals and read them on the spot. He said he believed the French were determined to have the country;[2] asked many questions, gave me many polite invitations to return with him to his home, which, as he said he had no answer to return by me, and as I was determined to see Newport, I civilly declined. Pursuing my journey I found a great difficulty to get over the water, as the boats and men were gone upon their usual employment. One was found after a time very tedious to me, and I landed on the island and had a good opportunity to see the whole of it, as my road to Bristol lay through the whole length

1 The then small town of Worcester alone furnished, during the fifteen years that the war with the French continued, four hundred and fifty-three men. *Lincoln's Worcester*, p. 66.

2 "It is almost incredible that four or five thousand men, most of them Canadians and savages, should give such an alarm." *Hutchinson*, iii. p. 60.

of it. To me the whole island appeared a most beautiful garden, an ornamented farm; but hostile armies have since degarnished it of a principal embellishment, the noble rows and plantations of trees. Crossing over the ferry to Bristol, I spent a night with Colonel Green, whose lady was a Church, and sister to Mrs. John Chandler. Here I was happy, and felt myself at home. Next morning I pursued my journey to Worcester. The whole was accomplished in four days, one of which was Sunday. As I was obliged to ride all that day, I had an opportunity of observing the manners of Rhode Island; — much more gay and social than our Sundays in Massachusetts.

In 1758, my period with Mr. Putnam expired. Two gentlemen, by name Doolittle and Baldwin,[1] visited me in the office, and invited me to settle in Worcester. They said, as there were two sides to a question, and two lawyers were always wanted where there was one, I might depend upon business in my profession; they were pleased to add that my character was fair, and well esteemed by all sorts of people in the town and through the county; that they wished to get me chosen at the next election, which was very near, Register of Deeds, which would procure me something handsome for the present, and insure me employment at the bar; that, as the Chandler family had engrossed almost all the public offices and employment in the town and county, they wished to select some person qualified to share with them in those honors and emoluments. My answer was, that as the Chandlers were worthy people, and discharged the duties of their offices very well, I envied not their felicity, and had no desire to set myself in opposition to them, and especially to Mr. Putnam, who had married a beautiful daughter of that family, and had treated me with civility and kindness. But there was one motive with me which was decisive. I was in very ill health; and the air of Worcester appeared to be unfriendly to me to such a degree that I panted for want of the breezes from the sea, and the pure zephyrs from the rocky mountains of my native town; that my father and mother invited me to live with them; and, as there never had been a lawyer in any country part of the then county of Suffolk,

[1] Notices of these gentlemen, afterwards active in promoting the Revolution, will be found in *Lincoln's History of Worcester*, pp. 176, 281.

I was determined at least to look into it and see if there was any chance for me. They replied that the town of Boston was full of lawyers, and many of them of established characters for long experience, great abilities, and extensive fame, who might be jealous of such a novelty as a lawyer in the country part of their county, and might be induced to obstruct me. I returned, that I was not wholly unknown to some of the most celebrated of those gentlemen; that I believed they had too much candor and generosity to injure a young man; and, at all events, I could try the experiment, and if I should find no hope of success, I should then think of some other place or some other course.]

1758.

October 5. Braintree. Yesterday I arrived here from Worcester. I am this day about beginning Justinian's Institutions, with Arnold Vinnius's notes; I took it out of the library at college. It is intituled "D. Justiniani sacratissimi Principis Institutionum sive Elementorum Libri quatuor, Notis perpetuis multo, quam hucusque, diligentius illustrati, Cura et Studio Arnoldi Vinnii J. C. Editio novissima priori emendatior et Progressu Juris civilis Romani, Fragmentis XII. Tabularum et Rerum Nominumque Indice auctior, ut ex Præfatione nostra patet."

Now I shall have an opportunity of judging of a Dutch commentator, whom the dedicator calls, "Celeberrimus suâ ætate in hâc academiâ Doctor." Let me read with attention, deliberation, distinction. Let me admire with knowledge. It is low to admire a Dutch commentator merely because he uses Latin and Greek phraseology. Let me be able to draw the true character both of the text of Justinian and of the notes of his commentator, when I have finished the book. Few of my contemporary beginners in the study of the law have the resolution to aim at much knowledge in the civil law; let me, therefore, distinguish myself from them by the study of the civil law in its native languages, those of Greece and Rome. I shall gain the consideration, and perhaps favor, of Mr. Gridley and Mr. Pratt by this means. As a stimulus let me insert in this place, Justinian's "adhortationem ad studium juris:— Summâ itaque ope et alacri studio has leges nostras accipite; et vosmetipsos sic eruditos ostendite, ut spes

S.A.Schoff.

The birth places of John and of John Quincy Adams.

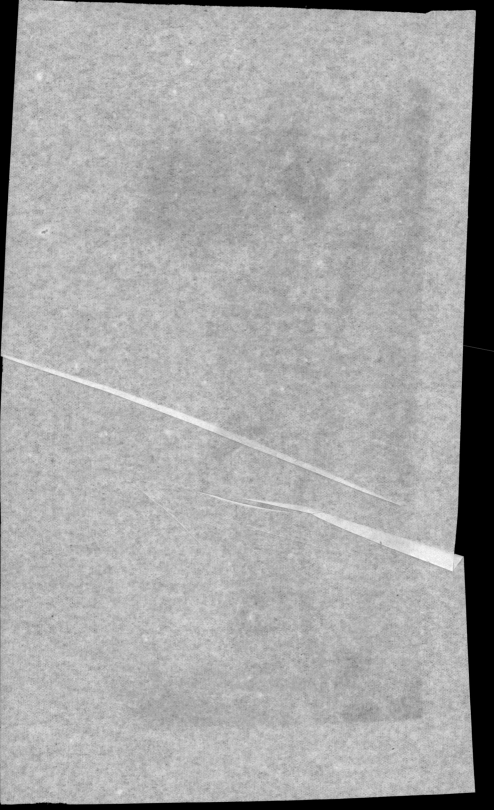

vos pulcherrima foveat, toto legitimo opere perfecto, posse etiam nostram Rempublicam in partibus ejus vobis credendis gubernari." Data Constantinopoli XI. Kalendas Decembris, Domino Justiniano perpetuo Augusto, tertiùm Consule.— *Cicero* 1 *de Orat.* "Pergite, ut facitis, adolescentes; atque in id studium, in quo estis, incumbite, ut et vobis honori, et amicis utilitati, et reipublicæ emolumento esse possitis." Arnoldus Vinnius in Academiâ Leydensi Juris Professor fuit celeberrimus.

I have read about ten pages in Justinian, and translated about four pages into English; this is the whole of my day's work. I have smoked, chatted, trifled, loitered away this whole day almost;—by much the greatest part of this day has been spent in unloading a cart, in cutting oven wood, in making and recruiting my own fire, in eating victuals and apples, in drinking tea, cutting and smoking tobacco, and in chatting with Dr. Savil's wife at their house and at this.[1] Chores,[2] chat, tobacco, tea, steal away time; but I am resolved to translate Justinian and his commentator's notes by daylight, and read Gilbert's Tenures by night, till I am master of both, and I will meddle with no other book in this chamber on a week day; on a Sunday I will read the Enquiry into the Nature of the Human Soul, and for amusement, I will sometimes read Ovid's Art of Love to Mrs. Savil. This shall be my method. I have read Gilbert's first section, of Feuds, this evening, but am not master of it.

6. Friday. Rose about sunrise, unpitched a load of hay, translated two leaves more of Justinian, and in the afternoon walked to Deacon Webb's, then around by the mill pond, home; smoked a pipe with Webb[3] at the Doctor's, and am now about reading over again Gilbert's section of Feudal Tenures.

8. Sunday. Read a few leaves in Baxter's Enquiry into the Nature of the Human Soul. He has explained with great exactness the resistance which matter makes to any change of its state or condition, whether of motion or of rest, the *vis inertiæ*,

1 The two houses were separated only by a cartway, and both belonged to the father of the author. In the one John Adams, in the other his son John Quincy, nine years after this date, was born. Both are still standing very much in their primitive state, as represented in the plate which accompanies the present volume.

2 Anglice—*chares* and *chewres*—the word, however spelt, is well understood and has the best authority for its use.

3 His cousin, Nathan Webb, before referred to.

the positive inactivity of matter, not barely its inactivity, but its antiactivity, for it not only is destitute of a power of changing its state from rest to motion or from motion to rest, but it has a positive power, — each single particle has a positive power of resisting any force that attempts to change its state. But a leaden ball held between my fingers, as soon as I withdraw my fingers will, of itself for aught I see, change its state from rest to motion and fall suddenly to the floor. This phenomenon is not *vis inertiæ;* it is by no reluctance or aversion to motion that it moves, but it seems to be a tendency to motion, an active principle. If it is passive, the agent that presses it downwards is invisible; but because matter, in all the experiments I have tried, resists a change from rest to motion upwards, will it follow that all matter essentially resists a change from rest to motion downwards? Is it *a posteriori* from experiments that he deduces this proposition that all matter essentially resists any change of state? or is it *a priori* from some property that is essentially included in our ideas of matter that he demonstratively argues this *vis inertiæ?* Is inactivity and anti-activity included in our ideas of matter? Are activity, perceptivity, &c., properties that we by only comparing ideas can see to be incompatible to any properties of matter? If nothing is matter which has not this anti-active principle, then human minds are not matter, for they have no such principle; we are conscious that we can begin and end motion of ourselves. If he argues *a posteriori* from experiments, he can pretend only to probability, for unless he was certain that he had made the experiment and found the property in every particle of matter that ever was created, he could not be certain that there was no particle in the world without this property, though he had tried all but one and found that they had it. We have tried but a few parcels of matter; the utmost we can say is, that all we have tried are inactive; but for argument's sake I will deny that all the parcels that we have tried have this property; on the contrary I will say that all have a motive power downwards; powder has an active power springing every way, &c. Thus experiment is turned against the doctrine. I cannot yet see how he will prove all matter anti-inactive *a priori* from properties of matter before known essential, with which he must show this to be necessarily connected.

9. Monday. Read in Gilbert's Tenures. I must and will make that book familiar to me.

10. Tuesday. Read in Gilbert. I read him slowly, but I gain ideas and knowledge as I go along, which I do not always when I read.

11. Wednesday. Rode to Boston; conversed with Ned Quincy[1] and Samuel, Peter Chardon, &c. By the way, Peter Chardon is a promising youth; he aspires and will reach to a considerable height; he has a sense of the dignity and importance of his profession, that of the law; he has a just contempt of the idle, incurious, pleasure-hunting young fellows of the town, who pretend to study law; he scorns the character, and he aims at a nobler; he talks of exulting in an unlimited field of natural, civil, and common law; talks of nerving, sharpening the mind by the study of law and mathematics; quotes Locke's Conduct of the Understanding; and transcribes points of law into a common-place book, on Locke's model. This fellow's thoughts are not employed on songs and girls, nor his time on flutes, fiddles, concerts, and card tables: he will make something.

12. Thursday. Examined the laws of this Province concerning roads, cattle, fences, &c., &c. Read in Gilbert. This small volume will take me a fortnight; but I will be master of it.

13. Friday. Read Gilbert. Went in the evening to Colonel Quincy's; heard a trial before him as a justice, between Jos. Field and Luke Lambert. The case was this: Lambert's horse broke into Field's inclosure and lay there some time, damage feasant.[2] When Lambert found that his horse was

[1] Edmund Quincy, the eldest of the three sons of Josiah Quincy, senior, died before the Revolution. Samuel Quincy, the second son, was afterwards Solicitor General of the Province under the Crown. He took the side of Government in the Revolution, left the country, and died in the island of Antigua, in 1789. Some interesting letters to and from this gentleman are to be found at the close of the supplement to Curwen's Journal, edited by Mr. Ward. Of the name of Chardon, one of the Huguenot families, whose transfer, under the edict of Nantes, proved as great a gain to America as it was a loss to France, no trace remains. The person named in the text was the last male of his family, and did not live long enough to verify the prediction. He went to the island of Barbadoes, where he died in 1766.

[2] The report of this, apparently the first case in which the writer became interested, though devoid of interest in itself, is retained on account of the light it throws upon his early formed habits of analytical investigation; and, because connected with the amusing incident of the defective writ, subsequently related. During many following years, not only reports of cases, but also the draughts of his own arguments are embodied in the Diary.

there, he entered the inclosure; and, although Field calls to him and forbids it, waved his hat, and screamed at the horse, and drove him away, without tendering Field his damages. This was a rescous of the horse out of Field's hands; for, although Lambert had a right to enter and take out his horse, tendering the damages, yet, as the words of the law are, "That whoever shall rescous any creature, &c., out of the hands of any person about to drive them to pound, whereby the party injured shall be liable to lose his damages, and the law be eluded, shall forfeit, &c.;" and as Field was actually about to drive them to pound, and Lambert offered him no damages, this was completely a rescous. Field, after the rescous, went to Colonel Quincy, made complaint against Lambert, and requested and obtained a warrant. The warrant was directed to the constable, who brought the offender before the justice, attended with the complainant and the witnesses ordered to be summoned.

Quincy,[1] for defendant, took exception on the warrant, to the jurisdiction of the justice; because the sum originally sued for, consisting of the forfeiture of forty shillings to the poor, and the parties' damages estimated at nine pence, which was forty shillings nine pence, was a greater sum than the justice can take cognizance of; and, because the words of this act of the province are, that this forty shillings to the poor and these damages to the party injured shall be recovered by action, &c., in any of his Majesty's courts of record;—now, as the court of a single justice is not one of his Majesty's courts of record, the forfeiture and damages prayed for in this complaint cannot be recovered in this court.

The justice adjourned his court till eight o'clock, Monday morning, in order to inform himself—1. Whether the court of a single justice of the peace was one of his majesty's courts of record? 2. Whether a single justice can take cognizance of any matter in which the sum originally prosecuted for is more than forty shillings?

If, upon examination, the Colonel shall find that a single justice has no authority to hear and determine such a rescous, at the adjournment the proceedings will be quashed, and the complainant must begin *de novo;* but if he finds that a single

[1] Samuel Quincy.

justice has authority to determine the matter, he will proceed to judgment. The questions that arise in my mind, on this case, are these.

1. What is the true idea and definition of a court of record? What courts in England, and what in this province, are courts of record, and what are not? Wood, Jacobs, &c.

2. Whether a justice has authority, by warrant, to hear and determine of any offence, the penalty of which, or the forfeiture of which, to the king, the poor, the informer, &c., is more than forty shillings?

3. Whether a court is denominated a court of record from its keeping records of its proceedings? Whether every court is a court of record whose president is a judge of record? For it seems plain in Dalton, that a justice of the peace is a judge of record.

4. On supposition the warrant should be quashed, who should pay the costs of the original warrant, of the defendant's attendance, and of witnesses' oaths and attendance? The complainant, who was mistaken, through ignorance, in going to the justice for a remedy, or the justice, who was mistaken in the same manner in acting upon the complaint beyond his authority?

5. What are the steps of prosecuting by information? Is not a motion made in court, that the information may be amended or filed? Are informations ever filed but by attorney-general? When the penalty, sued for by the information, is half to the king, or half to the poor, and the other half to the informer, is the defendant committed till he discharges the penalty, or is an execution ever issued?

6. It is said, courts of record alone have power to impose a fine or imprison. Quære, which?

7. A rescous is a breach of law, and a breach of the peace; and remedy for it may be by action of trespass, which is always *contra pacem.*

8. Are not justices' warrants confined to criminal matters? May a warrant be issued for a trespass *quare clausum fregit?* It may for a trespass of assault and battery.

Justices may punish by fine, imprisonment, stripes, &c. The Colonel inquired what punishment he could inflict on a constable for disobedience to his warrant, for not making return of his doings? He found a case ruled in King's Bench, that a constable is a subordinate officer to a justice of the peace, and is indictable at common law for neglect of duty. The malfeasance or nonfeasance of officers, are crimes and offences that may be inquired of, indicted, or presented by the grand jury at common law.

Field took Lambert's horses damage feasant in his close once before, and impounded them, and gave him verbal notice that his horses were in pound; but neglected to give either Lambert or the pound-keeper an account of the damages the horses had done him. Lambert went to the pound-keeper and demanded his horses, tendering the pound-keeper's fees, and the pound-keeper delivered them up. Now, quære, whether Field is enjoined by any law of the province to get his damages appraised, and to lodge an account of them with the pound-keeper?

2. Whether, as he neglected this, the pound-keeper cannot justify his resigning of them to the owner?

3. If Field had lodged an estimation of his damages with the pound-keeper, and the pound-keeper had nevertheless resigned the creatures up without taking the damages, would not an action lay against him, as an action lies against a prison-keeper, for a voluntary escape? and, quære, what action would be proper? I want a form of an action of escape now.

4. It cannot be called an indirect way of delivering his creatures out of pound, to pay or tender the pound-keeper his fees, and demand and receive his cattle of him when he has unlocked or opened the pound gate and turned the creatures out. So that it will not admit a query whether Lambert is liable to an action for receiving his horses of the pound-keeper. It is plain, I think, he is not.

16. Monday. Read a few pages in Gilbert. I proceed very slowly.

17. Tuesday. Read in Gilbert, went to Monatiquot[1] to see the raising of the new meeting house; no observations worth noting. I have not spirits and presence of mind to seek out scenes of observation and to watch critically the air, countenances, actions, and speeches of old men and young men, of

[1] That part of the town which has retained the name of Braintree. It constituted what was then called the middle precinct. The south precinct was afterwards set off as a town with the name of Randolph. The north precinct became the town of Quincy.

old women and young girls, of physicians and priests, of old maids and bachelors. I should chatter with a girl, and watch her behavior, her answers to questions, the workings of vanity and other passions in her breast. But objects before me do not suggest proper questions to ask and proper observations to make; so dull and confused at present is my mind.

Saw lawyer Thacher's father[1] at Mr. Niles's. He said, "old Colonel Thacher of Barnstable was an excellent man; he was a very holy man; I used to love to hear him pray; he was a counsellor and a deacon. I have heard him say that of all his titles that of a deacon he thought the most honorable." *Quære* — Is he a new light? Old age has commonly a sense of the importance and dignity of religion. I dare say he is not well pleased with his son's professing the law; he had rather have him a deacon.

18. Wednesday. Went to Boston.

Bob Paine.[2] "I have ruined myself by a too eager pursuit of wisdom. I have now neither health enough for an active life nor knowledge enough for a sedentary one."

Quincy. "We shall never make your great fellows."

Thus Paine and Quincy both are verging to despair.

Paine. "If I attempt a composition, my thoughts are slow and dull."

Paine is discouraged, and Quincy has not courage enough[3] to harbor a thought of acquiring a great character. In short, none of them have a foundation that will support them. Peter Chardon seems to me in the directest road to superiority. Paine's face has lost its bloom, and his eye its vivacity and fire; his eye is weak, his countenance pale, and his attention unsteady; and, what is worse, he suffers this decline of health to retard and

[1] Oxenbridge Thacher the elder, father of Oxenbridge the lawyer, often mentioned in this Diary. He lived at Milton, and died in 1772, at the age of ninety-three. *Eliot's Biographical Dictionary.*

[2] Robert Treat Paine. His father was for some time pastor of a church in Weymouth, the town adjoining Braintree. Eunice Paine, his sister, became an inmate of the hospitable dwelling of General Palmer, at Germantown. Hence his intimate acquaintance in Braintree. Notwithstanding this tone of despondency, the native energy of Paine's character ultimately opened to him a distinguished career in Massachusetts. A tolerably full account of him is found in Sanderson's Biography of the Signers of the Declaration of Independence.

[3] This prediction was fully verified twenty years afterwards.

almost to stop his studies; and Quincy's soul is afraid to aim at great acquisition.

Paine (to me.) "You don't intend to be a sage, I suppose?"

Oh, Paine has not penetration to reach the bottom of my mind. He don't know me; next time I will answer him, and say, "No. Knowledge enough to keep out of fire and water is all that I aim at."

19. Thursday. I borrowed yesterday of Quincy the first volume of Batista Angeloni's Letters,[1] and a "General Treatise of naval trade and commerce as founded on the laws and statutes of this realm, in which those" (laws and statutes, I suppose) "relating to his majesty's customs, merchants, masters of ships, mariners, letters of marque, privateers, prizes, convoys, cruisers, &c. are particularly considered and treated with due care under all the necessary heads, from the earliest time down to the present," second edition, in two volumes. Read Angeloni through, I believe, and studied carefully about a dozen pages in mercantile law. Angeloni's Letters are all of a piece. He has an odd system of faith, namely, that utility is truth,[2] and therefore that transubstantiation is true, and auricular confession is true, because they are useful, and promote the happiness of mankind. Therefore rain is true, because it is useful in promoting the growth of herbs and fruit and flowers, and consequently of animals, for man's use. This is very different from mathematical trûth, and this explanation of his meaning gives room to suspect that he disbelieves a revelation himself, though he thinks it useful for the world to believe it.

He reasons, Who can conceive that a being of infinite wisdom, justice, and goodness, would suffer the world to be governed two thousand years by a religion that was false? But may not this question be asked of the Mahomedans, the Chinese, in short, of every religion under heaven; and will not the argument equally prove these all to be true?

What passion is most active and prevalent in ——'s mind? The desire of money. He retails sugar by the pound, [3] by the bunch, pins, penknives, to save these articles in his family, and net a few shillings profit. He makes poor people who are

[1] This work, now deservedly forgotten, was the means of procuring for its author, Dr. Shebbeare, the distinction of the pillory in England.

[2] Vol. i. p. 91.

[3] Illegible.

in his debt pay him in labor He bargains with his debtors in the two other parishes for wood which he sends to the landing place and to Dr. Marsh's; thus by practice of physic, trading, and bargaining, and scheming, he picks up a subsistence for his family and gathers very gradually additions to his stock; but this is low. The same application and scheming in his profession would raise up and spread him a character, preserve him profitable business, and make him his fortune. But by this contemptible dissipation of mind among pins, needles, tea, snuffboxes, vendues, loads of wood, day labor, &c. he is negligent of the theory of his profession, and will live and die unknown. These drivelling souls, oh! He aims not at fame, only at a living and a fortune.

21. Saturday. Rose with the sun. I am now set down to the laws relating to naval trade and commerce. Let me inquire of the next master of a ship that I see, what is a bill of lading; what the log-book; what invoices they keep; what accounts they keep of goods received on board and of goods delivered out; what in other ports? &c.

22. Sunday. Conversed with Captain Thacher about commercial affairs.[1]

24. Tuesday. Rode to Boston; arrived about half after ten; went into the court house and sat down by Mr. Paine, at the lawyers' table. I felt shy, under awe and concern; for Mr Gridley, Mr. Pratt, Mr. Otis, Mr. Kent, and Mr. Thacher, were all present, and looked sour. I had no acquaintance with anybody but Paine and Quincy, and they took but little notice.

However, I attended court steadily all day, and at night went to consort with Samuel Quincy and Dr. Gardiner. There I saw the most spacious and elegant room, the gayest company of gentlemen, and the finest row of ladies that ever I saw; but the weather was so dull, and I so disordered, that I could not make one half the observations that I wanted to make.

25. Wednesday. Went in the morning to Mr. Gridley's* and asked the favor of his advice, what steps to take for an introduction to the practice of law in this county. He answered,

1 Here follows a minute abstract of the conversation; of bills of lading, invoices, accounts, &c.

* [Jeremiah Gridley, the father of the bar in Boston, and the preceptor of Pratt, Otis, Thacher, Cushing, and many others.]

"Get sworn." *Ego.* "But in order to that, sir, as I have no patron in this county"—— G. "I will recommend you to the court; mark the day the court adjourns to, in order to make up judgments; come to town that day, and, in the mean time, I will speak to the bar; for the bar must be consulted, because the court always inquires if it be with consent of the bar." Then Mr. Gridley inquired what method of study I had pursued, what Latin books I read, what Greek, what French? what I had read upon rhetoric? Then he took his common-place book and gave me Lord Hale's advice to a student of the common law; and when I had read that, he gave me Lord C. J. Reeve's advice to his nephew, in the study of the common law. Then he gave me a letter from Dr. Dickins, Regius Professor of Law at the University of Cambridge, to him, pointing out a method of studying the civil law; then he turned to a letter he wrote to Judge Lightfoot, Judge of the Admiralty in Rhode Island, directing to a method of studying the admiralty law. Then Mr. Gridley run a comparison between the business and studies of a lawyer, a gentleman of the bar in England and those of one here: A lawyer in this country must study common law, and civil law, and natural law, and admiralty law; and must do the duty of a counsellor, a lawyer, an attorney, a solicitor, and even of a scrivener; so that the difficulties of the profession are much greater here than in England. "The difficulties that attend the study may discourage some, but they never discouraged me." (Here is conscious superiority.) "I have a few pieces of advice to give you, Mr. Adams. One is, to pursue the study of the law, rather than the gain of it; pursue the gain of it enough to keep out of the briers,* but give your main attention to the study of it. The next is, not to marry early; for an early marriage will obstruct your improvement; and, in the next place, it will involve you in expense. Another thing is, not to keep much company, for the application of a man who aims to be a lawyer must be incessant; his attention to his books must be constant, which is inconsistent with keeping much company. In the study of law, the common law, be sure, deserves your first and last attention; and he has conquered all the difficulties of this law, who is

* [His advice made so deep an impression on my mind, that I believe no lawyer in America ever did so much business as I did afterwards, in the seventeen years that I passed in the practice at the bar, for so little profit.]

master of the Institutes. You must conquer the Institutes. The road of science is much easier now than it was when I set out; I began with Coke-Littleton, and broke through." I asked his advice about studying Greek. He answered, "It is a matter of mere curiosity." After this long and familiar conversation, we went to court, attended all day, and in the evening I went to ask Mr. Thacher's[1] concurrence with the bar; drank tea and spent the whole evening — upon original sin, origin of evil, the plan of the universe, and at last upon law. He says he is sorry that he neglected to keep a common-place book when he began to study law, and he is of half a mind to begin now. Thacher thinks this county is full.

26. Thursday. Went in the morning to wait on Mr. Pratt.[2] He inquired "if I had been sworn at Worcester?" "No." "Have you a letter from Mr. Putnam to the court?" "No." "It would have been most proper to have done one of these things first. When a young gentleman goes from me into another county, I always write in his favor to the court in that county; or, if you had been sworn there, you would have been entitled to be sworn here. But now, nobody in this county knows any thing about you, so nobody can say any thing in your favor but by hearsay. I believe you have made a proper proficiency in science, and that you will do very well, from what I have heard, but that is only hearsay."

(How different is this from Gridley's treatment! Besides, it is weak; for neither the court nor the bar will question the veracity of Mr. Gridley and Mr. Pratt. So that the only uncertainty that can remain is, whether Mr. Putnam was in earnest in the account he gave of my morals and studies to those gentlemen; which cannot be removed by a line from him, or by my being sworn at Worcester, or any other way than by getting Mr. Putnam sworn.) After this, he asked me a few short questions about the course

1 Oxenbridge Thacher. There was not a citizen of Boston more universally beloved for his learning, ingenuity, every domestic and social virtue, and conscientious conduct in every relation of life. — J. A. Mr. Tudor, who, in his Life of James Otis, has done much to embody the memory of these times, has given a happy sketch of his character. p. 57. A more particular account of him may be found in Dr. Eliot's Dictionary.

2 Benjamin Pratt is mentioned by Hutchinson as "of the first character in his profession." He was at this time a representative for Boston, the second instance of an election of a lawyer to that place. A few years after this he was made Chief Justice of New York.

of my studies, which I answered, and then came off as full of wrath as I was full of gratitude when I left Gridley the morning before. Pratt is infinitely harder of access than Gridley; he is ill-natured, and Gridley is good-natured.

Attended court all day, and at night waited on Otis,[1] at his office, where I conversed with him; and he with great ease and familiarity promised me to join the bar in recommending me to the court.* Mr. Gridley lent me Van Muyden's Compendiosa Institutionum Justiniani Tractatio in Usum Collegiorum, Editio tertia prioribus auctior et emendatior. Pax Artium Altrix. After I have mastered this, I must read Hoppius's Commentary on Justinian. The design of this book is to explain the technical terms, and to settle the divisions and distributions of the civil law. By the way, this is the first thing a student ought to aim at, namely, distinct ideas under the terms, and a clear apprehension of the divisions and distributions of the science. This is one of the principal excellencies of Hawkins's Pleas of the Crown, and it is the very end of this book of Van Muyden. Let me remark here one important neglect of the last week: I omitted minuting the names of the cases at trial in my ivory book; and I omitted to keep pen, ink and paper, at my lodgings, in order to commit to writing, at night, the cases and points of law that were argued and adjudged in the day. Let me remember to mark in my memorandum book the names of the cases, and the terms and points of law that occur in each case; to look these terms and points in the books at Otis's, Pratt's, or any other office, and to digest and write down the whole, in the evening, at my lodgings. This will be reaping some real advantage by my attendance on the courts; and without this, the observations which I may make will lie in total confusion in my mind.

27 – 30. Friday, Saturday, Sunday, Monday. All spent in absolute idleness, or, which is worse, gallanting the girls.

31. Tuesday. Sat down and recollected myself, and read a little in Van Muyden, a little in Naval Trade and Commerce.

November 2. Thursday. Rode as far as Smelt Brook, break-

1 James Otis the younger.

* [" There were so many lawyers in Boston," he said, " that it was not worth while to call upon more than three or four of them. I listened too willingly to this opinion; for I afterwards found there were several others well entitled to this respect from me, and some little offence was taken.]

fasted, made my fire, and am now set down to Van Muyden in earnest;—his Latin is easy, his definitions are pretty clear, and his divisions of the subject are judicious.

5. Sunday. Drank tea at Colonel Quincy's; he read to me a letter Colonel Gooch[1] wrote him in answer to his questions, whether a justice's court was a court of record? And then concluded: "So that Sammy was right, for he was all along of that opinion. I have forgot what your opinion was." (This must be false, or else partiality and parental affection have blotted out the remembrance, that I first started to his son Sam, and him too, the doubt whether he had jurisdiction as a justice. Sam made him really imagine what he wished had been true, namely, that he, Samuel, had started it. If he did remember, he knew it was insult to me; but I bore it. Was forgetfulness, was partiality, or was a cunning design to try if I was not vain of being the starter of the doubt, the true cause of his saying he forgot what my opinion was?)

6. Monday. Went to town; went to Mr. Gridley's office, but he had not returned to town from Brookline. Went again: not returned; attended court till after twelve, and began to grow uneasy, expecting that Quincy would be sworn, and I have no patron, when Mr. Gridley made his appearance, and on sight of me whispered to Mr. Pratt, Dana, Kent, Thacher, &c. about me. Mr. Pratt said, "Nobody knew me." "Yes," says Gridley, "I have tried him, he is a very sensible fellow." At last, he rose up, and bowed to his right hand, and said "Mr. Quincy,"—when Quincy rose up: then he bowed to me, "Mr. Adams,"—when I walked out. "May it please your honors, I have two young gentlemen, Mr. Quincy and Mr. Adams, to present for the oath of an attorney. Of Mr. Quincy, it is sufficient for me to say he has lived three years with Mr. Pratt; of Mr. Adams, as he is unknown to your honors, it is necessary to say that he has lived between two and three years with Mr. Putnam of Worcester, has a good character from him and all others who know him, and that he was with me the other day several hours, and I take it, he is qualified to study the law by his scholarship, and that he has made a very considerable, a very great proficiency

[1] See the record of the 9th August, 1760, note, for an account of this personage, in connection with a curious picture of the manners of the time.

in the principles of the law, and therefore, that the client's interest may be safely intrusted in his hands. I therefore recommend him, with the consent of the bar, to your honors for the oath." Then Mr. Pratt said two or three words, and the clerk was ordered to swear us; after the oath, Mr. Gridley took me by the hand, wished me much joy, and recommended me to the bar. I shook hands with the bar, and received their congratulations, and invited them over to Stone's to drink some punch, where the most of us resorted, and had a very cheerful chat.*

December 3 or 4. Tuesday. Bob Paine is conceited, and pretends to more knowledge and genius than he has. I have heard him say that he took more pleasure in solving a problem in algebra than in a frolic. He told me the other day, that he was as curious after a minute and particular knowledge of mathematics and philosophy as I could be about the laws of antiquity. By his boldness in company he makes himself a great many enemies; his aim in company is to be admired, not to be beloved. He asked me what Dutch commentator I meant? I said, Vinnius. "Vinnius!" says he, (with a flush of real envy, but pretended contempt,) "you cannot understand one page of Vinnius." He must know that human nature is disgusted with such incomplaisant behavior; besides, he has no right to say that I do not understand every word in Vinnius or even in [1] for he knows nothing of me. For the future let me act the part of a critical spy upon him; not that of an open, unsuspicious friend. Last superior court at Worcester, he dined in company with Mr. Gridley, Mr. Trowbridge, and several others, at Mr. Putnam's; and although a modest, attentive behavior would have best become him in such a company, yet he tried to

[1] One word illegible.

* [At this time the study of the law was a dreary ramble in comparison of what it is at this day. The name of Blackstone had not been heard, whose Commentaries, together with Sullivan's Lectures and Reeves's History of the Law, have smoothed the path of the student, while the long career of Lord Mansfield, his many investigations and decisions, the number of modern reporters in his time, and a great number of writers on particular branches of the science, have greatly facilitated the acquisition of it. I know not whether a set of the Statutes at Large or of the State Trials was in the country. I was desirous of seeking the law as well as I could in its fountains, and I obtained as much knowledge as I could of Bracton, Britton, Fleta and Glanville; but I suffered very much for want of books, which determined me to furnish myself at any sacrifice with a proper library; and accordingly, by degrees, I procured the best library of law in the State.]

engross the whole conversation to himself. He did the same in the evening, when all the judges of the superior court, with Mr. Winthrop, Sewall, &c., were present; and he did the same last Thanksgiving day at Colonel Quincy's, when Mr. Wibird, Mr. Cranch, &c. were present. This impudence may set the million agape at him, but will make all persons of sense despise him or hate him. That evening, at Putnam's, he called me a numskull and a blunderbuss before all the superior judges. I was not present indeed, but such expressions were indecent, and tended to give the judges a low opinion of me, as if I was despised by my acquaintances. He is an impudent, ill bred, conceited fellow; yet he has wit, sense, and learning, and a great deal of humor; and has virtue, and piety, except his fretful, peevish, childish complaints against the disposition of things. This character is drawn with resentment of his ungenerous treatment of me, and allowances must therefore be made; but these are unexaggerated facts.

Lambert sets up for a wit and a humorist. He is like a little knurly, ill-natured horse, that kicks at every horse of his own size, and sheers off from every one that is larger. I should mind what I say before him, for he is always watching for wry words to make into a droll story to laugh at. Such fellows are hated by all mankind; yet they rise and make a figure, and people dread them. But though men of bitter wit are hated and feared, yet they are respected by the world. *Quære*—Was there ever a wit who had much humanity and compassion, much tenderness of nature? Mr. Congreve was tender, extremely tender of giving offence to any man. Dr. Arbuthnot was a great wit and humorist, yet he was tender and prudent. Mr. Cranch has wit, and is tender and gentle.

The other night I happened to be at the Doctor's with Ben Veasey; he began to prate upon the presumption of philosophy in erecting iron rods to draw the lightning from the clouds. His brains were in a ferment, and he railed and foamed against those points and the presumption that erected them, in language taken partly from Scripture and partly from the disputes of tavern philosophy, in as wild, mad a manner as King Lear raves against his daughter's disobedience and ingratitude, and against the meanness of the storm in joining with his daughters against him, in Shakspeare's Lear. He talked of presuming upon God, as Peter attempted to walk upon the water; attempting to control the artillery of heaven — an execution that mortal man can't stay — the elements of heaven; fire, heat, rain, wind, &c.

Let me search for the clue which led great Shakspeare into the labyrinth of mental nature. Let me examine how men think. Shakspeare had never seen in real life persons under the influence of all those scenes of pleasure and distress which he has described in his works; but he imagined how a person of such a character would behave in such circumstances, by analogy from the behavior of others that were most like that character in nearly similar circumstances which he had seen.

18. Monday. I this evening delivered to Mr. Field a declaration in trespass for a rescue. I was obliged to finish it without sufficient examination. If it should escape an abatement, it is quite undigested and unclerk-like. I am ashamed of it, and concerned for it. If my first writ should be abated, if I should throw a large bill of costs on my first client, my character and business will suffer greatly; it will be said, I do not understand my business. No one will trust his interest in my hands. I never saw a writ on that law of the province. I was perplexed, and am very anxious about it. Now I feel the disadvantages of Putnam's insociability and neglect of me. Had he given me, now and then, a few hints concerning practice, I should be able to judge better at this hour than I can now. I have reason to complain of him; but it is my destiny to dig treasures with my own fingers; nobody will lend me or sell me a pickaxe. How this first undertaking will terminate, I know not; I hope the dispute will be settled between them, or submitted, and so my writ never come to an examination; but, if it should, I must take the consequences; I must assume a resolution to bear without fretting.

20. Wednesday. I am this forenoon resuming the study of Van Muyden; I begin at the ninety-ninth page.

21. Thursday. Yesterday and to-day I have read aloud Tully's four Orations against Catiline. The sweetness and grandeur of his sounds, and the harmony of his numbers, give pleasure enough to reward the reading, if one understood none of his meaning. Besides, I find it a noble exercise; it exercises

my lungs, raises my spirits, opens my pores, quickens the circulations, and so contributes much to health.

26. Tuesday. Being the evening after Christmas, the Doctor and I spent the evening with Mr. Cleverly and Major Miller. Mr. Cleverly was cheerful, alert, sociable, and complaisant; so much good sense and knowledge, so much good humor and contentment, and so much poverty, are not to be found in any other house, I believe, in this province. I am amazed, that a man of his ingenuity and sprightliness can be so shiftless. But what avails a noisy fame, a plentiful fortune, and great figure and consideration in this world? Neither Pratt nor Gridley, Mayhew nor Eliot, Stockbridge nor Hersey, appears more easy and happy, with all their wealth and reputation, than he with neither.

29. Friday. Let me see if Bob Paine don't pick up this story to laugh at.[1] Lambert will laugh, no doubt, and will tell the story to every man he sees, and will squib me about it whenever he sees me. He is impudent and unfair enough to turn this, on every occasion, to my disadvantage. Impudence, drollery, villany, in Lambert; indiscretion, inconsideration, irresolution, and ill luck in me; and stinginess, as well as ill luck, on the side of Field;—all unite in this case to injure me. Field's wrath waxed hot this morning, when he found himself defeated a second time. He wished the affair in hell, called Lambert a devil, and said, "that is always the way in this town; when any strange devil comes into town, he has all the privileges of the town."

Let me note the fatal consequences of precipitation. My first determination, what to do in this affair, was right; I determined not to meddle, but, by the cruel reproaches of my mother, by the importunities of Field, and by the fear of having it thought I was incapable of drawing the writ, I was seduced from that determination; and what is the consequence? the writ is defective. It will be said I undertook the case, but was unable to manage it; this nonsuit will be in the mouth of everybody; Lambert will proclaim it. Let me never undertake to draw a

[1] This refers to the failure of the writ, so strongly apprehended in the record of the 18th. Few of the profession have not experienced something of the state of feeling here so naturally portrayed, in connection with the first venture on a writ.

writ without sufficient time to examine and digest in my mind all the doubts, queries, objections, that may arise. But nobody will know of any abatement, except this omission of the county. An opinion will spread among the people that I have not cunning enough to cope with Lambert. I should endeavor, at my first setting out, to possess the people with an opinion of my subtlety and cunning. But this affair certainly looks like a strong proof of the contrary.

31. Sunday. Andrew Oliver[1] is a very sagacious trifler. He can decipher, with surprising penetration and patience, any thing wrote in signs, whether English, Latin, or French. But to what purpose? It is like great skill and dexterity in gaming, used only for amusement; with all his expertness he never wins any thing. But this is his way to fame. One man would be a famous orator; another a famous physician; another a famous philosopher; and a fourth a famous dancer; and he would be a famous decipherer. But I am quite content with the twenty-four letters, without inventing all the possible marks that might signify the same things. Ned Quincy is learning to be such another nugator sagax, — an artificial arrangement of dots and squares.

1759. January 3. Wednesday. Drank tea at Colonel Quincy's. Spent the evening there and the next morning. In the afternoon rode to Germantown.

H. Q.[2] or *O.* "Suppose you were in your study, engaged in the investigation of some point of law or philosophy, and your wife should interrupt you accidentally, and break the thread of your thoughts so that you never could recover it?"

Ego. "No man but a crooked Richard would blame his wife for such an accidental interruption; and no woman but a Xanthippe would insist upon her husband's company after he had given her his reasons for desiring to be alone."

O. "Should you like to spend your evenings at home in

Afterwards Judge of the Court of Common Pleas for the county of Essex. "He possessed fine talents, and was reckoned among our best scholars." *Eliot.*

2 Hannah Quincy, the daughter of Josiah, afterwards married to Dr. Lincoln, and subsequently to the late Ebenezer Storer, of Boston. A remarkable letter, addressed by her to her royalist brother, Samuel, upon his final separation from home and friends, is to be found in the supplement to Curwen's Journal, near the end.

reading and conversing with your wife, rather than spend them abroad in taverns or with other company?"

Ego. "Should prefer the company of an agreeable wife to any other company, for the most part, not always; I should not like to be imprisoned at home."

O. "Suppose you had been abroad, and came home fatigued and perplexed with business, or came out of your study wearied and perplexed with study, and your wife should meet you with an unpleasant or an inattentive face, how should you feel?"

—"I would flee my country, or she should."

O. "How shall a pair avoid falling into a passion or out of humor upon some occasions, and treating each other unkindly?"

Ego. "By resolving against it; every person knows that all are liable to mistakes and errors, and if a husband finds his wife in one, he should use reasoning and convince her of it, instead of being angry; and so, on the contrary. But if it happens that both get out of humor and an angry dispute ensues, yet both will be sorry when their anger subsides, and mutually forgive and ask forgiveness, and love each other the better for it for the future."

O. thinks more than most of her sex; she is always thinking or reading; she sits and looks steadily one way, very often several minutes together, in deep thought. E——[1] looks pert, sprightly, gay, but thinks and reads much less than O.

[2] exposed himself to ridicule by affectation, by pretensions to strength of mind and resolution, to depth and penetration. Pretensions to wisdom and virtue, superior to all the world, will not be supported by words only. If I tell a man I am wiser and better than he or any other man, he will either despise, or hate, or pity me, perhaps all three. I have not conversed enough with the world to behave rightly. I talk to Paine about Greek; that makes him laugh. I talk to Samuel Quincy about resolution, and being a great man, and study, and improving time; which makes him laugh. I talk to Ned about the folly of affecting to be a heretic; which makes him mad. I talk to Hannah and Esther about the folly of love; about despising it; about

1 Esther Quincy, the daughter of Edmund, elder brother of Josiah Quincy; afterwards married to Jonathan Sewall, frequently mentioned in this Diary.

2 One word illegible.

being above it; pretend to be insensible of tender passions; which makes them laugh. I talk to Mr. Wibird about the decline of learning; tell him I know no young fellow, who promises to make a figure; cast sneers on Dr. Marsh, for not knowing the value of old Greek and Roman authors; ask when will a genius rise that will shave his beard, or let it grow rather, and sink himself in a cell in order to make a figure? I talked to Parson Smith,[1] about despising gay dress, grand buildings and estates, fame, &c., and being contented with what will satisfy the real wants of nature.

All this is affectation and ostentation. It is affectation of learning, and virtue, and wisdom, which I have not; and it is a weak fondness to show all that I have, and to be thought to have more than I have. Besides this, I have insensibly fallen into a habit of affecting wit and humor; of shrugging my shoulders and moving and distorting the muscles of my face; my motions are stiff and uneasy, ungraceful; and my attention is unsteady and irregular. These are reflections on myself, that I make; they are faults, defects, fopperies, and follies, and disadvantages. Can I mend these faults and supply these defects?

O—— makes observations on actions, characters, events in Pope's Homer, Milton, Pope's Poems, any plays, romances, &c., that she reads; and asks questions about them in company—"What do you think of Helen? what do you think of Hector, &c.? what character do you like best? did you wish the plot had not been discovered in Venice Preserved?" These are questions that prove a thinking mind. E—— asks none such.

Thus, in a wild campaign, a dissipating party of pleasure, observations and improvements may be made; some foppery, and folly, and vice, may be discerned in one's self, and motives and methods may be collected to subdue it; some virtue or agreeable quality may be observed in one's self, and improved and cherished; or in another, and transplanted into one's self.

Though O—— knows and can practise the art of pleasing, yet she fails sometimes; she lets us see a face of ridicule and spying sometimes, inadvertently, though she looks familiarly and pleasantly for the most part. She is apparently frank, but

[1] The Rev. W. Smith, of Weymouth, to whose daughter he was subsequently married.

really reserved; seemingly pleased and almost charmed, when she is really laughing with contempt; her face and heart have no correspondence.

Hannah checks Parson Wibird with irony. "It was very saucy to disturb you, very saucy, I'm sure," &c.

I am very thankful for these checks. Good treatment makes me think I am admired, beloved, and my own vanity will be indulged in me; so I dismiss my guard, and grow weak, silly, vain, conceited, ostentatious. But a check, a frown, a sneer, a sarcasm, rouses my spirits, makes me more careful and considerate. It may, in short, be made a question, whether good treatment or bad is the best for me; that is, whether smiles, kind words, respectful actions, do not betray me into weaknesses and littlenesses that frowns, satirical speeches, and contemptuous behavior, make me avoid.

Popularity, next to virtue and wisdom, ought to be aimed at; for it is the dictate of wisdom, and is necessary to the practice of virtue in most.

Yesterday, went down to defend an action for an old horse *versus* Samuel Spear. This was undertaking the relief of distressed poverty; the defence of innocence and justice against oppression and injustice. Captain Thayer, and Major Crosby too, had told the plaintiff that he could not maintain his action, and advised him to drop it or agree it, and Thayer spoke out, "I would have these parties agree." I did not clearly understand the case, had no time to prepare, to fix in my mind, beforehand, the steps that I should take; and Captain Hollis, Major Miller, and Captain Thayer, were, all three, very active and busy, and interested themselves in the suit.

It was a scene of absolute confusion; — Major Crosby persuading an agreement; the parties raging and scolding; I arguing; and the three volunteers proposing each one his project; and all the spectators smiling, whispering, &c. My attention was dissipated, and I committed oversights, omissions, inexpert management. I should have adhered to the relation my client gave me, and believed nothing that came from the other side, without proof. I should have insisted upon the entry, and opposed any motion for an adjournment till next week, or continuance till next hour, to send for witnesses; for Madam Q. could not swear any thing that can support this action; I should have offered to admit all she could say. If I had strictly pursued the story that my client told me, I should have demanded an entry of the action, or else a dismission of the defendant with costs. It was equally idle and tame to continue the action, to send for a witness, and to submit it to referees; for the witness, if sent for, could not support the action; and to submit the original debt to referees, was to submit nothing; for, by the original agreement, nothing was due. The agreement was, to take the horse and keep him, and, if he lived till April, to pay two dollars for him; but, if he died before, to pay nothing; now, he actually died in February, and, therefore, nothing, by contract, was to be paid. The keeping of so old an horse was more than the service he could do was worth; the hay he ate would have had more riding and drawing than the horse did through that winter. If Spear had applied to such as knew, he would not have brought the writ; but deputy sheriffs, petit justices, and pettifogging meddlers, attempt to draw writs, and draw them wrong oftener than they do right. They are meddlers, hinters, and projectors. I should have made a motion to the justice, that either the defendant, or I, might be consulted in the settlement of this affair, and that ———, ———, and ———, who had no concern with it, might not determine it as they pleased.*

The other night the choice of Hercules came into my mind,

* [Looking about me, in the country, I found the practice of law was grasped into the hands of deputy sheriffs, pettifoggers, and even constables, who filled all the writs upon bonds, promissory notes, and accounts, received the fees established for lawyers, and stirred up many unnecessary suits. I mentioned these things to some of the gentlemen in Boston, who disapproved and even resented them very highly. I asked them whether some measures might not be agreed upon at the bar, and sanctioned by the court, which might remedy the evil. They thought it not only practicable, but highly expedient, and proposed meetings of the bar to deliberate upon it. A meeting was called, and a great number of regulations proposed, not only for confining the practice of law to those who were educated to it, and sworn to fidelity in it, but to introduce more regularity, urbanity, candor, and politeness, as well as honor, equity, and humanity, among the regular professors. Many of these meetings were the most delightful entertainments I ever enjoyed. The spirit that reigned was that of solid sense, generosity, honor, and integrity; and the consequences were most happy; for the courts and the bar, instead of scenes of wrangling chicanery, quibbling, and ill manners, were soon converted to order, decency, truth, and candor. Mr. Pratt was so delighted with these meetings and their effects, that when we all waited on him to Dedham, in his way to New York to take his seat as chief justice of that State, when we took leave of him, after dinner, the last words he said to us, were, "Brethren, above all things, forsake not the assembling of yourselves together."]

and left impressions there which I hope will never be effaced, nor long unheeded. I thought of writing a fable on the same plan, but accommodated, by omitting some circumstances and inserting others, to my own case.

Let Virtue address me: "Which, dear youth, will you prefer, a life of effeminacy, indolence and obscurity, or a life of industry, temperance and honor? Take my advice; rise and mount your horse by the morning's dawn, and shake away, amidst the great and beautiful scenes of nature that appear at that time of the day, all the crudities that are left in your stomach, and all the obstructions that are left in your brains. Then return to your studies, and bend your whole soul to the institutes of the law and the reports of cases that have been adjudged by the rules in the institutes; let no trifling diversion, or amusement, or company, decoy you from your book; that is, let no girl, no gun, no cards, no flutes, no violins, no dress, no tobacco, no laziness, decoy you from your books. (By the way, laziness, languor, inattention, are my bane. I am too lazy to rise early and make a fire; and when my fire is made, at ten o'clock my passion for knowledge, fame, fortune, for any good, is too languid to make me apply with spirit to my books, and by reason of my inattention my mind is liable to be called off from law by a girl, a pipe, a poem, a love-letter, a Spectator, a play, &c. &c.) But keep your law book or some point of law in your mind, at least, six hours in a day. (I grow too minute and lengthy.) Labor to get distinct ideas of law, right, wrong, justice, equity; search for them in your own mind, in Roman, Grecian, French, English treatises of natural, civil, common, statute law; aim at an exact knowledge of the nature, end, and means of government; compare the different forms of it with each other, and each of them with their effects on public and private happiness. Study Seneca, Cicero, and all other good moral writers; study Montesquieu, Bolingbroke, Vinnius, &c., and all other good civil writers."

What am I doing? shall I sleep away my whole seventy years? no, by every thing I swear I will renounce this contemplative, and betake myself to an active, roving life by sea or land, or else I will attempt some uncommon, unexpected enterprise in law; let me lay the plan, and arouse spirit enough to push boldly. I swear I will push myself into business; I'll watch my opportunity to speak in court, and will strike with surprise—surprise bench, bar, jury, auditors and all. Activity, boldness, forwardness, will draw attention. I'll not lean with my elbows on the table forever, like Read, Swift, Fitch, Skinner, Story, &c.; but I will not forego the pleasure of ranging the woods, climbing cliffs, walking in fields, meadows, by rivers, lakes, &c., and confine myself to a chamber for nothing. I'll have some boon in return, exchange; fame, fortune, or something.

Here are two nights and one day and a half spent in a softening, enervating, dissipating series of hustling, prattling, poetry, love, courtship, marriage; during all this time I was seduced into the course of unmanly pleasures that Vice describes to Hercules, forgetful of the glorious promises of fame, immortality and a good conscience, which Virtue makes to the same hero as rewards of a hardy, toilsome, watchful life in the service of mankind. I could reflect with more satisfaction on an equal space of time spent in a painful research of the principles of law, or a resolute attempt of the powers of eloquence. But where is my attention? Is it fixed from sunrise to midnight on Grecian, Roman, Gallic, British law, history, virtue, eloquence? I don't see clearly the objects that I am after; they are often out of sight; motes, atoms, feathers, are blown into my eyes and blind me. Who can see distinctly the course he is to take and the objects that he pursues, when in the midst of a whirlwind of dust, straws, atoms, and feathers?

Let me make this remark. In Parson Wibird's company something is to be learned of human nature, human life, love, courtship, marriage. He has spent much of his life from his youth in conversation with young and old persons of both sexes, married and unmarried, and yet has his mind stuffed with remarks and stories of human virtues and vices, wisdom and folly, &c. But his opinion, out of poetry, love, courtship, marriage, politics, war, beauty, grace, decency, &c., is not very valuable; his soul is lost in a dronish effeminacy. I'd rather be lost in a whirlwind of activity, study, business, great and good designs of promoting the honor, grandeur, wealth, happiness of mankind.

Pratt. "There is not a page in Flavel's works without several sentences of Latin; yet the common people admire him. They admire his Latin as much as his English and understand it as well."

[1] "preached the best sermon that I ever heard; it was plain common sense. But other sermons have no sense at all; they take the parts of them out of their concordances, and connect them together, head and tail." How greatly elevated above common people and above divines is this lawyer? Is not this vanity, littleness of mind?

February 1.* I intend a journey to Worcester to-morrow. How many observations shall I make on the people at Weston and Worcester, and how many new ideas, hints, rules of law and eloquence, shall I acquire before I return? Let my journal answer this question after my return.

2. At Weston, in Dr. Webb's chamber at Hammond's. His landlady is an odd woman; she seems good-natured and obliging too, but she has so many shrugs, grimaces, affectations of wit, cunning, and humor, as make her ridiculous. She is awkward, shamefaced, bashful, yet would fain seem sprightly, witty, &c. She is a squaddy, masculine creature, with a swarthy pale face, a great, staring, rolling eye, a rare collection of disagreeable qualities. I have read several letters this afternoon and evening in the Turkish Spy.[2]

11. Worcester. I have been in this town a week this night. How much have I improved my health by exercise, or my mind by study or conversation in this space? I have exercised little, eat, and drank, and slept intemperately; have inquired a little of Mr. Putnam and of Abel Willard concerning some points of practice in law; but dining once at Colonel Chandler's, once at Mr. Paine's, once at the Doctor's, drinking tea once at Mr. Paine's, once at the Doctor's, and spending one evening at the Doctor's, one at Gardner's, and several at Putnam's in company, has wasted insensibly the greatest and best part of my time since I have been in town.

Oh! how I have fulfilled the vain boast I made to Dr. Webb of reading twelve hours a day! What a fine scene of study

1 The name is illegible.

2 A work, once read with great avidity, but now entirely neglected.

* [The next year after I was sworn was the memorable year 1759, when the conquest of Canada was completed by the surrender of Montreal to General Amherst. This event which was so joyful to us, and so important to England, if she had seen her true interest, inspired her with a jealousy which ultimately lost her thirteen colonies, and made many of us at the time regret that Canada had ever been conquered.]

is this office![1] a fine collection of law, oratory, history, and philosophy! But I must not stay. I must return to Braintree; I must attend a long superior court at Boston. How shall I pursue my plan of study?

Braintree. *Mr. Marsh.* "Father Flynt[2] has been very gay and sprightly this sickness. Colonel Quincy went to see him a Fast day, and was or appeared to be, as he was about taking leave of the old gentleman, very much affected; the tears flowed very fast. 'I hope sir,' says he in a voice of grief, 'you will excuse my passions.' 'Ay, prithee,' says the old man, 'I don't care much for you nor your passions neither.' Morris said to him 'You are going, sir, to Abraham's bosom; but I don't know but I shall reach there first.' 'Ay, if you are going there I don't want to go.'"[3]

I spent one evening this week at Billy Belcher's. I sat, book in hand, on one side of the fire, while Doctor Wendell, Billy Belcher, and Stephen Cleverly, and another young gentleman, sat in silence round the card table all the evening. Two evenings I spent at Samuel Quincy's in the same manner. Doctor Gardiner, Henry Quincy, Ned Quincy, and Samuel Quincy, all playing cards the whole evening. This is the wise and salutary amusement that young gentlemen take every evening in this town. Playing cards, drinking punch and wine, smoking tobacco, and swearing, &c. &c., while a hundred of the best books lie on the shelves, desks, and chairs in the same room. This is not misspense of time; this is a wise a profitable improvement of time — cards and backgammon are fashionable diversions. I know not how any young fellow can study in this town. What pleasure can a young gentleman who is capable of thinking, take in playing cards? It gratifies none of the senses, neither sight, hearing, taste, smelling, nor feeling; it can

[1] Probably written in Mr. Putnam's office.

[2] Henry Flynt, a tutor in Harvard University upwards of fifty-five years, and about sixty years a fellow of the corporation, familiarly called *Father Flynt.* He lived a bachelor, and was noted for his facetiousness and humor mingled with gravity. His sister had married Judge Edmund Quincy of Braintree, in whose house, still standing, though gone out of the hands of the family, is a room which is yet known as Flynt's study. Peirce's *History of Harvard University*, quoted in Mr. Lunt's *Century Discourses.*

[3] Akin to this is the following anecdote: — In a company of gentlemen, where Father Flynt, who was a preacher, was present, Mr. Whitefield said "It is my opinion that Doctor Tillotson is now in hell for his heresy." Father Flynt replied, "It is my opinion that you will not meet him there." *Collections of the Massachusetts Historical Society*, vol. xiii. p. 211.

entertain the mind only by hushing its clamors. Cards, backgammon, &c. are the great antidotes to reflection, to thinking, that cruel tyrant within us! What learning or sense are we to expect from young gentlemen in whom a fondness for cards, &c. outgrows and chokes the desire of knowledge?

March 14. Reputation ought to be the perpetual subject of my thoughts, and aim of my behavior. How shall I gain a reputation? how shall I spread an opinion of myself as a lawyer of distinguished genius, learning, and virtue? Shall I make frequent visits in the neighborhood, and converse familiarly with men, women, and children, in their own style, on the common tittletattle of the town and the ordinary concerns of a family, and so take every fair opportunity of showing my knowledge in the law? But this will require much thought and time, and a very particular knowledge of the province law and common matters, of which I know much less than I do of the Roman law. Shall I endeavor to renew my acquaintance with those young gentlemen in Boston who were at college with me, and to extend my acquaintance among merchants, shopkeepers, tradesmen, &c., and mingle with the crowd upon Change, and traipse the town-house floor with one and another, in order to get a character in town? But this, too, will be a lingering method and will require more art, and address, and patience, too, than I am master of. Shall I, by making remarks and proposing questions to the lawyers at the bar, endeavor to get a great character for understanding and learning with them? But this is slow and tedious, and will be ineffectual; for envy, jealousy, and self-interest, will not suffer them to give a young fellow a free, generous character, especially me. Neither of these projects will bear examination, will avail. Shall I look out for a cause to speak to, and exert all the soul and all the body I own, to cut a flash, strike amazement, to catch the vulgar; in short, shall I walk a lingering, heavy pace, or shall I take one bold determined leap into the midst of fame, cash, and business? That is the question; — a bold push, a resolute attempt, a determined enterprise, or a slow, silent, imperceptible creeping; shall I creep or fly?

I feel vexed, fretted, chafed; the thought of no business mortifies, stings me. But let me banish these fears; let me assume a fortitude, a greatness of mind.

In such a slow, gradual ascent to fame and fortune and business, the pleasure that they give will be imperceptible; but by a bold, sudden rise, I shall feel all the joys of each at once. Have I genius and resolution and health enough for such an achievement?

"Means not, but blunders round about a meaning."

M—— has a very confused, blundering way of asking questions. She never knows distinctly what she is after, but asks, at random, any thing, and has a difficulty of recollecting the names of things. The names of things do not flow naturally into my mind when I have occasion to use them. I had the idea of the General Court in my mind when I said to Otis, the judges had some important business to do in, &c.; but the words, General Court, did not arise with the idea, and, therefore, Otis thought I made a silly speech. My aunt C—— has the same difficulty of recollecting words and ideas, too, especially of things that are some time past. A slothful memory, — a slow, heavy memory, in opposition to a quick, prompt memory.

Common people are not incapable of discerning the motives and springs of words and actions.

18. Monday. This whole day is dedicated to walking, riding, talk, &c.; no reading to-day.

It was avarice, not compassion, that induced —— to pass the last court; he was afraid that P—— would be provoked to appeal both to the superior court, if he put both in suit, and so keep him out of his money six or eight months; six months without interest! It is fear of losing the interest upon interest, that induces him to pass this court. Oh, love of money! oh, avarice, disguised under the show of compassion!

"Oh! but a wit can study in the streets,
And raise his mind above the mob he meets." [1]

[1] Here follow a series of desultory reflections unconnected with each other, and with any action, which seem, nevertheless, to have a bearing upon the general character of the writer.

Who can study in Boston streets? I am unable to observe the various objects that I meet, with sufficient precision. My eyes are so diverted with chimney-sweepers, sawyers of wood, merchants, ladies, priests, carts, horses, oxen, coaches, market-men and women, soldiers, sailors; and my ears with the rattle-gabble of them all, that I cannot think long enough in the street, upon any one thing, to start and pursue a thought. I cannot raise my mind above this mob crowd of men, women, beasts, and carriages, to think steadily. My attention is solicited every moment by some new object of sight, or some new sound. A coach, cart, a lady, or a priest, may at any time, by breaking a couplet, disconcert a whole page of excellent thoughts.

What is meant by "a nodding beam and pig of lead?"[1] He means that his attention is necessary to preserve his life and limbs, as he walks the street; for sheets of lead may fall from the roofs of houses. I know of no nodding beam, except at the hay market.

Shebbeare's dedication is in a strain of ironical, humorous satire. He reasons as warmly and positively as if in earnest, in his favor; but his reasoning is so manifestly weak, and, in some places, ambiguous, that every reader knows his true intention. This system of religion is indeed new. Religious institutions are mere means of increasing and preserving piety and virtue in the world; and any thing that will produce public and private advantages on the happiness and morals of a nation, however repugnant to common sense, as transubstantiation, e. g., is true.

April 8. Sunday. Spent the evening at Captain Bracket's. A case was proposed, and my opinion asked, which gave me opportunity to display some knowledge of law, but betrayed me into mistaken dogmatism. I am frequently exposing my ignorance of the province law, but things are started that put me upon examination.

It is in vain to expect felicity without an habitual contempt of fortune, fame, beauty, praise, and all such things; unaffected

[1] "And then a nodding beam, or pig of lead,
God knows, may hurt the very ablest head."
Pope's *Imitation of Horace's Second Epistle.*

benevolence to men, and conscious integrity, are sufficient supports. I have no money, but I have an easy heart, a quiet mind. God made us to be happy. I distress myself. This *animi magnitudo* and *rerum humanarum contemptio* are alone secure of happiness. Oh! stoics, you are wise.

What passions or affections, in human nature, are affected by satire, by humor, and drollery? There is some affection in human nature which is delighted with humor and satire; for a good deal of it is to be seen and heard in all nations, and among all ranks of people; it prevails in every country parish, may be found in every tavern, at every town meeting through the province.

F. Oh, blessed storm! the storm blowed me away; oh, blessed storm! This was spoken in person of one of the new selectmen, as Bracket, Thayer, &c.; and upon this secret principle, that an advantage had been meanly taken of the thinness of the meeting to get a change of town officers; so that it hinted at their meanness and want of influence in town. Their influence was not sufficient to have carried a vote, had the town been together; but they were mean enough to seize the opportunity, when three fourths of the town were detained at home by the storm, to assemble their crew of debtors and laborers, and accomplish their projects as they pleased.

Thus the wit of this lay in hinting at their meanness of soul and insignificancy in the town; it hinted that the point was carried, not by merit nor by real popularity, but by mean and clandestine artifice and plotting. How great is the dread of satire and ridicule in human nature! Mrs. S. is afraid of Colonel Quincy and his wife; he will laugh at her shape, dress, behavior. I used to dread J. O. and B. K., because I suspected they laughed at me; I used to dread Putnam, because of his satirical and contemptuous smiles.

Another reason, we were pleased to see the old gentleman diverting himself and laughing at the success of their artifices to depose him, instead of being angry and scolding. What passions are pleased in the reader or hearer, and what are vexed in the person ridiculed?

Ruggles's[1] grandeur consists in the quickness of his apprehension, steadiness of his attention, the boldness and strength of his thoughts and expressions, his strict honor, conscious superiority, contempt of meanness, &c. People approach him with dread and terror. Gridley's grandeur consists in his great learning, his great parts, and his majestic manner; but it is diminished by stiffness and affectation. Ruggles is as proud, as lordly, as Gridley, but he is more popular; he conceals it more, he times it better; and it is easy and natural in him, but is stiff and affected in Gridley. It is an advantage to Ruggles's character, but a disadvantage to Gridley's. Gridley has a bold, spirited manner of speaking, but is too stiff, has too little command of the muscles of his face; his words seem to pierce and search, to have something quick and animating; he is a great reasoner, and has a very vivid imagination. Pratt has a strong elastic spring, or what we call smartness, and strength in his mind; his ideas seem to lie deep and to be brought up with a strong effort of the mind; his ideas are vivid, and he sees their differences.

Otis is extremely quick and elastic; his apprehension is as quick as his temper. He springs and twitches his muscles about in thinking.

Thacher has not the same strength and elasticity; he is sensible but slow of conception and communication; he is queer and affected—he is not easy.

Colonel Quincy. "I learned to write letters of Pope, and Swift, &c. I should not have wrote a letter with so much correctness as I can, if I had not read and imitated them. The faculty has come to me strangely, without any formed design of acquiring it." There is a concealed encomium on himself, his

[1] Timothy Ruggles, a person, who, with the exception of Hutchinson, probably staked more of influence and property upon his activity on the loyal side than anybody in Massachusetts. At this time he was keeping a tavern and practising law in Sandwich, dividing the business of that section of the colony with the elder Otis; but he soon afterwards removed to Hardwick, in the county of Worcester, and became the political combatant of the younger Otis in the General Court. He was the President of the Congress of 1765, refused to sign the address which it adopted, and received, therefor, the censure of the House. He subsequently took an active part in organizing the loyalists in the field. He died in Nova Scotia in 1798. *Sabine's American Loyalists.*

own letters, in this remark; but there is an observation, too, which is worth considering. Men wear themselves by slow and imperceptible degrees into confirmed habits of thinking, speaking, and acting; he began early in life, I suppose, perhaps at college, to read those smooth soft writers, and although he never formed any design of imitating their ease and politeness, yet he gradually wore it into his mind. He learned to write as children learn to speak, without thinking what they do. Perhaps, had he formed a design in his youth of acquiring that faculty, and read authors with that design, he would have acquired it much sooner and more perfectly. The principle in nature is imitation, association of ideas, and contracting habits. How naturally we imitate, without design or with, modes of thinking, speaking, acting, that please us. Thus, we conform gradually to the manners and customs of our own family, neighborhood, town, province, nation, &c. At Worcester I learned several turns of mind of Putnam, and at Boston, I find myself imitating Otis, &c. But, *quære*—who will learn the art soonest and most perfectly, he who reads without a design of extracting beauties, or he who reads with? The last, undoubtedly. Design attends and observes nicely and critically. I learned with design to imitate Putnam's sneer, his sly look, and his look of contempt. This look may serve good ends in life, may procure respect.

To form a style, therefore, read constantly the best authors; get a habit of clear thinking, and strength, and propriety and harmony of expression. This one principle of imitation would lead me through the whole human system; a faculty acquired accidentally, without any endeavors or foresight of the effect. He read for amusement, not to learn to write. Let me recollect and con over all the phenomena of imitation, that I may take advantage of this principle in my own case; that I may learn easier and sooner.

The road is walled on each side with a grove of trees. The stillness, silence, and the uniformity of the prospect, put the mind into a stirring, thoughtful mood.

But the reflections that are made in a grove, are forgotten in the town; and the man who resembles a saint in his thoughts, in the first, shall resemble a devil, in his actions, in the last.

In such silent scenes as riding or walking through the woods, or sitting alone in my chamber, or lying awake in my bed, my thoughts commonly run upon knowledge, virtue, books, &c; though I am apt to forget these in the distracting bustle of the town, and ceremonious converse with mankind.

This morning rode to Moses French's, to get him to serve a writ for me. He told me he was not yet sworn, but was obliged to me for coming to him, and would be glad to serve me at any time, and would now, rather than it should be any damage to me.

Thus, he was pleased, I hope secured; men are only secured by falling in with their inclination, by favoring their hopes, clearing their prospects. Then I went to Wales's; he was not at home. I followed him to Germantown. He served the writ; we returned together. He seemed quite pleasant; told me the practice of the two ——. They drive a great stroke. There is ——, ——, are all pettifogging dabblers in iniquity and law. I might except ——, and, perhaps, ——, from the iniquitous part. I hope that Wales and French are secured to me. How they love —— I cannot say. I hope they will recommend me to persons that they hear speaking of business, as William Veasey did. Veasey knew me and mentioned me to S——.

The difference between a whole day, and a divided, scattered day. *Quære* — Can any man take a book into his hand, in the morning, and confine his thoughts to that till night? Is not such a uniformity tiresome? Is not variety more agreeable and profitable, too? Read one book one hour; then think an hour; then exercise an hour; then read another book an hour; then dine, smoke, walk, cut wood; read aloud another hour; then think, &c; and thus spend the whole day in perpetual variation, from reading to thinking, exercise, company, &c. But what is to be argued by this wavering life, but a habit of levity, and impatience of thought? I never spent a whole day upon one book in my life. What is the reason that I cannot remove all papers and books from my table, take one volume into my hands and read it, and then reflect upon it till night, without wishing for my pen and ink to write a letter, or take down any other book, or think of the girls? Because I can't command my attention. My thoughts are roving from girls to friends, from friends to court, to Worcester, Newbury, and then to Greece and Rome, then to law; from poetry to oratory, and law. Oh! a rambling imagination! Could I fix my attention, and keep off every fluttering thought that attempts to intrude upon the present subject, I could read a book all day.

> "Wisdom (curse on it) will come soon or late.
>
> . . . .
>
> I'll learn to smooth and harmonize my mind,
> Teach every thought within its bounds to roll,
> And keep the equal measure of the soul."

Accidents, as we call them, govern a great part of the world, especially marriages. S—— and E—— broke in upon H—— and me, and interrupted a conversation that would have terminated in a courtship, which would have terminated in a marriage, which marriage might have depressed me to absolute poverty and obscurity, to the end of my life; but that accident separated us, and gave room for ——'s addresses, which have delivered me from very dangerous shackles, and left me at liberty, if I will but mind my studies, of making a character and a fortune.

Now let me collect my thoughts, which have been long scattered among girls, father, mother, grandmother, brothers, matrimony, hustling, chat, provisions, clothing, fuel, servants for a family, and apply them with steady resolution and an aspiring spirit to the prosecution of my studies.

Now let me form the great habits of thinking, writing, speaking. Let my whole courtship be applied to win the applause and admiration of Gridley, Pratt, Otis, Thacher, &c. Let love and vanity be extinguished, and the great passions of ambition, patriotism, break out and burn. Let little objects be neglected and forgot, and great ones engross, arouse, and exalt my soul. The mind must be aroused, or it will slumber. I found a passion growing in my heart, and a consequent habit of thinking, forming and strengthening in my mind, that would have ate out every seed of ambition in the first, and every wise design or plan in the last.

Yesterday afternoon a plea *puis darein continuance* was argued, by Mr. Pratt for the plea, and Gridley and Otis against it. The plea was, that after the last continuance, and before the first day of the sitting of this court, this term, namely, on such a day, one Allen, one of the plaintiffs, died. Mr. Pratt argued that the writ must abate; for it was clear law that the writ, in this case, was *ipso facto* abated, and might be dismissed at the motion of any person as *amicus curiæ;* and of this opinion was the whole court. Gridley took an exception to the plea, as imperfect, in not giving the plaintiff a better writ. The whole afternoon was spent in arguing this point, and twenty volumes of Institutes and reporters, I suppose, were produced as authorities.

(*Otis*, aside. "It makes me laugh to see Pratt lug a cartload of books into court, to prove a point as clear as the sun. The action is as dead as a hub.")

Otis. "I will grant Mr. Pratt, very readily, that there has been a time, since William the Conqueror, when this plea would have abated this writ in England. But, I take it, that abatements at this day are rather odious than favored, and I don't believe that this plea could abate this writ, at any time within this century, in Westminster Hall."

Is it not absurd to study all arts but that of living in the world, and all sciences but that of mankind? Popularity is the way to gain and figure.

The arts of gain are necessary; you may get more by studying town meeting and training days, than you can by studying Justinian and all his voluminous and heavy commentators.

Mix with the crowd in a tavern, in the meeting-house, or the training field, and grow popular by your agreeable assistance in the tittletattle of the hour; never think of the deep hidden principles of natural, civil, or common law, for thoughts like these will give you a gloomy countenance and a stiff behavior.

I should talk with T——, L——, C——, &c. &c., about changing horses. Offer to change or sell, trade in any thing.

It is certain that retirement will lose its charms if it is not interrupted by business and activity. I must converse and deal with mankind, and move and stir from one scene of action and debate and business and pleasure and conversation to another, and grow weary of all, before I shall feel the strong desire of retiring to contemplation on men and business and pleasure and books.

After hard labor at husbandry, reading and reflection in retirement will be a relief and a high, refined pleasure; after attending a town meeting, watching the intrigues, arts, passions, speeches, that pass there, a retreat to reflect, compare, distinguish, will be highly delightful; so after a training day, after noting the murmurs, complaints, jealousies, impudence, envy, that pass in the field, I shall be pleased with my solitude.

Transitions from study to business, from business to conversation and pleasure, will make the revolution of study still more agreeable and perhaps not less profitable; for we are very apt in total retirement to forget the sciences and to smoke and trifle and drone it too much.

I have been very negligent and faulty in not treating Deacon S——, Nat B——, Deacon B——, &c., with more attention and sprightliness; I should bow and look pleasant to Deacon S——, and talk with him about news, war, ministers, sermons, &c.; should watch critically every word that Nat B—— says, and let him see by the motions of the muscles of my face that I have discernment between wise and foolish, witty and silly, candid and ill-natured, grave and humorous speeches, and let him know on proper occasions I can vent a smart repartee; should always speak and shake hands with the Deacon, inquire after his wife, sons, &c., and humor his talkative disposition. It is of no small importance to set the tongues of old and young men and women a prating in one's favor. As to Doctor Savil and his wife, I have dismissed all my guards before them, and acted and spoken at random. I might easily gain their warmest words and assiduous assistance, by visiting seldomer, by using tender and soothing, instead of rough and reproachful language, and by complying with their requests of riding out with her, and reading plays once in a while to them in the evening. But I have been rash, boastful, profane, uncivil, blustering, threatening, before them.

Let me remark Parson Wibird's popularity. He plays with babies and young children that begin to prattle, and talks with their mothers, asks them familiar, pleasant questions about their affection to their children; he has a familiar, careless way of conversing with people, men and women; he has wit and humor. Ripping, that is, using the words faith, devil, I swear, damnable, cursed, &c., displeases the Doctor, but especially his wife. Threatening to quarrel with Thayer, Penniman, Hollis, &c., disgusts them, especially her.

Asserting dogmatically on points of province law, which he knows more of than I by several years experience and conversation with people concerning their estates, lawsuits, &c., and being fretted, disgust them very much. I have more faults, mistakes, imprudences, follies, rashness, to answer for in the Doctor's house than in all the town besides.

I am to attend a vendue this afternoon at Lambert's; my father, Bracket, and Thayer, are a committee to lease out the town lands to the highest bidder. Let me remark the management of the sale and the behavior of persons, especially of Thayer and Bracket; watch his treatment of people and their treatment of him. Let me ask myself this question when I return: What have I seen, heard, learned? what hint observed to lift myself into business? what reputation or disgrace have I got by attending this vendue? My character will be spread and mended, or injured by it.

I was consulted by two men this afternoon, who would not have applied to me if I had not been at vendue;— E. Niles, and Elijah Belcher. And the questions they asked have led me into useful thoughts and inquiries. I find hints and inquiries arise sooner in the world than in my study.

It would be an agreeable and useful speculation to inquire into that faculty which we call imagination; define it, inquire the good ends it answers in the human system, and the evils it sometimes produces.

What is the use of imagination? It is the repository of knowledge. By this faculty are retained all the ideas of visible objects, all the observations we have made in the course of life, on men, and things, ourselves, &c.

I am conscious that I have the faculty of imagination; that I can at pleasure revive in my thoughts the ideas and assemblages of ideas that have been before in my mind; can revive the scenes, diversions, sports of childhood, youth; can recall my youthful rambles to the farms, frolics, dalliances, my lonely walks through the groves, and swamps, and fields, and meadows at Worcester;

can imagine myself with the wildest tribe of Indians in America, in their hunting, their wars, their tedious marches through wild swamps and mountains; can fly, by this faculty, to the moon, planets, fixed stars, unnumbered worlds; can cross the Atlantic and fancy myself in Westminster Hall, hearing causes in the courts of justice, or the debates in the House of Commons or Lords. As all our knowledge is acquired by experience, that is, by sensation or reflection, this faculty is necessary to retain the ideas we receive, and the observations we make, and to recall them for our use as occasion requires.

I am conscious, too, that this faculty is very active and stirring; it is constantly in action, unless interrupted by the presence of external objects, by reading, or restrained by attention; it hates restraint, it runs backward to past scenes, &c., or forward to the future; it flies into the air, dives in the sea, rambles to foreign countries, or makes excursions to foreign, planetary, starry worlds.

These are but hints, irregular observations, not digested into order; but what are the defects of this faculty? what are the errors, vices, habits, it may betray us into if not searched? what is the danger? I must know all the ends of this faculty and all its phenomena before I can know all its defects; its phenomena are infinitely various in different men, and its ends are different; therefore its defects must be almost infinitely various; but all its defects may be reduced to general laws. The sphere of imagination includes both actuality and possibility; not only what is, but what may be.

Thacher. "Pownal's style is better than Shirley's; Shirley never promoted any man for merit alone. If Satan himself were incarnate, and in competition with Parson Wells for the election, I would vote for old Harry. I can't think that any man of true good sense can be so vain and fond of talking of himself, as Parson Wells. Tully was not a vain man; the vainest thing that ever he said was in his Oration for Muræna; that if they provoked him he would profess himself a lawyer in three days. I wish myself a soldier; I look upon these private soldiers, with their guns upon their shoulders, as superior to me."

These are all wild, extravagant, loose opinions and expressions; he expresses himself as wildly as Colonel Chandler—wild flights;

he has not considered that these crude thoughts and wild expressions are catched and treasured as proofs of his character. He is extremely tender, and sensible of pleasure and of pain.

Kent[1] is for fun, drollery, humor, flouts, jeers, contempt. He has an irregular, immethodical head, but his thoughts are often good, and his expressions happy.

Thacher's passions are easily touched, his shame, his compassion, his fear, his anger, &c.

Fortune has burned Colonel Quincy's house and some of his furniture.[2] Fortune is a capricious goddess; she diverts herself with men; she bestows her favors sometimes with very great profusion on a man, and within a few years she strips him even of necessaries. It is a fluctuating state. We are tossed on the waves sometimes to heaven, and then sunk down to the bottom.

That house and furniture clung and twined round his heart, and could not be torn away without tearing to the quick. Is it possible to preserve a serene, undisturbed mind, through such a fire and the consequences of it? There is, in human nature, an attainable magnanimity which can see a valuable house full of furniture consuming in flames, a friend, a child, a wife, struggling in the agonies of death, without a sigh, a tear, or a painful sensation or reflection. The "*felicis animi immota tranquillitas*," the immovable tranquillity of a happy mind, unmoved by perils of water or of fire, unmoved by any losses, accidents, by loss of wealth, of fame, of friends, &c., — happy mind indeed! Cannot a mind be called happy unless its tranquillity, its ease, its rest, is immovable, invincible?

1 Benjamin Kent. An eccentric member of the bar, whose humor too often verged upon profanity to be acceptable to the people of his generation. Although early associated with the Whigs, he finally accompanied or followed his daughter, the wife of Sampson Salter Blowers, to Halifax; and for this has been set down, in late publications, as a loyalist; but a curious letter, which will be found in a note under date 5 November, 1771, in the present volume, seems to show that his mind had taken in all the principles of the Revolution, even in advance of the Declaration of Independence. We must, therefore, impute his emigration to some other cause than his loyalty.

2 Josiah Quincy met with this misfortune twice in the course of his life. At this period (17 May, 1759,) he occupied a house situated upon what is now called the Hancock lot, in the town of Quincy, noted as the spot where the Rev. John Hancock, the pastor of the parish, lived and died, and where his more celebrated son was born.

It is not at all surprising that the Colonel is more dejected than his brother was. For though his brother's reduction was more complete, yet the Colonel's was less expected. Ned was reduced to be worse than nothing. Josiah has a competency left. But Josiah's loss was entirely unforeseen, unexpected, and unprepared for. Ned's was, I presume, familiarly known and considered by him at least, beforehand.

Edmund lost a son as suddenly as the Colonel lost his house, and he showed as much anxiety, too; he could not sleep all night after he heard of it. The Colonel's grief is more eloquent than Ned's.

Disappointments are misery. If a man takes pride and pleasure in a house, or in rich furniture, or clothing, or in any thing, how is it possible for him to be satisfied when they are lost, destroyed, consumed?

> "Not to admire is all the art I know,
> To make men happy, and to keep them so."

Colonel admired his house; it is burned, he is unhappy, &c. They are burned, he is unhappy.

I made some observations on barberry bushes, sumach, caterpillars, &c.

Inquire the properties of isinglass and of carpenters' glue; how the first attracts all the pumice and sediment in cider to the bottom, and the latter to the top.

Inquire how the juice lies in the apple; what is the cause of its natural fermentation; and inquire the operation of artificial fermentation.

You regret your loss;[1] but why? Was you fond of seeing or of thinking that others saw and admired so stately a pile? or was you pleased with viewing the convenient and elegant contrivance of the inside, and with showing to others how neatly it was finished? Is it the pleasure of seeing, with your own eyes, the elegance and grandeur of your house, or is it the pleasure of imagining that others admired it, and admired or envied you

[1] This seems to have been part of a letter addressed to Josiah Quincy, upon the loss of his house by fire, as noticed in the preceding page.

for it, that you regret the loss of? Did you suppose that you was esteemed and regarded for the beauty and conveniency of your house? or are you mortified to think that your enemies will be gratified at your misfortune? If these are the sources of your grief, it is irrational, unmanly; for the friendship that is founded on your figure and estate, is not worth preserving; and the man who can rejoice at your loss, is not worth attention. But, if you consider it as a punishment of your vices and follies, as a frown that is designed to arouse your attention to things of a more permanent nature, you should not grieve, but rejoice that the great Parent of the world has thus corrected you for your good.

Figure and show may, indeed, attract the eyes and admiration of the vulgar, but are little, very little, regarded by wise men. Is it not rational, noble, to dote on the pleasure of viewing a fine horse, and being seen by others to ride such a one? A fine horse, riches, learning, make people stare at me and talk about me; and a mighty boon this, to be stared at, and talked of by people that I despise; and all that I regard will love and honor me for acquisitions, that I have power to make and which cannot be torn from me. Wisdom and virtue are not dependent on the elements of fire or water, air or earth.

How should I bear Bob Paine's detraction? Should I be angry, and take vengeance by scandalizing him? or should I be easy, undisturbed, and praise him as far as he is praiseworthy?—return good for evil? I should have been as well pleased, if he had said I was a very ingenious, promising young fellow; but, as it is, I am pretty easy.

[Sometime in 1761 or '62,[1] Mr. Samuel Quincy, with whom I sometimes corresponded, showed to Mr. Jonathan Sewall, a lawyer somewhat advanced before us at the bar, some juvenile letters of mine of no consequence, which, however, Sewall thought discovered a mind awake to the love of literature and law, and insisted on being acquainted with me and writing to me. His acquaintance and correspondence were readily embraced by me and continued for many years, till political disputes grew so warm as to separate us, a little before the war was commenced. His courtship of Miss Esther Quincy, a daughter of Edmund Quincy, brought him to Braintree commonly on Saturdays, where he remained till Monday, and gave us frequent opportunities of meeting, besides those at court in Boston, Charlestown, and Cambridge. He possessed a lively wit, a pleasing humor, a brilliant imagination, great subtlety of reasoning, and an insinuating eloquence. His sentiments of public affairs were for several years conformable to mine, and he once proposed to me to write in concert in the public prints to stir up the people to militia duty and military ardor, and was fully of my opinion, that the British Ministry and Parliament would force us to an appeal to arms; but he was poor, and Mr. Trowbridge and Governor Hutchinson contrived to excite him to a quarrel with Mr. Otis, because in the General Court Colonel Otis and his son had not very warmly supported a petition for a grant to discharge the debt of his uncle, the late chief justice, who died insolvent. To this artifice they added another which wholly converted him, by giving him the office of solicitor-general. I know not that I have ever delighted more in the friendship of any man, or more deeply regretted an irreconcilable difference in judgment in public opinions. He had virtues to be esteemed, qualities to be loved, and talents to be admired. But political principles were to me, in that state of the country, sacred. I could not follow him, and he could not follow me.]

1 The author, who appears to have written his Autobiography from recollection only, here makes a mistake of two or three years in the date, which should be 1759. Several letters of this correspondence have been preserved; some of them find their place in the Memoir.

Extract of a Letter to Jonathan Sewall.

This extract is copied upon the first page of one of the small paper books used for this Diary. It was placed here for a guide to the writer's studies, as appears from several subsequent references.

OCTOBER, 1759.

The true end which we ought to have in view is that *præclarum ac singulare quiddam*, which follows here.

'T is impossible to employ with full advantage the forces of our own minds in study, in council, or in argument, without examining with great attention and exactness all our mental faculties in all their operations, as explained by writers on the human understanding, and as exerted by geometricians.

'T is impossible to judge with much precision, of the true motives and qualities of human actions or of the propriety of rules contrived to govern them, without considering with like attention all the passions, appetites, affections, in nature, from which they flow. An intimate knowledge, therefore, of the intellectual and moral world is the sole foundation on which a stable structure of knowledge can be erected. And the structure of British laws is composed of such a vast and various collection of materials, taken partly from Saxony, Normandy, and Denmark, partly from Greece and Rome, and partly from the Canon and Feudal law, that 't is impossible for any builder to comprehend the whole vast design, and see what is well, and what is ill contrived or jointed, without acquainting himself with Saxon, Danish, Norman, as well as Greek and Roman history, with Civil, Feudal, and Canon law.

Besides all this, 't is impossible to avail ourselves of the genuine powers of eloquence, without examining in their elements and first principles, the force and harmony of numbers as employed by the poets and orators in ancient and modern times, and without considering the natural powers of imagination and the disposition of mankind to metaphor and figure, which will require the knowledge of the true principles of grammar and rhetoric and of the best classical authors.

Now, to what higher object, to what greater character, can any mortal aspire than to be possessed of all this knowledge well digested, and ready at command to assist the feeble and friendless, to discountenance the haughty and lawless, to procure redress of wrongs, the advancement of right, to assert and maintain liberty and virtue, to discourage and abolish tyranny and vice?[1]

October 12. Began, in pursuance of the foregoing plan, to transcribe, from Brightland's English Grammar, answers to Mr. Gridley's questions for that Grammar. I have begun, too, to compare Dr. Cowell's Institutes of the Laws of England, with Justinian's Institutes of the Laws of Rome, title by title, that

[1] The letter, to which this was an answer, has been preserved; it bears date, 29 September, 1759. The following extract, as showing the spirit of Mr. Sewall's part of the correspondence, is here subjoined. It is not so remarkable as that inserted in the Memoir, mainly, however, on account of the singular prediction respecting Mr. Adams, contained in the latter; but it does honor to the writer, who, we know from other sources, was one of the most accomplished men of his time in the colony. His controversial writings in the newspapers, at a period when the standard was very high, did all that could be done to uphold a feeble cause. Reputation, which in this world generally follows the maintenance of right principles and sometimes even that of wrong principles when attended with success, failed in his case from the want of both requisites.

JONATHAN SEWALL TO JOHN ADAMS.

It gives me the most sensible pleasure to find in my friend so becoming a resolution to persevere in the sublime study of the law, maugre all the difficulties and perplexing intricacies with which it *seems* embarrassed. I call it a sublime study; and what more sublime? What more worthy the indefatigable labors and pursuit of a reasonable man, than that science by which mankind raise themselves from the forlorn, helpless state, in which nature leaves them, to the full enjoyment of all the inestimable blessings of social union, and by which they (if you will allow the expression) triumph over the frailties and imperfections of humanity?

Though in my last I mentioned the greatness of the task we have voluntarily set ourselves, and the shortness of the time to which by the present constitution of things we are confined, as an apology for *my* attempting to assist *you* in your progress, and to justify you in making use of means so vastly disproportionate to the end; I say, though I hinted these things to these purposes, yet I would not have you conclude from hence that I am discouraged from the pursuit. No, my friend, I thank God, I am at present far from a state of despondency. The difficulties, 't is true, are great, but the motives to resolution and diligence are superior. The obstacles are surmounted by the industrious; are insurmountable only to the perversely indolent, and effeminately irresolute. For my own part, I am determined, as I have (to return you a Scripture metaphorical phrase,) put my hand to the plough, not to look back; and it is not the smallest encouragement that I have found in you a fellow traveller, who, if at any time through inattention, inability, or ignorance, I should stop short, or deviate, can, and I doubt not will, kindly lend a helping hand and set me right.

Your account of Mr. Blackstone's Lectures is entirely new to me, but I am greatly pleased with it. The embellishments of historical and critical learning, as well as the alluring ornaments of language, (too much neglected by law writers,) would undoubtedly render much more agreeable the study of the laws of England, in their present system too abstracted and dry. I could wish Mr. Blackstone, or some other friend to this invaluable branch of knowledge, would undertake to abridge the Reports, that we might not be forced to throw away so much of our time upon needless repetitions.

each may reflect light upon the other, and that I may advance my knowledge of civil and common law at the same time.

1760. May 26. Monday. Spent the evening at Mr. Edmund Quincy's, with Mr. Wibird and my cousin Zab. Mr. Quincy told a remarkable instance of Mr. Benjamin Franklin's activity and resolution to improve the productions of his own country; for from that source it must have sprung, or else from an unheard of stretch of benevolence to a stranger. Mr. Franklin happening, upon a visit to his Germantown friends, to be at Mr. Wibird's meeting, was asked after meeting in the afternoon to drink tea at Mr. Quincy's. The conversation turned upon the qualities of American soil, and the different commodities raised in these provinces. Among the rest, Mr. Franklin mentioned that the Rhenish grape vines had been introduced into Pennsylvania, and that some had been lately planted in Philadelphia, and succeeded very well. Mr. Quincy said, upon it, "I wish I could get some into my garden; I doubt not they would do very well in this province." Mr. Franklin replied, "sir, if I can supply you with some of the cuttings, I shall be glad to." Quincy thanked him and said, "I don't know but some time or other I shall presume to trouble you." And so the conversation passed off. Within a few weeks, Mr. Quincy was surprised with a letter from some of Franklin's friends in Boston, that a bundle of these Rhenish slips were ready for him; these came by water. Well, soon afterwards he had another message that another parcel of slips were left for him by the post. The next time Mr. Franklin was in Boston, Mr. Quincy waited on him to thank him for his slips; "but I am sorry, sir, to give you so much trouble." "O, sir," says Franklin, "the trouble is nothing to me, if the vines do but succeed in your province. However, I was obliged to take more pains than I expected, when I saw you. I had been told that the vines were in the city, but I found none, and was obliged to send up to a village, seventy miles from the city, for them." Thus, he took the trouble to hunt over the city, and not finding vines there, he sends seventy miles into the country, and then sends one bundle by water, and, lest they should miscarry, another by land, to a gentleman whom he owed nothing and was but little acquainted with, purely for the sake of doing good in the world by propagating the Rhenish vines through these provinces. And Mr. Quincy has some of them now growing in his garden. This is an instance, too, of his amazing capacity for business, his memory and resolution; amidst so much business as counsellor, postmaster, printer, so many private studies, and so many public avocations too, to remember such a transient hint and exert himself so in answer to it, is surprising.[1]

[1] Among the papers of Mr. Adams is found an original letter of Dr. Franklin, addressed to the same Mr. Quincy, in the following year, upon this subject. Unfortunately, it is not complete, one piece of it having been worn away and lost. Yet, as it does not seem to have been printed, and as every thing connected with the writer is interesting at this day, it is here appended in its fragmentary state.

TO EDMUND QUINCY.

London, 10 December, 1761.

SIR: — I should sooner have answered your obliging letter of January 9, but that I hoped from time to time I might be able to obtain some satisfactory answer to your queries. As yet, I have done little, that kind of information being looked upon as a part of the mysteries of trade, which the professors are very shy of communicating. But I think I am now in a train of obtaining more, of which I hope soon to give you a good account. In the mean time I may inform you that great quantities of wine are made, both here and at Bristol, from raisins, not by private families only, for their particular use, but, in the great way, by large dealers for the country consumption. As New England trades to Spain with their fish, it would, I imagine, be easy for you to furnish yourself, at the best hand, with plenty of raisins, and from thence produce a genuine wine of real worth, that might be sold with you for good profit. Being lately at a friend's house, where I drank some old raisin wine that I found to be very good, I requested the . . . .

. . sound and good. It is thought here, that by far the greatest part of the wine drank in England is made in England. Fine cider or perry is said to be the basis. Sloes afford roughness; elder berries, color; and brandy, a little more strength; but of this I have no certain account.

The porter now so universally drank here, is, I am assured, fined down with isinglass or fish-glue, for which sixty thousand pounds sterling, per annum, is paid to Russia. Of late, it has been discovered that this fish-glue is nothing more than the sounds of cod or other fish, extended and dried in the sun, without any other preparation. So you may make what quantity you please of it, and cheap, fish being with you so plenty.

I heartily wish you success in your attempts to make wine from American grapes. None has yet been imported here for the premium.

With great esteem, I am, sir,

Your most obedient, humble servant, B. FRANKLIN.

P. S. The negotiations for a peace, in which Canada was to be forever ceded to England, are at present broken off. But, whenever they are resumed, I am persuaded that will be made a point . . . .

N. B. One Ezekiel Hatch, near Greenwood's mast-yard, tells me that the cod sounds or other, may be saved by slinging up and drying; that, under this circumstance, they will not dissolve in any liquor, hot nor cold; but that, taken and wrapped up in clean linen cloth or other cloths, and covered up in embers, so as to roast them, they will then dissolve, and that they will answer the end of glue; but not so well of cod as the sounds of hake, which is caught in or near the fall. Those, many joiners, at distant places, use as glue for their cabinet work; roasted first, in order to dissolve, as glue.

This Rhenish wine is made of a grape that grows in Germany, upon the river Rhine, from which it receives its name, and is very famous all over Europe. Let me remember to look in Chambers, under Rhenish, and in Salmon's Geography, under the produce of the countries upon the Rhine, for more particulars of this vine, and grape, and wine; the soil it delights in, the method of cultivation, what digging, what manure, what pruning, &c. Let me ask Mr. Quincy whether the soil of his garden suits them, and what sorts and how many sorts of grapes he has? Don't they require more heat than we have for them? where he got his other slips? where he got his lime trees? &c.

28. Wednesday. Loitered the forenoon away upon this question in arithmetic.[1]

In the afternoon Zab[2] and I wandered down to Germantown on foot, running a parallel between the pleasures, profits, freedom, ease, and uses of the several professions, especially physic and divinity.

29. Thursday. Rose and breakfasted. Have done nothing yet to-day, and God only knows what I shall do. The question of the pipe.[3]

I must run over Fractions again, vulgar and decimal as well as algebraical, and now and then a few questions in Fenning and Hammond and Ward, or else I shall totally forget my numbers. I find that the art of numbering depends upon practice, and in a short disuse they will slip from the memory. A journal scrawled with algebraical signs, and interspersed with questions of law, husbandry, natural history, &c., will be a useful thing. The principal uses, however, will be to correct my style and assist my memory, give me a true compunction for the waste of time, and urge me of course to a better improvement of it. Besides, writing is one of the greatest pleasures, and it sooner rouses my ambition, warms my imagination, and fixes me in a train of thinking, than any other thing that I can do; than sitting still with my eyes shut, or than holding a book to

[1] This question, worked out by algebra, is omitted.

[2] The Rev. Zabdiel Adams, already once alluded to, was a cousin of the author, afterwards pastor of the church at Lunenburgh in Massachusetts. A biographical sketch of him may be found in Doctor Eliot's Collection. He used to say that by nature his kinsman and he should have exchanged callings. The two had many qualities of character in common.

[3] Another demonstration.

read. Mem. Last Sunday, after meeting, Mr. Cranch explained to us, at Doctor Tufts's, the machines that are used in the mines of coal in Newcastle, and of tin in Cornwall, to convey up water from the bottom of the mine. They go upon the principles of elastic air and rarefied vapor. They have hollow globes of plaited iron or of copper which will hold some barrels, which they heat with great fires, and have tubes and cocks, and can cast up great quantities of water, many hogsheads in a minute. But I have forgot the construction of the machines as well as the method of working them. Here is my failing, or one of my failings. My attention has not been keen enough to understand and fix in my memory the explications of many of these machines. Etter explained to me his stocking looms, but I could not, when I left him, have run from the first motion to the complete formation of a stocking; I did not see through it. Cranch once explained to me the machine that draws water from the Thames into the canals under the city of London, and that sends water up into their garrets, chambers, rooms, and cellars, so that by opening a cock you may draw a pail of water from the Thames in any house in the city almost; but I do not remember the construction of it. Let me remember to inquire of him about the construction of these two, that for water from the Thames, and that for water from the mines, and to go once more to see the stocking looms.

Few things, I believe, have deviated so far from the first design of their institution, are so fruitful of destructive evils, or so needful of a speedy regulation, as licensed houses. The accommodation of strangers, and, perhaps, of town inhabitants on public occasions, are the only warrantable intentions of a tavern; and the supply of the neighborhood with necessary liquors in small quantities,[1] and at the cheapest rates, are the only excusable designs of a retailer; and that these purposes may be effected, it is necessary that both should be selected from the most virtuous and wealthy people, who will accept the trust, and so few of each should be erected that the profits may enable them to make the best provision at a moderate price. But at

[1] "To be consumed at home," written and erased.

the present day, such houses are become the eternal haunt of loose, disorderly people of the same town, which renders them offensive and unfit for the entertainment of a traveller of the least delicacy; and it seems that poverty and distressed circumstances are become the strongest arguments to procure an approbation; and for these assigned reasons, such multitudes have been lately licensed that none can afford to make provision for any but the tippling, nasty, vicious crew that most frequent them. The consequences of these abuses are obvious. Young people are tempted to waste their time and money, and to acquire habits of intemperance and idleness, that we often see reduce many to beggary and vice, and lead some of them, at last, to prisons and the gallows. The reputation of our county is ruined among strangers, who are apt to infer the character of a place from that of the taverns and the people they see there. But the worst effect of all, and which ought to make every man who has the least sense of his privileges tremble, these houses are become in many places the nurseries of our legislators. An artful man, who has neither sense nor sentiment, may by gaining a little sway among the rabble of a town, multiply taverns and dram shops, and thereby secure the votes of taverner and retailer, and of all; and the multiplication of taverns will make many who may be induced by flip and rum to vote for any man whatever. I dare not presume to point out any method to suppress or restrain these increasing evils, but I think for these reasons, it would be well worth the attention of our legislature to confine the number and retrieve the character of licensed houses, lest that impiety and profaneness, that abandoned intemperance and prodigality, that impudence and brawling temper, which these abominable nurseries daily propagate, should arise at length to a degree of strength that even the legislature will not be able to control.

Pownal's remark, every other house a tavern. Twelve in this town. Call upon the selectmen not to grant approbation; upon the grand jurors to present all bad houses, &c.

30. Friday. Rose early. Several country towns, within my observation, have at least a dozen taverns and retailers. Here the time, the money, the health, and the modesty, of most that are young and of many old, are wasted; here diseases, vicious habits, bastards, and legislators, are frequently begotten. N——

would vote for any man for a little flip or a dram. B., &c., voted for T., for other reasons.

31. Saturday. Read in Naval Trade and Commerce, concerning factors, consuls, ambassadors, &c., and the South Sea Company, &c. Talked with William Veasey about church, &c. He will not allow that Dr. Mayhew has any uncommon parts; he had haughty spirits and vanity, &c. How the judgment is darkened and perverted by party passions! Drank tea with Zab; ran over the past passages of my life; — little boats, water-mills, windmills, whirligigs, birds' eggs, bows and arrows, guns, singing, pricking tunes, girls, &c.; ignorance of parents, masters Cleverly, Marsh, tutors Mayhew, &c. By a constant dissipation among amusements in my childhood, and by the ignorance of my instructors in the more advanced years of my youth, my mind has laid uncultivated; so that, at twenty-five, I am obliged to study Horace and Homer! — *proh dolor!*

June 1. Sunday. Read two Odes in Horace. Spent the evening at the Colonel's.

2. Monday. Wasted the day with a magazine in my hand. As it was artillery election, it seemed absurd to study; and I had no conveniences or companions for pleasure, either in walking, riding, drinking, hustling, or any thing else.

3. Tuesday. This day has been lost in much the same spiritless manner.

4. Wednesday. Read nothing but magazines, as, indeed, an indisposition rendered me unfit for any application. Discharged my venom to Billy Veasey against the multitude, poverty, ill government, and ill effects of licensed houses; and the timorous temper, as well as criminal design of the selectmen, who grant them approbations.[1] Then spent the evening with Zab at Mr. Wibird's.

5. Thursday. Arose late; feel disordered. Eight o'clock, three and a half hours after sunrise, is a sluggard's rising time; it is a stupid waste of so much time; it is getting a habit hard to conquer, and it is very hurtful to one's health; three and a half, one-seventh of the twenty-four, is thus spiritlessly dozed away. God grant me an attention to remark and a resolution

[1] These thoughts upon licensed houses appear to have fructified into the proceedings at the town meeting of May in the following year, as will hereafter be seen.

to pursue every opportunity for the improvement of my mind, and to save, with the parsimony of a miser, every moment of my time.

6. Friday. Arose very late. A cold, rainy, north-easterly storm, of several days continuance. Read Timon of Athens, the man-hater, in the evening, at the Doctor's.

7. Saturday. Arose late again. When shall I shake off the shackles of morning slumbers, and arise with the sun? Between sunrise and breakfast I might write, or read, or contemplate a good deal. I might, before breakfast, entirely shake off the drowsiness of the morning and get my thoughts into a steady train, my imagination raised, my ambition inflamed, in short, every thing within me and without into a preparation for improvement. I have some points of law to examine to-day.

8. Sunday. Spent the evening and night at the Colonel's, in ill-natured, invidious remarks upon Eb. Thayer and morals and General Courts, &c.

9. Monday. Attended Major Crosby's court, where Captains T. and H. made their appearance. T. had taken two accounts of Nathan Spear, in his own handwriting, and got the writs drawn by Niles. But, upon my making a defence for Hunt, Spear was afraid to enter, and so agreed to pay costs and drop. But poor T. had to say, several times, "I told him so, but he would have his own way." This little dirty pettifogging trade T. carries on yet.

10. Tuesday. Although my spirits were wasted yesterday by sitting so late the night before, (till one o'clock, I believe,) and rising so early yesterday morning, (by sunrise,) and walking in the dewy grass and damp air home to my father's, and then down to Major Crosby's, yet the thoughts of being employed, and of opposing Captain T., and punishing Nathan Spear, and spreading a reputation, roused my faculties, and rolled out thoughts and expressions with a strength and rapidity that I never expected. I remember something of the same sort when I first waited on Mr. Gridley. The awe of his presence, a desire of his esteem and of an introduction to practice, quickened my attention and memory, and sharpened my penetration. In short, I never shall shine till some animating occasion calls forth all my powers.[1] I find that the mind must be agitated with some

[1] Mr. Jefferson's description of his efforts in the Congress of 1776, will naturally occur to the reader.

passion, either love, fear, hope, &c., before she will do her best. I rambled this afternoon, with the Doctor, over the Commons, and amused myself by clearing the spring and climbing the ledges of rocks, through the apertures of which large trees had grown. But I spend too much time in these walks, these amusing rambles. I should be more confined to my chamber, should read and muse more; running to Dr. ——, to the barn, down to meals, and for pipes, and coals, and tobacco, &c., take up much of my time. I have grown habitually indolent and thoughtless. I have scarcely felt a glow, a pang, a transport of ambition, since I left Worcester; since I left my school, indeed, for there the mischievous tricks, the perpetual, invincible prate, and the stupid dulness of my scholars, roused my passions, and, with them my views and impatience of ambition. Let me remember to keep my chamber, not run abroad; my books, — Naval Trade, Coke, Andrews, Locke, Homer, — not fields, and groves, and springs, and rocks, should be the objects of my attention. Law, and not poetry, is to be the business of my life.

14. Saturday. This week has been spent in business; that is, filling writs, and journeys to Boston, Scadding,[1] Weymouth, Abington. The other night Cranch explained to Zab and me the fire-engine, with which they throw up water from the bottoms of their tin mines in Cornwall, and coal mines in New Castle.[2]

In my journey to Abington, my mind seemed to be confused with the dust, and heat, and fatigue. I had not spirit and attention to make any observations upon the land, corn, grass, grain, fences, orchards, houses, &c. I dined at Norton's, where the two military companies of the town were assembled to raise volunteers, recruits; but I had not spirits to make observations on the landlord or lady, or officers or soldiers, or house, or any thing.

15. Sunday. Rose early, five o'clock; a pleasant morning. The more I write the better. Writing is a most useful, improving exercise. Yesterday morning, before breakfast, I wrought my mind into a course of thinking, by my pen, which I should not have fallen into the whole day without it; and, indeed, not resuming my pen after breakfast, I insensibly lost my attention. Let me aim at perspicuity and correctness, more than ornament, in these papers.

1 The common name given to what is now the town of Randolph.
2 Here follows a long explanation.

16. Monday. Arose before the sun. Now I am ignorant of my future fortune, — what business, what reputation I may get, which is now far from my expectations. How many actions shall I secure this day? and what new client shall I have?

I found at evening I had secured six actions, but not one new client that I know of.

17. Tuesday. Arose before the sun again; this is the last day.[1] What and who to-day? Ebenezer Hayden was altogether new and unexpected; H. himself was altogether new and unexpected; and John Hayward was altogether new and unexpected; — three entirely new clients, all from Captain Thayer's own parish, one of whom is himself a pretender to the practice, are a considerable acquisition. I believe the writ and advice I gave Hayden, and the writ and advice and the lecture concerning idleness and pettifogging, given H. before Hayward, will spread me. H. is very near to beggary and imprisonment. His oxen are attached, and his cows, and pew; and a number of writs and executions are out against him, not yet extended. He owes more than his estate can pay, I believe; and I told him that, by neglecting his own proper business and meddling with law, which he did not understand, he had ruined himself — and it is true; for, if he had diligently followed his trade of making shoes, and lived prudently, he might at this day have been clear of debt and worth an handsome estate. But shoemaking, I suppose, was too mean and diminutive an occupation for Mr. T. H., as wigmaking was to Mr. N. G., or housebuilding to Mr. Daniel W.; and he, like them, in order to rise in the world, procured deputations from the sheriff, and, after serving long enough in that office to get a few copies of common writs and a most litigious disposition, left the sheriff[2] and commenced the writ-drawer. But poor H. is like to be stripped of all he has, if he should escape the jail, which D. W. was obliged to enter, and if he should not be forced to fly like N. G. These sudden transitions from shoemaking, wigmaking, and housebuilding, to the deputy sheriffwick, and from thence to the practice of law, commonly hurry men rapidly to destruction, to

[1] That is, of service.

[2] The practice of filling writs, by sheriffs and their deputies, was one of the grievances of this period. It became so fruitful of abuses that it was finally prohibited by a law passed through the agency, as it is said, of Timothy Ruggles. *Supplement to Curwen's Journal.*

beggary, and jails. Yet Colonel White has risen the same way; that is, by a deputation from the sheriff. But White had the advantage of a liberal education, and had no rival, no competitor to oppose him, so that he got quickly sworn. E. Taylor, too, was naturally smart, and had been long a sheriff, and had the patronage and encouragement of Mr. Trowbridge, who was his brother-in-law. Applin and Ruggles are in a higher class, men of genius and great resolution to combat the world, both by violence and stratagem. T., by his own abject slavery to Colonel P., got his affections, and he did every thing to encourage him. Dana has given him great numbers of writs to be served on people in this town; he takes seven shillings for the writ, and four shillings always, and some five, for the service; of this he gives Dana one shilling for his blank, and reserves ten or eleven to himself; great numbers of writs he has filled himself, and those which he durst not fill, he got Niles to fill for three shillings; so that he takes three and four are seven and, oftentimes, eight shillings to himself. Thus, from Colonel P., from Mr. Dana, and Elisha Niles, he has got his estate, as his legislative authority. As basely got as "Bestia's from the throne." A little longer experience will enable me to trace out the whole system of his policy and iniquity.

The office of a sheriff has dangers and temptations around it. Most of them decline in morals or estates, or both. P. is one.

18. Wednesday. Read but little, thought but little; for the north-east storm unstrung me.

19. Thursday.[1] I have been the longer in the argument of this cause, not for the importance of the cause itself, for in itself it is infinitely little and contemptible, but for the importance of its consequences. These dirty and ridiculous litigations have been multiplied, in this town, till the very earth groans and the stones cry out. The town is become infamous for them throughout the county. I have absolutely heard it used as a proverb in several parts of the province, — "As litigious as Braintree." This multiplicity is owing to the multiplicity of pettifoggers, among whom Captain H. is one, who has given out that he is

[1] Apparently a draught of the close of an argument, made three days later, in one of the trifling and vexatious suits which seem to have been commonly indulged in, at this period, by persons offended with each other in the country towns.

a sworn attorney, till nine tenths of this town really believe it. But I take this opportunity, publicly, to confront him and undeceive the town. He knows, in his conscience, that he never took the oath of an attorney, and that he dare not assume the impudence to ask to be admitted. He knows that the notion of his being a sworn attorney is an imposture, is an imposition upon this town. And I take this opportunity, publicly, to declare that I will take all legal advantages against every action brought by him, or by Captain T., or by any other pettifogger in this town. For I am determined, if I live in this town, to break up this scene of strife, vexation, and immorality. (Such suits as this, and most others that ever I have seen before a justice in this town, have a tendency to vex and embitter the minds of the people, to propagate an idle, brawling, wrangling temper; in short, such suits are an inlet to all manner of evils.)

And one of these suit managers, when I first came to this town, hearing that I had been through a regular course of study with a regular practitioner, and that I was recommended to the court in Boston by one of the greatest lawyers in America, concluded that I should be enabled by these advantages, and prompted by my own interest, if by no higher motive, to put an end to the illegal course of dirty, quacking practice in this town which he had been in, and thereby enslaved the minds and bodies and estates of his neighbors. And, to prevent this, he set himself to work to destroy my reputation, and prevent my getting business, by such stratagems as no honest mind can think of without horror; such stratagems as I always will resent, and never will forgive till he has made atonement by his future repentance and reformation. I thank God his malice has been defeated; he has not been able to enslave me, nor to drive me out of town. But people's eyes begin to open, and I hope they will open wider and wider, till they can see like other towns. Happy shall I be if I can rescue the souls and bodies, and estates of this town from that thraldom and slavery to which these pettifoggers have contributed to depress them; and if I can revive in them a generous love of liberty and sense of honor. After this long digression, your Honor will let me return to this cause; and I rely upon it, it is a vexatious one; I rely upon it, that many of these articles were borrowed and not bought, and that, therefore, this action cannot be maintained for them; I rely upon it, that the affair of the hat is a litigious thing; that it was a mere piece of tavern amusement, and, if there was any thing like bargain and sale in it, the bargain was completed, the hat delivered, and the money paid; and, with regard to the other articles, we have filed an account that more than balances them, and, therefore, I pray your Honor's judgment for costs.

20. Friday. I must not say so much about myself, nor so much about H. and T. by name. I may declaim against strife and a litigious spirit, and about the dirty dabblers in the law.

I have a very good regard for Lieutenant W., but he must allow me to have a much greater veneration for the law. To see the forms and processes of law and justice thus prostituted (I must say prostituted) to revenge an imaginary indignity offered in a tavern, over a cheerful bowl or enlivening mug; to have a mere piece of jocular amusement thus hitched into an action at law, a mere frolic converted into a lawsuit, is a degree of meanness that deserves no mercy, and shall have none from me. I don't think Lieutenant W. considered the nature and the consequences of this action before he brought it; if he had, he never would have brought it; he has too much honor to have brought it. But I suppose the case was this: Lieutenant W. was a little chagrined that my client had for once outwitted him, and in a miff or a bravado, I say a miff or a bravado, sees H. and asks his opinion; and H., glad of an opportunity to draw a writ, instantly encourages the suit, and the suit was brought, and when once brought it was too late to repent. But I dare say he has been severely sorry that he ever brought it, and will have still further occasion to be sorry before it ends.

23. Monday. A long, obstinate trial before Major Crosby, of the most litigious, vexatious suit, I think, that ever I heard. Such disputes begin with ill humor and scurrilous language, and end in a boxing bout or a lawsuit.

24. Tuesday. Arose early, a very beautiful morning. Zab seems to make insufficient distinctions between the vowels; he seems to swallow his own voice; he neither sounds the vowels nor articulates distinctly. The story of yesterday's trial spreads; Salisbury told my uncle, and my uncle told Colonel Quincy. They say I was saucy; that I whipped the old Major, &c.; that I ripped about the lawsuits of this town and of that house, and that I reminded the Major of his oath to be of counsel to neither

party, and to do justice equally between the parties according to law.

26. Thursday. I have began to read the Spirit of Laws, and have resolved to read that work through in order and with attention. I have hit upon a project that will secure my attention to it, which is to write, in the margin, a sort of index to every paragraph.[1]

27. Friday. Read one hundred pages in the Spirit of Laws. Rambled away to a fine spring in my cousin Adams's land, which gushes through a crack in a large flat rock, and gurgles down in a pretty rill. The water is clear, sweet, and cool, and is supposed to have a very wholesome quality, because it issues from a mountain and runs towards the north. What physical quality its northern direction may give it, I know not. By its sweetness, it flows through clean earth, and not minerals; its coolness may be owing to its rise from the bowels of the hill.

Zab's mind is taken up with arithmetical and geometrical problems, questions, paradoxes, and riddles. He studies these things that he may be able to gratify his vanity by puzzling all the vain pretenders to expertness in numbers, and that he may be too expert to be puzzled by any such questions from others. There is a set of people whose glory, pride, &c., it is to puzzle every man they meet with some question in the rule-of-three, or fractions, or some other branch of arithmetic.

July 5. Saturday. Cowen, and young Thayer the market-man, are full of W. and B. Cowen heard I tore W.'s account all to pieces, and Thayer thought that W. had a dirty case;—few justices' causes have been more famous than that. Isaac Tirrell had the story too, but he thought B. was to blame, was abusive.

6. Sunday. Heard Mr. Mayhew of Martha's Vineyard.

9. Wednesday. Gould has got the story of W. and B.

August 9. Saturday. Drank tea at Colonel Quincy's, with Colonel Gooch and Dr. Gardiner. I see Gooch's[2] fiery spirit, his

[1] A practice to which the author adhered ever after, as the volumes in his library abundantly show.

[2] Of Colonel Gooch, one of the singular characters of this period, Mr. Adams long afterwards, in a letter addressed to Jonathan Mason, a gentleman once his law pupil, gave the following curious account:—

"Joseph Gooch, a native, I believe, of Boston. He had considerable property, and was reported and reputed to be very rich. He had been educated at the Temple in England, and returned to Boston to practise law; he had very little

unguarded temper. He swears freely, boldly. He is a widower, and delights to dwell, in his conversation, upon courtship and

success. He had been a man of pleasure, and bore the indelible marks of it on his face to the grave. He was extremely ambitious, and the Rev. Mr. Niles of the second parish in Braintree, who was well acquainted with him, told me he was the most passionate man he ever knew. Not succeeding much at the bar in Boston, he had recourse to religion to assist him; joined the Old South Church, to avail himself of the influence of the sisterhood, and set up for representative for the town of Boston, but failed; and disappointed of his hopes in law and politics, he renounced the city, came up to Quincy, hired a house, turned Churchman, and set himself to intriguing for promotion, both in the military and civil departments. He interceded with the favorites of Governor Shirley, in this place, to procure him the commission of Colonel in the regiment of militia, and an election for representative of the town in the General Court. He promised to build a steeple to their church, at his own expense.

"Assiduous importunity was employed with Governor Shirley to procure him the command of the regiment; but this could not be obtained without cashiering the Colonel then in possession, and who had long been in possession of that office and given universal satisfaction in it.

"Colonel John Quincy had been in public life from his early youth. He had been near twenty years speaker of the House of Representatives, and many years a member of his Majesty's Council; and was as much esteemed and respected as any man in the province. He was not only an experienced and venerated statesman, but a man of letters, taste, and sense. Shirley was, with great difficulty, prevailed on to perform the operation of dismissing so faithful a servant of the public, and adopting one of so equivocal a character; and he said, some years afterwards, that nothing he had ever done in his administration had given him so much pain, as removing so venerable a magistrate and officer as Colonel Quincy. But the church party had insisted upon it so peremptorily, that he could not avoid it. Probably he dreaded their remonstrances to the Archbishop of Canterbury.

"These facts were currently reported and universally believed, and never contradicted.

"Gooch was appointed Colonel, and Quincy dismissed. The next thing to be done, was to new-model the subordinate officers in the regiment. Application was made to all the captains, lieutenants, and ensigns, in that part of the regiment which lies within three parishes of the ancient town of Braintree, to see if they would accept commissions under Colonel Gooch, and agree to vote for him as representative for the town. The then present officers were men among the most respectable of the inhabitants, in point of property, understanding, and character. They rejected the proposition with scorn.

"My father was among them; he was offered a captain's commission. He spurned the offer with disdain; would serve in the militia under no Colonel but Quincy. Almost, or quite an entire set of new officers were appointed through the whole town. These were of a very different character from those who were dismissed. Men of little property or no property at all; men of frivolous characters in understanding and morals.

"It was at this time the corrupt practice of treating, as they called it, at trainings and at elections was introduced, which so long prevailed in the town of Braintree. All this corruption, young as I was, I attributed to the King of Great Britain and his Governor and their bigoted Episcopal party; and, young as I was, I was thoroughly disgusted before I was ten years of age.

"Gooch, under the influence of all this machinery, obtained an election as representative; but the next year all the substantial people of the town aroused themselves and turned him out, which so enraged him that he swore he would no longer live in Braintree; renounced the church, refused to build their steeple, built him a house on Milton hill, and there passed the remainder of his days."

marriage. Has a violent aversion to long courtship. "He's a fool that spends more than a week," &c., &c.

A malignant wit; a fiery, fierce, outrageous enemy. He quarrels with all men. He quarrelled with Colonel Quincy, and intrigued to dispossess him of his regiment, by means of Dr. Miller and Mr. Apthorp. He now quarrels with Colonel Miller and Dr. Miller and Eb. Thayer. He curses all Governors. Pownal was a servant, door-keeper, pimp to Lord Halifax, and he contracted with Lord Halifax to give him fifteen shillings out of every pound of his salary; so that Pownal had twenty-five per cent. commissions, for his agency under Lord Halifax.

Thersites in Homer, was

> "Awed by no shame, by no respect controlled,
> In scandal busy, in reproaches bold;
> With witty malice, studious to defame;
> Scorn all his joy, and laughter all his aim.
> But chief he gloried with licentious style,
> To lash the great, and monarchs to revile."

Thus, we see that Gooches lived as long ago as the siege of Troy.

> "Spleen to mankind his envious heart possessed,
> And much he hated all, but most the best.
> Long had he lived the scorn of every Greek,
> Vext when he spoke, yet still they heard him speak."

His daughters have the same fiery temper, the same witty malice. They have all, to speak decently, very smart tempers, quick, sharp, and keen.

An insinuation of Mr. Pownal's giving three fourths of his salary for his commission.

This is,

> "with licentious style,
> Governors to revile."

"Colonel Miller can serve the devil with as much cunning as any man I know of, but for no other purpose is he fit."

This is,

> "In scandal busy, in reproaches bold."

"Gardiner has a thin, grasshopper voice, and an affected squeak; a meagre visage, and an awkward, unnatural complaisance. He is fribble."

Q. Is this a generous practice, to perpetuate the shrugs of wit and the grimaces of affectation?

12. Tuesday. Remonstrated at the Sessions against licensing Lambard; because the selectmen had refused to approbate him; because he never was approbated by the selectmen to keep a tavern in the house he now lives in; because there are already three, and his would make four taverns, besides retailers, within three quarters of a mile; and because he obtained a license from that court at April Sessions by artfully concealing his removal from the place where he formerly kept, and so by an imposition on the court. These reasons prevailed. Major Miller, Colonel Miller, and Ruddock were the only justices on Lambard's side; while I had eight or nine, Wendells, Colonel Phillips, Mr. Dana, Mr. Storer, &c., &c., &c. Mr. Dana inquired, whether those landing places at Braintree and Weymouth, or the road where these four taverns stand was not a great stage for travellers. I answered no, and rightly; for the greatest stage that I knew of from Boston to Plymouth, is in the north precinct of Braintree, where Mr. Bracket, but especially where Mr. Bass now keeps. Where Mr. Bass now keeps there has been a tavern always since my remembrance, and long before. It is exactly ten miles from town, and therefore, a very proper stage for gentlemen who are going from Boston down to Plymouth and to the Cape, and for people who come from the Cape towards this town; and there are very few travellers, either bound to or from Boston but what stop here; but this stage is two or three miles from the place in question. These things I should have said, but they did not then occur. Dana asked next, what number of carters, boatmen, ship-builders, &c., were ever employed at a time at that landing place? I answered, half a dozen carters, perhaps. But my answer should have been this: at some times there are three or four or half a dozen ship carpenters, and it is possible there may have been two or three boats at that wharf at a time, which will require half a dozen boatmen, and there have been perhaps forty carts in a day with stones, and wood, and lumber; but these carts are coming and going all day long, so that it is a rare thing to see half a dozen carts there at a time; in short, there is so much business done there as to render one tavern necessary, but there is not so much business, there is no such concourse of travellers, no such multi-

tude of busy people at that landing as to need all this cluster of taverns. One tavern and one retailer was thought by the selectmen quite sufficient for that place. They have licensed one of each, and pray that your Honors would recognize no more.

19. Tuesday. I began Pope's Homer, last Saturday night was a week, and last night, which was Monday night, I finished it. Thus I found that in seven days I could have easily read the six volumes, notes, preface, essays — that on Homer, and that on Homer's battles, and that on the funeral games of Homer and Virgil, &c. Therefore, I will be bound that in six months I would conquer him in Greek, and make myself able to translate every line in him elegantly.

Pratt. "It is a very happy thing to have people superstitious. They should believe exactly as their minister believes; they should have no creeds and confessions; they should not so much as know what they believe. The people ought to be ignorant; and our free schools are the very bane of society; they make the lowest of the people infinitely conceited."

These words I heard Pratt utter; they would come naturally enough from the mouth of a tyrant, or of a king or ministry about introducing an arbitrary power, or from the mouth of an ambitious ecclesiastic; but they are base, detestable principles of slavery. He would have ninety-nine hundredths of the world as ignorant as the wild beasts of the forest, and as servile as the slaves in a galley, or as oxen yoked in a team. He, a friend to liberty! He an enemy to slavery! He has the very principles of a Frenchman — worse principles than a Frenchman; for they know their belief and can give reasons for it.

Pratt. "It grieves me to see any sect of religion extinguished. I should be very sorry to have the Tract Society dissolved; so I should be sorry to have Condy's Anabaptist Society dissolved. I love to see a variety. A variety of religions has the same beauty in the moral world, that a variety of flowers has in a garden, or a variety of trees in a forest."

This fine speech was Pratt's; yet he is sometimes of opinion that all these sectaries ought to turn Churchmen, and that a uniform establishment ought to take place through the whole nation. I have heard him say that we had better, all of us, come into the church than pretend to overturn it, &c. Thus it is, that fine speech-makers are sometimes for uniformity, sometimes for variety and toleration. They don't speak for the truth or weight, but for the smartness, novelty and singularity of the speech. However, I heard him make two observations that pleased me much more;—one was, that "people in years never suppose that young people have any judgment." Another was, (when a deposition was produced, taken by Parson Wells with a very incorrect caption; a caption without mention of the cause in which it was to be used, or certifying that the adverse party was present or notified,) he observed that "the Parson could not take a caption to save his life; and that he knew too much to learn any thing."

October 7. Tuesday. Waited on Mr. Gridley for his opinion of my declaration, Lambard *versus* Tirrell, and for his advice whether to enter the action or not. He says the declaration is bad, and the writ, if advantage is taken, will abate. For it is a declaration on a parol lease, not on a deed; and, therefore, the lessee's occupancy ought to be set forth very exactly; for it is his occupancy, not any contract, that supports the action.[1]

9. Thursday. In support of complaint, in case Neal's action is not entered.[2]

I do not know, nor is it possible for your Honors to determine, what reason induced the plaintiff to renounce this suit. Whether it was because the estate is insolvent, or because he had no cause of action, or because his action was mislaid, or because his writ was bad—which by the way is very probable, considering who drew it—that determined the plaintiff not to enter this action, I cannot say, and your Honors cannot determine. It appears to your Honors that the defendant has been vexed and distressed by this summons; that she has been obliged to take a journey to this town and to attend upon this court, when it appears there is nothing for her to answer to;—all this appears. What motive induced the plaintiff to drop his action, does not appear; and, therefore, we have a right to costs. As things are circumstanced, I will own, that, had this action been commenced by any gentleman at this bar, I would have dispensed with this complaint; but it was drawn by a pettifogging deputy sheriff, against whom I know it is my duty, and I think it is my interest, to

[1] Here follows a legal opinion of Mr. Gridley, which is omitted.
[2] That is, a sketch of what he intended to say.

take all legal advantages; and he himself cannot think it hard, as he has taken both illegal and iniquitous advantages against me. Therefore I pray your Honor's judgment for costs. *Q.* If this action should be entered, what must be done with it? — continued or dismissed? A motion must be made for a continuance or a dismission.

11. Saturday. Neal's action is entered, so that I have two actions to defend by pleas in bar, and three of the actions I entered are to be defended. Clark is to plead in abatement, and Tirrell and Thayer are, I suppose, to plead to issue.

November 5. Wednesday. Messrs. I presume,[1] upon the common sense of the world, that no offence will be taken at the freedom of the following sentiments, while the utmost deference for authority and decency of language is preserved. As persons of obscure birth and station and narrow fortunes, have no other way but through the press to communicate their thoughts abroad, either to the high or the low.

The vacancy in the highest seat of justice in the province, occasioned by the death of Judge Sewall, naturally stirs the minds of all who know the importance of a wise, steady, and legal administration of justice, to inquire for a fit person to fill that place.

Such persons know that the rules of the common law are extremely numerous; the acts of parliament are numerous; — some taken from, or at least in spirit, from the civil law, others from the canon and feudal law. Such persons know that the histories of cases and resolutions of judges have been preserved from a very great antiquity; and they know also, that every possible case being thus preserved in writing and settled in a precedent, leaves nothing, or but little, to the arbitrary will or uninformed reason of prince or judge.

And it will be easy for any man to conclude what opportunities, industry, and genius employed from early youth, will be necessary to gain a knowledge from all these sources sufficient to decide the lives, liberties, and fortunes of mankind with safety to the people's liberties as well as the king's prerogative; that

[1] This appears to be the rough draft of an article designed for publication in the newspapers. It is retained on account of its bearing upon the question of the appointment to fill the vacancy in the post of Chief Justice; a question, the decision of which in favor of Hutchinson, largely contributed to bring on the Revolution. The allusions to his former life make it plain that the writer did not, even at this period, favor him.

happy union in which the excellence of British government consists, and which has often been preserved by the deep discernment and noble spirit of English judges.

It will be easy for any man to conclude that a man whose youth and spirits and strength have been spent in husbandry, merchandise, politics, nay, in science or literature, will never master so immense and involved a science; for it may be taken for a never-failing maxim, that youth is the only time for laying the foundation of a great improvement in any science or profession, and that an application in advanced years, after the mind is crowded, the attention divided or dissipated, and the memory in part lost, will make but a tolerable artist at best.

14. Friday. Another year is now gone, and upon recollection I find I have executed none of my plans of study. I cannot satisfy myself that I am much more knowing, either from books or men, from this chamber or the world, than I was at least a year ago, when I wrote the foregoing letter to Sewall.[1] Most of my time has been spent in rambling and dissipation. Riding and walking, smoking pipes and spending evenings, consume a vast proportion of my time; and the cares and anxieties of business damp my ardor and scatter my attention. But I must stay more at home, and commit more to writing. A pen is certainly an excellent instrument to fix a man's attention and to inflame his ambition. I am, therefore, beginning a new literary year in the twenty-sixth of my life.

I am just entered on the fifth year of my studies in law; and I think it is high time for a reformation, both in the man and the lawyer. Twenty-five years of the animal life is a great proportion to be spent to so little purpose; and four years, the space that we spend at college, is a great deal of time to spend for no more knowledge in the science and no more employment in the practice of law. Let me keep an exact journal, therefore, of the authors I read, in this paper. This day I am beginning my Lord Hale's History of the Common Law, a book borrowed of Mr. Otis and read once already, analysis and all, with great satisfaction. I wish I had Mr. Blackstone's Analysis, that I might compare and see what improvements he has made upon Hale's. But what principally pleased me in the first reading

[1] See page 79.

of Hale's History, was his Dissertation upon Descents and upon Trials by a Jury. Hale's Analysis, as Mr. Gridley tells me, is an improvement of one first planned and sketched by Noy, an attorney-general in the reign of Charles I.; and Mr. Blackstone's is an improvement upon Hale's. The title is "The History of the Common Law of England." The frontispiece I cannot comprehend;[1] it is this:

'Ισχυρὸν ὁ ΝΌΜΟΣ ἐστὶν ἄρχοντα.

His great distribution of the laws of England is, into *Leges Scriptæ* and *Leges non Scriptæ.* The first are acts of Parliament, which are originally reduced to writing before they are enacted or receive any binding power, every such law being in the first instance formally drawn up in writing, and made as it were a *tripartite* indenture between the king, the lords, and commons. The *Leges non Scriptæ*, although there may be some monument or memorial of them in writing (as there is of all of them,) yet all of them have not their original in writing, but have obtained their force by immemorial usage or custom.

15. Saturday. Spent last evening at Colonel Quincy's, with Colonel Lincoln. Several instances were mentioned when the independency and superiority of the law in general over particular departments of officers, civil and military, have been asserted and maintained by the Judges at home:—Lord Coke's resolution in the case of ——, in opposition to the opinion, and even to the orders and passionate threatenings of the king; Lord Holt's refusal to give the house of lords his reasons for his judgment in the case of —— in an extra-judicial manner, that is, without being legally and constitutionally called before them by a writ of error, certiorari or false judgment; and C. J. Willes's resolute, spirited assertion of the rights of common law in opposition to the court martial, against the intercession of powerful friends and even of the ministry, if not the king himself.[2]

[1] The frontispiece has been omitted from the later editions. Stephanus quotes the following as a proverb,—

'Ισχυρὸν ὁ νόμος ἐστὶν, ἢν ἄρχοντ' ἔχῃ.

which he translates,—The law is powerful if it have an executor.

[2] The first of the cases mentioned is the noted one touching the force of royal proclamations to set aside the law. The second is the case of the king against Knowllys. Both are suitably dwelt upon in the volumes lately published by Lord Campbell, of Lives of the Chief Justices of England; vol. i. p. 275; vol. ii. p. 148.

21. Friday. This day has been spent to little purpose. I must confine my body, or I never shall confine my thoughts:

The third case, though it constitutes the most remarkable event in the judicial life of Sir John Willes, appears to have escaped the attention of the same author, who shows clearly enough in other ways the feeble interest he takes in this part of his work. An account of it seems necessary to explain the allusion in the text, even though it have no immediate connection with the purpose of the present volumes. This conversation, held in 1760, in which instances of the assertion of the supremacy of the law over arbitrary power in the hands of the monarch are so carefully recounted, is not without its influence upon what comes afterwards.

A lieutenant of marines, by the name of Frye, whilst serving in the West Indies in 1744, was accused of some offences, for which he was tried by a court martial, condemned and sentenced to imprisonment for fifteen years besides the loss of his commission. Being remanded home with the proceedings in the case, for ratification by the admiralty, the sentence, so far from proving satisfactory, was annulled, and Frye fully and honorably reinstated. Not content with this tardy reparation for the sufferings which he had been compelled to endure in the course of his trial, Frye immediately brought an action for false imprisonment against Sir Chaloner Ogle, the presiding officer. The cause came up before Chief Justice Willes, and such was the nature of the evidence, that the jury at once brought in a verdict for the plaintiff with damages of a thousand pounds sterling. Taking advantage of an intimation thrown out by the court, Frye followed up this verdict with suits against two more of his unjust judges. One of them, Admiral Mayne, was arrested at the moment when he was presiding over another court martial assembled at Deptford to decide upon the mutual grievances of Admirals Matthews and Lestock, which had destroyed the efficiency of the Mediterranean squadron when in presence of the enemy the year before.

The officers sitting on this trial took fire at what they deemed a gross insult to their head, and rashly adopted some resolutions which they sent to the Secretary of the Admiralty, together with a letter containing formal charges of misconduct against Chief Justice Willes and his court. The judge was not a man to suffer the dignity of his court to be thus infringed, and his authority called in question. No sooner did he hear of the resolutions that had been sent to the King, than he caused warrants to be issued to take each individual of the twenty-eight constituting the court martial into custody.

The King and the ministry sympathized with the officers. The former went so far in his answer as to express "great displeasure at the insult offered to the court martial, by which the military discipline of the navy was so much affected, and to promise that he would consider what steps it might be advisable to take on the occasion." In spite of this royal language, the officers soon felt their situation uncomfortable. Yet they could extricate themselves only by signing a most humble recantation of all their offensive language. This was publicly presented in form to the Chief Justice, who thereupon sealed his triumph with the following remarks. The intimation thrown out in the first sentence will at this day be considered not the least singular portion of the whole affair.

"Although the injury I have received might have required a private satisfaction, yet as the offence was of a public nature, and offered to the whole court of common pleas as well as myself, I thought it more consistent with my character and the dignity of the post I have the honor to fill, to have satisfaction in this public manner; and desire, with the concurrence of my brothers, that it may be registered in the remembrance office, as a memorial to the present and future ages, that whoever set themselves above the law will in the end find themselves mistaken; for we may with propriety say of the law as of truth, '*Magna est et prævalebit.*'" *London Magazine* for 1746. *Barrow's Life of Lord Anson*, p. 126. *Corresp. of the Duke of Bedford*, vol. i. pp. 107–110–163.

running to Doctor's, cutting wood, blowing fire, cutting tobacco — waste my time, scatter my thoughts, and divert my ambition. A train of thought is hard to procure; trifles light as air break the chain, interrupt the series.

Finished the History of the Common Law, the second time. The Dissertation on Hereditary Descents, and that on Trials by Juries, are really very excellent performances, and well worth repeated attentive reading.

26. Wednesday. Ten days are now elapsed since I began Hale the second time; and all the law I have read for ten days, is that book once through. I read Wood's Institute through the first time with Mr. Putnam, in twice that time, that is, in three weeks, and kept a school every day. My present inattention to law is intolerable and ruinous.

Night before Thanksgiving. I have read a multitude of law-books; mastered but few. Wood, Coke, two volumes Lilly's Abridgment, two volumes Salkeld's Reports, Swinburne, Hawkins's Pleas of the Crown, Fortescue, Fitz-Gibbon, ten volumes in folio I read, at Worcester, quite through, besides octavos and lesser volumes, and many others of all sizes that I consulted occasionally without reading in course, as dictionaries, reporters, entries, and abridgments, &c.

I cannot give so good an account of the improvement of my two last years spent in Braintree. However, I have read no small number of volumes upon the law the last two years; — Justinian's Institutes I have read through in Latin, with Vinnius's perpetual notes; Van Muyden's Tractatio Institutionum Justiniani I read through and translated mostly into English, from the same language. Wood's Institute of the Civil Law, I read through. These on the Civil Law. On the Law of England I read Cowell's Institute of the Laws of England, in imitation of Justinian, Doctor and Student, Finch's Discourse of Law, Hale's History, and some Reporters, Cases in Chancery, Andrews, &c., besides occasional searches for business; also a General Treatise of Naval Trade and Commerce, as founded on the laws and statutes. All this series of reading has left but faint impressions and a very imperfect system of law in my head. I must form a serious resolution of beginning and pursuing, quite through, the plans of my Lords Hale and Reeve. Wood's Institutes of Common Law I never read but once, and my

Lord Coke's Commentary on Littleton I never read but once; these two authors I must get and read over and over again, and I will get them, too, and break through, as Mr. Gridley expressed it, all obstructions.

Besides, I am but a novice in natural law and civil law. There are multitudes of excellent authors on natural law that I have never read; indeed, I never read any part of the best authors, Puffendorf and Grotius. In the civil law there are Hoppius and Vinnius, commentators on Justinian, Domat, &c., beside Institutes of Canon and Feudal Law that I have to read. Much may be done in two years, I have found already; and let it be my care that at the end of the next two years I be better able to show that no time has been lost, than I ever have been yet.

Let me practise the rule of Pythagoras:—

> *Μηδ' ὕπνον μαλακοῖσιν ἐπ' ὄμμασι προσδέξασθαι,*
> *Πρὶν τῶν ἡμερινῶν ἔργων τρὶς ἕκαστον ἐπελθεῖν·*
> *Πῆ παρέβην; τί δ' ἔρεξα; τί μοι δέον ὀυκ ἐτελέσθη;*

Thus let me, every night before I go to bed, write down in this book what book of law I have read.

28. Friday. I have not read one word of law this day; but several points and queries have been suggested to me by the consultors. In whom is the fee and freehold of our burying yard? What right has any man to erect a monument, or sink a tomb there, without the consent of the proprietors? [1]

29. Saturday. There is an anecdote in the Spectator of De Witt, the famous Dutch politician. Somebody asked him how he could rid his hands of that endless multiplicity and variety of business that passed through them without confusion? He answered, "By doing one thing at once." When he began any thing, he applied his whole attention to it till he had finished it. This rule should be observed in law. If any point is to be examined, every book should be consulted, and every light should be considered before you proceed to any other business or study. If any book is to be read, no other book should be taken up to divert or interrupt your attention till that book is finished.

Order, method, regularity in business or study, have excellent

[1] The examination of this point, at length, here follows in the Diary. It is omitted, as without interest at the present day.

effects, both in saving of time and in bettering and improving performance. Business done in order, is done sooner and better.

30. Sunday. Read no law; read Bolingbroke.

December 1. Monday. I am beginning a week and a month, and I arose by the dawning of the day, and by sunrise had made my fire and read a number of pages in Bolingbroke. Tuesday and Wednesday passed without reading any law.

6. Saturday. Talked with Zab about Newton, Bacon, Locke, Martin and Chambers, Rowning, Desaguliers, S' Gravesande, &c. I told him I had a low opinion of the compilers, abridgers, and abstract makers; we had better draw science from its fountain in original authors. These writers, the hirelings of the booksellers, only vend us the discoveries of other philosophers, in another form and under another title, in order to get bread to eat and raiment to put on. Zab says that Martin has made several discoveries, has invented new machines, improved and perfected old ones; nay, has even detected errors in Newton: e. g. Newton always thought the moon was surrounded by an atmosphere, but Martin proves it is not, because the stars that appear all round it, above, below, and on each side of it, are not diminished in their lustre, as they would appear if the rays passed from them through an atmosphere.

Then we transided to Dr. Simpson, Euclid, &c., and he asked me to demonstrate that the three angles of a triangle are equal to two right. I undertook it.[1] Then we attempted to demonstrate the forty-seventh of the first book.

I am astonished at my own ignorance in the French tongue; I find I can neither express my own thoughts in it, nor understand others who express theirs readily in it. I can neither give nor receive thoughts by that instrument.

14. Sunday. Hunt *v.* White; — complaint to Colonel Quincy of a scandalous lie made and published to Hunt's damage.[2]

16. Tuesday. Attended the trial all day between Hunt and White, before Colonel Quincy, at James Bracket's. What will be the consequence of this trial, — to me, to Hunt, and to White? White has been punished for his licentious tittletattle; but Hunt has gained neither recompense nor credit. Benjamin Thayer is enraged, and Pratt and Pitty were enraged at me for abusing

[1] Here follows, in the original, a diagram with a demonstration.
[2] Here follows a report of the proceedings and argument in this case.

them by asking them their thoughts. Ben Thayer continues so, for aught I know or care. I fear this unsuccessful prosecution, connected with that of Lovell and Reed, will occasion squibs, and injure my reputation in Weymouth. However, in both I am well assured I had good cause of action. The circumstances of suspicion against Hunt have taken such hold of men's minds, that no conviction of White would have retrieved Hunt's character at all. It would have been much better never to have stirred in this affair. A prosecution commenced with so much temper, pursued with so much resolution, then supported by so little evidence, and terminated by agreement, though in his favor, yet with so small advantage, will give occasion for Weymouth tongues to wanton in obloquy, and for their sides to riot in laughter.

Virtues, ambition, generosity, indulged to excess, degenerate into extravagance, which plunges headlong into villany and folly.

18. Thursday. Yesterday spent in Weymouth in settling the disputes between old W. and young F. W. has the remainder of his habitual trickish, lying, cheating disposition, strongly working to this day; — an infinity of jesuitical distinctions and mental reservations. He told me he never lost a cause at court in his life; — which W. and W. say is a downright lie.

He owned to me that his character had been that of a knave and a villain, and says, "every man of wit and sense will be called a villain; — my principle has been, to deal upon honor with all men so long as they deal upon honor with me; but as soon as they begin to trick me, I think I ought to trick them."

Thus, every knave thinks others as knavish or more knavish than himself. What an intrenchment against the attack of his conscience is this; — "the knavery of my neighbor is superior to mine." An old, withered, decrepit person, eighty-seven years of age, with a head full of all the wiles and guile and artifice of the infernal serpent, is really a melancholy sight. Ambition of appearing sprightly, cunning, smart, capable of outwitting younger men. In short, I never saw that guile and subtlety in any man of that age. Father Niles has a little of that same serpentine guile. I never felt the meaning of the words, stratagem, guile, subtlety, cunning wiles, &c., that Milton applies to the devil, as his plan to effect the ruin of our first parents, so forcibly, as since I knew that old man and his grandson, who seems to have the same subtlety, and a worse temper, under a total secrecy and dissembled intention. He has a smiling face and a flattering tongue, with a total concealment of his designs; though a devilish, malignant, fiery temper appears in his eyes. He is a Cassius, like B. T.; sees through the characters of men much further and clearer than ordinary; never laughs; now and then smiles, or half smiles. Father W., with all his subtlety and guile, may be easily overreached by men like himself. He is too open, too ostentatious of his cunning, and, therefore, is generally outwitted and worsted.

Five strange characters I have had concerns with very lately! Two fools and two knaves, besides Daniel N., a lunatic. F.'s joy, like that of the devil when he had completed the temptation and fall of man, was extravagant; but he broke out into too violent a passion; he broke his own seal of secrecy, and betrayed his villanous designs to me. On my resenting his declared intention, he grew sensible of his error, and attempted, by soothing, to retrieve it. "He was sorry he had broke out so." "The treatment he had suffered made him in a passion." "I raised your temper too, prodigiously."

Justice Dyer says there is more occasion for justices than for lawyers. Lawyers live upon the sins of the people. If all men were just, and honest, and pious, and religious, &c., there would be no need of lawyers. But justices are necessary to keep men just, and honest, and pious, and religious. — Oh, sagacity! But it may be said, with equal truth, that all magistrates, and all civil officers, and all civil government, are founded and maintained by the sins of the people. All armies would be needless if men were universally virtuous. Most manufacturers and tradesmen would be needless; nay, some of the natural passions and sentiments of human minds would be needless, upon that supposition. For example, resentment, which has for its objects wrong and injury. No man, upon that supposition, would ever give another a just provocation; and no just resentment would take place without a just provocation. Thus, our natural resentments are founded on the sins of the people, as much as the profession of the law, or that of arms, or that of divinity. In short, vice and folly are so interwoven in all human affairs, that they could not, possibly, be wholly separated from them without tearing and rending the whole system of human nature and state; nothing would remain as it is.

22. Monday. This day and to-morrow are the last. I have but one blank left that I can use.

---

27. Saturday. Governor Bernard's speech to the two houses at the opening of the present sessions, has several inaccuracies in it. "The glorious conclusion of the North American War." The North American War is not yet concluded; it continues obstinate and bloody with the Cherokees, and will be renewed, probably, against the French in Louisiana. However, with regard to this province, whose legislature the Governor was congratulating, it may, not very improperly, be called a conclusion. "The fair prospect of the security of your country being settled upon the most sure and lasting foundations." Is not this sentence filled with tautology? The security being secured upon secure foundations. *Emendation*, "and the fair prospect that now presents itself of tranquillity, established on lasting foundations." But it is not tranquillity, nor safety, nor preservation, nor peace, nor happiness; but it is "security." Then it is not established, fixed, placed, but it is "settled;" and then it is not stable, permanent, but "sure." Here are, certainly, words used merely for sound.

"This great contest," &c. *Q.* What does he mean; the war, or the conclusion of the war? If the latter, conquest should have been his word. If the former, what follows is not true: namely, that "we may date the firm establishment of the British Empire in North America." From our late successes and acquisitions we may date that establishment, but not from our misfortunes and losses, which make no unmemorable part of this great contest.

"We form these pleasing assurances, not only from the more striking instances of the superiority of its power, but also, from the less obvious observation of the improvement of its policy." Its power; that is, the British Empire's power. Instances; that is, particulars in which it has appeared. Obvious observation has a good meaning, but an inelegant and inartificial sound. A defect of elegance, variety, harmony, at least.

"The improving a country is a more pleasing task than the defending it." Improving and defending, participles, used as substantives with the article *the* before them, will never be used by a grammarian, much less by a rhetorician! I never could bear such expressions in others, and never could use them myself, unless in case of absolute necessity, where there is no substantive to express the same idea.

"As I have consulted your convenience in deferring calling you together until this, the most leisure time of your whole year," &c. "In deferring calling," would never have been used together by a discerning ear. He might have said "In deferring this session, until, &c." "Your whole year!" Why yours any more than mine or others? *Ans.* It is not the most leisure time of every man's whole year; it is the most busy time of some men's year.

Deacon Palmer's observation upon this speech, that "he talks like a weak, honest man," is childish; 't is superficial; 't is prejudice; 't is a silly, thoughtless repetition of what he has heard others say. For though there are no marks of knavery in it, there are marks of good sense, I think. Grammatical and rhetorical inaccuracies are by no means proofs of weakness or ignorance. They may be found in Bacon, Locke, Newton, &c.

1761. January 2. Friday. The representatives, in their address to the Governor, have told him that "Great Britain is the leading and most respectable power in the whole world." Let us examine this. Is she the leading power either in war or negotiation? In war? She has no army, not more than fifty or sixty thousand men, whereas France has a standing army of two hundred and fifty thousand men in camp and in garrison, and their officers are as gallant and skilful, their gunners and engineers the most accomplished of any in Europe.

Their navy, indeed, is now inconsiderable, and our navy alone has given us the advantage. But our navy alone will not make us the leading power. How we can be called the leading power, I cannot see. Holland, Spain, Portugal, Denmark, and all Italy have refused to follow us, and Austria, Russia, Sweden, and indeed almost all the States of Germany, the Prince of Hesse excepted, have followed France. The only power, independent power, that has consented to follow us, is Prussia; and indeed, upon recollection, it seems to me we followed Prussia, too, rather than the contrary. Thus, we are the leading power without followers.

And if we are not the leading power in war, we never have

been the leading power in negotiation. It is a common-place observation that the French have regained by treaty all the advantages which we had gained by arms. Now, whether this arose from the superior dexterity of the French plenipotentiaries, or from the universal complaisance of the other plenipotentiaries of Europe to France and Frenchmen, it equally proves that England is not the leading power in councils.

How, then, are we the most respectable? The most respected I am sure we are not! Else how came all Europe to remain neuters, or else take arms against us? How came foreigners from all countries to resort to France to learn their policy, military discipline, fortification, manufactures, language, letters, science, politeness, &c., so much more than to England? How comes the French language to be studied and spoken as a polite accomplishment all over Europe? And how come all negotiations to be held in French?

And if we consider every thing, the religion, government, freedom, navy, merchandise, army, manufactures, policy, arts, sciences, numbers of inhabitants, and their virtues, it seems to me that England falls short in more and more important particulars than it exceeds the kingdom of France.

To determine the character of "leading and respectable," as Doctor Savil does, from a few victories and successes,—by which rules he makes Charles XII. to have been in his day the leading and most respectable power, and Oliver Cromwell in his, and the king of Prussia in this,—is most ignorant and silly.

In short, "leading and respectable" is not to be determined either by the prince, the policy, the army, navy, arts, sciences, commerce, nor by any other national advantage, taken singly, and abstracted from the rest. But that power is to be denominated so, whose aggregate of component parts is most.

8. Thursday. Last Monday had a passionate wrangle with Eben Thayer, before Major Crosby. He called me *a petty lawyer*. This I resented.

Messrs. ——[1]

I am an old man, seventy odd; and as I had my education, so I have spent my whole life, a few weeks in a year excepted, when I commonly took a journey, in the country. I was naturally inquisitive and a little too talkative in my youth, which qualities have, perhaps, increased with my age, but as I remember I used to sneer at the vanity and impertinence of old Nestor, whose speeches I have often read formerly in Pope's Homer, (a book, of which I was then, and am still very fond,) I expect that younger men will laugh at the like vanity and impertinence in me, which it shall be my care therefore, in this paper at least, to avoid, because I would have the subject of it candidly weighed.

Indeed, scarcely any thing that I have observed in the course of a long life has a greater influence on the religion, morals, health, property, liberties, and tranquillity of the world;—I mean public houses.

The temper and passions, the profaneness and brutal behavior inspired by the low sort of company that frequent such houses, and by the liquors they drink there, are not very compatible with the pure and undefiled religion of Jesus — that religion, whose first principle is to renounce all filthiness and superfluity of naughtiness. That inattention to the public ordinances of religion, as well as to private devotion, which I have reasons to think so prevalent in these times, is no unnatural consequence of the very general resort to those licentious houses. The plentiful use of spirituous liquors begins with producing a strange confusion of mind, appetites and passions too violent for the government of reason; proceeds to involve men in debts, and of consequence, in lying, cheating, stealing, and sometimes in greater crimes; and ends in total and incurable dissolution of manners.

The effects of such intemperance upon health are of two kinds. It either throws them into some acute and inflammatory fever, which carries them from the midst of their vices and their follies, the mischiefs they do, and the distresses they suffer, at

[1] Here follows the draught of an article written in the character of an elderly man, and evidently intended for a newspaper, although it does not appear ever to have been printed. As it touches an existing abuse, to remedy which, at that time, the author made strenuous efforts for several years, and which has, of late years, again strongly roused the public attention, it is retained entire.

once into their graves, or else it leads them by insensible degrees through all the gloom and languor of a chronical distemper, despised by many, hated by more, and pitied by a few, to a long expected and desired death.

Thousands and thousands are every year expiring in Europe, and proportionable numbers in America, the miserable victims of their own imprudence, and the ill policy of rulers in permitting the causes of their ruin to exist. Allured by the smell of these infernal liquors, like the ghosts in romances allured by the scent of human blood, they resort to these houses, waste their time, their strength, and their money, which ought to be employed in the management of their own affairs and families, till by degrees, much expended, little earned, they contract habits of carelessness, idleness, and intemperance; their creditors demand, they promise to pay, but fail; writs issue, charges are multiplied for the maintenance of others as idle as themselves, and executions strip them of all they have, and cast their miserable bodies into loathsome prisons.

The number of these houses have been lately so much augmented and the fortunes of their owners so much increased, that an artful man has little else to do but secure the favor of taverners, in order to secure the suffrages of the rabble that attend these houses, which in many towns within my observation makes a very large, perhaps the largest number of voters.

The consequence is, that these offices and elections, which all the wisest legislators of the world, in humble imitation of God and nature, have allotted to probity and understanding, may in time, I dare not say have already, become the gratuity of tipplers for drams and slops. Good God! Where are the rights of Englishmen! Where is the spirit that once exalted the souls of Britons, and emboldened their faces to look even Princes and Monarchs in the face! But, perhaps, I am too anxious, and in truth I must own I so revere the true constitution of our government, founded in those great principles that accomplished in a great antiquity the destruction of Troy, that extended in a later period the bounds of the Roman Empire, and that produced in the English history so many events for the universe to admire, that I cannot think of its evaporating and passing from human breasts with flip and rum, of which event there is great danger, without rage.

Last of all, innumerable violations of the peace and order of society are every day occurring, that spring originally from the same sources. Quarrels, boxing, duels, oaths, curses, affrays, and riots, are daily hatching from eggs and spawns deposited in the same nests. In short, these houses, like so many boxes of Pandora, are sending forth every day innumerable plagues of every kind, natural, moral, and political, that increase and multiply fast enough to lay waste in a little while the whole world. How different is this from the state of things in my youth. Instead of an unmanly retreat to the chimney-corner of a tavern, the young fellows of my age were out in the air improving their strength and activity by wrestling, running, leaping, lifting, and the like vigorous diversions, and when satisfied with these, resorted every one to his mistress or his wife. Love, that divine passion which nature has implanted for the renovation of the species, and the greatest solace of our lives — virtuous love, I mean — from whence the greatest part of human happiness originates, and which these modern seminaries have almost extinguished, or at least changed into filthiness and brutal debauch, was then considered as God intended it, both a duty of our nature and the greatest source of our bliss. But it is melancholy to think that the present prevalent debauchery which tends so much to shorten the lives of the present generation, tends also to prevent the propagation of a succeeding one. I really am afraid that in another century, unless some wise precaution should intervene, a man of my age will be the rarest phenomenon.

I should be called talkative indeed, if I should attempt to develop the causes of that strange multiplication of such houses, that is lately grown up. But I fear that some selectmen are induced by a foolish complaisance, and others by designs of ambition, to give their approbation to too many persons who are improper, and, perhaps, too many that are proper for that trust. I am afraid that some justices may be induced by lucrative motives, by mercantile principles, to augment the manufactory or the importation of rum or molasses, without attending to the other consequences, which are plainly pernicious.

But let this paper be considered as a warning, from one who has seen better days, to magistrates, to suppress rather than increase within their department; to selectmen, to discountenance rather than encourage pretenders, in their sphere; to parents and masters, to restrain their children and servants from frequenting. And in short, let every man endeavor to keep one from suffering any injury from them in any respect.

I was too incautious and unartful in my proceeding; but practice makes perfect.[1] I should have first taken all the summonses into my own hands, or powers of attorney from the defendants. Then I should have moved that the sheriff should be directed to return his writs, that against White, and that against Hayden. Then I should have drawn a complaint on each of them and filed them all. Then I should have desired the justice to make a record of his judgment. This would have been regular, masterly management; but I had no time to think and prepare.

This is the third time I have been before Major Crosby with T. The first time, he was for John Spear; that action was demolished. The next time he appeared for Nathan Spear against Eph. Hunt and John Vinton. Those actions were demolished. The last time he appeared for Bayley against Niles, White, Hayden, &c. These actions were all demolished. Thus I have come off pretty triumphantly every time, and he pretty foolishly. Yet I have managed none of these cases in the most masterly manner. I see several inadvertent mistakes and omissions. But I grow more expert, less diffident, &c. I feel my own strength. I see the complacent countenances of the crowd, and I see the respectful face of the justice, and the fearful faces of pettifoggers, more than I did.

To Chardon.[2]

Lest a maiden nicety should prevent the correspondence proposed last week, I have taken my pen to open it upon the lofty subject of law. We shall be called silly and tasteless, &c., for aught I know or care. For, let the smart sayings of the gay, and the grave satires even of the wise and learned, be what they

[1] This alludes to several causes tried in December.

[2] This is the draught of a letter to Peter Chardon, the person spoken of, as of so great promise, in page 39. The date of it is uncertain, although it follows in this connection. Possibly it may have been written a year or two earlier.

will, I have, for my own part, and I thank God for it, no bad opinion of the law, either as a science or a profession.

Why the minute arteries and tendons of the human body, the organization of the human voice and mouth, and numberless other subjects of the like sort, should be thought worthy of the attention of a liberal mind, and the no less wonderful and much more important combination of passions, appetites, affections, in the human breast, that operate on society, too futile or too disagreeable for a wise man's examination, I cannot imagine. Nay, if we proceed to the positive institutions of the law, I cannot think them so extremely dull, uncouth, and unentertaining, as you and I have heard them represented by some whom we love and honor. Multitudes of needless matters, and some that are nonsensical, it must be confessed, have in the course of ages crept into the law. But I beg to know what art or science can be found in the whole circle, that has not been taught by silly, senseless pedants, and is not stuffed with their crudities and jargon.

The man who intends to become skilful in any science, must be content to study such authors as have written upon it.

No man will be an adept in grammar or rhetoric, or poetry, or music, or architecture, without laboring through a vast deal of nonsense and impertinence; in short, nonsense seems an unalienable property of human affairs; and it is as idle to expect that any author should write well upon any subject, without intermingling some proportion of it, as it is to expect that a rapid torrent should descend from the mountains without washing some dirt and earth along with it.

But, if the grandeur and importance of a subject have any share in the pleasure it communicates, I am sure the law has by far the advantage of most other sciences. Nothing less than the preservation of the health and properties, lives and tranquillity, morals and liberties of millions of the human species, is the object and design of the law; and a comparison of several constitutions of government invented for those purposes, an examination of the great causes of their danger, as well as those of their safety, must be as agreeable an employment as can exercise the mind.

But it is a science that comprises a multitude; and great industry, as well as many helps, are needful to subdue it.

And, in truth, I do not know a more agreeable help than the correspondence of a friend. Exchange of observation, proposing difficulties, stating cases, repeating arguments, examining sophisms, will both arouse and support our ambition, and wear by easy degrees a system of law into the mind.

The plan that I would propose, then, is this; — for you to write me a report of any case you hear argued before the courts of admiralty, court of probate, governor and council, court of sessions, justice of the peace, &c., that you think curious; propose questions for examination; and write me answers to letters from me on all the foregoing subjects. And if we will secrete each other's letters, we shall at least avoid the ridicule of others. But, if we should be detected, we can say that Tully and Atticus held some such correspondence before, that never raised a laugh in the world.

---

27. Tuesday. Last Friday I borrowed of Mr. Gridley the second volume of the Corpus Juris Canonici, notis illustratum, Gregorii XIII. Jussu editum: complectens, Decretum Gratiani; Decretales Gregorii Papæ IX.; Sextum Decretalium Bonifacii Papæ VIII.; Clementinas; Extravagantes Joannis Papæ XXII.; Extravagantes Communes.

Accesserunt Constitutiones novæ summorum Pontificum nunquam antea editæ, quæ 7 Decretalium loco esse possint: Annotationes Ant. Naldi, cum addit. novis: Et quæ in plerisque Editionibus desiderabantur, Petri Lancelotti Institutiones Juris Canonici; Regulæ cancellariæ Apostolicæ cum Indicibus, &c.

Mr. Gridley, about fifteen months since, advised me to read an Institute of the Canon Law; and that advice lay broiling in my head till last week, when I borrowed the book. I am very glad that he gave and I took the advice, for it will explain many things in ecclesiastical history, and open that system of fraud, bigotry, nonsense, impudence, and superstition, on which the papal usurpations are founded, besides increasing my skill in the Latin tongue, and my acquaintance with civil law; for, in many respects the canon is grafted on the civil.

February 6. Friday. I have now almost finished the first book of Peter Lancelott's Institutes; which first book is taken up *de Jure Personarum*, and is well analyzed in the twenty-ninth title *de Clericis non residentibus*.

9. Monday. This morning, as I lay abed, I recollected my last week's work. I find I was extremely diligent; — constantly in my chamber; spent no evenings abroad, not more than one at the Doctor's; have taken no walks; never on horseback the whole week excepting once, which was on Tuesday, when I went to Boston. Yet, how has this retirement and solitude been spent? In too much rambling and straggling from one book to another; from the Corpus Juris Canonici to Bolingbroke; from him to Pope; from him to Addison; from him to Yorick's Sermons, &c. In fine, the whole week and all my diligence have been lost, for want of observing De Witt's maxim, "One thing at once."

This reflection raised a determination to reassume the Corpus Juris, or rather Lancelott's Institutes; read nothing else, and think of nothing else, — till sometime.

With the week, then, I begin the second book Institutionum Juris Canonici. De Rerum Divisione, atque illarum Administratione. Titulus Primus. Res Ecclesiasticæ sunt aut spirituales aut temporales.

Res spirituales sunt aut incorporales aut corporales; et corporales dividuntur in sacramenta, in res sacras, sanctas, et religiosas.

This Institute is a curious monument of priestly ambition, avarice, and subtlety. 'T is a system of sacerdotal guile.

His Majesty has declared himself, by his speech to his Parliament, to be a man of piety and candor in religion, a friend of liberty and property in government, and a patron of merit.

"The blessing of heaven I devoutly implore;" "As the surest foundation of the whole" (that is, the loyalty and affection of his people, his resolution to strengthen the constitution, the civil, &c., rights of his subjects and the prerogatives of his crown, &c.) "and the best means to draw down the Divine favor on my reign, it is my fixed purpose to countenance and encourage the practice of true religion and virtue." These are proofs of his piety.

He promises to patronize religion, virtue, the British name and constitution, in church and state; the subjects' rights, liberty, commerce, military merit. These are sentiments worthy of a king; — a patriot king.[1]

March 3. Tuesday. Mem.* To inquire of Tufts, Gould, Whitmarsh, Hunts, Whites, &c., about their method of mending highways by a rate; and to inquire at Worcester, whenever I shall get there, of Chandlers, Putnam, Willard, Paine, Swan, &c., about their method. They mended their ways by a rate, I am sure.

Samuel Clark, Daniel Nash; — myrmidons of Thayer. Luke Lambard, Ben Hayden, Samuel Clark, &c.; — all the myrmidons of Thayer, &c. Myrmidons, bull dogs, hounds, creatures, tools.

Weymouth mends her ways by a rate; — each man is rated so much; and a day's work is estimated at so much; a horse, a cart, yoke of oxen, &c., at so much; so each man has his choice, — to pay his money or to work it out. I did not think to ask what sum they expended yearly to mend ways. *Quære* — How they mend their ways, streets, lanes, alleys, &c., in Boston? Whether by a rate? Is not the town taxed for pavement of streets, &c.? *Q.* Whether they ever permit those who choose it, to work it out themselves?

March 21. Saturday. Memorandum. To inquire more particularly into the practice in Weymouth; — how they estimate a day's work for a man, horse, yoke of oxen, carts, tools, pickaxes, spades, shovels, &c.? how much money, or what a sum they assess

[1] These were the sentiments of the writer at the accession of the new and young sovereign George the Third, in the very same year and within a few weeks of the argument in the cause of writs of assistance. See page 124, note.

* [In March, when I had no suspicion, I heard my name pronounced in a nomination of surveyors of highways. I was very wroth, because I knew no better, but said nothing. My friend, Dr. Savil, came to me and told me that he had nominated me, to prevent me from being nominated as a constable. "For," said the Doctor, "they make it a rule to compel every man to serve either as constable or surveyor, or to pay a fine." I said, "they might as well have chosen any boy in school, for I knew nothing of the business; but since they had chosen me at a venture, I would accept it in the same manner, and find out my duty as I could." Accordingly, I went to ploughing, and ditching, and blowing rocks upon Penn's hill, and building an entire new bridge of stone below Dr. Miller's and above Mr. Wibird's. The best workmen in town were employed in laying the foundation and placing the bridge, but the next spring brought down a flood that threw my bridge all into ruins. The materials remained, and were afterwards relaid in a more durable manner; and the blame fell upon the workmen, not upon me. For all agreed that I had executed my office with impartiality, diligence, and spirit.]

upon the whole town, annually, to amend their ways? whether the assessment is committed to the surveyor, of all within his district, &c.? Inquire, too, at Boston, of Cunningham, how they pave and repair the pavements of their great streets, and lanes, and alleys, &c.? Whether poor people are left, at their election, to work or to pay? and how they apportion their assessments? But I presume it is not according to the poll tax, but in proportion to the province tax or town and county; so that rich men may contribute, in proportion to their wealth, to repairing, as they contribute most, by their equipages, &c., to the wearing and spoiling the highways. But a tax upon the polls and real and personal estates of the town, will not bring the burthen to equality. We will suppose that John Ruggles and Caleb Hubbard are rated equally for heads, and real and personal estates. Caleb Hubbard carts down one thousand pounds' worth of wood and timber to the landing-places, and so reaps three or four hundred pounds a year profit by improving the ways; and by his heavy loads and wheels, he breaks, and cuts, and crushes the ways to pieces. But Mr. Ruggles, on the other hand, confines himself to his farm; and he neither receives benefit from any highways, or does any damage to them, further than riding to meeting on Sundays and town meetings. Now, what reason, what propriety can there be in taxing Ruggles and Hubbard equally to the highways? One gets his living by ruining the ways, the other neither gets a farthing by them, nor does them a farthing's damage.*

The power of a town; the proviso in the eleventh of George, chapter IV., — "That this act shall not extend to the preventing or altering the practice, in any town, of defraying the charge of repairing or amending the highways by a rate, or tax, or any other

* [There had been a controversy in town, for many years, concerning the mode of repairing the roads. A party had long struggled to obtain a vote that the highways should be repaired by a tax, but never had been able to carry their point. The roads were very bad and much neglected, and I thought a tax a more equitable method and more likely to be effectual, and, therefore, joined this party in a public speech, carried a vote by a large majority, and was appointed to prepare a by-law, to be enacted at the next meeting. Upon inquiry, I found that Roxbury, and, after them, Weymouth, had adopted this course. I procured a copy of their law, and prepared a plan for Braintree, as nearly as possible conformable to their model, reported it to the town, and it was adopted by a great majority. Under this law the roads have been repaired to this day, and the effects of it are visible to every eye.]

method they have or shall agree upon;" the words, "agreed upon," in this proviso, I presume, signify "determined by the major part of the voters;" for the same words, "agreed upon," are used in several other acts, where their meaning must be so. Thus, 6 W. & M., chapter V.—the act to enable towns, villages, proprietors in common and undivided lands, to sue and be sued.

Messrs.[1]

I am an old man, turned of seventy. When I was young, my common amusement was reading. I had some engagements in business, and was no enemy to innocent pleasure; but as my circumstances were easy, I gave a greater indulgence to my curiosity of conversing largely with the world than most persons of my age and rank. In this course of life I soon found that human nature, the dignity of which I heard extolled by some and debased by others, was far from deserving that reverence and admiration which is due to great virtue and intelligence. I found, as I thought in that day, a multitude of people who suffered themselves to be caught by hooks and snares covered over with such bait as would not have imposed even on fishes and birds; and I found, as I thought, a few others, the anglers of that day, whose constant attention and pursuit was to allure and take that multitude.

The first instances of this sort that fell under my observation raised my compassion and indignation alternately. I pitied poor deluded simplicity on one hand, and I raged against cruelty and wickedness on the other; and could not but think that to rescue the lamb from the jaws of the wolf would be a noble adventure. But on further consideration, the design seemed impracticable. The attempt was odious. The knaves would arise in a combination to ruin the reformer, and the fools would be managed in no other way than that of their appetites and passions. For this reason, and to avoid the pungent misery of a disappointed, despised patriot, I determined to make a total alteration in the course and nature of my ideas and sentiments. Whenever I heard or saw an instance of atrocious treachery, fraud, hypocrisy, injustice, and cruelty, the common effects of excessive ambition, avarice, and lust, instead of indulg-

[1] Another article written for the newspapers.

ing the sentiments of nature, which I found were a resentment bordering on rage, I resolved instantly to set up a laugh, and make myself merry. Whenever I saw a simple deluded creature brought by the craft of others to brutal debauchery, sickness, cold, hunger, prison, whipping-post, pillory, or gallows, instead of indulging sympathy and feeling, I set myself to laughing. I must own I found a good deal of difficulty to command myself at first in this bold attempt to alter the whole system of morality; and in spite of my attention, a flash of vengeance, or a thrill of pity, would sometimes escape me before I could bring my muscles into a risible posture.

But by long practice I have at last obtained a settled habit of making myself merry at all the wickedness and misery of the world. And the causes of ridicule have been every hour increasing and multiplying from the twenty-fifth year of my age, when I first attempted the alteration of my mind, to the present hour. And now, in spite of all the infirmities of old age, I am the most tittering, giggling mortal you ever saw. But the amplest source of my merriment, through the whole course of my life, has been the affair of English privileges, British liberty, and all that.

I have heard men every day for fifty years boasting, "Our constitution is the first under heaven. We are governed by our own laws. No tyrant can lord it over us. The king is as accountable for his conduct as the subject. No government that ever existed was so essentially free; every man is his own monarch; his will or the will of his agent, and no other, can bind him." All these gallant, blustering speeches I have heard in words, and I never failed to raise a horse laugh; for observe the pleasant course of these things.

The few who have real honor, temperance, and understanding, who are desirous of getting their bread and paying their debts by their own industry, apply their attention to their own business, and leave the affairs of towns and provinces to others. But a young fellow, who happens to be by nature, or by habit, indolent, and perhaps profligate, begins by laying schemes by himself or his friends, to live and get money without labor or care. His first step is, to procure a deputation from some sheriff. By the help of writs and executions, and drawing writs, or employing some child, &c. to draw them for a share, one third or one fourth of the fee, then serving them and executions, carrying tales and intelligence from one party to the other, and then settling disputes, vastly compassionating the party by taking twice lawful fees, he wheedles himself into some connection with the people, and considerable sums of money into his own pockets. He presently grows a capable man, very expert at calculations, and well acquainted with the real and personal estates of the town, and so, very fit for selectman; and after two or three years opposition from the most virtuous and independent part of a town, he obtains an election. After this his reputation increases very fast. He becomes, to those not already grappled to his interest by fear or affection, very assiduous and obliging. And when the season of the year approaches, a swarm of candidates for approbation to keep taverns or dram-shops surround him for his favor. For one, he will use his utmost interest; for another, he really thinks there is occasion for a public house where he lives; for a third, his circumstances are so needy, he really thinks he ought to be assisted; for a fourth, he is so unable to work that he needs to be assisted; and to a fifth, he likes it very well, for he thinks the more there are, the better, the more obliging they will be, and the cheaper they will sell. Taverns and dram-shops are therefore placed in every corner of the town, where poor mankind, allured by the smell of brandy and rum, resort and carouse, waste their time, spend their money, run in debt to tavern and others, grow attached to the taverner, who is attached to his patron both by gratitude and expectation. The hero of this romance is presently extolled as a public blessing, as the most useful man in town, as a very understanding man; and is, at the next May meeting, set up for a candidate as representative. The same body of wealthy and virtuous persons who opposed the first step of his exaltation, are still resolute to oppose the second, and for the first few years he fails. But by assiduity and impudence, by extending and fortifying the parts of the same system, he increases his interest, and the virtuous few begin to dread the consequences; they resolve not to be present and witnesses of the disgrace of the town. They stay at home, and the news is brought them that the person they despised, &c., &c., has obtained his election.

In this manner, men, who are totally ignorant of all law, human and divine, natural, civil, ecclesiastical, and common, are employed to make laws for their country, while others who have been led by their education to search to the bottom of human nature, and to examine the effect of all laws upon human affairs . . . .

It would be worth while to describe all the transformations of ——'s flattery; yet there is always a salvo, which shows his deceit and insincerity.

"If Mr. Adams should become, in two or three years, one of the most eminent lawyers in the county, and remove to Boston, there you would find persons who have daughters to dispose of, who have knowledge of the world, and prudence enough to look out the best characters for matches to their daughters. Twenty such men would have their eyes upon you; would dress out their daughters to the best advantage, contrive interviews, lay schemes; and, presently, some one more beautiful, or sensible, or witty, or artful than the rest, will take you in. We shall see you, in spite of your philosophy, and contempt for wife and mistress, and all that, sighing and dying with love." Here, under a specious pretext of raillery for my boasted and affected indifference to ladies, he is insinuating, or would make me believe that he designed to insinuate, that I am likely to be the ablest lawyer on the stage in two or three years; that twenty gentlemen will eye me for a match to their daughters, and all that. This is the flattery. Yet, in truth, he only said, *if* Mr. Adams should become, &c.; so that if his consequences should never take place, — "Oh! I never expected they would, for I did not expect you would be eminent." Besides, if he was to speak his real sentiments, — "I am so ill-bred, unpolished, &c., that I never shall succeed with ladies, or the world, &c., &c."

The same evening I showed him my draught of our licensed houses, and the remarks upon it.[1] Oh! he was transported! he

[1] This draught consists of a rough plan of the principal roads in the town, with the position of every licensed house marked upon it, and certain remarks made upon each. It has a local interest at this day, for more reasons than one. The following note is all that is worth inserting here:—

N. B. Place one foot of your dividers at Eb. Thayer's house, and extend the other about one mile and a half, and then sweep a circle; you will surround eight public houses, besides one in the centre. There is vastly more travelling and little less business in Milton, Dorchester, and Roxbury, where public houses are thinly scattered, than there is in Braintree; and why poor Braintree men,

was ravished! he would introduce that plan at the sessions, and read the remarks, and say they were made, as well as the plan, by a gentleman to whom there could be no exception, &c. He saw an abstract of the argument for and against writs of assistants;[1] and says, "did you take this from those gentlemen as

who have no virtue to boast of, should be solicited with more temptations than others, I can't imagine. This, I will say, that whoever is in fault, or whatever was the design, taverns and dram-shops have been systematically and scandalously multiplied in this town; and, like so many boxes of Pandora, they are hourly scattering plagues of every kind, natural, moral, and political, through the whole town.

1 Here is the only allusion, in the Diary, to this incident, which, according to the writer's own account, had so great an influence over his subsequent career. The Autobiography speaks of it more fully, as follows: —

[The king sent instructions to his custom house officers to carry the acts of trade and navigation into strict execution. An inferior officer of the customs, in Salem, whose name was Cockle, petitioned the justices of the superior court, at their session in November (1760) for the county of Essex, to grant him writs of assistants, according to some provision in one of the acts of trade which had not been executed, to authorize him to break open ships, shops, cellars, houses, &c., to search for prohibited goods and merchandises, on which duties had not been paid. Some objection was made to this motion; and Mr. Stephen Sewall, who was then Chief Justice of that court, and a zealous friend of liberty, expressed some doubts of the legality and constitutionality of the writ, and of the power of the court to grant it. The court ordered the question to be argued at Boston, in February Term, 1761. In the mean time Mr. Sewall died; and Mr. Hutchinson, then lieutenant-governor, a counsellor and judge of probate for the county of Suffolk, &c., was appointed, in his stead, Chief Justice. The first vacancy on that bench had been promised, in two former administrations, to Colonel James Otis, of Barnstable. This event produced a dissension between Hutchinson and Otis, which had consequences of great moment.

In February, Mr. James Otis, junior, a lawyer of Boston, and a son of Colonel Otis of Barnstable, appeared, at the request of the merchants in Boston, in opposition to the writ. This gentleman's reputation as a scholar, a lawyer, a reasoner, and a man of spirit, was then very high. Mr. Putnam, while I was with him, had often said to me that Otis was by far the most able, manly, and commanding character of his age at the bar; and this appeared to me, in Boston, to be the unanimous opinion of judges, lawyers, and the public. Mr. Oxenbridge Thacher, whose amiable manners and pure principles united to a very easy and musical eloquence made him very popular, was united with Otis; and Mr. Gridley alone appeared for Cockle, the petitioner, in support of the writ. The argument continued several days in the council chamber, and the question was analyzed with great acuteness and all the learning which could be connected with the subject. I took a few minutes in a very careless manner, which, by some means, fell into the hands of Mr. Minot, who has inserted them in his history. I was much more attentive to the information and the eloquence of the speaker than to my minutes, and too much alarmed at the prospect that was opened before me to care much about writing a report of the controversy. The views of the English government towards the colonies, and the views of the colonies towards the English government, from the first of our history to that time, appeared to me to have been directly in opposition to each other, and were now, by the imprudence of administration, brought to a collision. England, proud of its power, and holding us in contempt, would never give up its pretensions. The Americans, devoutly attached

they delivered it? You can do any thing! you can do as you please! Gridley did not use that language; he never was master of such a style! It is not in him," &c.

"I will lay one hundred guineas that, before twenty years, you will raise the fees of the bar threefold. If your eloquence should turn out equal to your understanding, you will, I know you will! You have Lord Bolingbroke by heart! with one cursory reading, you have a deeper understanding of him, and remember more of him, than I do after three or four readings, or than I should have after twenty readings."

"With all your merit, and learning, and wit, and sense, and spirit, and vivacity, and all that—"

These are the bold, gross, barefaced flatteries, that I hear every time I see that man. Can he think me such a ninny as to be allured and deceived by such gross arts? He must think me vastly vain, silly, stupid, if he thinks to impose on me; if he thinks I can't see the deceit. It must be deceit. It cannot be any thing else.

If you ride over this whole province, you will find that, although taverns are generally too numerous,[1] they are not half so numerous in any one county, in proportion to the numbers of people and the necessity of business and travelling, as in this. In most country towns in this county, you will find almost every other house with a sign of entertainment before it.

If you call, you will find dirt enough, very miserable accommodations of provision and lodging for yourself and your horse. Yet, if you sit the evening, you will find the house full of people

to their liberties, would never submit, at least without an entire devastation of the country and a general destruction of their lives. A contest appeared to me to be opened, to which I could foresee no end, and which would render my life a burden, and property, industry, and every thing insecure. There was no alternative left but to take the side which appeared to be just, to march intrepidly forward in the right path, to trust in Providence for the protection of truth and right, and to die with a good conscience and a decent grace, if that trial should become indispensable.]

Among the papers of Mr. Adams, some notes remain of the argument in the case of the writs of assistance, which seem to be the foundation of the sketch published by Minot. As the smallest particular relating to this commencement of the revolutionary struggle is interesting, they are placed in the Appendix (A.) to this volume.

[1] This is the latter part of a long paper upon licensed houses, which seems to have been intended for publication at the time.

drinking drams, flip, toddy, carousing, swearing; but especially plotting with the landlord, to get him, at the next town meeting, an election either for selectman or representative. Thus the multiplicity of these houses, by dividing the profits, renders the landlords careless of travellers, and allures the poor country people, who are tired with labor, and hanker after company, to waste their time and money, contract habits of intemperance and idleness, and, by degrees, to lose the natural dignity and freedom of English minds, and confer those offices, which belong by nature and the spirit of all government to probity and honesty, on the meanest, and weakest, and worst of human characters.

A good deal of this has happened, as I believe, partly from what I have seen, and partly from credible information, in the country. But who is most to blame? The court of sessions has made such rules for itself that the country justices can seldom attend. The selectmen of the several towns have been so often disappointed that they are discouraged. Some houses, to my knowledge, have been licensed which never had any approbation from any selectman. Other persons have been licensed, whom the selectmen have found, by experience, and certified to be guilty of misrule, and therefore unfit. Others have been recognized for seven years together, without any approbation from the selectmen through the whole time. Nay, a man has been recognized, though the selectmen certified good reasons for not approbating him; — that he was very intemperate, had poor accommodations, and was subject to fits of caprice, if not delirium, that made it dangerous to come near him; and although it was proved that the same man, in one of these fits, had, but a few days before, stabbed another with apparent design and great danger of murder.

Now I agree that ambitious spirits in the country, who have little honor, will soon see that such houses must be favored and multiplied, to promote their own designs; and therefore retailers and taverners are generally, in the country, assessors, or selectmen, or representatives, or esquires. But are not we more to blame? Are not some of our justices importers of molasses? Are not others distillers, and are not all of them fond of a lawful fee? In short, is it owing wholly to Boston justices, that those houses have been so shamefully multiplied in the country; multiplied so that decent entertainment for a traveller is nowhere to be had?

The freedom of censure is a matter of very great consequence under our government. There are certain vices and follies, certain indecencies of behavior, beneath the inspection and censure of law and magistracy, which must be restrained and corrected by satire. And, for this reason, every piece of just ridicule, in public or private, bestowed on any wrong or foolish conduct, gives me great pleasure, even although I am myself the object. From the same principle, I was glad to see some animadversion on the late inconsistent conduct of the ministers of this town;[1] and nothing but sacerdotal impudence and ecclesiastical pride can account for the surly, revengeful manner in which those pieces have been received.[2]

1 Boston. This alludes to a very sharp controversy, carried on in the Gazette, upon the subject of feasts at ordinations. In that paper, of the 2d March of this year, there appeared a long account of the ceremonies at the Ordination of the Rev. Mr. Cuming, as colleague of Dr. Sewall, in the Old South Church. The public solemnity being over, this account goes on to say, — "there was a very sumptuous and elegant entertainment for the elders and messengers that assisted; to which his Excellency the Governor, who honored the ceremonial of the Instalment with his presence, was also invited, together with a considerable number of the principal gentlemen of the town and some of the country. One house, though capacious, not being sufficient to accommodate so large a number of honorable and reverend guests on such an occasion, two or more were provided for the occasion. The principal entertainment, however, (which is said to have been very grand) and consequently the greatest concourse of people, was at the Rev. Dr. Sewall's own house."

Such being the newspaper notice of the 2d, there appeared in the next week's paper, some well written but severe strictures upon the proceedings, as not consistent with the character and pledges of the actors. Such an attack, directed against the most powerful class of the day, naturally excited resentment, which showed itself in harsh and violent rejoinder. This led to retort, and to a warm controversy. In no particular are opinions and customs more changed, than in this. The decline of ecclesiastical influence may have diminished the interest taken in similar ceremonies; but the doing away with convivial entertainments, upon such occasions, has a deeper and more creditable cause. A calm reader of the controversy, at this day, would not hesitate on which side to give his verdict.

2 At a town meeting held in Braintree, on the 18th May, 1761, the following article appears in the warrant: —

"*Secondly.* To consider and determine upon some effectual method whereby to reduce the number of licensed houses in this town, as it is thought the present number are unnecessary."

The record further states, —

"After a full debate upon the second article, it was, by a great majority of the members present,

Voted, That, although licensed houses, so far as they are conveniently situated, well accommodated, and under due regulation for the relief and entertainment of travellers and strangers, may be a useful institution, yet there is reason to apprehend that the present prevailing depravity of manners, through the land in general, and in this town in particular, and the shameful neglect of

June 11. Thursday.* I have been for a week or fortnight engaged in a project; have remarkably succeeded hitherto. Mr. Niles approved in all things. Major Crosby approved in all things. Deacon Palmer approved in all things. They have given, under their hands, a very full and handsome character and recommendation of my brother; — much more ample than I expected. They have really spoken in hyperbole; they have expressed themselves with warmth. I expected only a signification of their consent and approbation; but they have expressed themselves with zeal. I ought to consider these credentials gratefully, as a strong instance of friendship, and take the first opportunity of making some return. Mr. N. has the worst opinion of T.'s morals. He detests the base methods of debauchery, and lying, and duplicity, that he has been in. O. despises him.

But scheming seldom has success. I expect to come off but second best after all! I expect that T. will hear of my design, and, in order to defeat it, continue in the office himself. If he should, I shall be pretty cool. Intrigue, and making interest, and asking favors, is a new employment to me. I am unpractised in intrigues for power. I begin to feel the passions of the world; — ambition, avarice, intrigue, party, all must be guarded.

My fears of failing are at last vanished. The scheme succeeded in all things, and is completed. Boylston is constituted,

religious and civil duties, so highly offensive in the sight of God, and injurious to the peace and welfare of society, are in a great measure owing to the unnecessary increase of licensed houses.

Voted, That, for the future, there be no persons in this town licensed for retailing spirituous liquors; and that there be three persons only approbated by the selectmen as Innholders, suitably situated in each precinct."

It is not unreasonable to infer that the decision of the town was the result of the efforts of Mr. Adams, even if, as is altogether probable, the votes were not drawn up by him.

* [On the 25th of May, in this year, my venerable father died, in his seventy-first year, beloved, esteemed, and revered by all who knew him. Nothing that I can say or do, can sufficiently express my gratitude for his parental kindness to me, or the exalted opinion I have of his wisdom and virtue. It was a melancholy house. My father and mother were seized at the same time with the violent fever, a kind of influenza or an epidemic, which carried off seventeen aged people in our neighborhood. My mother remained ill in bed at my father's funeral; but, being younger than my father, and possessed of a stronger constitution, she happily recovered, and lived, to my inexpressible comfort, till the year 1797, when she died at almost ninety years of age.]

commissioned, sworn, and has this day undertaken to officiate. Now, a new train of anxieties begins to take place. Fears of imperfect services, imperfect and false returns, voluntary and negligent escapes, miscalculations, want of strength, courage, celerity, want of art and contrivance, &c.; rashness, indolence, timidity, &c.*

The project was so well planned, that success seemed certain; all the justices recommended; two other gentlemen of his acquaintance, men of honor and figure, also concurred and urged, and dropped hints, if not anecdotes, *vs.* the old one. Hints were dropped to him by others that I should employ constables, and so deprive him of his profits; — so that his interest, his vanity, his honor, were all touched.

It cost me much pains, — at least two journeys to Boston, one to Mr. Niles's, one to Germantown, one to Mr. Bullard's and Major Crosby's; the writing of a long bond; the solicitation of credentials, of sureties, and of the office; mere solicitation procured it and although it was not much disguised or concealed, yet it was so silently conducted, that I believe the adversary never once suspected it. All the wiles and malice of the old serpent would have been employed against it, if it had been known or suspected. But there was one particular, of mere luck, to which we were much indebted; namely, the complaint of Cudworth against T.; — that unfriendly, unbrotherly, unneighborly, as well as rash and unmannerly spurning of the execution, and then sending it to Gould, where it was lost, gave the great man an ill opinion of his sub., and made him more willing and ready, at my solicitation, to constitute another, and even without consulting T.

---

20. Saturday. I have latterly arisen much earlier than usual; arose at five and at six o'clock, instead of eight and nine. The mornings are very long, and fine opportunities for study; they

* [In pursuance of my plan of reforming the practice of sheriffs and pettifoggers in the country, I procured of all the justices in Braintree, — John Quincy, Edmund Quincy, Josiah Quincy, and Joseph Crosby, — a recommendation of my brother to Stephen Greenleaf, sheriff of the county, and a certificate of his character; upon receiving which, Mr. Greenleaf readily gave him a deputation. He was young, loved riding, and discharged his duties with skill and fidelity; but his disposition was so tender, that he often assisted his debtors with his own purse and credit, and upon the whole, to say the least, was nothing the richer for his office.]

are cool and pleasant. But I have not improved my time properly. I have dosed and sauntered away much of my time. This morning is very fine; the clear sky, the bright sun, the clean groves and grass, after so fine a rain, are very pleasant. But the books within this chamber have a much better title to my attention than any of the rural scenes and objects without it. I have been latterly too much in the world, and too little in this retreat. Abroad, my appetites are solicited, my passions inflamed, and my understanding too much perverted, to judge wisely of men or things; but in this retreat, when neither my senses, nor appetites, nor passions are excited, I am able to consider all things more coolly and sensibly. I was guilty of rash and profane swearing, of rash virulence against the characters of Goffe, J. Russell, lieutenant-governor, &c. Not but that there have been faults in their characters and conduct that every honest man ought to resent.

I have been interrupted from reading this Institute, ever since February. Amidst the dissipations of business, pleasure, conversation, intrigue, party, &c., what mortal can give attention to an old Latin Institute of the canon law? But it is certainly worth while to proceed and finish it, as I have already been two thirds through it.

August 1. Saturday. I am creating enemies in every quarter of the town. The Clarks hate; — Mother Hubbard, Thayer, Lamb, Tirrell, J. Brackett. This is multiplying and propagating enemies fast. I shall have the ill will of the whole town.

Daniel White. Moses Adams. This will not do.

Daniel Pratt *vs.* Thomas Colson. This action was brought by plaintiff against Colson as administrator on the estate of Mr. Bolter, for non-performance of a covenant of indenture. Pratt was a poor fatherless child, and his mother, unable to provide for him, bound him an apprentice to Mr. Bolter. He was then under ten years of age, and so was bound for eleven years and some odd months. In consideration of this very long and unusual term of apprenticeship, his master covenanted to teach him to read, write, and cipher, and to teach him the trade of a weaver. But we complain that he never taught us either to read, write, or cipher, or to weave. Call the proof.

The law, gentlemen, is extremely tender and indulgent to such actions as these. For such is the benignity and humanity of the English constitution, that all the weak and helpless and friendless part of our species are taken under its peculiar care and protection — women, children, and especially widows and fatherless children. And they have always, from the compassion of the law, peculiar privileges and indulgences allowed them. Therefore, as a poor, fatherless, and friendless child, the law would allow great indulgence and lenity to this plaintiff. But he is to be favored for another reason; because the English law greatly favors education. In every English country, some sort of education, some acquaintance with letters is necessary, that a man may fill any station whatever. In the countries of slavery and Romish superstition, the laity must not learn to read, lest they should detect the gross impostures of the priesthood, and shake off the yoke of bondage. But in Protestant countries, and especially in England and its colonies, freedom of inquiry is allowed to be not only the privilege, but the duty of every individual. We know it to be our duty to read, examine, and judge for ourselves, even of ourselves, what is right. No priest nor pope has any right to say what I shall believe, and I will not believe one word they say, if I think it is not founded in reason and in revelation. Now, how can I judge what my Bible justifies unless I can read my Bible?

The English constitution is founded, 't is bottomed and grounded, on the knowledge and good sense of the people. The very ground of our liberties is the freedom of elections. Every man has in politics as well as religion, a right to think and speak and act for himself. No man, either king or subject, clergyman or layman, has any right to dictate to me the person I shall choose for my legislator and ruler. I must judge for myself. But how can I judge, how can any man judge, unless his mind has been opened and enlarged by reading? A man who can read will find in his Bible, in his common sermon books that common people have by them, and even in the almanac, and the newspapers, rules and observations that will enlarge his range of thought, and enable him the better to judge who has, and who has not that integrity of heart and that compass of knowledge and understanding which forms the statesman.

September 10. Thursday. Spent the evening at Zab's with the Parson.

Wibird. "I have seen a picture of Oliver Cromwell, with this motto under it:

> 'Careat successibus opto,[1]
> Quisquis ab eventu facta notanda putat.'

'I pray that he may want success who thinks that deeds are to be estimated from their event, their success.' Oliver was successful, but not prudent nor honest, nor laudable, nor imitable."

October 17. Saturday. Read in Institute and Lancelott. Began Lancelott's Institute last January, and have read no further than lib. 3, tit. 8, De Exceptionibus et Replicationibus.

October 18. Sunday. Arose at six. Read in Pope's Satires. Nil Admirari, &c. I last night read through both of Dr. Donne's Satires versified by Pope. Was most struck with these lines:

> "Bear me, some god! Oh! quickly bear me hence,
> To wholesome solitude, the nurse of sense,
> Where contemplation prunes her ruffled wings,
> And the free soul looks down to pity kings."

"Prayer." A posture; hands uplifted, and eyes. A very proper prayer for me to make when I am in Boston. "Solitude" is a personage in a clean, wholesome dress, the "nurse" and nourisher of sense. "Contemplation," a personage. "Prunes," picks, smooths. Is she an angel or a bird? — "ruffled," rumpled, rugged, uneven, tumbled; — "free soul," not enslaved, unshackled, no bondage, no subjection; "looks down," pities George, Louis, Frederick, Philip, Charles, &c.

November 10. Tuesday. [2] Another year is come round, and I can recollect still less reading than I could last November; the increase of my business within twelve months has been nothing; I drew fewer writs last October court than I drew the October court before, though I drew an uncommon number at both. Yet I have advanced a few steps; have procured my brother his office, abated Nathan Spear's writ, battled it with Captain

[1] Ovid's Heroids — Phyllis to Demophoon. l. 85.

[2] In the original is the following direction: "Turn back five leaves." The entry is made in the paper book which begins with the letter to Jonathan Sewall, and the reference is to the record of 14th November, 1760, p. 100.

Thayer at Major Crosby's, recovered of Jo. Tirrell for Lambard, recovered of Lawrence for Tirrell, abated King's writ, conducted the petition against taverners. All these things have been done in one year. Besides, have bought some books &c., but have read but little law.

This morning I have been reading Archbishop Sharp's Sermon;—"To the upright there ariseth light in the darkness;" his character of the upright man, &c. Same day, read a number of his sermons in his first volume. He is a moving, affectionate preacher; devotional, more than Tillotson, but not so moral.

14. Saturday. Brother Quincy and I were sworn before the Superior Court. It is now more than five years since I began the study of the law; and it is about three years since I was sworn at the Inferior Court.*

30. Monday. This day removed to my chamber and made a fire; the forenoon was spent in conversation with Zab, in walking to Doctor Turner's and up Penn's hill, and this afternoon in conversation with Grindal Rawson and Zab at Mrs. Marsh's. Yet I have caught several snatches of reading and thinking in Blackstone, Gilbert, &c. But I, as usual, expect great things from this chamber, and this winter.[1]

[1] At this place it seems proper to introduce the following note on account of its characteristic postscript. It is the first occasion upon which any allusion occurs to the person who afterwards became Mrs. Adams. The note is directed to "Miss Polly Smith in Weymouth," and is written by Richard Cranch, to whom, in the November following, she was married.

Germantown, 30 December, 1761.

DEAR MISS POLLY,—

I was at Boston yesterday, and saw your brother who was well. I have but a moment's notice of an opportunity of sending to you the inclosed, which I took at your Uncle Edward's.

I am, with compliments to your family, your affectionate humble servant,

R. CRANCH.

DEAR DITTO,—

Here we are, Dick and Jack, as happy as the wickedness and folly of this world will allow philosophers to be; our good wishes are poured forth for the felicity of you, your family and neighbors. My—I don't know what—to Mrs. Nabby; tell her I hear she 's about commencing a most loyal subject to young George; and although my allegiance has been hitherto inviolate, I shall endeavor all in my power to foment rebellion. J. ADAMS.

[* About this time the project was conceived, I suppose by the Chief Justice, Mr. Hutchinson, of clothing the judges and lawyers with robes. Mr. Quincy and I were directed to prepare our gowns and bands, and tie wigs, and were admitted barristers, having practised three years at the inferior courts, according to one of our new rules.]

1762. June 5. Saturday. Rode from Bass's to Secretary Oliver's in company with Judge Oliver.[1] The Judge soon opened upon politics. Says he, "Major Stockbridge informs me that Colonel Ruggles makes a very good Speaker. He has behaved to universal approbation."

Soon afterwards the Judge said, "I never knew so easy an election in my life. Some of the bar interest themselves very much in the matter. One gentleman has interested himself most infamously; advanced that to be law in the House, which is not law. That the judges cannot sit in the House of Commons is certain, because there is an act of Parliament against it, but the judges may sit and vote in the House of Lords, that is, they may if they are peers. Lord Mansfield—think he don't sit and vote?

How can the bar expect protection from the court, if the bar endeavors to bring the court into contempt? He is forever abusing the court. He said, not long since in the representative's room, that 'take all the superior judges and every inferior judge in the Province, and put them all together, and they would not make one half of a common lawyer.' I said upon this, 'that was a distracted speech. It is a pity that gentleman was not better guided; he has many fine talents.' The judge replied quick, 'I have known him these twenty years, and I have no opinion of his head or his heart. If Bedlamism is a talent, he has it in perfection.'

He will one time say of the Lieutenant-Governor, that he had rather have him, than any man he knows, in any one office; and the next hour will represent him as the greatest tyrant and most despicable creature living.

I have treated him with as much friendship as ever I did a stranger in my life, and he knows very well how he has treated me. I blush even to think of what he has said to me. I have him in the utmost contempt. I have the utmost contempt of

[1] Peter Oliver, afterwards Chief Justice of Massachusetts. Dr. Eliot says of him "that when raised to the supreme bench, his was a very popular appointment, though he had not that knowledge of the law which others had who were of the profession, and looked up to the place." His political sentiments are visible enough in the conversation here reported. Like so many others of those mentioned in the early portion of this diary, he became a refugee and an exile and died in England, in 1791.

him. I had as lief say it to him as not. I have the utmost contempt of him.

I have been twelve years concerned in the executive courts, and I never knew so much ill usage given to the court by all the lawyers in the province, put it all together for all that time, as I have known him give in one term.

The origin of all his bustle is very well known. I heard a gentleman say he would give his oath, that Otis said to him, if his father was not made a judge he would throw the Province into flames if it cost him his life.[1] For that one speech, a thousand other persons would have been indicted."

8. Tuesday. Went to Taunton court—to the land of Leonards;—three judges of the common pleas of that name, each of whom has a son who was bred at a college. The Honorable George Leonard, the first Justice, seems to me arbitrary; he committed two old gentlemen who were near eighty years old to the custody of an officer, only for speaking loud, when they were both deaf, and not conscious that they did speak loud. A check, a reproof, an admonition, would have been enough.

He was unwilling that the Sessions should adjourn for an hour to take the verdict of the jury in a trial upon a presentment of a riot, but would have had that jury kept together all night, till the court should sit again next morning. No other court in the Province, superior and inferior, would have thought of keeping the jury up.

He broke in most abruptly upon Bob Paine, 'He did not think it was right to run out against the king's witnesses. For his part, he did not love to hear it,' three or four times over, &c. Thus the haughty tyrant treats the county.

I lodged the first night at Crosman's, the second at Major Leonard's of Rainham, and the third at Captain Cobb's with Paine. I dined the first day I was there, Wednesday, at Captain Cobb's with Colonel Otis and Paine, and the second at Colonel

1 This was the favorite charge made by the government partisans against the younger Otis. It is of course repeated by Hutchinson, and it has found its way even into the moderate pages of Gordon and of Eliot. The subject is well treated in the Biography by Tudor, page 55. That Otis was impulsive, and not uniform or steady in advocating his principles, must be admitted. But nobody can think of the fiery furnace through which he was compelled to pass, without comprehending the extent of his mental trials, and appreciating the heroism with which they were endured.

White's. Drank tea once at Colonel White's with the three young Leonards, George, Zeph., and Daniel, and I spent two evenings at Cobb's with Colonel Otis and Paine; and I rode from Taunton to Milton with Colonel Otis.[1] He is vastly easy and steady in his temper; he is vastly good-humored and sociable and sensible; learned he is not, but he is an easy, familiar speaker. He gave me many anecdotes, both of his law and politics.

August 15. Sunday. Reading, thinking, writing — have I totally renounced all three?

"Tempora mutantur et nos mutamur in illis."

October 22. Friday. Spent last Monday in taking pleasure with Mr. Wibird. Met him in the morning at Mr. Borland's, rode with him to Squantum, to the very lowest point of the peninsula; next to Thompson's Island, to the high steep rock, from whence the squaw threw herself who gave the name to the place. It is an hideous, craggy precipice, nodding over the ocean, forty feet in height; the rocks seem to be a vast collection of pebbles as big as hens' eggs thrown into melted cement and cooled in. You may pull them to pieces with your fingers as fast as you please. Various have been the conjectures of the learned concerning this sort of rocks. Upon this part of the peninsula is a number of trees which appear very much like the lime tree [2] of Europe, which gentlemen are so fond of planting in their gardens for their beauty. Returned to Mr. Borland's,[3] dined, and afternoon rode to Germantown,[4] where we spent our evening. Deacon palmer showed us his lucern growing in his garden, of which he has cut, as he tells us, four crops this year. The Deacon

1 James Otis, the elder.

2 The American nettle tree. One of these is still to be seen growing out of the top of the rock at this place.

3 This is the mansion afterwards purchased by the writer, in which he lived from the date of his last return from Europe until his death, in 1826.

4 A secluded and beautiful spot almost surrounded by water, in which Deacon, afterwards called General Palmer, well known at this time, as well as subsequently, as a member of the Committee of Safety in the Revolution, had established himself among a colony of glassblowers from Germany, come to undertake the manufacture of that article in America. Hence the name, (Germantown,) which has remained whilst the persons have either removed or been merged in the general population. A pretty full and interesting account of the life and singular misfortunes of General Palmer, the materials for which were furnished by his great grandson, Mr. C. J. Palmer, is found in the New Englander for January, 1845.

had his lucern seeds of Mr. Greenleaf of Abington, who had his of Judge Oliver. The Deacon watered his but twice this summer, and intends to expose it uncovered to all the weather of the winter, for a fair trial whether it will endure our winters or not. Each of his four crops had attained a good length. It has a rich fragrance for a grass. He showed us a cut of it in "Nature Displayed," and another of St. Foin, and another of trefoil. The cut of the lucern was exact enough; the pod in which the seeds are is an odd thing, a kind of ram's-horn or straw.

We had a good deal of conversation upon husbandry. The Deacon has about seventy bushels of potatoes this year on about one quarter of an acre of ground. Trees of several sorts considered. The wild cherry tree bears a fruit of some value; the wood is very good for the cabinet maker, and is not bad to burn. It is a tree of much beauty; its leaves and bark are handsome, and its shape. The locust; good timber, fattening to soil by its leaves, blossoms, &c.; good wood, quick growth, &c. The larch tree; there is but one[1] in the country, that in the Lieutenant-Governor's yard at Milton; it looks somewhat like an evergreen, but is not; sheds its leaves.

I read in Thompson's Travels in Turkey in Asia, mention of a turpentine called by the name of the turpentine of Venice, which is not the produce of Venice, but of Dauphiné, and flows from the larch tree. It is thick and balsamic, and used in several arts, particularly that of enamelling.

24. Sunday. Before sunrise. My thoughts have taken a sudden turn to husbandry. Have contracted with Jo. Field to clear my swamp, and to build me a long string of stone wall, and with Isaac to build me sixteen rods more, and with Jo. Field to build me six rods more. And my thoughts are running continually from the orchard to the pasture, and from thence to the swamp, and thence to the house and barn and land adjoining. Sometimes I am at the orchard ploughing up acre after acre, planting, pruning apple-trees, mending fences, carting dung; sometimes in the pasture, digging stones, clearing bushes, pruning trees, building wall to redeem posts and rails; and sometimes removing button trees down to my house; sometimes I am at the old swamp, burning bushes, digging stumps and roots, cutting ditches

[1] This tree still remains in fine condition on Milton hill.

across the meadows and against my uncle; and am sometimes at the other end of the town buying posts and rails to fence against my uncle, and against the brook; and am sometimes ploughing the upland with six yoke of oxen, and planting corn, potatoes, &c., and digging up the meadows and sowing onions, planting cabbages, &c. &c. Sometimes I am at the homestead, running cross fences, and planting potatoes by the acre, and corn by the two acres, and running a ditch along the line between me and Field, and a fence along the brook against my brother, and another ditch in the middle from Field's line to the meadows. Sometimes am carting gravel from the neighboring hills, and sometimes dust from the streets upon the fresh meadows, and am sometimes ploughing, sometimes digging those meadows to introduce clover and other English grasses.

November 5. Friday. The cause of Jeffries, town treasurer of Boston, and Sewall, and Edwards, and several others;—being suits for the penalties arising by the law of the Province, for building and covering their buildings not with slate nor tile, but with shingles.

Mr. Gridley made a motion that those actions should be dismissed, because the judges were all interested in the event of them. Two of the judges, to wit, Wells and Foster Hutchinson, being inhabitants of Boston, and the other two, to wit, Eliakim Hutchinson and Watts, having real estates in that town, to the poor of which those penalties are appropriated. After a long wrangle, as usual when Trowbridge is in a case, the court determined to continue the action, that application might be made to the Governor and council for special judges. Wells and Foster declining to sit, and Watts too.

The case of a witness was mentioned in the argument. A witness cannot depose, when he is interested; a juryman may be challenged who is interested.

But persons belonging to corporations are allowed, for the necessity, to testify in cases where those corporations are interested; and jurymen and judges, belonging to this Province, sat in the case of Gray and Paxton, though interested, for the necessity.

This motion, Mr. G. said, could not be reduced to a written plea. He could not plead to the jurisdiction of the court. The court of common pleas had undoubted jurisdiction of the cause;

but the judges could not sit, because interested. Their honors were not the court of common pleas, but the justices of the court of common pleas. The court of common pleas was a body politic, an invisible system, a frame in the mind, a fiction of the law. The president and fellows of Harvard College, are not Harvard College.

The case in Strange was produced, in which Lord Raymond went off the bench; the parish of Abbots Langley, in which his lordship lived, being interested; an order of two justices for the removal of a pauper confined by the Sessions, was carried to King's Bench by certiorari.

Authorities from Hobart's and Coke's reports were produced, to show the tenderness of the law for this maxim, — that a man shall not be judge in his own cause, and that an act of Parliament against natural equity, as that a man should be judge in his own cause, would be void.

Mem. After the court had given judgment, Mr. Gridley moved for a minute of the reasons of the judgment. Wells said the court were not accountable to the bar for their reasons. But Otis said, the courts at home never refused their reasons for any judgment, when the bar requested them; because, if the bar are left ignorant of the reasons the court go upon, they will not know how to advise and direct their clients. And, after some debate, the clerk was ordered to minute the reason for the continuance; which was, that three of the judges apprehended themselves interested, and so not a court competent to try the cause.

G—— contended that, if the court should continue the causes, they could not refuse sitting on the trial, because an imparlance was a judicial act, and so an assumption of jurisdiction. Foster Hutchinson said, that dismissing the actions would be a judicial act, as much as continuing.

Q. The humanity, the utility, the policy, the piety of the sanguinary laws against robbery and stealing.

Boston. December 30. Thursday. At Goldthwait's [1] office spent one quarter of an hour with Lieutenant-Governor Hutch-

[1] Ezekiel Goldthwait was the register of deeds for the county of Suffolk. Although at first inclining to the opposition, his reverence for Hutchinson carried the day in the end. His name appears attached to the servile address presented to that officer on his final departure, in 1774.

inson. The first thing he said, was a question to Goldthwait,—what was the date of the earliest records of the county court? Goldthwait answered 1670. His Honor replied, there were county courts for forty years before that; and said, he wanted to settle something in his own mind concerning the origin and constitution of the courts; that adultery was punished with death by the first settlers, and many other offences were made capital, that are not now so; that commissioners were sent over by King Charles, in 1665, to inquire into the constitution of the Colonies, though their authority was not owned. Goldthwait said, there were a great many odd entries; one of a prosecution of a man for taking sixpence for an horse, (a Braintree man too,) as unjust and unrighteous. His Honor told of a record of a woman condemned for adultery, because a man had debauched her when she was drunk; and of another, of a boy imprisoned for a capital trial for some of their trifling capital crimes—stealing from his master or something—which boy was liberated by the commissioners of 1665. The story of Pratt's death was told. His Honor said it would be a loss to his family; he was in a fair way to have raised it. But the New Yorkers will be glad of it. This, to be sure, was familiarity and affability! But Goldthwait cringed down, and put on the timid, fawning face and air and tone.

1763. Braintree. February 1. Tuesday. Last Thursday afternoon, rode to Germantown and there stayed at my friend Cranch's till the last night,—four nights and four days. Those two families[1] well deserve the character they hold, of friendly, sensible, and social. The men, women, and children, are all sensible and obliging.

Mem. The anecdote of Mr. Erving. He has prophesied so long, and with so much confidence, that Canada would be restored to the French, that, because he begins to see his prediction will not be fulfilled, he is now straining his invention for reasons why we ought not to hold it. He says, the restoration of that province can alone prevent our becoming luxurious, effeminate, inattentive to any danger, and so an easy prey to an

[1] The two families referred to, were those of General Palmer and of Judge Cranch, whose sister the former had married. They had emigrated from England together, in 1746. Judge Cranch was just married to one of the daughters of the Rev. W. Smith, of Weymouth.

invader. He was so soundly bantered the other day in the council chamber, that he snatched his hat and cloak, and went off in a passion.

Mem. The other, of a piece, sent to Fleet to be printed, upon the unfitness of Mr. Mauduit to represent this Province at the British court, both in point of age and knowledge. He is, as that writer says, seventy years old; an honest man, but avaricious; a woollen draper, a mere cit; so ignorant of Court and public business, that he knew not where the public offices were, and that he told Mr. Bollan that he was agent for New England. He says that all the other agents laugh at this Province for employing him, and that all persons on that side of the water are surprised at us. That the "Considerations on the present German War," were written by a person unknown, who hired or persuaded Mr. Mauduit to father it.[1]

Books, — we read five sermons in Dr. Sherlock, and several chapters in the Inquiry into the Origin of our Ideas of the Sublime and the Beautiful. The chapter upon sympathy they all disapprove. The author says, — we have a real pleasure in the distresses and misfortunes of others. Mem. To write a letter to Sewall, or Quincy, or Lowell, on the subject of that chapter. I employed, however, too little of my time in reading and in thinking; I might have spent much more. The idea of M. de Vattel indeed, scowling and frowning, haunted me.

Q. Do we take pleasure in the real distress of others? What is my sensation when I see Captain Cunningham laid up with the gout, and hear his plaintive groans? What are the feelings of the women at groanings? What is my feeling when I hear of an honest man's losing a ship at sea?

[1] There had been a good deal of management on all sides, in the General Court of the last year, in the selection of an agent for the Colony. Mr. Bollan, who had acted in this capacity, was set aside by a union of opposite interests against him; finding difficulty in choosing a successor, a majority, as is not uncommon in such cases, combined upon Jasper Mauduit, esteemed more for his private worth, than for his competency for the post. But, soon discovering the mistake, Israel Mauduit, his brother, of far more capacity, and the author of the celebrated pamphlet referred to, would probably have been substituted, had it not been for Governor Bernard, whose influence was at its height, and whose views it suited that no change should then be made. Probably he kept the post in his eye for Mr. Jackson, as stated hereafter in this Diary. Hutchinson was again so popular as to be soon afterwards elected almost unanimously by the General Court, as a special agent. It was the hour of James Otis's weakness, and of compromise and reaction, ultimately stopped only by the energy of Oxenbridge Thacher. *Minot*, ii. p. 142. *Hutchinson*, iii. p. 105, note. *Tudor's Life of Otis*, p. 170.

5. Saturday. Memorabilia of this week

The bar agreed upon these four rules;—

1. That the clerk call the plaintiff, and if anybody answer except the plaintiff or some sworn attorney, his power be demanded, and no general power in such case be admitted.

2. That no attorney's fee be taxed for the future, where the declaration was not drawn by the plaintiff himself or some sworn attorney.

3. That no attendance be taxed, unless the party attend personally, or by some sworn attorney.

4. That no attorney be allowed to practise here, unless sworn in this court or in the superior court.

Mr. Gridley read these rules to the court, as unexceptionable regulations agreed upon by the bar.

Mr. Otis arose and said, he had the credit of the motion, but he never had moved for any such rules as these; for they were against the Province law, against the rights of mankind, and he was amazed that so many wise heads as that bar was blessed with, could think them practicable; and concluded that he was, for one, entirely against them; and said, that all schemes to suppress pettifoggers must rest on the honor of the bar. Foster Hutchinson asked, why then was the court troubled with the motion? Judge Watts said, if the bar was not agreed, the court could do nothing. And, at last, they determined to consider till April.

Thus, with a whiff of Otis' pestilential breath,
Was this whole system blown away.

But the bar was in a great rage! Thacher said to Kent, Auchmuty, and me,—"whoever votes for him to be any thing more than a constable, let him be *anathema maranatha*. I pamphleteer for him again? No! I'll pamphleteer against him." Kent damned him, and said he had been abused by him, personally, in such a manner as he never would forgive, unless he made him more satisfaction than he imagined was in his power.

Thacher moved, that, in the cards to be sent to the judges, the expression should be, "the bar, exclusively of Mr. Otis, invites,"—and Auchmuty, Kent, Gridley, and I, as well as Thacher, voted for it.

Auchmuty and Fitch[1] were equally warm; they talked about renouncing all commerce or connection with him. Gridley talked about treating him dryly and decently. Auchmuty said, the two principles of all this were popularity and avarice. He made the motion, at first, to get some of these understrappers into his service. He could not bear that Quincy and Auchmuty should have underworkers and he none, and he objected to the rules to save his popularity with the constables, Justices Story and Ruddock, &c., and pettifoggers of the town, and with the pettifoggers that he uses as tools and myrmidons in the house.

Mr. G. said he went off to avoid a quarrel; for he could not bear it;—such tergiversation, such trimming, such behavior! Kent and Auchmuty said they had borne with his insolence, thinking him honest, though hot and rash and passionate; but now he appeared to act against his conscience.[2]

Recipe to make a Patriot.[3]

Take of the several species of malevolence, as revenge, malice, envy, equal quantities; of servility, fear, fury, vanity, profaneness, and ingratitude, equal quantities; and infuse this composition into the brains of an ugly, surly, brutal mortal, and you have the desideratum.

The Life of Furio.

In Croatia. His descent, education at school, college, at the bar. Historians relate his wrath at Plymouth, at Boston; he heads the trade, brings actions, fails; is chosen representative, quarrels with Governor, Lieutenant, Council, House, custom-

[1] It is a curious fact, that, of eight persons here named as actively engaged at the bar at this period, only one, the writer himself, lived through the Revolution as an advocate of American Independence. Five adhered to Great Britain. Mr. Thacher died in 1765. Mr. Otis became incapacitated for action in 1771.

[2] This remarkable scene and extraordinary harshness will scarcely detract much from the character of James Otis. It illustrates the extent to which the *esprit de corps* will sometimes carry the most sensible men, and nothing more. Few, at this day, will be disposed to doubt that Mr. Otis was more nearly right than his opponents, and his action, in this instance, consistent with his general principles, if not with his first impulse.

[3] These two lampoons seem to have been the offspring of the passions of the moment and copied on the spot. It is not clear by whom they were made.

house officers, gentlemen of the army, the bar; retails prosody, writes upon money, Province sloop.[1]

Boston. February. This day learned that the Caucus Club meets, at certain times, in the garret of Tom Dawes, the Adjutant of the Boston Regiment. He has a large house, and he has a movable partition in his garret which he takes down, and the whole club meets in one room. There they smoke tobacco till you cannot see from one end of the garret to the other. There they drink flip, I suppose, and there they choose a moderator, who puts questions to the vote regularly; and selectmen, assessors, collectors, wardens, fire-wards, and representatives, are regularly chosen before they are chosen in the town. Uncle Fairfield, Story, Ruddock, Adams, Cooper, and a *rudis indigestaque moles* of others are members.[2] They send committees to wait on the merchant's club, and to propose and join in the choice of men and measures. Captain Cunningham says, they have often solicited him to go to those caucuses; they have assured him benefit in his business, &c.

1 It is scarcely necessary to say that each of these points has a direct reference to some event in the life of Otis. The question raised as to the Governor's authority to fit out the Province sloop is spoken of by Tudor as "one of the preparatory causes of the Revolution." *Life of Otis*, p. 117.

2 Gordon assigns a very early date for this practice. He says, "More than fifty years ago," (from 1774,) "Mr. Samuel Adams's father and twenty others, one or two from the north end of the town, where all the ship business is carried on, used to meet, make a caucus, and lay their plan for introducing certain persons into places of trust and power. When they had settled it, they separated, and used each their particular influence within his own circle. He and his friends would furnish themselves with ballots, including the names of the parties fixed upon, which they distributed on the days of election. By acting in concert, together with a careful and extensive distribution of ballots, they generally carried the elections to their own mind. In like manner it was, that Mr. Samuel Adams first became a representative for Boston." *History of the American Revolution*, vol. i. p. 365, note.

An interval of two years occurs here in the Diary. One event took place of no trifling consequence to the subsequent life of the writer.

1764. [Here it may be proper to recollect something which makes an article of great importance in the life of every man. I was of an amorous disposition, and, very early, from ten or eleven years of age, was very fond of the society of females. I had my favorites among the young women, and spent many of my evenings in their company; and this disposition, although controlled for seven years after my entrance into college, returned and engaged me too much till I was married.

I shall draw no characters, nor give any enumeration of my youthful flames. It would be considered as no compliment to the dead or the living. This, I will say; — they were all modest and virtuous girls, and always maintained their character through life. No virgin or matron ever had cause to blush at the sight of me, or to regret her acquaintance with me. No father, brother, son, or friend, ever had cause of grief or resentment for any intercourse between me and any daughter, sister, mother, or any other relation of the female sex. These reflections, to me consolatory beyond all expression, I am able to make with truth and sincerity; and I presume I am indebted for this blessing to my education. This has been rendered the more precious to me, as I have seen enough of the effects of a different practice. Corroding reflections through life are the never failing consequence of illicit amours in old as well as in new countries. The happiness of life depends more upon innocence in this respect, than upon all the philosophy of Epicurus or of Zeno without it.

I passed the summer of 1764 in attending courts and pursuing my studies, with some amusement on my little farm, to which I was frequently making additions, until the fall, when, on the 25th of October, I was married to Miss Smith, second daughter of the Rev. William Smith, minister of Weymouth, granddaughter of the Honorable John Quincy of Braintree, a connection which has been the source of all my felicity, although a sense of duty, which forced me away from her and my children for so many years, produced all the griefs of my heart, and all that I esteem real afflictions in life.]

Sodalitas, a Club of Friends.

1765. January 24. Thursday. Soon after I got to Boston, at January Court, Mr. Fitch came to me, upon 'Change, and told me that Mr. Gridley and he had something to communicate to me that I should like — in sacred confidence, however. I waited on Mr. Gridley at his office, (after many conjectures what the secret might be,) and he told me that he and Mr. Fitch had proposed a law club, a private association for the study of law and oratory. As to the bar, he thought of them as he did think of them; — Otis, Thacher, Auchmuty. He was considering who was, for the future, to support the honor and dignity of the bar; and he was determined to bring me into practice, the first practice, and Fitch[1] too. He could easily do it by recommending. And he was very desirous of forming a junto, a small sodality of himself and Fitch and me, — and Dudley, if he pleased, might come, — in order to read in concert the Feudal Law and Tully's Orations; and for this purpose he lent me The "Corpus Juris Civilis in quatuor Partes distinctum, eruditissimis Dionysii Gothofredi J. C. clarissimi Notis illustratum;" at the end of which are the "Feudorum Consuetudines, partim ex Editione Vulgatâ, partim ex Cujacianâ Vulgatâ appositæ," as also the "Epitome Feudorum Dionysio Gothofredo authore." We agreed to meet, the next evening, in one of Ballard's back chambers, and determine upon times, places, and studies. We accordingly met, Mr. Gridley, Fitch and I, and spent the whole evening. Proposals were, to read a reign and the statutes of that reign; to read Hurd's Dialogues and any new pieces. But at last we determined to read the Feudal Law and Cicero only, lest we should lose sight of our main object by attending to too many. Thursday nights were agreed on, and to meet first at Mr. Gridley's office. There we accordingly met on the Thursday night following, and suffered our conversation to ramble upon Hurd's Dialogues, the Pandects, their discovery in Italy by Lotharius in 1135, in the reign of Stephen, upon Lambard De

[1] Mr. Fitch afterwards obtained the office of Solicitor to the Board of Commissioners, and hence naturally signed the address to Governor Hutchinson in 1774, which entailed upon him the consequences of adhering to the loyal side. Mr. Sabine has not succeeded in tracing him abroad, beyond the year 1783. *The American Loyalists*, p. 287.

Priscis Anglorum Legibus, in Saxon and Latin, upon Lord Kames, Mr. Blackstone, &c. But we agreed to meet the next Thursday night at Mr. Fitch's, and to read the three first titles of the Feudal Law, and Tully's Oration for Milo.

I rode to Boston on purpose to meet at Fitch's. Gridley came; — we read the three first titles of the Feudal Law, and we read Gothofred's notes, and we looked into Strykius for the explanation of many hard words in those three titles. The Valvasors, Capitanei, Guardia and Guastaldi. This Strykius wrote an Examen Juris Feudalis, by way of question and answer. His account of the original of the Consuetudines Feudorum is, that they were collected and written by Gerardus Niger and Obertus, the consuls of Milan. We read also part of Tully's Milo, and are to read the fourth and fifth titles of the Feudal Law, and the rest of that oration next Thursday night. The law of inheritances in England originates in the feudal law; Gilbert's Tenures originate there. Robertson's History of Scotland gives the clearest account of the feudal system, they say. Lord Kames has given us the introduction of the feudal law into Scotland. *Q.* What say the law tracts and Dalrymple on this subject?

Gridley. " Taylor observed to me when in England, that no books were more proper for *nisi prius* oratory, than the Examiner, Craftsman, and such controversial writings of the best hands."

I expect the greatest pleasure from this sodality, that I ever had in my life, and a pleasure, too, that will not be painful to my reflection.

Milo was condemned, and went into banishment at Marseilles. There he afterwards read the oration, which had been corrected and polished for his perusal, and sent to him by Cicero for a present and an amusement. Reading it, he broke out, — " *Si sic egisses, Marce Tulli, barbatos pisces non comedissem.*"

For he had been eating a sort of bearded fishes that he found at Marseilles.

31. Thursday. The snowy weather prevented me from going to Dudley's. The sodality, however, met and read the two titles assigned, and assigned the three next; namely, the sixth, Episcopum vel Abbatem vel Abbatissam vel Dominum, Plebis feudum

dare non posse; Tit. 7th, De Natura Feudi; and Tit 8th, De Successione Feudi.

February 21. Thursday. At Boston entertained the sodality at Blodget's. We were never in better spirits, or more social. We began the thirteenth title of the Feudal Law, De Alienatione Feudi, and read three titles. Gridley proposed that we should mark all those passages which are adopted by the English law, that when we come to read Lord Coke, we may recur back upon occasion to the originals of our law.

The fourteenth title is De Feudo Marchiæ vel Ducatus vel Comitatus. Here, therefore, we see the originals of English dignities, marquisates, dukedoms, counties, &c. The fifteenth title is, An maritus succedat uxori in Feudo. I quoted to my brothers the preface to the Historical Law Tracts;—"The feudal customs ought to be the study of every man who proposes to reap instruction from the history of the modern European nations, because, among these nations, public transactions, not less than private property, were, some centuries ago, regulated by the feudal system.

"Sovereigns formerly were, many of them, connected by the relation of superior and vassal. The King of England, for example, by the feudal tenure, held of the French king many fair provinces."

I quoted also the sentiments of Rousseau, which are very inimical to the feudal system. "The notion of representatives," says he, "is modern, descending to us from the feudal system, that most iniquitous and absurd form of government by which human nature was so shamefully degraded."[1]

Fitch. "The feudal system was military; it was a martial system; a set of regulations, (as Robertson calls it,) for the encampment of a great army; and it was a wise and good system for a martial people in such circumstances. For the feudal connections, and subordination, and services, were necessary for their defence against the inroads and invasions of their neighbors," &c.

Ego. "I think that the absurdity and iniquity lies in this;—that nations at peace and in plenty, who live by commerce and industry, have adopted such a system."

[1] Du Contrat Social, chap. xv.

Gridley. "There lies the absurdity and iniquity; and the observation you quote proves that Rousseau is shallow."

I might have quoted Lord Kames's British Antiquities, who says, — "It is the plan of the feudal law to bestow the whole land property upon the king, and to subject to him the bulk of the people in quality of servants and vassals; a constitution so contradictory to all the principles which govern mankind can never be brought about, one should imagine, but by foreign conquest or native usurpation." And in another place he calls the feudal connection — "the feudal yoke."

These epithets of "absurd," "iniquitous," "unnatural," &c., are not very agreeable to the opinion of Strykius, who says, in answer to the question — unde originem trahunt feuda? Certo modo et si formam feudorum genericam consideres, dici potest, ex jure gentium. Hoc enim ratio naturalis, junctâ necessitate publicâ, exigit ut militibus potissimum prædia, ab hostibus occupata, pro bene meritis concederentur sub conditione tamen fidelitatis, quo eo securior esset respublica et ad patriam defendendam magis allicerentur.

In Milo we read from the twenty-seventh to the thirty-fourth section in Davidson's translation. We begin the peroration next. We had Guthrie's and Davidson's translations. In point of accuracy and spirit, Davidson's is vastly superior.

Mr. Gridley produced a book entitled, In Herennium Commentarius, as an introduction to Tully de Oratore, and read the three sorts of orations, — the demonstrative, deliberative, and judicial, — and the several parts of an oration, — the exordium, &c.

Gridley. "Our plan must be, when we have finished the Feudal Law, to read Coke-Littleton, and after him a reign and the statutes of that reign. It should also be a part of our plan to improve ourselves in writing, by reading carefully the best English writers, and by using ourselves to writing. For it should be a part of our plan to publish pieces now and then. Let us form our style upon the ancients and the best English authors.

"I hope and expect to see at the bar, in consequence of this sodality, a purity, an elegance, and a spirit surpassing any thing that ever appeared in America."

Fitch said that he would not say he had abilities, but he would say he had ambition enough to hope for the same thing.

This sodality has given rise to the following speculation of my own, which I commit to writing as hints for future inquiries, rather than as a satisfactory theory![1]

August 15. Wednesday. I hope it will give no offence to inquire into the grounds and reasons of the strange conduct of yesterday and last night at Boston. Is there any evidence that Mr. Oliver[2] ever wrote to the ministry, or to anybody in England, any unfavorable representations of the people of this Province? Has he ever placed the character of the people, their manners, their laws, their principles in religion or government, their submission to order and magistracy, in a false light? Is it known that he ever advised the ministry to lay internal taxes upon us? that he ever solicited the office of distributer of stamps? or that he has ever done any thing to injure the people or to incur their displeasure, besides barely accepting of that office? If there is no proof at all of any such injury done to the people by that gentleman, has not the blind, undistinguishing rage of the rabble done him irreparable injustice? To be placed, only in pageantry, in the most conspicuous part of the town, with such ignominious devices around him, would be thought severity enough by any man of common sensibility. But to be carried through the town in such insolent triumph, and burned on a hill, to have his garden torn in pieces, his house broken open, his furniture destroyed, and his whole family thrown into confusion and terror, is a very atrocious violation of the peace, and of dangerous tendency and consequence.

But, on the other hand, let us ask a few questions. Has not his Honor the Lieutenant-Governor discovered to the people, in innumerable instances, a very ambitious and avaricious disposi-

[1] Here follows the first draught of the three papers published in the Boston Gazette, and afterwards collected and republished in London under the title of "A Dissertation on the Canon and Feudal Law." As the work is reserved for another portion of these volumes, some remarkable variations in this draught will find a more appropriate place there.

[2] Mr. Oliver was hung in effigy upon Liberty tree. "Before night the image was taken down, and carried through the town-house, in the chamber whereof the governor and council were sitting. Forty or fifty tradesmen, decently dressed, preceded; and some thousands of the mob followed down King street to Oliver's dock, near which Mr. Oliver had lately erected a building, which it was conjectured he designed for a stamp office. This was laid flat to the ground in a few minutes. From thence the mob proceeded for Fort Hill, but Mr. Oliver's house being in the way, they endeavored to force themselves into it, and, being opposed, broke the windows, beat down the doors, entered and destroyed part of his furniture, and continued in riot until midnight, before they separated." *Hutchinson*, vol. iii. p. 121.

tion? Has he not grasped four of the most important offices in the Province into his own hands? Has not his brother-in-law, Oliver, another of the greatest places in government? Is not a brother of the Secretary, a judge of the superior court? Has not that brother a son in the House? Has not the Secretary a son in the House, who is also a judge in one of the counties? Did not that son marry the daughter of another of the Judges of the Superior Court? Has not the Lieutenant-Governor a brother, a Judge of the pleas in Boston, and a namesake and near relation who is another Judge? Has not the Lieutenant-Governor a near relation who is register of his own court of probate, and deputy secretary? Has he not another near relation who is Clerk of the House of Representatives? Is not this amazing ascendency of one family foundation sufficient on which to erect a tyranny? Is it not enough to excite jealousies among the people?

Quære further. Has not many a member of both houses labored to the utmost of his ability to obtain a resolution to send home some petitions and remonstrances to the King, Lords, and Commons, against the impositions they saw were about to be laid upon us? Has not the Lieutenant-Governor, all along, been the very gentleman who has prevented it, and wiped every spirited if not every sensible expression out of those petitions?

Quære further. When the Court was about to choose an agent, did not the Governor, Lieutenant-Governor, and Secretary, make use of all their influence to procure an election for Mr. Jackson?[1] Was not Mr. Jackson a secretary to Mr. Grenville? Was not Mr. Grenville the author of the late measures relative to the Colonies? Was not Mr. Jackson an agent and a particular friend of the Governor? Was not all this, considering the natural jealousy of mankind, enough to excite suspicions among the vulgar that all these gentlemen were in a combination to favor the measures of the Ministry, at least to prevent any thing from being done here to discourage the Minister from his rash, mad, and dogmatical proceedings? Would it not be prudence then in those gentlemen, at this alarming conjuncture, and a condescension that is due to the present fears and distresses of the people, (in some manner consistent with the dignity of their stations and characters,) to remove these jealousies from the minds of the people by giving an easy solution of these difficulties?

[1] See page 141, note.

[After the fourteenth of August I went on a journey to Martha's Vineyard, on the trial of a cause before referees, between Jerusha Mayhew and her relations. The keen understanding of this woman, and the uncontrollable violence of her irascible passions, had excited a quarrel of the most invidious, inveterate, and irreconcilable nature between the several branches of the Mayhew family, which had divided the whole island into parties. The rancor of that fiend, the spirit of party, had never appeared to me in so odious and dreadful a light, though I had heard much of it in a contest between Roland Cotton and Parson Jackson, at Woburn; and had remarked enough of it in the trial between Hopkins and Ward[1] at Worcester. In all these cases it seemed to have wrought an entire metamorphosis of the human character. It destroyed all sense and understanding, all equity and humanity, all memory and regard to truth, all virtue, honor, decorum, and veracity. Never in my life was I so grieved and disgusted with my species. More than a week, I think, was spent in the examination of witnesses and the arguments of counsel, Mr. Paine on one side, and I on the other. We endeavored to argue the cause on both sides as well as we could, but which of us got the cause I have forgotten. It was indeed no matter; for it was impossible for human sagacity to discover on which side justice lay. We were pretty free with our vituperations on both sides, and the inhabitants appeared to feel the justice of them. I think the cause was compromised.

I forgot to mention that while we were at Falmouth, waiting to be ferried over to the island, the news arrived from Boston of the riots on the twenty-sixth of August, in which Lieutenant-Governor Hutchinson's house was so much injured.

This year, 1765, was the epoch of the Stamp Act. I drew up a petition to the selectmen of Braintree, and procured it to be signed by a number of the respectable inhabitants, to call a meeting of the town to instruct their representative in relation to the stamps. The public attention of the whole continent was

[1] The history of this lawsuit, growing out of a long and vehement political struggle in Rhode Island, is given by Professor Gammell in his Life of Samuel Ward. *Sparks's American Biography*, vol. xix. pp. 259 – 283.

alarmed, and my principles and political connections were well known. I prepared a draught of instructions at home, and carried them with me. The cause of the meeting was explained at some length, and the state and danger of the country pointed out; a committee was appointed to prepare instructions, of which I was nominated as one. We retired to Mr. Niles's house, my draught was produced, and unanimously adopted without amendment, reported to the town, and accepted without a dissenting voice. These were published in Draper's paper, as that printer first applied to me for a copy. They were decided and spirited enough. They rang through the State and were adopted in so many words, as I was informed by the representatives of that year, by forty towns, as instructions to their representatives. They were honored sufficiently, by the friends of government, with the epithets of inflammatory, &c. I have not seen them now for almost forty years, and remember very little of them. I presume they would now appear a poor trifle; but at that time they met with such strong feelings in the readers, that their effect was astonishing to me, and excited some serious reflections. I thought a man ought to be very cautious what kinds of fuel he throws into a fire, when it is thus glowing in the community. Although it is a certain expedient to acquire a momentary celebrity, yet it may produce future evils which may excite serious repentance. I have seen so many firebrands thrown into the flame, not only in the worthless and unprincipled writings of the profligate and impious Thomas Paine, and in the French Revolution, but in many others, that I think every man ought to take warning.

In the Braintree instructions, however, if I recollect any reprehensible fault, it was that they conceded too much to the adversary, not to say, enemy.[1] About this time I called upon my friend, Samuel Adams, and found him at his desk. He told me the town of Boston had employed him to draw instructions for their representatives; that he felt an ambition which was very apt to mislead a man, — that of doing something extraordinary; and he wanted to consult a friend who might suggest some thoughts to his mind. I read his instructions, and showed him

[1] These instructions, being the first public act of Mr. Adams, will be found in another volume. They bear date the twenty-fourth of September, 1765.

a copy of mine. I told him I thought his very well as far as they went, but he had not gone far enough. Upon reading mine, he said he was of my opinion, and accordingly took into his some paragraphs from mine.]

Braintree. December 18. Wednesday. How great is my loss in neglecting to keep a regular journal through the last Spring, Summer, and Fall! In the course of my business, as a surveyor of highways, as one of the committee for dividing, planning, and selling the North Commons, in the course of my two great journeys to Pownalborough and Martha's Vineyard, and in several smaller journeys to Plymouth, Taunton, and Boston, I had many fine opportunities and materials for speculation. The year 1765 has been the most remarkable year of my life. That enormous engine, fabricated by the British Parliament, for battering down all the rights and liberties of America, I mean the Stamp Act, has raised and spread through the whole continent a spirit that will be recorded to our honor with all future generations. In every colony, from Georgia to New Hampshire inclusively, the stamp distributers and inspectors have been compelled by the unconquerable rage of the people to renounce their offices. Such and so universal has been the resentment of the people, that every man who has dared to speak in favor of the stamps, or to soften the detestation in which they are held, how great soever his abilities and virtues had been esteemed before, or whatever his fortune, connections, and influence had been, has been seen to sink into universal contempt and ignominy.

The people, even to the lowest ranks, have become more attentive to their liberties, more inquisitive about them, and more determined to defend them, than they were ever before known or had occasion to be; innumerable have been the monuments of wit, humor, sense, learning, spirit, patriotism, and heroism, erected in the several colonies and provinces in the course of this year. Our presses have groaned, our pulpits have thundered, our legislatures have resolved, our towns have voted; the crown officers have everywhere trembled, and all their little tools and creatures been afraid to speak and ashamed to be seen.

This spirit, however, has not yet been sufficient to banish from persons in authority that timidity which they have discovered from the beginning. The executive courts have not yet dared to adjudge the Stamp Act void, nor to proceed with business as usual, though it should seem that necessity alone would be sufficient to justify business at present, though the act should be allowed to be obligatory. The stamps are in the castle. Mr. Oliver has no commission. The Governor has no authority to distribute or even to unpack the bales; the Act has never been proclaimed nor read in the Province; yet the probate office is shut, the custom-house is shut, the courts of justice are shut, and all business seems at a stand. Yesterday and the day before, the two last days of service for January Term, only one man asked me for a writ, and he was soon determined to wave his request. I have not drawn a writ since the first of November.

How long we are to remain in this languid condition, this passive obedience to the Stamp Act, is not certain. But such a pause cannot be lasting. Debtors grow insolent; creditors grow angry; and it is to be expected that the public offices will very soon be forced open, unless such favorable accounts should be received from England as to draw away the fears of the great, or unless a greater dread of the multitude should drive away the fear of censure from Great Britain.

It is my opinion that by this inactivity we discover cowardice, and too much respect to the Act. This rest appears to be, by implication at least, an acknowledgment of the authority of Parliament to tax us. And if this authority is once acknowledged and established, the ruin of America will become inevitable. This long interval of indolence and idleness will make a large chasm in my affairs, if it should not reduce me to distress, and incapacitate me to answer the demands upon me. But I must endeavor, in some degree, to compensate the disadvantage, by posting my books, reducing my accounts into better order, and by diminishing my expenses, — but, above all, by improving the leisure of this winter in a diligent application to my studies.

I find that idleness lies between business and study; that is, the transition from the hurry of a multiplicity of business to the tranquillity that is necessary for intense study, is not easy. There must be a vacation, an interval between them, for the mind to recollect itself.

The bar seem to me to behave like a flock of shot pigeons; they seem to be stopped; the net seems to be thrown over them, and they have scarcely courage left to flounce and to flutter. So sudden an interruption in my career is very unfortunate for me. I was but just getting into my gears, just getting under sail, and an embargo is laid upon the ship. Thirty years of my life are passed in preparation for business; I have had poverty to struggle with, envy and jealousy and malice of enemies to encounter, no friends, or but few, to assist me; so that I have groped in dark obscurity, till of late, and had but just become known and gained a small degree of reputation, when this execrable project was set on foot for my ruin as well as that of America in general, and of Great Britain.

19. Thursday. A fair morning, after a severe storm of three days and four nights; a vast quantity of rain fell.

About twelve o'clock came in Messrs. Crafts and Chase, and gave me a particular account of the proceedings of the Sons of Liberty, on Tuesday last,[1] in prevailing on Mr. Oliver to renounce his office of distributer of stamps, by a declaration under his hand and under his oath, taken before Justice Dana in Hanover Square, under the very tree of liberty, nay, under the very limb where he had been hanged in effigy, August 14th, 1765. Their absolute requisition of an oath, and under that tree, were circumstances extremely humiliating and mortifying, as punishments for his receiving a deputation to be distributer, after his pretended resignation, and for his faint and indirect declaration in the newspapers last Monday.

About one o'clock came in Mr. Clark, one of the constables

[1] "The Secretary (Oliver,) being informed that the people were assembled before the time, by a note directed to them, desired to make his resignation at the town-house; but this would not satisfy them, and they insisted on his coming to the tree. Several of his friends, at his desire, accompanied him; but Mackintosh, the chief actor in destroying the Lieutenant-Governor's house, attended him, at his right hand, through the streets to the tree, in a rainy, tempestuous day, a great number following. About two thousand people were assembled. Several of the selectmen, and many other persons of condition, were in the house before which the tree stood, with Richard Dana, Esq., a justice of peace and a lawyer of note, who administered an oath to the Secretary to this purpose: — 'That he had never taken any measures, in consequence of his deputation, to act in his office as distributer of stamps, and that he never would, directly or indirectly, by himself or any under him, make use of his deputation, or take any measures for enforcing the stamp act in America.' After three huzzas, he was at liberty to return home." *Hutchinson's History*, iii. p. 140.

of the town of Boston, with a letter from Mr. William Cooper, their town-clerk, in these words:

"SIR:—I am directed by the town to acquaint you, that they have this day voted unanimously that Jeremiah Gridley, James Otis, and John Adams, Esquires, be applied to as counsel to appear before his Excellency the Governor in council, in support of their memorial praying that the courts of law in this Province may be opened. A copy of said memorial will be handed you on your coming to town.

I am, sir, your most obedient, humble servant,

WILLIAM COOPER, *Town Clerk.*"

JOHN ADAMS, ESQ.[1]

Boston, December 18th, 1765.

The reasons which induced Boston to choose me, at a distance and unknown as I am, the particular persons concerned and measures concerted to bring this about, I am wholly at a loss to conjecture; as I am, what the future effects and consequences will be both with regard to myself and the public.

But when I recollect my own reflections and speculations yesterday, a part of which were committed to writing last night, and may be seen under December 18th, and compare them with the proceedings of Boston yesterday, of which the foregoing letter informed me, I cannot but wonder, and call to mind my Lord Bacon's observation about secret, invisible laws of nature, and communications and influences between places that are not discoverable by sense.

But I am now under all obligations of interest and ambition, as well as honor, gratitude, and duty, to exert the utmost of my abilities in this important cause. How shall it be conducted? Shall we contend that the Stamp Act is void—that the Parliament have no legal authority to impose internal taxes upon us, because we are not represented in it—and, therefore, that the Stamp Act ought to be waved by the judges as against natural equity and the constitution? Shall we use these as arguments for opening the courts of law? or shall we ground ourselves on necessity only?

[1] The original of this is preserved.

20. Friday. Went to Boston; dined with Mr. Rowe,[1] in company with Messrs. Gridley, Otis, Kent, and Dudley. After dinner, went to the town-house, and attended, with the committee of the town of Boston and many other gentlemen, in the representatives room till about dark, after candle-light, when Mr. Adams, the chairman of the committee, received a message from the Governor, by the deputy secretary, purporting that his Excellency and the council were ready to hear the memorial of the town of Boston, and their counsel in support of it; but that no other persons might attend.

We accordingly went in. His Excellency recommended it to us, who were of counsel for the town, to divide the points of law and topics of argument among ourselves, that repetition might, as much as possible, be avoided.

Mr. Gridley answered, that, as he was to speak last, he would endeavor to avoid repetition of what should be said by the two gentlemen who were to speak before him.

Mr. Otis added, that, as he was to speak second, he would observe the same rule.

Then it fell upon me, without one moment's opportunity to consult any authorities, to open an argument upon a question that was never made before, and I wish I could hope it never would be made again, that is, whether the courts of law should be open or not?

My old friend Thacher's *officina justitiæ*.

I grounded my argument on the invalidity of the Stamp Act, it not being in any sense our act, having never consented to it. But, lest that foundation should not be sufficient, on the present necessity to prevent a failure of justice, and the present impossibility of carrying that act into execution.*

[1] John Rowe, a merchant, active on the side of liberty. Gordon says that many influential persons, at this time, were thinking of him as a representative from Boston to the General Court; but Mr. Samuel Adams artfully nominated a different one, by asking, with his eyes looking to Mr. Hancock's house, "Is there not another John that may do better?"

* [With so little preparation, and with no time to look into any books for analogous cases, I went and introduced the argument, but made a very poor figure. Mr. Gridley and Mr. Otis more than supplied all my defects. But the Governor and council would do nothing.]

Among the papers of Mr. Adams, the following abstract remains of the authorities on which he relied upon this occasion:—

Mr. Otis reasoned with great learning and zeal on the judges' oaths, &c.

Mr. Gridley on the great inconveniences that would ensue the interruption of justice.

The Governor said, many of the arguments used were very good ones to be used before the Judges of the executive courts; but he believed there had been no instance in America of an application to the Governor and council; and said, that if the Judges should receive any directions from the King about a point of law, they would scorn to regard them, and would say that while they were in those seats, they only were to determine points of law.

The council adjourned to the morning, and I repaired to my lodgings.

21. Saturday. Spent the morning in sauntering about and chatting with one and another, — the sheriff, Mr. Goldthwait, brother Sewall, &c., — upon the times. Dined with brother Kent;

RIGHT, WRONG, AND REMEDY.

Common law is common right. 1 Inst. 142 a. Coke's Proem to 2 Inst.

The law is the subject's best birthright. 2 Inst. 56.

Want of right and want of remedy is all one; for where there is no remedy there is no right. 1 Inst. 95 b.

The law provides a remedy for every wrong. 1 Inst. 197 b. 2 Inst. 55, 56, 405. But see 1 Inst. 199 b.

The law hath a delight in giving of remedy. Lit. 323. 1 Inst. 54 b., 199 b., 100 a.

The act of law never doth wrong. 1 Inst. 88 b., 148 a. b., 379 a.

Where the construction of any act is left to the law, the law will never construe it to work a wrong. Wood's Inst. pp. 4, 5.

A statute must be construed that no innocent man may, by a literal construction, receive damage. Wood, p. 9.

An act of Parliament can do no wrong. Holt, 12 Mod. 687, 688. Hill, 13 Wm. III. B. R. City of London *v.* Wood.

Actus Dei nemini facit injuriam; actus legis nulli facit injuriam.

CASES OF NECESSITY AND IMPOSSIBILITY.

The law forces no one to that which is impossible or vain. 1 Inst. 79 a., 92 a., 127 b. To procure the stamp papers is impossible, and to stop justice would be vain.

Things of necessity are to be excepted out of a general law. 2 Inst. 168. There is nothing of greater necessity than the administration of justice. Justice cannot be administered at present but in the usual way. Therefore the present case and these times are excepted out of that general law, the Stamp Act.

Things for necessity' sake or to prevent a failure of justice, are excepted out of a statute. Wood's Inst. p. 9.

Acts of Parliament that are against reason, or impossible to be performed, shall be judged void. 8 Rep. 118, 128, 129. 2 Inst. 587, 588.

after dinner received a hint from the committee, that, as I was of counsel for the town, I not only had a right, but it was expected I should attend the meeting. I went accordingly. The committee reported the answer of the board to their petition, which was, in substance, that the board had no authority to direct the courts of law in the manner prayed for; that the memorial involved a question of law, namely, whether the officers of the government, in the present circumstances of the Province, could be justified in proceeding with business without stamps; that the board were desirous that the judges should decide that question freely, without apprehension of censure from the board; and that the board recommended it to the judges of the inferior court, for the county of Suffolk, and to the other judges of the other courts in the Province, to determine that question as soon as may be, at or before their next respective terms.

The question was put, whether that paper should be recorded? Passed in the affirmative.

The next question was, whether it was a satisfactory answer to their memorial? Unanimously in the negative.[1] Then several motions were made. The first was, that the meeting be adjourned to a future day, and that the town's counsel be desired to consult together and give the town their opinions, whether any other legal and constitutional steps can be taken by the town towards removing the obstructions to justice. The second motion was, that those of the town's counsel who were present should then give their opinion. The third was, that application should be made to the judges to determine the question speedily. The second prevailed, and I was called upon to give my opinion first. I agreed with Kent, that an application to the Judges might be out of character, both for the town and the Judges, and that no person could be in any danger of penalties on the one hand, or of having processes adjudged void on the other. But many persons might entertain fears and jealousies and doubts, which

[1] Hutchinson's comment on this decision and its consequences is as follows: —

"This was very improper, and tending to division, and to increase the flame; but no other way occurred to the council, of freeing themselves from trouble.

The town adjourned for two or three days to know the result; and, when they heard it, voted, 'that it was not satisfactory.'

Such votes became frequent, and had greater effect than can well be imagined." *History*, iii. 141.

would everlastingly be a grievance. So that I had heard no proposal yet made, for the future conduct of the town, which had not difficulties and objections attending it; so that I must conclude myself as yet in doubt, and that I dared not give any opinion positively, in a matter of so much importance, without the most mature deliberation.

Mr. Otis then gave his sentiments, and declared once for all that he knew of no legal and constitutional course the town could take, but to direct their representatives to request the Governor to call a convention of the members of both houses, as he could not legally call an assembly; and if his Excellency would not, to call one themselves, by requesting all the members to meet; but concluded with observing that, as one of their counsel was not present, and another was in doubt, he thought it would be best to take further time for consideration. And the town accordingly voted an adjournment to next Thursday, ten o'clock.

A consultation, therefore, I must have with Messrs. Gridley and Otis, and we must all attend the town meeting next Thursday. What advice shall we give them?

The question is, "what legal and constitutional measures the town can take to open the courts of law?"

The town, in their memorial to his Excellency in council, assert that the courts of law within the Province, in which alone justice can be distributed among the people so far as respects civil matters, are to all intents and purposes shut up; for which no just and legal reason can be assigned. The record of the board, sent down in answer, admits that the courts of law are to all intents and purposes shut up; and says that, before they can be opened, a point of law must be decided, namely, whether the officers of the government, in the present circumstances of the Province, can be justified in proceeding in their offices without stamps? — which the Judges are to determine.

Are the board then agreed with the town that the courts of law are shut up? But I hope the town will not agree with the board, that the judges are the proper persons to decide whether they shall be open or not. It is the first time, I believe, that such a question was ever put since William the Conqueror, nay, since the days of King Lear. Should the twelve judges of England, and all other officers of justice, judicial and ministerial, suddenly stop and shut up their offices, I believe the King in council would hardly recommend any points of law to the consideration of those judges. The King, it is true, of his prerogative, could not remove the judges, because in England a judge is quite another thing from what he is here. But I believe the Commons in Parliament would immediately impeach them all of high treason.

My advice to the town will be, to take the board at their word, and to choose a committee immediately; in the first place, to wait on the Governor in council, as the supreme court of probate, and request of them a determination of the point,—whether the officers of the probate courts in the Province can be justified in proceeding with business without stamps; in the next place, to wait on the honorable the judges of the superior court, to request their determination of the same question; and, in the third place, to wait on the judges of the inferior court for the county of Suffolk, with the same request, in pursuance of the recommendation of the honorable board; and, unless a speedy determination of the question is obtained in all these courts in this way, to request of the Governor a convention of the two houses, and, if that is refused, to endeavor to call one themselves.

What are the consequences of the supposition that the courts are shut up? The King is the fountain of justice, by the constitution; and it is a maxim of the law, that the King never dies.

Are not protection and allegiance reciprocal? and if we are out of the King's protection, are we not discharged from our allegiance? Are not all the ligaments of government dissolved? Is it not an abdication of the throne? In short, where will such a horrid doctrine terminate? It would run us into treason!

22. Sunday. At home with my family, thinking.

23. Monday. Went to Boston. After dinner rambled after Messrs. Gridley and Otis, but could find neither. Went into Mr. Dudley's, Mr. Dana's, Mr. Otis's office, and then to Mr. Adams's, and went with him to the Monday night club. There I found Otis, Cushing, Wells, Pemberton, Gray, Austin, two Waldos, Inches, Dr. Parker, and spent the evening very agreeably indeed. Politicians all at this club. We had many curious anecdotes about governors, counsellors, representatives, demagogues, merchants, &c.

The behavior of these gentlemen is very familiar and friendly to each other, and very polite and complaisant to strangers. Gray[1] has a very tender mind, is extremely timid. He says, when he meets a man of the other side, he talks against him; when he meets a man of our side, he opposes him; — so that he fears he shall be thought against everybody, and so everybody will be against him. But he hopes to prepare the way for his escape, at next May, from an employment that neither his abilities, nor circumstances, nor turn of mind, are fit for.

Cushing[2] is steady, and constant, and busy in the interest of liberty and the opposition, is famed for secrecy and his talent at procuring intelligence.

Adams[3] is zealous, ardent, and keen in the cause, is always for softness, and delicacy, and prudence, where they will do, but is staunch and stiff and strict and rigid and inflexible in the cause.

Otis is fiery and feverous; his imagination flames, his passions blaze; he is liable to great inequalities of temper; sometimes in despondency, sometimes in a rage. The rashnesses and imprudencies into which his excess of zeal have formerly transported him, have made him enemies, whose malicious watch over him occasion more caution, and more cunning, and more inexplicable passages in his conduct than formerly; and, perhaps, views at the chair or the board, or possibly more expanded views beyond the Atlantic, may mingle now with his patriotism.

The Penseroso, however, is discernible on the faces of all four.

Adams, I believe, has the most thorough understanding of liberty and her resources in the temper and character of the people, though not in the law and constitution; as well as the most habitual, radical love of it, of any of them, as well as the most correct, genteel, and artful pen. He is a man of refined policy, steadfast integrity, exquisite humanity, genteel erudition, obliging, engaging manners, real as well as professed piety, and

[1] Harrison Gray, Treasurer of the Province, whose vacillation, here depicted, terminated as it usually terminates in difficult public questions, in taking the side of authority.

[2] Thomas Cushing, at this time Speaker of the House, and subsequently a member of the first Congress at Philadelphia. He is the person whose name was used by Dr. Johnson, in "Taxation no Tyranny." "If their rights are inherent and underived, the Americans may by their own suffrages encircle with a diadem the brows of Mr. Cushing."

[3] Samuel Adams.

a universal good character, unless it should be admitted that he is too attentive to the public, and not enough so to himself and his family.

The gentlemen were warm to have the courts opened. Gridley had advised to wait for a judicial opinion of the judges. I was for requesting of the Governor that the General Court might assemble at the time to which they stood prorogued; and, if the town should think fit, to request the extrajudicial opinion of the judges. I was for petitioning the Governor and council to determine the question first as Supreme ordinary. Gridley will be absent, and so shall I. But I think the apparent impatience of the town must produce some spirited measures, perhaps more spirited than prudent.

24. Tuesday. Returned from Boston; spent the afternoon and evening at home.

25. Wednesday. Christmas. At home thinking, reading, searching, concerning taxation without consent; concerning the great pause and rest in business.

By the laws of England, justice flows with an uninterrupted stream! In that music the law knows of neither rests nor pauses. Nothing but violence, invasion, or rebellion, can obstruct the river or untune the instrument.

Concerning a compensation to the sufferers by the late riots in Boston. Statute of Winchester, chapter II.—"If the county will not answer the bodies of the offenders, the people there shall be answerable for all the robberies done, and also for the damages." Wingate's Abridgment, Title *Robberies*.

"Nulli vendemus, nulli negabimus, aut deferemus justitiam."

Every writ supposes the King present in all his courts of justice.

Lord Coke says, "Against this ancient and fundamental law, and in the face thereof, I find an act of Parliament made, that as well justices of assize, as justices of peace, without any finding or presentment of twelve men, upon a bare information for the King before them made, should have full power and authority, by their discretions, to hear and determine all offences and contempts against the form, ordinance, and effect of any statute, by color of which act shaking this fundamental law, it is not credible what horrible oppressions and exactions were committed by Sir Richard Empson and Edmund Dudley; and, upon this unjust and injurious act, a new office was created, and they made masters of the king's forfeitures. But at the Parliament, first Henry VIII., this act, 11 Henry VII., is recited, made void, and repealed. The fearful end of these two oppressors should deter others from committing the like, and admonish Parliaments that, instead of this ordinary and precious trial *per legem terræ*, they bring not in absolute and partial trials by discretion."

Went not to Christmas; dined at home; drank tea at grandfather Quincy's.[1] The old gentleman inquisitive about the hearing before the Governor and council; about the Governor's and Secretary's looks and behavior, and about the final determination of the board. The old lady as merry and chatty as ever, with her stories out of the newspapers.

Spent the evening at home with my partner, and no other company. Mr. Samuel Adams told me he was glad I was nominated, for several reasons; first, because he hoped that such an instance of respect from the town of Boston, would make an impression on my mind, and secure my friendship to the town from gratitude. Secondly, he was in hopes such distinction from Boston would be of service to my business and interest. Thirdly, he hoped that Braintree, finding the eyes of Boston were upon me, would fix theirs on me too, next May.

His hopes, in the two first particulars, may be well grounded, but I am sure not in the third.

A Dissertation upon Seekers—of Elections, of Commissions from the Governor, of Commissions from the Crown.

Of elections,—when they give your one hundred pounds, lawful money, towards building a new meeting-house, and one hundred, old tenor, towards repairing one, or fifty dollars towards repairing highways, or ten dollars to the treasury towards the support of

[1] Colonel John Quincy, for more than forty years an active person in the General Court of the Colony, now retired in that part of Braintree called Mount Wollaston, where he died, 13th July, 1767.

the poor of the town, or when they are very liberal of their drams of brandy and lumps of sugar, and of their punch, &c., on May meeting days. These are commonly persons who have some further views and designs. These largesses aim at something further than your votes. These persons aim at being justices, sheriffs, judges, colonels; and when they get to court, they will be hired and sell their votes, as you sold yours to them. But there is another sort of seekers worse than the other two,—such as seek to be Governors, Lieutenant-Governors, Secretaries, Custom-house officers of all sorts, Stamp-officers of all sorts,—in fine, such as seek appointments from the crown. These seekers are actuated by a more ravenous sort of ambition and avarice, and they merit a more aggravated condemnation. These ought to be avoided and dreaded as the plague, as the destroying angels; and the evil spirits are as good objects of your trust as they.

Let no such man ever have the vote of a freeholder or a representative. Let no such man be trusted.

---

27. Friday. "In unforeseen cases, that is, when the state of things is found such as the author of the disposition has not foreseen, and could not have thought of, we should rather follow his intention than his words, and interpret the act as he himself would have interpreted it, had he been present, or conformably to what he would have done if he had foreseen the things that happened. This rule is of great use to Judges. Vattel, p. 230; book 2, ch. 17, s. 297. If a case be presented in which one cannot absolutely apply the well known reason of a law or a promise, this case ought to be excepted. Book 2, ch. 17, s. 292. Every interpretation that leads to an absurdity, ought to be rejected." Page 222, book 2, ch. 17, s. 282. Every impossibility, physical and moral, is an absurdity.*

At home all day. Mr. Shute called in the evening, and gave

* [The Court of Common Pleas, however, were persuaded to proceed; and the Superior Court postponed and continued the question till the act was repealed. At an inferior court in Plymouth, Mr. Paine and I called a meeting of the bar, and we labored so successfully with our brothers that we brought them all to agree in an application to the Court to proceed without stamps, in which we succeeded.]

us a number of anecdotes about Governor Rogers[1] and Secretary Potter,—their persecution in Boston, their flight to Rhode Island, their sufferings there; their deliverance from jail, and voyage to Antigua and Ireland without money; their reception in Ireland, and voyage to England; their distresses in England till they borrowed money to get Rogers's Journal printed and present it to his Majesty, which procured each of them his appointment at Michilimackinac. Shute is a jolly, merry, droll, social Christian; he loves to laugh, tells a story with a good grace, delights in banter, but yet reasons well; is inquisitive and judicious; has an eye that plays its lightnings; sly, and waggish, and roguish; is for sinking every person who either favors the stamps or trims about them, into private station; expects a great mortality among the counsellors next May. In this, I think he is right. If there is any man, who from wild ideas of power and authority, from a contempt of that equality in knowledge, wealth, and power, which has prevailed in this country, or from any other cause, can upon principle desire the execution of the Stamp Act, those principles are a total forfeiture of the confidence of the people. If there is any one who cannot see the tendency of that Act to reduce the body of the people to ignorance, poverty, dependence, his want of eyesight is a disqualification for public employment. Let the towns and the representatives, therefore, renounce every stamp man and every trimmer next May.

28. Saturday. Went to Weymouth with my wife; dined at Father Smith's; heard much of the uneasiness among the people of Hingham, at a sermon preached by Mr. Gay,[2] on the day of

[1] Robert Rogers, of New Hampshire, was noted during the French war as a daring partisan officer. He was placed in command of a company of Rangers, and was engaged in much dangerous service on scouting parties around Lake George, when Ticonderoga and Fort William Henry were the head quarters of conflicting forces. His Journal of these transactions, first printed in London, in 1765, has been reprinted within a few years at Concord, N. H. It is a book of little merit, yet it contains some details of the mode of warfare at this period which will be read with more curiosity as time elapses. He obtained the appointment of Governor of Michilimackinac, as stated in the text, but was soon displaced and sent in irons to Montreal, on suspicion of treachery. His mode of life had not been favorable to the cultivation of any moral sense, so that after the Revolution broke out he seemed ready to serve either side or both. General Washington seized him as a spy, which he probably was; he nevertheless succeeded in gaining his liberty, which he improved by taking a commission of Colonel in the British service. *Sabine's American Loyalists. Sparks's Washington.*

[2] Reverend Dr. Ebenezer Gay, for sixty-nine years pastor of the first church in Hingham. His political sentiments, inclining to the side of authority, caused

Thanksgiving, from a text in James: "Out of the same mouth proceedeth blessing and cursing." In which he said that the ancient weapons of the church were prayers and tears, not clubs; and inculcated submission to authority in pretty strong expressions. His people said that Mr. Gay would do very well for a distributer, and they believed he had the stamps in his house, and even threatened, &c. This uneasiness, it seems, was inflamed by a sermon preached there the Sunday after, by Mr. Smith, which they admired very much, and talk of printing, as the best sermon they ever heard him preach. This sermon of Mr. Smith's was from — "Render therefore unto Cæsar the things that are Cæsar's, and unto God the things that are God's." The tenor of it was to recommend honor, reward, and obedience, to good rulers, and a spirited opposition to bad ones, interspersed with a good deal of animated declamation upon liberty and the times.

It seems there is a club, consisting of Colonel Lincoln, the two Captain Barkers, one of them an half-pay officer, Colonel Thaxter, &c., who visit the parson (Gay) every Sunday evening; and this club is wholly inclined to passive obedience, as the best way to procure redress. A very absurd sentiment indeed! We have tried prayers and tears, and humble begging, and timid, tame submission, as long as trying is good; and, instead of redress, we have only increased our burdens and aggravated our condemnation.

Returned and spent the evening at home.

29. Sunday. Heard Parson Wibird:—"Hear, O heavens, and give ear, O earth! I have nourished and brought up children, and they have rebelled against me." I began to suspect a Tory sermon, on the times, from this text, but the preacher confined himself to spirituals. But, I expect, if the tories should become the strongest, we shall hear many sermons against the ingratitude, injustice, disloyalty, treason, rebellion, impiety, and ill policy of refusing obedience to the Stamp Act. The church clergy, to be sure, will be very eloquent. The church people are, many of them, favorers of the Stamp Act at present. Major Miller, for-

him some trouble in a parish which sympathized with the popular party. But he was not averse to gratifying his people, occasionally, by an exchange with his neighbor of Weymouth, the Rev. William Smith, father-in-law of Mr. Adams, who generally seized the opportunity, as in the present instance, of inculcating more acceptable doctrines.

sooth, is very fearful that they will be *stomachful* at home, and angry and resentful. Mr. Veasey insists upon it, that we ought to pay our proportion of the public burdens. Mr. Cleverly is fully convinced that they, that is the Parliament, have a right to tax us; he thinks it is wrong to go on with business; we had better stop and wait till Spring, till we hear from home. He says we put the best face upon it; that letters have been received in Boston, from the greatest merchants in the nation, blaming our proceedings, and that the merchants don't second us. Letters from old Mr. Lane and from Mr. Deberdt. He says that things go on here exactly as they did in the reign of King Charles I., "that blessed saint and martyr."

Thus that unaccountable man goes about, sowing his pernicious seeds of mischief, instilling wrong principles in church and state into the people, striving to divide and disunite them, and to excite fears, to damp their spirits and lower their courage.

Etter is another of the poisonous talkers, but not equally so. Cleverly and Veasey are slaves in principle; they are devout, religious slaves, and a religious bigot is the worst of men. Cleverly converses of late at Mr. Lloyd's, with some of the seekers of appointments from the Crown — some of the dozen, in the town of Boston, who ought, as Hancock says, to be beheaded; or with some of those who converse with the Governor, who ought, as Tom Boylston says, to be sent home with all the other Governors on the continent, with chains about their necks.

30. Monday. We are now concluding the year 1765. Tomorrow is the last day of a year in which America has shown such magnanimity and spirit, as never before appeared in any country for such a tract of country. And Wednesday will open upon us a new year, 1766, which I hope will procure us innumerable testimonies from Europe in our favor and applause, and which we all hope will produce the greatest and most extensive joy ever felt in America, on the repeal both of the Stamp Act and Sugar Act, at least of the former.

Q. Who is it that has harangued the grand juries in every county, and endeavored to scatter party principles in politics? Who has made it his constant endeavor to discountenance the odium in which informers are held? Who has taken occasion, in fine-spun, spick and span, spruce, nice, pretty, easy, warbling declamations to Grand Inquests, to render the characters of informers honorable and respectable? Who has frequently expressed his apprehensions that the form of government in England was become too popular? Who is it that has said in public speeches that the most complete monarchy in Europe was the government of France? Who is it that so often enlarges on the excellency of the government of Queen Elizabeth, and insists upon it so often that the constitution, about the time of her reign, and under her administration, was nearest the point of perfection? Who is it that has always given his opinion in favor of prerogative and revenue, in every case in which they have been brought into question, without one exception? Who is it that has endeavored to bias simple juries, by an argument as warm and vehement as those of the bar, in a case where the Province was contending against a custom-house officer?[1] And what were the other means employed in that cause against the resolutions of the General Assembly? Who has monopolized almost all the power of the government to himself and his family; and who has been endeavoring to procure more, both on this side and the other side the Atlantic?

Read Shakspeare's Life of King Henry VIII.

31. Tuesday. Went to Mr. Jo. Bass's, and there read yesterday's paper; walked in the afternoon into the common, and quite through my hemlock swamp. I find many fine bunches of young maples, and nothing else but alders. Spent the evening at home with neighbor Field.

The national attention is fixed upon the colonies; the religion, administration of justice, geography, numbers, &c., of the colonies, are a fashionable study. But what wretched blunders do they make in attempting to regulate them. They know not the character of Americans.

1766. January 1. Wednesday. Severe cold, and a prospect of snow. We are now upon the beginning of a year of greater expectation than any that has passed before it. This year brings ruin or salvation to the British Colonies. The eyes of all America are fixed on the British Parliament. In short, Britain and America are staring at each other; and they will probably stare more and more for some time.

[1] Gray *vs.* Paxton. *Minot's History*, vol. ii. p. 87. It is scarcely necessary to say that Hutchinson is the person pointed at.

At home all day. Mr. Joshua Hayward, Jr. dined with me; Town politics the subject. Doctor Tufts here in the afternoon; American politics the subject. Read in the evening a letter from Mr. Deberdt,[1] our present agent, to Lord Dartmouth, in which he considers three questions. 1. Whether in equity or policy America ought to refund any part of the expense of driving away the French in the last war? 2. Whether it is necessary for the defence of the British plantations to keep up an army there? 3. Whether in equity the Parliament can tax us? Each of which he discusses like a man of sense, integrity, and humanity, well informed in the nature of his subject. In his examination of the last question, he goes upon the principle of the Ipswich instructions; namely, that the first settlers of America were driven by oppression from the realm, and so dismembered from the dominions, till at last they offered to make a contract with the nation, or the Crown, and to become subject to the Crown upon certain conditions, which contract, subordination, and conditions, were wrought into their charters, which gave them a right to tax themselves.[2] This is a principle which has been advanced long ago. I remember in the trial of the cause at Worcester, between Governor Hopkins of Rhode Island and Mr. Ward, one of the witnesses swore that he heard Governor Hopkins some years before, in a banter with Colonel Amy, advancing that we were under no subjection to the British Parliament; that our forefathers came from Leyden, &c. And, indeed, it appears from Hutchinson's History and the Massa-

[1] This letter was simultaneously printed in the supplements to the Boston Gazette, the Post-Boy, and the Evening Post, of 30 December, 1765.

[2] Extract from the instructions given to Dr. John Calef, representative, by the people of Ipswich, 2d October, 1765:

"When our forefathers left their native country, they left also the laws and constitution they had been under, in all respects and to all purposes, save what was secured by the charters; and it is manifest fact, that, from that day to this, the government at home have never considered the Colonies as under the force of that constitution or the laws of that realm. Three things were necessary to have made this otherwise; First, that their migrating and coming forth should have been a national act. Secondly, that it should have been at a national expense. Thirdly, that they should be sent to settle some place or territory that the nation had before, in some way or other, made their own, as was usually, if not always the case with the ancient Romans. But neither of them was the case here. It is well known they came out of their own accord, and at their own expense, and took possession of a country they were obliged to buy or fight for, and to which the nation had no more right than to the moon. Thence it follows that, abating the charter, they were as much dismembered from the government they came from, as the people of any other part of the world."

chusetts Records, that the Colonies were considered formerly, both here and at home, as allies rather than subjects. The first settlement, certainly, was not a national act; that is, not an act of the people nor the Parliament. Nor was it a national expense; neither the people of England nor their representatives contributed any thing towards it. Nor was the settlement made on a territory belonging to the people nor the Crown of England.

Q. How far can the concern the council at Plymouth had in the first settlement, be considered as a national act? How far can the discoveries made by the Cabots be considered as an acquisition of territory to the nation or the crown? And *quære*, whether the council at Plymouth, or the voyages of the Cabots, or of Sir Walter Raleigh, &c., were any expense to the nation?

In the paper there are also Remarks on the Proceedings of Parliament relating to the Stamp Act, taken from the London Magazine, September, 1765.[1] This remarker says, "as a great number of new offences, new penalties, and new offices and officers, are by this act created, we cannot wonder at its being extremely disgustful to our fellow subjects in America. Even the patient and long suffering people of this country would scarcely have borne it at once. They were brought to it by degrees; and they will be more inconvenient in America than they can be in England."

The remarker says further, that "the design of one clause in the Stamp Act seems to be, that there shall be no such thing as a practising lawyer in the country,—the case of the Saxons. This design, he says ludicrously, by compelling every man to manage and plead his own cause, would prevent many delays and perversions of justice, and so be an advantage to the people of America. But he seriously doubts whether the tax will pay the officers. People will trust to honor, like gamesters and stockjobbers. He says he will not enter into the question, whether the Americans are right or wrong in the opinion they have been indulged in ever since their establishment, that they could not be subjected to any taxes but such as should be imposed by their own respective assemblies. He thinks a land tax the most just and convenient of any; an extension of the British land tax to the American dominions. But this would have occasioned a new assessment

[1] This article is printed in the Evening Post alone.

of the improved value of the lands in England as well as here, which probably prevented the scheme of a land tax; for he hopes no views of extending the corruptive power of the ministers of the crown had any effect."

It is said at New York, that private letters inform, the great men are exceedingly irritated at the tumults in America, and are determined to enforce the act.

This irritable race, however, will have good luck to enforce it. They will find it a more obstinate war than the conquest of Canada and Louisiana.

2. Thursday. A great storm of snow last night; weather tempestuous all day. Waddled through the snow driving my cattle to water at Doctor Savil's;—a fine piece of glowing exercise. Brother spent the evening here in cheerful chat.

At Philadelphia, the Heart-and-Hand Fire Company has expelled Mr. Hughes, the stamp man for that colony. The freemen of Talbot county, in Maryland, have erected a gibbet before the door of the court-house, twenty feet high, and have hanged on it the effigies of a stamp informer in chains, *in terrorem* till the Stamp Act shall be repealed; and have resolved, unanimously, to hold in utter contempt and abhorrence every stamp officer, and every favorer of the Stamp Act, and to "have no communication with any such person, not even to speak to him, unless to upbraid him with his baseness." So triumphant is the spirit of liberty everywhere. Such a union was never before known in America. In the wars that have been with the French and Indians a union could never be effected. I pity my unhappy fellow subjects in Quebec and Halifax for the great misfortune that has befallen them. Quebec consists chiefly of Frenchmen, who [are mixed] with a few English, and awed by an army; though it seems the discontent there is so great that the Gazette is dropped. Halifax consists of a set of fugitives and vagabonds, who are also kept in fear by a fleet and an army. But can no punishment be devised for Barbadoes, and Port Royal in Jamaica, for their base desertion of the cause of liberty, their tame surrender of the rights of Britons, their mean, timid resignation to slavery? Meeching,[1] sordid, stupid creatures, below contempt, below pity, they deserve to be made slaves to their

[1] "Sure she has some *meeching* rascal in her house," &c.
The Scornful Lady. Beaumont and Fletcher.

15 *

own negroes! But they live under the scorching sun, which melts them, dissipates their spirits, and relaxes their nerves. Yet their negroes seem to have more of the spirit of liberty than they. I think we sometimes read of insurrections among their negroes. I could wish that some of their blacks had been appointed distributers and inspectors, &c., over their masters. This would have but a little aggravated the indignity.

3. Friday. Fair weather, and snow enough. Major Miller, Dr. Savil, and Mr. Joseph Penniman, spent the evening with me. Agriculture, commerce, fishery, arts, manufactures; town, provincial, American, and national politics, the subject.

4. Saturday. Edes and Gill's Gazette brought in. I find that somebody has published the very scene in Shakspeare's Henry VIII., which I have put into Lord Clarendon's letter to Pym.[1] This brings to my mind again Lord Bacon's doctrine of secret, invisible connections and communications, and unknown, undiscovered laws of nature.

Hampden writes to Pym on the failure of justice in America, on the shutting up of the courts of justice since October. He has given the public Mr. Otis's argument before the Governor and council, from Magna Charta, Lord Coke, the Judges' oaths, &c., and promises to give more.

7. Tuesday. At Boston. Hampden has given us, in yesterday's Gazette, a long letter to Pym upon shutting up the courts; in which he proves, from Holt's and Pollexfen's argument at the revolution conference, from Grotius *De Jure Belli*, (book 1, ch. 3, s. 2,) that shutting up the courts is an abdication of the throne, a discharge of the subjects from their allegiance, and a total dissolution of government, and reduction of all men to a state of nature; and he proves, from Bracton, that partial tumults, &c., are not a *tempus guerrium*, (*bellorum*,) a time of war.

Samuel Waterhouse has made a most malicious, ungenerous attack upon James Lovell, Jr., the usher of the grammar school; as Y. Z. and H. had attacked him about idleness, and familiar

[1] Act 1; scene 2. The controversial papers of this period are of the highest ability. William Pym was the singular choice of a name by a writer on the side of government, in the London Evening Post, 20th August, 1765, whose speculations were reprinted in the Boston Evening Post, of the 25th of November. John Adams, by way of offset, chose that of Clarendon in his reply; whilst James Otis addressed to his opponent a series of vigorous articles under the name of John Hampden. They appeared in the Gazette.

spirits, and zanyship, and expectancy of a deputation, &c. This way of reviling one another is very shocking to humanity, and very dangerous in its consequences. To pry into a man's private life, and expose to the world all the vices and follies of youth, to paint before the public eye all the blots and stains in a man's private character, must excite the commiseration of every reader to the object, and his indignation against the author of such abuse.[1]

Spent half an hour with Father Dana; another with Samuel Quincy; an hour with Mr. Otis, &c. Otis is in high spirits; is preparing for next Monday's paper; says that Mr. Trail brings very comfortable news; that Conway told him the Stamp Act must be repealed, that there was some difficulty about coming off with honor, and that America would boast that she had conquered Britain, but he hoped the Americans would petition; he longed to receive some petitions, &c. John Wentworth[2] writes his uncle Samuel, that the Marquis of Rockingham told him he would give his interest to repeal one hundred Stamp Acts, before he would run the risk of such confusions as would be caused by enforcing it; that he knew there were already ten thousand workmen discharged from business in consequence of the advices from America.

9. Thursday. At home.

"Tantone novorum
Proventu scelerum quærunt uter imperet urbi?
Vix tanti fuerat civilia bella moveri,
Ut neuter."

Must such a number of new crimes be committed to decide which of these two, Cæsar or Pompey, shall be master in Rome? One would hardly purchase, at that price, the good fortune of having neither of them for master.[3]

10. Friday. Went in the afternoon, with my wife, to her grandfather's. Mr. Cleverly here in the evening. He says he

[1] These articles, of virulence not exceeded even in the worst newspapers of later times, are to be found in the Evening Post and Gazette of this period.

[2] The last loyal governor of New Hampshire, a classmate at Cambridge and an intimate friend of the author. He was in England at this time, and procured the appointment which he held until 1775, when under the efforts to aid General Gage his great popularity at last gave way and he was compelled to fly. *Belknap's History of N. H., Farmer's Edit.* vol. i. p. 357, 358.

[3] Lucan's Pharsalia, l. 2, v. 60.

is not so clear as he was that the Parliament has a right to tax us; he rather thinks it has not. Thus the contagion of the times has caught even that bigot to passive obedience and non-resistance; it has made him waver. It is almost the first time I ever knew him converted, or even brought to doubt and hesitate about any of his favorite points,—as the authority of Parliament to tax us was one. Nay, he used to assert positively that the king was as absolute in the plantations as the Great Turk in his dominions.

Mr. Quincy gave me some anecdotes about John Boylston and Jo. Green, &c. Green[1] refused to sign the resolutions of merchants at first, but was afterwards glad to send for the paper. They were at first afraid of Salem, Newbury, Marblehead, and Plymouth, but these towns have agreed unanimously to the same resolutions.

What will they say in England, when they see the resolves of the American legislatures, the petitions from the united colonies, the resolutions of the merchants in Boston, New York, Philadelphia, &c.?

13. Monday. At Boston. The inferior court of common pleas opened; present, Mr. Wells, Mr. Watts, and Mr. Foster Hutchinson; more than one hundred new entries. The actions all called over, and many defaulted and some continued, so that the court has rushed upon the thick bosses of the buckler, and into the thickest of the penalties and forfeitures. Dined at brother Dudley's, with Gridley, Swift, Lowell, and Mr. Fayerweather. Fayerweather is one of the genteel folks; he said he was dressed in black as mourning for the Duke of Cumberland; he said he was wearing out his black clothes as fast as he could, and was determined to get no more till the Stamp Act was repealed; he designed to wear out all his old clothes and then go upon our own manufactures, unless the Stamp Act was repealed. One Thompson came to me at Cunningham's, in the evening, and engaged me in a cause of Sampson *vs.* Buttar, which is for entering a vessel at Louisburg and taking away ten

[1] The poet and the wit, whose patriotism, moderate at first and whilst the questions at issue seemed purely commercial, gradually evaporated until his sympathies became marked by the nomination made of him as one of the Mandamus council. He also signed the Merchants' Address to Hutchinson, and soon afterwards left the country. He died in England in 1780. *Sabine.*

barrels of rum. Buttar was, or pretended to be, a naval officer for the port of Louisburg, or secretary to Governor Whitmore, and, under color of that authority, entered the vessel, and seized and brought off the rum. Now Buttar pretended to give commissions to officers under him to attend the wharves and keys of the port, and to examine all goods imported and exported, and to stop the same, and report to him if illegal or contrary to the orders of the Governor, &c.

Mr. Gridley was in a very trifling humor to-day, after dinner, telling tales about Overing,[1] &c.; and judges of inferior courts formerly; and McCarty, who built the court by the town-house, &c.; and stories about Colonel Choate of Ipswich, &c.[2] The unsmotherable pride of his own heart broke out in his account of his disputes, &c., with Choate. "Choate was a tyrant; Choate attempted things too large for him; I have tumbled him over and over, and twisted and tossed and tumbled him, and yet he could say to me, 'Sir, I was here at nine o'clock, by agreement, and you was not come.' I answered him, 'I was here, sir, at a quarter after nine, and you was not here; sir, the honor of attending me might at any time dispense with a quarter of an hour.'" This is not pride. If Gridley had pride, he would scorn such gross vanity. A New England church, he said, was one object of dispute between them. The people in the pale, the deacons, and the minister, were the picture of a New England church. No idea of it in the New Testament. Platform, too, was a bone of contention.

Spent the evening at Mr. Adams's, with him and brother Swift,[3] very socially.

[1] John Overing, a native of England and Attorney-General of the Province in the early part of this century. He is noticed in the valuable contribution to the history of the law and lawyers in Massachusetts, made by Mr. Joseph Willard in his Address to the Bar of Worcester County, October 2, 1829. Some more comprehensive work on the same plan is now much needed.

[2] Representative of the town of Ipswich for fifteen years, a member of the Council five years, Justice of the Sessions and Common Pleas, and Judge of the Probate Court. Out of respect to him, the inhabitants called the bridge, over Ipswich river, by his name. *Felt's History of Ipswich, Essex, and Hamilton*, p. 180.

[3] This Mr. Swift is probably the same person mentioned in the newspapers of the time as having marched at the head of the north end, upon the occasion of the reconciliation that took place with the south end, on the preceding fifth of November. It had been customary in Massachusetts as in England to celebrate that day as the anniversary of the deliverance of the nation from the Gunpowder Plot. In Boston the occasion had by degrees degenerated into a trial of strength between the people of the opposite ends of the town, pro-

14. Tuesday. Dined at Mr. William Cooper's,[1] with Messrs. Cushing, Story, and John Boylston. Cushing silent and sly as usual. Story, I don't know what. Cooper and Boylston principal talkers. Boylston affecting a philosophical indifference about dress, furniture, entertainments, &c.; laughed at the affectation of nicely distinguishing tastes, such as the several degrees of sweet, till you come up to the first degree of bitter; laughed at the great expenses for furniture, as Nick Boylston's carpets, tables, chairs, glasses, beds, &c., which Cooper said were the richest in North America; the highest taste, and newest fashion, would soon flatten and grow old; a curse or two upon the climate—preferable however to Carolina, but every part of Europe preferable to this. *Q.* Is not this nicety of feeling, this indisposition to be satisfied with the climate, of the same nature with the delicacy of tastes and the curiosity about furniture just before exploded?

Spent the evening at Cunningham's.

15. Wednesday. Dined at Mr. Isaac Smith's;—no company; no conversation. Spent the evening with the Sons of Liberty, at their own apartment in Hanover Square near the tree of liberty. It is a counting-room in Chase and Speakman's distillery; a very small room it is.

John Avery, distiller or merchant, of a liberal education, John Smith, the brazier, Thomas Crafts, the painter, Edes, the printer, Stephen Cleverly, the brazier, Chase, the distiller,[2] Joseph Field, master of a vessel, Henry Bass, George Trott, jeweller, were present. I was invited by Crafts and Trott to go and spend an evening with them and some others. Avery

ductive of many disorders. Taking advantage of the common indignation against the abettors of the Stamp Act, some of the more politic citizens recommended a formal celebration, in King Street, of the establishment of a union, which was accordingly carried into effect with great ceremonies, the leaders, Mr. Mackintosh from the south, and Mr. Swift from the north, appearing in military habits, with small canes resting on their left arms, and music in front and flank. Mr. Tudor says, however, that peace was not fully established until November, 1774. See *Snow's History of Boston*, pp. 262–264. *Tudor's Life of Otis*, pp. 26–29.

[1] This is the town-clerk for forty-nine years, whose name is found attached to almost all the Boston papers of the Revolution. Story was the registrar of the Admiralty Court, and very unpopular; his house had suffered in the mob of the 26th of August.

[2] Six of these names are given by Gordon as of those who provided and hung up on the liberty tree the effigy of a stamp officer and a jack boot, upon the memorable fourteenth of August preceding. Vol. i. p. 175.

was mentioned to me as one. I went, and was very civilly and respectfully treated by all present. We had punch, wine, pipes and tobacco, biscuit and cheese, &c. I heard nothing but such conversation as passes at all clubs, among gentlemen, about the times. No plots, no machinations. They chose a committee to make preparations for grand rejoicings upon the arrival of the news of a repeal of the Stamp Act, and I heard afterwards they are to have such illuminations, bonfires, pyramids, obelisks, such grand exhibitions and such fireworks as were never before seen in America.[1] I wish they may not be disappointed.

16. Thursday. Dined at Mr. Nick Boylston's, with the two Mr. Boylstons, two Mr. Smiths, Mr. Hallowell, and their ladies — an elegant dinner indeed! Went over the house to view the furniture, which alone cost a thousand pounds sterling. A seat it is for a nobleman, a prince. The Turkey carpets, the painted hangings, the marble tables, the rich beds with crimson damask curtains and counterpanes, the beautiful chimney clock, the spacious garden, are the most magnificent of any thing I have ever seen.

The conversation of the two Boylstons and Hallowell is a curiosity. Hotspurs all. Tantivy Nick, is a warm friend of the Lieutenant-Governor, and inclining towards the Governor. Tom, a fire-brand against both. Tom is a perfect viper, a fiend a Jew, a devil, but is orthodox[2] in politics, however. Hallowell tells stories about Otis, and drops hints about Adams, &c., and about Mr. Dudley Atkins of Newbury. Otis told him, he says, that the Parliament had a right to tax the colonies, and he was a d—d fool who denied it; and that this people never

[1] Copies of two letters addressed to the author by the Sons of Liberty, will be found appended to the Diary at the close of the present month.

[2] He did not remain so, when the question ceased to be a commercial one. He left America during the Revolution, with the leave of the provincial government, involved his large but hardly earned accumulations of money in the concerns of a house that became insolvent, and died broken-hearted in London, in 1798. Benjamin Hallowell, who had married his sister, was one of the commissioners of the customs, and his house had suffered at the time when Hutchinson's was destroyed. Again he was harshly treated in the riot caused by the attempt to seize Mr. Hancock's Sloop Liberty, and once more when falling accidentally into the mob assembled at Cambridge, in 1774, for the purpose of forcing Lieutenant-Governor Oliver to resign his place of counsellor by mandamus. He also left the country. Nicholas Boylston died before the Revolution. He is enrolled among the benefactors of Harvard College, as founder of one of the professorships and in other ways. See *Quincy's History*, vol. ii. p. 214. The partisan spirit of all is sufficiently visible in the conversation.

would be quiet till we had a council from home, till our charter was taken away, and till we had regular troops quartered upon us. He says he saw Adams under the tree of liberty when the effigies hung there, and asked him who they were and what; he said he did not know — he could not tell — he wanted to inquire. He says, Mr. Dudley Atkins was too well acquainted with the secret of some riots there to be entirely depended on in his account, &c. Nick Boylston, full of stories about Jemmy and Solomon Davis. Solomon says, Countryman, I don't see what occasion there is for a Governor, and Council, and House; you and the town would do well enough.

Spent the evening at Bracket's with General Winslow,[1] Colonel Bradford, Mr. Otis, Father Danforth, Colonel Richmond, Mr. Brinley, Mr. Caldwell, and Captain Hayward. Mr. Otis gave us some account of Ruggles's behavior at the Congress;[2] and Winslow told us about catching bass with eel spears at the North river. Otis says that when they came to sign, Ruggles moved that none of them should sign, but that the petitions should be carried back to the Assemblies to see if they would adopt them. This would have defeated the whole enterprise. This Ruggles has an inflexible oddity about him which has gained him a character for courage and probity, but renders him a disagreeable companion in business.

20. Monday. Leonard[3] gave me an account of a club that he belongs to in Boston. It consists of John Lowell, Elisha Hutchinson, Frank Dana, Josiah Quincy, and two other young fellows, strangers to me. Leonard had prepared a collection of the arguments for and against the right of Parliament to tax the colonies, for said club. His first inquiry was, whether the subject could be taxed without his consent in person, or by his

[1] General John Winslow of Marshfield, who commanded, in 1755, in the removal of the neutral French in Acadia. He seems at this time to have been acquiescing in the course of the Whigs, as he was one of the committee which reported the sharp reply of the House to the message of Governor Bernard; but it would appear from what is said of him in the record of the twenty-sixth of April, that he did not approve of it. He died in 1774, and his widow and family afterwards took the loyal side. *Sabine.*

[2] Of 1765, held at New York.

[3] Probably Daniel Leonard, at this time a young member of the bar, and inclining to the colonial side. But like so many of his contemporaries, he subsequently became a loyalist, and as the author of the papers of Massachusettensis took the first rank in the controversies of the period. He left the country, and became Chief Justice of the Bermudas. He died in London, in 1829.

representative? Second, whether we Americans are represented in Parliament or not?

Leonard says that Lowell is a courtier; that he rips about all who stand foremost in their opposition to the Stamp Act; at your Otises and Adamses, &c.; and says that no man can scribble about politics without bedaubing his fingers, and every one who does is a dirty fellow. He expresses great resentment against that line in Edes and Gill, — "Retreat or you are ruined;" and says they ought to be committed for that single stroke. Thus it seems that the air of Newbury, and the vicinage of Farnham, Chipman, &c. have obliterated all the precepts, admonitions, instructions, and example of his master, Thacher. Lowell is, however, very warm, sudden, quick, and impetuous; and all such people are unsteady.[1] Too much fire. *Experientia docet.*

Leonard gave me also a relation of his going to Providence Court, and spending an evening with the political club there.[2] The club consists of Governor Hopkins, Judge Jenks, Downer, Cole, and others. They were impatient to have the courts opened in this Province, not choosing to proceed in business alone; were very inquisitive concerning all our affairs; had much to say of Hutchinson, Otis, &c.; admired the answer to the Governor's speech; admired the Massachusetts resolves. Hopkins said that nothing had been so much admired there, through the whole course of the controversy, as the answer to the speech, though the Massachusetts resolves were the best

[1] John Lowell went so far as to sign the Address to Governor Hutchinson in 1774, but he finally remembered his master, Thacher, and took the side of liberty and the Revolution in season to prove himself steady, faithful, and useful throughout the great struggle. In a later letter to the author of the Diary he assigns a dislike of political warfare as the cause of his hesitation. It was more probably that sort of fastidiousness which constantly operates to deter many of the most respectable citizens from trusting themselves in the arena of political contention.

[2] The gentlemen named as of the club in Rhode Island, were all of the highest character and respectability, and all took an active part in the Revolution. Governor Hopkins was one of the Signers of the Declaration of Independence, and his biography is found in Sanderson's Collection, vol. v. A biography of Judge Cole is inserted in Updike's Memoirs of the Rhode Island Bar. p. 124. Judge Daniel Jenks is numbered among the wealthy benefactors of the Baptist Church, in Benedict's History of that sect. Mr. Silas Downer was selected by the Sons of Liberty in Providence to make the Address on the dedication of the Liberty Tree, in 1768. *Collections Rhode Island Historical Society*, vol. v. *Staples's Annals of Providence*, p. 222.

digested, and the best of any on the continent; inquired who was the author of them.[1]

Inquired also who it was that burlesqued the Governor's speeches; who wrote Jemmy Bullero, &c. Thought Hutchinson's history did not shine; said his house was pulled down to prevent his writing any more, by destroying his materials. Thought Otis was not an original genius, nor a good writer, but a person who had done and would continue to do much good service.

Were very inquisitive about Mackintosh;[2] whether he was a man of abilities or not; whether he would probably rise, in case this contest should be carried into any length. Jo Green, Waterhouse, and Church, were talked of as capable of Bullero and the burlesques.[3]

[1] The authorship is not fully ascertained, but the speech and the resolutions were probably drawn by Samuel Adams.

[2] Mackintosh was the chief of the south end party upon the occasion of the reconciliation mentioned in the note on page 177. He was also arrested for participation in the mob of the twenty-sixth of August, but released. His notoriety ceased with the local disturbances in Boston. *Hutchinson*, iii. 121.

[3] These were the wits and literary adventurers of the day. Of Green, Dr. Eliot says that the following epitaph was composed for him so early as 1743:

"Siste viator, here lies one,
Whose life was whim, whose soul was pun;
And if you go too near his hearse
He'll joke you both in prose and verse."

Samuel Waterhouse was in the custom-house. He is described in a later letter of Mr. Adams, as "the most notorious scribbler, satirist, and libeller, in the service of the conspirators against the liberties of America." He was the author of "Jemmibullero," the song alluded to in the text, and of many of the most scurrilous papers of the time.

The other person, Dr. Church, starting as an active patriot, made himself known at an early stage of the contest by his treachery, which, notwithstanding the labor to palliate it on account of the bungling manner in which it was attempted, admits of no apology or excuse. After some difficulty he was set at large. He then embarked in a vessel bound for the West Indies, which never reached its destination.

The following letters were written to carry out the policy of association in resistance to the Stamp Act.

The Sons of Liberty to John Adams.

Boston, 5 February, 1766.

Sir: — You, doubtless, and every American, must be sensible that where there is a union happily established, we should endeavor to support it by all possible means, especially when the grand object in view is the preservation of our invaluable rights and privileges.

The colonies, (we mean New York and Connecticut) have entered into certain reciprocal and mutual agreements, concessions, and associations, a copy of which[1] we received (by an express) the last Sunday, with their desire to accomplish the like association with us; which deserves our most serious attention, as thereby it will be the means of strengthening this late union, and, in our humble opinion, of preventing the execution of an Act of Parliament, commonly known by the name of the Stamp Act. But, to avoid enlarging, permit us to single out a few words by which you will know their intentions.

" The worthy Sons of Liberty in New York and Connecticut, taking into their most serious consideration the melancholy and unsettled state of Great Britain and her North American Colonies, proceeding, as they are fully persuaded, from a design in her most inveterate enemies to alienate the affections of his Majesty's most loyal and faithful subjects in America from his person and government, which they are determined to maintain and support; — and for the preservation of which they have signified their resolution and determination to march with all despatch, at their own costs and expense, on the first proper notice, with their whole force (if required) to the relief of those who shall or may be in danger from the Stamp Act or its abettors, and to keep a watchful eye over all those who, from the nature of their offices, vocations, or dispositions, may be the most likely to introduce the use of stamped paper, to the total subversion of the British constitution and American liberty."

We address ourselves to you, as a gentleman well versed in

[1] Given in Gordon's History, vol. i. pp. 195 – 198.

the constitution of your country, and who consequently will do your utmost to oppose all measures detrimental to the welfare of it; and we should be glad if you would inform us as soon as possible of your sentiments on the above, and the disposition of the people in your town.

Please to direct to us under cover, to Messrs. Edes and Gill, printers, in Boston.

We are, sir, your most humble servants,

THE SONS OF LIBERTY.

Thomas Crafts, Jr. to John Adams.

Boston, 15 February, 1766.

Friday Night, 10 o'clock.

SIR: — Yesterday I wrote you a few lines, by Dr. Tufts, informing you the Sons of Liberty desired your company at Boston next Wednesday, and mentioned for what occasion. I would now desire it as a favor, if you can spare the time, to come on Monday next, because they want you to write those inscriptions that I mentioned to you when last at Boston; one in favor of liberty, not forgetting the true-born sons, and another with encomiums on King George, expressive of our loyalty; which, if you can do by Wednesday, we will excuse your coming sooner. Pray let them be as short and as expressive as possible. The stamped paper I informed you of in my last, was found straggling about this town, but on Thursday, at eleven o'clock, shall commit it to its proper element with no small parade.[1]

I am, with great respect, your friend,

THOMAS CRAFTS, JR.

Destroy this after reading it. Mr. Samuel Adams sends his compliments, and desires you would come.

P. S. We expect the news of the repeal of the Act commonly called the Stamp Act, in three weeks from this, by the news we have had by the last ships from London, which I doubt not you have heard of.

[1] This date should be the 14th, as, according to Snow, Thursday, the 20th, was fixed for burning one of the stamped papers in the principal towns in every colony. In Boston, the ceremony was conducted with great decency and good order, and the effigies of Bute and Grenville in full court dress, were added to the bonfire. *Snow's History of Boston*, p. 266.

N. B. An answer to a letter sent by the Sons of Liberty last Saturday, will be acceptable.

I had wrote this letter before I received yours, and hope you will be here on Thursday next.

March 1. Saturday. Spent a part of last evening with Mr. Jo Cleverly. He is a tiptoe for town meeting; he has many schemes and improvements in his head;—namely, for separating the offices of constable and collector; collecting taxes has laid the foundation for the ruin of many families. He is for five selectmen, and will vote for the old ones, Mr. Quincy and Major Miller. He hears they are for turning out all the old selectmen, and choosing a new set; they for having but three, &c. The only way is to oppose schemes to schemes, and so break in upon them. Cleverly will become a great town-meeting man, and a great speaker in town meeting. *Q.* What effect will this have on the town affairs?

Brother tells me that William Veasey, Jr. tells him he has but one objection against Jonathan Bass, and that is, Bass is too forward. When a man is forward, we may conclude he has some selfish view, some self ends. Brother asked him if he and his party would carry that argument through. It holds stronger against Captain Thayer and Major Miller, than it ever did against anybody in this town, excepting Colonel Gooch and Captain Mills. But I desire the proof of Bass's forwardness. Has he been more so than Major Miller? Come, come, Mr. Veasey, says Master Jo Cleverly, don't you say too much; I an't of that mind. *Ego.* Bass is an active, capable man, but no seeker by mean begging or buying of votes.

3. Monday. My brother Peter, Mr. Etter, and Mr. Field, having a number of votes prepared for Mr. Quincy and me, set themselves to scatter them in town meeting. The town had been very silent and still, my name had never been mentioned, nor had our friends ever talked of any new selectmen at all, excepting in the south precinct; but as soon as they found there was an attempt to be made, they fell in and assisted; and, although there were six different hats with votes for as many different persons, besides a considerable number of scattering votes, I had the major vote of the assembly the first time. Mr.

Quincy had more than one hundred and sixty votes. I had but one vote more than half. Some of the church people, — Mr. Jo Cleverly, his brother Ben and son, &c. and Mr. Ben Veasey, of the middle precinct, Mr. James Faxon, &c. — I found were grieved and chagrined for the loss of their dear Major Miller.[1] Etter and my brother took a skilful method; they let a number of young fellows into the design, John Ruggles, Peter Newcomb, &c. who were very well pleased with the employment, and put about a great many votes. Many persons, I hear, acted slyly and deceitfully; this is always the case.

I own it gave me much pleasure to find I had so many friends, and that my conduct in town has been not disapproved. The choice was quite unexpected to me. I thought the project was so new and sudden that the people had not digested it, and would generally suppose the town would not like it, and so would not vote for it. But my brother's answer was, that it had been talked of last year and some years before, and that the thought was familiar to the people in general, and was more agreeable than any thing of the kind that could be proposed to many, and for these reasons his hopes were strong.

But the triumph of the party was very considerable, though not complete; for Thayer, and Miller, and the late lessees of the north commons,[2] and many of the church people, and many others had determined to get out Deacon Penniman; but, instead of that, their favorite was dropped, and I, more obnoxious to that party than even Deacon Penniman or any other man, was chosen in his room, and Deacon Penniman was saved with more than one hundred and thirty votes, — a more reputable election than even Thayer himself had.

1 This indicates the first popular struggle of the Revolution in the town of Braintree. Major Miller inclined to the government. See the entry of the twenty-ninth of December, page 168.

2 Of the share which they had in the matter, the Autobiography explains the cause.

[In 1763 or 1764 the town voted to sell their common lands. This had been a subject of contention for many years. The south parish was zealous, and the middle parish much inclined to the sale; the north parish was against it. The lands in their common situation appeared to me of very little utility to the public or to individuals; under the care of proprietors where they should become private property, they would probably be better managed and more productive. My opinion was in favor of the sale. The town now adopted the measure, appointed Mr. Niles, Mr. Bass, and me, to survey the lands, divide them into lots, to sell them by auction, and execute deeds of them in behalf of the town.]

Mr. Jo Bass was extremely sorry for the loss of Major Miller; he would never come to another meeting. Mr. Jo Cleverly could not account for many things done at town meetings. His motion for choosing collectors was slighted; his motion for lessening his fine was thrown out; and he made no sort of figure as a speaker; so that I believe Mr. Cleverly will make no hand.

Elisha Niles says, set a knave to catch a knave. A few days before a former March meeting, he told Thayer that he had a mind to get in Deacon Penniman. Thayer asked him, who he would have with him? he answered, Captain Allen. Thayer made him no answer, but when the meeting came, was chosen himself. Mr. Thomas Faxon, of this end of the town, told my wife he never saw anybody chosen so neatly in his life, — not a word, not a whisper beforehand. Peter Newcomb gave him a vote; he had one before for Miller, and had heard nothing of me; but he thought I should have one. So he dropped that for Miller. Jo Nightingale asked my wife, "Mr. Adams will have too much business, will he not; the courts to attend, selectman, and representative at May, &c.?" Mr. John Baxter, the old gentleman, told me he was very well pleased with the choice at the north end, &c. Old Mr. John Ruggles voted for me; but says that Thayer will [be chosen] at May. If I would set up, he would vote for me, and I should go, but Mr. Quincy will not. Lieutenant Holbrook, I hear, was much in my favor, &c. Thus the town is pretty generally disputing about me, I find.

But this choice will not disconcert Thayer, at May, though it will weaken him. But, as I said before, the triumph was not complete; — Cornet Bass had the most votes the first time, and would have come in the second, but the north end people, his friends, after putting in their votes the first time, withdrew for refreshment, by which accident he lost it, to their great regret.

Mark the fruits of this election to me. Will the church people be angry, and grow hot and furious, or will they be cooler and calmer for it? Will Thayer's other precinct friends resent it and become more violent, or will they be less so? In short, I cannot answer these questions; many of them will be disheartened, I know; some will be glad.

10. Monday. Last week went to Boston, and to Weymouth, &c. I hear that Mr. Benjamin Cleverly has already bespoke Mr. John Ruggles, Jr. against May meeting, — promised him

as much as he can eat and drink of the best sort, if he will vote for Captain Thayer; told him he would not have acted as he did, at March, if it had not been for Thomas Newcomb, and that he would vote for Thayer, at May, if it was not for Thomas Newcomb. By this, the other side are alarmed; the craft, they think, is in danger; but I believe their fears are groundless, though I wish there was good reason for them.

Drank tea at Mr. Etter's. He says all the blame is laid to him, and that a certain man takes it very ill of him. By the way, I heard to-day that Major Miller and James Bracket, Jr. were heard, since March meeting, raving against Deacon Palmer, and said he was a knave, &c. *Q.* About this quarrel?

I find the late choice has brought upon me a multiplicity of new cares. The schools are one great object of my attention. It is a thing of some difficulty to find out the best, most beneficial method of expending the school money. Captain Adams says, that each parish's proportion of the school money has not been settled since my father's day. Thomas Faxon says, it would be more profitable to the children, to have a number of women's schools about than to have a fixed grammar school. *Q.* Whether he has not a desire that his wife should keep one? Jonathan Bass says the same. *Q.* His wife is a school-mistress. So that two points of examination occur; the portion between the parishes, that is, the sum which this parish ought to have; and whether a standing grammar school is preferable to a number of school-mistresses part of the year, and a grammar school part.

Another great object is the poor; persons are soliciting for the privilege of supplying the poor with wood, corn, meat, &c. The care of supplying at cash price, and in weight and measure, is something; the care of considering and deciding the pretensions of the claimants is something.

A third, and the greatest, is the assessment; here I am not so thorough; I must inquire a great while before I shall know the polls and estates, real and personal, of all the inhabitants of the town or parish. The highways, the districts to surveyors, and laying out new ways or altering old ones, are a fourth thing. Perambulations of lines are another thing. Dorchester, Milton, Stoughton, Bridgewater, Abington, Weymouth,— orders for services of many sorts to, &c.

It will increase my connections with the people.

11. Tuesday. Went to Boston. The Chief Justice not there; a piece of political finesse, to make the people believe he was under a necessity of going a journey this week, but would be here by the next, was put about, while care was taken to secure an agreement to an adjournment for three or four weeks; so that Hutchinson is to trim, and shift, and luff up, and bear away, and elude the blame of the ministry and the people. Cushing spoke out boldly, and said he was ready to go on; he had no difficulty about going on. Lynde said, we are here. Oliver said, here am I in duress, and if I must go on, I must. Thus popular compulsion, fear of violence of the Sons of Liberty, &c., was suggested to be the only motive with him to go on.[1]

12. Wednesday. Returned to Braintree.

14. Friday. Yesterday and to-day the severest storm of snow we have had this year.

15. Saturday. The snow is as deep, and in as mountainous banks, as it has been at any time this winter. The unanimous agreement of the court and bar was, to try a few civil causes, one at least, and then adjourn over.

17. Monday. Rain. A piece in Evening Post, March 10th; Remarks and Observations on Hutchinson's History. The writer seems concerned lest his countrymen should incur the censure of hissing from the stage all merit of their own growth.

But *quære*, allowing Mr. Hutchinson's great merit, what disposition have his countrymen discovered to hiss it from the stage? Has not his merit been sounded very high, by his countrymen, for twenty years? Have not his countrymen loved, admired, revered, rewarded, nay, almost adored him? Have not ninety-nine in a hundred of them really thought him the greatest and best man in America? Has not the perpetual language of many members of both houses, and of a majority of his brother counsellors been, that Mr. Hutchinson is a great man, a pious, a wise, a learned, a good man, an eminent saint, a philosopher, &c.; the greatest man in the Province, the greatest on the continent, &c.? Nay, have not the affection and admiration of his countrymen arisen so high as often to style him the

[1] This account may be compared with that given by *Gordon*, vol. i. p. 192, and *Hutchinson*, vol. iii. p. 146.

greatest and best man in the world, that they never saw, nor heard, nor read of such a man — a sort of apotheosis like that of Alexander, and that of Cæsar, while they lived?

As to rewards, have they not admitted him to the highest honors and profits in the Province? Have they not assisted him cheerfully in raising himself and his family to almost all the honors and profits, to the exclusion of much better men? Have they not rewarded him so far as to form invincible combinations to involve every man of any learning and ingenuity in general detestation, obloquy, and ruin, who has been so unfortunate as to think him rather too craving?

There is also another piece in the same paper, called Remarks on the Times, possibly by the same hand, about "political enthusiasm, disordered pulses, precipices, vertigoes, falling on rugged cliffs, men of hot, enthusiastical turn of mind," &c.[1]

Went to town meeting through a fierce wind, a soaking rain, and miry roads and banks of snow.

18. Tuesday. Went to Weymouth; found the family mourning the loss and preparing for the funeral of old Tom. After my return rode to Mr. Hall's, and in my return stopped at Mr. Jo Bass's for the papers. Major Miller soon afterwards came in, and he and I looked on each other without wrath or shame or guilt, at least without any great degree of either, though I must own I did not feel exactly as I used to in his company, and I am sure by his face and eyes that he did not in mine. We were very social, &c.

28. Friday. I have omitted writing a week. Dr. Tufts lodged here last night, with yesterday's paper. The January packet arrived at New York has brought the King's speech, the addresses of Lords and Commons, 14th of January, and many private letters, which inform that Mr. Pitt was in the House of Commons, and declared himself against Grenville and for a repeal of the Stamp Act, upon principle; called it the most impolitic, arbi-

1 The following brief extract from this article may serve as a specimen of the general tone of the government writers of this time:

"Remark II. The best plans of government and completest models of civil states will suffer by tumults, and are subject to be overthrown, when self-designing men, and men of a hot, enthusiastical turn of mind, are at the head of public commotions.

"At a time when the torrent runs high and the state is unsettled, self-designing men will push themselves forward at all adventures, hoping for nothing more than self-promotion, though at the ruin of the public."

trary, oppressive, and unconstitutional Act that ever was passed; denied that we were represented in the House of Commons, (*Q.* Whether the House of Commons or the Parliament?) and asserted that the House granted taxes in their representative capacity, not in their legislative, and, therefore, that the Parliament had not the right to tax the colonies.

Q. What has been said in America which Mr. Pitt has not confirmed? Otis, Adams, Hopkins, &c., have said no more. Hampden, F. A., the Feudal System, and Lord Clarendon,[1] have gone no further than Pitt. No epithets have been used in America worse than impolitic, arbitrary, oppressive, unconstitutional, — unless it be cursed, damned, supercursed, &c. What shall we think of Mr. Pitt? What shall we call him? The genius and guardian angel of Britain and British America, or what? Is it possible that Grenville, offensive to his King, disagreeable to the people, should prevail against the whole new ministry and Mr. Pitt?

April 10. Friday. At Plymouth. Court open and business proceeding.

15. Tuesday. Went to Boston. The superior court adjourned again, for a fortnight. Hutchinson, Cushing, and Oliver, present. What insolence and impudence and chicanery is this!

Fleet, of yesterday, gives us a piece from London Gazette, January 8th, signed *Vindex Patriæ.* The sole question, he says, is, if the Americans are represented in Parliament.

Colonists by charters shall have same privileges, as if born in England, that is, that England shall be reputed their *natale solum;* Massachusetts, by fiction, supposed to lie in England. *Q.* Whether this thought was not suggested by the Braintree instructions?[2] "A fiction of law, insensible in theory and injurious in practice." All England is represented, then Massachusetts is.

26. Saturday. The last Thursday's paper is full. The resolves of the House of Commons are the most interesting. The bill which is to be brought in upon the first resolve and the sixth, has excited my curiosity and apprehensions the most.

1 The signatures of writers on this topic in the Boston Gazette.

2 Drawn up by himself, in the September preceding, and which will be found elsewhere in these volumes. It is a little singular that no other allusion to them occurs in the Diary.

The first resolve is, that King, Lords, and Commons, have an undoubted right to make laws for the Colonies in all cases whatever. I am solicitous to know whether they will lay a tax in consequence of that resolution, or what kind of a law they will make.

The first resolve is in these words: "That the King's Majesty, by and with the advice and consent of the Lords spiritual and temporal, and Commons of Great Britain in Parliament assembled, had, hath, and of right ought to have, full power and authority to make laws and statutes of sufficient force and validity to bind the Colonies and people of America, subjects of the Crown of Great Britain, in all cases whatever." Now, upon this resolution, a bill is to be brought in. *Q.* What is the end and design of that bill?

Another resolution is, that all who have suffered damages for their desire to comply with any act of Parliament, or to assist in the execution of any, ought to be amply compensated. But who are they who have manifested a desire to comply with the Stamp Act or to assist in the execution of it? Winslow, Foster, Clap, Brown, &c., were for submission, in order to obtain a repeal. Everybody has disowned any desire to comply or assist. Who will lay claim to the character of dutiful and loyal subjects, and to the protection of the House of Commons, in consequence of the fifth resolution?

Prophecies are the most airy, visionary things in nature. I remember the time when Pratt was universally called by the Hutchinsonians a bad politician; and I never could hear any other reason given but this, — that his prophecies about the King of Prussia and General Amherst, did not turn out right.

Now Hutchinson himself, Olivers, Trowbridges, Ruggleses, Winslows, have been prophesying that fleets and armies would be sent to enforce the Stamp Act; but they are as false prophets as ever uttered oracles.

Foresight, judgment, sagacity, penetration, &c., are but very feeble, infirm things, in these great affairs of state and war. What Hutchinson said in the probate office was as good a way as any: "I never was more at a loss in my life about any thing future! What the new ministry will do I know not; if Mr. Pitt was in, I should be at no loss at all." In this way, an air of deep, important wisdom is preserved, without danger of being proved mistaken by time.

27. Sunday. Heard Mr. Smith. In the evening, yesterday, I had a great deal of conversation with Ezekiel Price about politics, &c. I provoked him to speak freely, by calling him a Hutchinsonian. "I swear," says he, "I think the Lieutenant-Governor an honest man, and I think he has been most damnably abused, and slandered, and belied, &c. I know all his violent opposers. I know them and what they are after, and their disciples in and about the Capital. There is no man in the Province would fill any one of his offices as he does. He is the best Judge of Probate," &c. Flings about Otis and Adams, and about being one of their disciples, &c.

29. Tuesday. At Boston. To this day the Superior Court was adjourned. Hutchinson, Lynde, and Cushing, were present. Two of the bar agreed to continue an action. Hutchinson leans over and orders Winthrop to minute an agreement to continue. We will consider of it, says he. Another of the bar moved for a continuance, and no opposition. Hutchinson orders the clerk to enter it, motion for a continuance, &c. Then the Court went to playing off a farce, and to trying to get a cause for the jury, but none was then ready. Then Hutchinson proposed,—"What if we should adjourn to the first Tuesday in June?" Then Otis and Swift moved that complaints might be read and passed upon or affirmed. Hutchinson said, "I shall be very open in my judgment; I am not for making up judgment on any complaints; I am upon principle in it; it would not be regular nor prudent at this critical juncture." Cushing thought, "that in some cases of necessity it might be done," with one of his most jesuitical looks. Lynde declared he would not belong to the General Court, in all advents, this year. Hutchinson seemed in tortures. "He wanted to be out of town, to be at home; he was never so easy as when he was there; he did not love to spend his time idly; if there was no business to be done, he was for being where he could be employed."

Thus the Chief Justice is now mustering up fortitude enough to make public, to manifest his desire to comply with the Stamp Act, and to assist in carrying it into execution, in order to lay claim to the protection of the House of Commons, and to claim a compensation for his damages. Ay, he is now assuming the character of a dutiful and loyal subject! I kept an obstinate silence the whole time; I said not one word for or against the adjournment; I saw the court were determined before I came in, and they had no right to expect that I would fall in with that determination; and I had no disposition to foment an opposition to it, because an opposition made with any warmth might have ended in the demolition of the earthly house of his Honor's tabernacle.

But let me look back to the sixth page in this book, that is, to Tuesday, 11th of March,[1] and read what was said by Cushing, Lynde, &c., and can we be sufficiently amazed at the chicanery, the finesse, the prevarication, the insincerity, the simulation, nay, the lies and falsehoods of the Judges of the superior court? These are harsh words, but true. The times are terrible, and made so at present by Hutchinson, Chief Justice. I cannot say that Oliver fibbed, but Cushing did, abominably, on 11th March. Nathaniel Hatch says, "they are right, for nothing hindered the repeal of the Stamp Act, but what has been done here,—the riots, and resolves, and doing business," &c.

Thus America will ring with riots, resolves, opening courts, instructions, Edes and Gill's Gazette, writers, &c.—all the evil will be laid upon them and the Congress too, and recalling orders for goods.

May 4. Sunday. Returning from meeting this morning, I saw for the first time a likely young button-wood tree, lately planted on the triangle made by the three roads, by the house of Mr. James Bracket. The tree is well set, well guarded, and has on it an inscription, "The Tree of Liberty, and cursed is he who cuts this tree!" *Q.* What will be the consequences of this thought? I never heard a hint of it till I saw it, but I hear that some persons grumble, and threaten to girdle it.

18. Sunday. Mem. To write some speculations upon the union of legislative and executive powers,[2] and upon the knot, the junto, the combination.

26. Monday. I have been very unfortunate in running the gauntlet through all the rejoicings for the repeal of the Stamp Act.

[1] Page 188–189.

[2] From the coincidence of phrase here used with that which Gordon quotes as applied to justify the proceedings on the 28th, only ten days later, it is fair to infer that the writer was already possessed of the design to exclude Hutchinson from the council, and was meditating how to prepare the public mind for the stroke. *Gordon's History*, vol. i. p. 208.

Monday last, at two o'clock,[1] was our town meeting; and the same evening were all the rejoicings in Boston and in Plymouth. After meeting I mounted for Plymouth, and reached Dr. Hall's of Pembroke. The only rejoicings I heard or saw, were at Hingham, where the bells rung, cannons were fired, drums beaten, and landlady Cushing, on the plain, illuminated her house.

The county of Plymouth has made a thorough purgation; Winslow, Clap, Foster, Howard, Keen, Oliver, Alden, are all omitted, and Warren, Sever, Thomas, Turner, Vinal, Edson, Sprout, are chosen. What a change!

A duller day than last Monday, when the Province was in a rapture for the repeal of the Stamp Act, I do not remember to have passed. My wife, who had long depended on going to Boston, and my little babe, were both very ill of an whooping cough. Myself under obligation to attend the superior court at Plymouth the next day, and therefore unable to go to Boston, and the town of Braintree insensible to the common joy!

28. Wednesday. General election. At Boston. After lecture, dined at Mr. Austin's, the wine-cooper, with the Rev. Messrs. Prentice of Charlestown and Adams[2] of Roxbury. Adams and Austin were the disputants in politics. Prentice a moderator.

This morning, Adams was chosen Clerk, and Otis Speaker. Governor Bernard negatived him. Cushing was chosen. In the afternoon they proceeded to choose counsellors, when Hutchinson and the two Olivers were dropped, and Trowbridge was dropped,[3] and Mr. Pitts, Colonel Gerrish, Colonel White, Bowers, Powell, and Mr. Saunders, and Dexter, were chosen. What a change! This day seems to be the literal accomplishment of a prophecy of Mr. Otis, published two or three winters ago in the newspaper: "The day is hastening on, with large strides, when a dirty, very dirty, witless rabble, I mean the great vulgar, shall go down with deserved infamy to all posterity." Thus the tri-

[1] On the sixteenth of May, a copy of the Act of Parliament for the repeal of the Stamp Act was brought to Boston. No rejoicings, since the Revolution, had been equal to those on this occasion. The general language from the friends of liberty to such as had differed from them, was this: "See what firmness and resolution will do." *Hutchinson*, iii. 147.

[2] Rev. Amos Adams, in high repute at this time for abilities and learning. Notices of him are to be found in Eliot and Allen. He died in 1775, during the prevalence around Boston of an epidemic dysentery, to which he fell a victim.

[3] The curious reader can compare this account with that in the third volume of *Hutchinson's History*, pp. 148, et seq.

umph of Otis and his party are complete. But what changes are yet to come? Will not the other party soon be uppermost?

29. Thursday. The Governor negatived Otis, Sparhawk, Dexter, Saunders, Gerrish, and Bowers, and made the two Houses a most nitrous, sulphureous speech.

What will be the consequence?

This morning, in Hatch's office, Mr. Paxton came in.

"This is the laziest town upon the globe; poor, proud and lazy is the character of this town; they won't work. If the neutrals[1] were gone, there would be nobody to throw the water out of the long boat in this town." Trowbridge told stories about the virtue of some neutrals, their strict justice, their aversion to profaneness, &c. Paxton said they were never drunk, never disorderly, never before a magistrate, &c. &c. &c. All this from Goffe[2] and Paxton was meant in favor of Roman Catholic religion and civil slavery, I doubt not.

Goffe said he had been reading the History of England, and he found that there had always arisen men to defend liberty in the same manner and from the same principles as they do here.

He said further, that for himself he felt so happily after his death,[3] that he was pretty sure he had behaved well during his lifetime; for himself, he was easy, but the poor Secretary is infirm; it will bear hard upon him; and for the Lieutenant-Governor, now the Act is repealed, and considering how he has been used, instead of doing any thing to make up his loss, to leave him out of council, and so to confirm in the minds of the people a suspicion that he has been an enemy to the country, is very hard, for a man who has behaved so well as he has.

July 18. Monday after Commencement. Last Saturday, I accidentally found a curious volume which Oakes Angier found in a chest of books belonging to an uncle of his who died forty-five years ago. The title-page and all the rest is gone till you come to the eighteenth page. It seems to be a collection of pamphlets, published in the memorable year 1640, bound up together in one quarto volume. Lord Digbie's Speech, 9 November, 1640, concerning grievances and the Triennial Parliament.

[1] The Acadian exiles.

[2] Mr. Goffe had changed his name to that of Trowbridge, by which he is designated in a preceding sentence.

[3] Political death, by being left out of the council.

Harbottle Grimstone's speech, 18th December, 1640, moving for an impeachment of the Archbishop. He calls him the great and common enemy of all goodness and good men. Pym's speech after the articles against Strafford were read. Pym's speech after the articles against Sir George Ratcliffe were read.[1]

24. Sunday. Thanksgiving for the repeal of the Stamp Act. Mr. Smith's text was, "The Lord reigneth, let the earth rejoice, and the multitude of the isles be glad thereof."

Mr. Wibird's was, Genesis 50th, 20th: "But, as for you, ye thought evil against me; but God meant it unto good, to bring to pass, as it is this day, to save much people alive." America is Joseph; the King, Lords, and Commons, Joseph's father and brethren. Our forefathers sold into Egypt, that is, persecuted into America, &c. Wibird shone, they say.

28. Monday. At Boston. A meeting of the bar at the Coffee House, for the admission of three young gentlemen, Mr. Oliver, Mr. Quincy,[2] and Mr. Blowers, and another meeting appointed next Friday sevennight, to consider of some measures for limitation, making a pause, &c. They swarm and multiply—*sed* the country grows amazingly, and the time will not be long ere many who are now upon the stage will be in their graves. Four years must pass before the three young gentlemen admitted this night will assume the gown, and four years will make a great alteration in the bar. It is not so long since Pratt and Thacher were in their glory at the bar; since Colonel Otis reigned in three southern counties, &c. Mr. Gridley and Mr. Dana are between sixty and seventy. Kent is near sixty. Fitch, Otis, Auchmuty, are about forty. Benjamin Gridley and Mr. Dudley are about thirty-five, and Sewall, S. Quincy, and I, about thirty. Within four years, possibly some of all these ranks may depart. But the bar has at last introduced a regular progress to the gown, and seven years must be the state of probation.

Gridley, Otis, and Auchmuty were the chief speakers. Gridley, however, was not in trim; I never saw him more out of spirits. Otis told some stories. Auchmuty told more, and scolded and railed about the lowness of the fees. This is Auchmuty's com-

[1] Here follows a long list of titles of speeches made during the great struggle in England. The volume must have been curious and valuable.

[2] Josiah Quincy, Junior.

monplace topic: In Jamaica, Barbadoes, South Carolina, and New York, a lawyer will make an independent fortune in ten years.

29. Tuesday. At Boston. Bought Gilbert's Law of Evidence. Auchmuty is employed in Sessions and everywhere; the same heavy, dull, insipid way of arguing everywhere; as many repetitions as a Presbyterian parson in his prayer. Volubility, voluble repetition and repeated volubility; fluent reiterations and reiterating fluency. Such nauseous eloquence always puts my patience to the torture. In what is this man conspicuous?—in reasoning, in imagination, in painting, in the pathetic, or what? In confidence, in dogmatism, &c. His wit is flat, his humor is affected and dull. To have this man represented as the first at the bar, is a libel upon it, a reproach and disgrace to it.

30. Wednesday. At Boston; the weather cloudy. Going to the common pleas to-day. Let me take minutes; let me remark the speakers, their action, their pronunciation, their learning, their reasoning, their art and skill; let me remark the causes, the remarkable circumstances, &c. and report.

August 12. Tuesday. Set out with my wife for Salem; dined at Boston; drank tea at Dr. Simon Tufts's, at Medford; lodged at Mr. Bishop's.

13. Wednesday. Set out from Mr. Bishop's, oated at Norwood's *alias* Martin's, and reached brother Cranch's at twelve o'clock; dined and drank tea, and then rode down to the Neck Gate, and then back through the Common and down to Beverly Ferry, then back through the Common and round the back part of the town home; then walked round the other side of the town to Colonel Browne's, who not being at home we returned. The town is situated on a plain, a level, a flat; scarce an eminence can be found anywhere to take a view. The streets are broad and straight, and pretty clean. The houses are the most elegant and grand that I have seen in any of the maritime towns.

14. Thursday. In the morning rode a single horse, in company with Mrs. Cranch and Mrs. Adams in a chaise, to Marblehead. The road from Salem to Marblehead, four miles, is pleasant indeed. The grass plats and fields are delightful, but Marblehead differs from Salem. The streets are narrow, and rugged,

and dirty, but there are some very grand buildings. Returned and dined at Cranch's; after dinner walked to Witchcraft hill, a hill about half a mile from Cranch's, where the famous persons formerly executed for witches were buried. Somebody within a few years has planted a number of locust trees over the graves, as a memorial of that memorable victory over the "prince of the power of the air."

This hill is in a large common belonging to the proprietors of Salem, &c. From it you have a fair view of the town, of the river, the north and south fields, of Marblehead, of Judge Lynde's pleasure-house, &c. of Salem village, &c.

18. Monday. Went to Taunton; lodged at McWhorter's.

19. Tuesday. Dined at Captain Cobb's with Colonel G. Leonard, Paine, Leonard, young Cobb, &c.

20. Wednesday. Spent evening at lodgings with Charles Cushing and Daniel Oliver of Middleborough, Paine, and Leonard, socially.

21. Thursday morning, fine weather; feel well.

November 3. Monday. Set off with my wife for Salem; stopped half an hour at Boston, crossed the ferry, and at three o'clock arrived at Hill's, the tavern in Malden, the sign of the Rising Eagle, at the brook near Mr. Emerson's meeting-house, five miles from Norwood's; where, namely, at Hill's, we dined. Here we fell in company with Kent and Sewall. We all oated at Martin's, where we found the new sheriff of Essex, Colonel Saltonstall. We all rode into town together. Arrived at my dear brother Cranch's about eight, and drank tea, and are all very happy. Sat and heard the ladies talk about ribbon, catgut, and Paris net, riding-hoods, cloth, silk, and lace. Brother Cranch came home, and a very happy evening we had. Cranch is now in a good situation for business, near the court-house and Mr. Barnard's meeting-house, and on the road to Marblehead; his house fronting the wharves, the harbor and shipping, has a fine prospect before it.

4. Tuesday. A fine morning. Attended court all day; heard the charge to grand jury, and a prayer by Mr. Barnard. Deacon Pickering was foreman of one of the juries. This man, famous for his writing in newspapers concerning church order and government, they tell me is very rich; his appearance is perfectly plain, like a farmer; his smooth combed locks flow behind him

like Deacon Cushing's, though not so gray; he has a quick eye like —; he has an hypocritical demure on his face like Deacon Foster; his mouth makes a semicircle when he puts on that devout face. Deacon Penniman is somewhat like him, though Penniman has more of the grave solemnity in his behavior than the other. The picture of Governor Endicott, &c. in the council chamber, is of this sort; they are puritanical faces.

At this court I also saw a young gentleman lately sworn in the inferior court, whose name is Samuel Porter; he lived with Mr. Farnham, took his second degree last year, and lives at Ipswich. Thus every county of the Province swarms with pupils, and students, and young practitioners of law.

5. Wednesday. Attended court; heard the trial of an action of trespass, brought by a mulatto woman, for damages, for restraining her of her liberty. This is called suing for liberty; the first action that ever I knew of the sort, though I have heard there have been many. Heard another action for assault and battery, of a mariner, by the master of a vessel; a little fellow was produced as a witness who is a Spaniard; speaks intelligible English; black eyes, thin, sharp features; has been among the English three or four years.

Here I saw Nathaniel Peaslee Sargeant, of Methuen,[1] two years an attorney of superior court, now commencing a barrister. He took his degree the year I entered college; he has the character of sense, ingenuity, &c., but not of fluency; he is a stout man, not genteel nor sprightly. This is the gentleman whom Thacher recommended for a justice, and admired for his correctness and conciseness, as another Father Read. Here I found the famous Joseph Eaton, at law as usual. I knew him when I lived at Worcester, where he had a suit, I believe, every court while I lived there. He now lives at Lynn End, on the borders between Essex and Middlesex. This is one of the stirring instruments that Goffe has patronized and encouraged for many years. I remember to have heard Goffe celebrate him for self-government, for a cool, steady command of his passions, and for firmness of mind, &c.

Eaton is now at law with the Harts, whose characters are as curious as his and more so.

[1] Afterwards Chief Justice of the Supreme Court of Massachusetts. He died in 1791.

This Eaton, Goffe set up, as Pynchon tells me, to be a justice, but Thacher got him indicted in the county of Essex for a barrator, which defeated the scheme of Goffe, and he came near conviction. Goffe grew warm, and said that Eaton's character was as good as any man's at the bar.

Spent the evening at Mr. Pynchon's, with Farnham, Sewall, Sargeant, Colonel Saltonstall, &c. very agreeably. Punch, wine, bread and cheese, apples, pipes and tobacco. Popes and bonfires this evening at Salem, and a swarm of tumultuous people attending them.

6. Thursday. A fine morning; oated at Martin's, where we saw five boxes of dollars, containing, as we were told, about eighteen thousand of them, going in a horse-cart from Salem custom-house to Boston, in order to be shipped for England. A guard of armed men, with swords, hangers, pistols, and muskets, attended it. We dined at Dr. Tufts's in Medford.

There I first heard that the old custom and privilege of electing orators, thesis collectors, &c. by the class, has been lately taken away, and that this invasion of their privileges contributed more than the butter towards the late spirit of insurrection there.[1]

Drank tea at Mrs. Kneeland's; got home before eight o'clock.

7. Friday. Went up to my common pasture to give directions about trimming the trees, that is, lopping and trimming the walnuts and oaks, and felling the pines and savins and hemlocks. An irregular, misshapen pine will darken the whole scene in some places. These I fell without mercy, to open the prospect and let in the sun and air, that the other wood may grow the faster, and that the grass may get in for feed. I prune all the trees; I leave buttonwoods, elms, maples, oaks, walnuts, savins, hemlocks, and all. The pines that grow in that pasture are, that is, the white pines are, very knotty, crooked, unthrifty things. I am desirous of clearing out the rocky gutter, that is, of clearing away the bushes and pruning all the trees, that we may see clearly the course of the water there, and judge whether it is worth while to dig up the rocks and make a ditch for the water; and for another reason, too, namely, to let in the sun and air, because that rocky gutter produces a great deal of feed, which I should be glad to sweeten.

1 Quincy's *History of Harvard University*, vol. ii. p. 99.

Afternoon, went to Major Crosby's, to see him execute a codicil to his will. The old gentleman is very desirous that the Province should comply with the King's recommendation to make up the damages to the sufferers.

8. Saturday. Fine weather still.

Yesterday, Clement Hayden came in to Major Crosby's. He seemed to hope, he said, that the Court would not vote to make up the losses;[1] but he heard, to-day that the King had requested it, and if that was true he knew not what to say. The King had been so gracious as to repeal the Stamp Act, and now to deny him such a trifle, would seem ungrateful and ungenerous; and it was our best interest to be always in favor with him, and if we should refuse his request, it might be ten times more damage to us than to pay it; and he believed if this town was to meet and to be fully informed about it, they would not vote against it. In short, Clem talked like a reasonable man. He said that in all the wars and all other times nothing ever happened that affected him like the Stamp Act; he said, if it had been insisted on, he knew it would not be borne, and that he expected dismal scenes; the repeal of it was great joy, and he should be willing to do any thing in reason, out of duty to the King.

This morning I asked John Clark some questions about it. He thinks if the King has requested it, it will be difficult to refuse it, but yet it will be hard upon us to pay it.

11. Tuesday. Rain. Deacon Webb here at tea, and put this strange question to me,—What do you think of the Lieutenant-Governor, sir?

I told him what I once thought of him, and that I now hoped I was mistaken in my judgment. I told him I once thought that his death, in a natural way, would have been a smile of Providence upon the public, and would have been the most joyful news to me that I could have heard.

The Deacon thought him a devout, pious man, a professor of religion, a good man, a Christian, &c. and a capable man, and the best Judge of probate that ever we had this forty years; and that he had been envied. This observation, of his being envied, I have heard made by Nat Thayer before now. "He was

[1] "Of the Lieutenant-Governor, (Hutchinson,) and others, who had lost their property by the fury of the people" in the riot of the twenty-sixth of August, 1765. See *Hutchinson's History*, iii. 157.

capable and greatly promoted, and therefore envied; at the same time a craving man."

I presume it will not be denied that this Province is, at present, in a state of peace, order, and tranquillity; that the people are as quiet and submissive to government, as any people under the sun, as little inclined to tumults, riots, seditions, as they were ever known to be since the first foundation of the government. The repeal of the Stamp Act has hushed into silence almost every popular clamor, and composed every wave of popular disorder into a smooth and peaceful calm.

As the indemnification, recommended by his Majesty, seems at present the reigning topic of conversation, a few thoughts upon that subject may not be improper.

After the repeal of the Stamp Act, every newspaper and pamphlet, every public and private letter, which arrived in America from England, seemed to breathe a spirit of benevolence, tenderness, and generosity. The utmost delicacy was observed in all the State papers in the choice of expressions, that no unkind impression might be left upon the minds of the people in America. The letters from the ministry to the Governor recommended the mildest, softest, most lenient and conciliating measures; and even the resolve of the House of Commons, and the recommendation from his Majesty concerning an indemnification to the sufferers, was conceived in the most alluring language. Oblivion of every disagreeable circumstance which had happened through the warmth of the people in the late unhappy times, was recommended in the strongest terms.

What kind of behavior might have been expected from a Governor, in consequence of such advices from home?

At such a time, when the House of Representatives, newly chosen by the people, and a house which thought like the people, had proceeded, with as much calm, composed deliberation as was ever known, to the choice of a speaker, would it be expected that the Governor should negative that speaker? Especially as that gentleman had been a long time in great esteem in the Province, had but just before been unanimously chosen upon the Congress at New York, and had executed that trust to the universal acceptance of the Province.

At such a time, when the two houses had proceeded with equal solemnity to the choice of counsellors, and had completed the election, could it be believed that a Governor should, by his mighty negative, slaughter six of the list at a blow; six of the most steady, capable, and active friends of the people in the whole board?

After all this, which was borne without a murmur, does it not exceed all credibility that this same Governor should meet the two houses, and open the session with a speech! — a speech! — a speech! I want words to express my sentiments of this speech!

December 8. Monday. Dined at Dr. Tufts's; drank tea at Dr. Hall's, Pembroke; lodged at Captain Little's, Kingston. I find a general opposition in the county of Plymouth to compensation. Jacobs tells me that Scituate voted against it with great warmth. Judge Cushing, moderator, did not see fit to say a word, nor was there a word said or a hand up in favor of the bill, though they had voted for it in October. Keen, of Pembroke was warm, and stumped Soule, the moderator, to lay down the money and prevent a tax upon the poor.

Kingston was so fixed against it, that they would not call a meeting. The more considerate and sensible people, however, in all these towns, are in favor of it.

Landlord and landlady Little are full of politics. Mr. Little could get in General Winslow, and did get in Mr. Sever, and Mr. Sever is sensible of it. We had over the affairs of collector of excise. Little does not like Judge Cushing nor Brigadier Ruggles, because they opposed his collectorship, &c.

"At Plymouth, the Province has been drawn in cleverly to make itself guilty of the riots. Everybody out of the Province will say so. The Province has been brought to pay what ought to have been paid by Boston, every farthing of it."

Paine. "The mystery of iniquity opens more now in time of peace than it did in time of confusion." Sever said he believed Goffe would be glad to punish all the transgressors in the late times. Hally said he had tried to persuade Goffe to enter a *nolle prosequi* against the rioters in Berkshire, but he would *not*, and was very high, &c. Paine said the continent ought to have paid the damage.

Nat. Clap. "These town-meeting laws are the most awful things, and the town of Boston ought to be stigmatized, for setting the example."

23. Tuesday. I heard yesterday, for the first time, that young Jonathan Hayward, the son of Lieutenant Joseph Hayward of the south precinct, had got a deputation from the sheriff. Captain Thayer was the person who went to the sheriff and procured it for him. Silas Wild, Thomas Penniman, Stephen Penniman, Lieutenant Hayward, and Zebulon Thayer, were his bondsmen. A goodly class! a clever group! a fine company! a bright cluster!

But what will be the consequences of this deputation, and what were the causes of it? My brother's disregard and neglect of the office, and his neglect to pay Greenleaf, were the causes.

1767. March. Saturday. Went with Captain Thayer to visit Robert Peacock and his poor, distressed family.

We found them in one chamber, which serves them for kitchen, cellar, dining-room, parlor, and bedchamber. Two beds, in one of which lay Peacock, where he told us he had lain for seven weeks without going out of it further than the fire. He had a little child in his arms; another bed stood on one side of the chamber, where lay three other children. The mother only was up, by a fire made of a few chips not larger than my hand; the chamber excessive cold and dirty.

These are the conveniences and ornaments of a life of poverty, these the comforts of the poor! this is want, this is poverty! these the comforts of the needy, the bliss of the necessitous.

We found, upon inquiry, that the woman and her two oldest children had been warned out of Boston, but the man had not, and three children had been born since.

Upon this discovery, we waited on Colonel Jackson, the first selectman of Boston, and acquainted him with the facts, and that we must be excused from any expense for their support.

When I was in that chamber of distress, I felt the meltings of commiseration. This office of overseer of the poor leads a man into scenes of distress, and is a continual exercise of the benevolent principles in his mind; his compassion is constantly excited, and his benevolence increased.

April 4. Saturday. Suits generally spring from passion Jones *vs.* Bigelow, Cotton and Nye, arose from ambition. Jones and Bigelow were competitors for elections in the town of Weston. Cotton and Nye were rivals at Sandwich. Such rivals have no friendship for each other; from such rivalries originate contentions, quarrels, and suits. Actions of defamation are the usual fruits of such competitions. What affection can there be between two rival candidates for the confidence of a town? The famous action of slander, at Worcester,[1] between Hopkins and Ward of Rhode Island, sprouted from the same stock. There the aim was at the confidence of the Colony.

Poor Nye, of Sandwich, seems dejected. I should suspect, by his concern, that Cotton gained ground against him. He seems to be hipped; it frets, and worries, and mortifies him; he can't sleep a nights; his health is infirm.

Cotton is insane, wild; his proposal of giving his house and farm, at Sandwich, to the Province, is a proof of insanity. He has relations that are poor. John Cotton is now poor enough. He has a brother, Josiah Cotton the minister, whom he procured to be removed to Woburn, and thereby to be ruined, who is very poor, maintained by charity. Roland was Josiah's ruin, yet he did not choose to give his estate to Josiah; besides, his behavior at Boston, upon that occasion, was wild: his sitting down at the council table, with his hat on, and calling for his deed and a justice to acknowledge it, when the council was sitting. Cotton's method of getting papers signed by members, in order to demolish poor Nye, is new. The certificate from Murray and Foster, if genuine, is a mean, scandalous thing. It was mean in Murray and Foster to sign that paper. For one representative to give a constituent a weapon to demolish another representative, is ungentlemanlike.

8. Wednesday. Mounted my horse, in a very rainy morning, for Barnstable, leaving my dear brother Cranch and his family at my house, where they arrived last night, and my wife, all designing for Weymouth this afternoon, to keep the Fast with my father Smith and my friend Tufts. Arrived at Dr. Tufts's, where I found a fine wild goose on the spit, and cranberries stewing in the skillet for dinner. Tufts, as soon as he heard that Cranch was at Braintree, determined to go over and bring him and wife and child, and my wife and child over, to dine upon wild goose, and cranberry sauce.

Proceeded, without baiting, to Jacobs's, where I dined; lodged

[1] See page 152.

at Howland's; rode next day; baited at Ellis's; dined at Newcomb's, and proceeded to Barnstable; lodged at Howes's, and feel myself much better than I did when I came from home; but I have had a very wet, cold, dirty, disagreeable journey of it. Now I am on the stage, and the scene is soon to open, what part shall I act? The people of the county, I find, are of opinion that Cotton will worry Nye. But Nye must come off with flying colors.

May. Saturday night. At Howland's, in Plymouth. Returned this day from Barnstable. The case of Cotton and Nye, at Sandwich, is remarkable. Cotton has been driving his interest. This driving of an interest seldom succeeds. Jones, of Weston, by driving his, drove it all away. Where two persons in a town get into such a quarrel, both must be very unhappy;—reproaching each other to their faces, relating facts concerning each other to their neighbors. These relations are denied, repeated, misrepresented, additional and fictitious circumstances put to them, passions inflamed; malice, hatred, envy, pride, fear, rage, despair, all take their turns.

Father and son, uncle and nephew, neighbor and neighbor, friend and friend, are all set together by the ears. My clients have been the sufferers in both these representative causes. The Court was fixed in the Sandwich case. Cotton is not only a tory, but a relation of some of the Judges, Cushing particularly. Cushing married a Cotton, sister of John Cotton, the Register of Deeds at Plymouth. Cushing was very bitter; he was not for my arguing to the jury the question, whether the words were actionable or not; he interrupted me; stopped me short; snapped me up:—"Keep to the evidence; keep to the point; don't ramble all over the world to ecclesiastical councils; don't misrepresent the evidence." This was his impartial language. Oliver began his speech to the jury with,—"A disposition to slander and defamation, is the most cursed temper that ever the world was plagued with, and I believe it is the cause of the greatest part of the calamities that mankind labor under." This was the fair, candid, impartial judge. They adjudged solemnly that I should not dispute to the jury, whether the words were actionable or not.

Spent the evening at Mr. Hovey's, with Deacon Foster and Dr. Thomas. The Deacon was very silent, the Doctor pretty sociable.

Monday morning. A fine sun and air.

Cushing, at Barnstable, said to me, — happy is he whom other men's errors render wise. Otis, by getting into the General Court, has lost his business.

Felix quem faciunt aliena pericula cautum.

Other men's dangers, errors, miscarriages, mistakes, misfortunes.

1768. January 30. Saturday night. To what object are my views directed? What is the end and purpose of my studies, journeys, labors of all kinds, of body and mind, of tongue and pen?

Am I grasping at money or scheming for power? Am I planning the illustration of my family or the welfare of my country? These are great questions. In truth, I am tossed about so much from post to pillar, that I have not leisure and tranquillity enough to consider distinctly my own views, objects, and feelings. I am mostly intent, at present, upon collecting a library; and I find that a great deal of thought and care, as well as money, are necessary to assemble an ample and well chosen assortment of books.

But, when this is done, it is only a means, an instrument. Whenever I shall have completed my library, my end will not be answered. Fame, fortune, power, say some, are the ends intended by a library. The service of God, country, clients, fellow men, say others. Which of these lie nearest my heart?

> "Self love but serves the virtuous mind to wake,
> As the small pebble stirs the peaceful lake;
> The centre moved, a circle straight succeeds,
> Another still, and still another spreads;
> Friend, parent, neighbor, first it will embrace,
> His country next, and next all human race."

I am certain, however, that the course I pursue, will neither lead me to fame, fortune, power, nor to the service of my friends. clients, or country. What plan of reading, or reflection, or business, can be pursued by a man who is now at Pownalborough, then at Martha's Vineyard, next at Boston, then at Taunton, presently at Barnstable, then at Concord, now at Salem, then at Cambridge, and afterwards at Worcester? Now at Sessions, then at Pleas, now in Admiralty, now at Superior Court, then in the gallery of the House? What a dissipation must this be! Is it possible to pursue a regular train of thinking in this desultory life? By no means. It is a life of "*here and everywhere*," to use the expression that is applied to Othello by Desdemona's father.[1] Here, and there, and everywhere, — a rambling, roving, vagrant, vagabond life; a wandering life. At Mein's book-store, at Bowes's shop, at Dana's house, at Fitch's, Otis's office, and the clerk's office, in the court chamber, in the gallery, at my own fire, I am thinking on the same plan.

1 This is said by Roderigo to Desdemona's father: —

"Your daughter, if you have not given her leave,
I say again, hath made a gross revolt;
Tying her duty, beauty, wit, and fortune,
In an extravagant and wheeling stranger
Of here and everywhere."

Extract from the Autobiography.

[In the beginning of the year 1768, my friends in Boston were very urgent with me to remove into town. I was afraid of my health; but they urged so many reasons, and insisted on it so much, that, being determined at last to hazard the experiment, I wrote a letter to the town of Braintree,[1] declining an election as one of their selectmen, and removed in a week or two with my family into the White House, as it was called, in Brattle Square, which several of the old people told me was a good omen, as Mr. Bollan had lived formerly in the same house for many years. The year before this, that is, in 1767, my son John Quincy Adams was born, on the eleventh day of July, at Braintree; and, at the request of his grandmother Smith, christened by the name of John Quincy, on the day of the death of his great grandfather, John Quincy of Mount Wollaston.

In the course of this year, 1768, my friend, Mr. Jonathan Sewall, who was then Attorney-General, called on me, in Brattle street, and told me he was come to dine with me. This was always an acceptable favor from him; for, although we were at antipodes in politics, we had never abated in mutual esteem, or cooled in the warmth of our friendship. After dinner, Mr. Sewall desired to have some conversation with me alone, and proposed adjourning to the office. Mrs. Adams arose, and chose to adjourn to her chamber. We were accordingly left alone. Mr. Sewall then said he waited on me, at that time, at the request of the Governor, Mr. Bernard, who had sent for him a few days before, and charged him with a message to me. The office of Advocate-General in the Court of Admiralty was then vacant, and the Governor had made inquiry of gentlemen the best qualified to give him information, and particularly of one of great authority, meaning Lieutenant-Governor and Chief Justice Hutchinson,[2]

[1] Extract from the town records of Braintree, 1768, 7 March: — "*Voted*, The thanks of the town be given to John Adams, Esquire, for his services as selectman in said town for two years past."

[2] And yet, Hutchinson, knowing all this, was not above putting the following version of this transaction into his third volume. It is proper, however, to keep in mind that a commission as a justice of peace was of far more value at this time than it now is.

"Mr. Adams is said to have been at a loss which side to take. Mr. Sewall, who was with the government, would have persuaded him to be on the same

and, although he was not particularly acquainted with me himself, the result of his inquiries was, that, in point of talents, integrity, reputation, and consequence at the bar, Mr. Adams was the best entitled to the office, and he had determined, accordingly, to give it to me. It was true, he had not power to give me more than a temporary appointment, till his Majesty's pleasure should be known; but that he would give immediately all the appointment in his power, and would write an immediate recommendation of me to his Majesty, and transmit it to his ministers, and there was no doubt I should receive the King's commission as soon as an answer could be returned from England; for there had been no instance of a refusal to confirm the appointment of a Governor in such cases.

Although this offer was unexpected to me, I was in an instant prepared for an answer. The office was lucrative in itself, and a sure introduction to the most profitable business in the Province; and what was of more consequence still, it was a first step in the ladder of royal favor and promotion. But I had long weighed this subject in my own mind. For seven years I had been solicited by some of my friends and relations, as well as others, and offers had been made me, by persons who had influence, to apply to the Governor or to the Lieutenant-Governor to procure me a commission for the peace. Such an officer was wanted in the country, where I had lived, and it would have been of very considerable advantage to me. But I had always rejected these proposals, on account of the unsettled state of the country and my scruples about laying myself under any restraints or obligations of gratitude to the government for any of their favors. The new statutes had been passed in Parliament, laying duties on glass, paint, &c. and a board of commissioners of the revenue was expected, which must excite a great fermentation in the country, of the consequences of which I could see no end.

My answer to Mr. Sewall was very prompt, "That I was sensible of the honor done me by the Governor; but must be excused from accepting his offer." Mr. Sewall inquired, "Why,

side, and promised him to desire Governor Bernard to make him a justice of peace. The Governor took time to consider of it, and having, as Mr. Adams conceived, not taken proper notice of him, or given him offence on some former occasion, he no longer deliberated, and ever after joined in opposition. *Hutchinson*, iii. 296.

what was my objection?" I answered, that he knew very well my political principles, the system I had adopted, and the connections and friendships I had formed in consequence of them. He also knew that the British government, including the King, his Ministers, and Parliament, apparently supported by a great majority of the nation, were persevering in a system wholly inconsistent with all my ideas of right, justice, and policy, and therefore I could not place myself in a situation in which my duty and my inclination would be so much at variance. To this Mr. Sewall returned, that he was instructed by the Governor to say that he knew my political sentiments very well, but they should be no objection with him. I should be at full liberty to entertain my own opinions, which he did not wish to influence by this office. He had offered it to me merely because he believed I was the best qualified for it, and because he relied on my integrity. I replied, This was going as far in the generosity and liberality of his sentiments as the Governor could go, or as I could desire, if I could accept the office, but that I knew it would lay me under restraints and obligations that I could not submit to, and therefore I could not in honor or conscience accept it.

Mr. Sewall paused, and, then resuming the subject, asked, "Why are you so quick and sudden in your determination? You had better take it into consideration, and give me an answer at some future day." I told him my answer had been ready, because my mind was clear, and my determination decided and unalterable. That my advice would be that Mr. Fitch should be appointed, to whose views the office would be perfectly agreeable. Mr. Sewall said he should certainly give me time to think of it. I said that time would produce no change, and he had better make his report immediately. We parted, and about three weeks afterwards he came to me again, and hoped I had thought more favorably on the subject; that the Governor had sent for him, and told him the public business suffered, and the office must be filled. I told him my judgment and inclination and determination were unalterably fixed, and that I had hoped that Mr. Fitch would have been appointed before that time. Mr. Fitch, however, never was appointed. He acted for the Crown, by the appointment of the Judge, from day to day, but never had any commission from the Crown, or appointment of the Governor.

This year, 1768, I attended the Superior Court at Worcester, and the next week proceeded to Springfield, in the county of Hampshire, where I was accidentally engaged in a cause between a negro and his master, which was argued by me, I know not how; but it seems it was in such a manner as engaged the attention of Major Hawley, and introduced an acquaintance which was soon after strengthened into a friendship that continued till his death.

During my absence on this circuit, a convention[1] sat in Boston, the commissioners of the customs had arrived, and an army landed.[2] On my return, I found the town full of troops, and, as Dr. Byles, of punning memory, expressed it, our grievances redressed. Through the whole succeeding Fall and Winter, a regiment was exercised by Major Small, in Brattle Square, directly in front of my house. The spirit-stirring drum and the ear-piercing fife aroused me and my family early enough every morning, and the indignation they excited, though somewhat soothed, was not allayed by the sweet songs, violins and flutes, of the serenading Sons of Liberty under my windows in the evening. In this way and a thousand others, I had sufficient intimations that the hopes and confidence of the people were placed in me as one of their friends; and I was determined that,

[1] This convention was proposed in a regular town meeting of the citizens of Boston, held on the 12th and continued on the 13th of September. A circular letter was addressed on the 14th, by the selectmen, to the selectmen of the other towns, proposing the 22d as the day of meeting for the convention. In this paper the error was committed of assigning among the really good reasons for the call, the obviously false one of "an apprehension of an approaching war with France." The consequence was, that an advantage was given to the loyalists, of which they availed themselves effectively to weaken the moral force of the measure, although more than a hundred towns were represented under only a week's notice. Gordon speaks of the convention as having been a failure, whilst Hutchinson, on the other hand, affirms that it made a greater advance towards a revolution in government than any preceding measures in any of the Colonies. There can be no doubt that the apprehension of it was the main reason for General Gage's change of orders, by which a greater proportion of the troops were stationed in the town, instead of at the castle. *Gordon*, i. 244. *Hutchinson*, iii. 205. *Bradford*, i. 165.

[2] "About one o'clock at noon, October the first, the troops began landing, under cover of the ship's cannon, without molestation; and, having effected it, marched into the Common with muskets charged, bayonets fixed, drums beating, fifes playing, &c. making, with the train of artillery, upward of seven hundred men." *Gordon*, i. 247.

The population of Boston, at this period, did not exceed sixteen thousand souls. It had been retrograde during the preceding twenty-five years. *Snow's History of Boston*, p. 254.

so far as depended on me, they should not be disappointed; and that if I could render them no positive assistance, at least I would never take any part against them.

My daily reflections for two years, at the sight of those soldiers before my door, were serious enough. Their very appearance in Boston was a strong proof to me, that the determination in Great Britain to subjugate us was too deep and inveterate ever to be altered by us; for every thing we could do was misrepresented, and nothing we could say was credited. On the other hand, I had read enough in history to be well aware of the errors to which the public opinions of the people were liable in times of great heat and danger, as well as of the extravagances of which the populace of cities were capable when artfully excited to passion, and even when justly provoked by oppression. In ecclesiastical controversies to which I had been a witness, in the contest at Woburn and on Martha's Vineyard, and especially in the trial of Hopkins and Ward, which I had heard at Worcester, I had learned enough to show me, in all their dismal colors, the deceptions to which the people in their passions are liable, and the total suppression of equity and humanity in the human breast, when thoroughly heated and hardened by party spirit.

The danger I was in appeared in full view before me; and I very deliberately, and, indeed, very solemnly, determined at all events to adhere to my principles in favor of my native country, which, indeed, was all the country I knew, or which had been known by my father, grandfather, or great grandfather; but, on the other hand, I never would deceive the people, nor conceal from them any essential truth, nor, especially, make myself subservient to any of their crimes, follies, or eccentricities. These rules, to the utmost of my capacity and power, I have invariably and religiously observed to this day.[1]

I was solicited to go to the town meetings and harangue there. This I constantly refused. My friend, Dr. Warren, the most frequently urged me to this. My answer to him always was, "That way madness lies." The symptoms of our great friend, Otis, at that time, suggested to Warren a sufficient comment on those words, at which he always smiled, and said, "It was true."

[1] 21 February, 1805.

Although I had never attended a meeting, the town was pleased to choose me upon their committee to draw up instructions to their representatives, this year, 1768, and the next, 1769. The committee always insisted on my preparing the draught, which I did, and the instructions were adopted without alteration by the town. They will be found in the Boston Gazette for those years,[1] and, although there is nothing extraordinary in them of matter or style, they will sufficiently show the sense of the public at that time.

In the fall of the year 1768, a great uproar was raised in Boston on account of the unlading in the night of a cargo of wines from the sloop Liberty, from Madeira, belonging to Mr. Hancock, without paying the customs. Mr. Hancock was prosecuted upon a great number of libels, for penalties upon acts of Parliament, amounting to ninety or an hundred thousand pounds sterling. He thought fit to engage me as his counsel and advocate, and a painful drudgery I had of his cause.[2] There were few days through the whole winter, when I was not sum-

1 They will be given in another portion of these volumes.

2 A full report of the proceedings in this cause, and of his own elaborate argument, remains among the papers of Mr. Adams. The most interesting point of the defence is here subjoined. The prosecution was based on the statute 4 Geo. 3, ch. 15, s. 87, to which allusion is made in the beginning.

"But among the group of hardships which attend this statute, the first that ought always to be mentioned, and that ought never to be forgotten, is,—

"1. That it was made without our consent. My client, Mr. Hancock, never consented to it; he never voted for it himself, and he never voted for any man to make such a law for him. In this respect, therefore, the greatest consolation of an Englishman suffering under any law, is torn from him; I mean the reflection that it is a law of his own making, a law that he sees the necessity of for the public. Indeed, the consent of the subject to all laws is so clearly necessary that no man has yet been found hardy enough to deny it. The patrons of these acts allow that consent is necessary; they only contend for a consent by construction, by interpretation, a virtual consent. But this is only deluding men with shadows instead of substances. Construction has made treasons where the law has made none. Constructions and arbitrary distinctions made, in short, only for so many by-words, so many cries to deceive a mob, have always been the instruments of arbitrary power, the means of lulling and ensnaring men into their own servitude; for whenever we leave principles and clear, positive laws, and wander after constructions, one construction or consequence is piled upon another, until we get at an immense distance from fact and truth and nature, lost in the wild regions of imagination and possibility, where arbitrary power sits upon her brazen throne, and governs with an iron sceptre. It is a hardship, therefore, scarcely to be endured, that such a penal statute should be made to govern a man and his property without his actual consent, and only upon such a wild chimera as a virtual and constructive consent."

See *Hutchinson's* account of this case of the Liberty, and the proceedings of the town thereon. Vol. iii. p. 189, et seq. Also *Gordon*, i. 231-236.

moned to attend the Court of Admiralty. It seemed as if the officers of the Crown were determined to examine the whole town as witnesses. Almost every day a fresh witness was to be examined upon interrogatories. They interrogated many of his near relations and most intimate friends, and threatened to summon his amiable and venerable aunt, the relict of his uncle Thomas Hancock, who had left the greatest part of his fortune to him. I was thoroughly weary and disgusted with the court, the officers of the Crown, the cause, and even with the tyrannical bell that dangled me out of my house every morning; and this odious cause was suspended at last only by the battle of Lexington, which put an end, forever, to all such prosecutions.]

1769. August 10. Boston. John Tudor, Esq. came to me, and for the third time repeated his request that I would take his son William into my office. I was not fond of the proposal, as I had but ten days before taken Jonathan Williams Austin for three years. At last, however, I consented, and Tudor is to come to-morrow morning.

What shall I do with two clerks at a time? and what will the bar and the world say? As to the last I am little solicitous, but my own honor, reputation, and conscience, are concerned in doing my best for their education and advancement in the world; for their advancement I can do little; for their education much, if I am not wanting to myself and them.

11. Friday. Mr. Tudor[1] came, for the first time, and attended the office all day, and paid me ten pounds sterling. In the morning I went to take a view of Mr. Copley's pictures, and afterwards to hear news of the letters arrived in Scot. The mystery of iniquity seems to be unravelled.

I spent the evening at Mr. William Cooper's. The Doctor came in and was very social. He came from a meeting of the Overseers of the College at Cambridge, which was called to advise the Corporation to proceed to the choice of a President.

14. Sunday. At Mr. Quincy's.[2] Here is solitude and retire-

[1] The late Judge William Tudor, an interesting notice of whom is inserted in the eighteenth volume of Collections of the Massachusetts Historical Society, p. 285.

[2] Mr. Norton Quincy, the uncle of Mrs. Adams. His father, Colonel John

ment. Still, calm, and serene, cool, tranquil, and peaceful,—the cell of the hermit; out at one window you see Mount Wollaston, the first seat of our ancestors, and beyond that, Stony Field Hill,[1] covered over with corn and fruits; out at the other window, an orchard, and, beyond that, the large marsh called the broad meadows; from the east window of the opposite chamber, you see a fine plain covered with corn, and beyond that the whole harbor and all the islands; from the end window of the east chamber, you may see with a prospect-glass every ship, sloop, schooner, and brigantine, that comes in or goes out.

Heard Mr. Wibird upon resignation and patience under afflictions, in imitation of the ancient prophets and apostles. A sermon calculated for my uncle's family, whose funeral was attended last week.

In the afternoon, Elizabeth Adams, the widow of Micajah Adams, lately deceased, was baptized and received into full communion with the church. She never knew that she was not baptized in her infancy, till since her husband's decease, when her aunt came from Lynn and informed her.

Mr. Wibird prayed that the loss of her husband might be sanctified to her. This she bore with some firmness; but when he came to pray that the loss might be made up to her little fatherless children, the tears could no longer be restrained. Then the congregation sang a hymn upon submission under afflictions, to the tune of the funeral thought. The whole, together, was a moving scene, and left scarcely a dry eye in the house. After meeting I went to Colonel Quincy's,[2] to wait on Mr. Fiske[3] of Salem, seventy-nine years old.

This Mr. Fiske, and his sister, Madam Marsh,[4] the former born in the very month of the revolution under Sir Edmund Andros, and the latter ten years before that, made a very venerable appearance.

Quincy, had died two years before, and had left him possessor of the farm here described, which he occupied until his death, in 1801.

[1] This makes part of the farm afterwards occupied by Mr. Adams, and where he died.

[2] Josiah Quincy.

[3] Samuel Fiske, pastor successively of the first and third churches at Salem. He died on the seventh of April of the following year, aged 81.

[4] Ann Fiske was married to Rev. Joseph Marsh, the successor of her father, (as pastor) in Braintree, 30 June, 1709. At this time she must have been ninety years old. *Rev. Mr. Lunt's Century Sermons.* Appendix, p. 106.

14. Monday.[1] Dined with three hundred and fifty Sons of Liberty, at Robinson's, the sign of Liberty Tree, in Dorchester. We had two tables laid in the open field, by the barn, with between three and four hundred plates, and an awning of sail-cloth over head, and should have spent a most agreeable day, had not the rain made some abatement in our pleasures. Mr. Dickinson, the farmer's brother, and Mr. Reed, the Secretary of New Jersey,[2] were there; both cool, reserved, and guarded, all day. After dinner was over and the toasts drunk, we were diverted with Mr. Balch's mimicry. He gave us the lawyer's head, and the hunting of a bitch fox. We had also the Liberty Song—that by the farmer, and that by Dr. Church, and the whole company joined in the chorus. This is cultivating the sensations of freedom. There was a large collection of good company. Otis and Adams are politic in promoting these festivals; for they tinge the minds of the people; they impregnate them with the sentiments of liberty; they render the people fond of their leaders in the cause, and averse and bitter against all opposers. To the honor of the Sons, I did not see one person intoxicated, or near it.[3]

Between four and five o'clock the carriages were all got ready, and the company rode off in procession,—Mr. Hancock first, in his chariot, and another chariot bringing up the rear. I took my leave of the gentlemen, and turned off for Taunton, oated at Doty's, and arrived long after dark at Noice's; there I put up. I should have been at Taunton, if I had not turned back, in the morning, from Roxbury, but I felt as if I ought not to lose this

1 The anniversary of the union and firmly combined association of the "TRUE SONS OF LIBERTY." A full account of this festivity is found in the Evening Post and the Gazette of 21 August.

2 Probably Joseph Reed of Philadelphia, and not Secretary of New Jersey. In the lately published biography of this gentleman it is stated that it was John Dickinson himself in whose company he came to Boston at this time. But it is scarcely possible that it should have been he who was present and toasted at this entertainment, without any notice in the newspapers of his presence. *Life of J. Reed*, by his grandson, vol. i. p. 40.

3 The following, among the forty-five regular toasts given upon the occasion, may serve as specimens of the temper of the assembly:

38. The speedy removal of all task-masters, and the redress of all grievances.
39. The republic of letters.
40. The oppressed and distressed protestants.
43. The abolition of all craft and low cunning in Church and State.
45. Strong halters, firm blocks, and sharp axes, to such as deserve either.

(*A discharge of cannon, and three cheers.*)

feast; as if it was my duty to be there. I am not able to conjecture of what consequence it was whether I was there or not. Jealousies arise from little causes, and many might suspect that I was not hearty in the cause, if I had been absent, whereas none of them are more sincere and steadfast than I am.

15. Tuesday. Rode to Taunton, sixteen miles, before nine o'clock, though I stopped and breakfasted at Hayward's, in Easton, nine miles from Taunton. Spent all the leisure moments I could snatch, in reading a Debate in Parliament, in 1744, upon a motion to inquire into the conduct of Admiral Matthews and Vice-Admiral Lestock in the Mediterranean, when they had, and neglected, so fine an opportunity of destroying the combined fleets of France and Spain off Toulon.

September 2. Saturday night. Though this book has been in my pocket this fortnight, I have been too slothful to make use of it. Dined at Mr. Smith's. Heard that Messrs. Otis and Adams went yesterday to Concert Hall, and there had each of them a conference with each of the commissioners, and that all the commissioners met Mr. Otis this morning, at six o'clock, at the British Coffee House.[1] The cause and end of these conferences are subjects of much speculation in town.

3. Sunday. Heard Dr. Cooper in the forenoon, Mr. Champion of Connecticut in the afternoon, and Mr. Pemberton in the evening at the charity lecture. Spent the remainder of the evening and supped with Mr. Otis, in company with Mr. Adams, Mr. William Davis, and Mr. John Gill. The evening spent in preparing for the next day's newspaper, — a curious employment, cooking up paragraphs, articles, occurrences, &c., working the political engine! Otis talks all; he grows the most talkative man alive; no other gentleman in company can find a space to put in a word; as Dr. Swift expressed it, he leaves no elbow room. There is much sense, knowledge, spirit, and humor in his conversation; but he grows narrative, like an old man; abounds with stories.

4. Monday. Spent the evening at Dr. Pecker's, with the club.

[1] The Commissioners of the Customs, Henry Hutton, Charles Paxton, William Burch, and John Robinson, The probable cause of this meeting will be found explained in Tudor's Life of James Otis, p. 360. The publication by Mr. Otis, which led to the personal assault by Robinson, was made in the Boston Gazette of the fourth of September. The difficulty took place on the evening of the fifth.

Mr. Otis introduced a stranger, a gentleman from Georgia, recommended to him by the late Speaker of the House in that Province. Otis indulged himself in all his airs; attacked the selectmen, Inches and Pemberton, for not calling a town meeting to consider the letters of the Governor, General, Commodore, Commissioners, Collector, Comptroller, &c. Charged them with timidity, haughtiness, arbitrary dispositions, and insolence of office. But not the least attention did he show to his friend the Georgian. No questions concerning his Province, their measures against the Revenue Acts, their growth, manufactures, husbandry, commerce. No general conversation concerning the continental opposition; nothing but one continued scene of bullying, bantering, reproaching, and ridiculing the selectmen, airs and vapors about his moderatorship and membership, and Cushing's speakership. There is no politeness nor delicacy, no learning nor ingenuity, no taste or sense in this kind of conversation.

6. Wednesday. Mr. Cudworth told me, on the town-house steps, that Mr. Charles Paxton, the commissioner, told him this day that it was possible he might be sent with some process on board a man of war, and he advised him, as a friend, not to attempt to take any man from on board the man of war, for "you have no right to, and if you attempt it you will never come away alive, and I want to see Otis, the deputy sheriff, to give him the same advice." Cudworth told this to Otis, in my hearing, and Otis went directly to Mr. Paxton's, as I since hear, and Mr. Paxton gave him the same advice.

October 19. Thursday. Last night I spent the evening at the house of John Williams, Esq. the revenue officer, in company with Mr. Otis, Jonathan Williams, Esq. and Mr. McDaniel, a Scotch gentleman, who has some connection with the commissioners, as clerk or something. Williams is as sly, secret, and cunning a fellow as need be. The turn of his eye and cast of his countenance is like T. of Braintree. In the course of the evening he said, that he knew that Lord Townsend borrowed money of Paxton when in America, to the amount of five hundred pounds sterling at least, that is not paid yet; he also said, in the course of the evening, that if he had drank a glass of wine that came out of a seizure, he would take a puke to throw it up; he had such a contempt for the thirds of seizures. He affects to speak slightly of the commissioners, and of their conduct, though guardedly, and to insinuate that his connections, and interest, and influence at home with the Boards, &c. are greater than theirs.

McDaniel is a composed, grave, steady man to appearance; but his eye has its fire still, if you view it attentively. Otis bore his part very well; conversible enough, but not extravagant, not rough, nor sour.

The morning at Bracket's, upon the case of the whale. The afternoon, at the office, posting books.

24. Sunday last I rode to Braintree, in the morning, and heard Mr. Gay of Hingham, forenoon and afternoon, upon these words in the Proverbs: "The hoary head is a crown of glory, if it be found in the way of righteousness."

The good old gentleman had been to the funeral of his aged brother, at Dedham, and seemed to be very much affected. He said, in his prayer, that God in the course of his Providence was admonishing him that he must very soon put off this tabernacle, and prayed that the dispensation might be sanctified to him; and he told the people, in the introduction to his sermon, that this would probably be the last exhortation they would ever hear from him, their old acquaintance.[1] I have not heard a more affecting or more rational entertainment, on any Sabbath, for many years.

Dined with my friend and uncle, Mr. Quincy, and returned after meeting to Boston.

November. Saturday, after attending Court in the morning, I dined by particular invitation at Mr. Winthrop's, the Clerk of the Superior Court, with all the bar,—Messrs. Dana, Kent, Otis, Fitch, Reed, S. Quincy, B. Gridley, Cazneau, Blowers.

Otis, B. Gridley, Kent, and S. Quincy, were the principal talkers. Otis talked the most, B. Gridley next, Kent the next, and S. Quincy next; the rest of the company said very little.

B. Gridley told us a story of his uncle Jeremiah, the late head of the bar: "When I was a school-boy at Master Lovell's, Mr. Gridley, my uncle, used to make me call at his office sometimes

[1] He lived to preach, thirteen years later, a sermon from the text in Joshua xiv. 10: "I am this day fourscore and five years old;" which has been reprinted within a few years, bearing the title of the "Old Man's Calendar." Dr. Gay died in 1787, at the age of ninety.

to repeat my lesson to him. I called there one day for that purpose. 'Well, Ben! what have you to say, Ben?' says he.

"'I am come to say my lesson, sir, to you,' says I.

"'Ay, Ben, what book have you there under your arm?'

"'Virgil, sir.'

"'Ay, Ben, is that the poet Virgil?'

"'Yes, sir.'

"'Well, Ben, take it and read to me, Ben; read in the beginning of the Æneid, Ben.'

"'Yes, sir.' So I opened my book and began:

"'Arma, virumque cāno, Trojæ qui primus ab oris.'

"'Arma, virumque cāno, Ben! you blockhead! Does John Lovell teach you to read so? — read again.'

"So I began again, 'Arma virumque cāno —'

"'Cāno, you villain! canō,' and gave me a tremendous box on the ear.

"'Arma virumque canō, you blockhead, is the true reading.'

"Thinks I, what is this? I have blockheading and boxing enough at Master Lovell's, I won't have it repeated here; and in a great passion, I threw the Virgil at his head, hit him in the face, and bruised his lip, and ran away.

"'Ben! Ben! you blockhead! you villain! you rascal, Ben!'

"However, away I went, and went home.

"That evening uncle Jeremy came to our house, and sat down with my father.

"'Brother, I have something to say to you about that young rogue of a son of yours, that Ben. He came to my office, I bid him read a line in Virgil, and he read it wrong, and I boxed him; and he threw his Virgil in my face and wounded me, he bruised me in my lip, — here is the mark of it! You must lick him, you must thrash him, brother!'

"I was all this time a listening, and heard my father justify me.

"'Ben did right,' says he; 'you had no right to box him, you was not his master, and if he read wrong, you should have taught him how to read right, not have boxed him.'

"'Ay, then I find you justify the rogue.'

"'Yes,' says father, 'I think he did right.'

"'Ay, then you wont thrash him for it, will you?'

"'No! I think he ought not to be thrashed; I think you ought not to have boxed him.'

"'What, justify the young villain in throwing his book at me, and wounding me in this manner!'

"About two or three evenings afterwards, uncle Jeremy was at club with Jo Green, and John Lovell, and others, and began with great solemnity and sobriety,—'Jo, what shall I do? two or three days ago I was guilty of a bad action, and I don't know how to repair it. I boxed a little boy, a nephew of mine, very unrighteously, and he is so little, so mere a child, that I can't ask his pardon.' And so in solemn sadness he told the whole story to the club."

Whether there is truth in any part of this story or not, I can't say; but if it is mere fiction, there are certainly strong marks of ingenuity in the invention. The pride, obstinacy, and sauciness of Ben, are remembered in Ben, in the circumstance of throwing the Virgil. The same temper in his father is preserved in the circumstance of his justifying it. The suddenness and imperiousness of Jeremiah, in the boxing; and his real integrity, candor, benevolence, and good-nature, in repenting of it at club and wishing to make reparation.

B. Gridley, after this, gave us another story of Colonel Byfield, and his marrying a sailor, which occasioned a great laugh.

Upon the whole, this same Ben Gridley discovered a capacity, a genius, real sentiment, fancy, wit, humor, judgment, and observation; yet he seems to be totally lost to the world. He has no business of any kind, lies abed till ten o'clock, drinks, laughs and frolics, but neither studies nor practises in his profession.[1]

Otis spent almost all the afternoon in telling two stories. One, of Gridley's offending the Suffolk Inferior Court, in the dispute about introducing demurrers, and of his making the *amende honorable*, making concessions, &c. before that contemptible tribunal; and another about a conversation between Pratt, Kent, and him;—Kent's asking the question, What is the chief end of man? and Pratt's answer, To provide food, &c. for other animals. Before dinner, Kent proposed his project of an act of parliament against devils, like to that against witches. Otis catched at it, and proposed the draught of a bill. Be it enacted, &c. that whereas many of the subjects of this realm

[1] Benjamin Gridley signed the Addresses to Hutchinson and to Gage, in 1774, 1775; was proscribed in 1778, and went to England. Six of the ten members of the bar, mentioned in this day's record, became loyalists.

have heretofore, time out of mind, believed in certain imaginary beings called devils, therefore be it enacted, that no one shall mention the devil hereafter, &c. on pain of high treason, &c.

Thus are men's brains eternally at work, according to the proclamation of King James. I don't think the world can furnish a more curious collection of characters than those that made up this company. Otis, Kent, Dana, Gridley, Fitch, Winthrop, &c.

December 23. Saturday night. At my office, reading Sydney. I have been musing, this evening, upon a report of the case of the four sailors who were tried last June, before the special Court of Admiralty, for killing Lieutenant Panton.* A publication

* [During my last residence in Boston, two cases occurred of an extraordinary character, in which I was engaged, and which cost me no small portion of anxiety. That of the four sailors who killed Lieutenant Panton of the Rose frigate. These were both before special courts of admiralty, held in consequence of the statute. The four sailors were acquitted, as their conduct was adjudged to be in self-defence, and the action justifiable homicide. The other was the trial of Ansell Nickerson, for the murder of three or four men on board a vessel. This was, and remains still, a mysterious transaction. I know not, to this day, what judgment to form of his guilt or innocence; and this doubt, I presume, was the principle of acquittal. He requested my assistance, and it was given.]

These cases are both of them mentioned by Hutchinson. The first, in pages 231, 232, the other, in pages 419, 420, of his third volume. It may not be without its value to the curious, to have the opportunity to contrast with his version of Corbet's case the following account written at a late period in the life of the author, and without any knowledge of what had been said in the history. It is contained in a letter addressed to Judge William Tudor, dated 30 December, 1816:

'I cannot say whether I ought to laugh, or cry, or scold, in reporting the trial of Michael Corbet and his three comrades. You must remember it. A volume would be necessary to relate this cause as it ought to be, but never will be related. The trial was before a special court of vice-admiralty, instituted by a special act of Parliament for the trial of piracy and murder on the high seas. The court consisted of Governors Bernard and Wentworth, Lieutenant-Governor and Chief Justice Hutchinson, Judge of Admiralty Auchmuty, Commodore Hood, and certain counsellors from Massachusetts Bay, New Hampshire, and Rhode Island, to the number of fifteen.

Mr. Otis had been engaged with me in behalf of the prisoners; but his unhappy distemper was then in one of its unlucid intervals, and I could hardly persuade him to converse with me a few minutes on the subject; and he constantly and finally refused to appear publicly in the cause.

The whole burden of responsibility was thus cast upon me. You may easily believe I was anxious; the lives of four honest men in my hands, and a sympathizing world looking to me for exertions to preserve them. I determined to plead to the jurisdiction of the Court, and, if that should be overruled, demand a trial by jury. As each of my clients must plead for himself, I was obliged to write four pleas, one for each, and each consisting of sheets of paper setting forth charters, acts of parliament, common law, and ancient usages, which compelled me to sit up more than one night to transcribe. The Court met; prison-only of the record, (I mean the articles, plea to the jurisdiction, testimonies of witnesses, &c.) would be of great utility. The arguments that were used are scarcely worth publishing; those which might be used, would be well worth the perusal of the public. A great variety of useful learning might be brought into a history of that case, and the great curiosity of the world after the case, would make it sell. I have half a mind to undertake it.

The great questions concerning the right of juries in the Colonies, upon a comparison of the three statutes, and concerning the right of impressing seamen for his Majesty's service, whether with or without warrants from the Lords of the Admiralty, upon

ers ordered to the bar. I presented and read my pleas. No counsel for the Crown ordered to answer these pleas, not a word said at the bar or on the bench for them or against them, when Hutchinson, not slow-rising, but starting up, moved that the Court should adjourn to the council chamber. Every vote was ready, and away went their Excellencies, Honors, and learned Judges, to secret conclave. They sat late, and it was propagated through the town that they had determined to summon a jury. Jonathan Sewall himself, the Advocate-General, said he believed they would grant a jury.

The next morning, however, the judgment was pronounced by the President, Governor Bernard, that the Court had overruled the plea to the jurisdiction; no reason was given, not another word was said by the President or any other member of the court, in justification or explication of the decree. The cause was opened and stated by the Advocate-General in a very honorable manner; the witnesses called, examined, and cross-examined; and here I ought to observe, in honor of the morals of seamen, there was no contradiction or variation in the testimonies. British and American sailors, all agreed in every circumstance.

It then became my turn to speak in defence of the prisoners. I had taken more pains in that case than in any other, before or since; I had appealed to Heaven and earth; I had investigated all laws, human and divine; I had searched all the authorities in the civil law, the law of nature and nations, the common law, history, practice, and every thing that could have any relation to the subject. All my books were on the table before me, and I vainly felt as if I could shake the town and the world. A crowded audience attending, still as midnight, in eager expectation.

I had scarcely risen and said, —

"May it please your Excellencies and your Honors,

"My defence of the prisoners, is, that the melancholy action for which they stand accused is justifiable homicide, and therefore no crime at all," and produced one authority very plump to that purpose, — when Hutchinson again darted up, and moved that the Court should adjourn to the council chamber! No reason was given; not a word was said; the Pope's bull was implicitly and unanimously obeyed, and away marched their Excellencies and Honors to the council chamber. Dismal was the anxiety of the town, dreading a sentence of death the next morning. Alas, for me, my glass bubble was burst! my *boule de savon* was dissolved! all the inflammable gas was escaped from my balloon, and down I dropt like Pilâtre des Rosiers.

Never was a more gloomy assembly of countenances painted with terror and

orders of the King in council, are very important. Such a pamphlet might suggest alterations in the statutes, and might possibly procure us, for the future, the benefit of juries in such cases; and the world ought to know, at least the American part of it, more than it does of the true foundation of impresses, if they have any.

1770. January 16. At my office all day.

Last evening at Dr. Pecker's, with the club.

Otis is in confusion yet; he loses himself; he rambles and wanders like a ship without a helm; attempted to tell a story which took up almost all the evening; the story may, at any time, be told in three minutes with all the graces it is capable

horror, than appeared in the audience next morning. The Court appeared; the prisoners were ordered to the bar. The President arose, and pronounced the unanimous sentence of the court, — that the killing Lieutenant Panton was justifiable homicide in necessary self-defence. Auchmuty squealed out, "The judgment of the Court is unanimous," and not another word was said.

Now, sir, was the conduct of Hutchinson that of a "good judicial character?" You may say I write romance and satire. I say that true history, in this case, is the most surprising romance and the keenest satire. But I have not yet explained the secret. First and last, it was FEAR. Hutchinson dreaded, (and the apprehension of Hutchinson was the apprehension of all,) the public investigation, before the people, of the law applicable to that case. They dared not pronounce judgment in favor of impressment in any possible case. Such a judgment would, at that time, have been condemned, reprobated, and execrated, not only in New England and all the other Colonies, but throughout the three kingdoms. It would have accelerated the revolution more than even the impeachment of the judges, or Hutchinson's foolish controversy about the omniscience and omnipotence and infinite goodness of Parliament did afterwards. It would have spread a wider flame than Otis's ever did, or could have done.

But there is a secret behind, that has never been hinted in public, and that Hutchinson dreaded should be produced before the public. *You* know, Mr. Tudor, that I had imported from London, and then possessed, the only complete set of the British Statutes at Large, that then existed in Boston, and, as I believe, in all the Colonies. In that work is a statute which expressly prohibits impressments in America; almost the only statute in which the word or idea of impressment is admitted. The volume which contains that statute, doubled down in dog's ears, I had before me, on the table, with a heap of other books. I was determined that if the law of God, of nature, of nations, of the common law of England, and our American prescriptions and charters, could not preserve the lives of my clients, that statute should, if it could. The conclave dreaded the publication of that statute, which they intended to get repealed, and which they and their successors have since procured to be repealed.'

In the book of admiralty cases, kept by Mr. Adams, is an abstract of all the authorities collected by him in his preparation for this case, as well as a minute account of Lieutenant-Governor Hutchinson's action in the cause. As very few law proceedings, prior to the Revolution, have been preserved in Massachusetts, and as they may be interesting to the profession at this day, the notes, just as they stand in the original, have been placed in the Appendix to this volume. B.

of, but he took an hour. I fear he is not in his perfect mind. The nervous, concise, and pithy, were his character till lately; now the verbose, round-about, and rambling, and long-winded. He once said he hoped he should never see T. H. in heaven. Dan Waldo took offence at it, and made a serious affair of it; said Otis very often bordered upon profaneness, if he was not strictly profane. Otis said, if he did see H. there, he hoped it would be behind the door. "In my father's house are many mansions," some more and some less honorable.

In one word, Otis will spoil the club. He talks so much, and takes up so much of our time, and fills it with trash, obsceneness, profaneness, nonsense, and distraction, that we have none left for rational amusements or inquiries.

He mentioned his wife; said she was a good wife, too good for him; but she was a tory,[1] a high tory; she gave him such curtain lectures, &c. In short, I never saw such an object of admiration, reverence, contempt, and compassion, all at once, as this. I fear, I tremble, I mourn, for the man and for his country; many others mourn over him, with tears in their eyes.

Monday. February 26, or thereabouts. Rode from Weymouth;—stopped at my house, Veasey's blacksmith shop, my brother's, my mother's, and Robinson's.

These five stops took up the day. When I came into town, I saw a vast collection of people near Liberty Tree; inquired, and found the funeral of the child lately killed by Richardson[2]

[1] Miss Ruth Cunningham sympathized with the loyalists, and married her daughter to a British officer. Of course, this was a root of bitterness to James Otis, and aggravated his tendencies. See *Tudor's Life*, p. 20.

[2] In the mob collected before the house of one of the shopkeepers, who had determined to violate the non-importation agreement. Hutchinson's version of the affair is as follows:—

"One of the neighbors (Ebenezer Richardson) found fault with the proceedings, which provoked the mob to drive him into his house for shelter. Having been a land-waiter or inferior custom-house officer, and, before that, an informer against illicit traders, he was peculiarly obnoxious to the people. The mob surrounded his house, threw stones and brickbats through the windows, and, as it appeared upon trial, were forcing their way in, when he fired upon them and killed a boy of eleven or twelve years of age. He was soon seized, and another person with him who happened to be in the house. They were in danger of being sacrificed to the rage of the people, being dragged through the streets, and a halter having been prepared; but some, more temperate than the rest, advised to carry them before a justice of peace, who committed them to prison.

"The boy that was killed, was the son of a poor German. A grand funeral was, however, judged very proper for him. Young and old, some of all ranks was to be attended. Went into Mr. Rowe's and warmed me, and then went out with him to the funeral. A vast number of boys walked before the coffin; a vast number of women and men after it, and a number of carriages. My eyes never beheld such a funeral; the procession extended further than can be well imagined.

This shows there are many more lives to spend, if wanted, in the service of their country.

It shows, too, that the faction is not yet expiring; that the ardor of the people is not to be quelled by the slaughter of one child and the wounding of another.

At club, this evening, Mr. Scott and Mr. Cushing gave us a most alarming account of Otis. He has been, this afternoon, raving mad; raving against father, wife, brother, sister, friend, &c.

and orders, attended in a solemn procession from liberty tree to the town-house, and then to the common burying-ground."

This account should be compared with that of *Gordon*, i. 276, and *Bradford*, i. 205.

It is a little remarkable that no notice is taken in the Diary of the case of Captain Preston and the soldiers, for several years after the time at which it occurred. Here recourse must be had to the Autobiography, which gives the following narrative.

[The year 1770 was memorable enough in these little annals of my pilgrimage. The evening of the fifth of March I spent at Mr. Henderson Inches's house, at the south end of Boston, in company with a club with whom I had been associated for several years. About nine o'clock we were alarmed with the ringing of bells, and, supposing it to be the signal of fire, we snatched our hats and cloaks, broke up the club, and went out to assist in quenching the fire, or aiding our friends who might be in danger. In the street we were informed that the British soldiers had fired on the inhabitants, killed some and wounded others, near the town-house. A crowd of people was flowing down the street to the scene of action. When we arrived, we saw nothing but some field-pieces placed before the south door of the town-house, and some engineers and grenadiers drawn up to protect them. Mrs. Adams was then in circumstances to make me apprehensive of the effect of the surprise upon her, who was alone, excepting her maids and a boy, in the house. Having therefore surveyed round the town-house, and seeing all quiet, I walked down Boylston Alley into Brattle Square, where a company or two of regular soldiers were drawn up in front of Dr. Cooper's old church, with their muskets all shouldered, and their bayonets all fixed. I had no other way to proceed but along the whole front in a very narrow space which they had left for foot passengers. Pursuing my way, without taking the least notice of them, or they of me, any more than if they had been marble statues, I went directly home to Cole Lane.

My wife having heard that the town was still and likely to continue so, had recovered from her first apprehensions, and we had nothing but our reflections to interrupt our repose. These reflections were to me disquieting enough. Endeavors had been systematically pursued for many months, by certain busy characters, to excite quarrels, rencounters, and combats, single or compound, in the night, between the inhabitants of the lower class and the soldiers, and at all risks to enkindle an immortal hatred between them. I suspected that this was the explosion which had been intentionally wrought up by designing men, who knew what they were aiming at better than the instruments employed. If these poor tools should be prosecuted for any of their illegal conduct, they must be punished. If the soldiers in self-defence should kill any of them, they must be tried, and, if truth was respected and the law prevailed, must be acquitted. To depend upon the perversion of law, and the corruption or partiality of juries, would insensibly disgrace the jurisprudence of the country and corrupt the morals of the people. It would be better for the whole people to rise in their majesty, and insist on the removal of the army, and take upon themselves the consequences, than to excite such passions between the people and the soldiers as would expose both to continual prosecution, civil or criminal, and keep the town boiling in a continual fermentation. The real and full intentions of the British government and nation were not yet developed; and we knew not whether the town would be supported by the country; whether the Province would be supported by even our neighboring States of New England; nor whether New England would be supported by the continent. These were my meditations in the night.

The next morning, I think it was, sitting in my office, near the steps of the town-house stairs, Mr. Forrest came in, who was then called the Irish Infant. I had some acquaintance with him. With tears streaming from his eyes, he said, "I am come with a very solemn message from a very unfortunate man, Captain Preston, in prison. He wishes for counsel, and can get none. I have waited on Mr. Quincy, who says he will engage, if you will give him your assistance; without it, he positively will not. Even Mr. Auchmuty declines, unless you will engage." I had no hesitation in answering, that counsel ought to be the very last thing that an accused person should want in a free country; that the bar ought, in my opinion, to be independent and impartial, at all times and in every circumstance, and that persons whose lives were at stake ought to have the counsel they preferred. But he must be sensible this would be as important a cause as was ever tried in any court or country of the world; and that every lawyer must hold himself responsible not only to his country, but to the highest and most infallible of all tribunals, for the part he should act. He must, therefore, expect from me no art or address, no sophistry or prevarication, in such a cause, nor any thing more than fact, evidence, and law would justify. "Captain Preston," he said, "requested and desired no more; and that he had such an opinion from all he had heard from all parties of me, that he could cheerfully trust his life with me upon those principles." "And," said Forrest, "as God Almighty is my judge, I believe him an innocent man." I replied, "that must be ascertained by his trial, and if he thinks he cannot have a fair trial of that issue without my assistance, without hesitation, he shall have it."

Upon this, Forrest offered me a single guinea as a retaining fee, and I readily accepted it. From first to last I never said a word about fees, in any of those cases, and I should have said nothing about them here, if calumnies and insinuations[1] had not been propagated that I was tempted by great fees and enormous sums of money. Before or after the trial, Preston sent me ten guineas, and at the trial of the soldiers afterwards, eight guineas more, which were all the fees I ever received or were offered to me, and I should not have said any thing on the subject to my clients if they had never offered me any thing. This was all the pecuniary reward I ever had for fourteen or fifteen days labor in the most exhausting and fatiguing causes I ever tried, for hazarding a popularity very general and very hardly earned, and for incurring a clamor, popular suspicions and prejudices,[2] which are not yet worn out, and never will be forgotten as long as the history of this period is read.

It was immediately bruited abroad that I had engaged for Preston and the soldiers, and occasioned a great clamor, which the friends of government delighted to hear, and slily and secretly

[1] Hutchinson, who in his third volume has done much to embody, in a permanent form, these floating insinuations of the day against the leading men of the patriotic party, alludes to this affair in the following insidious manner:

"Captain Preston had been well advised to retain two gentlemen of the law, who were strongly attached to the cause of liberty, *and to stick at no reasonable fees for that purpose;* and this measure proved of great service to him."

[2] A remarkable proof of the extent to which these were carried, and the effect which they had even upon the nearest relatives of the parties engaged for Captain Preston, is to be found in a letter addressed to Josiah Quincy, Jr. by his father. 22 March, 1770. See *Memoir of Josiah Quincy, Jr.* by his son, p. 34.

fomented with all their art. The trial of the soldiers was continued for one term, and in the mean time an election came on for a representative of Boston. Mr. Otis had resigned. Mr. Bowdoin was chosen in his stead. At the general election, Mr. Bowdoin was chosen into the council, and Mr. Hutchinson, then Governor, did not negative him. A town meeting was called for the choice of a successor to Mr. Bowdoin. Mr. Ruddock, a very respectable justice of the peace, who had risen to wealth and consequence by a long course of industry as a master shipwright, was set up in opposition to me. Notwithstanding the late clamor against me, and although Mr. Ruddock was very popular among all the tradesmen and mechanics in town, I was chosen by a large majority.

I had never been at a Boston town meeting, and was not at this, until messengers were sent to me to inform me that I was chosen. I went down to Faneuil Hall, and in a few words expressive of my sense of the difficulty and danger of the times, of the importance of the trust, and of my own insufficiency to fulfil the expectations of the people, I accepted the choice. Many congratulations were offered, which I received civilly, but they gave no joy to me. I considered the step as a devotion of my family to ruin, and myself to death; for I could scarce perceive a possibility that I should ever go through the thorns and leap all the precipices before me and escape with my life.

At this time I had more business at the bar than any man in the Province. My health was feeble. I was throwing away as bright prospects as any man ever had before him, and I had devoted myself to endless labor and anxiety, if not to infamy and to death, and that for nothing, except what indeed was and ought to be all in all, a sense of duty. In the evening, I expressed to Mrs. Adams all my apprehensions. That excellent lady, who has always encouraged me, burst into a flood of tears, but said she was very sensible of all the danger to her and to our children, as well as to me, but she thought I had done as I ought; she was very willing to share in all that was to come, and to place her trust in Providence.

I immediately attended the General Court at Cambridge, to which place the Governor had removed it, to punish the town of Boston, in obedience however, as he said I suppose truly, to an instruction he had received from the King. The proceedings of the legislature, at that time and place, may be seen in their journals, if they are not lost. Among other things will be found a labored controversy, between the House and the Governor, concerning these words: "In General Court assembled, and by the authority of the same." I mention this merely on account of an anecdote, which the friends of government circulated with diligence, of Governor Shirley, who then lived in retirement at his seat in Roxbury. Having read this dispute, in the public prints, he asked, "Who has revived those old words? They were expunged during my administration." He was answered, "The Boston seat." "And who are the Boston seat?" "Mr. Cushing, Mr. Hancock, Mr. Samuel Adams, and Mr. John Adams." "Mr. Cushing I knew, and Mr. Hancock I knew," replied the old Governor, "but where the devil this brace of Adamses came from, I know not." This was archly circulated by the ministerialists, to impress the people with the obscurity of the original of the *par nobile fratrum*, as the friends of the country used to call us, by way of retaliation.

This was to me a fatiguing session;[1] for they put me upon all

[1] A brief recital of the political movements of this session will show not only the active part taken in them by the writer, but also the extent of the influence exerted by the "Boston seat," which from small beginnings had grown to a great height. It had been customary for years to rely upon some one person as a guide in the legal and constitutional questions that might come up in the controversies with the Executive. Thus, although Samuel Adams was now the master mover, John Adams seems to have this year succeeded to the post of legal adviser, which had been filled by Oxenbridge Thacher and James Otis. The following abstract, taken from the journal of the House for the year, will serve to show the share which he took in the proceedings:—

1770. June 6. John Adams, Esq. returned a member from Boston, in the room of the Honorable James Bowdoin, Esq. now a member of the council board, making his appearance in the House; Ordered, That Mr. Hancock attend Mr. Adams to the gentlemen appointed to administer the oaths,

Who reported that he had taken the oaths and subscribed the declaration required by act of parliament, and then Mr. Adams took his seat in the House.

June 8. A committee appointed to state the reasons for adhering to the resolution that it is not expedient to proceed to business while the General Court is held out of the town-house in Boston. The members were,—

Major Hawley, Mr. Samuel Adams, John Adams, Esq. Mr. Pickering, Mr. Leonard, Capt. Mitchel, Capt. Sumner, Mr. Hobson, and Capt. Denny.

June 14. A committee to prepare a message to his Honor the Lieutenant-Governor, setting forth that the House cannot recede from its resolution, and praying his Honor, if determined not to remove the assembly to Boston, that he would give the members leave to go home. The members were,—

Mr. Speaker (Cushing), Major Hawley, Samuel Adams, Capt. Sheaffe, and John Adams.

(Of this committee, three of the five persons belonged to the Boston seat.)

the drudgery of managing all the disputes; and an executive court had a long session, which obliged me to attend almost

June 15. A committee to present the draft of the message reported by the preceding committee. The members, Mr. Hancock, Mr. Samuel Adams, Capt. Brown, John Adams, and David Ingersoll. (Three out of five from Boston.)

After the Recess.

July 25. A committee to wait on his Honor the Lieutenant-Governor, and to solicit him to remove the General Assembly to the town-house in Boston. The members, Mr. Hancock, Mr. Adams, Capt. Keene, Mr. Hall, and Mr. John Adams. (Three out of five from Boston.)

July 26. A committee to prepare an answer to the Speech of his Honor the Lieutenant-Governor. The members, Mr. Speaker, Mr. Hancock, Mr. Leonard, Mr. S. Adams, Mr. John Adams, Capt. Dennie, and Major Gallison. (This includes all four of the Boston seat.)

The House prorogued until

September 27. A committee to consider what is proper to be done respecting the speech of the Lieutenant-Governor. The members, Mr. Speaker, Mr. Samuel Adams, Major Foster, Mr. Dennie, Mr. John Adams, Mr. Hancock, Major Godfrey, Colonel Warren, and Mr. Hobson. (All the Boston seat.)

October 4. A committee to prepare a message to his Honor the Lieutenant-Governor. The members, Mr. Hancock, Mr. John Adams, Mr. David Ingersol, Mr. Samuel Adams, and Capt. Fuller. (Three of the Boston seat.)

October 5. A committee to consider the message of his Honor, of the fourth instant. The members, Colonel Murray, Colonel Gerrish, Mr. John Adams, Brigadier Preble, and Mr. Samuel Adams. (Two from the Boston seat.)

This was in the morning. After dinner, Colonel Murray reported, from this committee, its unanimous opinion that his Honor's message was not satisfactory.

Read and accepted, and ordered, That Mr. John Adams, Mr. S. Adams, Mr. Hancock, Mr. David Ingersol, and Mr. Bullen, be a committee to prepare an address.

(Yet, immediately after this vote, a change of feeling manifests itself, which the journal does not explain, neither is it quite clear what the form was, upon which the decision was made. The language of the journal is, —)

The House took into *further* consideration the report of the committee on his Honor's speech, and the question being put, it passed in the negative.

(But, whatever may have been the precise shape of the question, there can be little doubt that it involved the alternative of an utter and absolute refusal to legislate, or of a surrender to the Lieutenant-Governor. The writer of the Diary elsewhere says, that, throughout this session, the parties in the General Court were almost equal. And it is very certain that the majority was not prepared at this moment to go a step further towards disorganization. Apart from this, however, a change of policy, on the part of the opposition, had grown out of the fact that they now learnt that the Lieutenant-Governor was involved, by the government at home, in a difficulty of a still more important character. Orders had come that the fort at Castle William should be occupied by the King's troops, and the provincial garrison dismissed. A suspension of the legislative functions, at such a moment, would have been a relief to the Executive, who had assumed the responsibility of the transfer. All these considerations united to recommend procrastination, so the majority, by a vote of fifty-nine to twenty-nine, contented themselves with entering a protest and proceeding to business. In the minority, however, are found the names of most of the leading men of the patriotic party. John Adams's is not in the lists. The omission is explained in the record of the next day, by which it seems that an unusual privilege of explanation was accorded to him.)

constantly there upon a number of very disagreeable causes. Not long after the adjournment of the General Court, came on

October 16. A committee to consider the state of the Province. The members were, Mr. S. Adams, Major Hawley, Mr. J. Adams, Mr. Hancock, Colonel Worthington, Mr. Pickering, Colonel Warren, and Colonel Whitcomb. (Three Boston members.)

Colonel Warren moved to the House, that the members, who were absent when the resolution passed to proceed to business out of the town-house in Boston, might have leave to declare their opinion thereon in the House.

And the question being put, it passed in the affirmative.

Whereupon Colonel Warren and Mr. John Adams, *who had been absent*, declared their opinions against the resolution.

The House was moved that his Honor be addressed, praying that he would appoint a day of solemn prayer and humiliation.

Ordered, That Mr. John Adams, Mr. Danielson, and Colonel Warren, be a committee to prepare an address accordingly.

October 17. His Honor's message of this forenoon was read again, according to order, and thereupon

Ordered, That Mr. Samuel Adams, Mr. John Adams, Colonel Warren, Mr. Hancock, and Colonel Prescott, be a committee to prepare another message, to request a more explicit answer to the message of the 15th.

The committee, of the 16th, reported. Report read and recommitted.

Mr. Adams was excused from serving, and Dr. Holten appointed in his place.

November 2. Ordered, That Mr. Leonard, Mr. Samuel Adams, Mr. John Adams, Major Hawley, and Mr. Ingersol of Great Barrington, consider the message of his Honor, and report.

(This is the controversy referred to in the text, relating to the words, "In General Court assembled.") *Bradford*, i. 237.

November 7. A committee of correspondence with the agent *and others*, in Great Britain, and also with the Speakers of the several assemblies or committees of correspondence. The members, Mr. Speaker, Mr. Hancock, Mr. Hall, Mr. Samuel Adams, Mr. John Adams. (This embraces the four Boston members.)

November 13. A committee to prepare a remonstrance against the allowance of the Treasurer's accounts. The members, Mr. John Adams, Mr. Samuel Adams, Dr. Wheaton, Dr. Holten, and Mr. Gardner.

November 14. A committee on burning the securities redeemed by the Treasurer. The members, Mr. Speaker, Mr. Hancock, Mr. John Adams, Mr. Samuel Adams.

November 15. A committee to present the answer of the House to the message of his Honor, of the 8th instant. The members, Mr. J. Adams, Major Hawley, Captain Thayer, Mr. Porter, and Mr. Gardner.

November 16. *Resolved*, That Mr. Speaker, Mr. Hancock, Captain Heath, Mr. Samuel Adams, Mr. John Adams, Captain Thayer, Mr. Bachelor, Mr. Howe, and Mr. White, be a committee to prepare a plan for the encouragement of arts, agriculture, manufactures, and commerce, and report at the next session.

1771. April 16. Mr. J. Adams, Mr. Leonard, Major Hawley, Mr. Ingersol, and Mr. Samuel Adams, be a committee to inquire into the validity of the bonds usually given by the Treasurer.

(The committees specified, embrace all but one of those raised during the year upon questions of any public importance. Although a person wholly new to legislation, and at the time very much engaged in his professional duties, including the defence of Captain Preston and the soldiers, it appears that John Adams was placed upon as many committees as his more experienced associate and kinsman. The great preponderance of the Boston members, in the con-the trials of Captain Preston and the soldiers. I shall say little of these cases. Preston's trial was taken down, in short hand, and sent to England, but was never printed here. I told the court and jury, in both causes, that, as I was no authority, I would propose to them no law from my own memory, but would read to them all I had to say of that nature from books, which the court knew, and the counsel on the other side must acknowledge, to be indisputable authorities. This rule was carefully observed, but the authorities were so clear and full, that no question of law was made. The juries in both cases, in my opinion, gave correct verdicts. It appeared to me, that the greatest service which could be rendered to the people of the town, was to lay before them the law as it stood, that they might be fully apprized of the dangers of various kinds which must arise from intemperate heats and irregular commotions. Although the clamor was very loud among some sorts of people, it has been a great consolation to me, through life, that I acted in this business with steady impartiality, and conducted it to so happy an issue.]

Ipswich, June 19. Tuesday morning. Rambled with Kent round Landlord Treadwell's pastures, to see how our horses fared. We found them in the grass up to their eyes;—excellent pastures. This hill, on which stand the meeting-house and court-house, is a fine elevation, and we have here a fine air, and the pleasant prospect of the winding river at the foot of the hill.

25. Boston. *Blowers.* "In the reign of Richard II. or Henry VI. you may find precedents for any thing." This observation was echoed from some tory, who applied it to a late quotation of the House of Representatives.

It is true, Richard II. and Henry VI. were weak and worthless princes, and their parliaments were bold and resolute; but weak princes may arise hereafter, and then there will be need of daring and determined parliaments. The reigns of Richard II. and Henry VI. were the reigns of evil counsellors and favorites, and they exhibit notable examples of the public mischiefs

struction of all of them, is also remarkable, considering the low ratio which the population of the town then bore to that of the Province.

The questions involved in the controversies of this session cannot be explained here. They will be found fully detailed in *Hutchinson*, vol. iii. pp. 291 – 307. *Gordon*, vol. i. pp. 304 – 306. *Bradford*, vol. i. pp. 218 – 239.)

arising from such administrations, and of national and parliamentary vengeance on such wicked minions.

26. Last of service; very little business this court; the bar and the clerks universally complain of the scarcity of business; so little was, perhaps, never known at July Term.[1] The cause must be the non-importation agreement, and the declension of trade. So that the lawyers lose as much by this patriotic measure as the merchants and tradesmen.

Stephens, the Connecticut hemp man, was at my office, with Mr. Counsellor Powell and Mr. Kent. Stephens says, that the whole colony of Connecticut has given more implicit observance to a letter from the selectmen of Boston than to their Bibles for some years; and that, in consequence of it, the country is vastly happier than it was; for every family has become a little manufactory-house, and they raise and make within themselves many things for which they used to run in debt to the merchants and traders. So that nobody is hurt but Boston and the maritime towns.

"I wish there was a tax of five shillings sterling on every button from England. It would be vastly for the good of this country, &c. As to all the bustle and bombast about tea, it has been begun by about half a dozen Holland tea-smugglers, who could not find so much profit in their trade since the ninepence was taken off in England." Thus he. Some sense and some nonsense!

27. Wednesday morning. Very fine, likely to be hot; at my office early. The only way to compose myself and collect my

[1] In connection with a Diary, minute points of personal history are not out of place. Among the papers of Mr. Adams remains a series of accounts of the clerks' fees in the common pleas and superior courts, which are now curious, as showing the rate of advance of a prospering lawyer at that day, and also the fluctuations caused by the times. They commence in 1761, and continue until Mr. Adams was drawn off from practice. An abstract of those in the inferior court, being complete, is given. The others show less variation.

		l.	*s.*	*d.*			*l.*	*s.*	*d.*
1761.	Eight entries, &c.	5	17	4	1768.	Seventy-seven do.	54	8	10
1762.	Thirty-six do.	25	13	2	1769.	One hundred and nine entries.	82	19	6
1763.	Seventy-nine do.	55	3	0	1770.	Ninety-four do.	68	8	6
1764.	Forty-three do.	29	13	10	1771.	Seventy-five do.	65	16	4
1765.	Seventy-three do.	52	9	8	1772.	Sixty-three do.	52	4	2
1766.	Sixty-two do.	42	13	4	1773.	Ninety-seven do.	67	4	3
1767.	Fifty-nine do.	47	2	2					

thoughts, is to sit down at my table, place my Diary before me, and take my pen into my hand. This apparatus takes off my attention from other objects. Pen, ink, and paper, and a sitting posture, are great helps to attention and thinking.

Took an airing in the chaise with my brother, Samuel Adams, who returned and dined with me. He says he never looked forward in his life; never planned, laid a scheme, or formed a design of laying up any thing for himself or others after him.

I told him I could not say that of myself. "If that had been true of me, you would never have seen my face." And I think this was true; I was necessitated to ponder in my youth, to consider of ways and means of raising a subsistence, food and raiment, and books, and money to pay for my education to the bar. So that I must have sunk into total contempt and obscurity, if not perished for want, if I had not planned for futurity; and it is no damage to a young man to learn the art of living early, if it is at the expense of much musing, and pondering, and anxiety.

28. Thursday. *Mr. Goldthwait.* "Do you call to-morrow and dine with us at Flax Pond, near Salem. Rowe, Davis, Brattle, and half a dozen as clever fellows as ever were born, are to dine there under the shady trees by the pond, upon fish, and bacon, and pease, &c.; and as to the Madeira, nothing can come up to it. Do you call. We 'll give a genteel dinner, and fix you off on your journey."

Rumors of ships and troops, a fleet and an army, ten regiments, and a number of line-of-battle ships, were talked of today. If an armament should come, what will be done by the people? will they oppose them?

"If, by supporting the rights of mankind, and of invincible truth, I shall contribute to save from the agonies of death one unfortunate victim of tyranny, or of ignorance equally fatal, his blessing and tears of transport will be a sufficient consolation to me for the contempt of all mankind." *Essay on Crimes and Punishments,*[1] page 42.

[1] This passage was used in the December following with much force in the introduction of the argument in defence of Captain Preston and the soldiers. His son, John Quincy Adams, said of it: —

"The writer has often heard from individuals, who had been present among the crowd of spectators at the trial, the electrical effect produced upon the jury

I have received such blessing, and enjoyed such tears of transport; and there is no greater pleasure or consolation. Journeying to Plymouth, at a tavern, I found a man who either knew me before, or by inquiring of some person then present, discovered who I was. He went out and saddled my horse and bridled him, and held the stirrup while I mounted. "Mr. Adams," says he, "as a man of liberty, I respect you; God bless you! I'll stand by you while I live, and from hence to Cape Cod you wont find ten men amiss."

A few years ago, a person arraigned for a rape at Worcester, named me to the court for his counsel. I was appointed, and the man was acquitted, but remanded in order to be tried on another indictment for an assault with intention to ravish. When he had returned to prison, he broke out, of his own accord, "God bless Mr. Adams; God bless his soul. I am not to be hanged, and I don't care what else they do to me." Here was his blessing and his transport, which gave me more pleasure when I first heard the relation, and when I have recollected it since, than any fee would have done.

This was a worthless fellow; but *nihil humanum, alienum.* His joy, which I had in some sense been instrumental in procuring, and his blessings and good wishes, occasioned very agreeable emotions in the heart.

This afternoon Mr. William Frobisher gave me a narration of his services to the Province, in introducing the manufacture of potashes and pearlashes; and of his unsuccessful petitions to the General Court for a compensation. He says he has suffered in his fortune by his labors and expenses, and has been instrumental of introducing and establishing the manufacture, and can obtain nothing; that twenty-five thousand pounds' worth of potashes have been exported from this town yearly for five years past, and more than that quantity for the last two years, as appears by the custom-house books, and Mr. Sheaff, the collector, was his informer; that he has invented a method of making potashes in much greater quantity and better quality than heretofore has been done from the same materials, without

and upon the immense and excited auditory, by the first sentence with which he opened his defence, which was the following citation from the then recently published work of Beccaria." *National Portrait Gallery*, article, *John Adams.*

any augmentation of expense; that he went to Hingham and worked with Mr. Lincoln a month, and has a certificate from him to the foregoing purpose; that his new method separates from the potash a neutral salt that is very pure, and of valuable use in medicine, &c.; and that if his method was adopted, no Russian potash would sell at any market where American was to be had. Thus projectors, ever restless.

29. Friday. Began my journey to Falmouth in Casco Bay. Baited my horse at Martin's in Lynn, where I saw T. Fletcher and his wife, &c. Dined at Goodhue's, in Salem, where I fell in company with a stranger, his name I knew not; he made a genteel appearance, was in a chair himself with a negro servant; seemed to have a general knowledge of American affairs; said he had been a merchant in London; had been at Maryland, Philadelphia, New York, &c. One year more, he said, would make Americans as quiet as lambs; they could not do without Great Britain, they could not conquer their luxury, &c. Oated my horse, and drank balm tea at Treadwell's in Ipswich, where I found Brother Porter, and chatted with him half an hour, then rode to Rowley, and lodged at Captain Jewett's Jewett "had rather the House should sit all the year round, than give up an atom of right or privilege. The Governor can't frighten the people with, &c."

30. Saturday. Arose not very early, and drank a pint of new milk, and set off; oated my horse at Newbury, rode to Clark's, at Greenland meeting-house, where I gave him hay and oats, and then set off for Newington; turned in at a gate by Colonel March's, and passed through two gates more before I came into the road that carried me to my uncle's.[1] I found the old gentleman, in his eighty-second year, as hearty and alert as ever, his son and daughter well, their children grown up, and

[1] "My father's eldest brother, Joseph Adams, minister of that town. My uncle had been a great admirer of Doctor Mather and was said to affect an imitation of his voice, pronunciation, and manner in the pulpit. His sermons, though delivered in a powerful and musical voice, consisted of texts of Scripture, quoting chapter and verse, delivered *memoriter*, and without notes. In conversation, he was vain and loquacious, though somewhat learned and entertaining." *Extract of a Letter to David Sewall*, 31 December, 1821.

Joseph Adams lived until he was ninety-three. Notices of him are found in Allen's Biographical Dictionary, and in Doctor Belknap's History of New Hampshire.

every thing strange to me. I find I had forgot the place; it is seventeen years, I presume, since I was there. My reception was friendly, cordial, and hospitable, as I could wish; took a cheerful, agreeable dinner, and then set off for York over Bloody Point Ferry, a way I never went before, and arrived at Woodbridge's half an hour after sunset.

I have had a very unsentimental journey excepting this day at dinner time; have been unfortunate enough to ride alone all the way, and have met with very few characters or adventures.

Soon after I alighted at Woodbridge's in York, Mr. Winthrop, Mr. Sewall, and Mr. Farnham, returned from an excursion they had made to Agamenticus, on a party of pleasure. It is the highest mountain in this part of the world; seen first by sailors, coming in from sea. It is in the town of York, about seven miles from the court-house. They talk much this evening of erecting a beacon upon it.

I forgot yesterday to mention, that I stopped and inquired the name of a pond in Wenham, which I found was Wenham Pond, and also the name of a remarkable little hill at the mouth of the pond, which resembles a high loaf of our country brown bread, and found that it is called Peters's Hill to this day from the famous Hugh Peters, who about the year 1640 or before preached from the top of that hillock to the people who congregated round the sides of it, without any shelter for the hearers, before any buildings were erected for public worship.[1]

By accidentally taking this new route, I have avoided Portsmouth, and my old friend the Governor of it. But I must make my compliments to him as I return. It is a duty; — he is my friend, and I am his. I should have seen enough of the pomps and vanities and ceremonies of that little world, Portsmouth, if I had gone there; but formalities and ceremonies are an abomination in my sight; — I hate them in religion, government, science, life.

July 1. Sunday. Arose early; at Paul Dudley Woodbridge's. A cloudy morning. Took a walk to the pasture, to see how my horse fared. Saw my old friend and classmate, David Sewall,[2]

[1] See Dr. Bentley's description of Salem, in *Mass. Hist. Soc. Collections*, vol. vi. p. 254.

[2] For the following account of this gentleman, the Editor is indebted to the Rev. S. Sewall, of Burlington, in Massachusetts. It will be seen by it that Mr.

walking in his garden. My little mare had provided for herself, by leaping out of a bare pasture into a neighboring lot of mowing-ground, and had filled herself with grass and water. *These are important materials for history, no doubt. My biographer will scarcely introduce my little mare and her adventures in quest of food and water. The children of the house have got a young crow, a sight I never saw before; — the head and bill are

Sewall's hesitation, hinted at in the next paragraph, was only momentary. He died a few months before the author of this Diary, with whom he kept up quite a lively correspondence until a late period:

"Hon. David Sewall, of York, was a lineal descendant of the third generation from Mr. Henry Sewall, who came to this country in 1634, aided in the settlement of Newbury, 1635, and was the common ancestor of all the Sewalls, generally speaking, in New England and Lower Canada, as was Mr. John Sewall of Newbury, his second son, of most if not all the numerous families and individuals of the name of Sewall in the State of Maine. Samuel Sewall, Esq. of York, a son of John of Newbury, was a ruling elder in the church of that town, and a gentleman of distinguished wisdom, piety, and compassion toward the poor and distressed. He died April 28, 1769, aged eighty-one; leaving seven sons, of whom David, the subject of this notice, was the fifth. He was born at York, October 7, 1735, old style; was graduated at Harvard College, 1755, and followed the profession of the law, which he practised with fidelity and reputation several years. He was appointed a justice of the peace, 1762, and register of probate, 1766. In the revolutionary contest, he cordially espoused the cause of his country, and was chosen by the people, in 1776, a member of the legislative council of this then Province of Massachusetts Bay. In 1777, he was appointed a justice of the supreme judicial court of Massachusetts, (then styled the 'superior court of judicature;') and shortly after the federal constitution went into operation, in 1789, he was nominated district judge of the United States court for Maine, an office which he accepted, and continued to sustain till 1818, when he resigned. And it has been remarked concerning him, that, during the long period of forty years and upwards that he was a judge, he never failed of attending court and discharging the duties of his high station a single term. He died October 22, 1825, when he had just entered the ninety-first year of his age. President Allen, in his American Biographical and Historical Dictionary, gives him the character of 'an honest lawyer, a learned and upright judge, a sincere patriot, and an exemplary Christian.' And an obituary notice, in the Boston Columbian Centinel of November 2, 1825, observes of him, — 'He was a member of the church from about the year 1768, and the latter part of his life one of its officers. He enjoyed an uncommon degree of health, of calmness, and serenity. He was a rare instance of a long, uniform, and steady life, and unspotted character and reputation. His religion was not ostentatious, but of a serious and practical nature, which shone forth in works of piety, charity and benevolence. Though he left no children to mourn his loss, yet many orphans and widows will remember his kindness and charities to them, and will call him blessed.'

"The esteem and profound veneration cherished for his character, where he was best known, were manifested at his funeral. On this solemn occasion, his remains were conveyed into the meeting-house in York, where a large concourse of people was assembled to pay him their last respects; and where, prayer being offered by Rev. Mr. Chandler of Eliot, an appropriate discourse was delivered by his minister, Rev. Mr. Dow, from Psalm xii. 1: 'Help, Lord; for the godly man ceaseth; for the faithful fail from among the children of men.'"

monstrous; the legs and claws are long and sprawling. But the young crow and the little mare are objects that will not interest posterity.

Landlord says, "David Sewall is not of the liberty side; the Moultons, Lymans, and Sewalls, and Sayward, are all of the prerogative side. They are afraid of their commissions; and rather than hazard them they would ruin the country. We had a fair trial of them when we met to return thanks to the ninety-two anti-rescinders;[1] none of them voted for it, though none of them but Sayward[2] and his book-keeper had courage enough to hold up his hand, when the vote was put the contrary way."

This same landlord, I find, is a high son; he has upon his sign-board, "*Entertainment for the Sons of Liberty*," under the portrait of Mr. Pitt. Thus the spirit of liberty circulates through every minute artery of the Province.

Heard Mr. Lyman all day. They have four deacons and three elders in this church. Bradbury is an elder, and Sayward is a deacon. Lyman preached from—"Which things the angels desire to look into."

Drank coffee at home with Mr. Farnham, who came in to see me; and then went to D. Sewall's, where I spent an hour with Farnham, Winthrop, Sewall, and when I came away, took a view of the comet, which was then near the north star; a large bright nucleus in the centre of a nebulous circle.

Came home and took a pipe after supper with landlord, who is a staunch, zealous son of liberty. He speaks doubtfully of the new counsellor, Gowing of Kittery; says he always runs away, till he sees how a thing will go; says he will lean to the other side; says that he (the landlord) loves peace, and should be very glad to have the matter settled upon friendly terms, without bloodshed; but he would venture his own life, and spend all he had in the world, before he would give up.

He gives a sad account of the opposition and persecution he has suffered from the tories, for his zeal and firmness against their schemes; says they, that is, the Moultons, Sewalls, and

[1] Those members of the General Court who refused to rescind the resolution of the preceding House, directing a circular letter to be sent to the several assemblies on the continent. This had given so great offence to the government at home, that it demanded some act of recantation. The vote stood ninety-two against, and seventeen for, rescinding.

[2] Jonathan Sayward was one of the seventeen rescinders.

Lymans, contrived every way to thwart, vex, and distress him, and have got a thousand pounds sterling from him, at least; but he says that Providence has seemed to frown upon them,— one running distracted, and another, &c.— and has favored him in ways that he did not foresee.

2. Monday morning. In my sulky before five o'clock, Mr. Winthrop, Farnham, and D. Sewall with me on horseback; rode through the woods, the tide being too high to go over the beach and to cross Cape Neddick River; came to Littlefield's, in Wells, a quarter before eight o'clock; stopped there and breakfasted. Afterwards, Sewall and I stopped at the door of our classmate, Hemmenway,[1] whom we found well and very friendly, complaisant, and hospitable; invited us to alight, to stop on our return and take a bed with him; and he inquired of me where I lived in Boston; said he would make it his business to come and see me, &c. Rode to Patten's, of Arundel, and Mr. Winthrop and I turned our horses into a little close, to roll and cool themselves, and feed upon white honeysuckle. Farnham and Sewall are gone forward to James Sullivan's,[2] to get dinner ready.

Stopped at James Sullivan's, at Biddeford, and drank punch; dined at Allen's, a tavern at the bridge. After dinner, Farnham, Winthrop, Sewall, Sullivan, and I, walked a quarter of a mile down the river to see one Poke, a woman at least one hundred and ten years of age, some say one hundred and fifteen. When we came to the house, nobody was at home but the old woman, and she lay in bed asleep under the window. We looked in at the window and saw an object of horror;— strong muscles withered and wrinkled to a degree that I never saw before. After some time her daughter came from a neighbor's house, and we went in. The old woman roused herself, and looked round very composedly upon us, without saying a word. The daughter told her, "here is a number of gentlemen come to see you." "Gentlemen," says the old antediluvian, "I am glad

[1] Of the Rev. Dr. Hemmenway, for a long period of time settled over this parish in Wells, a notice is given in Greenleaf's Ecclesiastical History of Maine, p. 22. Also in the Appendix, No. 2, of the same volume, is an extract from a funeral sermon preached by the Rev. Mr. Buckminster, of Portsmouth, N. H.

[2] Afterwards the Governor of Massachusetts. A brief notice of his life is inserted in the Collections of the Massachusetts Historical Society, of which he was the first President, vol. ii. p. 252.

to see them; I want them to pray for me; my prayers, I fear, are not answered; I used to think my prayers were answered, but of late I think they are not; I have been praying so long for deliverance;— Oh, living God, come in mercy! Lord Jesus, come in mercy! Sweet Christ, come in mercy! I used to have comfort in God, and set a good example; but I fear, &c."

Her mouth was full of large, ragged teeth, and her daughter says, since she was one hundred years old, she had two new double teeth come out. Her hair is white as snow, but there is a large quantity of it on her head; her arms are nothing but bones covered over with a withered, wrinkled skin and nerves; in short, any person will be convinced, from the sight of her, that she is as old as they say, at least. She told us she was born in Ireland, within a mile of Derry; came here in the reign of King William. She remembers the reign of King Charles II., James II., William and Mary; she remembers King James's wars, &c. but has got quite lost about her age. Her daughter asked her how old she was? She said, "upwards of threescore, but she could not tell."

Got into my chair, after my return from the old woman; rode with Elder Bradbury through Sir William Pepperell's woods; stopped and oated at Milliken's, and rode into Falmouth, and put up at Mr. Jonathan Webb's,[1] where I found my classmate, Charles Cushing, Mr. George Lyde, the collector here, and Mr. Johnson, and one Mr. Crocker.

8. Sunday. This week has been taken up in the hurry of the court, and I have not been able to snatch a moment to put down any thing. The softly people where I lodge, Don Webb and his wife, are the opposites of every thing great, spirited, and enterprising. His father was a dissenting parson, and a relation of mine; a zealous puritan and famous preacher. This son, however, without the least regard to his education, his connections, relations, reputation, or examination into the controversy, turns about and goes to church, merely because a handful of young, foolish fellows here took it into their heads to go. Don never was, or aimed to be, any thing at college but a silent hearer of a few rakes, and he continues to this day the same

[1] Some notice of this person is found in Mr. William Willis's recent republication of the *Journal of the Rev. Thomas Smith*, p. 164, note. Also of Mr. Lyde.

man, — rather the same softly living thing that creepeth upon the face of the earth. He attempted trade, but failed in that; now keeps school and takes boarders, and his wife longs to be genteel, to go to dances, assemblies, dinners, suppers, &c. but cannot make it out for want thereof. Such imbecility of genius, such poverty of spirit, such impotence of nerve, is often accompanied with a fribbling affectation of politeness, which is to me completely ridiculous. "Green tea, if we could but get it." "Madeira wine, if I could but get it." Collectors, genteel company, dances, late suppers, and clubs, &c. &c.

12. Thursday afternoon, 3 o'clock. Got into my désobligeant, to go home. Two or three miles out of town I overtook two men on horseback; they rode sometimes before me, then would fall behind, and seemed a little unsteady; at last one of them came up. "What is your name?" "Why; of what consequence is it what my name is?" "Why," says he, "only as we are travelling the road together, I wanted to know where you came from, and what your name was." I told him my name. "Where did you come from?" "Boston." "Where have you been?" "To Falmouth." "Upon a frolic, I suppose?" "No, upon business." "What business, pray?" "Business at Court."

Thus far I humored his impertinence. "Well now," says he, "do you want to know my name?" "Yes." "My name is Robert Jordan; I belong to Cape Elizabeth, and am now going round there. My forefathers came over here and settled a great many years ago." After a good deal more of this harmless impertinence, he turned off and left me. I baited at Milliken's, and rode through Saco woods, and then rode from Saco Bridge, through the woods, to Patten's, after night. Many sharp, steep hills, many rocks, many deep ruts, and not a footstep of man, except in the road; it was vastly disagreeable. Lodged at Patten's.

13. Friday. Arose and walked with Patten to see the neighboring fields of English grass and grain and Indian corn consuming before the worms. A long black worm crawls up the stalk of rye or grass and feeds upon the leaves. The Indian corn looked stripped to a skeleton, and that was black with the worms. I found that they prevail very much in Arundel and Wells, and so all along to Portsmouth and to Hampton.

Stopped two hours at Mr. Hemmenway's, and then rode

through the woods in excessive heat to York. Dined at Woodbridge's, who was much elated with his new license, and after dinner was treating his friends, — some of them. Spent an hour at Mr. Sewall's with Elder Bradbury, and then went to Portsmouth, crossed the ferry after nine o'clock, and put up at Tilton's, the sign of the Marquis of Rockingham. A very good house. I will call no more at Stavers's. I found very good entertainment and excellent attendance, a very convenient house, a spacious yard, good stables, and an excellent garden, full of carrots, beets, cabbages, onions, cauliflowers, &c. This Tilton's is just behind the State House.

14. Saturday. Arose at four; got ready as soon as I could, and rode out of town a few miles to breakfast. Breakfasted at Lovett's in Hampton, ten miles from Portsmouth and twelve from Newbury. Threatened with a very hot day. I hope I shall not be so overcome with heat and fatigue as I was yesterday. I fully intended to have made a long visit to Governor Wentworth upon this occasion; but he was unluckily gone to Wolfborough. So that this opportunity is lost.

August 19. Sunday. Last Friday went to the light-house with the committee of both Houses.

Mr. Royal Tyler began to pick chat with me. "Mr. Adams, have you ever read Doctor South's sermon upon the Wisdom of this World?" "No." "I'll lend it to you." "I should be much obliged." "Have you read the Fable of the Bees?" "Yes, and the Marquis of Halifax's Character of a Trimmer, and Hurd's Dialogue upon Sincerity in the Commerce of Life, and Machiavel, and Cæsar Borgia — Hard if these are not enough." *Tyler.* "The author of the Fable of the Bees understood human nature and mankind better than any man that ever lived; I can follow him as he goes along. Every man in public life ought to read that book, to make him jealous and suspicious, &c."

Yesterday he sent the book, and excellent sermons they are; concise, and nervous, and clear. Strong ebullitions of the loyal fanaticism of the times he lived in, at and after the restoration; but notwithstanding those things, there is a degree of sense and spirit and taste in them which will ever render them valuable. The sermon which Mr. Tyler recommended to my perusal is a sermon preached at Westminster Abbey, April 30, 1676, from 1 Corinthians, iii. 19: "For the wisdom of this world is foolishness with God." The Doctor undertakes to show what are those rules or principles of action, upon which the policy or wisdom in the text proceeds, and he mentions four rules or principles. 1. A man must maintain a constant, continued course of dissimulation in the whole tenor of his behavior. 2. That conscience and religion ought to lay no restraint upon men at all, when it lies opposite to the prosecution of their interest. Or, in the words of Machiavel, "That the show of religion was helpful to the politician, but the reality of it, hurtful and pernicious." 3. That a man ought to make himself, and not the public, the chief, if not the sole end of all his actions. 4. That in showing kindness or doing favors, no respect at all is to be had to friendship, gratitude, or sense of honor; but that such favors are to be done only to the rich or potent, from whom a man may receive a farther advantage, or to his enemies, from whom he may otherwise fear a mischief.

Mr. Winthrop, Mr. Adams, and myself, endeavored to recollect the old distich, —

"Gutta cavat lapidem non vi, sed sæpe cadendo."

So far we got, but neither of these gentlemen had ever heard the other part; I, who had some years ago been very familiar with it, could not recollect it; but it is, —

"Sic homo fit doctus, non vi, sed sæpe legendo."

Mr. Mason led us a jaunt over sharp rocks to the point of the island opposite to Nantasket, where, in a hideous cavern formed by a great prominent rock, he showed us the animal plant or flower, a small, spongy, muscular substance, growing fast to the rock, in figure and feeling resembling a young girl's breast, shooting out at the top of it a flower, which shrinks in and disappears upon touching the substance.

20. Monday. The first maxim of worldly wisdom, constant dissimulation, may be good or evil as it is interpreted; if it means only a constant concealment from others of such of our sentiments, actions, desires, and resolutions, as others have not a right to know, it is not only lawful, but commendable; because when these are once divulged, our enemies may avail themselves of the knowledge of them to our damage, danger, and confusion. So that some things, which ought to be com-

municated to some of our friends, that they may improve them to our profit, or honor, or pleasure, should be concealed from our enemies and from indiscreet friends, lest they should be turned to our loss, disgrace, or mortification. I am under no moral or other obligation to publish to the world, how much my expenses or my incomes amount to yearly. There are times when, and persons to whom, I am not obliged to tell what are my principles and opinions in politics or religion. There are persons whom in my heart I despise; others I abhor. Yet I am not obliged to inform the one of my contempt, nor the other of my detestation. This kind of dissimulation, which is no more than concealment, secrecy, and reserve, or in other words, prudence and discretion, is a necessary branch of wisdom, and so far from being immoral and unlawful, that it is a duty and a virtue. Yet even this must be understood with certain limitations, for there are times when the cause of religion, of government, of liberty, the interest of the present age and of posterity, render it a necessary duty for a man to make known his sentiments and intentions boldly and publicly; so that it is difficult to establish any certain rule, to determine what things a man may, and what he may not lawfully conceal, and when. But it is no doubt clear, that there are many things which may lawfully be concealed from many persons at certain times, and on the other hand, there are things, which at certain times, it becomes mean and selfish, base and wicked, to conceal from some persons.

22. Wednesday. Rode to Cambridge, in company with Colonel Severn Ayers and Mr. Hewitt, from Virginia, Mr. Bull and Mr. Trapier, from South Carolina, Messrs. Cushing, Hancock, Adams, Tom Brattle, Dr. Cooper, and William Cooper. Mr. Professor Winthrop showed us the college, the hall, chapel, philosophy-room, apparatus, library, and museum.

We all dined at Stedman's, and had a very agreeable day. The Virginia gentlemen are very full and zealous in the cause of American liberty. Colonel Ayers is an intimate friend of Mr. Patrick Henry, the first mover of the Virginia Resolves in 1765, and is himself a gentleman of great fortune, and of great figure and influence in the House of Burgesses. Both he and Mr. Hewitt were bred at the Virginia College, and appear to be men of genius and learning. Ayers informed me, that in the reign of Charles II. an act was sent over from England, with an instruction to the Governor, and he procured the Assembly to pass it, granting a duty of two shillings a hogshead upon all tobacco exported from the Colony,[1] to his Majesty forever. This duty amounts now to a revenue of five thousand pounds sterling a year, which is given, part to the Governor, part to the Judges, &c. to the amount of about four thousand pounds, and what becomes of the other one thousand is unknown. The consequence of this is, that the Governor calls an Assembly when he pleases, and that is only once in two years.

These gentlemen are all valetudinarians, and are taking the northern tour for their health.

"If I would but go to hell, for an eternal moment or so, I might be knighted."
Shakspeare.

The good of the governed is the end, and rewards and punishments are the means, of all government. The government of the supreme and all-perfect Mind, over all his intellectual creation, is by proportioning rewards to piety and virtue, and punishments to disobedience and vice. Virtue, by the constitution of nature, carries in general its own reward, and vice its own punishment, even in this world. But, as many exceptions to this rule take place upon earth, the joys of heaven are prepared, and the horrors of hell in a future state, to render the moral government of the universe perfect and complete. Human government is more or less perfect, as it approaches nearer or diverges further from an imitation of this perfect plan of divine and moral government.

In times of simplicity and innocence, ability and integrity will be the principal recommendations to the public service, and the sole title to those honors and emoluments which are in the power of the public to bestow. But when elegance, luxury, and effeminacy begin to be established, these rewards will begin to be distributed to vanity and folly; but when a government becomes totally corrupted, the system of God Almighty in the government of the world, and the rules of all good government upon earth, will be reversed, and virtue, integrity, and ability, will become the objects of the malice, hatred, and revenge of the

1 See *Chalmers's Introd. to the History of the Revolt of the American Colonies*, vol. i. p. 101.

men in power, and folly, vice, and villany will be cherished and supported. In such times you will see a Governor of a Province, for unwearied industry in his endeavors to ruin and destroy the people, whose welfare he was under every moral obligation to study and promote, knighted and ennobled.[1] You will see a "Philanthrop," for propagating as many lies and slanders against his country as ever fell from the pen of a sycophant, rewarded with the places of Solicitor-General,[2] Attorney-General, Advocate-General, and Judge of Admiralty, with six thousands a year.

You will see seventeen rescinders,[3] wretches without sense or sentiment, rewarded with commissions to be justices of peace, justices of the common pleas, and presently justices of the King's Bench. The consequence of this will be that the iron rod of power will be stretched out against the poor people in every[4] . . .

1771. January 10. Thursday. Dined at the Honorable John Erving's,[5] with Gray, Pitts, Hancock, Adams, Townsend, J. Erving, Jr., G. Erving, Boardman. We had over the nominations of Nat Hatch, to be judge of the common pleas, and Edmund Quincy, to be a justice of the quorum, and H. Gray's story of a letter from a repentant whig to him.

H. Gray. "The General Court is a good school for such conversation as this." That is, *double-entendre*, affectation of wit, pun, smut, or at least distant and delicate allusions to what may bear that name.

Gray said he could sometimes consent to a nomination, when he could not advise to it, and, says he, "I can illustrate it to you, Mr. Hancock;— Suppose a young gentleman should ask his father's consent, that he should marry such a young woman, or

1 Sir Francis Bernard.

2 Jonathan Sewall, author of certain articles in the newspapers, signed Philanthropos, defending Governor Bernard.

3 See page 243, note.

4 This article remains imperfect.

5 John Erving, and his son John Erving, Jr. were men of influence in the Province, before the Revolution. The former was for many years a member of the Council, and has already been once mentioned in this Diary. All three of the name for a while accommodated themselves to the revolutionary spirit; but, when they came to a pinch, they all ranged themselves on the side of the Crown. John Erving, the younger, received the distinction of a nomination by mandamus to the Council, was banished and proscribed. He died in England, in 1816. *Sabine.*

a young lady should ask her father's consent that she should marry such a young man. The father says, I cannot advise you to have a person of his or her character, but, if you have a desire, I wont oppose it; you shall have my consent. Now, Mr. Hancock, I know this simile will justify the distinction to a young gentleman of your genius."

A light brush happened, too, between Pitts and Gray. Pitts hinted something about the strongest side. Gray said, there were two or three of us, last May, that were midwives, I know; but you have been always of the strongest side; you have been so lucky.

February 7. Friday. Met a committee of the House, at the representatives' room,[1] to consider of a plan for a society for encouraging arts, agriculture, manufactures, and commerce, within the Province.

Such a plan may be of greater extent and duration, than at first we may imagine. It might be useful at any time. There are, in this Province, natural productions enough. Hemp, silk, and many other commodities, might be introduced here and cultivated for exportation. The mulberry tree succeeds as well in our climate and soil as in any.

12. Wednesday. At a time when the barriers against popery, erected by our ancestors, are suffered to be destroyed, to the hazard even of the Protestant religion; when the system of the civil law, which has for so many ages and centuries been withstood by the people of England, is permitted to become fashionable; when so many innovations are introduced, to the injury of our constitution of civil government, it is not surprising that the great securities of the people should be invaded, and their fundamental rights drawn into question. While the people of all the other great kingdoms in Europe have been insidiously deprived of their liberties, it is not unnatural to expect that such as are interested to introduce arbitrary government, should see with envy, detestation, and malice, the people of the British empire, by their sagacity and valor, defending theirs to the present times.

[There is nothing to distinguish the government of Great Britain from that of France or of Spain, but the part which the people are, by the constitution, appointed to take in the passing

[1] See page 235, note.

and execution of laws. Of the legislature, the people constitute one essential branch; and, while they hold this power unlimited, and exercise it frequently, as they ought, no law can be made, and continue long in force, that is inconvenient, hurtful, or disagreeable to the mass of the society. No wonder, then, that attempts are made to deprive the freeholders of America, and of the county of Middlesex, of this troublesome power, so dangerous to tyrants, and so disagreeable to all who have vanity enough to call themselves the better sort. In the administration of justice, too, the people have an important share. Juries are taken, by lot or by suffrage, from the mass of the people, and no man can be condemned of life, or limb, or property, or reputation, without the concurrence of the voice of the people. As the constitution requires that the popular branch of the legislature should have an absolute check, so as to put a peremptory negative upon every act of the government, it requires that the common people, should have as complete a control, as decisive a negative, in every judgment of a court of judicature. No wonder, then, that the same restless ambition of aspiring minds, which is endeavoring to lessen or destroy the power of the people in legislation, should attempt to lessen or destroy it in the execution of laws. The rights of juries and of elections were never attacked singly in all the English history. The same passions which have disliked one, have detested the other, and both have always been exploded, mutilated, or undermined together.

The British empire has been much alarmed, of late years, with doctrines concerning juries, their powers and duties, which have been said, in printed papers and pamphlets, to have been delivered from the highest tribunals of justice. Whether these accusations are just or not, it is certain that many persons are misguided and deluded by them to such a degree, that we often hear in conversation doctrines advanced for law, which, if true, would render juries a mere ostentation and pageantry, and the Court absolute judges of law and fact. It cannot, therefore, be an unseasonable speculation, to examine into the real powers and duties of juries, both in civil and criminal cases, and to discover the important boundary between the power of the court and that of the jury, both in points of law and of fact.

Every intelligent man will confess that cases frequently occur in which it would be very difficult for a jury to determine the question of law. Long chains of intricate conveyances, obscure, perplexed, and embarrassed clauses in writings, researches into remote antiquity for statutes, records, histories, judicial decisions, which are frequently found in foreign languages, as Latin and French, which may be all necessary to be considered, would confound a common jury, and a decision by them would be no better than a decision by lot; and, indeed, juries are so sensible of this, and of the great advantages the judges have to determine such questions, that, as the law has given them the liberty of finding the facts specially, and praying the advice of the court in the matter of law, they very seldom neglect to do it when recommended to them, or when in any doubt of the law.

But it will by no means follow from thence, that they are under any legal, or moral, or divine obligation, to find a special verdict, when they themselves are in no doubt of the law.

The oath of a juror, in England, is to determine causes "according to your evidence." In this Province, "according to law and the evidence given you." It will be readily agreed, that the words of the oath, at home, imply all that is expressed by the words of the oath here; and, whenever a general verdict is found, it assuredly determines both the fact and the law.

It was never yet disputed or doubted that a general verdict, given *under the direction of the court* in point of law, was a legal determination of the issue. Therefore, the jury have a power of deciding an issue upon a general verdict. And, if they have, is it not an absurdity to suppose that the law would oblige them to find a verdict according to the direction of the court, against their own opinion, judgment, and conscience?

It has already been admitted to be most advisable for the jury to find a special verdict, where they are in doubt of the law. But this is not often the case; a thousand cases occur in which the jury would have no doubt of the law, to one in which they would be at a loss. The general rules of law and common regulations of society, under which ordinary transactions arrange themselves, are well enough known to ordinary jurors. The great principles of the constitution are intimately known; they are sensibly felt by every Briton; it is scarcely extravagant to say they are drawn in and imbibed with the nurse's milk and first air.

Now, should the melancholy case arise that the judges should give their opinions to the jury against one of these fundamental principles, is a juror obliged to give his verdict generally, according to this direction, or even to find the fact specially, and submit the law to the court? Every man, of any feeling or conscience, will answer, no. It is not only his right, but his duty, in that case, to find the verdict according to his own best understanding, judgment, and conscience, though in direct opposition to the direction of the court. A religious case might be put, of a direction against a divine law.

The English law obliges no man to decide a cause upon oath against his own judgment, nor does it oblige any man to take any opinion upon trust, or to pin his faith on the sleeve of any mere man.

14. Thursday. Dined at Mr. Hancock's, with the members, Warren, Church, Cooper, &c. and Mr. Harrison, and spent the whole afternoon, and drank green tea, from Holland, I hope, but don't know.

15. Friday evening. Going to Mr. Pitts's, to meet the Kennebec company, — Bowdoin, Gardiner, Hallowell, and Pitts. There I shall hear philosophy and politics, in perfection, from H.; high flying, high church, high state, from G.; sedate, cool moderation, from B.; and warm, honest, frank whiggism, from P. I never spent an evening at Pitts's. What can I learn to-night? Came home, and can now answer the question; — I learned nothing. The company was agreeable enough.

[The complicated cares of my legal and political engagements, the slender diet to which I was obliged to confine myself, the air of the town of Boston, which was not favorable to me, who had been born and passed almost all my life in the country, but especially the constant obligation to speak in public, almost every day for many hours, had exhausted my health, brought on a pain in my breast, and a complaint in my lungs, which seriously threatened my life, and compelled me to throw off a great part of the load of business, both public and private, and return to my farm in the country. Early in the Spring of 1771, I removed my family to Braintree, still holding, however, an office in Boston. The air of my native spot, and the fine breezes from the sea on one side, and the rocky mountains of pine and savin on the other, together with daily rides on horseback and the amusements of agriculture, always delightful to me, soon restored my health in a considerable degree.]

April 16. Tuesday evening. Last Wednesday, my furniture was all removed to Braintree. Saturday I carried up my wife and youngest child, and spent the Sabbath there, very agreeably On the 20th or 25th of April, 1768, I removed into Boston. In the three years I have spent in that town, have received innumerable civilities from many of the inhabitants; many expressions of their good will, both of a public and private nature. Of these I have the most pleasing and grateful remembrance. I wish all the blessings of this life, and that which is to come, to the worthy people there, who deserve from mankind, in general, much better treatment than they meet with. I wish to God it was in my power to serve them, as much as it is in my inclination. But it is not; — my wishes are impotent, my endeavors fruitless and ineffectual to them, and ruinous to myself. What are to be the consequences of the step I have taken, time only can discover. Whether they shall be prosperous or adverse, my design was good, and therefore I never shall repent it.

Monday morning I returned to town, and was at my office before nine. I find that I shall spend more time in my office than ever I did. Now my family is away, I feel no inclination at all, no temptation, to be anywhere but at my office. I am in it by six in the morning, I am in it at nine at night, and I spend but a small space of time in running down to my brother's to breakfast, dinner, and tea. Yesterday, I rode to town from Braintree, before nine, attended my office till near two, then dined and went over the ferry to Cambridge. Attended the House the whole afternoon, returned and spent the whole evening in my office alone, and I spent the time much more profitably, as well as pleasantly, than I should have done at club. This evening is spending the same way. In the evening, I can be alone at my office, and nowhere else; I never could in my family.

18. Thursday. Fast day. Tuesday I staid at my office in town; yesterday, went up to Cambridge; returned at night to Boston, and to Braintree, — still, calm, happy Braintree, — at nine o'clock at night. This morning, cast my eyes out to see what my workmen had done in my absence, and rode with my wife over to Weymouth; there we are to hear young Blake — a pretty fellow.

20. Saturday. Friday morning by nine o'clock arrived at my office in Boston, and this afternoon returned to Braintree; arrived just at tea time; drank tea with my wife. Since this hour, a week ago, I have led a life active enough: have been to

Boston twice, to Cambridge twice, to Weymouth once, and attended my office, and the court too.

But I shall be no more perplexed in this manner. I shall have no journeys to make to Cambridge, no General Court to attend; but shall divide my time between Boston and Braintree, between law and husbandry; — farewell politics. Every evening I have been in town, has been spent till after nine at my office. Last evening, I read through a letter from Robert Morris, barrister at law and late secretary to the supporters of the Bill of Rights, to Sir Richard Aston, a judge of the King's Bench; a bold, free, open, elegant letter it is; annihilation would be the certain consequence of such a letter here, where the domination of our miniature infinitesimal deities far exceeds any thing in England. This mettlesome barrister gives us the best account of the unanimity of the King's Bench, that I have ever heard or read. According to him, it is not uncommon abilities, integrity and temper, as Mr. Burrow would persuade us, but sheer fear of Lord Mansfield, the Scottish chief, which produces this miracle in the moral and intellectual world; that is, of four judges agreeing perfectly in every rule, order, and judgment for fourteen years together. Four men never agreed so perfectly in sentiment for so long a time before. Four clocks never struck together a thousandth part of the time; four minds never thought, reasoned, and judged alike before for a ten thousandth part.

21. Sunday. Last night went up to Braintree, and this evening down to Boston. Called at S. Adams's, and found Mr. Otis, Colonel Warren, and Doctor Warren. Otis is steady and social and sober as ever, and more so.

22. Monday. In the morning mounted for Worcester with Pierpont, Caleb and Robert Davis, Josiah Quincy, &c.; baited the horses at Brewer's and at Colonel Buckminster's.

25. Thursday. Dined last Monday at Brigham's in Southborough, and lodged at Furnasse's in Shrewsbury; next day dined at Mr. Putnam's, in Worcester, and at same place dined on Wednesday; this day, dined at Mr. Paine's with much company. At about two o'clock this day we finished the famous cause of Cutler *vs.* Pierpont and Davis — an action of trespass for compelling the plaintiff to store his goods with the committee at Boston, and carting him, &c. We had stories

about Fort George, the Duke of York, and a warm gentleman at Cambridge, Bob Temple.

The Duke of York was in a battle at sea; a cannon ball hit a man's head, and dashed his blood and brains in the Duke's face and eyes. The Duke started and leaped quite out of the rank. The officer who commanded said "Pray, your Highness, don't be frightened." The Duke replied, "Oh sir, I am not frightened, but I wonder *what business that fellow had here with so much brains in his head.*" The warm gentleman at Cambridge was Bob Temple. A number of gentlemen at Cambridge, his friends, got into a quarrel and squabble, and somebody knowing that all had a great esteem of Temple, begged him to interpose and use his influence to make peace. At last he was persuaded, and went in among the persons; and one of the first steps he took to make peace was to give one of the persons a blow in the face with his fist.

Thus the defendants are to be laughed and storied out of large damages, no doubt. However, the jury gave none; they could not agree; eight were for defendant, four for plaintiff.[1]

May 1. Wednesday. Saturday I rode from Martin's in Northborough to Boston on horseback, and from thence to Braintree in a chaise; and when I arrived at my little retreat, I was quite overcome with fatigue. Next morning felt better, and arose early, and walked up Penn's Hill, and then round by the meadow home. After meeting in the afternoon, Mr. Tudor and I rambled up the western common and took a view of a place which I have never seen since my removal to Boston. I felt a joy, I enjoyed a pleasure, in revisiting my old haunts, and recollecting my old meditations, among the rocks and trees, which was very intense indeed. The rushing torrent, the purling stream, the gurgling rivulet, the dark thicket, the rugged ledges and precipices, are all old acquaintances of mine. The young trees, walnuts and oaks, which were pruned and trimmed by me, are grown remarkably. Nay, the pines have grown the better for lopping.

This evening at the bar meeting, I asked and obtained the unanimous consent of the bar to take Mr. Elisha Thayer of Braintree, son of Captain Ebenezer Thayer, Jr., as a clerk. How

1 The verdict ultimately obtained was for the defendants.

few years are gone since this gentleman was pleased to call me a *petty lawyer* at Major Crosby's Court![1] now is soliciting me to take his son, and complimenting, &c. me with being the first lawyer in the Province, as he did in express words, though it was but a compliment, and if sincere in him was not true, but a gross mistake; nay, what is more remarkable still, complimenting me with his seat in the House of Representatives, as he did by assuring me in words, that if I had an inclination to come from Braintree, he would not stand in my way. Such are the mistakes we are apt to make in the characters of men, and in our conjectures of their future fortune. This, however, is a wretched triumph, a poor victory, a small antagonist to defeat; and I have very few of this kind of conquests to boast of. The Governor tells of a vast number of these changes in sentiment concerning him, and will be able to tell of many more.

2. Thursday. The triumphs and exultation of Ezekiel Goldthwait and his pert pupil, Price, at the election of a Registrar of Deeds, are excessive.[2] They crow like dung-hill cocks; they are rude and disgusting. Goldthwait says he would try the chance again for twenty dollars, and he would get it by a majority of one hundred votes, even in this town. Nay more, he says if he would be representative, and would set up, he would be chosen representative before Adams. Adams the lawyer don't succeed in the interest he makes for people; he is not successful. N. B. Very true!

Price says to me, if you was to go and make interest for me to be clerk in the room of Cook, I should get it, no doubt. These are the insults that I have exposed myself to, by a very small and feeble exertion for S. Adams, to be Registrar of Deeds. Thus are the friends of the people, after such dangerous efforts, and such successful ones too, left in the lurch even by the people themselves. I have acted my sentiments with the utmost frankness at the hazard of all, and the certain loss of ten times more than it is in the power of the people to give me, for the sake of the people; and now I reap nothing but insult, ridicule,

1 See page 110.

2 On Tuesday last the Court of General Sessions of the peace for the county of Suffolk opened the votes of the freeholders of the several towns in said county for the choice of registrar of deeds and conveyances of land, and upon sorting and counting the votes, there were 1590; of which number there were for Ezekiel Goldthwait, Esq., 1123. Mr. Samuel Adams, 467. *Gazette.*

and contempt for it, even from many of the people themselves.

However, I have not hitherto regarded consequences to myself. I have very cheerfully sacrificed my interest, and my health, and ease and pleasure, in the service of the people. I have stood by their friends longer than they would stand by them. I have stood by the people much longer than they would stand by themselves. But I have learned wisdom by experience; I shall certainly become more retired and cautious; I shall certainly mind my own farm and my own office.

3. Friday. Last evening I went in to take a pipe with Brother Cranch, and there I found Zab Adams. He told me he heard that I had made two very powerful enemies in this town, and lost two very valuable clients, Treasurer Gray and Ezekiel Goldthwait; and that he heard that Gray had been to me for my account, and paid it off, and determined to have nothing more to do with me. Oh, the wretched, impotent malice! they show their teeth, they are eager to bite; but they have not strength! I despise their anger, their resentment, and their threats. But I can tell Mr. Treasurer that I have it in my power to tell the world a tale, which will infallibly unhorse him, whether I am in the House or out. If this Province knew that the public money had never been counted these twenty years, and that no bonds were given last year, nor for several years before, there would be so much uneasiness about it, that Mr. Gray would lose his election another year.[1]

It may be said that I have made enemies by being in the General Court. The Governor, Lieutenant-Governor, Gray, Goldthwait, the gentry at Cambridge, &c., are made my bitter foes. But there is nothing in this. These people were all my foes before, but they thought it for their interest to disguise it, but now they think themselves at liberty to speak it out. But there is not one of them but would have done me all the harm in his power secretly before.

This evening Mr. Otis came into my office and sat with me most of the evening; more calm, more solid, decent and cautious than he ever was, even before his late disorders. I have this week had an opportunity of returning an obligation, of

[1] This probably explains the motive of the motion made by the writer in the General Court. See page 236, note.

repaying an old debt to that gentleman, which has given me great pleasure. Mr. Otis was one of the three gentlemen, Mr. Gridley and Mr. Thacher were the other two, who introduced me to practice in this county. I have this week strongly recommended fourteen clients from Wrentham, and three or four in Boston, to him, and they have accordingly, by my persuasion, engaged him in their causes; and he has come out to court, and behaved very well. So that I have now introduced him to practice. This indulgence to my own grateful feelings was equally my duty and my pleasure.

He is a singular man. It will be amusing to observe his behavior, upon his return to active life, in the senate and at the bar, and the influence of his presence upon the public councils of this Province.[1] I was an hour with him this morning at his office; and there he was off his guard and reserve with me. I find his sentiments are not altered, and his passions are not eradicated, the fervor of his spirit is not abated, nor the irritability of his nerves lessened.

9. Thursday. From Saturday to Wednesday morning I staid at Braintree, and rode walked, rambled, and roamed. Enjoyed a serenity and satisfaction to which I have been three years a stranger.

This day, arrived Hall from London with news of the commitment of the Mayor and Mr. Alderman Oliver to the Tower by the House of Commons.

I read this morning in the English papers and the Political Register for April, all the proceedings against the printers, Thompson and Wheble, and against the Mayor and Aldermen, Wilkes and Oliver.[2] What the consequence will be of these movements, it is not easy to foresee or conjecture.[3] A struggle, a battle so serious and determined, between two such bodies as the House and the City, must produce confusion and carnage,

1 He was elected this year to the House in place of the writer, who had removed to Braintree. But it was only to show the flickering of the expiring lamp. The public career of James Otis was already run.

2 Annual Register, 1771, pp. 63 – 70.

3 The immediate consequence was the complete removal of all future restriction upon the publication of the parliamentary debates. The effect of this in changing the British constitution is yet in process of development. A brief but clear account of this struggle is given in a note to Woodfall's edition of the Letters of Junius, vol iii. p. 345.

without the most delicate management on both sides, or the most uncommon concurrence of accidents.

14. Tuesday. Yesterday came to town with my wife; a fine rain all night. Captain Bradford sent his compliments, and desired me to meet the club at his house this evening, which I did. Doctor Cooper, Mr. Lathrop, Otis, Adams, Doctor Greenleaf, William Greenleaf, Doctor Warren, Thomas Brattle, William Cooper, C. Bradford. A very pleasant evening. Otis gave us an account of a present from Doctor Cumings of Concord to Harvard College chapel, of a brass branch of candlesticks, such as Isaac Royal, Esq. gave to the Representatives' room, and that it was sent to N. Hurd's to have an inscription engraved on it. The inscription is, —

> In sacelli hujusce ornatum et splendorem
> Phosphoron hoc munus, benigne contulit
> Cumings, armiger, medicus, Concordiensis.[1]

Danforth. "The inscription was much faulted by the wits at club, and as it was to be a durable thing for the criticisms of strangers and of posterity, it was thought that it ought to be altered." Doctor Cooper mentioned an old proverb, that an ounce of mother wit is worth a pound of clergy. Mr. Otis mentioned another, which he said conveyed the same sentiment, — An ounce of prudence is worth a pound of wit. This produced a dispute, and the sense of the company was, that the word wit in the second proverb meant, the faculty of suddenly raising pleasant pictures in the fancy; but that the phrase, mother wit, in the first proverb, meant natural parts, and clergy-acquired learning — book learning. Doctor Cooper quoted another proverb from his Negro Glasgow, — A mouse can build an house without trouble. And then told us another instance of Glasgow's intellect, of which I had before thought him entirely destitute. The Doctor was speaking to Glasgow about Adam's Fall, and the introduction of natural and moral evil into the world, and Glasgow said, they had in his country a different account of this matter. The tradition was, that a dog and a toad were to run a race, and if the dog reached the goal first, the world was to

[1] This article was destroyed by fire a few years ago, with many other curious relics belonging to the University, that had been temporarily stored in a building in Cambridge.

continue innocent and happy; but if the toad should outstrip the dog, the world was to become sinful and miserable. Everybody thought there could be no danger; but in the midst of the career the dog found a bone by the way, and stopped to gnaw it; and while he was interrupted by his bone, the toad, constant in his malevolence, hopped on, reached the mark, and spoiled the world.

15. Wednesday. Argued before the Sessions the question, whether the Court had authority by law to make an allowance of wages and expenses, above the fees established by law, to the jurors who tried Captain Preston and the soldiers. The two Quincys, Otis, and Adams, argued. Otis is the same man he used to be.

> "He spares not friend nor foe, but calls to mind,
> Like doomsday, all the faults of all mankind."

He will certainly soon relapse into his former condition. He trembles; his nerves are irritable; he cannot bear fatigue. "Brother A. has argued so prodigiously like a representative, that I can't help considering him as the ghost of one, &c."

22. Wednesday. At Plymouth; put up at Witherell's, near the county-house; lodged with Mr. Angier, where we had a chamber wholly to ourselves,—very still and retired, very serene and happy. Mrs. Howland and her family, I hear, are very much grieved and hurt and concerned about my passing by their house. But my health is my excuse for all my removals. I am not strong enough to bear the smoke and dirt and noise of Howland's, and their late hours at night.

Heard of the election of Colonel Edson, at Bridgewater, and Colonel Gilbert, of Freetown,[1] which proves to me that the system of the Province will be different this year from what it was the last. The House was very near equally divided the whole of the last session, and these two members will be able to make a balance in favor of timidity, artifice, and trimming. How

[1] These were of the government side, but the general remark, which follows, is hardly just, if we may credit Hutchinson, who says of this period:

"This year, particularly, *except in two or three instances*, the new members in the House were in opposition. Several gentlemen remained in the House, who, in common times, would have had great weight on the other side; but now, the great superiority in number against them caused them to despair of success from their exertions, and in most cases they were inactive." Vol. iii. p. 338.

easily the people change, and give up their friends and their interest!

29. Wednesday. General election. Went to Boston and to Cambridge, and returned to Boston at night.

30. Thursday. Mounted my horse for Connecticut.* Stopped and chatted an hour with Tom Crafts, who is very low with rheumatism and an hectic, but the same honest, good humored man as ever. Stopped again at little Cambridge, at the house by the meeting-house, and gave my horse hay and oats at Mr. Jackson's. Rode alone. My mind has been running chiefly upon my farm and its inhabitants and furniture, my horses, oxen, cows, swine, walls, fences, &c. I have, in several late rambles, very particularly traced and pursued every swamp and spring upon the north side of Penn's hill, from its source to its outlet; and I think if I owned the whole of that side of the hill, I could make great improvements upon it by means of springs, and descents, and falls of water.

31. Friday. Lodged at Mr. Putnam's, in Worcester.

June 1. Saturday. Spent the day at Worcester, in riding about with Mr. Putnam to see his farm. He does what he pleases with meadows and rivers of water; he carries round the streams wherever he pleases.

Took one ride up to Bogachoag Hill one way, and another up the lane by Doolittle's shop; and I found that great alterations have been made, and many improvements, in thirteen years,—for it is so long since I was in either of those parts of the town of Worcester before. In the latter road I missed many objects of my former acquaintance, many shady thickets and gloomy grottos, where I have sat by the hour together to ruminate and listen to the falls of water.

This pleasure of revisiting an old haunt is very great. Mr. Putnam says he was lately at Danvers, and visited the very path where he used to drive the cows to pasture when he was seven years old. It gave him a strange feeling; it made him feel young—seven years old.

* [I was advised to take a journey to the Stafford Springs, in Connecticut, then in as much vogue as any mineral springs have been in since. I spent a few days in drinking the waters, and made an excursion through Somers and Windsor down to Hartford, and the journey was of use to me, whether the waters were or not.]

I visited Dr. Willard. I see little alteration in him or his wife in sixteen years. His sons are grown up; Sam, the eldest, who has been to college, is settled at Uxbridge, in the practice of physic; Levi is at home.

I met Colonel Gardner Chandler. He said he heard I was in quest of health; if I found more than I wanted, he begged a little. No poor creature ever suffered more for want of it. Thus he is the same man. Sixteen years I have been a witness to his continual complaints of weakness and want of health.

2. Sunday. Heard Mr. Wheeler, late minister of Harvard, at Worcester all day. Here I saw many faces much altered, and many others not at all, since I first knew this place, which is now sixteen years. Here I saw many young gentlemen who were my scholars and pupils when I kept school here; — John Chandler, Esq. of Petersham, Rufus Chandler, the lawyer,[1] Dr. William Paine, who now studies physic with Dr. Holyoke of Salem, Nat. Chandler, who studies law with Mr. Putnam, and Dr. Thad. Maccarty, who is now in the practice of physic at Dudley; most of these began to learn Latin with me.

Mem. Gardner Chandler, yesterday, said that many regulations were wanting, but the town of Boston more than any thing; and that, after election, everybody used to be inquiring who were chosen counsellors, — very anxious and inquisitive to know; but now, nobody asked any thing about it, nobody cared any thing about it. And Putnam said, yesterday, he did not like the town of Boston, he did not like their manners, &c. I record these curious speeches, because they are characteristic of persons and of the age.

Drank tea at Mr. Putnam's, with Mr. Paine, Mrs. Paine, Dr. Holyoke's lady, and Dr. Billy Paine. The Doctor is a very civil, agreeable, and sensible young gentleman. Went, in the evening, over to G. Chandler's, and chatted with him an hour. He is very bitter against the town of Boston. "I hate them, from my soul," says he. "Great patriots! were for non-importation, while their old rags lasted; and, as soon as they were sold at enormous prices, they were for importing; no more to be heard about manufactures, and now, there is a greater flood of

[1] Interesting notices of both these Chandlers, as well as of Mr. Putnam, will be found in *Mr. Willard's Address to the Bar of Worcester County*, in 1829, pp. 58 – 61, 73, 75. They all took the side of government.

goods than ever were known; and as to tea, those who were most strenuous against it are the only persons who have any to sell."

John Chandler, Esq. of Petersham, came into P.'s in the evening, from Boston, yesterday, and gave us an account of Mr. Otis's conversion to toryism.[1] Adams was going on in the old road, and Otis started up and said, they had gone far enough in that way; the Governor had an undoubted right to carry the court where he pleased, and moved for a committee to represent the inconveniences of sitting there, and for an address to the Governor. He was a good man; the ministers said so, the justices said so, and it must be so; and moved to go on with business; and the House voted every thing he moved for. Boston people say he is distracted, &c.

3. Monday. Oated in Spencer; turned my horse to grass at Wolcott's, in Brookfield. I ride alone; I find no amusement, no conversation, and have nothing to think about; but my office and farm frequently steal into my mind, and seem to demand my return; they must both suffer for want of my presence.

The road to Stafford turns off by Brookfield meeting-house into Brimfield, in the county of Hampshire. Dined at Cheney's, of Western, in the county of Hampshire. An old man came in, and after some conversation with the old landlady, she asked him if he was not the man who called here about seventeen years ago, and was intrusted with a gill of West India rum? He said, "Yes; Han't you had your money?" "No." "Well, I sent it by a Brimfield man, within a fortnight after. I'll at him about it; I'm desperate glad you mentioned it. I had the rum; I was driving down a drove of hogs; my two boys were with me,—I lost them both, in the year 1759, one at Crown Point, and one about eighteen miles from Albany;—they drinked the rum with me. I am glad you mentioned it; the money is justly your due. I'll pay you now; how much is it?" "Two shillings and four pence." "But," says I, interposing for curiosity, "that will hardly do justice; for the interest is as much as the principal; the whole debt is four shillings and eight pence." "I'm a poor man," says he, "landlady wont ask me

[1] How much hope Governor Hutchinson built upon this speech of James Otis, is visible in his History, vol. iii. p. 339; but Otis at this time had ceased to be a responsible agent.

interest." I was much amused with the old woman's quick and tenacious memory, and with the old man's honesty. But it seems to me that the whole anecdote shows that these are but twopenny people.

This honest man, whose name is Frost, hearing that I was bound to the Springs, and unacquainted with the way, very obligingly waited for me, to show me the way as far as he went, which was several miles. His father came from Billerica to Springfield. Mrs. Cheney says her husband came from Roxbury. I found that Frost was a great partisan of the mineral spring. He said he had been weakly these thirty years, and the spring had done him more good in a few days than all the doctors had done in thirty years; and he went on and told of a great number of marvellous instances of cure wrought by washing and drinking, while he was there.

Oated at Silas Hodges's, in Brimfield, near the Baptist meeting-house. There I find they have not so much faith in the spring. Lodged at Colburn's, the first house in Stafford. There I found one David Orcutt, who came from Bridgewater thirty years ago, a relation of the Orcutts in Weymouth. He, I find, is also a great advocate for the spring. He was miserable many years with rheumatism, &c. and, by means of the spring, was now a comfortable man. The landlord came with his father, thirty years ago, from Roxbury. He has a farm of two hundred acres of land, one hundred under improvement; keeps near thirty head of neat cattle, three horses, fifty sheep, and yet offers to sell me his place for five hundred pounds, lawful money.

4. Tuesday. Rode over to the spring. One Child had built a small house within a few yards of the spring, and there some of the lame and infirm people keep. The spring rises at the foot of a steep, high hill, between a cluster of rocks, very near the side of a river. The water is very clear, limpid, and transparent; the rocks and stones and earth, at the bottom, are tinged with a reddish yellow color, and so is the little wooden gutter, that is placed at the mouth of the spring to carry the water off; indeed, the water communicates that color, which resembles that of the rust of iron, to whatever object it washes. Mrs. Child furnished me with a glass mug broken to pieces and puttied together again, and with that I drank pretty plentifully of the water; it has the taste of fair water with an infusion of some

preparation of steel in it, which I have taken heretofore, *Sal Martis*, somewhat like copperas. They have built a shed over a little reservoir made of wood, about three feet deep, and into that have conveyed the water from the spring; and there people bathe, wash, and plunge, for which Child has eight pence a time. I plunged in twice, but the second time was superfluous, and did me more hurt than good; it is very cold indeed.

Mrs. Child directed me to one Green's, about half a mile from the spring, as a place to lodge at; and when I got there I found it was my old acquaintance, John Green, who lived with Colonel Chandler, at Worcester, while I lived with Putnam.

The place where I now sit, in the chamber in Green's house, has the command of a great view. This is a mountainous country; this house stands upon very high land, and here is a fine, spacious road laid out very wide, and of great length, and quite straight, which lies right before me now, with the meeting-house in the middle of it, more than half a mile off.

Colonel Abijah Willard and Sam Ward and another bought of William Browne, of Salem or Virginia, seven thousand acres of land in this town, and they are about erecting iron mills here, furnaces, &c. and there is a talk of making this a shire town, &c. Unimproved land is to be bought in this town, in great plenty, for six shillings an acre. At night, Green called to his wife, "come, put by your work and come in;" and takes his family Bible and reads a chapter, and then makes a long prayer of half an hour, and we all go to bed.

5. Wednesday. Rode to the spring; drank and plunged; dipped but once; sky cloudy. Activity and industry, care and economy, are not the characteristics of this family. Green was to set out upon a journey to Providence to-day, to get stores, &c. and stock for trade; but he lounged and loitered away hour after hour, till nine o'clock, before he mounted. The cow, whose teats strut with milk, is unmilked till nine o'clock. My horse would stand by the head hour after hour if I did not put him out myself, though I call upon the father and the sons to put him out.

Looking into a little closet in my chamber, this morning, I found a pretty collection of books;—The Preceptor, Douglass's History, Paradise Lost, the Musical Miscellany in two volumes, the Life of the Czar Peter the Great, &c. I laid hold of the second volume of the Preceptor, and began to read the Elements of

Logic, and considered the fourfold division of the subject,— simple apprehension or perception, judgment or intuition, reasoning, and method. This little compendium of logic I admired at college; I read it over and over; I recommended it to others, particularly to my chum, David Wyer, and I took the pains to read a great part of it to him and with him. By simple apprehension or perception, we get ideas; by sensation and by reflection, the ideas we get are simple, &c. Mem. I hope I shall not forget to purchase these Preceptors, and to make my sons transcribe this treatise on logic entirely with their own hands, in fair characters, as soon as they can write, in order to imprint it on their memories. Nor would it hurt my daughter to do the same; I have a great opinion of the exercise of transcribing in youth.

About eleven o'clock arrived Dr. McKinstry of Taunton, and spoke for lodgings for himself and Co. Barrell and his wife. "It is not you, is it?" says he. "Persons in your way are subject to a certain weak muscle and lax fibre, which occasions glooms to plague you; but the spring will brace you." I joy and rejoice at his arrival. I shall have opportunity to examine him about this mineral, medicinal water.

I have spent this day in sauntering about down in the pasture to see my horse, and over the fields in the neighborhood; took my horse after noon and rode away east, a rugged, rocky road, to take view of the lands about the town, and went to the spring. Thirty people have been there to-day, they say;—the halt, the lame, the vapory, hypochondriac, scrofulous, &c. all resort here. Met Dr. McKinstry at the spring. We mounted our horses together, and turned away the western road toward Somers, to see the improvements that I saw yesterday from the mountain by the spring, and returned to our lodgings. The Doctor, I find, is a very learned man. He said that the Roman empire came to its destruction as soon as the people got set against the nobles and commons, as they are now in England, and they went on quarrelling till one Brutus carried all before him, and enslaved 'em all. "Cæsar, you mean, Doctor." "No, I think it was Brutus, wan't it?" Thus we see the Doctor is very book-learned. And when we were drinking tea, I said, five hundred years hence there would be a great number of empires in America, independent of Europe and of each other. "Oh," says he, "I have no idea that the world will stand so long, — not half five hundred years. The world is to conform to the Jewish calculations; — every seventh day was to be a day of rest, every seventh year was to be a jubilee, and the seventh thousand years will be a thousand years of rest and jubilee; no wars, no fightings, and there is but about two hundred and thirty wanting to complete the six thousand years; till that time, there will be more furious wars than ever." Thus I find I shall have in the Doctor a fund of entertainment. He is superficial enough, and conceited enough, and enthusiastical enough to entertain.

6. Thursday. Spent this fine day in rambling on horseback and on foot with Dr. McKinstry, east and west, north and south; went with him twice to the spring and drank freely of the waters, and rode about to hire a horse to carry me to Springfield and Northampton; at last obtained one. The Doctor is alert and cheerful, and obliging and agreeable.

In the afternoon, Colburn Barrell and his wife and daughter, came and took lodgings at our house; drank tea and spent the evening with them. When the Doctor took his hat to go out to a neighbor's to lodge, Colburn sprung out of his chair and went up to the Doctor, took him by the hand, and kissed him before all the company in the room. This is sandemanianism.

Rode this day beyond the meeting-house, and found my old acquaintance the parson, John Willard, at his own door. He lives in a little, mean-looking hut. How many of my contemporaries at college, worthy men, live in poor and low circumstances! Few of them have so much of this world's goods as have fallen even to my share, though some of them have much more. Let me enjoy, then, what I have, and be grateful.

Mr. Barrell confirms the account of Mr. Otis's behavior in the House, which Mr. Chandler gave me at Worcester, but says he cannot reconcile this to Mr. Otis's whole conduct for a course of years.

7. Friday. Went to the spring with the Doctor, and drank a glass and a half, that is, a gill and a half. My horse was brought very early; my own mare I shall leave in a very fine pasture, with oats for her twice a day, that she may rest and recruit.

Rode to Somers, over a very high, large mountain, which the people here call Chesnut hill. It is five miles over, very bad road, very high land; it is one of a range of great mountains which runs north and south parallel with Connecticut River, about ten miles to the east of it, as another similar range runs on the Western side of it. There is a mountain which they call the bald mountain, which you pass by as you cross Chesnut hill, much higher, from whence you can see the great river and many of the great towns upon it, as they say. Dined at Kibby's; met people going over to the spring.

In Kibby's bar-room, in a little shelf within the bar, I espied two books. I asked what they were. He said Every Man his own Lawyer, and Gilbert's Law of Evidence. Upon this I asked some questions of the people there, and they told me that Kibby was a sort of a lawyer among them; that he pleaded some of their home cases before justices and arbitrators, &c. Upon this I told Kibby to purchase a copy of Blackstone's Commentaries. Rode from Kibby's over to Enfield, which lies upon Connecticut River; oated and drank tea at Pease's; — a smart house and landlord truly; well dressed, with his ruffles, &c. and upon inquiry I found he was the great man of the town; their representative, &c. as well as tavern-keeper, and just returned from the General Assembly at Hartford. Somers and Enfield are upon a level; a fine champaign country. Suffield lies over the river on the west side of it. Rode along the great river to Windsor, and put up at Bissell's, that is, in East Windsor; for the town of Windsor, it seems, lies on the west side of the river.

The people in this part of Connecticut make potash, and raise a great number of colts, which they send to the West Indies and barter away for rum, &c. They trade with Boston and New York, but most to New York. They say there is a much greater demand for flax-seed, of which they raise a great deal, at New York than there is at Boston, and they get a better price for it. Kibby, at Somers, keeps a shop, and sells West India goods and English trinkets; keeps a tavern and pettifogs it.

At Enfield, you come into the great road upon Connecticut River, which runs back to Springfield, Deerfield, Northampton, &c. northward, and down to Windsor and Hartford, Wethersfield, and Middletown southward. The soil, as far as I have ridden upon the river, if I may judge by the road, is dry and sandy; but the road is three quarters of a mile from the river, and the interval land lies between.

I begin to grow weary of this idle, romantic jaunt; I believe it would have been as well to have staid in my own country and amused myself with my farm, and rode to Boston every day. I shall not suddenly take such a ramble again merely for my health. I want to see my wife, my children, my farm, my horse, oxen, cows, walls, fences, workmen, office, books, and clerks; I want to hear the news and politics of the day. But here I am at Bissell's, in Windsor, hearing my landlord read a chapter in the kitchen, and go to prayers with his family in the genuine tone of a puritan.

8. Saturday. Bissell says there are settlements upon this river for three hundred miles, that is, from Seabrook, where it discharges itself. The river, in the spring, when the snow melts, swells prodigiously, and brings down the washings of mountains and old swamps, rotten wood and leaves, &c. to enrich the interval lands upon its banks.

At eleven o'clock, arrived at Wright's, in Wethersfield. I have spent this morning in riding through paradise; my eyes never beheld so fine a country; from Bissell's, in Windsor, to Hartford ferry, eight miles, is one continued street, houses all along, and a vast prospect of level country on each hand; the lands very rich, and the husbandry pretty good. The town of Hartford is not very compact; there are some very handsome and large houses, some of brick. The State House is pretty large, and looks well. I stopped only to oat my horse and get my head and face shaved, and then rode to Wethersfield, four miles, on the west side of the river. Here is the finest ride in America, I believe; nothing can exceed the beauty and fertility of the country. The lands upon the river, the flat lowlands, are loaded with rich, noble crops of grass and grain and corn. Wright says some of their lands will yield two crops of English grass, and two tons and a half at each crop, and plenty of after-feed besides; but these must be nicely managed and largely dunged. They have, in Wethersfield, a large brick meeting-house, Lockwood the minister. A gentleman came in and told me that there was not such another street in America, as this at Wethersfield, excepting one at Hadley; and that Mr. Ingersol, the stamp-master, told him he had never seen, in Philadelphia nor in England, any place equal to Hartford and Wethersfield.

Dined at the widow Griswold's in Wethersfield, about three

miles from Wright's. The road and country are equally pleasant all the way. Sat down to table with the old woman and another woman, and a dirty, long, gray-bearded carpenter who was at work for landlady, and might be smelled from one room to the other; so that these republicans are not very decent or neat. Landlady and her housewright, very, very chatty about Boston, Providence, Newport, Martha's Vineyard, and Nantucket. Landlady says the Deputy-Governor calls here, and always has some comical story to tell her. He asked her the other day to come down and see his wife make cheese. He has twenty-two cows, and his women make cheese in the forenoon, and then dress up and go out, or receive company at home.

Rode to Middletown and put up, for the Sabbath, at Shaler's, near the court-house. Middletown, I think, is the most beautiful town of all. When I first came into the town, which was upon the top of a hill, there opened before me the most beautiful prospect of the river, and the intervals and improvements on each side of it, and the mountains, at about ten miles distance, both on the east and west side of the river, and of the main body of the town at a distance. I went down this hill and into a great gate which led me to the very banks of the river; and on the right hand is a fine level track of interval land, as rich as the soil of Egypt. The lots are divided by no fence, but here are strips running back at right angles from the river; — on one is Indian corn; on another, parallel to it, is rye; on another, barley; on another, flax; on another, a rich burden of clover and other English grasses. And, after riding in this enchanting meadow for some time, you come to another gate which lets you into the main body of the town, which is ornamented, as is the meadow I just mentioned, with fine rows of trees, and appears to me as populous, as compact, and as polite as Hartford. The air all along from Somers to Middletown appears to me to be very clear, dry, and elastic, and therefore, if I were to plan another journey for my health, I would go from Boston to Lancaster and Lunenburg, thence to No. 4,[1] and thence down to Northampton, Deerfield, Hadley, Springfield, then to Enfield, and along the river down to Seabrook, and from thence over to Rhode Island, and from thence to Braintree. And here I might possibly, that is, at No. 4, look up some land to purchase for my benefit or the ben-

[1] Now Charlestown, N. H.

efit of my children. But I hope I shall not take another journey merely for my health very soon; I feel sometimes sick of this; I feel guilty; I feel as if I ought not to saunter, and loiter, and trifle away this time; I feel as if I ought to be employed for the benefit of my fellow men in some way or other. In all this ramble from Stafford I have met with nobody that I knew excepting Jo. Trumbull, who, with his father, the Governor, was crossing the ferry for the east side when I was for the west.

Bespoke entertainment for the Sabbath at Shaler's, and drank tea. She brought us in the finest and sweetest of wheat bread, and butter as yellow as gold, and fine radishes, very good tea and sugar. I regaled without reserve. But my wife is one hundred and fifty miles from me, at least, and I am not yet homeward bound. I wish Connecticut River flowed through Braintree. But the barren, rocky mountains of Braintree are as great a contrast as can be conceived to the level, smooth, fertile plains of this country; yet Braintree pleases me more; I long to be foul of Deacon Belcher's orchard; I am impatient to begin my canal and bank, to convey the water all round by the road and the house; I must make a pool in the road by the corner of my land, at the yard in front of the house for the cool spring water to come into the road there, that the cattle and hogs and ducks may regale themselves there.

Looking into the almanac, I am startled. Supreme Court, Ipswich, is the 18th day of June; I thought it a week later, 25th; so that I have only next week to go home, one hundred and fifty miles; I must improve every moment. It is twenty-five miles a day if I ride every day next week.

9. Sunday. Feel a little discomposed this morning; rested but poorly last night, anxious about my return, fearful of very hot or rainy weather; I have before me an uncomfortable journey to Casco Bay, little short of three hundred miles. Looking into a little bedroom in this house, Shaler's, I found a few books, the Musical Miscellany, Johnson's Dictionary, the Farmer's Letters, and the ninth volume of Dr. Clarke's Sermons. This last I took for my Sabbath-day book, and read the sermon on the fundamentals of Christianity, which he says are the doctrines concerning the being and providence of God, the necessity of repentance and obedience to His commands, the certainty of a life to come, a resurrection from the dead, and a future judgment.

Read also another sermon on the reward of justice. "There is," says the Doctor, "a duty of justice towards the public. There is incumbent upon men the very same obligation not to wrong the community as there is not to violate any private man's right, or defraud any particular person of his property. The only reason why men are not always sufficiently sensible of this, so that many who are very just in their dealings between man and man will yet be very fraudulent or rapacious with regard to the public, is because in this latter case it is not so obviously and immediately apparent upon whom the injury falls as it is in the case of private wrongs. But so long as the injury is clear and certain, the uncertainty of the persons upon whom the injury falls in particular, or the number of the persons among whom the damage may chance to be divided, alters not at all the nature of the crime itself."

Went to meeting in the morning, and tumbled into the first pew I could find. Heard a pretty sensible Yalensian Connecticutensian preacher. At meeting I first saw Dr. Eliot Rawson, an old school-fellow; he invited me to dine. His house is handsome without, but neither clean nor elegant within, in furniture or any thing else. His wife is such another old puritan as his cousin, Peter Adams's wife at Braintree. His children are dirty and ill-governed. He first took me into his physic room and showed me a number of curiosities which he has collected in the course of his practice. His dining-room is crowded with a bed and a cradle, &c. &c. We had a picked up dinner. Went to meeting with him in the afternoon, and heard the finest singing that ever I heard in my life; the front and side galleries were crowded with rows of lads and lasses, who performed all their parts in the utmost perfection. I thought I was wrapped up; a row of women all standing up and playing their parts with perfect skill and judgment, added a sweetness and sprightliness to the whole which absolutely charmed me.

The more I see of this town the more I admire it. I regret extremely that I can't pursue my tour to New Haven.

The Doctor thinks Hancock vain; told a story; — "I was at school with him, and then upon a level with him; my father was richer than his. But I was not long since at his store, and said to Mr. Glover, whom I knew, 'This I think is Mr. Hancock.' Mr. Hancock just asked my name and nothing more; it was such a piece of vanity! There is not the meanest creature that comes from your way, but I take notice of him, and I ought. What though I am worth a little more than they? I am glad of it, and that I have it, that I may give them some of it." I told the Doctor that Mr. Hancock must have had something upon his mind, that he was far from being arrogant, &c.

Drank tea with landlady and her son, Mr. Shaler, in pretty western room; but they are not very sociable. In short, I have been most miserably destitute of conversation here. The people here all trade to New York, and have very little connection with Boston. After tea went over to the Doctor's and found him very social and very learned. We talked much about history, &c. He says that Boston lost the trade of this colony by the severe laws against their old tenor; but they may easily regain the trade; for the people here are much disgusted with New York, for their defection from the non-importation agreement, and for some frauds and unfair practices in trade. He says they have found out that New York merchants have wrote home to the manufacturers in England to make their goods narrower and of a meaner fabric, that they might sell cheaper and undersell Boston.

Landlady has an only son, Nat. Shaler, and she is very fond and very proud of him. He lived with a merchant; is now twenty-five or twenty-six, and contents himself still to keep that merchant's books, without any inclination to set up for himself; is a great proficient in music, plays upon the flute, fife, harpsichord, spinet, &c.; associates with the young and the gay, and is a very fine Connecticut young gentleman. Oh, the misery, the misfortune, the ruin of being an only son! I thank my God that I was not, and I devoutly pray that none of mine may ever be!

10. Monday. Took my departure from Middletown homewards the same way I went down; very hot; oated at Hartford, and reached Bissell's of Windsor, twenty-three miles, before dinner, just as they had got their Indian pudding and their pork and greens upon the table, one quarter after twelve. After dinner attempted to cut off an angle by striking over by Goshen, that is, Ellington, to Kibby's at Somers, but lost my way, and got bewildered among woods and cross paths, and after riding ten miles to no purpose, returned to Bissell's, and took the old

road to Enfield; excessive hot; lodged at Pease's, but passed a very restless, uncomfortable night; overcome with fatigue and inflamed with heat, I could not sleep, and my meditations on my pillow were unhappy.

11. Tuesday. Rode to Kibby's at Somers, but got caught in the rain; very heavy, plentiful, showers; I was much wet. Thus I have hitherto had not very good luck upon my homeward bound voyage. Dined at Kibby's, and then rode over the mountain to Stafford; went to the Spring and drank of the waters with a gentleman from New Jersey, who was there with a servant. Dr. McKinstry was gone to Brookfield to accompany Mr. Barrell so far in his way home.

12. Wednesday. Set out upon my return home. Oated at Warrener's in Brimfield; caught in a cold rain; obliged to stop at Cheney's in Western, in order to dine; landlord very sick of a pleurisy. While I was at Cheney's five chaises went by: Jonathan Amory and wife, Deacon Newhall and wife, Ned Paine and wife, and sister, and servants, &c. Oated at Spencer; drank tea and put up at Serjeant's in Leicester; a very good house, neat, and clean, and convenient, &c.

I have had a naked, barren journey; my brains have been as barren the whole time as a sandy plain or a gravelly knoll; my soul has been starved. Came off just when company began to collect. This week and the next would have brought together a curious collection of characters from all parts of New England, and some, perhaps, from the southern Provinces, and some from the West Indies.

13. Thursday. Remarkable! the change of thoughts, and feelings, and reasonings, which are occasioned by a change of objects; a man is known by his company, and evil communications corrupt good manners. "Man is a social creature, and his passions, his feelings, his imaginations are contagious." We receive a tincture of the character of those we converse with.

Stopped at Mr. Putnam's, and at the court-house. Went in and bowed to the court and shook hands with the bar; said how d'ye, and came off. Dined at Colonel Williams's; drank tea at Munn's with Dr. Cooper and his lady, Captain Jonathan Freeman and his lady, and Mr. Nat. Barrett and his lady, who were upon their return from a tour to Lancaster. Rode this day from Worcester to Munn's, in company with one

Green, of Leicester, who was very social and good company,—an honest, clever man. By him I learn that Thomas Faxon, of Braintree, has removed with his family to Leicester, and hired a house near the meeting-house. And I met Joseph Crane, to-day, in Marlborough, going to Rutland. He is about removing his family there. But I find that people in Rutland and Leicester and Worcester, &c. are more disposed to emigrate still further into the wilderness, than the inhabitants of the old towns.

I hear much, to-day and yesterday, of the harmony prevailing between the Governor and the House. Cushing is unanimously Commissary, not negatived, and Goldthwait is Truckmaster. "Behold how good and pleasant it is for brethren to dwell together in unity." It seems to be forgotten entirely by what means Hutchinson procured the government; by his friendship for Bernard, and by supporting and countenancing all Bernard's measures, and the commissioners, and army, and navy, and revenue, and every other thing we complain of.

I read to-day an address from the convention of ministers, and from the clergy in the northern part of the county of Hampshire, and from the town of Almsbury, all conceived in very high terms of respect and confidence and affection. Posterity will scarcely find it possible to form a just idea of this gentleman's character; but if this wretched journal should ever be read by my own family, let them know that there was upon the scene of action with Mr. Hutchinson, one determined enemy to those principles and that political system to which alone he owes his own and his family's late advancement; one who thinks that his character and conduct have been the cause of laying a foundation for perpetual discontent and uneasiness between Britain and the colonies; of perpetual struggles of one party for wealth and power at the expense of the liberties of this country, and of perpetual contention and opposition in the other party to preserve them, and that this contention will never be fully terminated, but by wars and confusions and carnage. Cæsar, by destroying the Roman republic, made himself perpetual dictator. Hutchinson, by countenancing and supporting a system of corruption and all tyranny, has made himself Governor, and by the mad idolatry of the people, always the surest instruments of their own servitude, laid prostrate at the feet of both. With great anxiety and hazard, with continual application to business, with loss of health, reputation, profit, and as fair prospects and opportunities of advancement as others who have greedily embraced them, I have, for ten years together, invariably opposed this system and its fautors. It has prevailed, in some measure, and the people are now worshipping the authors and abettors of it, and despising, insulting, and abusing the opposers of it. Edward and Alfred—

> "Closed their long glories with a sigh, to find
> Th' unwilling gratitude of base mankind."

As I came over Sudbury causey, I saw a chaplain of one of the King's ships fishing in the river;—a thick, fat man, with rosy cheeks and black eyes. At night he came in with his fish. I was in the yard, and he spoke to me and told me the news. "The Governor gave a very elegant entertainment to the gentlemen of the army and navy and revenue, and Mrs. Gambier, in the evening, a very elegant ball; as elegant a cold collation as, perhaps, you ever see; all in figures, &c. &c. &c."

Read this day's paper. The melodious harmony, the perfect concords, the entire confidence and affection that seem to be restored, greatly surprise me. Will it be lasting?[1] I believe there is no man in so curious a situation as I am;—I am, for what I can see, quite left alone in the world.

17. Monday. Set out upon the eastern circuit. Stopped at Boston, at my office, and nowhere else. Came over Charlestown ferry and Penny ferry, and dined at Kettel's, in Malden, by the meeting-house. Kettel is a deputy sheriff; the meeting-house is Mr. J. Thacher's.

I mounted my horse and rode to Boston, in a cloth coat and waistcoat, but was much pinched with a cold, raw, harsh, north-east wind. At Boston, I put on a thick flannel shirt, and that made me comfortable, and no more; so cold am I, or so cold is the weather,—17th June.

Overtook Judge Cushing in his old curricle and two lean horses, and Dick, his negro, at his right hand, driving the curricle.

[1] It was not lasting. The difference which took place at this time, between John Hancock and Samuel Adams, inspired Governor Hutchinson with the hope that the former could be gained over. But it proved delusive. See *Hutchinson's History*, iii. 346.

This is the way of travelling in 1771; — a judge of the circuits, a judge of the superior court, a judge of the King's bench, common pleas, and exchequer for the Province, travels with a pair of wretched old jades of horses in a wretched old dung-cart of a curricle, and a negro on the same seat with him driving. But we shall have more glorious times anon, when the sterling salaries are ordered out of the revenue, to the judges, &c. as many most ardently wish, and the judges themselves, among the rest, I suppose. Stopped at Martin's, in Lynn, with Judge Cushing; oated and drank a glass of wine, and heard him sigh and groan the sighs and groans of seventy-seven, though he kept active. He conversed in his usual, hinting, insinuating, doubting, scrupling strain.

Rode with King, a deputy sheriff, who came out to meet the judges, into Salem; put up at Goodhue's. The negro that took my horse soon began to open his heart; — he did not like the people of Salem; wanted to be sold to Captain John Dean, of Boston; he earned two dollars in a forenoon, and did all he could to give satisfaction, but his mistress was cross, and said he did not earn salt to his porridge, &c. and would not find him clothes, &c. Thus I find discontents in all men; — the black thinks his merit rewarded with ingratitude, and so does the white; the black estimates his own worth and the merit of his services higher than anybody else, so does the white. This flattering, fond opinion of himself, is found in every man.

I have hurt myself to-day, by taking cold in the forenoon, and by drinking too much wine at Kettel's, and at Martin's. I drank half a pint at Kettel's, and two glasses at Martin's.

Just after I had drank tea and got my fire made in my chamber, my old neighbor, Jo. Barrell, came and lodged at Goodhue's in the same chamber with me. His grief is intense indeed. He spent the whole evening and a long time after we got to bed, in lamenting the loss of his wife,[1] in enumerating her excellencies, &c.; heartily wishes himself with her; would have been very glad to have gone with her. He married from pure regard, utterly against the will of his mother and all his friends, because

[1] From the Gazette, 22 April, 1771: — "Last Wednesday, died here, greatly lamented, Mrs. Anna Barrell, aged twenty-seven, the virtuous and amiable consort of Mr. Joseph Barrell, merchant, and daughter of the late Hon. Joseph Pierce, Esq. of Portsmouth, in New Hampshire."

she was poor; but she made him happy. She was the best of women; the world has lost all its charms to him. She beckoned to me but a few minutes before she died, when her hands were as cold as clods. She whispered to me, "I love you now; if I could but carry you and the children with me, I should go rejoicing."

In this eloquent strain of grief did he run on. Millions of thoughts did this conversation occasion me. I thought I should have had no sleep all night; however, I got to sleep and slept well.

18. Tuesday. Rode with Mr. Barrell to Ipswich, and put up at Treadwell's. Every object recalls the subject of grief. Barrell, all the way to Ipswich, was like the turtle bemoaning the loss of his mate. "Fine season and beautiful scenes, but they did not charm him as they used to. He had often rode this way a courting with infinite pleasure," &c. "I can't realize that she has left me forever. When she was well, I often thought I could realize the loss of her, but I was mistaken; I had no idea of it." In short, this man's mournings have melted and softened me beyond measure.

22. Saturday. Spent this week at Ipswich, in the usual labors and drudgery of attendance upon court. Boarded at Treadwell's; have had no time to write. Landlord and landlady are some of the grandest people alive; landlady is the great granddaughter of Governor Endicott, and has all the great notions of high family that you find in Winslows, Hutchinsons, Quincys, Saltonstalls, Chandlers, Leonards, Otises, and as you might find with more propriety in the Winthrops. Yet she is cautious and modest about discovering it. She is a new light; continually canting and whining in a religious strain. The Governor was uncommonly strict and devout, eminently so in his day; and his great, great granddaughter hopes to keep up the honor of the family in hers, and distinguish herself among her contemporaries as much. "Terrible things sin causes," sighs and groans, "the pangs of the new birth. The death of Christ shows above all things the heinous nature of sin! How awfully Mr. Kent talks about death! how lightly and carelessly! I am sure a man of his years, who can talk so about death, must be brought to feel the pangs of the new birth here, or made to repent of it forever. How dreadful it seems to me to hear him, I that am so afraid of death, and so concerned lest I an't fit and

prepared for it! What a dreadful thing it was that Mr. Gridley died so!—too great, too big, too proud to learn any thing; would not let any minister pray with him; said he knew more than they could tell him; asked the news, and said he was going where he should hear no news," &c.

Thus far landlady. As to landlord, he is as happy, and as big, as proud, as conceited as any nobleman in England; always calm and good-natured and lazy; but the contemplation of his farm and his sons and his house and pasture and cows, his sound judgment, as he thinks, and his great holiness, as well as that of his wife, keep him as erect in his thoughts as a noble or a prince. Indeed, the more I consider of mankind, the more I see that every man seriously and in his conscience believes himself the wisest, brightest, best, happiest, &c. of all mankind.

I went this evening, spent an hour and took a pipe with Judge Trowbridge, at his lodgings. He says, "you will never get your health, till your mind is at ease. If you tire yourself with business, but especially with politics, you won't get well." I said, "I don't meddle with politics nor think about them"—"except," says he, "by writing in the papers." "I'll be sworn," says I, "I have not wrote one line in a newspaper these two years," &c. The Judge says he had a hint that Foster Hutchinson was appointed Judge, because of the judgment of the Court in the case of Spear *vs.* Keen. The merchants took the alarm, and said, that, instead of lawyers, they ought to have merchants, upon the bench; and Mr. Hutchinson being both a lawyer and a merchant, he was the man, against the Governor's determination a little time before. [But this is one instance among a thousand of the Governor's disguise before those that he induces to believe have his entire familiarity and confidence. He made Mr. Goffe understand he intended to make Worthington or some other lawyer a judge, when he fully designed to make his brother; not indeed to please the merchants, or because Foster was a merchant, but because he was his brother, and that the family might have a majority in that court. He is impenetrable to those who don't desire to reach any imperfection in him, and who are determined not to fathom him where they may. The bigoted, the superstitious, the enthusiastical, the tools, the interested, the timid, are all dazzled with his glare, and can't see clearly when he is in the horizon.

23. Sunday. In the morning my horse was gone. Went to meeting all day, and heard old Mr. Rogers, a good, well-meaning man, I believe. After meeting rode to Newbury and visited Brother Lowell, Brother Farnham, and then went and supped with Mr. Jonathan Jackson in company with Captain Tracy, Mr. Hooper, Mr. Williams, Mr. Frazier, and Brother Lowell; then went and lodged with Lowell.

24. Monday. Reached Portsmouth with Lowell and walked half an hour with him on the town-house floor with Mr. Livius and Mr. Jonathan Warner, &c. Put up at Tilton's, and intend to visit the Governor this afternoon.

Had a good deal of chat with Lowell on the road. He practises much in New Hampshire, and gave me an account of many strange judgments of the superior court at Portsmouth; that an infant, if allowed to trade by his parents, is bound by his contract, &c.; and he gave me an account, also, of the politics of the Province. A controversy is arising or has arisen in the Wentworth family. The old Governor, by his will, gave all his estate to his wife, and she is since married to one Michael Wentworth, which has a little disappointed the Governor, and he not long since asked the advice of his Council, whether he might not reassume the lands which were formerly granted by the late Governor to himself, or at least reserved to himself in each grant of a township, and grant them over again to a third person, from whom he might take a conveyance of them to himself. All the council, except Livius, advised him to the reassumption, he having laid before them the opinion of S. Fitch of Boston, that the Governor could not grant land to himself. Livius dissented and entered his protest, and gave his reasons, for which the Governor has displaced him as a judge of one of their courts.

At Tilton's, in Portsmouth, I met with my cousin, Joseph Adams, whose face I was once as glad to see as I should have been to see an angel. The sight of him gave me a new feeling. When he was at college, and used to come to Braintree with his brother Ebenezer, how I used to love him! He is broken to pieces with rheumatism and gout now. To what cause is his ruin to be ascribed? After dinner a gentleman came to Tilton's to inquire me out, and it proved to be Mr. Pickering, a lawyer. He treated me with great politeness, and seems a very sensible and well accomplished lawyer. After dinner rode to York, and put up at Ritchie's with Lowell and Bradbury.

25. Tuesday. At York court. Dined with the judges, and spent the evening at Ritchie's with Bradbury, and Hale of Portsmouth — a sensible young lawyer.

26. Wednesday. Yesterday I had a good deal of conversation with Judge Trowbridge. He seems alarmed about the powers of the court of probate. He says if Judge Danforth was to die to-morrow, and the Governor was to offer that place to him, he would not take it, because he thinks it ought always to be given to some judge of the inferior court, and then some one lawyer might be found in each county who would take a seat upon the inferior bench if he could be made a judge of probate at the same time. He says he is utterly against Foster Hutchinson's holding the probate office in Boston, if he takes his place upon the superior bench; and if the Governor is an integral part of the court of probate, the supreme ordinary, that is, if he is not, with the members of the council, only *primus inter pares*, but has a negative upon all their decrees, as Governor Shirley, Governor Bernard, and the late Secretary were of opinion, he thinks we may be in great danger from the court of probate; and Judge Russell always opposed every attempt to extend the power of the court of probate. He used to say we might have bishops here, and the court of probate might get into their hands, and therefore we ought to be upon our guard.

28. Friday. At York. Yesterday I spent in walking one way and another to view the town. I find that walking serves me much; it sets my blood in motion much more than riding. Had some conversation this week with Chadburn of Berwick. He says that Jo. Lee came to him on the election-day morning, and said, "I know you are a peaceable man. Why can't you vote for a few gentlemen who would be agreeable to the Governor, and then perhaps some gentleman may not be negatived who would be agreeable to you. Why can't you promote a coalition?" Chadburn answered, "I don't know who would be agreeable to the Governor; I have not had a list." Lee then mentioned Mr. Ropes, Lieutenant Governor Oliver, and some of the judges. "Why can't you choose some of those old statesmen who have been long and intimately acquainted with the policy of the Province? &c." Thus the Governor's emis-

saries are busy, instilling, insinuating their notions and principles, &c.

Had a little chat this week with Colonel Sparhawk of Kittery.[1] He says, "Now you are come away they are become peaceable. You kept up a shocking clamor while you was there." This he said laughing, but there was rather too much truth in it to be made a jest. "They do you the justice to say that no man ever spoke more freely than you did, and in opposition to the rising sun. But in order to take off from your virtue, they say there is some private pique between the Governor and you." I told him there was none; he had always treated me well, personally; if I had been actuated by private pique, I would not have left the General Court, but I would have remained there on purpose to plague him. I could at least have been a thorn in his side &c. But that I had been fully convinced in my own mind these ten years that he was determined to raise himself and family at all hazards, and even on the ruins of the Province, and that I had uniformly expressed that opinion these ten years.

Sparhawk mentioned the intrepidity of Samuel Adams, a man, he says, of great sensibility, of tender nerves, and harassed, dependent, in their power. Yet he had borne up against all; it must have penetrated him very deeply, &c.

July 2. Tuesday. At Falmouth, at Mr. Jonathan Webb's, who has removed to a house very near the court house. Last Friday morning I mounted with Brother Bradbury and his Brother Bradbury, at York for Falmouth; went over the sands, but could not ford Cape Neddick, and so was obliged to go round over the bridge by the mill. Dined at Littlefield's, in Wells; drank tea and lodged at Allen's, in Biddeford. Colonel Tyng and his son in law Jo. Tyler, came along and lodged there; Tyng being the owner of the house and farm there, forty-seven rods wide upon the river and four miles and a half long. Next day, Saturday, it rained, and Jonathan Sewall, Mr. Lowell, and Mr. Leonard Jarvis came in; and after noon, Judges Lynch and Cushing, with their servants; but the house had not lodgings for them. The Judges went back to Ladd's, Sewall and Lowell went to James Sullivan's. Sunday morning the weather was

[1] The grandson of Sir William Pepperell. He signed the addresses to Hutchinson and Gage. *Sabine.*

fair, and we set off for Scarborough, put up at Millikin's, went to meeting forenoon and afternoon; heard Mr. Briggs, a young gentleman, and after meeting rode to Falmouth, and I put up at Webb's, where I have been ever since, reading the achievements of Don Quixote.

This has been the most flat, insipid, spiritless, tasteless journey that ever I took, especially from Ipswich. I have neither had business, nor amusement, nor conversation; it has been a moping, melancholy journey upon the whole. I slumber and mope away the day. Tyng, Tyler, Sewall, Lowell, Jarvis, were all characters which might have afforded me entertainment, perhaps instruction, if I had been possessed of spirits to enjoy it.

Saturday afternoon. I projected making a backgammon table, and about it Sewall, Lowell, and Jarvis and Jo. Tyler went, got pieces of cedar, &c., and while they were playing, I went to sleep.

Sunday. Jarvis was telling of an instance of cruelty and inhumanity in Hall, the wharfinger, in Boston, in ordering a poor widow to be taken with a single writ when her daughter was dying, and of his being bail for her. Sewall said, "Hall would certainly be damned, and you will certainly go to Heaven, let you do what you will."

I feel myself weary of this wandering life; my heart is at home. It would be more for my health to ride to Boston every fair morning, and to Braintree every fair afternoon. This would be riding enough, and I could then have one eye to my office, and another to my farm. After my return I shall try the experiment.

In the evening went to the Club or Friendly Society, as they call themselves, where I found William Cushing, Wyer, with whom I went, that is, at his invitation, Mr. Lyde, Child, Simmons, Jarvis, Dr. Coffin, Captain Wait, and Don Webb. Conversation decent, but upon trifles and common matters.

Saw Mr. Simmons at court, a gentleman from England who has been at Falmouth a number of years as a factor for several merchants in England, purchasing deals.

4. Thursday. Dined with D. Wyer in company with his father, Farnham, Sewall, Cushing, Lowell, &c. Conversation turns upon revelations, prophecies, Jews, &c. Spent the evening with the bar at Shattuck's, the tavern, in high spirits.

Agreed unanimously to recommend Tim. Langdon to be sworn. All in good spirits, very cheerful and chatty, many good stories, &c. This day argued the cause of Freeman and Child, a suit for ten pounds penalty for taking greater fees in the custom-house than those allowed by the Province law.

5. Friday. Cadwallader Ford came to me this morning, and congratulated me on the verdict for Freeman. "Sir," says he, "I shall think myself forever obliged to you for the patriotic manner in which you conducted that cause. You have obtained great honor in this county by that speech. I never heard a better, &c." All this is from old Cadwallader. Langdon told me that a man came running down, when I had done speaking, and said, "That Mr. Adams has been making the finest speech I ever heard in my life. He's equal to the greatest orator that ever spoke in Greece or Rome." What an advantage it is to have the passions, prejudices, and interests of the whole audience in a man's favor! These will convert plain common sense into profound wisdom, nay, wretched doggerel into sublime heroics. This cause was really, and in truth, and without partiality or affectation of modesty, very indifferently argued by me. But I have often been surprised with claps and plaudits and hosannas, when I have spoken but indifferently, and as often met with inattention and neglect when I have thought I spoke very well;—how vain and empty is breath!

Tuesday went to Boston with my wife, and the next day to Commencement at Cambridge; was only at three chambers,—Palmer's, French's, and Rogers's.

22. Monday. After rambling about my farm and giving some directions to my workmen, I went to Boston. There soon came into my office Ruddock[1] and Story. It seems that Andrew Belcher's widow has sued Story as deputy register of the admiralty under her husband in his lifetime, and Ruddock as his bondsman, upon the bond given for the faithful discharge of his office. Three or four hundred pounds sterling of the King's third of a seizure is not accounted for, and Ruddock is in trouble. This Ruddock is as curious a character as any of his age, a fin-

[1] John Ruddock, already spoken of, page 232. He was active as a justice of the peace and of the quorum at this period when much business was transacted before those magistrates. He had been a selectman of the town, and captain of the North Battery. He died on the second of September of the next year.

ished example of self-conceit and vanity. "I am plunged! I never was concerned in any affair before that I could not have any thoughts of my own upon it. I know there are several laws; by one law, the sheriff's bonds are not to be put in suit after two years, and the treasurer's are limited to three years; but whether these precedents will govern this case I cannot tell. I consulted Mr. Pratt once about an affair, and he advised me to do something. I told him I was of a different opinion; every line in his face altered when I said this. 'You are certainly wrong,' said he. 'Well,' says I, 'you will be my lawyer when we come to court?' 'Yes,' said he. But next morning he told me, 'Brother Ruddock, I have been ruminating your affair on my pillow, and I find you was right and I was wrong.'" Thus Mr. Justice Ruddock is mighty in counsel.

"I told Andrew Belcher, if he would not do so and so, he should never be chosen counsellor again; he would not do it, and the next year he was left out. I told him further that I would not accept of any post in the world to stop my mouth about liberty, but I would write home and get away his post of register of the admiralty." Thus Squire Ruddock thinks himself powerful at court. The instances of this man's vanity are innumerable; his soul is as much swollen as his carcass.

I dined at my lodgings, came early to my office, went home and drank tea at six o'clock, and returned to my office, and here I am. What a multitude passes my window every day! Mr. Otis's servant brought his horse to the door at seven, and he took a ride. Treasurer Gray stalked along from New Boston, where his daughter Otis[1] lives, down to the British Coffee House, where the club meets, as I suppose, about half after seven. Spent an hour or two in the evening at Mr. Cranch's. Mr. Jo. Greenleaf came in, and Parson Hilliard[2] of Barnstable; and we were very chatty. Sister Cranch says, she has had an opportunity of making many observations this year at Commencement; and she has quite altered her mind about dancing and dancing-schools; and Mr. Cranch seems convinced, too, and says, it seems that all such as learn to dance are so taken up with it,

[1] The wife of Samuel Allyne Otis, afterwards the first clerk of the Senate of the United States.

[2] Rev. Timothy Hilliard, afterwards settled in Cambridge. An account of him is found in *Mass. Hist. Society's Collections*, vol. vii. p. 63–67.

that they can't be students. So that if they should live to bring up their son to college, they would not send him to dancing-school, nor their daughters neither.

What a sudden and entire conversion is this! That Mrs. C. should change so quick is not so wonderful; but that his mathematical, metaphysical, mechanical, systematical head should be turned round so soon by her report of what she saw at Cambridge is a little remarkable. However, the exchange is for the better; it is from vanity to wisdom, from foppery to sobriety and solidity. I never knew a good dancer good for any thing else. I have known several men of sense and learning who could dance,—Otis, Sewall, Paine,—but none of them shone that way, and neither of them had the more sense, or learning, or virtue for it. I would not, however, conclude peremptorily against sending sons or daughters to dancing, or fencing, or music, but had much rather they should be ignorant of them all than fond of any one of them.

23. Tuesday. The court sat; nothing remarkable. It is a pity that a day should be spent in the company of courts, &c., and nothing be heard or seen worth remembering; but this is the case. Of all that I have heard from judges, lawyers, jurors, clients, clerks, I cannot recollect a word, a sentence, worth committing to writing. Took a pipe in the beginning of the evening with Mr. Cranch, and then supped with Dr. Warren.

The Indian preacher cried, Good God! that ever Adam and Eve should eat that apple, when they knew in their own souls it would make good cider.

25 and 26. Thursday and Friday. Both these days spent in the trial of Mr. Otis's case, against Mr. Robinson.

27. Saturday. The jury this morning delivered their verdict for two thousand pounds sterling damages, and costs.[1] I have spent this morning in reading the Centinels. There is a profuse collection of knowledge in them, in law, history, government, that indicates to me the only author, I think; a great variety of knowledge.[2]

1 This was an action instituted by Mr. Otis for the assault made upon him by Mr. Robinson, 5 September, 1769. Mr. Otis at this time appealed from the verdict; but he subsequently released the damages, and Mr. Robinson confessed his wrong. He had no power to repair the grievous evil he had inflicted!

It is a little singular that the finding of the jury is dated August Term, 1772. See *Tudor's Life of James Otis*, Appendix, p. 503.

2 The publication of these papers was commenced in the Massachusetts Spy

The subject of the Governor's independency is a serious, a dangerous, and momentous thing. It deserves the utmost attention.

J. Q. says Mr. O. was quite wild at the bar meeting; cursed the servants for not putting four candles on the table, swore he could yet afford to have four upon his own, &c. &c.

August 13 or 14. Spent the evening at Cordis's, the British Coffee House, in the front room towards the Long Wharf where the Merchants' Club has met this twenty years. It seems there is a schism in that church, a rent in that garment, a mutiny in that regiment, and a large detachment has decamped and marched over the way to Ingersol's. This evening the Commissary and Speaker, and Speaker and Commissary, Mr. Cushing, was present. The clerk of the House Mr. Adams, Mr. Otis, Mr. John Pitts, Dr. Warren, Mr. Molineux, Mr. Josiah Quincy, and myself were present.

22 and 23. Thursday and Friday. At the office.

Mr. Otis's gestures and motions are very whimsical, his imagination is disturbed, his passions all roiled. His servant he orders to bring up his horse, and to hold him by the head at the stone of his door an hour before he is ready to mount; then he runs into one door and out at another, and window, &c. &c. &c.

November 5. Tuesday. At Salem; fine weather. Deacon Thurston of Rowley came in last night; a venerable old man, with his snowy, hoary locks. Kent and the Deacon soon clashed upon religion. "Don't you think, sir," says the Deacon, "we are here probationers for eternity?" "No, by no means," says Kent. "We are here probationers for the next state, and in the next we shall be probationers for the next that is to follow, and so on through as many states as there are stars or sands, to all eternity. You have gone through several states already before this." "Ay," says the Deacon, "where do you get this; don't you believe the Scriptures?" I put in my oar. "He made it, Deacon, out of the whole cloth; it never existed out of his imagination." *Kent.* "I get it from analogy." It is the delight of this Kent's heart to tease a minister or deacon with his wild conceits about religion.[1]

on the second of May, and was continued to the 26th of March, 1772, making in all forty numbers. They are written with much ability and varied learning.

[1] Ben Kent began life as a clergyman in Marlborough. Doctor Franklin says of him, "He was an honest man, and had his virtues. If he had any hypocrisy

9. Saturday. At Salem all this week, at court. Dined one day at Chief Justice Lynde's, all the rest of the week till this day with the court. Dined this day, spent the afternoon, and drank tea, at Judge Ropes's, with Judges Lynde, Oliver and Hutchinson, Sewall, Putnam and Winthrop. Mrs. Ropes is a fine woman, very pretty and genteel. Our Judge Oliver is the best bred gentleman of all the judges by far; there is something in every one of the others indecent and disagreeable at times in company — affected witticisms, unpolished fleers, coarse jests, and sometimes, rough, rude attacks; — but these you don't see escape Judge Oliver. Drank tea at Judge Ropes's, spent the

it was of that inverted kind, with which a man is not so bad as he seems to be." The following letter written by him to Mr. Adams, in 1776, is in singular contrast with the fact that he afterwards became a refugee, and is now ranked among the Tories. See page 74, note. *Sabine. Curwen's Journal*, p. 481. *Sparks's Franklin*, vol. x. p. 366.

BENJAMIN KENT TO JOHN ADAMS.

BROTHER ADAMS: Boston, 24 April, 1776.

When I had last the pleasure of your company at Watertown, I told you I would write you when our attack upon the King's troops should afford matter of some importance. But alas, their fears of their demerits made them flee when no man pursued them; and may they eat of the fruit of their doings, and be filled with their own devices.

But to the purpose. What in the name of *Common Sense* are you gentlemen of the Continental Congress about? A few words and spiteful is my maxim, that is, what will be so called. Saint Paul, though sometimes a little inclined to Toryism, was a very sensible gentleman, and he expressly damns the fearful as well as the unbelieving. And though I know all your counsels are overruled by the wonderful Counsellor, and even our chicane, (I allude to the last pityful address,*) nay, our downright blunders, are and have been most happily overruled for the good of our most righteous cause, and I doubt not the same happy government will continue; but that same overruling Providence, (at the kind instance of Brother Joseph Greenleaf, Esq.) orders that I should write even this, I won't say (though you may) insignificant letter. It appears to me from a hundred things which I have no need to mention to you, that it is as certain that the Colonies will be wholly divorced from that accursed kingdom called Great Britain, as that there will be any eclipses of the sun or moon this year.

Pray tell the fearful of your members, if you have any such, and prove it to them, that a separation first or last must be the necessary consequence of a hundred facts that have turned up already; then you will have nothing to do but to convince them that the present time to make a final Declaration of Independence is the best. But as I know you must come to it, I think the same of you as I should of a sinner who I knew would repent of his sins before he dies. So that I am perfectly resigned to whatever you great little gods shall do. "Forasmuch as the Lord reigns I will rejoice." One thing I must rely upon, that is, that Congress will tolerate all religions, both natural and revealed, and establish none; and I have infallible proof that it is your duty, namely, that the Lord of lords and the God of gods doth the same thing.

Farewell — these for your friend, B. K.

* The second petition to the King.

evening at Colonel Pickman's. He is very sprightly, sensible, and entertaining, talks a great deal, tells old stories in abundance about the witchcraft, paper money, Governor Belcher's administration, &c.

10. Sunday. Heard Mr. Cutler of Ipswich Hamlet; dined at Dr. Putnam's, with Colonel Putnam and lady, and two young gentlemen, nephews of the Doctor, and Colonel ——, and a Mrs. Scollay. Colonel Putnam told a story of an Indian upon Connecticut River, who called at a tavern, in the fall of the year, for a dram. The landlord asked him two coppers for it. The next spring, happening at the same house, he called for another, and had three coppers to pay for it. "How is this, landlord?" says he; "last fall, you asked but two coppers for a glass of rum, now you ask three." "Oh!" says the landlord, "it costs me a good deal to keep rum over winter. It is as expensive to keep a hogshead of rum over winter as a horse." "Ay!" says the Indian, "I can't see through that; he wont eat so much hay;—*Maybe he drink as much water*." This was *sheer wit*, *pure satire*, and *true humor*. Humor, wit, and satire, in one very short repartee.

Kent brought with him, "Utopia, or the Happy Republic; a philosophical romance, by Sir Thomas More, translated by Bishop Burnet." There is a sensible preface, by the translator, prefixed, and some testimonies concerning More, by great and learned men of different nations and religions,—Cardinal Pole, Erasmus, Jo. Cochlæus, Paulus Jovius, Jo. Rivius, Charles V. &c. The translation, I think, is better than mine, which is by another hand. The romance is very elegant and ingenious, the fruit of a benevolent and candid heart, a learned and strong mind. The good humor, hospitality, humanity, and wisdom of the Utopians, is charming; their elegance and taste is engaging; their freedom from avarice and foppery and vanity is admirable.

1772. February 2. Sunday. Have omitted now, for three months almost, to keep any "note of time or of its loss."

Thomas Newcomb dined with me. He says that Etter, the stocking-weaver, told him, about a fortnight ago, that he saw the Governor, within these three months, and told him he hoped the people would be contented and easy, now they had a Governor from among themselves. The Governor said, "There were some discontents remaining, occasioned by continual clamors in the newspapers, and that a great part of those clamors came from his, Etter's, town, (Braintree.)" This was partly, I suppose, to pump Etter and get something out of him, and partly to put Etter upon the right scent; as the Governor thought that he might hunt down the seditious writer at Braintree. This conversation shows that the Governor is puzzled, and wholly ignorant of the real writers that molest him. The Centinel has puzzled him.

Mr. Thomas Edwards, our school-master, and Mr. Joseph Crosby, a senior sophister at college, spent the evening with me. Our conversation was upon Austin, Tudor, Bulkley, Morton, Thayer, Angier, Colonel Thayer, the settlement of the militia, algebra, Fenning, Dr. Sanderson, &c. &c. Edwards is balancing in his mind the several professions, in order to choose one. Is at a loss between divinity and law, but his inclination is to the latter. Asked me to take him. I only answered, there were such swarms of young ones, that there was no encouragement.

4. Tuesday. Took a ride in the afternoon, with my wife and little daughter, to make a visit to my brother; but finding him and sister just gone to visit my mother, we rode down there and drank tea all together. Chatted about the new promotions in the militia, and speculated about the future officers of this company, upon supposition that the old officers should resign;—Billings, brother, &c. &c. It is curious to observe the effect these little objects of ambition have upon men's minds. The commission of a subaltern in the militia, will tempt these little minds as much as crowns and stars and garters will greater ones. These are things that strike upon vulgar, rustic imaginations, more strongly than learning, eloquence, and genius, of which common persons have no idea.

My brother seems to relish the thought of a commission, and, if Rawson and Bass resign, I hope he will have one under Billings.

9. Sunday.

> "If I would but go to hell, for an eternal moment or so, I might be knighted."
>
> *Shakspeare.*

Shakspeare, that great master of every affection of the heart and every sentiment of the mind, as well as of all the powers of expression, is sometimes fond of a certain pointed oddity of language, a certain quaintness of style that is an imperfection in his character. The motto prefixed to this paper may be considered as an example to illustrate this observation.

Abstracted from the point and conceit in the style, there is sentiment enough in these few words to fill a volume. It is a striking representation of that struggle which I believe always happens between virtue and ambition, when a man first commences a courtier. By a courtier, I mean one who applies himself to the passions and prejudices, the follies and vices of great men, in order to obtain their smiles, esteem, and patronage, and consequently their favors and preferment. Human nature, depraved as it is, has interwoven in its very frame a love of truth, sincerity, and integrity, which must be overcome by art, education, and habit, before the man can become entirely ductile to the will of a dishonest master. When such a master requires of all who seek his favor an implicit resignation to his will and humor, and these require that he be soothed, flattered, and assisted in his vices and follies, perhaps the blackest crimes that men can commit, the first thought of this will produce in a mind not yet entirely debauched, a soliloquy something like my motto, as if he should say,—

"The Minister of State or the Governor would promote my interest, would advance me to places of honor and profit, would raise me to titles and dignities that will be perpetuated in my family; in a word, would make the fortune of me and my posterity forever, if I would but comply with his desires, and become his instrument to promote his measures. But still I dread the consequences. He requires of me such compliances, such horrid crimes, such a sacrifice of my honor, my conscience, my friends, my country, my God, as the Scriptures inform us must be punished with nothing less than hell-fire, eternal torment; and this is so unequal a price to pay for the honors and emoluments in the power of a Minister or Governor, that I cannot prevail upon myself to think of it. The duration of future punishment terrifies me. If I could but deceive myself so far as to think eternity a moment only, I could comply and be promoted."

Such as these are probably the sentiments of a mind as yet pure and undefiled in its morals; and many and severe are the pangs and agonies it must undergo, before it will be brought to yield entirely to temptation.

Notwithstanding this, we see every day that our imaginations are so strong, and our reason so weak, the charms of wealth and power are so enchanting, and the belief of future punishment so faint, that men find ways to persuade themselves to believe any absurdity, to submit to any prostitution, rather than forego their wishes and desires. Their reason becomes at last an eloquent advocate on the side of their passions, and they bring themselves to believe that black is white, that vice is virtue, that folly is wisdom, and eternity a moment.

The Brace of Adamses.[1]

Q. Is it not a pity that a brace of so obscure a breed should be the only ones to defend the household, when the generous mastiffs and best-blooded hounds are all hushed to silence by the bones and crumbs that are thrown to them, and even Cerberus himself is bought off with a sop?

The malice of the court and its writers seems to be principally directed against these two gentlemen. They have been steadfast and immovable in the cause of their country from the year 1761, and one of them, Mr. Samuel Adams, for full twenty years before. They have always, since they were acquainted with each other, concurred in sentiment that the liberties of this country had more to fear from one man, the present Governor Hutchinson, than from any other man, nay, than from all other men in the world. This sentiment was founded in their knowledge of his character, his unbounded ambition, and his unbounded popularity. This sentiment they have always freely, though decently, expressed in their conversation and writings, which the Governor well knows, and which will be remembered as long as his character and administration.

It is not, therefore, at all surprising that his indignation and that of all his creatures should fall upon these gentlemen. Their Maker has given them nerves that are delicate; and of consequence their feelings are exquisite, and their constitutions tender, and their health, especially of one of them, very infirm; but, as a compensation for this, He has been pleased to bestow upon them spirits that are unconquerable by all the art and all the

[1] Here is the same anecdote, respecting Governor Shirley's inquiry, which is told in the passage of the Autobiography, already inserted in page 233. It is therefore omitted. The remarks which follow it are, however, retained.

power of Governor Hutchinson and his political creators and creatures on both sides of the Atlantic. That art and power which have destroyed a Thacher, a Mayhew, an Otis, may destroy the health and the lives of these gentlemen, but can never subdue their principles or their spirit. They have not the cheering, salubrious prospect of honors and emoluments before them to support them under all the indignities and affronts, the insults and injuries, the malice and slander that can be thrown upon men: they have not even the hope of those advantages that the suffrages of the people only can bestow; but they have a sense of honor and a love of their country, the testimony of a good conscience, and the consolation of philosophy, if nothing more, which will certainly support them, in the cause of their country, to their last gasp for breath, whenever that may happen.

10. Monday. Went to Boston to the Court of Admiralty, and returned at night. I went upon the first appeal that has been yet made and prosecuted before Judge Auchmuty; and, as it is a new thing, the Judge has directed an argument and a search of books concerning the nature of appeals by the civil law. I found time to look into Calvin's Lexicon, Title *Appellatio et Provocatio*, and into Maranta, who has treated largely of appeals; borrowed Ayliff, but there is no table, and could find nothing about the subject; Domat I could not find.[1]

June 30. Tuesday. Falmouth, Casco Bay. My office at Boston will miss me this day; it is the last day of arresting for July court. What equivalent I shall meet with here is uncertain.

It has been my fate to be acquainted in the way of my business with a number of very rich men, — Gardiner, Bowdoin, Pitts, Hancock, Rowe, Lee, Sargent, Hooper, Doane. Hooper, Gardiner, Rowe, Lee, and Doane have all acquired their wealth by their own industry; Bowdoin and Hancock received theirs by succession, descent, or devise; Pitts by marriage.[2] But

1 The following entry appears in the book of records of the town of Braintree, in the interval between this and the next date. 2d March, 1772.

Voted, An oration relative to the civil and religious rights and privileges of the people be delivered on the day the annual meeting for the choice of a representative shall be appointed in May next.

Voted, The Selectmen be desired to wait on John Adams, Esquire, with the above vote, and request his assistance therein, and in case of his refusal, to engage some other gentleman of the town to assist in that affair.

No further notice of the matter occurs in the records.

2 Mr. Pitts had married Mr. Bowdoin's sister.

there is not one of all these who derives more pleasure from his property than I do from mine; my little farm, and stock, and cash afford me as much satisfaction as all their immense tracts, extensive navigation, sumptuous buildings, their vast sums at interest, and stocks in trade yield to them. The pleasures of property arise from acquisition more than possession, from what is to come rather than from what is. These men feel their fortunes; they feel the strength and importance which their riches give them in the world; their courage and spirits are buoyed up, their imaginations are inflated by them. The rich are seldom remarkable for modesty, ingenuity, or humanity. Their wealth has rather a tendency to make them penurious and selfish.

I arrived in this town on Sunday morning; went to meeting all day, heard Mr. Smith and Mr. Deane. Drank tea with Brother Bradbury, and spent the evening with him at Mr. Deane's; sat in the pew with Mr. Smith, son of the minister in the morning, and with William Tyng,[1] Esquire, sheriff and representative, in the afternoon. Lodged at Mrs. Stover's; a neat, clean, clever woman, the wife of a sea captain at sea.

Have spent my idle time in reading my classmate Hemmenway's, "Vindication of the Power, Obligation, and Encouragement of the Unregenerate to attend the Means of Grace," and the "Clandestine Marriage," by Colman and Garrick.

July 1. Wednesday.

> He who contends for freedom
> Can ne'er be justly deemed his sovereign's foe;
> No, 'tis the wretch that tempts him to subvert it,
> The soothing slave, the traitor in the bosom,
> Who best deserves that name; he is a worm
> That eats out all the happiness of kingdoms.[2]

[1] Some account of this gentleman is found in Mr. Sabine's valuable work, and also in the tenth volume of the Massachusetts Historical Society's Collections. The name is one of the oldest and most respectable in the State; but in the male line it has long since run out. It may be as well, however, to correct a slight error of fact in the volume of Collections already quoted, which states that one of the two brothers, who first came to the country, William Tyng, and spent his life at Braintree, left no posterity. He left four daughters, one of whom married the Rev. Thomas Shepard, of Charlestown, and through her the children of the author of this Diary traced their descent from him.

[2] These lines are taken from a play, now little read: Thomson's Edward and Eleanora, act i. sc. 2, and act ii. sc. 2.

When life or death
Become the question, all distinctions vanish;
Then the first monarch, and the lowest slave,
On the same level stand; in this, the sons
Of equal nature all.

September 22. At Boston. Paid Dr. Gardiner and took up my last note to him. I have now got completely through my purchase of Deacon Palmer, Colonel Quincy, and all my salt marsh, being better than twenty acres, and have paid two hundred and fifty pounds old tenor towards my house in Boston, and have better than three hundred pounds left in my pocket. At thirty-seven years of age almost, this is all that my most intense application to study and business has been able to accomplish, an application that has more than once been very near costing me my life, and that has so greatly impaired my health.

[I am now writing in my own house in Queen Street,* to which I am pretty well determined to bring my family this fall. If I do, I shall come with a fixed resolution to meddle not with public affairs of town or Province. I am determined my own life and the welfare of my whole family, which is much dearer to me, are too great sacrifices for me to make. I have served my country and her professed friends, at an immense expense to me of time, peace, health, money, and preferment, both of which last have courted my acceptance and been inexorably refused, lest I should be laid under a temptation to forsake the sentiments of the friends of this country. These last are such politicians as to bestow all their favors upon their professed and declared enemies. I will devote myself wholly to my private business, my office and my farm, and I hope to lay a foundation for better fortune to my children, and a happier life than has fallen to my share.

This the last training day for the year. Have been out to view

* [Finding my health much improved, and finding great inconvenience in conducting my business in Boston, in my office there, while my family was in the country, I began to entertain thoughts of returning. Having found it very troublesome to hire houses, and be often obliged to remove, I determined to purchase a house, and Mr. Hunt offering me one in Queen Street near the scene of my business, opposite the Court House, I bought it, and inconvenient and contracted as it was, I made it answer, both for a dwelling and an office, till a few weeks before the 19th of April, 1775, when the war commenced.]

the regiment, the cadets, the grenadiers, the train, &c. A great show indeed.

EPITAPH.

Algernon Sidney fills this tomb,
An Atheist, for disdaining Rome;
A rebel bold, for striving still
To keep the laws above the will.
Of Heaven, he sure must needs despair,
If holy Pope be turnkey there.
And hell him ne'er will entertain,
For there is all tyrannic reign.
Where goes he then? Where he ought to go;—
Where Pope, nor Devil have to do.

October 5. Monday. Rode to Plymouth with my sister, Miss Betsey Smith; most agreeably entertained at the house of Colonel Warren. The Colonel, his lady, and family, are all agreeable. They have five sons,—James, now at college, Winslow, Charles, Henry, and George. Five fine boys.

At Taunton. This week has been a remarkable one.

19. Monday. Boston. The day of the month reminds me of my birthday, which will be on the 30th. I was born October 19, 1735.[1] Thirty-seven years, more than half the life of man, are run out. What an atom, an animalcule I am! The remainder of my days I shall rather decline in sense, spirit, and activity. My season for acquiring knowledge is past, and yet I have my own and my children's fortunes to make. My boyish habits and airs are not yet worn off.

27. Tuesday. At the printing office this morning. Mr. Otis came in, with his eyes fishy and fiery, looking and acting as wildly as ever he did. "You, Mr. Edes, you, John Gill, and you, Paul Revere, can you stand there three minutes?" "Yes." "Well, do. Brother Adams, go along with me." Up chamber we went; he locks the door and takes out the key; sit down, *tête-à-tête*. "You are going to Cambridge to-day?" "Yes." "So am I, if I please. I want to know, if I was to come into court and ask the court if they were at leisure to hear a motion, and they should say, yes, and I should say,—'May it please your Honors, I have heard a report and read an account that your Honors are to be paid your salaries, for the future, by the

[1] O. S.

Crown out of a revenue raised from us without our consent; as an individual of the community, as a citizen of the town, as an attorney and barrister of this court, I beg your Honors would inform me whether that report is true, and if it is, whether your Honors determine to accept of such an appointment;' or suppose the substance of this should be reduced to a written petition, would this be a contempt? Is mere impertinence a contempt?" In the course of this curious conversation, it oozed out that Cushing, Adams, and he, had been in consultation but yesterday, in the same chamber, upon that subject. In this chamber, Otis was very chatty. He told me a story of Colonel Erving, whose excellency lies, he says, not in military skill, but in humbugging. "Erving met Parson Moorhead[1] near his meeting-house. 'You have a fine steeple and bell,' says he, 'to your meeting-house now.' 'Yes; by the liberality of Mr. Hancock, and the subscriptions of some other gentlemen, we have a very handsome and convenient house of it at last.' 'But what has happened to the vane, Mr. Moorhead? it don't traverse; it has pointed the same way these three weeks.' 'Ay, I did not know it. I'll see about it.' Away goes Moorhead, storming among his parish and the tradesmen who had built the steeple, for fastening the vane so that it could not move. The tradesmen were alarmed, and went to examine it, but soon found that the fault was not in the vane, but the weather, the wind having set very constantly at east for three weeks before." He also said there was a report about town that Moorhead had given thanks publicly, that, by the generosity of Mr. Hancock and some other gentlemen, they were enabled to worship God as *genteelly* now as any other congregation in town. After we came down stairs, something was said about military matters. Says Otis to me, "You will never learn military exercises." "Ay, why not?" "That you have a head for it, needs no commentary, but not a heart." "Ay, how do you know? you never searched my heart." "Yes, I have;—tired with one year's service, dancing from Boston to

1 A Presbyterian, who came out from Ireland, in 1727, with a number of families of Scotch origin, and established a church in Long Lane, now called Federal Street. It seems to have lived and died with him. For most of the members' names have not been perpetuated in Boston, and the building has passed into the hands of another denomination. The bell and vane of the old meeting-house in Brattle street, when pulled down, were presented to this Society. See *Coll. Hist. Society Mass.* vol. iii. p. 262.

Braintree, and from Braintree to Boston; moping about the streets of this town as hipped as Father Flynt at ninety, and seemingly regardless of every thing but to get money enough to carry you smoothly through this world."

This is the rant of Mr. Otis concerning me, and I suppose of two thirds of the town. But, be it known to Mr. Otis, I have been in the public cause as long as he, though I was never in the General Court but one year. I have sacrificed as much to it as he. I have never got my father chosen Speaker and Counsellor by it; my brother-in-law chosen into the House and chosen Speaker by it; nor a brother-in-law's brother-in-law into the House and Council by it; nor did I ever turn about in the House, betray my friends, and rant it on the side of prerogative for a whole year, to get a father into a probate office and a first justice of a court of common pleas, and a brother into a clerk's office. There is a complication of malice, envy, and jealousy in this man, in the present disordered state of his mind, that is quite shocking.[1]

I thank God my mind is prepared for whatever can be said of me. The storm shall blow over me in silence.

Rode to Cambridge, and made a morning's visit to Judge Trowbridge, in his solitary, gloomy state. He is very dull, talks about retiring from court; says he cannot fix his attention as he could; is in doubt whether he ought to sit in a capital case, lest he should omit something that is material, &c. &c. Was inquisitive, however, about politics, and what the town of Boston was likely to do about the Judges' salaries. Said he heard they were about to choose a committee to wait upon the court, to inquire of them, &c. &c. Comparing this with Otis's distracted proposal to me about a motion or petition, I concluded that something of this kind had been talked of in town, though I never heard a hint of it from any but these two. Trowbridge thought there never was a time when every thing was so out of joint; — our General Court gave Cushing, for a fortnight's work, as much as the Judges for two years; the Ministry gave six hundred pounds

[1] Otis was scarcely an object for indignation at this period. Neither does the remark made by him seem to merit so harsh a comment as it receives. There can be no doubt that the state of Mr. Adams's health, and the extensive professional practice to which he had after long labor arrived, combined to make him averse to political life. Hutchinson assigns the same reasons. Vol. iii. p. 296.

a year to the Admiralty Judges, for doing no more business than the Superior Court did in one term, though the latter had a control over the former. For his part, he could not look upon it in any other light than as an affront. This is nearly the same that he said to Colonel Warren.

Attended court all day. Dined with the judges, &c. at Bradish's. Brattle was there, and was chatty. Fitch came in blustering when dinner was half over.

November 21. Next Tuesday I shall remove my family to Boston, after residing in Braintree about nineteen months. I have recovered a degree of health by this excursion into the country, though I am an infirm man yet. I hope I have profited by retirement and reflection, and learned in what manner to live in Boston. How long I shall be able to stay in the city, I know not; if my health should again decline, I must return to Braintree and renounce the town entirely. I hope, however, to be able to stay there many years. To this end I must remember temperance, exercise, and peace of mind; above all things, I must avoid politics, political clubs, town meetings, General Court, &c. &c. I must ride frequently to Braintree, to inspect my farm; and, when in Boston, must spend my evenings in my office or with my family, and with as little company as possible.

Eleven years have passed since I minuted any thing in this book.[1] What an admirable advantage it would have been if I had recorded every step in the progress of my studies for these eleven years! If I had kept an exact journal of all my journeys on the circuit, of all the removes of my family, my buildings, purchases, the gradual increase of my library and family, as well as of the improvement of my mind by my studies, the whole would have composed entertaining memoirs to me in my old age, and to my family after my decease.

One thing in this book shall be a lesson to me. The gentleman to whom the letter is directed,[2] an extract of which is in the beginning of this book, eleven years ago I thought the best friend I had in the world. I loved him accordingly, and corres-

[1] This is that particular portion of the Diary which commences with the copy of a letter to Jonathan Sewall, in October, 1759. The entries, made at times long apart from each other, are, in this publication, inserted in their regular chronological order.

[2] See page 79.

ponded with him many years without reserve. But the scene is changed. At this moment I look upon him as the most bitter, malicious, determined, and implacable enemy I have. God forgive him the part he has acted, both in public and private life! It is not impossible that he may make the same prayer for me.

I am now about removing, a second time, from Braintree to Boston. In April, 1768, I removed to Boston, to the white house in Brattle Square. In the spring, 1769, I removed to Cole Lane, to Mr. Fayerweather's house. In 1770, I removed to another house in Brattle Square, where Dr. Cooper now lives. In 1771, I removed from Boston to Braintree, in the month of April, where I have lived to this time. I hope I shall not have occasion to remove so often for four years and a half to come. The numerous journeys and removes that I have taken in this period, have put my mind into an unsettled state. They have occasioned too much confusion and dissipation. I hope to pass a more steady, regular life, for the future, in all respects. When I chance to meet with any of my own compositions, of ten years old, I am much inclined to think I could write with more accuracy and elegance then than I can now, and that I had more sense and knowledge then, than I have now. My memory and fancy were certainly better then, and my judgment, I conjecture, quite as good.

28. Friday. This week, namely, last Tuesday, my family and goods arrived at Boston, where we have taken possession of my house in Queen Street, where I hope I shall live as long as I have any connection with Boston. This day, Major Martin came into the office and chatted an hour very sociably and pleasantly. He says that politics are the finest study and science in the world, but they are abused; real patriotism, or love of one's country, is the greatest of moral virtues, &c. He is a man of sense, and knowledge of the world. His observation upon politics is just; they are the grandest, the noblest, the most useful and important science in the whole circle.

A sensible soldier is as entertaining a companion as any man whatever. They acquire an urbanity, by travel and promiscuous conversation, that is charming. This Major Martin has conversed familiarly in Scotland, in England, and in America, and seems to understand every subject of general conversation very well.

I have now got through the hurry of my business. My father-in-law, Mr. Hall, and my mother, are well settled in my farm at Braintree. The produce of my farm is all collected in; my own family is removed and well settled in Boston; my wood and stores are laid in for the winter; my workmen are nearly all paid; I am disengaged from public affairs, and now have nothing to do but to mind my office, my clerks, and my children. But this week, which has been so agreeable to me in the course of my own affairs, has not been so happy for my friends. Beware of idleness, luxury, and all vanity, folly, and vice!

The conversation of the town and country has been about the strange occurrence of last week, a piracy said to have been committed on a vessel bound to Cape Cod; three men killed, a boy missing, and only one man escaped to tell the news. A mysterious, inexplicable affair![1] about Wilkes's probable mayoralty, and about the salaries to the Judges. These are the three principal topics of conversation at present.

December 16. Wednesday. Dined with the Rev. Mr. Simeon Howard of West Boston, in company with Dr. Chauncy, Captain Phillips, Dr. Warren, Mrs. Howard, Miss Betsey Mayhew, and a young gentleman whose name I don't know. Had a very agreeable conversation.

Mr. Howard was silent. Dr. Chauncy very sociable; glories much in his inflexible adherence to rules of diet, exercise, study, sleep, &c. If he had not lived as regularly as the sun moves in the heavens, he should long ago have mouldered to dust, so as not to be distinguished from common earth. Never reads nor studies after eight o'clock. He would not, for all the commissions in the gift of all the potentates upon earth, become the tool of any man alive. Told us of his writing to England and Scotland, and of the politics he wrote. Among the rest, that, in twenty-five years, there would be more people here than in the three kingdoms, &c.—the greatest empire on earth. Our freeholds would preserve us, for interest would not lie. If ever he should give the charge at an ordination, he would say, "We Bishops," &c. &c. He told us of Mr. Temple's keeping a fair journal of all the proceedings of the board of commissioners, &c. and that the ministry provided for him, to prevent his raising a

[1] This was the singular case of Ansell Nickerson, alluded to page 224 Hutchinson's account of it is quite full. Vol. iii. p. 419.

clamor. Captain Phillips would not have got his appointment, if Mr. Temple had not been his friend, &c. Phillips says they are all still and quiet at the southward, and at New York they laugh at us.

20. Sunday. Heard Dr. Chauncy in the morning upon these words: "As Paul reasoned of righteousness, temperance, and judgment to come, Felix trembled." The Doctor dilated upon the subject of Paul's discourse,—the great moral duties of justice and temperance as they are connected with the future judgment; upon the Apostle's manner,—he reasoned, &c.; and upon the effect that such reasoning had upon Felix,—it made him tremble. In the afternoon, Dr. Cooper sounded harmoniously upon the deceitfulness of sin. The Doctor's air and action are not graceful; they are not natural and easy. His motions with his head, body, and hands, are a little stiff and affected; his style is not simple enough for the pulpit; it is too flowery, too figurative; his periods too much or rather too apparently rounded and labored. This however, *sub rosâ*, because the Doctor passes for a master of composition and is an excellent man.

23. Wednesday. Major Martin at the office. He is very gracious with the first man in the Province. "The Governor spoke very handsomely of all my counsel. He did you justice," &c. &c. The Major is to dine with me to-morrow. He wishes for war. Wants to be a Colonel, to get one thousand pounds sterling for eight or ten years, that he may leave something to his children, &c. &c. An Ensign in the army is company for any nobleman in England. A Colonel in the army, with one thousand pounds a year, will spend an evening with an Ensign who can but just live upon his pay, and make him pay his club. The company that the officers are obliged to keep, makes them poor, as bare as a scraped carrot, &c. &c.

The manners of these gentlemen are very engaging and agreeable.

Took a walk this morning to the south end, and had some conversation with my old friends, Crafts and Trott.[1] I find they are both cooled, both flattened away. They complain, especially Crafts, that they are called Tories, &c. &c. Crafts has got Swift's "Contests and Dissensions of the Nobles and Commons of

[1] See page 178.

Athens and Rome," and is making extracts from it about Clodius and Curio, popular leaders, &c. &c.

My wife says her father never inculcated any maxim of behavior upon his children so often as this,— never to speak ill of any body; to say all the handsome things she could of persons, but no evil; and to make things, rather than persons, the subjects of conversation. These rules he always impressed upon us, whenever we were going abroad, if it was but to spend an afternoon. He was always remarkable for observing these rules in his own conversation. Her grandfather Quincy was remarkable for never praising any body; he did not often speak evil, but he seldom spoke well.

24. Thursday. Major Martin, Mr. Blowers, and Mr. Williams dined with me. All agreeable. This day I heard that Mr. Hancock had purchased twenty writs for this court of Mr. S. Quincy. Oh, the mutability of the legal, commercial, social, political, as well as material world! For about three or four years I have done all Mr. Hancock's business, and have waded through wearisome, anxious days and nights, in his defence; but farewell!

29. Tuesday. Spent the last Sunday evening with Dr. Cooper at his house, with Justice Quincy and Mr. William Cooper. We were very social, and we chatted at large upon Cæsar, Cromwell, &c.

Yesterday, Parson Howard and his lady, lately Mrs. Mayhew, drank tea with Mrs. Adams.

Heard many anecdotes from a young gentleman in my office of Admiral Montague's manners. A coachman, a jack-tar before the mast, would be ashamed, nay, a porter, a shoeblack, or chimney sweeper, would be ashamed of the coarse, low, vulgar dialect of this sea officer, though a rear admiral of the blue, and though a second son of a genteel if not a noble family in England. An American freeholder, living in a log house twenty feet square without a chimney in it, is a well-bred man, a polite accomplished person, a fine gentleman, in comparison of this beast of prey. This is not the language of prejudice, for I have none against him, but of truth. His brutal, hoggish manners are a disgrace to the royal navy and to the King's service. His lady is very much disliked, they say, in general. She is very full of her remarks at the assembly and concert. "Can this lady afford the jewels and dress she wears ?" "Oh, that ever my son should come to dance with a mantuamaker!"

The high commission court, the star chamber court, the court of inquisition, for the trial of the burners of the Gaspee at Rhode Island are the present topic of conversation. The Governor of that Colony has communicated to the assembly a letter from the Earl of Dartmouth.[1] The Colony are in great distress, and have applied to their neighbors for advice how to evade or sustain the shock.

29. Tuesday. This afternoon I had a visit from Samuel Pemberton, Esquire, and Mr. Samuel Adams. Mr. P. said they were a sub-committee deputed by the standing committee of the town of Boston to request that I would deliver an oration in public upon the ensuing 5th of March. He said that they two were desirous of it, and that the whole committee was unanimously desirous of it. I told them that the feeble state of my health rendered me quite willing to devote myself forever to private life; that, far from taking any part in public, I was desirous to avoid even thinking upon public affairs, and that I was determined to pursue that course, and therefore that I must beg to be excused. They desired to know my reasons. I told them that so many irresistible syllogisms rushed into my mind and concluded decisively against it, that I did not know which to mention first. But I thought the reason that had hitherto actuated the town was enough, namely, the part I took in the trial of the soldiers. Though the subject of the oration was quite compatible with the verdict of the jury in that case, and indeed, even with the absolute innocence of the soldiers, yet I found the world in general were not capable or not willing to make the distinction, and therefore, by making an oration upon

1 This was a special commission issued from the Crown. Hutchinson derives the authority for such an act from the power to order the royal navy to any colony, and considers this paramount to any charter whatever. Yet he says, "such a commission became an additional article of grievance," as if this were a matter of surprise. Vol. iii. p. 365, note.

The proceeding came to nothing, as might very naturally have been expected. The substitution of a novel and foreign tribunal with no additional powers of compulsion, was not likely to elicit more frank communications than were to be obtained through the process of the ordinary courts. But the British ministry throughout the American quarrel never stopped to study human nature. There is a very warm letter of John Dickinson on this subject in the Life and Correspondence of R. H. Lee, vol. i. p. 91.

this occasion I should only expose myself to the lash of ignorant and malicious tongues on both sides of the question. Besides that, I was too old to make declamations. The gentlemen desired I would take time to consider of it. I told them, no; that would expose me to more difficulties; I wanted no time; it was not a thing unthought of by me, though this invitation was unexpected; that I was clearly, fully, absolutely, and unalterably determined against it, and therefore that time and thinking would answer no end. The gentlemen then desired that I would keep this a secret, and departed.

30. Wednesday. Spent this evening with Mr. Samuel Adams at his house. Had much conversation about the state of affairs, Cushing, Phillips, Hancock, Hawley, Gerry, Hutchinson, Sewall, Quincy, &c. Adams was more cool, genteel, and agreeable than common; concealed and restrained his passions, &c. He affects to despise riches, and not to dread poverty; but no man is more ambitious of entertaining his friends handsomely, or of making a decent, an elegant appearance than he. He has lately new-covered and glazed his house, and painted it very neatly, and has new-papered, painted, and furnished his rooms; so that you visit at a very genteel house, and are very politely received and entertained.

Mr. Adams corresponds with Hawley, Gerry, and others. He corresponds in England, and in several of the other Provinces. His time is all employed in the public service.

31. Thursday. This evening at Mr. Cranch's. I found that my constitutional or habitual infirmities have not entirely forsaken me. Mr. Collins, an English gentleman, was there, and in conversation about the high commission court for inquiring after the burners of the Gaspee at Providence, I found the old warmth, heat, violence, acrimony, bitterness, sharpness of my temper and expression, was not departed. I said there was no more justice left in Britain than there was in hell; that I wished for war, and that the whole Bourbon family was upon the back of Great Britain; avowed a thorough disaffection to that country; wished that any thing might happen to them, and, as the clergy prayed of our enemies in time of war, that they might be brought to reason or to ruin.

I cannot but reflect upon myself with severity for these rash, inexperienced, boyish, raw, and awkward expressions. A man who has no better government of his tongue, no more command of his temper, is unfit for every thing but children's play and the company of boys.

A character can never be supported, if it can be raised, without a good, a great share of self-government. Such flights of passion, such starts of imagination, though they may strike a few of the fiery and inconsiderate, yet they lower, they sink a man with the wise. They expose him to danger, as well as familiarity, contempt, and ridicule.

[It was, I believe, in 1772, that Governor Hutchinson, in an elaborate speech to both Houses, endeavored to convince them, their constituents, and the world, that Parliament was our sovereign legislature, and had a right to make laws for us in all cases whatsoever, to lay taxes on all things external and internal, on land as well as on trade. The House appointed a committee to answer this speech. An answer was drawn, prettily written.

. . . .

The draught of a report was full of very popular talk, and of those democratical principles which have done so much mischief in this country. I objected to them all, and got them all expunged which I thought exceptionable, and furnished the committee with the law authorities, and the legal and constitutional reasonings that are to be seen on the part of the House in that controversy. How these papers would appear to me or to others at this day, I know not, having never seen them since their first publication; but they appeared to me, at that time, to be correct.]

This statement of the authorship of the most elaborate state-paper of the revolutionary controversy in Massachusetts, corresponds, with the exception of the date, which was January, 1773, with the account given by Hutchinson, who says: "Mr. Hawley and Mr. Samuel Adams were the persons who had the greatest share in preparing it, being assisted by Mr. John Adams, who was not at this time a member, but whose character, as a man of strong natural powers and of good knowledge in the laws, was established." Yet, — since a claim has been very confidently made in behalf of Mr. Samuel Adams, and as Mr. Webster, in his celebrated eulogy of John Adams and Thomas Jefferson, incidentally notices what he denominates the "singular ability" of the discussion, without appearing conscious of the part had in it by one of the persons of whose public services he was then speaking, — it seems not irrelevant here to introduce the fullest account of the matter which the author left behind him. This is found in a letter addressed by him to Judge Tudor, on the eighth of March, 1817. In order to make way for this, a portion of the same narrative, found in the Autobiography, has been omitted as needless repetition. The probability is, that Mr. Samuel Adams incorporated all the legal and constitutional reasoning, furnished by his namesake, into the fair draught made by him as the report of the committee, and that the existence of this paper in the handwriting of the former constituted the evidence upon which the claim of authorship in his behalf was advanced. But, — apart from the internal evidence in the paper of the mind of a jurist, which Samuel Adams was not, and over and above the sub-

My dear Sir

If you have had Leisure to commit your thoughts to writing agreeable to my Request I shall be obligd if you will send them by the Bearer — The Govr says the House have *incautiously* applied a Rule of the Common Law (see the 4th Coll. of his Speech). The Objection is *mine*, upon *your* Authority as I thought. If it be vindicable, pray give me your Aid in that as briefly as you please. I am sorry to trouble you at a time when I know you must be much engagd but to tell you a Secret, if there be a Lawyer in the house in Major Hawleys Absence, there is no one whom I incline to confide in

Your friend

S. Adams

Monday Evg

To John Adams Esqr

joined narrative, — there is among the papers of John Adams a brief note from his kinsman, which seems to set the question at rest. An exact imitation of this note accompanies the present volume. It was written because Governor Hutchinson, in his reply to the House, denied one of the main positions of their answer, and because it became necessary that the person who had originally advanced that position should be called upon, when disputed, to make it good. The letter to Judge Tudor now follows.

"Vanity of vanities, all is vanity." The French have a distinction between eulogy and apology. I know not under which of these heads to class the following anecdote.

Governor Hutchinson, in the plenitude of his vanity and self-sufficiency, thought he could convince all America and all Europe that the Parliament of Great Britain had an authority supreme, sovereign, absolute, and uncontrollable over the Colonies, in all cases whatsoever. In full confidence of his own influence, at the opening of a session of the legislature, he made a speech to both Houses, in which he demonstrated, as he thought, those mighty truths beyond all contradiction, doubt, or question.

The public stood astonished! The two Houses appointed committees to take into consideration the Governor's speech. If any honest historian should ever appear, he will search these records. The proceedings of the Council I shall leave to the historian.

The House appointed a committee to take into consideration the Governor's speech. Major Hawley, who, far from assuming the character of commander-in-chief of the House, pretended to nothing, still, however, insisted with the committee in private that they should invite John Adams to meet with them, and to take his opinion and advice upon every question. So critical was the state of affairs, that Samuel Adams, John Hancock, Thomas Cushing, and all their friends and associates, could carry no question upon legal and constitutional subjects in the House, without the countenance, concurrence, and support of Major Hawley. John Adams was, therefore, very civilly invited, requested, and urged to meet the committee; which he did every evening till their report was finished.

When I first met the gentlemen, they had an answer to his Excellency's speech already prepared, neatly and elegantly composed, which I then believed had been written by Samuel Adams, but which I have since had some reasons to suspect was drawn at his desire, and with his coöperation, by my friend, Dr. Joseph Warren. It was full of those elementary principles of liberty, equality, and fraternity, which have since made such a figure in the world; principles which are founded in nature, and eternal, unchangeable truth, but which must be well understood and cautiously applied. It is not safe at all times, and in every case, to apply the *ratio ultima rerum*,—resort to club law and the force of arms. There was no answer nor attempt to answer the Governor's legal and constitutional arguments, such as they were.

I found myself in a delicate situation, as you may well suppose. In the first place, the self-love of the composer, who I believed to be Samuel Adams, having then no suspicion of Warren, would be hurt by garbling his infant. In the second place, to strike out principles which I loved as well as any of the people, would be odious and unpopular.

We read that West would give five hundred dollars for a red lion that he painted for a sign post. I, poor as I am, would give as much for a copy of that answer to Governor Hutchinson. But I fear it is lost forever.[1] It may, however, be hereafter found; and I wish it may.

Can I describe to you, my dear Tudor, the state of my mind at that time? I had a wife—and what a wife! I had children—and what children! I was determined never to accept any office, place, or employment, from the government of Great Britain or its representatives, governors in America. On the other hand, I knew here was nothing for me to depend on but popular breath, which I knew to be as variable and uncertain as any one of the thirty-two points of the compass.

In this situation I should have thought myself the happiest man in the world, if I could have retired to my little hut and forty acres, which my father left me in Braintree, and lived on potatoes and sea-weed for the rest of my life. But I had taken a part, I had adopted a system, I had encouraged my fellow-citizens, and I could not abandon them in conscience nor in honor. I determined, therefore, to set friends and enemies at

1 At this time it seems not a little strange to find all knowledge of the existence of this now celebrated paper so completely lost in the mind of the person most interested in it. But nothing is more marked in the whole of Mr. Adams's life, than his disregard of those memorials which go far more to form posthumous reputation than the most brilliant actions of a life.

defiance, and follow my own best judgment, whatever might "fall thereon," to borrow a phrase from our old legal formulary.

We read the answer, paragraph by paragraph. I suggested my doubts, scruples, and difficulties. The committee seemed to see and to feel the force of them. The gentlemen condescended to ask my opinion, what answer would be proper for them to report? I modestly suggested to them the expediency of leaving out many of those popular and eloquent periods, and of discussing the question with the Governor upon principles more especially legal and constitutional. The gentlemen very civilly requested me to undertake the task, and I agreed to attempt it.

The committee met from evening to evening, and I soon made my report. I drew a line over the most eloquent parts of the oration they had before them, and introduced those legal and historical authorities which appear on the record. It is more than forty years since I have seen any one of those papers which composed that controversy, and I know not how they would appear to the present generation, nor, indeed, how they would appear to myself. They stand upon record, and were printed together in a pamphlet, and no doubt in the newspapers. They ought to be looked up, for the effect of them upon public opinion was beyond expectation. The Governor's reasoning, instead of convincing the people that Parliament had sovereign authority over them in all cases whatsoever, seemed to convince all the world that Parliament had no authority over them in any case whatsoever. Mr. Hutchinson really made a meagre figure in that dispute. He had waded beyond his depth. He had wholly misunderstood the legal doctrine of allegiance.

In all great affairs there is always something ridiculous; et, malheureusement, j'ai toujours été trop incliné a saisir les ridicules. I had quoted largely from a law authority which no man in Massachusetts, at that time, had ever read. Hutchinson and all his law counsels were in fault; they could catch no scent. They dared not deny it, lest the book should be produced to their confusion. It was humorous enough to see how Hutchinson wriggled to evade it. He found nothing better to say than that it was "the artificial reasoning of Lord Coke." The book was Moore's Reports. The owner of it, for, alas! master, it was borrowed, was a buyer, but not a reader, of books. It had been Mr. Gridley's.

1773. January the first, being Friday. I have felt very well and been in very good spirits all day. I never was happier in my whole life than I have been since I returned to Boston. I feel easy and composed and contented. The year to come will be a pleasant, a cheerful, a happy, and a prosperous year to me. At least, such are the forebodings of my mind at present. My resolutions to devote myself to the pleasures, the studies, the business, and the duties of private life, are a source of ease and comfort to me that I scarcely ever experienced before. Peace, be still, my once anxious heart. A head full of schemes, and a heart full of anxiety, are incompatible with any degree of happiness.

I have said above, that I have the prospect before me of a happy and prosperous year, and I will not retract it, because I feel a great pleasure in the expectation of it, and I think that there is a strong probability and presumption of it. Yet fire may destroy my substance, diseases may desolate my family, and death may put a period to my hopes and fears, pleasures and pains, friendships and enmities, virtues and vices.

This evening, my friend Mr. Pemberton invited me, and I went with him, to spend the evening with Jere. Wheelwright. Mr. Wheelwright is a gentleman of a liberal education, about fifty years of age, and constantly confined to his chamber by lameness. A fortune of about two hundred pounds a year enables him to entertain his few friends very handsomely, and he has them regularly at his chamber every Tuesday and Friday evening.

The Speaker, Dr. Warren, and Mr. Swift were there, and we six had a very pleasant evening. Our conversation turned upon the distress of Rhode Island, upon the Judges' dependency, the late numerous town-meetings, upon Brattle's publication in Draper's paper of yesterday, and upon each other's characters. We were very free, especially upon one another. I told Cushing, as Ruggles told Tyler, that I never knew a pendulum swing so clear. Warren told me that Pemberton said I was the proudest and cunningest fellow he ever knew. We all rallied Pemberton upon the late appointment of Tommy Hutchinson[1] to be a Judge of the common bench, and pretended to insist upon it that he

[1] Thomas Hutchinson, Jr. the son of the Governor, who made no scruple of providing for his relations.

was disappointed and had lost all his late trimming, and lukewarmness, and toryism. Warren thought I was rather a cautious man, but that he could not say I ever trimmed; when I spoke at all, I always spoke my sentiments. This was a little soothing to my proud heart, no doubt.

Brattle has published a narration of the proceedings of the town of Cambridge at their late meeting, and he has endeavored to deceive the world.

March 4. Thursday. The two last months have slided away. I have written a tedious examination of Brattle's absurdities. The Governor and General Court have been engaged, for two months, upon the greatest question ever yet agitated. I stand amazed at the Governor for forcing on this controversy. He will not be thanked for this. His ruin and destruction must spring out of it, either from the Ministry and Parliament on one hand, or from his countrymen on the other. He has reduced himself to a most ridiculous state of distress. He is closeting and soliciting Mr. Bowdoin, Mr. Denny, Dr. Church, &c. &c. and seems in the utmost agony.

The original of my controversy with Brattle is worthy to be committed to writing in these memoranda. At the town meeting in Cambridge, called to consider of the Judges' salaries, he advanced for law that the judges, by this appointment, would be completely independent; for that they held estates for life in their offices, by common law, and their nomination and appointment. And he said, "This I aver to be law, and I will maintain it against anybody; I will dispute it with Mr. Otis, Mr. Adams, (Mr. John Adams, I mean,) and Mr. Josiah Quincy. I would dispute it with them here in town meeting; nay, I will dispute it with them in the newspapers."

He was so elated with that applause which this inane harangue procured him from the enemies of this country, that in the next Thursday's Gazette he roundly advanced the same doctrine in print, and, the Thursday after, invited any gentleman to dispute with him upon his points of law.

These vain and frothy harangues and scribblings would have had no effect upon me, if I had not seen that his ignorant doctrines were taking root in the minds of the people, many of whom were, in appearance, if not in reality, taking it for granted that the Judges held their places during good behavior.

Upon this, I determined to enter the lists, and the General was very soon silenced;[1] whether from conviction, or from policy, or contempt, I know not.

It is thus that little incidents produce great events. I have never known a period in which the seeds of great events have been so plentifully sown as this winter. A Providence is visible in that concurrence of causes, which produced the debates and controversies of this winter. The Court of Inquisition at Rhode Island, the Judges' salaries, the Massachusetts Bay town meetings,[2] General Brattle's folly, all conspired in a remarkable, a wonderful manner. My own determination had been to decline all invitations to public affairs and inquiries. But Brattle's rude, indecent, and unmeaning challenge, of me in particular, laid me under peculiar obligations to undeceive the people, and changed my resolution. I hope that some good will come out of it—God knows.

[In the year 1773, arose a controversy concerning the independence of the Judges. The King had granted a salary to the Judges of our Superior Court, and forbidden them to receive their salaries, as usual, from the grants of the House of Representatives, and the Council and Governor, as had been practised till this time. This, as the Judges' commissions were during pleasure, made them entirely dependent on the Crown for bread as well as office. The friends of government were anxious to persuade the people that their commissions were during good behavior. Brigadier-General Brattle, who had been a practitioner of law, and was at this time in his Majesty's Council, after some time came out with his name in one of the Gazettes, with a formal attempt to prove that the Judges held their offices for life. Perhaps I should not have taken any public notice of this, if it had not been industriously circulated among the people that the General had, at a town meeting in Cambridge the week before, advanced this doctrine, and challenged me, by name, to dispute the point with him. His challenge I should have disre-

[1] The papers written during this controversy, not being entirely temporary in their character, will be found in another volume.

[2] This measure, which greatly contributed to accelerate the Revolution by the organization of committees of correspondence throughout the Province, is fully dwelt upon by *Hutchinson*, vol. iii. p. 361–370; by *Gordon*, i. 314–320; and by *Bradford*, i. 258–262.

garded; but as his appeal to me was public, if I should remain silent, it would be presumed that my opinion coincided with his. It was of great importance that the people should form a correct opinion on this subject; and therefore I sent to the press a letter in answer, which drew me on to the number of eight letters, which may be seen in the Boston Gazette for this year. The doctrine and the history of the independence of Judges, was detailed and explained as well as my time, avocations, and information enabled me; imperfect and unpolished as they were, they were well-timed. The minds of all men were awake, and every thing was eagerly read by every one who could read. These papers accordingly contributed to spread correct opinions concerning the importance of the independence of the Judges to liberty and safety, and enabled the Convention of Massachusetts, in 1779, to adopt them into the constitution of the Commonwealth, as the State of New York had done before partially, and as the constitution of the United States did afterwards, in 1787. The principles developed in these papers have been very generally, indeed, almost universally, prevalent among the people of America from that time.]

---

5. Friday. Heard an oration, at Mr. Hunt's[1] meeting-house, by Dr. Benjamin Church, in commemoration of the massacre in King Street three years ago. That large church was filled and crowded in every pew, seat, alley, and gallery, by an audience of several thousands of people, of all ages and characters, and of both sexes.

I have reason to remember that fatal night. The part I took in defence of Captain Preston and the soldiers procured me anxiety and obloquy enough. It was, however, one of the most gallant, generous, manly, and disinterested actions of my whole life, and one of the best pieces of service I ever rendered my country. Judgment of death against those soldiers would have been as foul a stain upon this country as the executions of the quakers or witches anciently. As the evidence was, the verdict of the jury was exactly right.

This, however, is no reason why the town should not call the action of that night a massacre; nor is it any argument in favor

[1] Commonly known as the "Old South."

of the Governor or Minister who caused them to be sent here. But it is the strongest of proofs of the danger of standing armies

22. Monday. This afternoon received a collection of seventeen letters written from this Province, Rhode Island, Connecticut, and New York, by Hutchinson, Oliver, Moffat, Paxton, and Rome, in the years 1767, 1768, 1769.[1]

They came from England under such injunctions of secrecy,— as to the person to whom they were written, by whom and to whom they are sent here, and as to the contents of them, no copies of the whole or any part to be taken,— that it is difficult to make any public use of them.

These curious projectors and speculators in politics, will ruin this country. Cool, thinking, deliberate villain, malicious and vindictive, as well as ambitious and avaricious. The secrecy of these epistolary genii is very remarkable; profoundly secret, dark, and deep.

April 7. Wednesday. At Charlestown. What shall I write, say, do? Sterility, vacuity, barrenness of thought and reflection. What news shall we hear?

24. Saturday. I have communicated to Mr. Norton Quincy and to Mr. Wibird the important secret. They are as much affected by it as any others. Bone of our bone, born and educated among us! Mr. Hancock is deeply affected; is determined, in conjunction with Major Hawley, to watch the vile serpent, and his deputy serpent, Brattle. The subtlety of this serpent is equal to that of the old one. Aunt is let into the secret, and is full of her interjections!

[1] These are the celebrated letters transmitted by Dr. Franklin from London to Mr. Thomas Cushing at Boston, then Speaker of the House, the publication of which caused a duel between Messrs. Temple and Whately, in England. The source from which they came has never yet been fully ascertained. A complete copy of Governor Hutchinson's principal letter, made in the handwriting of Mr. Adams, remains among his papers. In a letter written to Dr. Hosack, 28 January, 1820, he says, "I was one of the first persons to whom Mr. Cushing communicated the great bundle of letters of Hutchinson and Oliver," &c. Mr. Cushing's letter of acknowledgment bears date the 24th of March, and begins thus: "I have *just* received your favor of the 2d December last, with the several papers enclosed, for which I am much obliged to you." It would seem, from this entry in the Diary of two days earlier, that no time had been lost in making them known to the confidential circle. Those who are disposed to place reliance upon Hutchinson's account of any thing appertaining to the action of the leading patriots, will do well to contrast his narrative of this proceeding, vol. iii. pp. 394–396, including the garbled letter in the note, with the correspondence published in the fourth volume of Mr. Sparks's edition of Franklin's writings.

But Cushing tells me that Powell told him, he had it from a tory, or one who was not suspected to be any thing else, that certain letters were come, written by four persons, which would show the causes and the authors of our present grievances. This tory, we conjecture to be Bob Temple, who has received a letter,[1] in which he is informed of these things: if the secret[2] — out by this means, I am glad it is not to be charged upon any of us, to whom it has been committed in confidence.

Fine, gentle rain, last night and this morning, which will lay a foundation for a crop of grass. My men at Braintree have been building me a wall this week, against my meadow. This is all the gain that I make by my farm, to repay me my great expense. I get my land better secured and manured.

April 25. Sunday. Heard Dr. Chauncy in the morning, and Dr. Cooper this afternoon. Dr. Cooper was upon Revelations, xii. 9: — "And the great dragon was cast out, that old serpent called the Devil and Satan, which deceiveth the whole world; he was cast out into the earth, and his angels were cast out with him." *Q.* Whether the Doctor had not some political allusions in the choice of this text?

May 24. Tuesday. To-morrow is our general election. The plots, plans, schemes, and machinations of this evening and night will be very numerous. By the number of ministerial, governmental people returned, and by the secrecy of the friends of liberty relating to the grand discovery of the complete evidence of the whole mystery of iniquity, I much fear the elections will go unhappily. For myself, I own, I tremble at the thought of an election. What will be expected of me? What will be required of me? What duties and obligations will result to me from an election? What duties to my God, my king, my country, my family, my friends, myself? What perplexities,

[1] In the letter to Dr. Hosack, already mentioned, Mr. Adams distinctly states that Sir John Temple told him, in Holland, that he had furnished these letters to Dr. Franklin. He adds, however, his belief that they were delivered through the hands of a third person, a member of Parliament. This precisely corresponds with the impression of Governor Hutchinson himself, soon after the time, derived from sources wholly distinct, but only known to the world since the publication of his third volume, in 1828, two years after Mr. Adams's death. If, in addition to this evidence, any credence at all be given to the rumor mentioned in the text, scarcely a doubt can remain that Sir John Temple was the man who procured them, although the way he did it remains hidden as ever.

[2] The words "should leak" erased in the original, and none substituted.

and intricacies, and difficulties shall I be exposed to? What snares and temptations will be thrown in my way? What self-denials and mortifications shall I be obliged to bear?

If I should be called in the course of providence to take a part in public life, I shall act a fearless, intrepid, undaunted part at all hazards, though it shall be my endeavor likewise, to act a prudent, cautious, and considerate part. But if I should be excused by a non-election, or by the exertions of prerogative [1] from engaging in public business, I shall enjoy a sweet tranquillity in the pursuit of my private business, in the education of my children, and in a constant attention to the preservation of my health. This last is the most selfish and pleasant system, the first, the more generous, though arduous and disagreeable. But I was not sent into this world to spend my days in sports, diversions, and pleasures; I was born for business, for both activity and study. I have little appetite or relish for any thing else. I must double and redouble my diligence. I must be more constant to my office and my pen; constancy accomplishes more than rapidity; continual attention will do great things; frugality of time is the greatest art, as well as virtue. This economy will produce knowledge as well as wealth.

Spent this evening at Wheelwright's, with Parson Williams of Sandwich, Parson Lawrence of Lincoln, Mr. Pemberton, and Swift. Williams took up the whole evening with stories about Colonel Otis, and his son, the Major.[2] "The Major employed the Treasurer and Parson Walter to represent him to the Governor as a friend to government, in order to get the commission of lieutenant-colonel. The Major quarrels and fights with Bacon; they came to, 'you lie,' and 'you lie;' and often very near to blows, sometimes quite. The Major has 'Liberty' written over his manufactory house, and the Major enclosed the exceptionable passages in the Governor's proclamation in crotchets. Colonel Otis reads to large circles of the common people Allen's Oration on the Beauties of Liberty, and recommends it as an excellent production."

[1] This alludes to the nomination of him by the friends of liberty, as a member of the Council. Two days afterwards he was chosen by the House of Representatives, and on the next, the Governor sent down a message, interposing his negative. In his History, he assigns as a reason for this negative, the "very conspicuous part Mr. Adams had taken in opposition." Vol. iii. p. 396.

[2] The father, and brother of James Otis

Stories of Colonel Otis's ignorance of law, about joint-tenancies. Criticizing upon the word household-goods in a will of the Parson's writing, and saying it was a word the law knew nothing of; it should have been household-stuff. Colonel Otis's orthodoxy, and yet some years ago, his arguing in the strain of Tindal against Christianity.

Yet some years ago Otis and Williams were very friendly. These prejudices against Otis and his family are very carefully cultivated by the Tories in that county, and by the Judges of the Superior Court. They generally keep Sabbath there. The Chief Justice went to spend the evening with him this year when I was at Sandwich, in order to keep up his spirits and fill his head with malicious stories. After I got home my wife surprised me; she had been to Justice Quincy's. Mr. Hancock came in, and gave, before a large company of both sexes, to Mr. Cooper, a particular account of all the plans of operation for to-morrow,[1] which he and many others had been concerting. Cooper, no doubt, carried it directly to Brattle, or at least, to his son Thomas; — such a leaky vessel is this worthy gentleman.

June 8. Parson Turner's sermon, the spirited election, Parson Howard's artillery sermon, the seventeen letters, Dr. Shipley's sermon, the Bishop of Saint Asaph, before the Society for Propagating the Gospel, discover the times to be altered. But how long will the tides continue to set this way?

July 16. Drank tea at Dr. Cooper's with Mr. Adams, Mr. S. Elliot, Mr. T. Chase, and with Mr. Mifflin, of Philadelphia, and a French gentleman. Mr. Mifflin[2] is a grandson, his mother was the daughter, of Mr. Bagnall of this town, who was buried the day before yesterday. Mr. Mifflin is a representative of the city of Philadelphia; a very sensible and agreeable man. Their academy emits from nine to fourteen graduates annually. Their grammar school has from ninety to one hundred scholars in all. Mr. Mifflin is an easy and a very correct speaker.

Mr. F. Dana came to me with a message from Mr. Henry Marchant, of Rhode Island, and to ask my opinion concerning the measures they are about to take with Rome's and Moffat's[3]

[1] The day of election. Hancock's allusion was probably to the selection already made of counsellors, of whom Mr. Adams was one.

[2] Thomas Mifflin, afterwards the Governor of Pennsylvania. His history is well known.

[3] These were in the package sent from England by Dr. Franklin. See page

letters. They want the originals, that they may be prosecuted as libels, by their attorney-general and grand jury. I told him I thought they could not proceed without the originals, nor with them, if there was any material obliteration or erasure, though I had not examined, and was not certain of this point, nor did I remember whether there was any obliteration on Rome's and Moffat's letters. Mr. Dana says the falsehoods and misrepresentations in Rome's letters are innumerable and very flagrant. Spent the evening with Cushing, Adams, Pemberton, and Swift, at Wheelwright's; nobody very chatty but Pemberton.

July 19. Monday.

To Thomas Hutchinson.[1]

SIR:—You will hear from us with astonishment. You ought to hear from us with horror. You are chargeable before God and man, with our blood. The soldiers were but passive instruments, mere machines; neither moral nor voluntary agents in our destruction, more than the leaden pellets with which we were wounded. You was a free agent. You acted, coolly, deliberately, with all that premeditated malice, not against us in particular, but against the people in general, which, in the sight of the law, is an ingredient in the composition of murder. You will hear further from us hereafter. CHRISPUS ATTUCKS.

August 23. Monday. Went this morning to Mr. Boylston's to make a wedding visit to Mr. Gill[2] and his lady. A very cordial, polite, and friendly reception, I had. Mr. Gill showed me Mr. Boylston's garden, and a large, beautiful, and agreeable one it is; a great variety of excellent fruit, plums, pears, peaches, grapes, currants, &c. &c.; a fig tree, &c.

318. Mr. George Rome was a gentleman of large property who came from the mother country and established himself in Rhode Island. His letter contained charges of the worst kind against the principal persons in that colony. Dr. Moffat was a Scotchman, and had been one of the officers appointed under the Stamp Act. See *Updike's History of the Narragansett Church*, pp. 252, 332–343.

[1] This address, in the name of the mulatto who was shot by the soldiers in the riot of the 5th of March, 1770, seems to have been intended for publication in a newspaper.

[2] Moses Gill, afterwards Lieutenant-Governor of Massachusetts, married a sister of Thomas and Nicholas Boylston.

Mr. and Mrs. Gill both gave me a very polite invitation to sup and spend the evening there, with Mr. Lynch and his lady, which I promised to do. At noon, I met Mr. Boylston upon 'Change, and he repeated the invitation in a very agreeable manner.

In the evening I waited on my wife there, and found Mr. Lynch[1] and his lady and daughter, Mr. Smith, his lady and daughter, and Miss Nabby Taylor; and a very agreeable evening we had. Mr. Lynch is a solid, sensible, though a plain man; a hearty friend to America and her righteous cause. His lady has the behavior and appearance of a very worthy woman, and the daughter seems to be worthy of such parents.

30. Monday. Spent the evening with my wife at her uncle Smith's, in company with Mr. Lynch, his lady and daughter, Colonel Howarth, his sister and daughter, Mr. Edward Green and his wife, &c. The young ladies, Miss Smith and Miss Lynch, entertained us upon the spinet, &c. Mr. Lynch still maintains the character. Colonel Howarth attracted no attention, until he discovered his antipathy to a cat.

December 17. Last night, three cargoes of Bohea tea were emptied into the sea. This morning a man-of-war sails. This is the most magnificent movement of all.[2] There is a dignity, a majesty, a sublimity, in this last effort of the patriots, that I greatly admire. The people should never rise without doing something to be remembered, something notable and striking. This destruction of the tea is so bold, so daring, so firm, intrepid and inflexible, and it must have so important consequences, and so lasting, that I cannot but consider it as an epocha in history. This, however, is but an attack upon property. Another similar exertion of popular power may produce the destruction of lives Many persons wish that as many dead carcasses were floating in the harbor, as there are chests of tea. A much less number of lives, however, would remove the causes of all our calamities. The malicious pleasure with which Hutchinson the Governor, the consignees of the tea, and the officers of the customs, have

[1] Thomas Lynch, of South Carolina, elected a delegate to the first and succeeding Congress. His son, Thomas Lynch, Jr., was a signer of the Declaration of Independence. A biography of the latter, including a notice of the father, is found in Mr. Sanderson's valuable collection.

[2] In the general correspondence, will be found a letter of this date directed to General James Warren, of Plymouth, showing some degree of acquaintance with this movement.

stood and looked upon the distresses of the people and their struggles to get the tea back to London, and at last the destruction of it, is amazing. 'T is hard to believe persons so hardened and abandoned.

What measures will the Ministry take in consequence of this? Will they resent it? Will they dare to resent it? Will they punish us? How? By quartering troops upon us? by annulling our charter? by laying on more duties? by restraining our trade? by sacrifice of individuals? or how?

The question is, Whether the destruction of this tea was necessary? I apprehend it was absolutely and indispensably so. They could not send it back. The Governor, Admiral, and Collector and Comptroller would not suffer it. It was in their power to have saved it, but in no other. It could not get by the castle, the men-of-war, &c. Then there was no other alternative but to destroy it or let it be landed. To let it be landed, would be giving up the principle of taxation by parliamentary authority, against which the continent has struggled for ten years. It was losing all our labor for ten years, and subjecting ourselves and our posterity forever to Egyptian task-masters; to burthens, indignities; to ignominy, reproach and contempt; to desolation and oppression; to poverty and servitude. But it will be said, it might have been left in the care of a committee of the town, or in Castle William. To this many objections may be made.

Deacon Palmer and Mr. Isaac Smith dined with me, and Mr. Trumbull came in. They say the Tories blame the consignees as much as the Whigs do, and say that the Governor will lose his place, for not taking the tea into his protection before, by means of the ships of war, I suppose, and the troops at the castle. I saw him this morning pass my window in a chariot, with the Secretary; and by the marching and countermarching of counsellors, I suppose they have been framing a proclamation, offering a reward to discover the persons, their aiders, abettors, counsellors, and consorters, who were concerned in the riot last night. Spent the evening with Cushing, Pemberton, and Swift, at Wheelwright's. Cushing gave us an account of Bollan's letters, of the quantity of tea the East India Company had on hand, forty millions weight, that is, seven years consumption,—two millions weight in America.

18. Saturday. J. Quincy met me this morning, and, after him, Kent, and told me that the Governor said, yesterday, in council, that the people had been guilty of high treason, and that he would bring the Attorney-General, on Monday, to convince them that it was so. And that Hancock said, he was for having a body meeting[1] to take off that brother-in-law of his.[2]

In the interval between these entries in his Diary, that is, on the twenty-fifth of January, 1774, the following letter was received by Mr. Adams.

London Tavern, 21 September, 1773.

Supporters of the Bill of Rights.

SIR: — In pursuance of a resolution of this Society, I am to signify to you that you have this day been duly elected a member thereof.[3]

I am, sir, your most humble servant,

THOMAS WILSON, *Chairman.*

Signed by his order,

JOHN WILKES.

London, 15 October, 1773.

SIR: — I have the honor of transmitting you the inclosed resolution of the Society of the Bill of Rights, which was unanimous.

It affords me great pleasure to find so very respectable a gentleman of America, disposed to unite with the Friends of Liberty in England for our mutual safety and defence.

I am, most respectfully,

Your very obedient, humble servant,

STEPHEN SAYRE.[4]

1 Contradistinguished from a town meeting which was called by authority of the town officers, and in which none but citizens of the town could take part. Body meetings more resemble what is now called a mass meeting.

2 Jonathan Sewall and John Hancock married sisters.

3 This election and that of Joseph Warren were made on the recommendation of Samuel Adams, through Arthur Lee, who was then in London. See the letter of the former, dated 9th April, 1773, in the Life of Arthur Lee, by R. H. Lee, vol. ii. p. 203, and the reply of the latter, on the 23d of June, in vol. i. p. 222. There is a mistake of one year in the date of this last. It is much to be regretted that the Biography of both the Lees should have been so much disfigured as it is by errors of haste, as well in arrangement as in typography.

4 Of the singular career of this gentleman, in England, Prussia, Russia, and America, an interesting account has been given by Mr. Reed, in his Biography of Joseph Reed, vol. i. p. 27, note.

1774. February 28. I purchased of my brother my father's homestead, and house where I was born. The house, barn, and thirty-five acres of land, of which the homestead consists, and eighteen acres of pasture in the North Common, cost me four hundred and forty pounds. This is a fine addition to what I had there before of arable and meadow. The buildings and the water I wanted very much; that beautiful, winding, meandering brook, which runs through this farm, always delighted me. How shall I improve it? Shall I try to introduce fowl-meadow, and herds-grass into the meadows? or still better, clover and herds-grass? I must ramble over it and take a view.

March 2. Wednesday. Last evening at Wheelwright's with Cushing, Pemberton, and Swift. Lieutenant-Governor Oliver, senseless and dying; the Governor sent for, and Oliver's sons. Flucker[1] has laid in to be Lieutenant-Governor, and has persuaded Hutchinson to write in his favor. This will make a difficulty. Chief Justice Oliver and Flucker will interfere. Much said of the impeachment against the Chief Justice, and upon the question whether the Council have the power of judicature in Parliament, which the Lords have at home, or whether the Governor and Council have this power. It is said by some that the Council is too precarious a body to be intrusted with so great a power. So far from being independent, and having their dignities and power hereditary, they are annually at the will, both of the House and the Governor, and therefore are not sufficiently independent to hold such powers of judicature over the lives and fortunes of mankind. But the answer is this: they may be intrusted with the powers of judicature as safely as with the powers of legislation, and it should be remembered that the Council can in no case here be triers of fact as well as law, as the Lords are at home, when a peer is impeached, because the Council are all Commoners and no more. The House of Representatives are the triers of the facts, and their vote impeaching is equivalent to a bill of indictment, and their vote demanding judgment is equivalent to a verdict of a jury, according to Selden. Are not the life, and liberty, and property of the subject thus guarded as secure as they ought to be, when no

[1] Thomas Flucker, Secretary of the colony, a mandamus counsellor, and afterwards an exile in England, where he died in 1783. *Sabine.*

man can be punished without the vote of the Representatives of the whole people, and without the vote of the Council Board, if he can be without the assent of the Governor? But it is said that there is no court of judicature in the Province, erected by the charter only; that in the charter a power is given to the General Court to erect courts; that the General Court has not made the Governor and Council a court of judicature, and therefore it is not one, only in cases of marriage and probate. To this it may be answered, by inquiring how the Council came by their share in the legislative.[1] The charter says, indeed, that the General Court shall consist of Governor, Council, and House, and that they shall make laws; but it nowhere says the Council shall be an integral part of this General Court—that they shall have a negative voice. It is only from analogy to the British legislative, that they have assumed this importance in our constitution. Why, then, may they not derive from the same analogy the power of judicature? About nine at night I stepped over the way, and took a pipe with Justice Quincy, and a Mr. Wendell of Portsmouth. Mr. Wendell seems a man of sense and education, and not ill affected to the public cause.

[1] The common form at this period of designating the law-making department of government.

[At this period the universal cry among the friends of their country was, "what shall we do to be saved?" It was by all agreed, as the Governor was entirely dependent on the Crown, and the Council in danger of becoming so, if the judges were made so too, the liberties of the country would be totally lost, and every man at the mercy of a few slaves of the Governor; but no man presumed to say what ought to be done, or what could be done. Intimations were frequently given, that this arrangement should not be submitted to. I understood very well what was meant, and I fully expected that if no expedient could be suggested, the judges would be obliged to go where Secretary Oliver had gone, to Liberty Tree, and compelled to take an oath to renounce the royal salaries. Some of these judges were men of resolution, and the Chief Justice,[1] in particular, piqued himself so much upon it and had so often gloried in it on the bench, that I shuddered at the expectation that the mob might put on him a coat of tar and feathers, if not put him to death. I had a real respect for the judges; three of them, Trowbridge, Cushing, and Brown, I could call my friends. Oliver and Ropes, abstracted from their politics, were amiable men, and all of them were very respectable and virtuous characters. I dreaded the effect upon the morals and tempers of the people, which must be produced by any violence offered to the persons of those who wore the robes and bore the sacred characters of judges; and moreover, I felt a strong aversion to such partial, and irregular recurrences to original power. The poor people themselves, who by secret manœuvres are excited to insurrection, are seldom aware of the purposes for which they are set in motion, or of the consequences which may happen to themselves; and, when once heated and in full career, they can neither manage themselves nor be regulated by others.

Full of these reflections I happened to dine with Mr. Samuel Winthrop at New Boston, who was then clerk of the Superior Court, in company with several members of the General Court of both Houses, and with several other gentlemen of the town.

[1] Peter Oliver.

Dr. John Winthrop, philosophical professor at college, and Dr. Cooper of Boston, both of them very much my friends, were of the company. The conversation turned wholly on the topic of the day, and the case of the Judges. All agreed that it was a fatal measure, and would be the ruin of the liberties of the country. But what was the remedy? It seemed to be a measure that would execute itself. There was no imaginable way of resisting or eluding it. There was lamentation and mourning enough, but no light and no hope. The storm was terrible, and no blue sky to be discovered. I had been entirely silent, and in the midst of all this gloom, Dr. Winthrop, addressing himself to me, said, "Mr. Adams, we have not heard your sentiments on this subject; how do you consider it?" I answered that my sentiments accorded perfectly with all that had been expressed. The measure had created a crisis; and if it could not be defeated, the liberties of the Province would be lost. The stroke was levelled at the essence of the constitution, and nothing was too dear to be hazarded in warding it off. It levelled the axe at the root, and if not opposed, the tree would be overthrown from the foundation. It appeared so to me at that time, and I have seen no reason to suspect that I was in an error to this day.

"But," said Dr. Winthrop, "what can be done?" I answered that I knew not whether any one would approve of my opinion, yet I believed there was one constitutional resource; but I knew not whether it would be possible to persuade the proper authority to have recourse to it. Several voices at once cried out, "A constitutional resource! what can it be?" I said it was nothing more nor less than an impeachment of the Judges, by the House of Representatives, before the Council. "An impeachment! why, such a thing is without precedent." I believed it was, in this Province; but there had been precedents enough, and by much too many, in England; it was a dangerous experiment at all times, but it was essential to the preservation of the constitution in some cases that could be reached by no other power but that of impeachment. "But whence can we pretend to derive such a power?" From our charter, which gives us in words as express, as clear, and as strong as the language affords, all the rights and privileges of Englishmen; and if the House of Commons in England is the grand inquest of the nation, the House of Representatives is the grand inquest of this Province, and the Council must have the powers of judicature of the House of Lords in Great Britain. This doctrine was said by the company to be wholly new; they knew not how far it could be supported, but it deserved to be considered and examined. After all, if it should be approved by the House, the Council would not convict the judges. That, I said, was an after consideration; if the House was convinced that they had the power and that it was their duty to exercise it, they ought to do it, and oblige the Council to inquire into their rights, and powers, and duties. If the Council would not hearken to law or evidence, they must be responsible for the consequences, and the guilt and blame must lie at their door. The company separated, and I knew that the Governor and the Judges would soon have information of this conversation, and as several members of both Houses were present, and several gentlemen of the town, I was sensible that it would soon become the talk of the legislature, as well as of the town.

The next day, I believe, Major Hawley came to my house, and told me he heard I had broached a strange doctrine. He hardly knew what an impeachment was; he had never read any one, and never had thought on the subject. I told him he might read as many of them as he pleased; there stood the State Trials on the shelf, which was full of them, of all sorts, good and bad. I showed him Selden's works, in which is a treatise on judicature in Parliament, and gave it him to read. I added, that judicature in Parliament was as ancient as common law and as Parliament itself; that without this high jurisdiction it was thought impossible to defend the constitution against princes, and nobles, and great ministers, who might commit high crimes and misdemeanors which no other authority would be powerful enough to prevent or punish; that our constitution was a miniature of the British; that the charter had given us every power, jurisdiction, and right within our limits which could be claimed by the people or government of England, with no other exceptions than those in the charter expressed. We looked into the charter together, and after a long conversation and a considerable research, he said he knew not how to get rid of it. In a day or two another lawyer in the House came to me, full of doubts and difficulties; he said he heard I had shown Major Hawley some books relative to the subject, and desired to see them.

I showed them to him, and he made nearly the same comments upon them. It soon became the common topic and research of the bar.

Major Hawley had a long friendship for Judge Trowbridge, and a high opinion of his knowledge of law, which was indeed extensive. He determined to converse with the Judge upon the subject; went to Cambridge on Saturday and staid till Monday. On this visit he introduced this subject, and appealed to Lord Coke and Selden, as well as to the charter, and advanced all the arguments which occurred to him. The Judge, although he had renounced the salary, we may suppose was not much delighted with the subject on account of his brothers. He did, however, declare to the Major that he could not deny that the constitution had given the power to the House of Representatives, the charter was so full and express, but that the exercise of it in this case would be vain, as the Council would undoubtedly acquit the judges, even if they heard and tried the impeachment. Hawley was not so much concerned about that as he was to ascertain the law. The first time I saw Judge Trowbridge he said to me, "I see, Mr. Adams, you are determined to explore the constitution, and bring to life all its dormant and latent powers, in defence of your liberties as you understand them." I answered, "I should be very happy if the constitution could carry us safely through all our difficulties without having recourse to higher powers not written." The members of the House becoming soon convinced that there was something for them to do, appointed a committee to draw up articles of impeachment against the Chief Justice Oliver. Major Hawley, who was one of this committee, would do nothing without me, and insisted on bringing them to my house to examine and discuss the articles, paragraph by paragraph, which was readily consented to by the committee. Several evenings were spent in my office upon this business until very late at night. One morning, meeting Ben Gridley, he said to me, "Brother Adams, you keep late hours at your house; as I passed it last night long after midnight, I saw your street door vomit forth a crowd of senators."

The articles, when prepared, were reported to the House of Representatives, adopted by them, and sent up to the Council Board. The Council would do nothing, and there they rested,

The friends of administration thought they had obtained a triumph, but they were mistaken. The articles were printed in the journals of the House, and in the newspapers, and the people meditated on them at their leisure. When the Superior Court came to sit in Boston, the grand jurors and petit jurors, as their names were called over, refused to take the oaths. When examined and demanded their reasons for this extraordinary conduct, they answered to a man that the Chief Justice of that court stood impeached of high crimes and misdemeanors before his Majesty's Council, and they would not sit as jurors while that accusation was depending. At the Charlestown Court the jurors unanimously refused in the same manner. They did so at Worcester and all the other Counties. The court never sat again until a new one was appointed by the Council exercising the powers of a Governor under the charter, after the battle of Lexington on the 19th of April, 1775.]

March 5. Saturday. Heard the oration, pronounced by Colonel Hancock, in commemoration of the massacre. An elegant, a pathetic, a spirited performance. A vast crowd, rainy eyes, &c. The composition, the pronunciation, the action, all exceeded the expectations of everybody. They exceeded even mine, which were very considerable. Many of the sentiments came with great propriety from him. His invective,[1] particularly, against a preference of riches to virtue, came from him with a singular dignity and grace.[2] Dined at neighbor Quincy's with my wife. Mr. John Denny and son there. Denny gave a few hints of vacating the charter and sending troops, and depriving the Province of advantages, quartering troops, &c. but all pretty faint. The happiness of the family where I dined, upon account of the Colonel's justly applauded oration, was complete. The Justice and his daughters were all joyous.[3]

6. Sunday. Heard Dr. Cooper in the morning. Paine drank coffee with me. Paine is under some apprehensions of troops,

[1] "Despise the glare of wealth. That people who pay greater respect to a wealthy villain, than to an honest, upright man in poverty, almost deserve to be enslaved; they plainly show that wealth, however it may be acquired, is in their esteem, to be preferred to virtue." *Extract from Mr. Hancock's Oration.*

[2] Mr. Hancock was considered the richest man in the Province.

[3] Edmund Quincy, whose daughter was married to Mr. Hancock.

on account of the high proceedings. He says there is a ship in to-day with a consignment of tea from some private merchants at home, &c.

Last Thursday morning, March 3d, died Andrew Oliver, Esq. Lieutenant-Governor. This is but the second death which has happened among the conspirators,[1] the original conspirators against the public liberty, since the conspiracy was first regularly formed and begun to be executed, in 1763 or 1764. Judge Russell, who was one, died in 1766. Nat Rogers, who was not one of the originals, but came in afterwards, died in 1770. This event will have considerable consequences; — Peter Oliver will be made Lieutenant-Governor. Hutchinson will go home, and probably be continued Governor, but reside in England, and Peter Oliver will reside here and rule the Province. The duty on tea will be repealed. Troops may come, but what becomes of the poor patriots? They must starve and mourn as usual. The Hutchinsons and Olivers will rule and overbear all things as usual.

An event happened last Friday that is surprising. At a General Council, which was full, as the General Court was then sitting, Hutchinson had the confidence to nominate for justices of the peace, George Bethune, Nat Taylor, Ned Loyd, Benjamin Gridley, and Sam. Barrett, and informed the Board that they had all promised to take the oath. The Council had the pusillanimity to consent, by their silence at least, to these nominations. Nothing has a more fatal tendency than such prostitution of the Council. They tamely, supinely, timorously acquiesce in the appointment of persons to fill every executive department in the Province with tools of the family who are planning our destruction. Neighbor Quincy spent the evening with me.

7. Monday. This morning brought us news from South Carolina, of the destruction of the tea there, and from England, of a duel between Mr. Temple and Mr. Whately, and Mr. Franklin's explicit declaration that he alone sent the Governor's letters to Boston, and that both Temple and Whately were ignorant and innocent of it; and that three regiments are ordered to Boston and New York; that the Judges' opinions are required, and the Board of Trade in motion, and great things are to be laid

[1] Hutchinson's lamentation over this gentleman is in singular and remarkable contrast with this notice in the text. Vol. iii. p. 456, note.

before Parliament, &c. &c. Twenty-eight chests of tea arrived yesterday, which are to make an infusion in water at seven o'clock this evening.[1] This evening there has been an exhibition in King Street, of the portraits of the soldiers and the massacre, and of Hutchinson and C. J. Oliver in the horrors—reminded of the fate of Empson and Dudley, whose trunks were exposed with their heads off, and the blood fresh streaming after the axe.[2]

8. Tuesday. Last night twenty-eight chests and a half of tea were drowned.

9. Wednesday. Returned from Charlestown Court with Colonel Tyng of Dunstable, who told me some anecdotes of Bernard and Brattle, Otis, Hutchinson, &c. "Bernard said, he never thought of Pratt. He would find a place for him now upon the bench. Brattle shall be Colonel and Brigadier, &c. Bernard

[1] It is very clear that the author knew what was going to be done. But he never knew the names of the actors.

The following letter, written to Mr. Niles, Editor of the Weekly Register, is suitable for insertion in this connection. The writer was mistaken in his recollection of where he was at the moment. See the record of the 17th December, page 323, and the letter to James Warren, of the same date, in the general correspondence.

Quincy, 10 May, 1819.

In one of your letters, you ask me whether I can give the names of the Mohawks, who were concerned in the noyade of the tea in Boston harbor? I now tell you in truth, and upon honor, that I know not and never knew the name of any one of them. During the week of that transaction, I was employed in the discharge of my duty, as a barrister of law in the Court of Judicature, in the town and county of Plymouth. When I returned to Boston the deed was done. I never inquired who did it. Whenever any person discovered an inclination to give me a history of it, as many did, I constantly stopped him short, and said, say not a word to me on that subject; name not to me one person concerned in it. My reason for this caution was, that I expected every day an indictment against the authors of it, and that I should be called upon to defend them in a court of justice; and I was determined that no judge or juror, attorney-general or solicitor-general, should have it in his power to compel me to testify as a witness to any fact relative to the transaction; and to this day, I know not the name of one man concerned in it. Within two years past, a gentleman, an entire stranger to me, on a visit he was pleased to make, blurted out the name of one gentleman, who, he said, told him that he was one of the "Mohawks;" but this name I will not commit to writing.

You may depend upon it they were no ordinary Mohawks. The profound secrecy in which they have held their names, and the total abstinence from plunder, are proofs of the characters of the men. I believe they would have tarred and feathered any one of their number who should have been detected in pocketing a pound of Hyson.

[2] Hutchinson betrays his sense of this insult by the affected contempt with which he treats it, and quotes Tacitus, to prove that such things when left without notice are forgotten, at the very moment when he is giving it all the permanency in his power, by recording it in his History. Vol. iii. p. 457.

said, afterwards, this miff broke out into a blaze. Jemmy Russell was as sociable and familiar with Dix and Gorham and Stone, and with all the members of the House, as possible. An artful fellow, deeply covered." He told a saying of the Admiral at the funeral yesterday. "There was never any thing in Turkey, nor in any part of the world, so arbitrary and cruel as keeping old Mr. Clarke at the castle all this winter, an old man[1] from his family." This day the General Court prorogued in anger by the Governor.

11. Friday. Dined at Charlestown with Mr. Thomas Russell, with Mr. Temple, Mr. Jacob Rowe, Mr. Nichols, Mr. Bliss, and several other gentlemen and ladies to me unknown. No politics, but Mr. Temple's duel and the pieces in the London papers relative to it. A young brother of Mr. Russell came in. Conversation about making porter here, our barley, hops, &c. The right of private judgment and the liberty of conscience were claimed by the papists, and allowed them in the reign of James II., but have been prohibited by law ever since. The advocates for the administration now in America, claim the right of private judgment to overthrow the constitution of this Province, the privileges of all America, and British liberties into the bargain. *Sed non allocatur.*

12. Saturday. There has been and is a party in the nation, a very small one indeed, who have pretended to be conscientiously persuaded that the pretender has a right to the throne. Their principles of loyalty, hereditary right, and passive obedience, have led them to this judgment and opinion; and as long as they keep these opinions to themselves, there is no remedy against them. But as soon as they express these opinions publicly, and endeavor to make proselytes, especially if they take any steps to introduce the pretender, they become offenders, and must suffer the punishment due to their crimes. Private judgment might be alleged in excuse for many crimes. A poor enthusiast might bring himself to believe it lawful for him to steal from his rich neighbor, to supply his necessities. But the law will not allow of this plea; the man must be punished for his theft. Ravaillac and Felton probably thought they were

[1] Richard Clarke and sons were consignees of the tea, who took refuge in the castle, from the excited feelings of the community in Boston. *Hutchinson*, vol. iii. p. 430.

doing their duty, and nothing more, when they were committing their vile assassinations; but the liberty of private conscience did not exempt them from the most dreadful punishment that civil authority can inflict or human nature endure. Hutchinson and Oliver might be brought, by their interested views and motives, sincerely to think that an alteration in the constitution of this Province, and an "abridgment of what are called English liberties," would be for the good of the Province, of America, and of the nation. In this they deceived themselves, and became the bubbles of their own avarice and ambition. The rest of the world are not thus deceived. They see clearly that such innovations will be the ruin, not only of the Colonies, but of the empire, and therefore think that examples ought to be made of these great offenders *in terrorem*.

The enmity of Governor Bernard, Hutchinson, and Oliver, and others, to the constitution of this Province, is owing to its being an obstacle to their views and designs of raising a revenue by parliamentary authority, and making their own fortunes out of it. The constitution of this Province has enabled the people to resist their projects so effectually, that they see they shall never carry them into execution while it exists. Their malice has, therefore, been directed against it, and their utmost efforts have been employed to destroy it. There is so much of a republican spirit among the people, which has been nourished and cherished by their form of government, that they never would submit to tyrants or oppressive projects. The same spirit spreads like a contagion into all the other colonies, into Ireland and into Great Britain too, from this single Province of Massachusetts Bay, that no pains are too great to be taken, no hazards too great to be run, for the destruction of our charter.

13. Sunday. Heard Mr. Lathrop in the forenoon, and Dr. Cooper in the afternoon. Last evening, Justice Pemberton spent with me. He says that Moses Gill has made many justices by lending money.

28. Monday. Rode with brother Josiah Quincy to Ipswich Court. Arrived at Piemont's, in Danvers, in good order and well conditioned. Spent the evening, and lodged agreeably. Walked out in the morning to hear the birds sing. Piemont says there is a report that the Sons of Liberty have received some advices from England, which makes them look down; that

Watertown 23d Septr 1775

[Ma]dm Adams

The Publick have [g]reat need of two Vols of Mr Adams [E]nglish Statutes at large — the [E]dition which Mr Adams owns is (if I dont mistake) Ruffheads [T]he one Vol. which is wanted is that [w]hich contains the Statutes of [2]7th of Edward the third and the [o]ther which is Needed contains the [S]tatutes of the 23d of Henry 8th — I would not ask such a favour [M]adam, if the publick was not much [in]terested — I shall desire Col Thayer [to] be particularly careful in bringing [th]em — after their arrival — I will [u]ndertake that they be most carefully [u]sed and will be responsible for ye [s]peedy return of them — I dont know [w]here else they can be Obtaind —

I am madme your most respectful and Obedient Servt

Joseph Hawley

they have received a letter from Mr. Bollan, that they must submit; and other letters which they keep secret.

29. Tuesday. Rode to Ipswich, and put up at the old place, Treadwell's. The old lady has got a new copy of her great grandfather Governor Endicott's picture hung up in the house. The old gentleman is afraid they will repeal the excise upon tea, and then that we shall have it plenty; wishes they would double the duty, and then we should never have any more. The question is, Who is to succeed Judge Ropes? whether Brown, or Pynchon, or Lee, or Hatch? The bar here are explicit against the two last, as unfit. Lowell says Pynchon would take it, because he wants to make way for Wetmore, who is about marrying his daughter. Pynchon says Judge Ropes was exceedingly agitated, all the time of his last sickness, about the public affairs in general, and those of the superior court in particular; afraid his renunciation would be attributed to timidity; afraid to refuse to renounce; worried about the opinion of the bar, &c. Mr. Farnham is exceedingly mollified; is grown quite modest and polite, in comparison with what he used to be, in politics. Lowell is so, too; seems inclined to be admitted among the liberty men.

At a meeting of the bar, a doubt of Brother Lowell was mentioned, upon the law of the Province for the relief of poor prisoners for debt. Questions were asked, whether appealing an action was not fraud? whether trading without insuring was not fraud? &c. A question also about the duty of the sheriff. Whether a party plaintiff could control the King's precept, &c. by ordering the sheriff not to serve it? &c. Mr. Wetmore was agreed to be recommended for the oath, &c.

30. Wednesday. A dull day. My head is empty, but my heart is full. I am wanted at my office, but not wanted here; there is business there, but none here. My wife, perhaps, wants to see me. I am anxious about her; I cannot get the thoughts of her state of health out of my mind; I think she must remove to Braintree, and the family, at least for the season.

31. Thursday. Let me ask my own heart, have I patience and industry enough to write a history of the contest between Britain and America? It would be proper to begin at the Treaty of Peace, in 1763, or at the commencement of Governor Bernard's administration, or at the accession of George III. to

the throne; the Reign, or the Peace. Would not it be proper to begin with those articles in the Treaty of Peace which relate to America? The cession of Canada, Louisiana, and Florida, to the English. Franklin, Lee, Chatham, Camden, Grenville, and Shelburne, Hillsborough, Dartmouth, Whately, Hutchinson, Oliver, Judge Oliver, Bernard, Paxton, Otis, Thacher, Adams, Mayhew, Hancock, Cushing, Phillips, Hawley, Warren, with many other figures, would make up the group.

June 20. Monday. At Piemont's, in Danvers; bound to Ipswich. There is a new and a grand scene open before me; a Congress. This will be an assembly of the wisest men upon the continent, who are Americans in principle, that is, against the taxation of Americans by authority of Parliament. I feel myself unequal to this business. A more extensive knowledge of the realm, the colonies, and of commerce, as well as of law and policy, is necessary, than I am master of. What can be done? Will it be expedient to propose an annual congress of committees? to petition? Will it do to petition at all?—to the King? to the Lords? to the Commons? What will such consultations avail? Deliberations alone will not do. We must petition or recommend to the Assemblies to petition, or—

The ideas of the people are as various as their faces. One thinks, no more petitions,—former having been neglected and despised; some are for resolves, spirited resolves, and some are for bolder counsels. I will keep an exact diary of my journey, as well as journal of the proceedings of Congress.

25. Saturday. Since the Court adjourned without day this afternoon, I have taken a long walk through the Neck, as they call it, a fine tract of land in a general field. Corn, rye, grass, interspersed in great perfection this fine season. I wander alone and ponder. I muse, I mope, I ruminate. I am often in reveries and brown studies. The objects before me are too grand and multifarious for my comprehension. We have not men fit for the times. We are deficient in genius, in education, in travel, in fortune, in every thing. I feel unutterable anxiety. God grant us wisdom and fortitude! Should the opposition be suppressed, should this country submit, what infamy and ruin! God forbid. Death in any form is less terrible!

Extract from the Autobiography.

[It is well known that in June, 1774, the General Court at Cambridge[1] appointed members to meet with others from the other States in Congress, on the 5th of August.[1] Mr. Bowdoin, Mr. Cushing, Mr. Samuel Adams, Mr. John Adams, and Mr. Robert Treat Paine, were appointed. After this election, I went for the tenth and last time on the eastern circuit. At York, at dinner with the court, happening to sit at table next to Mr. Justice Sayward, a representative of York, but of the unpopular side, we entered very sociably and pleasantly into conversation, and, among other things, he said to me, "Mr. Adams, you are going to Congress, and great things are in agitation. I recommend to you the doctrine of my former minister, Mr. Moody. Upon an occasion of some gloomy prospects for the country, he preached a sermon from this text: 'They know not what they do.' After a customary introduction, he raised this doctrine from his text, that in times of great difficulty and danger, when men know not what to do, it is the duty of a person or a people to be very careful that they do not do they know not what." This oracular jingle of words, which seemed, however, to contain

[1] These are mistakes of haste. Governor Gage had adjourned the General Court from Boston to Salem, as a place exercising a less unfavorable influence upon its members. Here, on the 17th of June, the last act of the body, done whilst the Secretary was standing on the outside of the locked doors with a proclamation dissolving it in his hand, was to appoint the five gentlemen named in the text a committee (as it was called) to meet committees from the other colonies, at Philadelphia, on the first day of September following. The resolution, authorizing this appointment, was adopted with twelve dissenting voices out of a hundred and twenty-nine then present.

On the same day, what is described as a legal and very full adjourned meeting of the citizens of Boston was held at Faneuil Hall, at which the author of the Diary presided as moderator. The object was to consult upon the measures made necessary by the Boston Port Bill. Of this meeting it is said, that, "it was as full and respectable as ever was known; — their unanimity and firmness was never exceeded; not one, though often called upon, had any thing to offer in favor of paying for the tea, in compliance with the Boston Port Bill; all appeared disposed to stand the utmost efforts of tyranny, rather than make a free surrender of the rights of America. The speeches made on the state of American affairs would do honor to any Assembly. The resolutions were adopted with a single dissenting vote."

American Archives, 4th series, vol. i. 423.

some good sense, made us all very gay. But I thought the venerable preacher, when he had beat the drum ecclesiastic to animate the country to undertake the expedition to Louisburg, in 1745, and had gone himself with it as a chaplain, had ventured to do he knew not what, as much as I was likely to do in the expedition to Congress. I told the Deacon that I must trust Providence, as Mr. Moody had done when he did his duty, though he could not foresee the consequences.[1]

To prepare myself as well as I could for the storm that was coming on, I removed my family to Braintree. They could not, indeed, have remained in safety in Boston; and when the time arrived, Mr. Bowdoin having declined the appointment, Mr. Cushing, Mr. Adams, Mr. Paine, and myself, set out on our journey together in one coach.]

Boston. August 10. Wednesday. The committee for the Congress[2] took their departure from Boston, from Mr. Cushing's house, and rode to Coolidge's, where they dined in company with a large number of gentlemen, who went out and prepared an entertainment for them at that place. A most kindly and affectionate meeting we had, and about four in the afternoon we took our leave of them, amidst the kind wishes and fervent

[1] The prophet of York has not prophesied in vain. There is, in this town and county, a Laodiceanism that I have not found in any other place. I find more persons here who call the destruction of the tea mischief and wickedness, than anywhere else; more persons who say that the duty upon tea is not a tax nor an imposition, because we are at liberty to use it or not, than anywhere else. I am told that the Deacon insinuates sentiments and principles into the people here in a very subtle manner; a manner so plausible that they scarcely know how they come by them.

When I got to the tavern, on the eastern side of Piscataqua river, I found the sheriff of York and six of his deputies, all with gold laced hats, ruffles, swords, and very gay clothes, and all likely young men, who had come out to that place, ten miles, to escort the court into town. This unusual parade excited my curiosity, and I soon suspected that this was to show respect, and be a guard to the Chief Justice if he had been coming to Court.

The foreman of the grand jury told Judge Trowbridge, that, if the Chief Justice had been here, not a man of their jury would have refused to be sworn. However, I have been told by others that the foreman is mistaken; that it was universally known he was not at Ipswich, and would not be here; but if he had been here, there would have been a difficulty. *J. A. to his wife*, 29 June, 1774.

[2] The list of persons elected by the respective Provinces to the Congress of 1774, is omitted, because it is found in every copy of the journals.

prayers of every man in the company for our health and success. This scene was truly affecting, beyond all description affecting.[1] I lodged at Colonel Buck's.

15. Monday. Mr. Silas Deane,[2] of Wethersfield, came over to Hartford to see us. He is a gentleman of a liberal education, about forty years of age; first kept a school, then studied law, then married the rich widow of Mr. Webb, since which he has been in trade. Two young gentlemen, his sons-in-law, Messrs. Webbs, came over with him. They are genteel, agreeable men, largely in trade, and are willing to renounce all their trade.

Mr. Deane gave us an account of the delegates of New York. Duane and Jay are lawyers. Livingston, Low, and Alsop are merchants. Livingston is very popular. Jay married a Livingston, Peter's daughter,[3] and is supposed to be of his side.

Mr. Deane says the sense of Connecticut is, that the resolutions of the Congress shall be the laws of the Medes and Persians; that the Congress is the grandest and most important assembly ever held in America, and that the *all* of America is intrusted to it and depends upon it.

Last evening, after spending the evening at the meeting-house to hear the singing, we were invited into Mr. Church's. Mr. Seymour, Mr. Payne, lawyers, and Mr. Bull, merchant, came to see us, and invited us to dine with them this day, with the principal gentlemen of the place.

This morning, Mr. Deane and two young gentlemen, Messrs. Webbs, came to see us from Wethersfield. Mr. Deane says, there are thirty thousand bushels of flax-seed sent to New York yearly, in exchange for salt; that it would be no loss to stop this, as the seed may be made into oil more profitably. They

[1] Boston, August 15. Wednesday morning, the Hon. Thomas Cushing, Esq. Mr. Samuel Adams, John Adams, and Robert Treat Paine, Esquires, — the delegates appointed by the Hon. Commons House of Assembly, for this Province, to attend the General Congress to be holden at Philadelphia, some time next month, — set out from hence, attended by a number of gentlemen, who accompanied them to Watertown, where they were met by many others, who provided an elegant entertainment for them. After dinner, they proceeded on their journey, intending to reach Southborough that evening. *Boston Gazette.*

[2] According to Gordon's account, confirmed hereafter by the author, Mr. Deane's introduction to public life was not altogether out of character with its termination. It was effected by his own vote for himself. *History*, vol. i. pp. 369 – 370.

[3] This is a mistake. Mrs. Jay was the daughter of William Livingston, afterwards Governor of New Jersey.

have many oil mills in the colony. Connecticut sends great quantities of provisions, cattle, and horses, to the West Indies, and brings great quantities of rum, as well as sugar and molasses, to New York. Some lumber they send; — staves, hoops, heading, &c. There is a stream of provisions continually running from Connecticut. Mr. Deane and Messrs. Webbs are intimately acquainted and closely connected with people at New York.

We dined at the tavern with upwards of thirty gentlemen of the first character in the place, at their invitation; the Secretary, Wyllys, the Treasurer, Judge Talcott, Mr. Alsop, merchant, Mr. Payne and Mr. Seymour, lawyers, two Mr. Bulls, and many others. The company appeared to be determined to abide by the resolutions of the Congress. After dinner, at four o'clock, we set out for Middletown. A number of gentlemen in carriages, and a number on horseback, insisted upon attending us, which they did, to our brother Deane's in Wethersfield. There we stopped, and were most cordially and genteelly entertained with punch, wine, and coffee.

We went up the steeple of Wethersfield meeting-house, from whence is the most grand and beautiful prospect in the world, at least that I ever saw. Then we rode to Middletown, and lodged at Bigelow's. There Mr. Hobby and another gentleman came to see us.

16. Tuesday. This morning, Dr. Eliot Rawson, Mr. Alsop, Mr. Mortimer, and others, the committee of correspondence, Mr. Henshaw and many other gentlemen, came to pay their respects to us, and to assure us that they thought we had their all in our hands, and that they would abide by whatever should be determined on, even to a total stoppage of trade to Europe and the West Indies.

This morning rode to Wallingford, to Johnson's, where we dined. We wrote a card to Dr. Dana to dine with us. He came, and informed us that he had wrote some cards for us to put up with him this night. The Doctor dined with us, and was very sociable and agreeable.

At four we made for New Haven. Seven miles out of town, at a tavern, we met a great number of carriages and of horsemen who had come out to meet us. The sheriff of the county, and constable of the town, and the justices of peace, were in the train. As we were coming, we met others to the amount of I know not what number, but a very great one. As we came into the town, all the bells in town were set to ringing, and the people, men, women, and children, were crowding at the doors and windows, as if it was to see a coronation. At nine o'clock the cannon were fired, about a dozen guns, I think.

These expressions of respect to us, are intended as demonstrations of the sympathy of this people with the Massachusetts Bay and its capital, and to show their expectations from the Congress, and their determination to carry into execution whatever shall be agreed upon. No Governor of a Province, nor General of an army, was ever treated with so much ceremony and assiduity as we have been throughout the whole colony of Connecticut, hitherto, but especially all the way from Hartford to New Haven inclusively.

Nothing shows to me the spirit of the town of New Haven in a stronger point of light, than the politeness of Mr. Ingersoll, Judge of Admiralty for the Pennsylvanian Middle District, who came over with his neighbors this evening, and made his compliments very respectfully to Tom Cushing, Sam Adams, John Adams, and Bob Paine. The numbers of gentlemen who have waited on us from Hartford to this place, the heat of the weather and the shortness of the time have made it impossible for me to learn their names.

17. Wednesday. At New Haven. We are told here that New York is now well united and very firm. This morning, Roger Sherman, Esquire, one of the delegates for Connecticut, came to see us at the tavern, Isaac Bears's. He is between fifty and sixty, a solid, sensible man. He said he read Mr. Otis's Rights, &c. in 1764, and thought that he had conceded away the rights of America. He thought the reverse of the declaratory act was true, namely, that the Parliament of Great Britain had authority to make laws for America in no case whatever. He would have been very willing that Massachusetts should have rescinded that part of their Circular Letter[1] where they allow Parliament to be the supreme Legislative over the Colonies in any case.

Mr. Jones, Mr. Douglass, and several other gentlemen, accompanied us to take a view of the town. It is very pleasant;— there are three Congregational meeting-houses, and one Episco-

[1] The letter of the 11th February, 1768, already alluded to, which the British government required the Legislature to rescind. See page 243, note.

pal church, near together. Went to view the grave-stone of Dixwell, the regicide, in the burying-yard. Went to college, and saw their library, their apparatus, and chapel, &c. Mr. Dwight, and Mr. Davenport, two of the tutors, waited on us with great civility. We dined with Mr. Douglass, with Mr. Babcock, son of Dr. Babcock of Westerly, Mr. Odell, Mr. Smith, Mr. Sherman, and a number of ladies; were very genteelly entertained, and spent the whole afternoon in politics, the depths of politics. Mr. Douglass showed us his garden, which is a very good one; fine fruit, and muskmelons and watermelons, such as I never saw before; a muskmelon seventeen inches long, and a watermelon whose inside looked as if it was painted.

An inquiry was started, who were the members of the House of Commons who had plantations in the West Indies, and who were returned by the interest of the West India planters? No one could tell. None could pretend to foresee the effect of a total non-exportation to the West Indies. Jamaica was said to be the most independent part of the world. They had their plantain for bread; they had vast forests, and could make their own heading, staves, and hoops; they could raise their own provisions. This afternoon and evening we had a plentiful rain.

18. Thursday. Mr. Babcock is of the same mind with Major Hawley, that a non-importation and non-consumption agreement will not be faithfully observed; that the Congress have not power to enforce obedience to their laws; that they will be like a legislative without an executive.

We had a good deal of chat last evening with Mr. Bears, our landlord. By his account, the parade which was made to introduce us into town was a sudden proposal, in order to divert the populace from erecting a liberty pole, &c. Ingersoll's friends were at the bottom of it.

Breakfasted at Bryant's, in Milford, where there are two meeting-houses and a church. We visited the burying-yard and the tomb of Paine's great grandfather, R. Treat, thirty years Governor and Deputy-Governor; died 1710, eighty-seven years of age. There is an old venerable monument over him, with an inscription. About ten, we passed the Housatonic River, at Stratford, a river which runs up one hundred and fifty miles and more, though it is not navigable above ten miles. We stopped at Curtis's. The people here all say, Boston is suffering persecution; that now is the time for all the rest to be generous, and that Boston people must be supported. Dined at Fairfield, at Bulkeley's. Mr. Eliot, the new minister of this town, came to see us. This is a county town, and has an elegant court-house, meeting-house, and church, as well as many very elegant private houses. Mr. Burr came to see us. After noon we rode to Quintard's, of Norwalk, where we are to put up, having rode thirty-six miles, and having fifty miles to New York.

19. Friday. Rode to Fitch's, of Stamford, where we breakfasted. Rode to Haviland's, of Rye, the first town in the Province of New York. The barber says that religion don't flourish in this town. The Congregational society have no minister. The Church minister has forty-five pounds from the Society. They have a school for writing and ciphering, but no grammar school. There is no law of this Province that requires a minister or schoolmaster.

20. Saturday. Lodged at Cock's, at Kingsbridge; a pretty place, Uncas river running before the door, and verdant hills all round. This place is about fifteen miles from New York. Uncas River is the bound between the county of Westchester and the county of New York. This place is ten miles from Hell Gate, which is supposed to be occasioned by a large cavern under the rocks, into which the water rushes at certain times of the tide. This whirlpool is five miles from the city.

We breakfasted at Day's, and arrived in the city of New York at ten o'clock, at Hull's, a tavern, the sign the Bunch of Grapes. We rode by several very elegant country seats before we came to the city. This city will be a subject of much speculation to me. From Hull's, we went to private lodgings at Mr. Tobias Stoutenberg's, in King Street, very near the City Hall one way, and the French Church the other. Mr. McDougall and Mr. Platt came to see us. Mr. Platt asked us to dinner next Monday. Mr. McDougall staid longer and talked a good deal. He is a very sensible man, and an open one.[1] He has none of the mean cunning which disgraces so many of my countrymen. He offers to wait on us this afternoon to see the city.

[1] General Alexander McDougall, early engaged in the revolutionary movement, and well known for his civil and military services throughout the war that ensued. He earned from Washington the commendation of being "a brave soldier and a disinterested patriot." See *Writings of Washington*, ix. p. 186.

After dinner, Mr. McDougall and Mr. Platt came, and walked with us to every part of the city. First we went to the fort, where we saw the ruins of that magnificent building, the Governor's house.[1] From the Parade, before the fort, you have a fine prospect of Hudson River, and of the East River, or the Sound, and of the harbor; of Long Island, beyond the Sound River, and of New Jersey beyond Hudson's River. The walk round this fort is very pleasant, though the fortifications are not strong. Between the fort and the city is a beautiful ellipsis of land, railed in with solid iron, in the centre of which is a statue of his majesty on horseback, very large, of solid lead gilded with gold, standing on a pedestal of marble, very high. We then walked up the Broad Way, a fine street, very wide, and in a right line from one end to the other of the city. In this route we saw the old church and the new church. The new is a very magnificent building, cost twenty thousand pounds, York currency. The prison is a large and a handsome stone building; there are two sets of barracks. We saw the New York college, which is also a large stone building. A new hospital is building, of stone. We then walked down to a ship-yard, where a Dutch East India ship is building of eight hundred tons burthen. Then we walked round through another street, which is the principal street of business. Saw the several markets. After this we went to the coffee-house, which was full of gentlemen; read the newspapers, &c. Here were introduced to us Mr. Morin Scott and a Mr. Litchfield, who invited us to Hull's tavern, where we went and staid till eleven o'clock. We supped together, and had much conversation. Mr. Scott is a lawyer, of about fifty years of age; a sensible man, but not very polite. He is said to be one of the readiest speakers upon the continent. It was he who harangued the people, and prevailed upon them to discard the resolves of their committee of fifty-one, as void of vigor, sense, and integrity.[2]

Mr. Scott was censuring McDougall, in a friendly, free way, for not insisting upon choosing delegates by ballot, &c. Mr.

[1] This was burnt on the night of the 29th December preceding, and the inmates with difficulty escaped.

[2] It was remarked by George Clymer, in a letter addressed to Josiah Quincy, Jr. in the year 1773, that patriotism "then seemed to have taken but shallow root in some places, particularly at New York, where political principles are truly as unfixed as the wind. One year sees the New Yorkers champions for

Platt said but little; but McDougall was talkative, and appears to have a thorough knowledge of politics. The two great families in this Province, upon whose motions all their politics turn, are the Delanceys and Livingstons. There is virtue, and abilities as well as fortune, in the Livingstons, but not much of either of the three in the Delanceys, according to him.

The streets of this town are vastly more regular and elegant than those in Boston, and the houses are more grand, as well as neat. They are almost all painted, brick buildings and all. In our walks they showed us the house of Mr. William Smith, one

liberty, and the next hugging their chains." This characteristic of instability has remained through all the vicissitudes of subsequent times. Divided as the population was in sentiment at this period, (1774,) the conservative and aristocratic interest maintained a preponderance in the Province at large, and prevented its Legislature from acting at all, whilst in the city it was waging a more doubtful struggle with the feeling which had, for years, manifested decided popular tendencies. This conflict developed the tendency to political manœuvering, for which the people of New York have ever since been noted. Nowhere, perhaps, have a greater number of persons shaped their action by the rule of the celebrated Bussy Rabutin, in the days of faction in France: "Je suis, autant que je puis, du parti le plus fort." Hence arose the ludicrous embarrassment of its provincial assembly in the next year, 1775, upon receiving the news that General Washington and Governor Tryon were both on their way to the city at the same time, and hence their order "that the militia should stand ready to receive the one or the other, as he might first arrive, and should wait on both as well as circumstances would allow." Hence the facts related by Gordon, in the second volume of his History, p. 120. See also the *Life of Charles Lee*, *Sparks's American Biography*, vol. xviii. pp. 96 – 105.

At the moment alluded to in the text, the news of the passage of the Boston Port Bill had given a force to the popular side in the city, which threatened to carry every thing before it. Sensible of the hazard attending open resistance, the conservative interest adopted the more prudent policy of falling in with the public sentiment so far as to secure the control of all action. This was the origin of the plan to reorganize the committee of correspondence, and to place upon it, in conjunction with some of the popular leaders, a large number of lukewarm, if not hostile, persons. The history of this committee of fifty-one, is the record of a struggle between opposite forces, between skilful management on the part of a few, and blind power on the part of the many. Thus it happened, that whilst at one moment the former met with a complete defeat in the rejection of a series of temporizing resolutions, characterized "as void of vigor, sense, and integrity," at another the latter secured the more substantial advantage of preventing the choice of John Morin Scott, through whose energy they had been worsted, as stated in the text, and of Alexander McDougall, as delegates to the Congress of 1774. There can be no disputing that throughout the Revolution a large proportion of the population, including most of the property-holders of New York, sympathized with the mother country. Neither did the effect of this cease with the establishment of the national independence. The history yet remains as the work for a discriminating and thoroughly unbiased pen. As a guide to the movements here indicated, it may be well to read with attention a letter of Gouverneur Morris to Mr. Penn, and the correspondence of Lieutenant-Governor Colden with Lord Dartmouth. *Life of G. Morris*, by J. Sparks, vol. i. p. 23. Force's *American Archives*, 1774.

of their Council and the famous lawyer, Mr. Thomas Smith, &c. Mr. Rivington's store, &c.

21. Sunday. Went to meeting at the old Presbyterian Society, where Dr. Pemberton formerly preached. We heard Dr. Rogers on "Seek first the kingdom of God and His righteousness, and all other things shall be added unto you." After service, Mr. Peter Vanbrugh Livingston and Mr. Thomas Smith came to our lodgings, introduced to us by Mr. McDougall.

Mr. Livingston is an old man, extremely staunch in the cause, and very sensible. He tells us that Dr. Chandler and Dr. Cooper, and other Episcopal clergymen, were met together about the time of the news of the Boston Port Bill, and were employed night and day writing letters and sending despatches to the other Colonies and to England. This he thinks was to form an union of the Episcopal party, through the continent, in support of ministerial measures. He says they have never been able to obtain a charter for their burying-yard, or the ground on which their Presbyterian church stands! They have solicited their Governors, and have solicited at home without success.

In the afternoon we went to the same meeting, and heard Mr. Treat from "These shall go away into everlasting punishment." Both these clergymen are good speakers, and without notes. The psalmody is an exact contrast to that of Hartford; it is in the *old way*, as we call it—all the drawling, quavering, discord in the world. After meeting, Mr. McDougall introduced me and Mr. Paine to Mr. William Smith, the historian of New York,[1] a gentleman a little turned of forty, a plain, composed man, to appearance. He very politely invited us to tea at his house; but we were engaged. He then inquired where we lodged, and said he would wait on us. After meeting we went to Mr. McDougall's, where we saw his lady, a charming woman, and his daughter, an agreeable Miss. Mrs. Clymer was there from Philadelphia, who inquired very kindly after Mr. Hancock and his aunt, and Mr. Jonathan Mason and his family. This is a very facetious and social lady. At Mr. McDougall's, Colonel Folsom and Major Sullivan, the delegates from New Hampshire, came to see us; they were hastening over the ferry for

[1] Though much connected with the men of the popular party, he finally decided for the royal side in 1778. He afterwards became a Chief Justice of Canada. *Sabine's American Loyalists.*

fear of the smallpox, neither of them having had that distemper. Also Mr. Low, a relation of the delegate from New York of that name, Mr. Lamb, Mr. Hughes, a schoolmaster, and many others whose names I cannot recollect. We then went to Mr. David Van Horne's, who sent his compliments to Mr. McDougall, and requested him to introduce us to his house, as he was sick and unable to come out. He seems well affected to the public cause, and speaks very sensibly about it.

22. Monday. This morning we took Mr. McDougall into our coach, and rode three miles out of town to Mr. Morin Scott's to breakfast — a very pleasant ride. Mr. Scott has an elegant seat there, with Hudson's River just behind his house, and a rural prospect all around him. Mr. Scott, his lady and daughter, and her husband, Mr. Litchfield, were dressed to receive us. We sat in a fine airy entry till called into a front room to breakfast. A more elegant breakfast I never saw — rich plate, a very large silver coffee-pot, a very large silver tea-pot, napkins of the very finest materials, toast, and bread, and butter, in great perfection. After breakfast a plate of beautiful peaches, another of pears, and another of plums, and a muskmelon, were placed on the table.

Mr. Scott, Mr. William Smith, and Mr. William Livingston, are the triumvirate who figured away in younger life against the Church of England, who wrote the Independent Reflector, the Watch Tower, and other papers.[1] They are all of them children of Yale College. Scott and Livingston are said to be lazy; Smith improves every moment of his time. Livingston is lately removed into New Jersey, and is one of the delegates for that Province.

Mr. Scott is an eminent lawyer; he drew the answer of the Council to Governor Colden's Reasons in favor of an Appeal in the case of Forsey *vs.* Cunningham.[2] He is said to be one of the readiest speakers on the continent. Scott told me that the state of the New York claim, Massachusetts claim, New Hampshire claim, and Canada claim, which is printed in the Journal of the House in New York, 1763, to the lands contested between Connecticut and Hudson's River, was principally drawn by Mr

[1] A full account of these publications is given in the third chapter of *Sedgwick's Memoir of W. Livingston.*

[2] See the same Memoir, pp. 121 – 124.

Duane, who has unhappily involved almost all his property in those lands. He has purchased patents of government, and claims of soldiers, &c., to the amount of one hundred thousand acres. Mr. Duane is an Episcopalian; so are all the delegates from New York excepting Mr. Livingston. Mr. Jay is a young gentleman of the law, of about twenty-six; Mr. Scott says, a hard student and a good speaker. Mr. Alsop is a merchant, of a good heart, but unequal to the trust in point of abilities, as Mr. Scott thinks. Mr. Low, the chairman of the Committee of Fifty-one, they say, will profess attachment to the cause of liberty, but his sincerity is doubted. Mr. William Bayard, Mr. McEvers, and Mr. Beech, are gentlemen who were very intimate with General Gage when he was here. Mr. Bayard has a son and a son-in-law in the army, and a son in the service of the East India Company. These are connected with Mr. Apthorp and his contracts, and are lookers-up to government for favors, are correspondents of General Gage, and will favor his measures, though they profess attachment to the American cause.

Mr. McDougall gave a caution to avoid every expression here which looked like an allusion to the last appeal. He says there is a powerful party here who are intimidated by fears of a civil war, and they have been induced to acquiesce by assurances that there was no danger, and that a peaceful cessation of commerce would effect relief. Another party, he says, are intimidated lest the levelling spirit of the New England Colonies should propagate itself into New York.[1] Another party are prompted by Episcopalian prejudices against New England. Another party are merchants largely concerned in navigation, and therefore afraid of non-importation, non-consumption, and non-exportation agreements. Another party are those who are looking up to Government for favors. About eleven o'clock, four of the delegates for the city and county of New York came to make their compliments to us; — Mr. Duane, Mr. Livingston, Mr. Low, and Mr. Alsop. Mr. Livingston is a downright, straightforward man. Mr. Alsop is a soft, sweet man. Mr. Duane has a sly, surveying eye, a little squint-eyed; between forty and forty-five, I should guess; very sensible, I think, and very artful. He says, their private correspondence and their

1 This leading idea deserves to be kept steadily in mind throughout the history of the early stages of the Revolution.

agent's letters, Mr. Burke,[1] are that the nation is against us; that we cannot depend upon any support of any kind from thence; that the merchants are very much against us; that their pride is touched, and what they call their rights, by our turning away their ships from our ports. A question arose, whether it was a prerogative of the Crown at common law, to license wharves. I thought it was, by statutes at home, which were never extended to America before the Boston Port Bill. Mr. Duane was of my opinion. Mr. Livingston thought it was a prerogative of the Crown at common law; said it had been so understood here; that all the public wharves in this town were by charter from the Governor. He questioned whether the officers of the customs were obliged to attend any wharves but licensed ones.

Mr. Morin Scott called upon us at our lodgings, and politely insisted upon our taking a seat in his chariot to Mr. Platt's. We accepted the invitation, and, when we came there, were shown into as elegant a chamber as ever I saw—the furniture as rich and splendid as any of Mr. Boylston's. Mr. Low, Mr. Peter Vanbrugh Livingston, Mr. Philip Livingston, Dr. Treat, a brother of the minister, and Mr. McDougall, Mr. Scott, and Mr. Litchfield, dined with us and spent the afternoon.

P. V. Livingston is a sensible man and a gentleman. He has been in trade, is rich, and now lives upon his income. Phil. Livingston is a great, rough, rapid mortal. There is no holding any conversation with him. He blusters away; says, if England should turn us adrift, we should instantly go to civil wars among ourselves, to determine which Colony should govern all the rest; seems to dread New England, the levelling spirit, &c. Hints were thrown out of the Goths and Vandals; mention was made of our hanging the Quakers, &c. I told him, the very existence of the Colony was at that time at stake—surrounded with Indians at war, against whom they could not have defended the Colony if the Quakers had been permitted to go on.

23. Tuesday. We went upon the new Dutch church steeple, and took a view of the city. You have a very fine view of the whole city at once, the harbor, East River, North River, Long Island, New Jersey, &c. The whole city is upon a level, a flat. The houses in general are smaller than in Boston, and the city

[1] The letter referred to has been preserved in the *Life of Peter Van Schaack* by his son, pp. 18–20.

occupies less ground. We breakfasted with Mr. Low, a gentleman of fortune and in trade. His lady is a beauty. Rich furniture again for the tea table. Mr. Lott, the treasurer of the Province, did us the honor to breakfast with us, and politely asked us to dine or to breakfast with him; but we were engaged for all the time we were to stay. The conversation turned upon the constitution of the city. The mayor and recorder are appointed by the Governor; the aldermen and common council are annually elected by the people. The aldermen are the magistrates of the city, and the only ones; they have no justices of the peace in the city; so that the magistracy of the city are all the creatures of the people. The city cannot tax itself; the constables, assessors, &c., are chosen annually; they petition the assembly every year to be empowered by law to assess the city for a certain sum. The whole charge of the Province is annually between five and six thousand pounds, York money. Mr. Cushing says the charge of the Massachusetts is about twelve thousand, lawful money, which is sixteen thousand, York currency. The support of Harvard College, and of forts and garrisons and other things, makes the difference. About eleven o'clock, Mr. Low, Mr. Curtenius, Mr. Pascall Smith, Mr. Van Schaack, and others, a deputation from the committee of correspondence from this city, waited on us with an invitation to dine with them Thursday next, which we accepted. One of the gentlemen said he was in England at the time of a former non-importation agreement, and it was not much felt among the merchants or manufacturers. Another of them replied, the true cause of that was the German contract, and the demand from Russia. Mr. Ebenezer Hazard waited on me with a letter, requesting my assistance in making his collection of American State papers. I recommended him to Mr. S. Adams, and Dr. Samuel Mather. I advised him to publish from Hackluyt, the Voyage of Sebastian Cabot, in this collection. He thought it good advice. Hazard is certainly very capable of the business he has undertaken; he is a genius. Went to the Coffee House and saw the Virginia Paper; the spirit of the people is prodigious; their resolutions are really grand. We then went to Mr. Peter Vanbrugh Livingston's, where, at three o'clock, we dined, with Scott, McDougall, Philip Livingston, Mr. Thomas Smith, and a young gentleman, son of Mr. Peter Livingston.

Smith and young Livingston seem to be modest, decent, and sensible men.

The way we have been in, of breakfasting, dining, drinking coffee, &c., about the city, is very disagreeable on some accounts. Although it introduces us to the acquaintance of many respectable people here, yet it hinders us from seeing the college, the churches, the printers' offices, and booksellers' shops, and many other things which we should choose to see.

With all the opulence and splendor of this city, there is very little good breeding to be found. We have been treated with an assiduous respect; but I have not seen one real gentleman, one well-bred man, since I came to town. At their entertainments there is no conversation that is agreeable; there is no modesty, no attention to one another. They talk very loud, very fast, and altogether. If they ask you a question, before you can utter three words of your answer, they will break out upon you again, and talk away.

24. Wednesday. This day Cushing and Paine went over to Long Island to dine with Phil Livingston. Adams and I sent our excuse, that we were not very well; it was raw and wet.

25. Thursday. Mr. Mathew Cushing came and escorted us into Trinity Church and churchyard. Under the chancel of this church Mr. Pratt was buried. This is an old building. We then went into Saint Paul's. This is a new building, which cost eighteen thousand pounds, York money. It has a piazza in front, and some stone pillars, which appear grand; but the building, taken altogether, does not strike me like the Stone Chapel, or like Dr. Cooper's meeting-house, either on the inside or outside. We then went to see Mr. Cushing work his new constructed pumps, which work easier, he says, and convey more water, than any other. We then went to college; were introduced to Mr. Harper, who showed us the library, the books, and curiosities. We were then introduced to Dr. Clossy, who was exhibiting a course of experiments to his pupils to prove the elasticity of the air.

There is but one building at this college, and that is very far from full of scholars; they never have had forty scholars at a time. We then made a visit of ceremony to Mr. William Smith, a counsellor at law, and a counsellor by mandamus. This gentleman has the character of a great lawyer, a sensible and learned man, and yet a consistent, unshaken friend to his country and her liberties. He entertained us with an account of his negotiating between the Governor (Colden), the General (Gage), and the people, in the year 1765, when the people attacked the fort to obtain the stamped papers, in which he acted an intrepid, an honest, and a prudent part. Mr. McDougall told me of the part he acted in the affair of the prosecution of him for a libel.[1] The Governor asked him if he would not act for the Crown. Mr. Smith said, he would not do the dirty jobs of government; he would not hold any thing under the Crown upon such terms.

Mr. Smith expressed his sentiments of General Gage and his new station and character very freely. He said he had a great personal regard for the General; that he was a good-natured, peaceable, and sociable man here; but that he was altogether unfit for a Governor of the Massachusetts; that he would lose all the character he had acquired as a man, a gentleman, and a general, and dwindle down into a mere scribbling Governor, a mere Bernard or Hutchinson.

Mr. Smith received us very politely. We afterwards made a visit to friend Holt, the liberty printer, and to Noel and Hazard's. We afterwards dined in the Exchange Chamber, at the invitation of the Committee of Correspondence, with more than fifty gentlemen, at the most splendid dinner I ever saw; a profusion of rich dishes, &c. &c.

I had a great deal of conversation with Mr. Duane, who is a sensible, an artful, and an insinuating man. He talked of Mr. Pratt; said he had the greatest memory of any man he ever saw; that he had read a great deal, but that he had not a clear head. One of the bar used to say that Mr. Pratt thickened the clear; that he knew Mr. Pratt try eight criminals in a forenoon upon different indictments, and with the same jury; that he took no notes, but summed the evidence with great exactness, remembered every circumstance of every testimony, and the names of all the witnesses, although the witnesses were Dutch people, and their names such as Mr. Pratt never could have heard. After dinner the Connecticut delegates came in. In the evening several gentlemen came to our lodgings, and among others, Mr. Sears.

26. Friday. This morning we went to see the city hall, the

[1] This history is given by Gordon, vol. i. pp. 301–303.

chamber where the Supreme Court sits, and that where the Mayor and Recorder sit. Afterwards we went down to the new Dutch Church, which is a much more elegant building than Saint Paul's; it is the most elegant building in the city. The pillars are smaller than Dr. Cooper's, and the pews are all painted, but the building is not so handsome. At nine o'clock we crossed Paulus Hook Ferry to New Jersey, then Hackinsack Ferry, then Newark Ferry, and dined at Elizabethtown. After dinner we rode twenty miles, crossed Brunswick ferry, and put up at Farmer's in the city of Brunswick. That part of the Province of New Jersey which we have passed is all upon a level, as fine a road as ever was trod; yet the lands seem to be good.

27. Saturday. Went to view the city of Brunswick. There is a Church of England, a Dutch Church, and a Presbyterian Church, in this town; there is some little trade here; small craft can come up to the town. We saw a few small sloops. The river is very beautiful. There is a stone building for barracks, which is tolerably handsome; it is about the size of Boston jail. Some of the streets are paved, and there are three or four handsome houses; only about one hundred and fifty families in the town; rode ten miles to Jones's, where we stopped to blow our horses. This whole Colony of New Jersey is a champaign. About twelve o'clock we arrived at the tavern in Princeton, which holds out the sign of Hudibras, near Nassau Hall College. The tavern keeper's name is Hire. The college is a stone building, about as large as that at New York; it stands upon rising ground, and so commands a prospect of the country. After dinner, Mr. Pigeon, a student of Nassau Hall, son of Mr. Pigeon of Watertown, from whom we brought a letter, took a walk with us and showed us the seat of Mr. Stockton, a lawyer in this place, and one of the Council, and one of the trustees of the college; as we returned we met Mr. Euston, the professor of mathematics and natural philosophy, who kindly invited us to his chamber. We went. The college is conveniently constructed; instead of entries across the building, the entries are from end to end, and the chambers are on each side of the entries. There are such entries, one above another, in every story; each chamber has three windows, two studies with one window in each, and one window between the studies to enlighten the chamber. Mr. Euston then showed us the library;

it is not large, but has some good books. He then led us into the apparatus; here we saw a most beautiful machine — an orrery or planetarium, constructed by Mr. Rittenhouse, of Philadelphia. It exhibits almost every motion in the astronomical world; the motions of the sun and all the planets, with all their satellites, the eclipses of the sun and moon, &c. He showed us another orrery, which exhibits the true inclination of the orbit of each of the planets to the plane of the ecliptic. He then showed us the electrical apparatus, which is the most complete and elegant that I have seen. He charged the bottle and attempted an experiment, but the state of the air was not favorable. By this time the bell rang for prayers; we went into the chapel; the President soon came in, and we attended. The scholars sing as badly as the Presbyterians at New York. After prayers the President attended us to the balcony of the college, where we have a prospect of an horizon of about eighty miles diameter. We went into the President's house, and drank a glass of wine. He is as high a son of liberty as any man in America. He says it is necessary that the Congress should raise money and employ a number of writers in the newspapers in England, to explain to the public the American plea, and remove the prejudices of Britons. He says, also, we should recommend it to every Colony to form a society for the encouragement of Protestant emigrants from the Three Kingdoms. The Doctor waited on us to our lodgings, and took a dish of coffee. He is one of the committee of correspondence, and was upon the Provincial Congress for appointing delegates from this Province to the General Congress. Mr. William Livingston and he labored, he says, to procure an instruction that the tea should not be paid for. Livingston, he says, is very sincere and very able in the public cause, but a bad speaker, though a good writer. Here we saw a Mr. Hood, a lawyer of Brunswick, and a Mr. Jonathan Dickinson Sergeant, a young lawyer of Princeton, both cordial friends to American liberty. In the evening young Whitwell, a student at this college, son of Mr. Whitwell at Boston, to whom we brought a letter, came to see us. By the account of Whitwell and Pigeon, the government of this college is very strict, and the scholars study very hard. The President says they are all sons of liberty.

28. Sunday. Heard Dr. Witherspoon all day; a clear, sen-

sible preacher. Mr. Mason came to see us. We sent a card to Mr. Sergeant, a lawyer; he dined, drank coffee, and spent the evening with us. He is a young gentleman of about twenty-five, perhaps; very sociable. He gave us much light concerning the characters of the delegates from New York, Philadelphia, Virginia, &c., and concerning the characters of the principal lawyers in all these Provinces. Smith, he says, is the oracle of New York for chamber counsel; Scott is a character very much like that of old Mr. Auchmuty; sit up all night at his bottle, yet argue to admiration next day; an admirable speaker, according to him. Duane is a plodding body, but has a very effeminate, feeble voice. He says the Virginians speak in raptures about Richard Henry Lee and Patrick Henry, one the Cicero, and the other the Demosthenes of the age.[1] Jo Reed is at the head of his profession in Philadelphia; Fisher is next. Waln and Dickinson have retired.

29. Monday. Rode to Trenton upon Delaware River to breakfast. At Williams's, the tavern at Trenton ferry, we saw four very large black walnut trees standing in a row behind the house. It seems that these trees are plenty in these southern Provinces; all the black-walnut timber which is used by our cabinet makers in Boston is brought from the southern Provinces. This town of Trenton is a pretty village; it appears to be the largest town that we have seen in the Jerseys, larger than Elizabethtown, Brunswick, or Princeton.

We then crossed the ferry over Delaware River, to the Province of Pennsylvania. We then rode across an elbow and came to the Delaware again, a beautiful river, navigable up as far as Trenton; the country on each side is very level. We arrived at Bristol about eleven o'clock;—a village on the Delaware, opposite to which is Burlington. The scenes of nature are delightful here. This is twenty miles from Philadelphia. Here we saw two or three passage wagons, a vehicle with four wheels, contrived to carry many passengers and much baggage. We then rode to the Red Lion and dined. After dinner we stopped at Frankfort, about five miles out of town. A number of carriages and gentlemen came out of Philadelphia to meet

1 From this it is plain that these titles were already made in Virginia, before these gentlemen ever appeared on the floor of the Continental Congress. But see *Wirt's Life of Henry*, p. 107.

us, — Mr. Thomas Mifflin, Mr. McKean, of the lower counties, one of their delegates, Mr. Rutledge of Carolina, and a number of gentlemen from Philadelphia, Mr. Folsom and Mr. Sullivan, the New Hampshire delegates. We were introduced to all these gentlemen, and most cordially welcomed to Philadelphia. We then rode into town, and dirty, dusty, and fatigued as we were, we could not resist the importunity to go to the tavern, the most genteel one in America. There we were introduced to a number of other gentlemen of the city: Dr. Shippen, Dr. Knox, Mr. Smith, and a multitude of others, and to Mr. Lynch and Mr. Gadsden of South Carolina. Here we had a fresh welcome to the city of Philadelphia, and after some time spent in conversation, a curtain was drawn, and in the other half of the chamber a supper appeared as elegant as ever was laid upon a table. About eleven o'clock we retired.

By a computation made this evening by Mr. McKean, there will be at the Congress about fifty-six members, twenty-two of them lawyers. Mr. McKean gave me an account this evening of the behavior of Ruggles at the former Congress, 1765. He was treated pretty cavalierly. His behavior was very dishonorable.

A gentleman who returned into town with Mr. Paine and me in our coach, undertook to caution us against two gentlemen particularly; one was Dr. Smith, the provost of the college, who is looking up to government for an American episcopate, and a pair of lawn sleeves. Soft, polite, insinuating, adulating, sensible, learned, industrious, indefatigable; he has had art enough, and refinement upon art, to make impressions even upon Mr. Dickinson and Mr. Reed.[1]

30. Tuesday. Walked a little about town; visited the market, the State House, the Carpenters' Hall, where the Congress is to sit, &c.; then called at Mr. Mifflin's; a grand, spacious, and elegant house. Here we had much conversation with Mr. Charles Thomson, who is, it seems, about marrying a lady, a relation of Mr. Dickinson's, with five thousand pounds sterling. This Charles Thomson is the Sam Adams of Philadelphia, the life of the cause of liberty,[2] they say. A Friend, Collins, came

[1] Mr. Reed, if he ever fell into this delusion, must have been very soon rescued from it. See his Life, by his grandson, vol. ii. p. 169 – 170.

[2] Mr. W. B. Reed quotes the description given of him by the Abbé Robin, a French priest who came out with Rochambeau. " Sa figure maigre, sillonneux,

to see us, and invited us to dine on Thursday. We returned to our lodgings, and Mr. Lynch, Mr. Gadsden, Mr. Middleton, and young Mr. Rutledge came to visit us. Mr. Lynch introduced Mr. Middleton to us; Mr. Middleton was silent and reserved; young Rutledge was high enough. A promise of the King was mentioned. He started! "I should have no regard to his word; his promises are not worth any thing," &c. This is a young, smart, spirited body. Mr. Blair came to visit us with another gentleman; Mr. Smith, an old gentleman, was introduced to us by his son; another Mr. Smith came in with our Mr. Paine. The regularity and elegance of this city are very striking. It is situated upon a neck of land about two miles wide between the river Delaware and the river Schuylkill; the streets are all exactly straight and parallel to the river; Front Street is near the river, then 2d Street, 3d, 4th, 5th, 6th, 7th, 8th, 9th. The cross streets which intersect these are all equally wide, straight, and parallel to each other, and are named from forest and fruit trees, — Pear Street, Apple Street, Walnut Street, Chestnut Street, &c.

Towards the evening, Mr. Thomas Smith, son of the old gentleman who made us a visit, who is a brother of Mr. Smith the minister of Casco Bay, and Dr. Shippen and his brother, and Mr. Reed, went with us to the Hospital. We saw, in the lower rooms under ground, the cells of the lunatics, a number of them, some furious, some merry, some melancholy, and, among the rest, John Ingham, whom I once saved at Taunton Court from being whipped and sold for horse-stealing. We then went into the sick-rooms, which are very long, large walks, with rows of beds on each side, and the lame and sick upon them; a dreadful scene of human wretchedness. The weakness and languor, the distress and misery of these objects, is truly a woful sight. Dr. Shippen then carried us into his chamber, where he showed us a series of anatomical paintings, of exquisite art. Here was a great variety of views of the human body, whole and in parts. The Doctor entertained us with a very clear, concise, and comprehensive lecture upon all the parts of the human frame. This entertainment charmed me. He first showed us a set of paintings of bodies, entire and alive, then of others with the skin taken

ses yeux caves et étincelans, ses cheveux blancs, droits, ne descendant pas à ses oreilles fixèrent et surprirent tous nos regards." *Life of J. Reed*, vol. ii. p. 307.

off, then with the first coat of muscles taken off, then with the second, then with all — the bare bones. Then he showed us paintings of the insides of a man, seen before, all the muscles of the belly being taken off; the heart, lungs, stomach, &c.

31. Wednesday. Breakfasted at Mr. Bayard's, of Philadelphia, with Mr. Sprout, a Presbyterian minister.

Made a visit to Governor Ward, of Rhode Island, at his lodgings. There we were introduced to several gentlemen. Mr. Dickinson, the farmer of Pennsylvania, came in his coach with four beautiful horses to Mr. Ward's lodgings, to see us. He was introduced to us, and very politely said he was exceedingly glad to have the pleasure of seeing these gentlemen; made some inquiry after the health of his brother and sister, who are now in Boston; gave us some account of his late ill health and his present gout. This was the first time of his getting out. Mr. Dickinson has been subject to hectic complaints. He is a shadow; tall, but slender as a reed; pale as ashes; one would think at first sight that he could not live a month; yet, upon a more attentive inspection, he looks as if the springs of life were strong enough to last many years. We dined with Mr. Lynch, his lady and daughter, at their lodgings, Mrs. McKenzie's; and a very agreeable dinner and afternoon we had, notwithstanding the violent heat. We were all vastly pleased with Mr. Lynch. He is a solid, firm, judicious man. He told us that Colonel Washington made the most eloquent speech at the Virginia Convention that ever was made. Says he, "I will raise one thousand men, subsist them at my own expense, and march myself at their head for the relief of Boston."

Mr. Lynch says, they shall export this year twelve thousand weight of indigo, and one hundred and fifty thousand tierces of rice from South Carolina. About three hundred ships are employed. Mrs. Lynch inquired kindly after Mrs. Adams's health, and Mrs. Smith and family, and Mr. Boylston, and Mr. and Mrs. Gill, &c.

September 1. Thursday. This day we breakfasted at Mr. Mifflin's. Mr. C. Thomson came in, and soon after, Dr. Smith, the famous Dr. Smith, the provost of the college. He appears a plain man, tall and rather awkward; there is an appearance of art. We then went to return visits to the gentlemen who had visited us. We visited a Mr. Cadwallader, a gentleman of large fortune, a grand and elegant house and furniture. We then visited Mr. Powell, another splendid seat. We then visited the gentlemen from South Carolina, and, about twelve, were introduced to Mr. Galloway, the Speaker of the House in Pennsylvania.

We dined at Friend Collins's, Stephen Collins's,[1] with Governor Hopkins, Governor Ward, Mr. Galloway, Mr. Rhoades, &c. In the evening, all the gentlemen of the Congress who were arrived in town, met at Smith's, the new city tavern, and spent the evening together. Twenty-five members were come. Virginia, North Carolina, Maryland, and the city of New York, were not arrived. Mr. William Livingston, from the Jerseys, lately of New York, was there. He is a plain man, tall, black, wears his hair; nothing elegant or genteel about him. They say he is no public speaker, but very sensible and learned, and a ready writer. Mr. Rutledge, the elder, was there, but his appearance is not very promising. There is no keenness in his eye, no depth in his countenance; nothing of the profound, sagacious, brilliant, or sparkling, in his first appearance.

Yesterday we removed our lodgings to the house of Miss Jane Port, in Arch Street, about half way between Front Street and Second Street. I find that there is a tribe of people here exactly like the tribe, in the Massachusetts, of Hutchinsonian Addressers. There is, indeed, a set in every colony. We have seen the revolutions of their sentiments. Their opinions have undergone as many changes as the moon. At the time of the Stamp Act, and just before it, they professed to be against the parliamentary claim of right to tax Americans, to be friends to our constitutions, our charter, &c. Bernard was privately, secretly, endeavoring to procure an alteration of our charter. But he concealed his designs until his letters were detected. Hutchinson professed to be a staunch friend to liberty and to our charter, until his letters were detected. A great number of good people thought him a good man, and a sincere friend to the

[1] "This gentleman is of figure and eminence, as well as fortune, in this place. He is of the profession of the Friends, but not stiff nor rigid. He is a native of Lynn, in New England, a brother of Ezra Collins in Boston. I have been treated by him in this city, both in the former Congress and the present, with unbounded civility and friendship. His house is open to every New England man. I never knew a more agreeable instance of hospitality." *J. A. to his Wife*, 4 July, 1775.

Congregational interest in religion, and to our charter privileges. They went on with this Machiavelian dissimulation, until those letters were detected. After that, they waited until the Boston Port Bill was passed, and then, thinking the people must submit immediately and that Lord North would carry his whole system triumphantly, they threw off the mask. Dr. Smith, Mr. Galloway, Mr. Vaughan, and others in this town, are now just where the Hutchinsonian faction were in the year 1764, when we were endeavoring to obtain a repeal of the Stamp Act.

2. Friday. Dined at Mr. Thomas Mifflin's, with Mr. Lynch, Mr. Middleton, and the two Rutledges with their ladies. The two Rutledges are good lawyers. Governor Hopkins and Governor Ward were in company. Mr. Lynch gave us a sentiment: "The brave Dantzickers, who declare they will be free in the face of the greatest monarch in Europe." We were very sociable and happy. After coffee, we went to the tavern, where we were introduced to Peyton Randolph, Esquire, Speaker of Virginia, Colonel Harrison, Richard Henry Lee, Esquire, and Colonel Bland. Randolph is a large, well looking man; Lee is a tall, spare man; Bland is a learned, bookish man.

These gentlemen from Virginia appear to be the most spirited and consistent of any. Harrison said he would have come on foot rather than not come. Bland said he would have gone, upon this occasion, if it had been to Jericho.

3. Saturday. Breakfasted at Dr. Shippen's; Dr. Witherspoon was there. Col. R. H. Lee lodges there; he is a masterly man. This Mr. Lee is a brother of the sheriff of London, and of Dr. Arthur Lee, and of Mrs. Shippen; they are all sensible and deep thinkers. Lee is for making the repeal of every revenue law,—the Boston Port Bill, the bill for altering the Massachusetts constitution, and the Quebec Bill, and the removal of all the troops, the end of the Congress, and an abstinence from all dutied articles, the means,—rum, molasses, sugar, tea, wine, fruits, &c. He is absolutely certain that the same ship which carries home the resolution will bring back the redress. If we were to suppose that any time would intervene, he should be for exceptions. He thinks we should inform his Majesty that we never can be happy, while the Lords Bute, Mansfield, and North, are his confidants and counsellors. He took his pen and attempted a calculation of the numbers of people represented by

the Congress, which he made about two millions two hundred thousand; and of the revenue, now actually raised, which he made eighty thousand pounds sterling. He would not allow Lord North to have great abilities; he had seen no symptoms of them; his whole administration had been blunder. He said the opposition had been so feeble and incompetent hitherto, that it was time to make vigorous exertions.

Mrs. Shippen is a religious and a reasoning lady. She said she had often thought that the people of Boston could not have behaved through their trials with so much prudence and firmness at the same time, if they had not been influenced by a superior power. Mr. Lee thinks that to strike at the Navigation Acts would unite every man in Britain against us, because the kingdom could not exist without them, and the advantages they derive from these regulations and restrictions of our trade are an ample compensation for all the protection they have afforded us, or will afford us. Dr. Witherspoon enters with great spirit into the American cause. He seems as hearty a friend as any of the natives, an animated Son of Liberty. This forenoon, Mr. Cæsar Rodney of the lower counties on Delaware River, two Mr. Tilghmans from Maryland, were introduced to us. We went with Mr. William Barrell to his store, and drank punch, and eat dried smoked sprats with him; read the papers and our letters from Boston; dined with Mr. Joseph Reed, the lawyer, with Mrs. Deberdt and Mrs. Reed, Mr. Willing, Mr. Thomas Smith, Mr. Dehart, &c.; spent the evening at Mr. Mifflin's, with Lee and Harrison from Virginia, the two Rutledges, Dr. Witherspoon, Dr. Shippen, Dr. Steptoe, and another gentleman; an elegant supper, and we drank sentiments till eleven o'clock. Lee and Harrison were very high. Lee had dined with Mr. Dickinson, and drank Burgundy the whole afternoon.

Harrison gave us for a sentiment, "A constitutional death to the Lords Bute, Mansfield, and North." Paine gave us, "May the collision of British flint and American steel produce that spark of liberty which shall illumine the latest posterity." "Wisdom to Britain, and firmness to the Colonies; may Britain be wise, and America free." "The friends of America throughout the world." "Union of the Colonies." "Unanimity to the Congress." "May the result of the Congress answer the expectations of the people." "Union of Britain and the

Colonies on a constitutional foundation," and many other such toasts. Young Rutledge told me he studied three years at the Temple. He thinks this a great distinction; says he took a volume of notes which J. Quincy transcribed; says that young gentlemen ought to travel early, because that freedom and ease of behavior which is so necessary cannot be acquired but in early life. This Rutledge is young, sprightly, but not deep; he has the most indistinct, inarticulate way of speaking; speaks through his nose; a wretched speaker in conversation. How he will shine in public, I don't yet know. He seems good-natured, though conceited. His lady is with him, in bad health. His brother still maintains the air of reserve, design, and cunning, like Duane and Galloway and Bob Auchmuty. Cæsar Rodney is the oddest looking man in the world; he is tall, thin and slender as a reed, pale; his face is not bigger than a large apple, yet there is sense and fire, spirit, wit, and humor in his countenance. He made himself very merry with Ruggles and his pretended scruples and timidities at the last Congress. Mr. Reed told us, at dinner, that he never saw greater joy than he saw in London when the news arrived that the non-importation agreement was broke. They were universally shaking hands and congratulating each other. He says that George Hayley is the worst enemy to America that he knew there. Swore to him that he would stand by government in all its measures, and was always censuring and cursing America.

4. Sunday. Went to the Presbyterian meeting, and heard Mr. Sprout in the forenoon. He uses no notes; don't appear to have any; opens his Bible and talks away. Not a very numerous nor very polite assembly. Dined at our lodgings, at Mrs. Yard's, with Major De Bure, a French gentleman, a soldier, Mr. Webb and another. Went in the afternoon to Christ Church, and heard Mr. Coombe. This is a more noble building, and a genteeler congregation. The organ and a new choir of singers were very musical. Mr. Coombe is celebrated here as a fine speaker; he is sprightly, has a great deal of action, speaks distinctly. But I confess I am not charmed with his oratory; his style was indifferent; his method confused. In one word, his composition was vastly inferior to the ordinary sermons of our How, Hunt, Chauncy, Cooper, Eliot, and even Stillman. Mr. Mifflin spent the Sunday evening with us at our lodgings.

5. Monday. At ten the delegates all met at the City Tavern, and walked to the Carpenters' Hall, where they took a view of the room, and of the chamber where is an excellent library; there is also a long entry where gentlemen may walk, and a convenient chamber opposite to the library. The general cry was, that this was a good room, and the question was put, whether we were satisfied with this room? and it passed in the affirmative. A very few were for the negative, and they were chiefly from Pennsylvania and New York. Then Mr. Lynch arose, and said there was a gentleman present who had presided with great dignity over a very respectable society, greatly to the advantage of America, and he therefore proposed that the Honorable Peyton Randolph, Esquire, one of the delegates from Virginia, and the late Speaker of their House of Burgesses, should be appointed Chairman, and he doubted not it would be unanimous.

The question was put, and he was unanimously chosen.

Mr. Randolph then took the chair, and the commissions of the delegates were all produced and read.

Then Mr. Lynch proposed that Mr. Charles Thomson, a gentleman of family, fortune, and character in this city, should be appointed Secretary, which was accordingly done without opposition, though Mr. Duane and Mr. Jay discovered at first an inclination to seek further.

Mr. Duane then moved that a committee should be appointed to prepare regulations for this Congress. Several gentlemen objected.

I then arose and asked leave of the President to request of the gentleman from New York an explanation, and that he would point out some particular regulations which he had in his mind. He mentioned particularly the method of voting, whether it should be by Colonies, or by the poll, or by interests.

Mr. Henry then arose, and said this was the first General Congress which had ever happened; that no former Congress could be a precedent; that we should have occasion for more general congresses, and therefore that a precedent ought to be established now; that it would be great injustice if a little Colony should have the same weight in the councils of America as a great one, and therefore he was for a committee.[1]

[1] The above very simple narrative, of the action of Mr. Henry upon this occasion, strangely contrasts with the picture painted by the florid imagination of

Major Sullivan observed that a little Colony had its all at stake as well as a great one.

This is a question of great importance. If we vote by Colonies, this method will be liable to great inequality and injustice; for five small Colonies, with one hundred thousand people in each, may outvote four large ones, each of which has five hundred thousand inhabitants. If we vote by the poll, some Colonies have more than their proportion of members, and others have less. If we vote by interests, it will be attended with insuperable difficulties to ascertain the true importance of each Colony. Is the weight of a Colony to be ascertained by the number of inhabitants merely, or by the amount of their trade, the quantity of their exports and imports, or by any compound ratio of both? This will lead us into such a field of controversy as will greatly perplex us. Besides, I question whether it is possible to ascertain, at this time, the numbers of our people or the value of our trade. It will not do in such a case to take each other's word; it ought to be ascertained by authentic evidence from records.

The following brief notes of the discussion this day, upon the method of voting, are found in a separate sheet.

DEBATES.

Mr. Henry. Government is dissolved. Fleets and armies and the present state of things show that government is dissolved. Where are your landmarks, your boundaries of Colonies? We are in a state of nature, sir. I did propose that a scale should be laid down; that part of North America which was once Massachusetts Bay, and that part which was once Virginia, ought to be considered as having a weight. Will not people complain? Ten thousand Virginians have not outweighed one thousand others.

I will submit, however; I am determined to submit, if I am overruled.

A worthy gentleman (ego) near me seemed to admit the necessity of obtaining a more adequate representation.

I hope future ages will quote our proceedings with applause. It is one of the great duties of the democratical part of the con-

Mr. Wirt, as does also the abstract of the speech, with his idea of it. *Life of Patrick Henry*, p. 106.

stitution to keep itself pure. It is known in my Province that some other Colonies are not so numerous or rich as they are. I am for giving all the satisfaction in my power.

The distinctions between Virginians, Pennsylvanians, New Yorkers, and New Englanders, are no more. I am not a Virginian, but an American.

Slaves are to be thrown out of the question, and if the freemen can be represented according to their numbers, I am satisfied.[1]

Mr. Lynch. I differ in one point from the gentleman from Virginia, that is, in thinking that numbers only ought to determine the weight of Colonies. I think that property ought to be considered, and that it ought to be a compound of numbers and property that should determine the weight of the Colonies.

I think it cannot be now settled.

Mr. Rutledge. We have no legal authority; and obedience to our determinations will only follow the reasonableness, the apparent utility and necessity of the measures we adopt. We have no coercive or legislative authority. Our constituents are bound only in honor to observe our determinations.

Governor Ward. There are a great number of counties, in Virginia, very unequal in point of wealth and numbers, yet each has a right to send two members.

Mr. Lee. But one reason, which prevails with me, and that is, that we are not at this time provided with proper materials. I am afraid we are not.

Mr. Gadsden. I can't see any way of voting, but by Colonies.

Colonel Bland. I agree with the gentleman (ego) who spoke near me, that we are not at present provided with materials to ascertain the importance of each Colony. The question is, whether the rights and liberties of America shall be contended for, or given up to arbitrary powers.

Mr. Pendleton. If the committee should find themselves unable to ascertain the weight of the Colonies, by their numbers and property, they will report this, and this will lay the foundation for the Congress to take some other steps to procure evidence of numbers and property at some future time.

Mr. Henry. I agree that authentic accounts cannot be had, if by authenticity is meant attestations of officers of the Crown.

[1] This is probably all that has been saved of the celebrated speech of Patrick Henry at the opening of the Congress, which earned for him the national reputation he has ever since enjoyed.

I go upon the supposition that government is at an end. All distinctions are thrown down. All America is thrown into one mass. We must aim at the minutiæ of rectitude.

Mr. Jay. Could I suppose that we came to frame an American constitution, instead of endeavoring to correct the faults in an old one — I can't yet think that all government is at an end. The measure of arbitrary power is not full, and I think it must run over, before we undertake to frame a new constitution.

To the virtue, spirit, and abilities of Virginia, we owe much. I should always, therefore, from inclination as well as justice, be for giving Virginia its full weight.

I am not clear that we ought not to be bound by a majority, though ever so small, but I only mentioned it as a matter of danger, worthy of consideration.[1]

---

6. Tuesday. Went to Congress again; received by an express an intimation of the bombardment of Boston,[2] a confused account, but an alarming one indeed; God grant it may not be found true.

7. Wednesday. Went to Congress again, heard Mr. Duché read prayers; the collect for the day, the 7th of the month, was most admirably adapted, though this was accidental, or rather providential. A prayer which he gave us of his own composition was as pertinent, as affectionate, as sublime, as devout, as I ever heard offered up to Heaven.[3] He filled every bosom present.[4]

1 "The mode of voting in this Congress was first resolved upon; which was, that each Colony should have one voice; but, as this was objected to as unequal, an entry was made on the journals to prevent its being drawn into precedent in future." *Letter of Connecticut Delegates to Governor Trumbull*, 10 October, 1774.

2 This rumor grew out of the seizure made by an armed force under orders from General Gage, of the gunpowder belonging to the Province, stored in Charlestown. See *Frothingham's History of the Siege of Boston*, p. 13.

3 The subsequent conduct of Mr. Duché did not prove him worthy of the commendation here awarded. In his letter to General Washington he most pointedly sneers at the New England delegates, to whom he was indebted for the distinction of being selected. Their motive is explained in Samuel Adams's letter to Dr. Joseph Warren, dated 9 September. See *Force's American Archives*, 1774, c. 802. *Sparks's Washington*, vol. v. p. 476.

4 This is more fully spoken of by the writer in a private letter to his wife, dated the 16th instant, of which, the following is the substance: —

"When the Congress first met, Mr. Cushing made a motion that it should be opened with prayer. It was opposed by Mr. Jay of New York, and Mr. Rut-

Dined with Mr. Miers Fisher, a young Quaker and a lawyer. We saw his library, which is clever. But this plain Friend and his plain though pretty wife, with her Thees and Thous, had provided us the most costly entertainment; ducks, hams, chickens, beef, pig, tarts, creams, custards, jellies, fools, trifles, floating islands, beer, porter, punch, wine, and a long &c. We had a large collection of lawyers at table; Mr. Andrew Allen, the Attorney-General, a Mr. Morris, the Prothonotary, Mr. Fisher, Mr. McKean, Mr. Rodney; besides these, we had Mr. Reed, Governor Hopkins, and Governor Ward. We had much conversation upon the practice of law in our different Provinces, but at last we got swallowed up in politics, and the great question of parliamentary jurisdiction. Mr. Allen asks me, from whence do you derive your laws? How do you entitle yourselves to English privileges? Is not Lord Mansfield on the side of power?

8. Thursday. Attended my duty on the committee all day,

ledge of South Carolina, because we were so divided in religious sentiments; some Episcopalians, some Quakers, some Anabaptists, some Presbyterians, and some Congregationalists, that we could not join in the same act of worship. Mr. Samuel Adams arose and said, 'he was no bigot, and could hear a prayer from a gentleman of piety and virtue, who was at the same time a friend to his country. He was a stranger in Philadelphia, but had heard that Mr. Duché (Dushay they pronounce it,) deserved that character, and therefore he moved that Mr. Duché, an episcopal clergyman, might be desired to read prayers to the Congress to-morrow morning.' The motion was seconded and passed in the affirmative. Mr. Randolph, our President, waited on Mr. Duché and received for answer that, if his health would permit, he certainly would. Accordingly, next morning he appeared with his clerk and in his pontificals, and read several prayers in the established form, and then read the collect for the seventh day of September, which was the thirty-fifth Psalm. You must remember, this was the next morning after we heard the horrible rumor of the cannonade of Boston. I never saw a greater effect upon an audience. It seemed as if Heaven had ordained that Psalm to be read on that morning.

"After this, Mr. Duché, unexpectedly to every body, struck out into an extemporary prayer, which filled the bosom of every man present. I must confess, I never heard a better prayer, or one so well pronounced. Episcopalian as he is, Dr. Cooper himself never prayed with such fervor, such ardor, such earnestness and pathos, and in language so elegant and sublime, for America, for the Congress, for the Province of Massachusetts Bay, and especially the town of Boston. It has had an excellent effect upon every body here. I must beg you to read that Psalm. If there was any faith in the sortes Virgilianæ, or sortes Homericæ, or especially the sortes Biblicæ, it would be thought providential.

"It will amuse your friends to read this letter and the thirty-fifth Psalm to them. Read it to your father and Mr. Wibird. I wonder what our Braintree churchmen would think of this. Mr. Duché is one of the most ingenious men, and best characters, and greatest orators in the episcopal order upon this continent; yet a zealous friend of liberty and his country."

and a most ingenious, entertaining debate we had. The happy news were brought us from Boston, that *no blood had been spilled*, but that General Gage had taken away the provincial powder from the magazine at Cambridge. This last was a disagreeable circumstance. Dined at Mr. Powell's, with Mr. Duché, Dr. Morgan, Dr. Steptoe, Mr. Goldsborough, Mr. Johnson, and many others; a most sinful feast again! every thing which could delight the eye or allure the taste; curds and creams, jellies, sweetmeats of various sorts, twenty sorts of tarts, fools, trifles, floating islands, whipped sillabubs, &c. &c., Parmesan cheese, punch, wine, porter, beer, &c. At evening we climbed up the steeple of Christ Church with Mr. Reed, from whence we had a clear and full view of the whole city, and of Delaware River.

DEBATES.

September 8. In the Committee for stating rights, grievances, and means of redress.

Colonel Lee. The rights are built on a fourfold foundation; on nature, on the British constitution, on charters, and on immemorial usage. The Navigation Act, a capital violation.

Mr. Jay. It is necessary to recur to the law of nature, and the British constitution, to ascertain our rights. The constitution of Great Britain will not apply to some of the charter rights.

A mother country surcharged with inhabitants, they have a right to emigrate. It may be said, if we leave our country, we cannot leave our allegiance. But there is no allegiance without protection, and emigrants have a right to erect what government they please.

Mr. J. Rutledge. Emigrants would not have a right to set up what constitution they please. A subject could not alienate his allegiance.

Lee. Can't see why we should not lay our rights upon the broadest bottom, the ground of nature.[1] Our ancestors found here no government.

1 From this declaration it is clear that the delegation from Virginia was not unanimous in the policy imputed to them by Mr. Rutledge and the Carolinians. See the next note.

Mr. Pendleton. Consider how far we have a right to interfere with regard to the Canada constitution. If the majority of the people there should be pleased with the new constitution, would not the people of America and of England have a right to oppose it, and prevent such a constitution being established in our neighborhood?

Lee. It is contended that the Crown had no right to grant such charters as it has to the Colonies, and therefore, we shall rest our rights on a feeble foundation, if we rest them only on charters; nor will it weaken our objections to the Canada bill.

Mr. Rutledge. Our claims, I think, are well founded on the British constitution, and not on the law of nature.

Colonel Dyer. Part of the country within the Canada bill is a conquered country, and part not. It is said to be a rule that the King can give a conquered country what law he pleases.

Mr. Jay. I can't think the British constitution inseparably attached to the person of every subject. Whence did the constitution derive its authority? from compact; might not that authority be given up by compact?

Mr. William Livingston. A corporation cannot make a corporation; charter governments have done it. King can't appoint a person to make a justice of peace; all governors do it. Therefore it will not do for America to rest wholly on the laws of England.

Mr. Sherman. The ministry contend that the Colonies are only like corporations in England, and therefore subordinate to the legislature of the kingdom. The Colonies not bound to the King or Crown by the act of settlement, but by their consent to it. There is no other legislative over the Colonies but their respective assemblies.

The Colonies adopt the common law, not as the common law, but as the highest reason.

Mr. Duane. Upon the whole, for grounding our rights on the laws and constitution of the country from whence we sprung, and charters, without recurring to the law of nature; because this will be a feeble support. Charters are compacts between the Crown and the people, and I think on this foundation the charter governments stand firm.

England is governed by a limited monarchy and free constitution. Privileges of Englishmen were inherent, their birthright and inheritance, and cannot be deprived of them without their consent.

Objection; that all the rights of Englishmen will make us independent. I hope a line may be drawn to obviate this objection.

James was against Parliament interfering with the Colonies. In the reign of Charles II. the sentiments of the Crown seem to have been changed. The Navigation Act was made; Massachusetts denied the authority, but made a law to enforce it in the Colony.

Lee. Life, and liberty which is necessary for the security of life, cannot be given up when we enter into society.

Mr. Rutledge. The first emigrants could not be considered as in a state of nature; they had no right to elect a new king.

Mr. Jay. I have always withheld my assent from the position that every subject discovering land (does it) for the state to which he belongs.

Mr. Galloway. I never could find the rights of Americans in the distinction between taxation and legislation, nor in the distinction between laws for revenue and for the regulation of trade. I have looked for our rights in the law of nature, but could not find them in a state of nature, but always in a state of political society.

I have looked for them in the constitution of the English government, and there found them. We may draw them from this source securely.

Power results from the real property of the society. The states of Greece, Macedon, Rome were founded on this plan. None but landholders could vote in the comitia or stand for offices.

English constitution founded on the same principle. Among the Saxons, the landholders were obliged to attend, and shared among them the power. In the Norman period, the same. When the landholders could not all attend, the representatives of the freeholders came in. Before the reign of Henry IV. an attempt was made to give the tenants *in capite* a right to vote. Magna Charta — archbishops, bishops, abbots, earls, and barons, and tenants *in capite* held all the lands in England.

It is of the essence of the English constitution that no laws shall be binding, but such as are made by the consent of the proprietors in England.

How then, did it stand with our ancestors when they came over here? They could not be bound by any laws made by the British Parliament, excepting those made before. I never could see any reason to allow that we are bound to any law made since, nor could I ever make any distinction between the sorts of law.

I have ever thought we might reduce our rights to one—an exemption from all laws made by British Parliament since the emigration of our ancestors. It follows, therefore, that all the acts of Parliament made since, are violations of our rights.

These claims are all defensible upon the principles even of our enemies,—Lord North himself, when he shall inform himself of the true principles of the constitution, &c.

I am well aware that my arguments tend to an independency of the Colonies, and militate against the maxims that there must be some absolute power to draw together all the wills and strength of the empire.

9. Friday. Attended my duty upon committees; dined at home.

Extract from the Autobiography.

[The more we conversed with the gentlemen of the country, and with the members of Congress, the more we were encouraged to hope for a general union of the continent. As the proceedings of this Congress are in print, I shall have occasion to say little of them. A few observations may not be amiss.

After some days of general discussions, two committees were appointed of twelve members each, one from each state, Georgia not having yet come in. The first committee was instructed to prepare a bill of rights, as it was called, or a declaration of the rights of the Colonies; the second, a list of infringements or violations of those rights. Congress was pleased to appoint me on the first committee, as the member for Massachusetts.

It would be endless to attempt even an abridgment of the discussions in this committee, which met regularly every morning for many days successively, till it became an object of jealousy to all the other members of Congress. It was, indeed, very much against my judgment that the committee was so soon appointed, as I wished to hear all the great topics handled in Congress at large in the first place. They were very deliberately considered and debated in the committee, however. The two points which labored the most were: 1. Whether we should recur to the law of nature, as well as to the British constitution, and our American charters and grants. Mr. Galloway and Mr. Duane were for excluding the law of nature. I was very strenuous for retaining and insisting on it, as a resource to which we might be driven by Parliament much sooner than we were aware. 2. The other great question was, what authority we should concede to Parliament; whether we should deny the authority of Parliament in all cases; whether we should allow any authority to it in our internal affairs; or whether we should allow it to regulate the trade of the empire with or without any restrictions. These discussions spun into great length, and nothing was decided. After many fruitless essays, the committee determined to appoint a sub-committee to make a draught of a set of articles that might be laid in writing before the grand committee, and become the foundation of a more regular debate and final decision. I was appointed on the sub-committee, in which, after going over the ground again, a set of articles were drawn and debated one by one. After several days deliberation, we agreed upon all the articles excepting one, and that was the authority of Parliament, which was indeed the essence of the whole controversy; some were for a flat denial of all authority; others for denying the power of taxation only; some for denying internal, but admitting external, taxation. After a multitude of motions had been made, discussed, negatived, it seemed as if we should never agree upon any thing. Mr. John Rutledge of South Carolina, one of the committee, addressing himself to me, was pleased to say, "Adams, we must agree upon something; you appear to be as familiar with the subject as any of us, and I like your expressions, — '*the necessity of the case*,' and '*excluding all ideas of taxation, external and internal;*' I have a great opinion of that same idea of the necessity of the case, and I am determined against all taxation for revenue. Come, take the pen and see if you can't produce something that will unite us." Some others of the committee seconding Mr. Rutledge, I took a sheet of paper and drew up an article. When it was read, I believe not one of the committee was fully satisfied with it; but they all soon acknowledged that there was no hope of hitting on any thing in which we could all agree with more satisfaction. All therefore agreed to this, and upon this depended the union of the Colonies. The sub-committee reported their draught to the grand committee, and another long debate ensued, especially on this article, and various changes and modifications of it were attempted, but none adopted.[1]

[1] This account, written in 1804, evidently from recollection only and without consulting the record, appears by comparison, though substantially corresponding with it, not to be precisely accurate in the details. And, inasmuch as every step in this commencement of the federative union, of which so little is now known, is of some interest, it may not be deemed out of place to subjoin here what it has been found possible to gather together concerning the formation and objects of these first committees.

The Journal of 1774, for Tuesday, September 6, has the following entry:

"Resolved, unanimously, That a committee be appointed to state the rights of the Colonies in general, the several instances in which these rights are violated or infringed, and the means most proper to be pursued for obtaining a restoration of them.

"Resolved, That a committee be appointed to examine and report the several Statutes which affect the trade and manufactures of the Colonies."

On the next day, Wednesday 7th, the Journal says:—

"The Congress taking into consideration the appointment of the Committees, a vote was taken on the number of which the first committee should consist, and by a great majority agreed that it consist of two from each of the Colonies."

As the delegates from North Carolina did not come in until a week later, it follows that this committee was at first composed of twenty-two members, of whom those selected from Massachusetts, were Samuel and John Adams. But on the 14th instant the two delegates of North Carolina were added, making up the number of twenty-four.

The Journal proceeds:—

"Agreed, That the second committee consist of one chosen from each Colony."

Hence it follows that the second committee was only half as large as the first. Major John Sullivan, of New Hampshire, is the first named person in both; he, Governor Hopkins of Rhode Island, and latterly, William Hooper of North Carolina, are the only persons who served in both committees, the small number delegated from those Colonies making this step unavoidable.

It further appears that the second of these committees was first ready to report; for the Journal of Saturday, 17th September, has the following entry:—

"The committee appointed to examine and report the several statutes which affect the trade and manufactures of the Colonies, brought in their report, which was ordered to lie on the table."

On Monday, 19 September:—

"The report brought in on Saturday being read, as follows:—

. . . .

"Ordered, That the same be referred to the committee appointed to state the rights of the Colonies, &c. to which committee the Honorable Thomas Cushing, Patrick Henry, and Thomas Mifflin, Esquires, were added."

The report does not seem to have been inserted in the Journal, although space was left for it. It is not difficult, however, to identify it in the final draught of the resolutions, as will presently appear.

On the 19th, there was then only one committee left to which the whole of the subject, which had originally been distributed between two, was now referred.

The articles were then reported to Congress, and debated, paragraph by paragraph. The difficult article was again attacked and defended. Congress rejected all amendments to it, and the general sense of the members was, that the article demanded as little as could be demanded, and conceded as much as could be conceded with safety, and certainly as little as would be accepted by Great Britain; and that the country must take its fate, in

This committee consisted of twenty-seven members, or about one half of the whole assembly, every Colony having two representatives, with the exception of Virginia, Massachusetts, and Pennsylvania, to each of which another had been conceded, thus framing a species of compromise between the two principles of federation and population presented in the first day's debate.

The abstract of the discussion which took place in this committee on the eighth and ninth instant, is inserted in its place. It will be examined with more interest from the light shed upon it by the preceding extract from the Autobiography. The subject seems to have been elaborately discussed by Mr. Adams himself, as well as by the other gentlemen, though, whilst taking notes of their remarks, he neglected to make any record of his own. On the tenth, twelfth, and thirteenth of September, his Diary shows him to have been acting on the *sub*-committee, which sat whilst the Congress and the full committee did nothing, in order to give it room. On the last named day, it agreed upon a report to the larger body. But it was not until nine days afterwards, to wit, Thursday, the 22d, that the grand committee itself was ready to report, and then it did so only in part, as follows: —

"The committee appointed to state the rights of the Colonies, &c. having brought in a report of the rights, the same was read, and the consideration of it referred till Saturday next.

"Ordered, That a copy of this report be made out for each Colony."

On Saturday, 24 September, the record says, —

"The Congress entered upon the consideration of the report referred to this day, and after some debate, upon motion, —

"Resolved, That the Congress do confine themselves, at present, to the consideration of such rights only as have been infringed by acts of the British Parliament since the year 1763, postponing the further consideration of the general state of American rights to a future day."

This decision was not arrived at without much difference of opinion. From the report of the South Carolina delegates, it appears that the limitation was fixed by the influence of Virginia combining with the least resolute party, desirous of avoiding abstract principles on which a difference would admit of no reconciliation, and keeping the issue exclusively upon the temporary action of the existing ministry at home.

This point being definitively settled, in favor of the narrow construction, the committee appointed to state the rights, &c. brought in the other part of their report upon the infringements and violations of American rights, which being read, upon motion, —

"Resolved, That the consideration of this report be referred till Monday, and that the Congress, in the meanwhile, deliberate on the means most proper to be pursued for a restoration of our rights." *

* "Committees were then appointed to state American rights and grievances, and the various acts of the British Parliament which affect the trade and manufactures of these Colonies. On these subjects the committees spent several days, when the Congress judged it necessary, previous to completing and resolving on these subjects, to take under consideration that of ways and means for redress." *Letter of Connecticut Delegates to Governor Trumbull*, 10 October, 1774.

consequence of it. When Congress had gone through the articles, I was appointed to put them into form and report a fair draught for their final acceptance. This was done, and they were finally accepted.

The committee of violations of rights reported a set of articles which were drawn by Mr. John Sullivan of New Hampshire; and these two declarations, the one of rights and the other of violations, which are printed in the journals of Congress for 1774, were two years afterwards recapitulated in the Declaration of Independence, on the Fourth of July, 1776.]

---

10. Saturday. Attended my duty upon the sub-committee. Dined at home. Dr. Morgan, Dr. Cox, Mr. Spence, and several other gentlemen, Major Sullivan and Colonel Folsom, dined with us upon salt fish. Rambled in the evening with Jo Reed, and fell into Mr. Sprout's meeting, where we heard Mr. Spence preach. Mr. Reed returned with Mr. Adams and me to our lodgings, and a very sociable, agreeable, and communicative

This second report of the large committee is the one which, from its being made separately, Mr. Adams in his later recollection appears to have blended with the action of the second committee.

On Monday and Tuesday, the 26th and 27th of September, the Congress proceeded to deliberate on the question, as stated above, and the result was the adoption of a non-importation agreement, as it stands upon the journals. The notes taken by Mr. Adams of this discussion will be found appended to the record of the 27th.

On the 28th, Mr. Galloway, of Pennsylvania, made his celebrated motion, and proposed his plan of union, which he prefaced with a speech. The notes of that speech, and of a part of the debate which is known to have been the critical one in the career of this assembly, are appended to the record of that day. The plan is said to have been defeated only by a majority of one State.

The Congress did not resume the consideration of the subject of rights and grievances until Wednesday, October 12; and on Friday, the 14th, they adopted the resolutions as they are found in the Journals of that day. Among the papers of Mr. Adams there is, in handwriting somewhat resembling that of Major Sullivan, a draught of the articles as they were doubtless first submitted to the committee. So little is known of the proceedings of this Congress, that it may not be deemed superfluous, in the Appendix C. to this volume, to place this draught in contrast with the resolutions as they were ultimately passed. From this comparison it will appear that the critical article alluded to by Mr. Adams, as finally drawn up by himself, is the fourth in the series. It was this article against which Mr. Galloway afterwards, in his pamphlet, directed his main attack, on the ground that it aimed at independence. It will likewise be seen that all after the tenth resolution constitutes that portion of the report which had its origin in the labors of the second committee, before it was merged in the larger one, and which was reported afterwards, to wit, on the 24th of September.

evening we had. He says we never were guilty of a more masterly stroke of policy, than in moving that Mr. Duché might read prayers; it has had a very good effect, &c. He says the sentiments of people here are growing more and more favorable every day.

11. Sunday. There is such a quick and constant succession of new scenes, characters, persons, and events, turning up before me, that I can't keep any regular account. This Mr. Reed is a very sensible and accomplished lawyer, of an amiable disposition, soft, tender, friendly, &c.; he is a friend to his country and to liberty. Mr. Reed was so kind as to wait on us to Mr. Sprout's meeting, where we heard Mr. Spence. These ministers all preach without notes. We had an opportunity of seeing the custom of the Presbyterians in administering the sacrament. The communicants all come to a row of seats, placed on each side of a narrow table spread in the middle of the alley, reaching from the deacons' seat to the front of the house. Three sets of persons of both sexes came in succession. Each new set had the bread and the cup given them by a new minister. Mr. Sprout first, Mr. Treat next, and Mr. Spence last. Each communicant has a token which he delivers to the deacons or elders, I don't know which they call them. As we came out of meeting, a Mr. Webster joined us, who has just come from Boston, and has been a generous benefactor to it in its distresses. He says he was at the town meeting, and he thinks they managed their affairs with great simplicity, moderation, and discretion. Dined at Mr. Willing's, who is a judge of the supreme court here, with the gentlemen from Virginia, Maryland, and New York. A most splendid feast again, — turtle and every thing else. Mr. Willing told us a story of a lawyer here, who the other day gave him, upon the bench, the following answer to a question, Why the lawyers were so increased?

"You ask me why lawyers so much are increased,
Tho' most of the country already are fleeced;
The reason, I'm sure, is most strikingly plain; —
Tho' sheep are oft sheared, yet the wool grows again;
And tho' you may think e'er so odd of the matter,
The oftener they're fleeced, the wool grows the better.
Thus downy chin'd boys, as oft I have heard,
By frequently shaving, obtain a large beard."

By Mr. Peters,[1] written at the bar, and given to a judge, Mr. Willing, who had asked the question at dinner in pleasantry. Mr. Willing is the most sociable, agreeable man of all. He told us of a law of this place, that whereas oysters, between the months of May and September, were found to be unwholesome food, if any were brought to market they should be forfeited and given to the poor. We drank coffee, and then Reed, Cushing, and I strolled to the Moravian evening lecture, where we heard soft, sweet music, and a Dutchified English prayer and preachment.

12. Monday. Attended my duty on the committee until one o'clock, and then went with my colleagues and Messrs. Thomson and Mifflin to the Falls of Schuylkill, and viewed the Museum at Fort St. David's; a great collection of curiosities. Returned and dined with Mr. Dickinson at his seat at Fair Hill, with his lady, Mrs. Thomson, Miss Norris, and Miss Harrison. Mr. Dickinson has a fine seat, a beautiful prospect of the city, the river, and the country, fine gardens, and a very grand library. The most of his books were collected by Mr. Norris, once Speaker of the House here, father of Mrs. Dickinson. Mr. Dickinson is a very modest man, and very ingenious as well as agreeable; he has an excellent heart, and the cause of his country lies near it. He is full and clear for allowing to Parliament the regulation of trade, upon principles of necessity, and the mutual interest of both countries.

13. Tuesday. Attended my duty all day on the sub-committee. Agreed on a report.

14. Wednesday. Visited Mr. Gadsden, Mr. Deane, Colonel Dyer, &c. at their lodgings. Gadsden is violent against allowing to Parliament any power of regulating trade, or allowing that they have any thing to do with us. "Power of regulating trade," he says, "is power of ruining us; as bad as acknowledging them a supreme legislative in all cases whatsoever; a right of regulating trade is a right of legislation, and a right of legislation in one case is a right in all; this I deny." Attended the Congress and committee all the forenoon; dined with Dr.

[1] Richard Peters, long celebrated in Philadelphia for his wit, as well as for other and higher qualities. He served as Secretary of the Board of War, until 1781, and as Judge of the District Court of the United States until his death, in 1828, at an advanced age.

Cox. Dr. Morgan, Dr. Rush, Mr. Bayard, and old Mr. Smith, dined with us. Dr. Rush lives upon Water Street, and has, from the window of his back room and chamber, a fine prospect of Delaware River and of New Jersey beyond it. The gentlemen entertained us with absurdities in the laws of Pennsylvania, New Jersey, and Maryland. This, I find, is a genteel topic of conversation here. A mighty feast again; nothing less than the very best of Claret, Madeira, and Burgundy; melons, fine beyond description, and pears and peaches as excellent. This day Mr. Chase introduced to us a Mr. Carroll, of Annapolis, a very sensible gentleman, a Roman Catholic, and of the first fortune in America. His income is ten thousand pounds sterling a year now, will be fourteen in two or three years, they say; besides, his father has a vast estate which will be his after his father.

16. Friday. Dined with Mr. Wallace with a great deal of company at an elegant feast again.

17. Saturday. This was one of the happiest days of my life. In Congress we had generous, noble sentiments, and manly eloquence. This day convinced me that America will support the Massachusetts or perish with her.[1] Dined with old Mr. Smith, with much company; visited the Bettering House, a large building, very clean, neat, and convenient for the poor; viewed the gardens, &c.

18. Sunday. Went to church and heard Mr. Coombe read prayers, and Mr. Duché preach — a fine preacher indeed; dined at home. Went to Dr. Allison's meeting in the afternoon; heard Mr. ——, a very ingenious preacher of benevolence and humanity. Spent the evening at home with General Lee, Captain Dagworthy, Mr. McDougall and others; wrote many letters to go by Mr. Paul Revere.

[1] On this day the celebrated resolutions of Suffolk County, in Massachusetts, had been laid before Congress, and resolutions were adopted by the Congress expressive of sympathy and support. See the *Journals*.

"The proceedings of the Congress are all a profound secret as yet, except two votes which were passed yesterday, and ordered to be printed. You will see them from every quarter. These votes were passed in full Congress with perfect unanimity. The esteem, the affection, the admiration for the people of Boston and the Massachusetts, which were expressed yesterday, and the fixed determination that they should be supported, were enough to melt a heart of stone. I saw the tears gush into the eyes of the old, grave, pacific Quakers of Pennsylvania." *J. A. to his Wife*, 18 Sept. Compare the letter of S. Adams to Dr. Chauncy. *Quincy's Life of Quincy*, p. 180.

19. Monday. Dined with Dr. Rush, in company with Dr. Shippen and many others, Folsom and Sullivan from New Hampshire, Mr. Blair, &c. &c.

20. Tuesday. Had cards a week ago to dine with Mr. Mease, but forgot it and dined at home. After we had dined, after four o'clock, Mr. Mease's brother came to our lodgings after us. We went, after dinner, and found Mr. Dickinson, Mifflin, Dr. Rush, Mr. West, Mr. Biddle, and Captain Allen, and Mr. Mease's brother; a very agreeable company. Our regret at the loss of this company was very great. Mr. Dickinson was very agreeable. A question was started about the conduct of the Bostonian merchants, since the year 1770, in importing tea and paying the duty. Mr. Hancock, it is said, has received the freight of many chests of tea. I think the Bostonian merchants are not wholly justifiable, yet their conduct has been exaggerated; their fault and guilt have been magnified. Mr. Hancock, I believe, is justifiable, but I am not certain whether he is strictly so. He owned a ship in partnership with George Hayley, who is agreed here to be a ministerial man, and Hayley, I suppose, sent the tea in the ship.

21. Wednesday. Captain Callender came to breakfast with us. Colonel Dagworthy and his brother, Captain Dagworthy, breakfasted with us. Mrs. Yard entertained us with muffins, buckwheat cakes, and common toast. Buckwheat is an excellent grain, and is very plenty here. Attended Congress from nine to after three. Rode out of town six miles, to Mr. Hill's, where we dined with Mr. Hill and lady, Mr. Dickinson and his lady, Mr. Thomson and his lady, old Mr. Meredith, father of Mrs. Hill, Mr. Johnson of Maryland, and Mr. Jo Reed.

22. Thursday. Dined with Mr. Chew, Chief Justice of the Province, with all the gentlemen from Virginia, Dr. Shippen, Mr. Tilghman, and many others. We were shown into a grand entry and stair-case, and into an elegant and most magnificent chamber, until dinner. About four o'clock, we were called down to dinner. The furniture was all rich. Turtle, and every other thing, flummery, jellies, sweetmeats of twenty sorts, trifles, whipped sillabubs, floating islands, fools, &c. and then a dessert of fruits, raisins, almonds, pears, peaches. Wines most excellent and admirable. I drank Madeira at a great rate, and found no inconvenience in it. In the evening, General Lee and Colonel

Lee, and Colonel Dyer, and Mr. Deane, and half a score friends from Boston came to our lodgings. Colonel Lee staid till twelve o'clock, and was very social and agreeable.

23. Friday. Walked along Second Street, southward, until I got out of the city into the country. The uniformity of this city is disagreeable to some. I like it. Dined with the late Chief Justice Allen, with all the gentlemen from North Carolina, and Mr. Hamilton, late Governor, and Mr. Andrew Allen, Attorney-General. We had much conversation about Mr. Franklin. The Chief Justice and Attorney-General had much droll chat together.

24. Saturday. Dined with Mr. Charles Thomson, with only Mr. Dickinson, his lady and niece in company. A most delightful afternoon we had; sweet communion, indeed, we had. Mr. Dickinson gave us his thoughts and his correspondence very freely.

25. Sunday. Went in the evening to Quaker meeting, and afterwards went to supper at Stephen Collins's.

26. Monday. Dined at old Dr. Shippen's, with Mr. and Mrs. Blair, young Dr. Shippen, the Jersey delegates, and some Virginians.[1] Afterwards went to the hospital, and heard another lecture upon anatomy from young Dr. Shippen.

27. Tuesday. Dined at Mr. Bayard's, with Dr. Cox, Dr. Rush, Mr. Hodge, Mr. Deane, Colonel Dyer. Dr. Cox gave us a toast: "May the fair dove of liberty, in this deluge of despotism, find rest to the sole of her foot in America."

The notes which follow appear to have been taken in a discussion which terminated in the adoption of the non-importation resolution recorded in the Journal of the 27th.[2]

DEBATES.

Mr. Lee made a motion for a non-importation.

Mr. Mifflin. The first of November ought to be fixed; for no

[1] The following extract from the writer's letter of this date, to the late Judge Tudor, is of importance to elucidate the motives of action at this time.

"We have had numberless prejudices to remove here. We have been obliged to act with great delicacy and caution. We have been obliged to keep ourselves out of sight, and to feel pulses and sound the depths; to insinuate our sentiments, designs, and desires, by means of other persons; sometimes of one Province, and sometimes of another."

[2] "Resolved, unanimously, That from and after the first day of December next, there be no importation into British America, from Great Britain or Ire-

honest orders were sent after the first of June. Orders are generally sent in April and May. But the intention was known of a non-importation.

Colonel Bland. I think the time ought to be fixed, when goods are shipped in Great Britain, because a ship may have a long voyage.

Mr. Gadsden. For the first of November; we may be deceived and defrauded if we fix the time, when goods are shipped.

Colonel Lee. Invoices have been antedated.

Mr. John Rutledge. I think all the ways and means should be proposed.

Mr. Mifflin proposes stoppage of flax-seed and lumber to the West Indies, and non-importation of dutied articles; to commence 1 August, 1775.

Mr. Chase. Force, I apprehend, is out of the question in our present inquiry. In 1770, the annual tax was thirteen millions; last year it was only ten millions. Land tax, malt tax, perpetual funds, amount to only ten millions. They are compelled to raise ten millions in time of peace.

The emigrations from Great Britain prove that they are taxed as far as they can bear. A total non-importation and non-exportation to Great Britain and the West Indies must produce a national bankruptcy, in a very short space of time.[1] The foreign trade of Great Britain is but four millions and a half; as great a man as ever Britain produced calculated the trade with the Colonies at two millions. I believe the importation to the Colonies now represented, may be three millions. A non-exportation amounts to three millions more, and the debt due to four millions. Two thirds in the Colonies are clothed in British manufactures. Non-exportation of vastly more importance than a non-importation; it affects the merchants as well as manufacturers, the trade as well as the revenue. Sixty thousand hogsheads of tobacco. Two hundred and twenty-five British ships employed.

land, of any goods, wares, or merchandises whatsoever, or from any other place, of any such goods, wares, or merchandises, as shall have been exported from Great Britain or Ireland, and that no such goods, wares, or merchandises imported after the said first day of December next, be used or purchased."

A non-exportation rule was also adopted on Friday, the 30th.

[1] This was a common impression of the times. The whole action of this Congress was predicated upon the error. Yet the commercial position of China could not have been entirely unknown, even at that period.

I am for a non-exportation of lumber to the West Indies immediately.

The importance of the trade of the West Indies to Great Britain almost exceeds calculation. The sugar carries the greatest revenue; the rum a great deal. If you don't stop the lumber immediately, you can't stop it at all. If it takes place immediately, they can't send home their next year's crop.

A non-exportation at a future day cannot avail us. What is the situation of Boston and the Massachusetts?

A non-exportation at the Virginia day will not operate before the fall of 1776. I would not affect the trade of the Colonies to the Mediterranean or other parts of the world.

I am for a more distant day than the first of November.

Mr. Lynch. We want not only redress, but speedy redress. The mass can't live without government, I think, one year. Nothing less than what has been proposed by the gentleman last speaking, will put the Colonies in the state I wish to see them in. I believe the Parliament would grant us immediate relief. Bankruptcy would be the consequence if they did not.

Mr. Gadsden. By saving our own liberties, we shall save those of the West Indies. I am for being ready, but I am not for the sword. The only way to prevent the sword from being used, is to have it ready.

Though the Virginians are tied up,[1] I would be for doing it without them. Boston and New England can't hold out. The country will be deluged in blood, if we don't act with spirit.

[1] In the account, given by Judge Drayton, of the report made by the South Carolina delegates of the proceedings of this Congress, there is a little obscurity, which appears to grow out of a confounding of two separate positions taken by the Virginia delegates. The one related to the limitation of the statement of grievances to the period of the present reign. The other to the hesitation to come into a measure of non-exportation, on the ground of insufficient powers. The first case, however decided, would scarcely present sufficient cause for serious division. The second seems at one time to have threatened seriously to impair the harmony of the union. The language of Judge Drayton, if applied to this, receives some illustration from the remarks attributed in the text to Messrs. Gadsden and Chase. It runs thus:—

"It was then pressed in Congress that the other Colonies should, in this measure, act independently of Virginia; but Maryland and North Carolina represented, that as their exports were similar to those of Virginia, so they could not, with any advantage to the common cause, act independently of her; for their own commodities would be carried to the Virginia ports, which would run away with all their trade." *Memoirs of the American Revolution*, vol. i. p. 168.

The delegates from Virginia finally signed the agreement in its fullest extent.

Don't let America look at this mountain and let it bring forth a mouse.

Mr. Chase. We can't come into a non-exportation, immediately, without Virginia.

Mr. Cushing for a non-importation, non-exportation, and non-consumption; and immediately.

Colonel Bland. It has been our glory —

Mr. Hooper. We make some tobacco. I was instructed to protest against petitioning alone. Tar, pitch, and turpentine, we can ship nowhere but to Great Britain. The whole of the subsistence of the people in the southern ports is from naval stores. Great Britain cannot do without naval stores from North Carolina.

Mr. Edward Rutledge. A gentleman from the other end of the room talked of generosity. True equality is the only public generosity. If Virginia raises wheat, instead of tobacco, they will not suffer. Our rice is an enumerated commodity. We shall, therefore, lose all our trade.[1] I am both for non-importation and non-exportation, to take place immediately.

Mr. Henry. We don't mean to hurt even our rascals, if we have any. I move that December may be inserted instead of November.

Mr. Jay. Negotiation, suspension of commerce, and war, are the only three things. War is, by general consent, to be waved at present. I am for negotiation and suspension of commerce.

[1] This article of rice proved another great stumbling-block in the way of union, which was at last removed only by consenting to except it from the agreement of non-exportation to Europe. In the first instance, the bare proposition of excepting that and indigo, is stated by Mr. Gadsden, who disagreed with the rest of his colleagues, to have occasioned a cessation from business for several days, in order to give the refractory deputies time to recollect themselves, although it is difficult now to tell exactly when this cessation could have taken place. He further says, that even when the association was completing, without any exception, and the members were signing it, all the deputies from South Carolina, but himself, withdrew; and that State was on the point of being excluded, when a compromise was proposed, by which indigo being surrendered on the one side, the exception was admitted of rice on the other.

This compromise was not, however, altogether relished by their constituents in Carolina, and especially by the cultivators of indigo, who considered their interests sacrificed for the benefit of the rice planters. An account of the violent struggle between these two parties in the provincial legislature, is given by Judge Drayton in his interesting Memoirs, vol. i. pp. 168 – 174. Ramsay says nothing of it, but leaves a directly contrary impression on the mind of the reader. *History*, vol. i. p. 24.

Colonel Lee. All considerations of interest, and of equality of sacrifice, should be laid aside.

Produce of the other Colonies is carried to market in the same year when it is raised, even rice. Tobacco is not until the next year.

Mr. Sullivan. We export masts, boards, plank, fish, oil, and some potash. Ships we load with lumber for the West Indies, and thence carry sugar to England, and pay our debts that way. Every kind of lumber we export to the West Indies. Our lumber is made in the winter. Our ships sail in January or February for the West Indies.

Colonel Dyer. They have now drawn the sword, in order to execute their plan of subduing America; and I imagine they will not sheathe it, but that next summer will decide the fate of America. To withdraw all commerce with Great Britain at once, would come upon them like a thunderclap. By what I heard yesterday, Great Britain is much more in our power than I expected;—the masts from the northward, the naval stores from North Carolina.

We are struggling for the liberties of the West Indies and of the people of Great Britain, as well as our own, and perhaps of Europe.

Stopping the flax-seed to Ireland would greatly distress them.

Mr. Cushing. Whoever considers the present state of Great Britain and America, must see the necessity of spirited measures. Great Britain has drawn the sword against us, and nothing prevents her sheathing it in our bowels, but want of sufficient force.

I think it absolutely necessary to agree to a non-importation and non-exportation immediately.

---

28. Wednesday. Dined with Mr. R. Penn; a magnificent house, and a most splendid feast, and a very large company. Mr. Dickinson and General Lee were there, and Mr. Moylan, besides a great number of the delegates. Spent the evening at home, with Colonel Lee, Colonel Washington, and Dr. Shippen, who came in to consult with us.[1]

[1] This meeting, and the motives which induced it, are alluded to by General Washington in a letter to Captain Mackenzie, of the 9th of October following. See *Sparks's Washington*, vol. ii. p. 401.

DEBATES.

Among all the difficulties in the way of effective and united action, in 1774,—and they were far greater than the members of the Congress were, at the time, for very obvious reasons, willing to admit, or than the people of the present generation, who judge only from results, are apt to imagine,—no more alarming one happened than the "plan of a proposed union between Great Britain and the Colonies," presented, on the 28th of September, by Mr. Joseph Galloway, a delegate from Pennsylvania. Himself a gentleman of abilities, of property, and of extensive influence on the popular side, he seems to have accepted a seat in this Congress rather for the purpose of "sitting on the skirts of the American advocates," than of promoting any valuable end. He prefaced his formidable motion with a speech, of which the outline is now to be given. How near he came to success, may be judged not only from his own account, which he afterwards gave in a pamphlet, but still more from the extreme earnestness of his opponents to expunge from the record all traces of the proceedings, and to discredit his statements as those of a renegade and a traitor. Nevertheless, there is no good reason for doubting his substantial accuracy. He says of the fate of his scheme:—

"The plan read, and warmly seconded by several gentlemen of the first abilities, after a long debate, was so far approved as to be thought worthy of further consideration, and referred, under a rule for that purpose, by a majority of the Colonies. Under this promising aspect of things, and an expectation that the rule would have been regarded, or at least that something rational would take place to reconcile our unhappy differences, the member proposing it was weakly led to sign the non-importation agreement, although he had uniformly opposed it; but in this he was disappointed. The measures of independence and sedition were soon after preferred to those of harmony and liberty, and no arguments, however reasonable and just, could prevail on a majority of the Colonies to desert them." *Candid Examination of the Mutual Claims of Great Britain and the Colonies.*

The plan was not a new one. It had been suggested to Governor Hutchinson, and opposed by him, early in the controversy. Though it does not appear in the Journals, its details were published by Mr. Galloway himself in the pamphlet from which the preceding extract is taken, and it has been inserted in its place in the republication made by Mr. Force in the American Archives of 1774. It was defeated by the close vote of six Colonies to five. The mover continued, nevertheless, to act with the majority, and he actually signed the non-importation agreement and the Address to the King. But in the next year he got himself excused from further service in Congress, and, in 1776, he openly joined the royalist forces in New York.

Mr. Galloway. The proposal I intended to make having been opposed, I have waited to hear a more effectual one. A general non-importation from Great Britain and Ireland has been adopted, but I think this will be too gradual in its operation for the relief of Boston. A general non-exportation I have ever looked on as an undigested proposition. It is impossible America can exist under a total non-exportation. We, in this Province, should have tens of thousands of people thrown upon the cold hand of charity. Our ships would lie by the walls, our seamen would be thrown out of bread, our shipwrights, &c. out of employ, and it would affect the landed interest. It would weaken us in another struggle, which I fear is too near.

To explain my plan, I must state a number of facts relative to Great Britain and relative to America. I hope no facts which I shall state will be disagreeable.

In the last war, America was in the greatest danger of destruction. This was held up by the Massachusetts, and by the Congress in 1754. They said we are disunited among ourselves. There is no indifferent arbiter between us.

Requisitions came over. A number of the Colonies gave most extensively and liberally; others gave nothing or late. Pennsylvania gave late, not for want of zeal or loyalty, but owing to their disputes with proprietors, their disunited state. These delinquencies were handed up to the parent State, and these gave occasion to the Stamp Act. America, with the greatest reason and justice, complained of the Stamp Act.

Had they proposed some plan of policy, some negotiation been set afoot, it would have terminated in the most happy harmony between the two countries. They repealed the Stamp Act, but they passed the Declaratory Act.

Without some supreme legislature, some common arbiter, you are not, say they, part of the State.

I am as much a friend of liberty as exists; and no man shall go further in point of fortune, or in point of blood, than the man who now addresses you.

Burlamaqui, Grotius, Puffendorf, Hooker. There must be a union of wills and strength; distinction between a State and a multitude; a State is animated by one soul.

As we are not within the circle of the supreme jurisdiction of the Parliament, we are independent States. The law of Great Britain does not bind us in any case whatever.

We want the aid and assistance and protection of the arm of our mother country. Protection and allegiance are reciprocal duties. Can we lay claim to the money and protection of Great Britain upon any principles of honor or conscience? Can we wish to become aliens to the mother state?

We must come upon terms with Great Britain.

Some gentlemen are not for negotiation. I wish I could hear some reason against it.

The minister must be at twenty or thirty millions [expense] to enforce his measures.

I propose this proposition. The plan, — two classes of laws. 1. Laws of internal policy. 2. Laws in which more than one Colony are concerned, — raising money for war. No one act can be done without the assent of Great Britain. No one without the assent of America. A British American Legislature.

Mr. Duane. As I mean to second this motion, I think myself bound to lay before the Congress my reasons. New York thought it necessary to have a Congress for the relief of Boston and Massachusetts, and to do more, to lay a plan for a lasting accommodation with Great Britain.

Whatever may have been the motive for departing from the first plan of the Congress, I am unhappy that we have departed from it. The Post-office Act was before the year 1763. Can we expect lasting tranquillity? I have given my full assent to a non-importation and non-exportation agreement.

The right of regulating trade, from the local circumstances of the Colonies, and their disconnection with each other, cannot be exercised by the Colonies. Massachusetts disputed the Navigation Act, because not represented, but made a law of their own, to inforce that Act. Virginia did the same nearly.

I think justice requires that we should expressly cede to Parliament the right of regulating trade. In the Congress of 1754, which consisted of the greatest and best men in the Colonies, this was considered as indispensable.

A civil war with America would involve a national bankruptcy.

Colonel Lee. How did we go on for one hundred and sixty years before the year 1763? We flourished and grew. This plan would make such changes in the Legislature of the Colonies, that I could not agree to it without consulting my constituents.

Mr. Jay. I am led to adopt this plan. It is objected that this plan will alter our constitutions, and therefore cannot be adopted without consulting constituents. Does this plan give up any one liberty, or interfere with any one right?

Mr. Henry. The original constitution of the Colonies was founded on the broadest and most generous base. The regulation of our trade was compensation enough for all the protection we ever experienced from her.

We shall liberate our constituents from a corrupt House of Commons, but throw them into the arms of an American Legislature, that may be bribed by that nation which avows, in the face of the world, that bribery is a part of her system of government.

Before we are obliged to pay taxes as they do, let us be as free as they; let us have our trade open with all the world.

We are not to consent by the representatives of representatives.

I am inclined to think the present measures lead to war.

Mr. Edward Rutledge. I came with an idea of getting a bill of rights and a plan of permanent relief. I think the plan may be freed from almost every objection. I think it almost a perfect plan.

Mr. Galloway. In every government, patriarchal, monarchial, aristocratical, or democratical, there must be a supreme legislature.

I know of no American constitution; a Virginia constitution, a Pennsylvania constitution we have; we are totally independent of each other.

Every gentleman here thinks the Parliament ought to have the power over trade, because Britain protects it and us. Why then will we not declare it?

Because Parliament and Ministry is wicked and corrupt, and will take advantage of such declaration to tax us, and will also reason from this acknowledgment to further power over us.

Answer. We shall not be bound further than we acknowledge it.

Is it not necessary that the trade of the empire should be regulated by some power or other? Can the empire hold together without it? No. Who shall regulate it? Shall the Legislature of Nova Scotia or Georgia regulate it? Massachusetts, or Virginia? Pennsylvania or New York? It can't be pretended. Our legislative powers extend no further than the limits of our governments. Where then shall it be placed? There is a necessity that an American Legislature should be set up, or else that we should give the power to Parliament or King.

Protection. Acquiescence. Massachusetts. Virginia.

Advantages derived from our commerce.

---

29. Thursday. Dined at home, with the delegates from North Carolina and a number of other gentlemen.[1]

30. Friday. Dined at Mr. Jonathan Smith's. Dr. Allison, Mr. Sprout, and many other gentlemen.[2]

[1] "Patience, forbearance, long suffering, are the lessons taught here for our Province, and, at the same time, absolute and open resistance to the new government. I wish I could convince gentlemen of the danger or impracticability of this, as fully as I believe it myself. The art and address of ambassadors from a dozen belligerent powers of Europe, nay, of a conclave of cardinals at the election of a Pope, or of the princes in Germany at the choice of an Emperor, would not exceed the specimens we have seen; yet the Congress all profess the same political principles. They all profess to consider our Province as suffering in the common cause, and indeed they seem to feel for us, as if for themselves. We have had as great questions to discuss as ever engaged the attention of men, and an infinite multitude of them." *J. A. to his wife*, 29 September.

[2] Among the papers of Mr. Adams is the draught of the following resolutions, on which, in the handwriting of another person, is indorsed "J. Adams's motion, September 30th." No such motion is recorded in the journal, although some of the language is found incorporated into the resolution, adopted on the seventh of October, instructing a committee to prepare a letter to General Gage. The probability is, that the Congress was not at the moment ready to pledge all the Colonies quite so deeply as these resolutions would have done, although some of the measures recommended were ultimately adopted.

"*Resolved*, That the Province of the Massachusetts Bay and the town of Boston are now suffering and struggling in the common cause of American freedom, and, therefore, that it is the indispensable duty of all the Colonies to support them by every necessary means, and to the last extremity."

"Whereas hostilities have been already commenced against the Province of Massachusetts Bay, and through them against all the Colonies, and whereas this Congress have already advised the people of that Province by no means to submit to the late Act of Parliament for altering their government, —

"*Resolved*, That in case hostilities should be further pursued against that Province, and submission be attempted to be compelled by force of arms, as soon as intelligence of this shall be communicated to the several Colonies, they ought immediately to cease all exportations of goods, wares, and merchandise, to Great Britain, Ireland, and the West Indies."

"*Resolved*, That in case any person or persons should be arrested, in the Massachusetts Bay or any other Colony, by General Gage or any other person, in order to be sent to Great Britain to be there tried for any crime whatsoever, committed in America, under pretence of authority of the statute of Henry VIII. or that of the present reign, this ought to be considered as a declaration of war and a commencement of hostilities against all the Colonies, and reprisals ought to be made in all the Colonies and held as hostages for the security of the person or persons so arrested; and all exportations of merchandise to Great Britain, Ireland, and the West Indies, ought immediately to cease."

October 1. Saturday. Dined with Mr. Webster; spent the evening with Stephen Collins; went to see the election at the State House. Mr. Dickinson was chosen.

2. Sunday. Went to Christ Church and heard Mr. Coombe upon "Judge not according to the appearance, but judge righteous judgment." Went to Mr. Sprout's, in the afternoon, and heard Mr. Tennent. Spent the evening at home with Mr. McDougall, Mr. Cary of Charlestown, Mr. Reed, and Colonel Floyd.

3. Monday. Breakfasted at home with Colonel Dagworthy, of Maryland, Captain Dagworthy, his brother, Major De Bois, Mr. Webb, Dr. Clopton, &c. The hurry of spirits I have been in, since my arrival in this city, has prevented my making remarks in my journal, as I wished to have done. The quick succession of objects, the variety of scenes and characters, have rendered it impracticable. Major De Bois says he will drink dispute this morning. The Congress not come to decision yet. Dined at home. This day, Charles Thomson and Thomas Mifflin were chosen burgesses for this city. The change in the elections for this city and county is no small event. Mr. Dickinson and Mr. Thomson, now joined to Mr. Mifflin, will make a great weight in favor of the American cause.

4. Tuesday. Dined with Mr. Alexander Wilcox, with all the delegates from New York, and several other gentlemen. This evening, General Lee came to my lodgings and showed me an Address from the C. to the people of Canada, which he had.[1]

5. Wednesday. Dined with Dr. Cadwallader, in company with Governor Hamilton, General Lee, Mr. Henry, Mr. Pendleton, Mr. De Hart, and many others. Spent the evening at home, with Mr. McDougall and Mr. Sherman, in sad and solemn consultation about the miseries and distresses of our dear town of Boston.

6. Thursday. Dined with Mr. Hodge, father-in-law to Mr. Bayard.

[1] It is worthy of notice that this is more than a fortnight before the resolution, directing such a memorial to be prepared, passed in Congress, and, further, that it is in the hands of General Lee. The committee afterwards appointed consisted of Mr. Cushing, R. H. Lee, and J. Dickinson. They reported on the 24th, and their report was recommitted. They again reported, on the 26th, the paper which was adopted.

DEBATES.

The following brief and fragmentary report of a discussion upon the proposition of a non-importation agreement has no date attached to it. The probability is that it took place on or before the 6th of October, when the committee appointed to consider and report upon the subject were finally instructed to insert the following clause:—

"That from and after the first day of December next, no molasses, coffee, or pimento, from the British plantations or from Dominica, or wines from Madeira and the Western Islands, or foreign indigo, be imported into these Colonies."

Mr. Gadsden. There are numbers of men who will risk their all. I shudder at the thought of the blood which will be spilled, and would be glad to avoid it.

Mr. Pendleton. How is the purchaser to know whether the molasses, sugar, or coffee, has paid the duty or not? It can't be known. Shan't we by this hang out to all the world our intentions to smuggle?

Don't we complain of these acts as grievances, and shan't we insist on the repeal?

But this will give an advantage to the West Indians, and will make it their interest to oppose our obtaining any redress.

Colonel Dyer. This subject, as every part of our deliberations, is important. The question is, how far to extend the non-importation of dutiable articles.

Mr. Chase. I am against the question before you. What are the ways and means of obtaining redress? In the manner it is penned it would not answer the end. How shall the buyer know whether the duties have been paid or not?

Our enemies will think that we mean to strike at the right of Parliament to lay duties for the regulation of trade.

I am one of those who hold the position that Parliament has a right to make laws for us in some cases to regulate the trade, and in all cases where the good of the whole empire requires it.

My fears were up when we went into the consideration of a bill of rights. I was afraid we should say too little or too much.

It is said, this is not a non-importation resolution. But it is; for there is no importation of goods but according to the law of the land.

Mr. Lynch. I came here to get redress of grievances, and to adopt every means for that end which could be adopted with a good conscience.

In my idea, Parliament has no power to regulate trade. But these duties are all for revenue, not for regulation of trade.

Many gentlemen in this room know how to bring in goods, sugars and others, without paying duties.

Will any gentleman say he will never purchase any goods until he is sure that they were not smuggled?

Mr. Mifflin. We shall agree, I suppose, to a non-exportation of lumber to the West Indies. They cannot send their sugars to England nor to America, therefore they can't be benefited.

Mr. Low. Gentlemen have been transported, by their zeal, into reflections upon an order of men, who deserve it the least of any men in the community.

We ought not to deny the just rights of our mother country. We have too much reason, in this Congress, to suspect that independency is aimed at.

I am for a resolution against any tea, Dutch as well as English.

We ought to consider the consequences, possible as well as probable, of every resolution we take, and provide ourselves with a retreat or a resource.

What would be the consequence of an adjournment of the Congress for six months? or a recommendation of a new election of another, to meet at the end of six months? Is not it possible they may make it criminal, as treason, misprision of treason, or felony, or a *præmunire*, both in the assemblies who choose and in the members who shall accept the trust? Would the assemblies or members be intimidated? Would they regard such an act?

Will, can the people bear a total interruption of the West India trade? Can they live without rum, sugar, and molasses? Will not this impatience and vexation defeat the measure? This would cut up the revenue by the roots, if wine, fruit, molasses, and sugar were discarded as well as tea.

But a prohibition of all exports to the West Indies will annihilate the fishery, because that cannot afford to lose the West India market, and this would throw a multitude of families in our fishing towns into the arms of famine.

October 7. Friday. Dined with Mr. Thomas Smith, with a large company, the Virginians and others.[1]

8. Saturday. Dined with Mr. George Clymer, Mr. Dickinson, and a large company again.

9. Sunday. Went to hear Dr. Allison, an aged gentleman. It was Sacrament day, and he gave us a sacramental discourse. This Dr. Allison is a man of abilities and worth; but I hear no preachers here like ours in Boston, excepting Mr. Duché. Coombe indeed is a good speaker, but not an original, but a copy of Duché. The multiplicity of business and ceremonies and company that we are perpetually engaged in, prevents my writing to my friends in Massachusetts as I ought, and prevents my recording many material things in my journal. Philadelphia, with all its trade and wealth and regularity, is not Boston. The morals of our people are much better; their manners are more polite and agreeable; they are purer English; our language is better, our taste is better, our persons are handsomer; our spirit is greater, our laws are wiser, our religion is superior, our education is better. We exceed them in every thing but in a market, and in charitable, public foundations. Went, in the afternoon, to the Romish chapel, and heard a good discourse upon the duty of parents to their children, founded in justice and charity. The scenery and the music are so calculated to take in mankind, that I wonder the Reformation ever succeeded. The paintings, the bells, the candles, the gold and silver; our Saviour on the Cross, over the altar, at full length, and all his wounds bleeding. The chanting is exquisitely soft and sweet.

10. Monday. The deliberations of the Congress are spun out to an immeasurable length. There is so much wit, sense, learning, acuteness, subtlety, eloquence, &c. among fifty gentlemen, each of whom has been habituated to lead and guide in his own Province, that an immensity of time is spent unnecessarily. Johnson of Maryland has a clear and a cool head, an extensive knowledge of trade as well as law. He is a deliber-

[1] "There is a great spirit in the Congress. But our people must be peaceable. Let them exercise every day in the week, if they will; the more the better. Let them furnish themselves with artillery, arms, and ammunition. Let them follow the maxim, which you say they have adopted, 'In times of peace prepare for war.' But let them avoid war, *if possible — if possible*, I say." *J. A. to his wife*, 7 October.

ating man, but not a shining orator; his passions and imagination don't appear enough for an orator; his reason and penetration appear, but not his rhetoric. Galloway, Duane, and Johnson are sensible and learned, but cold speakers. Lee, Henry, and Hooper, are the orators; Paca is a deliberator too; Chase speaks warmly; Mifflin is a sprightly and spirited speaker; John Rutledge don't exceed in learning or oratory, though he is a rapid speaker; young Edward Rutledge is young and zealous, a little unsteady and injudicious, but very unnatural and affected as a speaker;[1] Dyer and Sherman speak often and long, but very heavily and clumsily.

11. Tuesday. Dined with Mr. McKean in Market Street, with Mr. Reed, Rodney, Chase, Johnson, Paca, Dr. Morgan, Mr. R. Penn, &c. Spent the evening with Mr. Henry at his lodgings, consulting about a petition to the King.[2] Henry said he had no public education; at fifteen he read Virgil and Livy, and has not looked into a Latin book since. His father left him at that age, and he has been struggling through life ever since. He has high notions, talks about exalted minds, &c. He has a horrid opinion of Galloway, Jay, and the Rutledges. Their system, he says, would ruin the cause of America. He is very impatient, to see such fellows, and not be at liberty to describe them in their true colors.

12. Wednesday. Dined with Captain Richards, with Dr. Coombe.

[1] This opinion is in marked opposition to that ascribed by Mr. Wirt to Mr. Henry, which is the more singular as, a few paragraphs below, the same gentleman betrays any thing but enthusiasm for, or admiration of the Rutledges. The truth must be told of Mr. Wirt's volume. It is little to be relied on, excepting for the information directly obtained from witnesses of facts. How narrowly he escaped lauding Mr. Henry as a deep classical scholar, is shown in Mr. Jefferson's letter lately published in Kennedy's Biography, vol. i. p. 409. His own frank and playful admissions of his unfitness to write mere facts redeem a world of error. "What the deuce has a lawyer to do with truth?" See his letter in the same work, vol. i. page 388.

[2] On the first day of the month, R. H. Lee, J. Adams, T. Johnson, Patrick Henry, and Mr. J. Rutledge, were appointed a committee to prepare an address to his Majesty.

The history of the action of this committee is little known. The fact seems well established that the first report was drawn up by Mr. Lee, that it did not satisfy the Assembly, who recommitted it on the 21st October, at the same time adding Mr. Dickinson, who had taken his seat on the 17th, to the committee. They reported, three days later, the paper which has ever since been ascribed to Mr. Dickinson. It is included in the collection of his writings, made during his lifetime, and published at Wilmington, in Delaware.

13. Thursday. Dined with Mr. Dickinson, with Chase, Paca, Low, Mifflin, Mr. Penn, and General Lee, at six o'clock. From ten o'clock until half after four, we were debating about the parliamentary power of regulating trade. Five Colonies were for allowing it, five against it, and two divided among themselves, that is, Massachusetts and Rhode Island. Mr. Duane has had his heart set upon asserting in our bill of rights the authority of Parliament to regulate the trade of the Colonies. He is for grounding it on compact, acquiescence, necessity, protection, not merely on our consent.

14. Friday. Went in the morning to see Dr. Chovet and his skeletons and wax-works — most admirable, exquisite representations of the whole animal economy. Four complete skeletons; a leg with all the nerves, veins, and arteries injected with wax; two complete bodies in wax, full grown; waxen representations of all the muscles, tendons, &c. of the head, brain, heart, lungs, liver, stomach, &c. This exhibition is much more exquisite than that of Dr. Shippen at the hospital. The Doctor reads lectures for two half joes a course, which takes up four months. These wax-works are all of the Doctor's own hands.[1] Dined with Dr. Morgan, an ingenious physician and an honest patriot. He showed us some curious paintings upon silk which he brought from Italy, which are singular in this country, and some bones of an animal of enormous size found upon the banks of the river Ohio. Mr. Middleton, the two Rutledges, Mr. Mifflin, and Mr. William Barrell dined with us. Mrs. Morgan is a sprightly, pretty lady. In the evening we were invited to an interview, at Carpenters' Hall, with the Quakers and Anabaptists. Mr. Backus is come here from Middleborough with a design to apply to the Congress for a redress of grievances of the anti-pedobaptists in our Province. The cases from Chelmsford, the case of Mr. White of Haverhill, the case of Ashfield and Warwick were mentioned by Mr. Backus. Old Israel Pemberton was quite rude, and his rudeness was resented; but the conference, which held till eleven o'clock, I hope will produce good.

[1] In the appendix B to Mr. Duane's publication of "Passages from the Remembrancer of Christopher Marshall," is a somewhat curious account of Dr. Chovet and his lectures.

[There is an anecdote which ought not to be omitted, because it had consequences of some moment at the time, which have continued to operate for many years, and, indeed, are not yet worn out, though the cause is forgotten, or rather was never generally known. Governor Hopkins and Governor Ward, of Rhode Island, came to our lodgings and said to us, that President Manning, of Rhode Island College, and Mr. Backus, of Massachusetts, were in town, and had conversed with some gentlemen in Philadelphia who wished to communicate to us a little business, and wished we would meet them at six in the evening at Carpenters' Hall. Whether they explained their affairs more particularly to any of my colleagues, I know not; but I had no idea of the design. We all went at the hour, and to my great surprise found the hall almost full of people, and a great number of Quakers seated at the long table with their broad-brimmed beavers on their heads. We were invited to seats among them, and informed that they had received com plaints, from some Anabaptists and some Friends in Massachusetts, against certain laws of that Province, restrictive of the liberty of conscience, and some instances were mentioned, in the General Court, and in the courts of justice, in which Friends and Baptists had been grievously oppressed. I know not how my colleagues felt, but I own I was greatly surprised and somewhat indignant, being, like my friend Chase, of a temper naturally quick and warm, at seeing our State and her delegates thus summoned before a self-created tribunal, which was neither legal nor constitutional.

Israel Pemberton, a Quaker of large property and more intrigue, began to speak, and said that Congress were here endeavoring to form a union of the Colonies; but there were difficulties in the way, and none of more importance than liberty of conscience. The laws of New England, and particularly of Massachusetts, were inconsistent with it, for they not only compelled men to pay to the building of churches and support of ministers, but to go to some known religious assembly on first days, &c.; and that he and his friends were desirous of engaging us to assure them that our State would repeal all those laws, and place things as they were in Pennsylvania.

A suspicion instantly arose in my mind, which I have ever

believed to have been well founded, that this artful Jesuit, for I had been before apprized of his character, was endeavoring to avail himself of this opportunity to break up the Congress, or at least to withdraw the Quakers and the governing part of Pennsylvania from us; for, at that time, by means of a most unequal representation, the Quakers had a majority in their House of Assembly, and, by consequence, the whole power of the State in their hands. I arose, and spoke in answer to him. The substance of what I said, was, that we had no authority to bind our constituents to any such proposals; that the laws of Massachusetts were the most mild and equitable establishment of religion that was known in the world, if indeed they could be called an establishment; that it would be in vain for us to enter into any conferences on such a subject, for we knew beforehand our constituents would disavow all we could do or say for the satisfaction of those who invited us to this meeting. That the people of Massachusetts were as religious and conscientious as the people of Pennsylvania; that their consciences dictated to them that it was their duty to support those laws, and therefore the very liberty of conscience, which Mr. Pemberton invoked, would demand indulgence for the tender consciences of the people of Massachusetts, and allow them to preserve their laws; that it might be depended on, this was a point that could not be carried; that I would not deceive them by insinuating the faintest hope, for I knew they might as well turn the heavenly bodies out of their annual and diurnal courses, as the people of Massachusetts at the present day from their meeting-house and Sunday laws. Pemberton made no reply but this: "Oh! sir, pray don't urge liberty of conscience in favor of such laws!" If I had known the particular complaints which were to be alleged, and if Pemberton had not broken irregularly into the midst of things, it might have been better, perhaps, to have postponed this declaration. However, the gentlemen proceeded, and stated the particular cases of oppression, which were alleged, in our general and executive courts. It happened that Mr. Cushing and Mr. Samuel Adams had been present in the General Court when the petitions had been under deliberation, and they explained the whole so clearly that every reasonable man must have been satisfied. Mr. Paine and I had been concerned at the bar in every action in the executive courts which was complained of, and we explained them all to the entire satisfaction of impartial men, and showed that there had been no oppression or injustice in any of them. The Quakers were not generally and heartily in our cause; they were jealous of independence; they were then suspicious, and soon afterwards became assured, that the Massachusetts delegates, and especially John Adams, were advocates for that obnoxious measure, and they conceived prejudices which were soon increased and artfully inflamed, and are not yet worn out.]

October 15. Saturday. Dined at Mr. West's, with the Rutledges and Mr. Middleton; an elegant house, rich furniture, and a splendid dinner.

16. Sunday. Staid at home all day; very busy in the necessary business of putting the proceedings of the Congress into order.[1]

20. Thursday. Dined with the whole Congress, at the City Tavern, at the invitation of the House of Representatives of the Province of Pennsylvania. The whole House dined with us, making near one hundred guests in the whole; a most elegant entertainment. A sentiment was given: "May the sword of the parent never be stained with the blood of her children." Two or three broad-brims over against me at table; one of them said, this is not a toast, but a prayer; come, let us join in it. And they took their glasses accordingly.

21. Friday. Dined at the Library Tavern, with Messrs. Markoe and a dozen gentlemen from the West Indies and North Carolina. A fine bowling-green here; fine turtle, and admirable wine.

22. Saturday. Dined in the country with Mr. Dickinson, with all the delegates from New England, Mr. Duane, Mr. Reed, Mr. Livingston, &c.

23. Sunday. Heard Mr. Percy, at Mr. Sprout's. He is chaplain to the Countess of Huntingdon, comes recommended to Mr. Cary, of Charlestown, from her, as a faithful servant of the Lord; no genius, no orator.

[1] No direction to perform this duty appears on the Journal. Undoubtedly it refers to the declaration of rights, as explained in the close of the extract from the Autobiography, in page 377.

In the afternoon I went to the Baptist Church, and heard a trans-Alleghanian, a preacher from the back parts of Virginia, behind the Alleghany mountains. He preached an hour and a half; — no learning, no grace of action or utterance, but an honest zeal. He told us several good stories. One was, that he was once preaching in Virginia, and said that those ministers who taught the people that salvation was to be obtained by good works or obedience, were leading them to ruin. Next day he was apprehended by a warrant from a magistrate for reviling the clergy of the Church of England. He asked for a prayer-book, and had it, turned to the eighteenth or twentieth article, where the same sentiment is strongly expressed; he read it to the magistrate; the magistrate, as soon as he heard it, dashed the warrant out of his hand, and said, Sir, you are discharged. In the evening, I went to the Methodist meeting, and heard Mr. Webb, the old soldier, who first came to America in the character of quarter-master under General Braddock. He is one of the most fluent, eloquent men I ever heard; he reaches the imagination and touches the passions very well, and expresses himself with great propriety. The singing here is very sweet and soft indeed; the first music I have heard in any society, except the Moravians, and once at church with the organ. Supped and spent the remainder of the evening at Mr. Jo Reed's, with Colonel Lee, Dr. Shippen, Mr. Cary, Dr. Loring, &c.

24. Monday. In Congress, nibbling and quibbling as usual. There is no greater mortification than to sit with half a dozen wits, deliberating upon a petition, address, or memorial. These great wits, these subtle critics, these refined geniuses, these learned lawyers, these wise statesmen, are so fond of showing their parts and powers, as to make their consultations very tedious. Young Ned Rutledge is a perfect Bob-o-Lincoln, — a swallow, a sparrow, a peacock; excessively vain, excessively weak, and excessively variable and unsteady; jejune, inane, and puerile. Mr. Dickinson is very modest, delicate, and timid. Spent the evening at home. Colonel Dyer, Judge Sherman, and Colonel Floyd came in, and spent the evening with Mr. Adams and me. Mr. Mifflin and General Lee came in. Lee's head is running upon his new plan of a battalion.

25. Tuesday. Dined with Mr. Clymer; General Lee, &c. there.

26. Wednesday. Dined at home. This day the Congress fin-

ished. Spent the evening together at the City Tavern; all the Congress, and several gentlemen of the town.

27. Thursday. Went this morning, with Mr. Tudor, to see the Carpenters' Hall and the library, and to Mr. Barrell's, and Bradford's, and then to the State House, to see the Supreme Court sitting. Heard Mr. Wilcox and Mr. Reed argue a point of law, concerning the construction of a will. Three judges,—Chew, Willing, and Morton.

28. Friday. Took our departure, in a very great rain, from the happy, the peaceful, the elegant, the hospitable, and polite city of Philadelphia. It is not very likely that I shall ever see this part of the world again, but I shall ever retain a most grateful, pleasing sense of the many civilities I have received in it, and shall think myself happy to have an opportunity of returning them. Dined at Anderson's, and reached Priestly's, of Bristol, at night, twenty miles from Philadelphia, where we are as happy as we can wish.

29. Saturday. Rode to Princeton, where we dine, at the sign of Hudibras. Vacation at Nassau Hall. Dr. Witherspoon out of town. Paine recollected the story of Mr. Keith's joke upon him at Howland's, of Plymouth, in the time of the Stamp Act. Paine said he would go to making brass buckles. Keith said he might do that to great advantage, for his stock would cost him nothing. Lodged at Farmer's, in Brunswick.

30. Sunday. My birthday; I am thirty-nine years of age. Rode to Elizabethtown, in New Jersey, where we are to dine; rode down to Elizabethtown Point, and put our carriage and all our horses into two ferry-boats; sailed, or rather rowed, six miles to a point on Staten Island, where we stopped and went into a tavern; got to Hull's, in New York, about ten o'clock at night.

31. Monday. Mr. McDougall, Mr. Scott, Captain Sears, Mr. Platt, Mr. Hughes, came to see us; all but the last dined with us. Walked to see the new hospital; a grand building. Went to the Coffee House. Mr. Cary and Dr. Loring dined with us. The Sons of Liberty are in the horrors here; they think they have lost ground since we passed through this city. Their delegates have agreed with the Congress, which I suppose they imagine has given additional importance to their antagonists.[1]

[1] This judgment was not without foundation. The provincial legislature refused to sanction the proceedings of the Congress, declined to send any dele-

November 1. Tuesday. Left Brother Paine at New York, to go by the packet to Newport; rode to Cock's, at Kingsbridge, to breakfast, to Haviland's, at Rye, to dinner, and to Knap's, at Horse Neck, in Greenwich, to lodge.

2. Wednesday. Rode to Bulkeley's, at Fairfield, to dinner, and to Captain Benjamin's, of Stratford, to lodge.

3. Thursday. We design to Great Swamp to-day, forty-two miles. At New Haven, Colonel Dyer, Deane, and Sherman, Mr. Parsons, the new Speaker, Williams, Mr. Trumbull, and many other gentlemen came to see us, at Bears's, as soon as we got in. Colonel Dyer presented the compliments of the Governor and Council to the Massachusetts delegates, and asked our company to spend the evening. I begged Colonel Dyer to present my duty to the Governor and Council, and my gratitude for the high honor they did us, but that we had been so long from home, and our affairs were so critical, we hoped they would excuse us if we passed through the town as fast as possible. Mr. Sherman invited us to dine, but Mr. Babcock claimed a promise, so we dined with him. Two or three carriages accompanied us a few miles out of town in the afternoon. We had the most pressing invitations from many gentlemen to return through New London, Windham, &c. &c. &c. but excused ourselves. The people had sent a courier to New Haven, on purpose to wait for our arrival and return to inform the people we were coming. Twenty miles from Middletown, we met two gentlemen from thence, who came on purpose to meet us and invite us to dine to-morrow at Middletown. We excused ourselves with great earnestness.

4. Friday. Dined at Hartford, at Bull's, where we had the pleasure of seeing Mr. Adams's minister, Mr. Howe,[1] who is supposed to be courting here. Lodged at Dr. Chafy's, in Windsor; very cordially entertained.

5. Saturday. Breakfasted at Austin's, of Suffield. Went to see a company of men exercising upon the hill, under the com-

gates to the next, and adopted a half way policy of its own, intended to satisfy the popular feeling without irritating the government at home. This led to a reaction in the city, where, after a trial of physical strength between the parties, the old committee of fifty-one was dissolved and a new one created, consisting of sixty members, through whom the patriots finally succeeded in effecting an independent organization in the Colony.

[1] This gentleman died at this place in the following year.

mand of a green-coated man, lately a regular; a company of very likely, stout men. Dined at Parsons's, of Springfield. Captain Pynchon and another Pynchon and Mr. Bliss, came in to see us, and at last Colonel Worthington. Worthington behaved decently and politely.[1] Said he was in hopes we should have staid the Sabbath in town, and he should have had the pleasure of waiting on us, &c. Captain Pynchon was of the late Provincial Congress, and gave us some account of their proceedings. Arrived, about seven o'clock, at Scott's, of Palmer, *alias* Kingston, where we are to lodge. Scott and his wife are at *this instant* great patriots — zealous Americans. Scott's faith is very strong that they will repeal all the acts this very winter. Dr. Dana told us all America and Great Britain and Europe owed us thanks, and that the ministry would lay hold of our consent that they should regulate trade, and our petition, and grant us relief this winter. But neither the Doctor's nor Scott's faith is my faith.

6. Sunday. Went all day to hear Mr. Baldwin, a Presbyterian minister at Kingston. We put up at Scott's. Mr. Baldwin came in the evening to see us. Horat., book 3, ode 2: "Pueros ab ineunte ætate assuefaciendos esse rei militari et vitæ laboriosæ."[2] We walked to meeting above two miles at noon; we walked a quarter of a mile, and staid at one Quintain's, an old Irishman; and a friendly, cordial reception we had; the old man was so rejoiced to see us he could hardly speak; more glad to see us, he said, than he should to see Gage and all his train. I saw a gun; the young man said, that gun marched eight miles towards Boston on the late alarm; almost the whole parish marched off, and the people seemed really disappointed when the news was contradicted.

7. Monday. Dined at Rice's, of Brookfield. Major Foster came to see us, and gave us an account of the proceedings of the Provincial Congress. Lodged at Hunt's, in Spencer.

8. Tuesday. Breakfasted at Colonel Henshaw's, of Leicester; dined at Woodburn's, of Worcester. Furnival made the two young ladies come in and sing us the new Liberty Song.

Lodged at Colonel Buckminster's, of Framingham.

9. Wednesday. Breakfasted at Reeve's, of Sudbury.

[1] Colonel Worthington was a moderate adherent of the government.
[2] This is a caption given to that Ode of Horace in some editions.

[Upon our return to Massachusetts, I found myself elected by the town of Braintree into the Provincial Congress, and attended that service as long as it sat.[1] About this time, Draper's paper in Boston swarmed with writers, and among an immense quantity of meaner productions appeared a writer under the signature of Massachusettensis, suspected, but never that I knew ascertained, to be written by two of my old friends, Jonathan Sewall and Daniel Leonard.[2] These papers were well written, abounded with wit, discovered good information, and were conducted with a subtlety of art and address wonderfully calculated to keep up the spirits of their party, to depress ours, to spread intimidation, and to make proselytes among those whose principles and judgment give way to their fears; and these compose at least one third of mankind. Week after week passed away, and these papers made a very visible impression on many minds. No answer appeared, and indeed some who were capable, were too busy, and others too timorous. I began at length to think seriously of the consequences, and began to write under the signature of Novanglus, and continued every week in the Boston Gazette, till the 19th of April, 1775.[3] The last number was prevented from impression by the commencement of hostilities, and Mr. Gill gave it to Judge William Cushing, who now has it in manuscript. An abridgment of the printed numbers was made by some one in England, unknown to me, and published in Almon's Remembrancer, for the year 1775, and afterwards reprinted in a pamphlet, in 1783, under the title of "History of the Dispute with America." In New England, they had the effect of an antidote to the poison of Massachusettensis; and the battle of Lexington, on the 19th of April, changed the instruments of warfare from the pen to the sword.

A few days after this event, I rode to Cambridge, where I

1 Wednesday, 23 November, 1774. "*Resolved*, That John Adams, Esq. be desired to favor this Congress with his presence as soon as may be." *Extract from the Journals of the Provincial Congress.*

28 November. "*Voted*, John Adams, Esq. be joined to the members of the Provincial Congress, as a member for this town." *Extract from the Braintree Town Records.*

2 Massachusettensis is now understood to have been the work of Judge Leonard, although Mr. Adams, until a very late period of his life, supposed it to have come from the other gentleman named.

3 The papers will be found in another portion of these volumes.

saw General Ward, General Heath, General Joseph Warren, and the New England army. There was great confusion and much distress. Artillery, arms, clothing were wanting, and a sufficient supply of provisions not easily obtained. Neither the officers nor men, however, wanted spirits or resolution. I rode from thence to Lexington, and along the scene of action for many miles, and inquired of the inhabitants the circumstances. These were not calculated to diminish my ardor in the cause; they, on the contrary, convinced me that the die was cast, the Rubicon passed, and, as Lord Mansfield expressed it in Parliament, if we did not defend ourselves, they would kill us. On my return home, I was seized with a fever, attended with alarming symptoms; but the time was come to repair to Philadelphia to Congress, which was to meet on the fifth of May. I was determined to go as far as I could, and instead of venturing on horseback, as I had intended, I got into a sulky, attended by a servant on horseback, and proceeded on the journey. This year, Mr. Hancock was added to our number. I overtook my colleagues before they reached New York.[1] At Kingsbridge we were met by a great number of gentlemen in carriages and on horseback, and all the way their numbers increased, till I thought the whole city was come out to meet us. The same ardor was continued all the way to Philadelphia.[2]

Congress assembled and proceeded to business, and the members appeared to me to be of one mind, and that mind after my own heart. I dreaded the danger of disunion and divisions among us, and much more among the people. It appeared to me that all petitions, remonstrances, and negotiations, for the future, would be fruitless, and only occasion a loss of time, and give opportunity to the enemy to sow divisions among the States and the people. My heart bled for the poor people of Boston, imprisoned within the walls of their city by a British army, and we knew not to what plunders or massacres or cruelties they might be exposed. I thought the first step ought to be to recommend to the people of every State in the Union,

[1] The following entry is found by itself in a small book of accounts: —

1775. April 30. Sunday. Heard Mr. Strong all day. At night a man came in and informed us of the death of Josiah Quincy. *Proh Dolor!*

[2] May 10. "This day arrived the Hon. John Hancock, and Thomas Cushing, Esquire, Samuel Adams, John Adams, and Robert Treat Paine, Esquires, delegates from the Colony of Massachusetts Bay." *Pennsylvania Gazette.*

to seize on all the Crown officers, and hold them with civility, humanity, and generosity, as hostages for the security of the people of Boston, and to be exchanged for them as soon as the British army would release them; that we ought to recommend to the people of all the States to institute governments for themselves, under their own authority, and that without loss of time; that we ought to declare the Colonies free, sovereign, and independent States, and then to inform Great Britain we were willing to enter into negotiations with them for the redress of all grievances, and a restoration of harmony between the two countries, upon permanent principles. All this I thought might be done before we entered into any connections, alliances, or negotiations with foreign powers. I was also for informing Great Britain, very frankly, that hitherto we were free; but, if the war should be continued, we were determined to seek alliances with France, Spain, and any other power of Europe that would contract with us. That we ought immediately to adopt the army in Cambridge as a continental army, to appoint a General and all other officers, take upon ourselves the pay, subsistence, clothing, armor, and munitions of the troops. This is a concise sketch of the plan which I thought the only reasonable one; and, from conversation with the members of Congress, I was then convinced, and have been ever since convinced, that it was the general sense at least of a considerable majority of that body. This system of measures I publicly and privately avowed without reserve.

The gentlemen in Pennsylvania, who had been attached to the proprietary interest, and owed their wealth and honors to it, and the great body of the Quakers, had hitherto acquiesced in the measures of the Colonies, or at least had made no professed opposition to them; many of both descriptions had declared themselves with us, and had been as explicit and as ardent as we were. But now these people began to see that independence was approaching, they started back. In some of my public harangues, in which I had freely and explicitly laid open my thoughts, on looking round the assembly I have seen horror, terror, and detestation, strongly marked on the countenances of some of the members, whose names I could readily recollect; but as some of them have been good citizens since, and others went over afterwards to the English, I think it unnecessary to record them here. There is one gentleman, however, whom I must mention in self-defence; I mean John Dickinson, then of Philadelphia, now of Delaware. This gentleman had been appointed a member of Congress, by the Legislature of Pennsylvania, about a week before the close of the Congress of 1774, and now, in 1775, made his appearance again at the opening of the Congress of 1775.

In some of the earlier deliberations in May, after I had reasoned at some length on my own plan, Mr. John Rutledge, in more than one public speech, approved of my sentiments, and the other delegates from that State, Mr. Lynch, Mr. Gadsden, and Mr. Edward Rutledge, appeared to me to be of the same mind. Mr. Dickinson himself told me, afterwards, that when we first came together the balance lay with South Carolina. Accordingly, all their efforts were employed to convert the delegates from that State. Mr. Charles Thomson, who was then rather inclined to our side of the question, told me that the Quakers had intimidated Mr. Dickinson's mother and his wife, who were continually distressing him with their remonstrances. His mother said to him, "Johnny, you will be hanged; your estate will be forfeited and confiscated; you will leave your excellent wife a widow, and your charming children orphans, beggars, and infamous." From my soul I pitied Mr. Dickinson. I made his case my own. If my mother and my wife had expressed such sentiments to me, I was certain that if they did not wholly unman me and make me an apostate, they would make me the most miserable man alive. I was very happy that my mother and my wife and my brothers, my wife's father and mother, and grandfather Colonel John Quincy and his lady, Mr. Norton Quincy, Dr. Tufts, Mr. Cranch, and all her near relations, as well as mine, had uniformly been of my mind, so that I always enjoyed perfect peace at home.

The proprietary gentlemen, Israel Pemberton and other principal Quakers now united with Mr. Dickinson, addressed themselves with great art and assiduity to all the members of Congress whom they could influence, even to some of the delegates of Massachusetts; but most of all to the delegates from South Carolina. Mr. Lynch had been an old acquaintance of the Penn family, particularly of the Governor. Mr. Edward Rutledge had brought his lady with him, a daughter of our former President

Middleton. Mr. Arthur Middleton, her brother, was now a delegate in place of his father. The lady and the gentlemen were invited to all parties, and were visited perpetually by the party, and we soon began to find that Mr. Lynch, Mr. Arthur Middleton, and even the two Rutledges, began to waver and to clamor about independence. Mr. Gadsden was either, from despair of success, never attempted, or, if he was, he received no impression from them. I became the dread and terror and abhorrence of the party. But all this I held in great contempt. Arthur Middleton became the hero of Quaker and proprietary politics in Congress. He had little information, and less argument; in rudeness and sarcasm his forte lay, and he played off his artillery without reserve. I made it a rule to return him a Roland for every Oliver, so that he never got, and I never lost, any thing from these rencounters. We soon parted, never to see each other more,—I believe, without a spark of malice on either side; for he was an honest and generous fellow, with all his zeal in this cause.

The party made me as unpopular as they could, among all their connections, but I regarded none of those things. I knew and lamented that many of these gentlemen, of great property, high in office, and of good accomplishments, were laying the foundation, not of any injury to me, but of their own ruin; and it was not in my power to prevent it. When the party had prepared the members of Congress for their purpose, and indeed had made no small impression on three of my own colleagues, Mr. Dickinson made or procured to be made a motion for a second petition to the King, to be sent by Mr. Richard Penn, who was then bound on a voyage to England. The motion was introduced and supported by long speeches. I was opposed to it, of course, and made an opposition to it in as long a speech as I commonly made, not having ever been remarkable for very long harangues, in answer to all the arguments which had been urged. When I sat down, Mr. John Sullivan arose, and began to argue on the same side with me, in a strain of wit, reasoning, and fluency, which, although he was always fluent, exceeded every thing I had ever heard from him before. I was much delighted, and Mr. Dickinson, very much terrified at what he said, began to tremble for his cause. At this moment I was called out to the State House yard, very much to my regret, to some one who had business with me. I took my hat, and went out of the door of Congress Hall. Mr. Dickinson observed me, and darted out after me. He broke out upon me in a most abrupt and extraordinary manner; in as violent a passion as he was capable of feeling, and with an air, countenance, and gestures, as rough and haughty as if I had been a school-boy and he the master. He vociferated, "What is the reason, Mr. Adams, that you New-Englandmen oppose our measures of reconciliation? There now is Sullivan, in a long harangue, following you in a determined opposition to our petition to the King. Look ye! If you don't concur with us in our pacific system, I and a number of us will break off from you in New England, and we will carry on the opposition by ourselves in our own way."[1] I own I was shocked with this magisterial salutation. I knew of no pretensions Mr. Dickinson had to dictate to me, more than I had to catechize him. I was, however, as it happened, at that moment, in a very happy temper, and I answered him very coolly. "Mr. Dickinson, there are many things that I can very cheerfully sacrifice to harmony, and even to unanimity; but I am not to be threatened into an express adoption or approbation of measures which my judgment reprobates. Congress must judge, and if they pronounce against me, I must submit, as, if they determine against you, you ought to acquiesce." These were the last words which ever passed between Mr. Dickinson and me in private. We continued to debate, in Congress, upon all questions publicly, with all our usual candor and good humor. But the friendship and acquaintance was lost forever by an unfortunate accident, which must now be explained.

The more I reflected on Mr. Dickinson's rude lecture in the State House yard, the more I was vexed with it; and the determination of Congress in favor of the petition did not allay the irritation. A young gentleman from Boston, Mr. Hichborn, whom I had known as a clerk in Mr. Fitch's office, but with whom I had no particular connection or acquaintance, had been for some days soliciting me to give him letters to my friends in the Massachusetts. I was so much engaged in the business of

[1] Mr. Dickinson's fear of the New-Englandmen was of early date, and his apprehensions were shared by almost all persons in the Middle, and by many in the Southern, States. Compare two letters in *Quincy's Life of Quincy*, pp. 164–170.

Congress, in the daytime, and in consultations with the members, on evenings and mornings, that I could not find time to write a line. He came to me at last, and said he was immediately to set off on his journey home, and begged I would give him some letters. I told him I had not been able to write any. He prayed I would write, if it were only a line, to my family, for, he said, as he had served his clerkship with Mr. Fitch, he was suspected and represented as a Tory, and this reputation would be his ruin, if it could not be corrected, for nobody would employ him at the bar. If I would only give him the slightest letters to any of my friends, it would give him the appearance of having my confidence, and would assist him in acquiring what he truly deserved, the character of a Whig. To get rid of his importunity, I took my pen and wrote a very few lines to my wife, and about an equal number to General James Warren. Irritated with the unpoliteness of Mr. Dickinson, and more mortified with his success in Congress, I wrote something like what has been published, but not exactly. The British printers made it worse than it was in the original.[1] Mr. Hichborn was inter-

[1] These letters produced a great effect at the moment on both sides of the Atlantic. They were thought by the timid and hesitating in America to justify the suspicions that had been entertained of the designs of the New-Englandmen to make the breach irreparable, whilst the government at home considered them grossly inconsistent with the professions of the second petition to the King, received from Congress at about the same moment. The originals are now in the State paper office in London. The following copies were found among Mr. Adams's papers, but they are not in his handwriting. There is also a long letter of apology from Mr. Hichborn, for suffering them to be taken in his hands, which saves his honesty only at the expense of his character for presence of mind.

TO JAMES WARREN.

Philadelphia, 24 July, 1775.

DEAR SIR: — I am determined to write freely to you this time. A certain great fortune and piddling genius, whose fame has been trumpeted so loudly, has given a silly cast to our whole doings. We are between hawk and buzzard. We ought to have had in our hands, a month ago, the whole legislative, executive, and judicial of the whole continent, and have completely modelled a constitution; to have raised a naval power, and opened all our ports wide; to have arrested every friend of government on the continent and held them as hostages for the poor victims in Boston, and then opened the door as wide as possible for peace and reconciliation. After this, they might have petitioned, negotiated, addressed, &c. if they would. Is all this extravagant? Is it wild? Is it not the soundest policy? One piece of news, seven thousand pounds of powder arrived last night. We shall send you some of it as soon as we can, but you must be patient and frugal. We are lost in the extensiveness of our field of business. We have a continental treasury to establish, a paymaster to choose, and a committee of correspondence, or safety, or accounts, or something, I know not what, that has confounded us all this day.

cepted in crossing Hudson's River, by the boats from a British man-of-war, and my letters, instead of being destroyed, fell into the hands of the enemy, and were immediately printed with a little garbling. They thought them a great prize. The ideas of independence, to be sure, were glaring enough, and they thought they should produce quarrels among the members of Congress and a division of the Colonies. Me they expected utterly to ruin, because, as they represented, I had explicitly avowed my designs of independence. I cared nothing for this. I had made no secret, in or out of Congress, of my opinion that independence was become indispensable, and I was perfectly sure that in a little time the whole continent would be of my mind. I rather rejoiced in this as a fortunate circumstance, that the idea was held up to the whole world, and that the people could not avoid contemplating it and reasoning about it. Accordingly, from this time at least, if not earlier, and not from the publication of "Common Sense," did the people in all parts of the continent turn their attention to this subject. It was, I know, considered in the same light by others. I met Colonel

Shall I hail you Speaker of the House, or counsellor, or what? What kind of an election had you? What sort of magistrates do you intend to make? Will your new legislative or executive feel bold or irresolute? Will your judicial hang and whip and fine and imprison without scruple? I want to see our distressed country once more, yet I dread the sight of devastation. You observe in your letter the oddity of a great man. He is a queer creature, but you must love his dogs if you love him, and forgive a thousand whims for the sake of the soldier and the scholar.

TO MRS. ADAMS.

My Dear:—It is now almost three months since I left you, in every part of which, my anxiety about you and the children, as well as our country, has been extreme. The business I have had upon my mind has been as great and important as can be entrusted to man, and the difficulty and intricacy of it prodigious. When fifty or sixty men have a constitution to form for a great empire, at the same time that they have a country of fifteen hundred miles extent to fortify, millions to arm and train, a naval power to begin, an extensive commerce to regulate, numerous tribes of Indians to negotiate with, a standing army of twenty-seven thousand men to raise, pay, victual, and officer, I really shall pity those fifty or sixty men. I must see you ere long. Rice has written me a very good letter, so has Thaxter, for which I thank them both. Love to the children.

J. A.

P. S. I wish I had given you a complete history, from the beginning to the end of the journey, of the behavior of my compatriots. No mortal tale can equal it. I will tell you in future, but you shall keep it secret. The fidgets, the whims, the caprice, the vanity, the superstition, the irritability of some of us is enough to ——.

Yours.

Reed, soon afterwards, who was then General Washington's secretary, who mentioned those letters to me, and said that Providence seemed to have thrown those letters before the public for our good; for independence was certainly inevitable, and it was happy that the whole country had been compelled to turn their thoughts upon it, that it might not come upon them presently by surprise.[1]

There were a few expressions which hurt me, when I found the enemy either misunderstood them or wilfully misrepresented them. The expressions were, "Will your judiciary whip and hang without scruple?" This they construed to mean to excite cruelty against the Tories, and get some of them punished with severity. Nothing was further from my thoughts. I had no reference to Tories in this. But as the exercise of judicial power, without authority from the Crown, would be probably the most offensive act of government to Great Britain, and the least willingly pardoned, my question meant no more than,—"Will your judges have fortitude enough to inflict the severe punishments, when necessary, as death upon murderers and other capital criminals, and flagellation upon such as deserve it?" Nothing could be more false and injurious to me, than the imputation of any sanguinary zeal against the Tories; for I can truly declare, that, through the whole Revolution, and from that time to this, I never committed one act of severity against the Tories. On the contrary, I was a constant advocate for all the mercy and indulgence consistent with our safety. Some acts of treachery, as well as hostility, were combined together in so atrocious a manner that pardon could not be indulged, but, as it happened, in none of these had I any particular concern.

In a very short time after the publication of these letters, I received one from General Charles Lee, then in the army in the neighborhood of Boston, in which, after expressing the most obliging sentiments of my character, he said some gentlemen had hinted to him that I might possibly apprehend that he would take offence at them; but he assured me he was highly pleased with what was said of him in them. The acknowledgment from me, that he was a soldier and a scholar, he esteemed as an honor done to him; and as to his attachment to his dogs,

[1] The same sentiment is expressed in Mr. Reed's letter to Thomas Bradford, dated 21 August, and published in the Life written by his grandson, vol. i. p. 118.

when he should discover in men as much fidelity, honesty, and gratitude, as he daily experienced in his dogs, he promised to love men as well as dogs. Accordingly the cordiality between him and me continued till his death.[1]

[1] The writer does not seem to have relied upon any thing but his own recollection in this sketch. As General Lee's letter remains, and is highly characteristic, it is here given in full. Considering the course which Mr. Adams took in opposing his nomination as the second Major-General, it is creditable to him, although he was really under obligations to him for his final appointment as the third. See *Mr. Adams's Letter to J. Quincy — Quincy's Memoir of Quincy*, p. 482.

Camp, 5 October, 1775.

My Dear Sir: — As you may possibly harbor some suspicions that a certain passage in your intercepted letters (may) have made some disagreeable impressions on my mind, I think it necessary to assure you that it is quite the reverse. Until the bulk of mankind is much altered, I consider the reputation of being whimsical and eccentric rather as a panegyric than sarcasm, and my love of dogs passes with me as a still higher compliment. I have, thank Heaven, a heart susceptible of friendship and affection. I must have some object to embrace. Consequently, when once I can be convinced that men are as worthy objects as dogs, I shall transfer my benevolence, and become as staunch a philanthropist as the canting Addison affected to be. But you must not conclude from hence that I give in to general misanthropy. On the contrary, when I meet with a biped endowed with generosity, valor, good sense, patriotism, and zeal for the rights of humanity, I contract a friendship and passion for him amounting to bigotry or dotage; and let me assure you without compliments that you yourself appear to me possessed of these qualities. I give you my word and honor that I am serious; and I should be unhappy to the greatest degree if I thought you would doubt of my sincerity. Your opinion, therefore, of my attainments as a soldier and scholar is extremely flattering. Long may you continue in this, to me, gratissimus error. But something too much of this.

Before this reaches you, the astonishing and terrifying accusation, or rather detection, of Dr. Church, will be reported to the Congress. I call it astonishing, for, admitting his intentions not to be criminal, so gross a piece of stupidity in so sensible a man is quite a portent; and, supposing him guilty, it is terrifying to the last degree, as such a revolt must naturally infect with jealousy all political affiance. It will spread an universal diffidence and suspicion, than which nothing can be more pernicious to men embarked in a cause like ours, the corner stone of which is laid not only on honor, virtue, and disinterestedness, but on the persuasion that the whole are actuated by the same divine principles. I devoutly wish that such may not be the effects.

We long here to receive some news from the Congress. Now is the time to show your firmness. If the least timidity is displayed, we and all posterity are ruined; on the contrary, at this crisis, courage and steadiness must infuse the blessings of liberty not only to Great Britain but perhaps to all mankind. Do not go hobbling on, like the Prince of Lilliput, with one high-heeled shoe, one low one, for you will undoubtedly fall upon your noses every step you take. It is my humble opinion that you ought to begin by confiscating (or at least laying under heavy contributions) the estates of all the notorious enemies to American liberty through the continent. This would lighten the burthen which must otherwise fall heavy on the shoulders of the community. That afterwards you should invite all the maritime towns of the world into your ports. If they are so dull as not to accept the invitation, wean yourselves from all ideas of foreign commerce, and become entirely a nation of ploughmen and soldiers. A little

This measure of imbecility, the second petition to the King, embarrassed every exertion of Congress; it occasioned motions and debates without end for appointing committees to draw up a declaration of the causes, motives, and objects of taking arms, with a view to obtain decisive declarations against independence, &c. In the mean time the New England army investing Boston, the New England legislatures, congresses, and conventions, and the whole body of the people, were left without munitions of war, without arms, clothing, pay, or even countenance and encouragement. Every post brought me letters from my friends, Dr. Winthrop, Dr. Cooper, General James Warren, and sometimes from General Ward and his aids, and General Heath and many others, urging in pathetic terms the impossibility of keeping their men together without the assistance of Congress. I was daily urging all these things, but we were embarrassed with more than one difficulty, not only with the party in favor of the petition to the King, and the party who were jealous of independence, but a third party, which was a Southern party against a Northern, and a jealousy against a New England army under the command of a New England General. Whether this jealousy was sincere, or whether it was mere pride and a haughty ambition of furnishing a southern General to command the northern army, (I cannot say); but the intention was very visible to me that Colonel Washington was their object, and so many of our staunchest men were in the plan, that we could carry nothing without conceding to it. Another embarrassment, which was never publicly known, and which was carefully concealed by those who knew it, the Massachusetts and other New England delegates were divided. Mr. Hancock and Mr. Cushing hung back; Mr. Paine did not come forward, and even Mr. Samuel Adams was irresolute. Mr. Hancock himself had an

habit, and I am persuaded you will bless yourselves for the resolution. But I am running into an essay; shall, therefore, to prevent pedantry and impertinence, stop short with once more assuring you that I am,

Most truly and affectionately yours,

C. LEE.

My respects to your namesake, and let me hear from you. Spada sends his love to you, and declares, in very intelligible language, that he has fared much better since your allusion to him, for he is caressed now by all ranks, sexes, and ages.

ambition to be appointed commander-in-chief.[1] Whether he thought an election a compliment due to him, and intended to have the honor of declining it, or whether he would have accepted, I know not. To the compliment he had some pretensions, for, at that time, his exertions, sacrifices, and general merits in the cause of his country had been incomparably greater than those of Colonel Washington. But the delicacy of his health, and his entire want of experience in actual service, though an excellent militia officer, were decisive objections to him in my mind. In canvassing this subject, out of doors, I found too that even among the delegates of Virginia there were difficulties. The apostolical reasonings among themselves, which should be greatest, were not less energetic among the saints of the ancient dominion than they were among us of New England. In several conversations, I found more than one very cool about the appointment of Washington, and particularly Mr. Pendleton was very clear and full against it. Full of anxieties concerning these confusions, and apprehending daily that we should hear very distressing news from Boston, I walked with Mr. Samuel Adams in the State House yard, for a little exercise and fresh air, before the hour of Congress, and there represented to him the various dangers that surrounded us. He agreed to them all, but said, "What shall we do?" I answered him, that he knew I had taken great pains to get our colleagues to agree upon some plan, that we might be unanimous; but he knew that they would pledge themselves to nothing; but I was determined to take a step which should compel them and all the other members of Congress to declare themselves for or against something. "I am determined this morning to make a direct motion that Congress should adopt the army before Boston, and appoint Colonel Washington commander of it." Mr. Adams seemed to think very seriously of it, but said nothing.

Accordingly, when Congress had assembled, I rose in my place, and in as short a speech as the subject would admit,

[1] This will scarcely surprise those who know that Mr. Hancock's prevailing foible was a fondness for official distinction. But the writer never was among those disposed on this account to depreciate the merit of this gentleman's services in the Revolution. In the general correspondence will be found a letter addressed to Judge William Tudor, particularly on this subject. The Biography of Hancock, in Sanderson's Collection, is a curious specimen of unfavorable judgment in the guise of eulogy.

represented the state of the Colonies, the uncertainty in the minds of the people, their great expectation and anxiety, the distresses of the army, the danger of its dissolution, the difficulty of collecting another, and the probability that the British army would take advantage of our delays, march out of Boston, and spread desolation as far as they could go. I concluded with a motion, in form, that Congress would adopt the army at Cambridge, and appoint a General; that though this was not the proper time to nominate a General, yet, as I had reason to believe this was a point of the greatest difficulty, I had no hesitation to declare that I had but one gentleman in my mind for that important command, and that was a gentleman from Virginia who was among us and very well known to all of us, a gentleman whose skill and experience as an officer, whose independent fortune, great talents, and excellent universal character, would command the approbation of all America, and unite the cordial exertions of all the Colonies better than any other person in the Union. Mr. Washington, who happened to sit near the door, as soon as he heard me allude to him, from his usual modesty, darted into the library-room. Mr. Hancock, — who was our President, which gave me an opportunity to observe his countenance while I was speaking on the state of the Colonies, the army at Cambridge, and the enemy, — heard me with visible pleasure; but when I came to describe Washington for the commander, I never remarked a more sudden and striking change of countenance. Mortification and resentment were expressed as forcibly as his face could exhibit them. Mr. Samuel Adams seconded the motion, and that did not soften the President's physiognomy at all.[1] The subject came under debate, and several gentlemen declared themselves against the appointment of Mr. Washington, not on account of any personal objection against him, but because the army were all from New England, had a General of their own, appeared to be satisfied with him, and had proved themselves able to imprison the British army in Boston, which was all they expected or desired at that time.

[1] The emotion was smothered enough by the second day to enable him in writing to Mr. Gerry, in Massachusetts, to call Washington "a fine man." But there can be little doubt that neither Hancock nor Ward was ever afterwards cordial towards him. Mr. Adams's own letters of the same date will be found elsewhere. *Austin's Life of Gerry*, vol. i. p. 82.

Mr. Pendleton, of Virginia, Mr. Sherman, of Connecticut, were very explicit in declaring this opinion; Mr. Cushing and several others more faintly expressed their opposition, and their fears of discontents in the army and in New England. Mr. Paine expressed a great opinion of General Ward and a strong friendship for him, having been his classmate at college, or at least his contemporary; but gave no opinion upon the question. The subject was postponed to a future day. In the mean time, pains were taken out of doors to obtain a unanimity, and the voices were generally so clearly in favor of Washington, that the dissentient members were persuaded to withdraw their opposition, and Mr. Washington was nominated, I believe by Mr. Thomas Johnson of Maryland, unanimously elected, and the army adopted.

The next question was, who should be the second officer. General Lee was nominated, and most strenuously urged by many, particularly Mr. Mifflin, who said that General Lee would serve cheerfully under Washington, but, considering his rank, character, and experience, could not be expected to serve under any other. That Lee must be, *aut secundus, aut nullus*. To this I as strenuously objected, that it would be a great deal to expect of General Ward that he should serve under any man, but that under a stranger he ought not to serve; that though I had as high an opinion of General Lee's learning, general information, and especially of his science and experience in war, I could not advise General Ward to humiliate himself and his country so far as to serve under him. General Ward was elected the second, and Lee the third.[1] Gates and Mifflin, I believe, had some appointments, and General Washington took with him Mr. Reed, of Philadelphia, a lawyer of some eminence, for his private Secretary; and the gentlemen all set off for the camp. They had not proceeded twenty miles from Philadelphia, before they met a courier with the news of the battle of Bunker's Hill, the death of General Warren, the slaughter among the British officers and men, as well as among ours, and the burning of Charlestown.

[1] Mr. Adams was one of the committee of three (Mr. Henry and Mr. Lynch) appointed to wait upon General Lee, to inform him of his appointment, and request his answer, whether he would accept the command. They reported immediately his words of acceptance. *Journals of Congress*, 19 June, 1775.

I have always imputed the loss of Charlestown, and of the brave officers and men who fell there, and the loss of a hero of more worth than all the town, I mean General Warren, to Mr. Dickinson's petition to the King; and the loss of Quebec and Montgomery to his subsequent, unceasing, though finally unavailing efforts against independence. These impeded and paralyzed all our enterprises. Had our army been acknowledged in season, which acknowledgment ought to have been our first step, and the measures taken to comfort and encourage it, which ought to have been taken by Congress, we should not have lost Charlestown; and if every measure for the service in Canada, from the first projection of it to the final loss of the Province, had not been opposed and obstinately disputed by the same party, so that we could finally carry no measure but by a bare majority —.[1] And every measure was delayed, till it became ineffectual.

In the fall of the year, Congress was much fatigued with the incessant labors, debates, intrigues, and heats of the summer, and agreed on a short adjournment. The delegates from Massachusetts returned home, and as, the two houses of the legislature had chosen us all into the Council, we went to Watertown and took our seats for such times as we could spare before our return to Congress. I had been chosen before, two years successively, that is, in 1773 and 1774, and had been negatived by the Governor, the first time by Hutchinson, and the second by Gage. My friend, Dr. Cooper, attempted to console me under the first negative, which he called a check; but I told him I considered it not as a check, but as a boost, a word of John Bunyan which the Doctor understood. These negatives were, indeed, no mortification to me, for, knowing that neither honor nor profit was to be obtained, nor good to be done in that body in those times, I had not a wish to sit there. When a person came running to my office to tell me of the first of them, I cried out, laughing, "Now I believe, in my soul, I am a clever fellow, since I have the attestation of the three branches of the Legislature." This vulgar, familiar little sally, was caught as if it had been a prize, and immediately scattered all over the Province.

I went to head-quarters, and had much conversation with

[1] There seems to be an accidental omission to carry out the sense with some such words as these, "we should not have lost Canada."

Generals Washington, Ward, Lee, Putnam, Gates, Mifflin, and others, and went with General Lee to visit the outposts and the sentinels nearest the enemy at Charlestown. Here Lee found his dogs inconvenient, for they were so attached to him that they insisted on keeping close about him, and he expected he should be known by them to the British officers in the fort, and he expected every moment a discharge of balls, grape, or langrage about our ears. After visiting my friends and the General Court, the army and the country, I returned to Philadelphia, but not till I had followed my youngest brother to the grave. He had commanded a company of militia all summer, at Cambridge, and there taken a fatal dysentery, then epidemic in the camp, of which he died, leaving a young widow and three young children, who are all still living. My brother died greatly lamented by all who knew him, and by none more than by me, who knew the excellence of his heart, and the purity of his principles and conduct. He died, as Mr. Taft, his minister, informed me, exulting, as his father had done, in the exalted hopes of a Christian.

An event of the most trifling nature in appearance, and fit only to excite laughter in other times, struck me into a profound reverie, if not a fit of melancholy. I met a man who had sometimes been my client, and sometimes I had been against him. He, though a common horse-jockey, was sometimes in the right, and I had commonly been successful in his favor in our courts of law. He was always in the law, and had been sued in many actions at almost every court. As soon as he saw me, he came up to me, and his first salutation to me was, "Oh! Mr. Adams, what great things have you and your colleagues done for us! We can never be grateful enough to you. There are no courts of justice now in this Province, and I hope there never will be another." Is this the object for which I have been contending? said I to myself, for I rode along without any answer to this wretch. Are these the sentiments of such people, and how many of them are there in the country? Half the nation, for what I know; for half the nation are debtors, if not more, and these have been, in all countries, the sentiments of debtors. If the power of the country should get into such hands, and there is great danger that it will, to what purpose have we sacrificed our time, health, and every thing else? Surely we must guard against this spirit and these principles, or we shall repent of all our conduct. However, the good sense and integrity of the majority of the great body of the people came into my thoughts, for my relief, and the last resource was after all in a good Providence.]

Single Entry in Account Book.

September 3. At Woodstock.[1] Heard Mr. Learned, from Isaiah xxxii. 16: "The work of righteousness is peace, and the effect of righteousness quietness and assurance forever."

---

15. Friday.[2] Archibald Bullock and John Houston, Esquires, and the Rev. Dr. Zubly, appear as delegates from Georgia. Dr. Zubly is a native of Switzerland, and a clergyman of the independent persuasion, settled in a parish in Georgia. He speaks, as it is reported, several languages, English, Dutch, French, Latin, &c.; is reported to be a learned man. He is a man of a warm

[1] On his way to the Congress, at Philadelphia, after the recess. The fashion of travelling is now so completely changed, that it may be of some interest to the curious to know the course that was taken by Mr. Adams at this time. He was on horseback, and accompanied by a man-servant also mounted. The account book, from which the above entry is taken, gives the following list of his stops:—

28 August.
At Davis's at Roxbury.
At Watertown.
At Baldwin's.
At Buckminster's at Framingham.
At Bowman's at Oxford.
At Sherman's in Grafton.
4 September.
At Hide's in Woodstock from Saturday to Monday.
At Clark's at Pomfret.
At Cary's at Windham.
At Gray's at Lebanon.
At Taynter's in Colchester.
At Smith's of Haddam.
At Camp's in Durham.
At Bears's of New Haven.
At Bryant's of Milford.
At Stratford Ferry.
At Stratfield.
At Penfield's of Fairfield.
At Betts's of Norwalk.
At Fitch's of Stamford.
At Knap's of Horseneck.
At Bull's of White Plains.
At Dobb's Ferry.
At Hackensack.
At Pierson's of Newark.
At Graham's, Elizabethtown.
At Dawson's, Woodbridge.
At Brunswick.
At Jones's at Ten Mile Inn.
At Princeton.
At Trenton.
At Priestley's at Bristol.
At Wilson's.
At Shammony Ferry.

[2] For the sake of preserving the continuity of the narrative in the Autobiography, embracing the remainder of Mr. Adams's congressional life, it is placed by itself at the end of that portion of the Diary and Debates covering the same period.

and zealous spirit; it is said that he possesses considerable property. Houston is a young gentleman, by profession a lawyer, educated under a gentleman of eminence in South Carolina. He seems to be sensible and spirited, but rather inexperienced. Bullock is clothed in American manufacture. Thomas Nelson, Esq., George Wythe, Esq., and Francis Lightfoot Lee, Esq., appeared as delegates from Virginia. Nelson is a fat man, like the late Colonel Lee of Marblehead. He is a speaker, and alert and lively for his weight. Wythe is a lawyer, it is said, of the first eminence. Lee is a brother of Dr. Arthur, the late sheriff of London, and of our old friend Richard Henry, sensible and patriotic, as the rest of the family.

Deane says that two persons of the name of De Witt, of Dutch extraction, one in Norwich, the other in Windham, have made saltpetre with success, and propose to make a great deal. That there is a mine of lead, at Middletown, which will afford a great quantity; that works are preparing to smelt and refine it, which will go in a fortnight. There is a mine at Northampton, which Mr. W. Bowdoin spent much money in working, with much effect, though little profit.

Langdon and Bartlett came in this evening from Portsmouth. Four hundred men are building a fort on Pierce's Island to defend the town against ships of war. Upon recollecting the debates of this day in Congress, there appears to me a remarkable want of judgment in some of our members. Chase is violent and boisterous, asking his pardon; he is tedious upon frivolous points. So is E. Rutledge. Much precious time is indiscreetly expended; points of little consequence are started and debated with warmth. Rutledge is a very uncouth and ungraceful speaker; he shrugs his shoulders, distorts his body, nods and wriggles with his head, and looks about with his eyes from side to side, and speaks through his nose, as the Yankees sing. His brother John dodges his head too, rather disagreeably, and both of them spout out their language in a rough and rapid torrent, but without much force or effect.[1] Dyer is long-winded and

[1] This account of Edward Rutledge is not flattering. But it derives some confirmation from the report of the rule which he is said to have adopted in speaking. In Sanderson's Collection of Lives of the Signers, is the following account: —

"Mr. Rutledge often remarked, that, in the early period of his career, he had been more than once in the awkward predicament of being oppressed with his

round-about, obscure and cloudy, very talkative and very tedious, yet an honest, worthy man, means and judges well. Sherman's air is the reverse of grace; there cannot be a more striking contrast to beautiful action, than the motions of his hands; generally he stands upright, with his hands before him, the fingers of his left hand clenched into a fist, and the wrist of it grasped with his right. But he has a clear head and sound judgment; but when he moves a hand in any thing like action, Hogarth's genius could not have invented a motion more opposite to grace; — it is stiffness and awkwardness itself, rigid as starched linen or buckram; awkward as a junior bachelor or a sophomore.

Mr. Dickinson's air, gait, and action are not much more elegant.

16. Saturday. Walking to the State House, this morning, I met Mr. Dickinson, on foot, in Chesnut Street. We met, and passed near enough to touch elbows. He passed without moving his hat or head or hand. I bowed, and pulled off my hat. He passed haughtily by. The cause of his offence is the letter, no doubt, which Gage has printed in Draper's paper.[1] I shall, for the future, pass him in the same manner; but I was determined to make my bow, that I might know his temper. We are not to be upon speaking terms nor bowing terms for the time to come. This evening had conversation with Mr. Bullock, of Georgia. I asked him whether Georgia had a charter? What was the extent of the Province? What was their constitution? How justice was administered? Who was chancellor? who ordinary? and who judges? He says they have county courts for the trial of civil causes under eight pounds; and a Chief Justice appointed from home, and three other judges appointed by the Governor, for the decision of all other causes, civil and criminal, at Savannah; that the Governor alone is both chancellor and ordinary. Parson Gordon, of Roxbury,[2] spent the evening

own incoherency, but, — reflecting that few of a large audience could immediately perceive what was sense or the reverse, that those who were capable of thus discriminating were probably the most generous and indulgent to youthful orators, and that it was necessary at all events to succeed in his profession, — he made it a positive rule never to sit down *or to hesitate or halt, but to talk on, and brave it out with the best countenance he could assume.*"

[1] The intercepted letter in which allusion is made to him, as "a certain great fortune and piddling genius." See page 411, note.

[2] The author of the History, which with some marked defects contains a great deal that is of value, and that can with difficulty be found in any other quarter.

here. I fear his indiscreet prate will do harm in this city. He is an eternal talker, and somewhat vain, and not accurate nor judicious; very zealous in the cause, and a well-meaning man, but incautious, and not sufficiently tender of the character of our Province, upon which at this time much depends; fond of being thought a man of influence at head-quarters, and with our Council and House, and with the general officers of the army, and also with gentlemen in this city and other Colonies. He is a good man, but wants a guide.

17. Sunday. Mr. Smith, Mr. Imlay, and Mr. Hanson, breakfasted with us. Smith is an Englishman. Imlay and Hanson New Yorkers. Heard Sprout on Titus iii. 5: "Not by works of righteousness which we have done, but according to his mercy he saved us, through the washing of regeneration and the renewing of the Holy Ghost." There is a great deal of simplicity and innocence in this worthy man, but very little elegance or ingenuity. In prayer, he hangs his head in an angle of forty-five over his right shoulder; in sermon, which is delivered without notes, he throws himself into a variety of indecent postures, bends his body, points his fingers, and throws about his arms without any rule or meaning at all. He is totally destitute of the genius and eloquence of Duffield; has no imagination, no passions, no wit, no taste, and very little learning, but a great deal of goodness of heart.

18. Monday. This morning, John McPherson, Esq. came to my lodgings, and requested to speak with me in private. He is the owner of a very handsome country seat, about five miles out of this city; is the father of Mr. McPherson, an aid-de-camp to General Schuyler. He has been a captain of a privateer, and made a fortune in that way the last war; is reputed to be well skilled in naval affairs. He proposes great things; is sanguine, confident, positive, that he can take or burn every man-of-war in America.[1] It is a secret, he says, but he will communicate it to any one member of Congress, upon condition that it be not divulged during his life at all, nor after his death, but for the

[1] In the letters of General Washington, printed in the Life of Joseph Reed, by far the most natural and characteristic productions of his that have come down to this generation, is a sly hit at this gentleman's fancy, which carried him all the way to Cambridge, in the November following, to submit his project to the approbation of the commander-in-chief. Vol. i. p. 126.

service of this country. He says it is as certain as that he shall die, that he can burn any ship. In the afternoon, Mr. S. A. and I made a visit, at Mrs. Bedford's, to the Maryland gentlemen. We found Paca and Chase, and a polite reception from them. Chase is ever social and talkative; he seems in better humor than he was before the adjournment. His Colony have acted with spirit in support of the cause; they have formed themselves into a system and enjoined an association, if that is not an absurdity.

19. Tuesday. This morning, Mr. Henry Hill, with his brother, Nat Barrett, came to visit us. Paine introduced him to Mrs. Yard as one of the poor of Boston. He is here with his wife on a visit to her brother. Paine cries, "You, H. Hill, what did you come here for? Who did you bring with you?—ha! ha! ha!"

20. Wednesday. Took a walk, in company with Governor Ward, Mr. Gadsden and his son, and Mr. S. Adams, to a little box in the country belonging to old Mr. Marshall,[1] the father of three sons who live in the city; a fine, facetious old gentleman, an excellent Whig. There we drank coffee; a fine garden; a little box of one room; very cheerful and good-humored.

21. Thursday. The famous partisan, Major Rogers, came to our lodgings to make us a visit. He has been in prison; discharged by some insolvent or bankrupt act. He thinks we shall have hot work, next Spring. He told me an old half-pay officer, such as himself, would sell well next Spring; and when he went away, he said to S. A. and me, "If you want me, next Spring, for any service, you know where I am, send for me; I am to be sold."[2] He says, "the Scotchmen at home say, 'd—n that Adams and Cushing; we must have their heads,' &c. Bernard used to damn that Adams;—'Every dip of his pen stung like

[1] This is Christopher Marshall, in whose Diary is the following entry, under same date.

"Past three went to the place, where Samuel Adams, Governor Ward, John Adams, and Christopher Gadsden and son came, drank coffee, and spent the afternoon in free conversation."

[2] A true Captain Dalgetty. See page 167, note. Major Rogers was arrested on the next day by order of the Pennsylvania Committee of Safety, and submitted to the disposal of Congress, which ordered his release on his giving parole that he would not serve against America during the war. He proceeded to New York, and took a commission as Colonel in the British service. Force's *American Archives*, fourth series, p. 865–866.

a horned snake.' Paxton made his will in favor of Lord Townsend, and by that manœuvre got himself made a commissioner. There was a great deal of beauty in that stroke of policy. We must laugh at such sublime strokes of politics," &c. &c. &c. In the evening, Mr. Jonathan Dickinson Sergeant of Princeton, made a visit to the Secretary and me. He says he is no idolater of his namesake; that he was disappointed when he first saw him. Fame had given him an exalted idea; but he came to New Jersey upon a particular cause, and made such a flimsy, effeminate piece of work of it, that he sunk at once in his opinion. Sergeant is sorry to find such a falling off in this city;—not a third of the battalion men muster, who mustered at first. D. he says, sinks here, in the public opinion; that many gentlemen chime in with a spirited publication in the paper of Wednesday which blames the conduct of several gentlemen of fortune, D., Cad., R., and J. Allen, &c.

22. Friday. Mr. Gordon spent the evening here.

23. Saturday. Mr. Gordon came and told us news, opened his budget. Ethan Allen with five hundred Green Mountain boys was intrenched half way between St. Johns and Montreal, and had cut off all communication with Carlton, and was kindly treated by the French. A council of war had been held, and it was their opinion that it was practicable to take Boston and Charlestown; but as it would cost many lives, and expose the inhabitants of Boston to destruction, it was thought best to postpone it for the present. Major Rogers came here too this morning; said he had a hand and a heart, though he did not choose by offering himself, to expose himself to destruction. I walked a long time, this morning, backward and forward in the State House yard with Paca, McKean, and Johnson. McKean has no idea of any right or authority in Parliament. Paca contends for an authority and right to regulate trade, &c. Dyer, and Sergeant of Princeton, spent the evening here. S. says, that the Irish interest in this city has been the support of liberty. Mease, &c. are leaders in it. The Irish and the Presbyterian interest coalesce.

24. Sunday. Dyer is very sanguine that the two De Witts, one of Windham, the other of Norwich, will make saltpetre in large quantities. He produces a sample, which is very good. Harrison is confident that Virginia alone will do great things

from tobacco houses; but my faith is not strong as yet. Lord North is at his old work again, sending over his anodynes to America; deceiving one credulous American after another into a belief that he means conciliation, when in truth he means nothing but revenge. He rocks the cradle and sings lullaby, and the innocent children go to sleep, while he prepares the birch to whip the poor babes. One letter after another comes, that the people are uneasy, and the ministry are sick of their systems, but nothing can be more fallacious. Next Spring we shall be jockied by negotiation, or have hot work in war; besides, I expect a reinforcement to Gage and to Carlton this fall or winter. Heard Mr. Smith, of Pecquea, about forty miles towards Lancaster, a Scotch clergyman of great piety, as Colonel Roberdeau says. The text was, Luke xiv. 18: "And they all, with one consent, began to make excuse." This was at Duffield's meeting. In the afternoon, heard our Mr. Gordon, in Arch Street: "The Lord is nigh unto all that call upon him." Called upon Stephen Collins, who has just returned. Stephen has a thousand things to say to us, he says; a thousand observations to make. One thing he told me for my wife, who will be peeping here some time or other, and come across it. He says, when he called at my house, an English gentleman was with him; a man of penetration, though of few words; and this silent, penetrating gentleman was pleased with Mrs. Adams, and thought her the most accomplished lady he had seen since he came out of England. Down, vanity, for you don't know who this Englishman is.

Dr. Rush came in. He is an elegant, ingenious body, a sprightly, pretty fellow. He is a republican; he has been much in London; acquainted with Sawbridge, Macaulay, Burgh, and others of that stamp. Dilly sends him books and pamphlets, and Sawbridge and Macaulay correspond with him. He complains of D.; says the Committee of Safety are not the representatives of the people, and therefore not their legislators; yet they have been making laws, a whole code, for a navy. This committee was chosen by the House, but half of them are not members, and therefore not the choice of the people. All this is just. He mentions many particular instances in which Dickinson has blundered; he thinks him warped by the Quaker interest and the church interest too; thinks his reputation past the meridian, and that avarice is growing upon him. Says that Henry and Mifflin both complained to him very much about him. But Rush, I think, is too much of a talker to be a deep thinker; elegant, not great. In the evening, Mr. Bullock and Mr. Houston, two gentlemen from Georgia, came into our room, and smoked and chatted the whole evening. Houston and Adams disputed the whole time in good humor. They are both dabs at disputation, I think. Houston, a lawyer by trade, is one of course, and Adams is not a whit less addicted to it than the lawyers. The question was, whether all America was not in a state of war, and whether we ought to confine ourselves to act upon the defensive only? He was for acting offensively, next spring or this fall, if the petition was rejected or neglected. If it was not answered, and favorably answered, he would be for acting against Britain and Britons, as, in open war, against French and Frenchmen; fit privateers, and take their ships anywhere. These gentlemen give a melancholy account of the State of Georgia and South Carolina. They say that if one thousand regular troops should land in Georgia, and their commander be provided with arms and clothes enough, and proclaim freedom to all the negroes who would join his camp, twenty thousand negroes would join it from the two Provinces in a fortnight. The negroes have a wonderful art of communicating intelligence among themselves; it will run several hundreds of miles in a week or fortnight. They say, their only security is this; that all the king's friends, and tools of government, have large plantations, and property in negroes; so that the slaves of the Tories would be lost, as well as those of the Whigs.

I had nearly forgot a conversation, with Dr. Coombe, concerning assassination, Henry IV., Buckingham, Sully, &c. &c. &c. Coombe has read Sully's Memoirs with great attention.

25. Monday. Rode out of town, and dined with Mr. McPherson. He has the most elegant seat in Pennsylvania, a clever Scotch wife, and two pretty daughters. His seat is on the banks of the Schuylkill. He has been nine times wounded in battle; an old sea commander; made a fortune by privateering; an arm twice shot off, shot through the leg, &c. He renews his proposals of taking or burning ships. Spent the evening with Lynch at the City Tavern. He thinks the row gallies and *vaisseaux de frise* inadequate to the expense.

27. Wednesday. Mr. Bullock and Mr. Houston, the gentlemen from Georgia, invited S. A. and me to spend the evening with them in their chamber, which we did very agreeably and sociably. Mr. Langdon, of New Hampshire was with us. Mr. Bullock, after dinner, invited me to take a ride with him in his phaeton, which I did. He is a solid, clever man. He was President of their Convention.

28. Thursday. The Congress and the Assembly of this Province were invited to make an excursion, upon Delaware River, in the new row gallies built by the Committee of Safety of this Colony. About ten in the morning we all embarked. The names of the gallies are the Washington, the Effingham, the Franklin, the Dickinson, the Otter, the Bull Dog, and one more whose name I have forgot. We passed down the river, by Gloucester, where the *vaisseaux de frise* are. These are frames of timber, to be filled with stones, and sunk in three rows in the channel. I went in the Bull Dog, Captain Alexander, commander, Mr. Hillegas, Mr. Owen Biddle, and Mr. Rittenhouse, and Captain Faulkner were with me. Hillegas is one of our continental treasurers; is a great musician; talks perpetually of the forte and piano, of Handel, &c. and songs and tunes. He plays upon the fiddle. Rittenhouse is a mechanic; a mathematician, a philosopher, and an astronomer. Biddle is said to be a great mathematician. Both are members of the American Philosophical Society. I mentioned Mr. Cranch to them for a member. Our intention was to have gone down to the fort, but the winds and tide being unfavorable, we returned by the city, and went up the river to Point-no-Point; a pretty place. On our return, Dr. Rush, Dr. Zubly, and Counsellor Ross, brother of George Ross, joined us. Ross is a lawyer of great eloquence, and heretofore of extensive practice; a great Tory, they say, but now begins to be converted. He said the Americans were making the noblest and firmest resistance to tyranny that ever was made by any people. The acts were founded in wrong, injustice, and oppression; the great town of Boston had been remarkably punished without being heard. Rittenhouse is a tall, slender man, plain, soft, modest, no remarkable depth or thoughtfulness in his face, yet cool, attentive, and clear.

October 25. Wednesday. Mr. Duane told me, at the funeral of our late virtuous and able President, that he, Mr. Duane, had accustomed himself to read the Year Books. Mr. De Lancey, who was Chief Justice of New York, he said, advised him to it, as the best method of imbibing the spirit of the law. De Lancey told him that he had translated a pile of cases from the Year Books, although he was a very lazy man. Duane says, that Jefferson is the greatest rubber off of dust that he has met with; that he has learned French, Italian, Spanish, and wants to learn German. Duane says he has no curiosity at all, not the least inclination, to see a city or a building, &c.; that his memory fails, is very averse to be burthened; that in his youth he could remember any thing; nothing but what he could learn; but it is very different now.

Last evening, Mr. Hewes, of North Carolina, introduced to my namesake and me a Mr. Hogg, from that Colony, one of the proprietors of Transylvania, a late purchase from the Cherokees upon the Ohio. He is an associate with Henderson, who was lately one of the associate judges of North Carolina, who is President of the Convention in Transylvania. These proprietors have no grant from the Crown, nor from any Colony; are within the limits of Virginia and North Carolina, by their charters, which bound those Colonies in the South Sea. They are charged with republican notions and Utopian schemes.[1]

29. Sunday. Paine brought in a large sample of saltpetre, made in this city by Mr. Ripsama. It is very good, large, and burns off, when laid upon a coal, like moist powder. I tried it. Heard Mr. Carmichael, at Mr. Duffield's, on "Trust in the Lord and do good, so shall you dwell in the land, and verily thou shalt be fed."

December 9. Saturday. Having yesterday asked and obtained leave of Congress to go home this morning, I mounted, with my own servant only, about twelve o'clock, and reached the Red Lion about two, where I dine. The roads very miry and dirty; the weather pleasant and not cold.

10. Sunday. Rode from Bristol to Trenton, breakfasted, rode to Princeton, and dined with a Captain Flahaven, in Lord Stirling's regiment, who has been express to Congress from his lordship. Flahaven's father lives in this Province. He has lived in

[1] An interesting report of this conference was made by Mr. Hogg, which is found in full in Force's *American Archives*, fourth series, vol. iv. p. 543.

Maryland. Says that the Virginia Convention, granting the Scotch petition to be neutral, has done all the mischief, and been the support of Lord Dunmore. He says the Scotch are, in some parts of Virginia, powerful; that, in Alexandria, he has heard them cursing the Congress, and vilifying not only their public proceedings, but their private characters. He has heard them decrying the characters of the Maryland delegates, particularly Chase, and the Virginia delegates, particularly Lee, Henry, and Washington. Last evening, when I dismounted at Bristol, the taverner showed me into a room where was a young gentleman very elegantly dressed, with whom I spent the evening; his name I could not learn. He told me he had been an officer in the army, but had sold out. I had much conversation with him, and some of it very free. He told me we had two valuable prizes among the prisoners taken at Chambly and St. Johns; a Mr. Barrington, nephew of Lord Barrington, and a Captain Williams, who, he says, is the greatest officer in the service. He gives a most exalted character of Williams as a mathematician, philosopher, engineer, and in all other accomplishments of an officer. In the evening, Mr. Baldwin came to see me. We waited on Dr. Witherspoon, the President of the college, where we saw Mr. Smith and two other of the light-horse, from Philadelphia, going to the camp with a wagon.

1776. January 24. Wednesday. Began my journey to Philadelphia. Dined at C. Mifflin's, at Cambridge, with G. Washington and Gates and their ladies, and half a dozen sachems and warriors of the French Caghnawaga tribe, with their wives and children. Williams is one who was captured in his infancy and adopted. There is a mixture of white blood, French or English, in most of them. Louis, their principal, speaks English and French, as well as Indian. It was a savage feast, carnivorous animals devouring their prey; yet they were wondrous polite. The General introduced me to them as one of the grand council fire at Philadelphia, upon which they made me many bows and a cordial reception.

25. Thursday. About ten, Mr. Gerry called me, and we rode to Framingham, where we dined. Colonel Buckminster, after dinner, showed us the train of artillery brought down from

Ticonderoga by Colonel Knox. It consists of iron, nine eighteen pounders, ten twelve, six six, four nine pounders; three thirteen inch mortars, two ten inch mortars; one eight inch and one six and a half howitzer; and one eight inch and a half, and one eight. Brass cannon: eight three pounders, one four pounder, two six pounders, one eighteen, and one twenty-four pounder; one eight inch and a half mortar, one seven inch and a half dts. and five cohorns.

After dinner, rode to Maynard's, and supped there very agreeably.

26. Friday. Stopped at Stearns's, in Worcester, and dined with Mr. Lincoln at Mr. Jonathan Williams's. In Putnam's office, where I formerly trimmed the midnight lamp, Mr. Williams keeps Law's works, and Jacob Behmen's, with whose mystical reveries he is much captivated.

28. Sunday. Mr. Upham informs that this town of Brookfield abounds with a stone, out of which alum, copperas, and sulphur are made. Out of one bushel of this stone, he made five pounds of copperas; — he put the stone into a tub, poured water on it, let it stand two or three days, then drew it off, and boiled the liquor away; let it stand and it shot into a kind of crystals adding chamber-lye and alkaline salts to the copperas, and that makes alum. "We made some sulphur by sublimation; we put four quarts of stone into an iron kettle, laid a wooden cover over the kettle, leaving a hole in the middle, then we put an earthern pot over the top of the kettle, and cemented it with clay, then made a fire under the kettle, and the sulphur sublimated; we got about a spoonful. We have found a bed of yellow ochre in this town. I got twelve hundred weight. We make Spanish brown by burning the yellow ochre."

29. Monday. Rode to Springfield. Dined at Scott's. Heard that the cannon at Kingsbridge, in New York, were spiked up; that dry goods, English goods, were sent round to New York from Boston, and from New York sold all over New England, and sent down to camp; that Tryon has issued writs for the choice of a new Assembly, and that the writs were likely to be obeyed, and the Tories were likely to carry a majority of members.

October 13.[1] Sunday. Set out from Philadelphia towards Boston. Oated at the Red Lion; dined at Bristol; crossed Trenton Ferry long before sunset; drank coffee at the ferry-house on the east side of the Delaware, where I put up, partly to avoid riding in the evening air, and partly because thirty miles is enough for the first day, as my tendons are delicate, not having been once on horseback since the eighth day of last February.

1777. February 6. Thursday. Lodged last night, for the first time, in my new quarters, at Mrs. Ross's, in Market Street, Baltimore, a few doors below the Fountain Inn.

The gentlemen from Pennsylvania and Maryland complain of the growing practice of distilling wheat into whiskey. They say it will become a question, whether the people shall eat bread or drink whiskey. The Congress sits in the last house at the west end of Market Street, on the south side of the street; a long chamber, with two fire-places, two large closets, and two doors. The house belongs to a Quaker, who built it for a tavern.

7. Friday. Dined about half a mile out of town, at Mr. Lux's, with Dr. Witherspoon, Mr. S. Adams, Mr. Lovel, Mr. Hall, Dr. Thornton, a Mr. Harrison, Dr.   , and Mr. George Lux, and two ladies, Mrs. Lux and her sister. This seat is named Chatworth, and an elegant one it is; has a large yard, enclosed with stone in lime, and before the yard two fine rows of large cherry trees, which lead out to the public road; there is a fine prospect about it. Mr. Lux and his son are sensible gentlemen. I had much conversation, with George, about the new form of government adopted in Maryland. George is the young gentleman by whom I sent letters to my friends, from Philadelphia, when the army was at Cambridge, particularly to Colonel Warren, whom, and whose lady, Lux so much admired. The whole family profess great zeal in the American cause. Mr. Lux lives like a Prince.

8. Saturday. Dined at the President's, with Mr. Lux, Messrs. Samuel and Robert Purviance, Captain Nicholson, of the Maryland frigate, Colonel Harrison, Wilson, Mr. Hall, upon New

[1] "I suppose your ladyship has been in the twitters, for some time, because you have not received a letter by every post, as you used to do. But I am coming to make my apology in person. I yesterday asked and obtained leave of absence." *J. A. to his Wife,* 11 October.

England salt fish. The weather was rainy, and the streets the muddiest I ever saw. This is the dirtiest place in the world. Our Salem and Portsmouth are neat in comparison. The inhabitants, however, are excusable, because they had determined to pave the streets, before this war came on, since which they have laid the project aside, as they are accessible to men-of-war. This place is not incorporated; it is neither a city, town, nor borough, so that they can do nothing with authority.

9. Sunday. Heard Mr. Allison. In the evening, walked to Fell's Point, the place where the ships lie; a kind of peninsula, which runs out into the basin, which lies before Baltimore town. This basin, thirty years ago, was deep enough for large tobacco ships, but since then has filled up ten feet; between the town and the point, we pass a bridge, over a little brook, which is the only stream which runs into the basin, and the only flux of water, which is to clear away the dirt which flows into the basin from the foul streets of the town, and the neighboring hills and fields. There is a breast-work thrown up upon the Point with a number of embrasures, for cannon, facing the entrance into the harbor. The Virginia frigate, Captain Nicholson, lies off in the stream. There is a number of houses upon this Point; you have a fine view of the town of Baltimore from this Point. On my return, I stopped and drank tea at Captain Smith's, a gentleman of the new Assembly.

16. Sunday. Last evening, I supped with my friends, Dr. Rush and Mr. Sergeant, at Mrs. Page's, over the bridge. The two Colonel Lees, Dr. Witherspoon, Mr. Adams, Mr. Gerry, Dr. Brownson, made the company. They have a fashion, in this town, of reversing the picture of King George III. in such families as have it. One of these topsy-turvy kings was hung up in the room where we supped, and under it were written these lines, by Mr. Throop, as we are told.

> Behold the man, who had it in his power
> To make a kingdom tremble and adore.
> Intoxicate with folly, see his head
> Placed where the meanest of his subjects tread.
> Like Lucifer, the giddy tyrant fell;
> He lifts his heel to Heaven, but points his head to Hell.

17. Monday. Yesterday, heard Dr. Witherspoon, upon re-

deeming time; an excellent sermon. I find that I understand the Doctor better since I have heard him so much in conversation, and in the Senate; but I perceive that his attention to civil affairs has slackened his memory; it cost him more pains than heretofore to recollect his discourse. Mr. Hancock told C. W., yesterday, that he had determined to go to Boston in April. Mrs. Hancock was not willing to go till May, but Mr. Hancock was determined upon April. Perhaps the choice of a Governor may come on in May. What aspiring little creatures we are! How subtle, sagacious, and judicious this passion is! How clearly it sees its object, how constantly it pursues it, and what wise plans it devises for obtaining it!

21. Friday. Dined, yesterday, at Mr. Samuel Purviance's. Mr. Robert, his brother and lady, the President and lady, the two Colonel Lees and their ladies, Mr. Page and his lady, Colonel Whipple, Mrs. K. Quincy, a young gentleman and a young lady, made the company; a great feast. The Virginia ladies had ornaments about their wrists which I don't remember to have seen before. These ornaments were like miniature pictures, bound round the arms with some chains. This morning, received a long card from Mr. H. expressing great resentment about fixing the magazine at Brookfield, against the bookbinder and the General. The complaisance to me, and the jealousy for the Massachusetts, in this message, indicate to me the same passion and the same design with the journey to Boston in April.

23. Sunday. Took a walk, with Mr. Gerry, down to a place called Ferry Branch; a point of land which is formed by a branch of the Patapsco on one side, and the basin, before the town of Baltimore, on the other. At the point is a ferry over to the road which goes to Annapolis; this is a very pretty walk. At the point you have a full view of the elegant, splendid seat of Mr. Carroll, barrister. It is a large and elegant house; it stands fronting looking down the river into the harbor; it is one mile from the water. There is a most beautiful walk from the house down to the water; there is a descent not far from the house; — you have a fine garden, then you descend a few steps and have another fine garden; you go down a few more and have another. It is now the dead of winter; no verdure or bloom to be seen; but in the spring, summer, and fall, this scene must be very pretty. Returned and dined with Mr. William

Smith, a new member of Congress. Dr. Lyon, Mr. Merriman, Mr. Gerry, a son of Mr. Smith, and two other gentlemen, made the company. The conversation turned, among other things, upon removing the obstructions and opening the navigation of Susquehannah River. The company thought it might easily be done, and would open an amazing scene of business. Philadelphia will oppose it, but it will be the interest of a majority of Pennsylvania to effect it.

This Mr. Smith is a grave, solid gentleman, a Presbyterian by profession; a very different man from the most of those we have heretofore had from Maryland.

The manners of Maryland are somewhat peculiar. They have but few merchants. They are chiefly planters and farmers; the planters are those who raise tobacco, and the farmers such as raise wheat, &c. The lands are cultivated, and all sorts of trades are exercised by negroes, or by transported convicts, which has occasioned the planters and farmers to assume the title of gentlemen; and they hold their negroes and convicts, that is, all laboring people and tradesmen, in such contempt, that they think themselves a distinct order of beings. Hence they never will suffer their sons to labor or learn any trade but they bring them up in idleness, or, what is worse, in horse-racing, cock-fighting, and card-playing.

28. Friday. Last evening, had a good deal of free conversation with Mr. R. Purviance. He seems to me to have a perfect understanding of the affairs of this State. Men and things are very well known to him.

The object of the men of property here, the planters, &c., is universally wealth. Every way in the world is sought to get and save money. Landjobbers, speculators in land; little generosity to the public, little public spirit.

September 15. Monday. Friday, the 12th, I removed from Captain Duncan's, in Walnut Street, to the Rev. Mr. Sprout's in Third Street, a few doors from his meeting-house. Mr. Marchant, from Rhode Island, boards here with me. Mr. Sprout is sick of a fever. Mrs. Sprout and the four young ladies, her daughters, are in great distress, on account of his sickness and the approach of Mr. Howe's army; but they bear their affliction with Christian patience and philosophic fortitude. The young ladies are Miss Hannah, Olive, Sally, and Nancy. The only son is an officer in the army; he was the first clerk in the American war-office.

We live in critical moments! Mr. Howe's army is at Middleton and Concord. Mr. Washington's, upon the western banks of Schuylkill, a few miles from him. I saw, this morning, an excellent chart of the Schuylkill, Chester River, the Brandywine, and this whole country, among the Pennsylvania files. This city is the stake for which the game is played. I think there is a chance for saving it, although the probability is against us. Mr. Howe, I conjecture, is waiting for his ships to come into the Delaware. Will Washington attack him? I hope so; and God grant him success.

16. Tuesday. No newspaper this morning. Mr. Dunlap has moved or packed up his types. A note from General Dickinson, that the enemy in New Jersey are four thousand strong. Howe is about fifteen miles from us, the other way. The city seems to be asleep, or dead, and the whole State scarce alive. Maryland and Delaware the same. The prospect is chilling on every side; gloomy, dark, melancholy, and dispiriting. When and where will the light spring up? Shall we have good news from Europe? Shall we hear of a blow struck by Gates? Is there a possibility that Washington should beat Howe? Is there a prospect that McDougall and Dickinson should destroy the detachment in the Jerseys? From whence is our deliverance to come? or is it not to come? Is Philadelphia to be lost? If lost, is the cause lost? No; the cause is not lost, but it may be hurt. I seldom regard reports, but it is said that Howe has marked his course from Elk with depredation. His troops have plundered hen-roosts, dairy-rooms, the furniture of houses, and all the cattle in the country. The inhabitants, most of whom are Quakers, are angry and disappointed, because they were promised the security of their property. It is reported, too, that Mr. Howe lost great numbers in the battle of the Brandywine.

18. Thursday. The violent north-east storm, which began the day before yesterday, continues. We are yet in Philadelphia, that mass of cowardice and Toryism. Yesterday, was buried Monsieur Du Coudray, a French officer of artillery, who was lately made an Inspector-General of artillery and military man-

ufactures, with the rank of Major-General. He was drowned in the Schuylkill, in a strange manner. He rode into the ferry-boat, and rode out at the other end into the river, and was drowned. His horse took fright. He was reputed the most learned and promising officer in France. He was carried into the Romish Chapel, and buried in the yard of that church. This dispensation will save us much altercation.[1]

19. Friday. At three, this morning, was waked by Mr. Lovel, and told that the members of Congress were gone, some of them, a little after midnight; that there was a letter from Mr. Hamilton, aid-de-camp to the General, informing that the enemy were in possession of the ford and the boats, and had it in their power to be in Philadelphia before morning, and that, if Congress was not removed, they had not a moment to lose. Mr. Marchant and myself arose, sent for our horses, and, after collecting our things, rode off after the others. Breakfasted at Bristol, where were many members determined to go the Newtown road to Reading. We rode to Trenton, where we dined. Colonel Harrison, Dr. Witherspoon, all the delegates from New York and New England, except Gerry and Lovel. Drank tea at Mr. Spencer's; lodged at Mr. S. Tucker's, at his kind invitation.

20. Saturday. Breakfasted at Mrs. J. B. Smith's. The old gentleman, his son Thomas, the loan officer, were here, and Mrs. Smith's little son and two daughters. An elegant breakfast we had, of fine Hyson, loaf sugar, and coffee, &c. Dined at Williams's, the sign of the Green Tree; drank tea with Mr. Thomson and his lady at Mrs. Jackson's; walked with Mr. Duane to General Dickinson's house, and took a look at his farm and gardens, and his greenhouse, which is a scene of desolation; the floor of the greenhouse is dug up, by the Hessians, in search for money; the orange, lemon, and lime trees, are all dead, with the leaves on; there is a spacious ball-room, above stairs, a drawing-room, and a whispering-room; in another apartment, a huge crash of glass bottles, which the Hessians had broke, I suppose. These are thy triumphs, mighty Britain! Mr. Law, Mr. Hancock, Mr. Thomson, Mr. ——, were here. Spent the evening at

[1] The difficulties, growing out of Mr. Deane's engagement with this officer, in France, were such that Congress refused to ratify it. See *Sparks's Washington*, vol. iv. p. 490.

Williams's, and slept again at Tucker's. Mrs. Tucker has about sixteen hundred pounds sterling, in some of the funds in England, which she is in fear of losing. She is, accordingly, passionately wishing for peace, and that the battle was fought once for all; says that private property will be plundered where there is an army, whether of friends or enemies; that if the two opposite armies were to come here, alternately, ten times, she would stand by her property until she should be killed; if she must be a beggar, it should be where she was known, &c. This kind of conversation shows plainly enough how well she is pleased with the state of things.

21. Sunday. It was a false alarm which occasioned our flight from Philadelphia. Not a soldier of Howe's has crossed the Schuylkill. Washington has again crossed it, which I think is a very injudicious manœuvre. I think his army would have been best disposed on the west side of the Schuylkill. If he had sent one brigade of his regular troops to have headed the militia, it would have been enough. With such a disposition, he might have cut to pieces Howe's army, in attempting to cross any of the fords. Howe will not attempt it. He will wait for his fleet in Delaware River; he will keep open his line of communication with Brunswick, and at last, by some deception or other, will slip unhurt into the city.

Burgoyne has crossed Hudson's River, by which General Gates thinks he is determined at all hazards to push for Albany, which General Gates says he will do all in his power to prevent him from reaching. But I confess I am anxious for the event, for I fear he will deceive Gates, who seems to be acting the same timorous, defensive part, which has involved us in so many disasters. O, Heaven! grant us one great soul! One leading mind would extricate the best cause from that ruin which seems to await it for the want of it. We have as good a cause as ever was fought for; we have great resources; the people are well tempered; one active, masterly capacity, would bring order out of this confusion, and save this country.

22. Monday. Breakfasted at Ringold's, in Quaker Town; dined at Shannon's, in Easton, at the Forks; slept at Johnson's, in Bethlehem.

23. Tuesday. Mr. Okeley, Mr. Hassey, and Mr. Edwine, came to see me. Mr. Edwine showed us the Children's Meet-

ing, at half after eight o'clock; music, consisting of an organ, and singing in the German language. Mr. Edwine gave a discourse in German, and then the same in English. Mrs. Langley showed us the Society of Single Women; then Mr. Edwine showed us the waterworks and the manufactures; — there are six sets of works in one building; a hemp-mill, an oil-mill, a mill to grind bark for the tanners; then the fullers-mill, both of cloth and leather, the dyer's house, and the shearer's house. They raise a great deal of madder. We walked among the rows of cherry trees, with spacious orchards of apple trees on each side of the cherry walk. The Society of Single Men have turned out for the sick.

24. Wednesday. Fine morning. We all went to meeting, last evening, where Mr. Edwine gave the people a short discourse in German, and the congregation sung, and the organ played. There were about two hundred women and as many men; the women sat together in one body, and the men in another; the women dressed all alike; the women's heads resembled a garden of white cabbage heads.

25. Thursday. Rode from Bethlehem through Allentown, yesterday, to a German tavern, about eighteen miles from Reading; rode this morning to Reading, where we breakfasted, and heard for certain that Mr. Howe's army had crossed the Schuylkill. Colonel Hartley gave me an account of the late battle between the enemy and General Wayne. Hartley thinks that the place was improper for battle, and that there ought to have been a retreat.

November 11. Tuesday. Set off from Yorktown; reached Lancaster. 12. From Lancaster to Reading; slept at General Mifflin's. 13. Reached Strickser's. 14. Dined at Bethlehem; slept at Easton, at Colonel Hooper's; supped at Colonel Dean's. Met Messrs. Ellery and Dana, and Colonel Brown, on the 15th, a few miles on this side of Reading. We have had five days of very severe weather; raw, cold, frosty, snowy; this cold comes from afar. The lakes, Champlain and George, have been boisterous, if not frozen.

Will the enemy evacuate Ticonderoga? Are they supplied with provisions for the winter? Can they bring them from Canada, by water or ice? Can they get them in the neighboring country? Can we take Mount Independence in the winter?

15. Saturday. At Willis's, at the Log Jail in New Jersey, twenty-eight miles from Easton.

17. Monday. Rode yesterday from Log Jail, Willis's; breakfasted at Hoffman's, at Sussex Court House, and supped and lodged at David McCambly's, thirty-four miles from Willis's. The taverners, all along, are complaining of the guard of light-horse which attended Mr. H. They did not pay, and the taverners were obliged to go after them to demand their dues. The expense, which is supposed to be the country's, is unpopular. The Tories laugh at the tavern keepers, who have often turned them out of their houses for abusing Mr. H. They now scoff at them for being imposed upon by their king, as they call him. Vanity is always mean; vanity is never rich enough to be generous. Dined at Brewster's, in Orange county, State of New York. Brewster's grandfather, as he tells me, was a clergyman, and one of the first adventurers to Plymouth; he died, at ninety-five years of age, a minister on Long Island; left a son who lived to be above eighty, and died leaving my landlord, a son who is now, I believe, between sixty and seventy. The manners of this family are exactly like those of the New England people; a decent grace before and after meat; fine pork and beef, and cabbage and turnip.

18. Tuesday. Lodged at Brooks's, five miles from the North River. Rode to the Continental Ferry, crossed over, and dined at Fishkill, at the Dr's. Mess, near the Hospital, with Dr. Samuel Adams, Dr. Eustis, Mr. Wells, &c. It was a feast; — salt pork and cabbage, roast beef and potatoes, and a noble suet pudding, grog, and a glass of Port.

Our best road home is through Litchfield and Springfield. Morehouse's is a good tavern, about twenty-four miles, three or four miles on this side of Bull's Iron Works; fifty miles to Litchfield; Captain Storm's, eight miles; Colonel Vandeborough's, five miles; Colonel Morehouse's, nine miles; Bull's Iron Works, four miles; no tavern; Cogswell's Iron Works, ten miles; a tavern; Litchfield, eight miles; cross Mount Tom to get to Litchfield.

19. Wednesday. Dined at Storm's. Lodged last night and breakfasted this morning at Loudoun's, at Fishkill. Here we are, at Colonel Morehouse's, a member of Assembly for Dutchess county.

20. Thursday. To Harrington, Phillips's, five miles; to Yale's, in Farmington, five miles; to Humphrey's, in Simsbury, seven miles; to Owen's, in Simsbury, seven miles; to Sheldon's, in Suffield, ten miles; Kent's, in Suffield, five miles; to Springfield, ten miles.

21. Friday. To Hays's, Salmon Brook, five miles; to Southwick, Loomis's, six miles; to Fowler's, three miles; to Westfield, Clap's, four miles; to Captain Clap's, four miles this side N. H.; to North Hampton, Lyman's or Clark's.

NOTES OF DEBATES

IN THE

CONTINENTAL CONGRESS,

IN 1775 AND 1776.

All the notes made by Mr. Adams, during these years, have been put together and set apart in the following pages, with the addition of such explanations, by the Editor, as seem necessary to make them readily understood. Whilst the interest attaching to some of the minor questions discussed has passed away, it is believed that what has been preserved, upon such subjects as the state of trade, the authority to institute governments, and the formation of the Articles of Confederation, fragmentary as it is, will not be without its value to those who desire to understand the true history of the Revolution.

DEBATES.

The following resolution appears upon the Journal of Congress, for the 23d of September, 1775: —

"*Resolved*, That a committee be appointed to purchase a quantity of woollen goods, for the use of the army, to the amount of five thousand pounds sterling.

"That the said goods, when bought, be placed in the hands of the Quarter-Masters-General of the Continental armies, and that the same be, by them, sold out to the private soldiers of said armies, at prime cost and charges, including a commission of five per centum, to the said Quarter-Masters-General, for their trouble.

"That the committee consist of five.

"The ballot being taken, and examined, the following members were chosen. Mr. Lewis, Mr. Alsop, Mr. Willing, Mr. Deane, Mr. Langdon."

Thomas Mifflin had just been appointed, by General Washington, Quarter-Master-General of the army at Cambridge. The debate, which follows, took place upon an application of his, but to whom does not clearly appear, and it terminated in the foregoing resolution.

1775. September 23. Saturday. *Samuel Adams* moved, upon Mifflin's letter, that a sum be advanced from the treasury for Mifflin and Barrell.

Mr. E. Rutledge wished the money might be advanced upon the credit of the Quarter-Master-General; wished that an inquiry might be made, whether goods had been advanced. If so, it was against the association. *Lynch* wished the letter read. *S. Adams* read it. *Jay* seconded the motion of E. Rutledge that a committee be appointed to inquire if goods are raised against the association. *Gadsden* wished the motion put off. We had other matters of more importance. *Willing* thought that goods might be purchased upon four months' credit. We should not intermix our accounts.

Paine. We have not agreed to clothe the soldiers, and the Quarter-Master-General has no right to keep a slop-shop, any more than anybody else. It is a private matter; very indigested applications are made here for money.

Deane. The army must be clothed, or perish. No preaching against a snow-storm. We ought to look out that they be kept warm, and that the means of doing it be secured.

Lynch. We must see that the army be provided with clothing. I intended to have moved, this very day, that a committee be appointed to purchase woollen goods in this city and New York for the use of the army. *E. Rutledge.* I have no objection to the committee. I meant only that the poor soldiers should be supplied with goods and clothing as cheap as possible.

Lewis. Brown, of Boston, bought goods at New York, and sent them up the North River, to be conveyed by land to Cambridge.

Dyer wanted to know whether the soldiers would be obliged to take these goods. Goods cheaper in New York than here.

Sherman. The sutlers, last war, sold to the soldiers, who were not obliged to take any thing. Many will be supplied by families with their own manufacture. The Quarter-Master-General did not apply to Congress, but to his own private correspondents.

Deane. The soldiers were imposed on by sutlers last war; the soldiers had no pay to receive.

Lynch. A soldier without clothing is not fit for service; but he ought to be clothed, as well as armed, and we ought to provide, as well as it can be done, that he may be clothed.

Nelson moved that five thousand pounds sterling be advanced to the Quarter-Master-General, to be laid out in clothing for the army. *Langdon* hoped a committee would be appointed. *Sherman* liked Nelson's motion, with an addition that every soldier should be at liberty to supply himself in any other way.

Read understood that Massachusetts Committee of Supplies had a large store that was very full. *Sherman,* for a committee to inquire what goods would be wanted for the army, and at what prices they may be had, and report. *Gadsden* liked that best. *Johnson* moved that the sum might be limited to five thousand pounds sterling. We don't know what has been supplied by Massachusetts, what from Rhode Island, what from New York, and what from Connecticut. *S. Adams* liked Nelson's motion. *Ward* objected to it, and preferred the motion for a committee. *Nelson.* The Quarter-Master is ordered, by the General, to supply the soldiers, &c.

Paine. It is the duty of this Congress to see that the army be supplied with clothing at a reasonable rate. I am for a committee. Quarter-Master has his hands full. *Zubly.* Would it not be best to publish proposals in the papers for any man who was willing to supply the army with clothing to make his offers?

Harrison. The money ought to be advanced in all events; content with a committee.

R. R. Livingston. . . . *Willing* proposed that we should desire the committee of this city to inquire after these goods, and this will lead them to an inquiry that will be beneficial to America.

Chase. The city of Philadelphia has broken the association, by raising the price of goods fifty per cent. It would not be proper to purchase goods here. The breach of the association here is general in the price of goods, as it is in New York with respect to tea. If we lay out five thousand pounds here, we shall give a sanction to the breaches of the association; the breach is too general to be punished. *Willing.* If the association is broken in this city, don't let us put the burden of examining into it upon a few, but the whole committee. New York have broken it entirely; ninety-nine in a hundred drink tea. I am not for screening the people of Philadelphia.

Sherman. I am not an importer, but have bought of New York merchants, for twenty years, at a certain advance on the sterling cost.

R. R. Livingston thought we ought to buy the goods where they were dearest, because if we bought them at New York, where they were cheapest, New York would soon be obliged to purchase in Philadelphia, where they are dearest, and then the loss would fall upon New York; whereas, in the other way, the loss would be general. *Jay.* We had best desire the committee of this city to purchase the quantity of goods, at the price stated by the association, and see if they were to be had here at that price.

This debate terminated in a manner that I did not foresee. A committee was appointed to purchase five thousand pounds sterling's worth of goods, to be sent to the Quarter-Master-General, and by him to be sold to the soldiers at first cost and charges. Quarter-Master to be allowed five per cent. for his trouble.

Mr. Lynch and Colonel Harrison and Colonel Nelson indulged their complaisance and private friendship for Mifflin and Washington, so far as to carry this.

It is almost impossible to move any thing, but you instantly see private friendships and enmities, and provincial views and prejudices, intermingle in the consultation.[1] These are degrees of corruption. They are deviations from the public interest and from rectitude. By this vote, however, perhaps the poor soldiers may be benefited, which was all I wished, the interest of Mr. Mifflin being nothing to me.

---

25. Monday. An uneasiness among some of the members, concerning a contract with Willing and Morris for powder, by which the House, without any risk at all, will make a clear profit of twelve thousand pounds at least.[2] Dyer and Deane spoke in public; Lewis, to me, in private about it. All think it exorbitant.

S. Adams desired that the Resolve of Congress, upon which the contract was founded, might be read; he did not recollect it.

De Hart. One of the contractors, Willing, declared to this Congress, that he looked upon the contract to be, that the first cost should be insured to them, not the fourteen pounds a barrel for the powder.

R. R. Livingston. I never will vote to ratify the contract in the sense that Morris understands it.

Willing. I am, as a member of the House, a party to that contract, but was not privy to the bargain. I never saw the contract, until I saw it in Dr. Franklin's hand. I think it

[1] The same complaint is made by General Washington, in a letter addressed to Richard Henry Lee, about this time. *Sparks's Washington*, vol. iii. p. 68.

[2] *Extract from the Secret Journals of Congress*, 18 September, 1775: —

"*Resolved*, That a secret committee be appointed to contract for the importation and delivery of a quantity of gunpowder, not exceeding five hundred tons.

"That the said committee consist of nine, any five of whom to be a quorum.

"19 September. The members chosen for the secret committee: —

"Mr. Willing, Mr. Franklin, Mr. P. Livingston, Mr. Alsop, Mr. Deane, Mr. Dickinson, Mr. Langdon, Mr. McKean, and Mr. Ward."

Extract from the Journals, 25 September: —

"The delegates, from Pennsylvania, produced an account of the powder imported, and how it has been disposed of."

insures only the first cost; my partner thinks it insures the whole. He says that Mr. Rutledge said, at the time, that Congress should have nothing to do with sea risk. The committee of this city offered nineteen pounds. I would wish to have nothing to do with the contract, but to leave it to my partner, who is a man of reason and generosity, to explain the contract with the gentlemen who made it with him.

J. Rutledge. Congress was to run no risk, only against men-of-war and custom-house officers. I was surprised, this morning, to hear that Mr. Morris understood it otherwise. If he won't execute a bond, such as we shall draw, I shall not be at a loss what to do.

Johnson. A hundred tons of powder was wanted. *Ross.* In case of its arrival, Congress was to pay fourteen pounds; if men-of-war or custom-house officers should get it, Congress was to pay first cost only, as I understood it. *Zubly.* We are highly favored; fourteen pounds we are to give, if we get the powder, and fourteen pounds, if we don't get it. I understand, persons enough will contract to supply powder at fifteen pounds and run all risks.

Willing. Sorry any gentleman should be severe. Mr. Morris's character is such that he cannot deserve it.

Lynch. If Morris will execute the bond, well; if not, the committee will report.

Deane. It is very well that this matter has been moved, and that so much has been said upon it.

Dyer. There are not ten men, in the Colony I came from, who are worth so much money as will be made, clear, by this contract. *Ross.* What has this matter to (do with) the present debate, whether Connecticut men are worth much or no; it proves there are no men there whose capital or credit is equal to such contracts; that is all. *Harrison.* The contract is made, and the money paid. How can we get it back?

Johnson. Let us consider the prudence of this contract. If it had not been made, Morris would have got nineteen pounds, and not have set forward a second adventure. *Gadsden* understands the contract as Morris does, and yet thinks it a prudent one, because Morris would have got nineteen pounds.

J. Adams. &c. &c. &c.

Cushing. I move that we take into consideration a method of keeping up an army in the winter.

Gadsden seconds the motion, and desires that a motion made in writing some days ago, and postponed, may be read as it was, as also passages of G. Washington's letter.

S. Adams. The General has promised another letter, in which we shall have his sentiments. We shall have it to-morrow, perhaps. *Lynch*. If we have, we shall only lose the writing of a letter.

J. Adams moved that the General's advice should be asked concerning barracks, &c. and that a committee be appointed to draught a letter. *Lynch* seconded the motion.

A committee was appointed. Lynch, J. Adams, and Colonel Lee, the men.

Sherman moved that a committee be appointed, of one member from each Colony, to receive and examine all accounts.[1] *S. Adams* seconded the motion.

Harrison asked, "Is this the way of giving thanks?"

S. Adams was decent to the Committee for Riflemen's Accounts; meant no reflections upon them; was sorry that the worthy gentleman from Virginia conceived that any was intended; he was sure there was no foundation for it.

Paine thought that justice and honor required that we should carefully examine all accounts and see to the expenditure of all public moneys; that the minister would find out our weakness, and would foment divisions among our people; he was sorry that gentlemen could not hear methods proposed to settle and pay accounts, in a manner that would give satisfaction to the people, without seeming to resent them. *Harrison*. Now the gentlemen have explained themselves, he had no objection; but when it was proposed to appoint a new committee, in the place of the former one, it implied a reflection. *Willing*. These

1 See Journals: "*Resolved*, That a Committee of Accounts or Claims be now appointed, to consist of one member from each of the United Colonies, to whom all accounts against the continent are to be referred, who are to examine and report upon the same in order for payment, seven of them to be a quorum."

The various topics here discussed do not appear in the Journals arranged in the same order that is kept in these notes.

accounts are for tents, arms, clothing, &c. as well as expenses of the riflemen, &c.

Nelson moved that twenty thousand dollars be voted into the hands of the other committee to settle the accounts. *S. Adams* seconded the motion, but still hoped that some time or other a committee would be appointed, of one member from each Colony, to examine all accounts, because he thought it reasonable.[1]

September 27. Wednesday. *Willing*, in favor of Mr. Purviance's petition.[2] *Harrison* against it.

Willing thinks the non-exportation sufficiently hard upon the farmer, the merchant, and the tradesman, but will not arraign the propriety of the measure.

Nelson. If we give these indulgences, I know not where they will end. Sees not why the merchant should be indulged more than the farmer. *Harrison.* It is the merchant in England that is to suffer. *Lynch.* They meant gain, and they ought to bear the loss.

Sherman. Another reason, the cargo is provisions, and will probably fall into the hands of the enemy.

R. R. Livingston. There is no resolve of Congress against exporting to foreign ports. We shall not give license to deceit by clearing out for England.

Lynch moves that the committee of this city be desired to inquire whether Dean's vessel, taken at Block Island, and another at Cape Cod, were not sent on purpose to supply the enemy.

Read. The committee of this city have inquired of the owners of one vessel. The owners produced their letter books, and were ready to swear; the conduct of the captain is yet suspicious. Thinks the other inquiry very proper.

1 The new committee consisted of the following members:—

Mr. Langdon, Mr. Cushing, Mr. Ward, Mr. Deane, Mr. Lewis, Mr. Smith, Mr. Willing, Mr. Rodney, Mr. Johnson, Mr. Nelson, Mr Gadsden, and Dr. Zubly.

2 *Extract from the Journals of Congress*, 27 September:—

"A memorial of Samuel and Robert Purviance was presented and read, setting forth that they had chartered a vessel to carry a load of wheat; that the said vessel, in going from Philadelphia to Chestertown, in Maryland, was lost in the late storm, by which they were prevented from exporting, before the 10th of September, the cargo which they had actually purchased; and, therefore, praying for liberty to export the cargo to a foreign port.

"Ordered, to lie on the table."

Lee thinks Lynch's motion proper; thinks the conduct detestable parricide, to supply those who have arms in their hands to deprive us of the best rights of human nature. The honest seamen ought to be examined, and they may give evidence against the guilty.

Hancock. Dean belongs to Boston; he came from West Indies, and was seized here and released; loaded with flour and went out.

Extract from the Journals of Congress.

Wednesday, 4 October, 1775.

"Agreeable to the order of the day, the Congress resolved itself into a committee of the whole, to take into consideration the state of the trade of the thirteen United Colonies."

1775. October 4. *Johnson.* I should be for the resolutions about imports and exports standing till further order. I should be against giving up the carriage. The grower, the farmer, gets the same, let who will be the exporter, but the community does not. The shipwright, rope-maker, hemp-grower, all shipbuilders, the profits of the merchant, are all lost, if foreigners are our sole carriers, as well as seamen, &c. I am for the report standing;[1] the association standing.

J. Rutledge. The question is, whether we shall shut our ports entirely, or adhere to the association. The resolutions we come to ought to be final.

Lee. North Carolina is absent; they are expected every hour; we had better suspend a final determination. I fear our determination to stop trade will not be effectual.

Willing. North Carolina promised to put themselves in the same situation with other Colonies. New York have done the same. Our gold is locked up at present; we ought to be decisive; interest is near and dear to men. The Committee of Secrecy find difficulties; merchants dare not trade.

Deane. Sumptuary laws, or a non-importation, were necessary, if we had not been oppressed; a non-export was attended with difficulty; my Colony could do as well as others. We

[1] On Saturday, the 30th September, the committee appointed to consider the trade of America brought in their report. See *Journals*.

The original agreement of non-exportation had fixed the tenth of September, 1775, as the period from which it was to begin. The resolutions, finally passed, will be found in the Journals of the 1st of November.

should have acquiesced in an immediate non-export, or a partial one. Many voted for it as an object *in terrorem.* Merchants, mechanics, farmers, all call for an establishment.

Whether we are to trade with all nations, except Britain, Ireland, and West Indies, or with one or two particular nations, we cannot get ammunition without allowing some exports; for the merchant has neither money nor bills, and our bills will not pass abroad.

R. R. Livingston. We should go into a full discussion of the subject; every gentleman ought to express his sentiments. The first question is, how far we shall adhere to our association; what advantages we gain, what disadvantages we suffer by it. An immediate stoppage last year would have had a great effect, but at that time the country could not bear it. We are now out of debt nearly; the high price of grain, in Boston, will be an advantage to the farmer. The price of labor is nearly equal in Europe; the trade will be continued, and Great Britain will learn to look upon America as insignificant. If we export to Britain, and don't import, they must pay us in money; of great importance that we should import. We employ our ships and seamen; we have nothing to fear but disunion among ourselves. What will disunite us more than the decay of all business? The people will feel, and will say, that Congress tax them and oppress them worse than Parliament.

Ammunition cannot be had, unless we open our ports. I am for doing away our non-exportation agreement entirely. I see many advantages in leaving open the ports, none in shutting them up. I should think the best way would be to open all our ports. Let us declare all those bonds illegal and void. What is to become of our merchants, farmers, seamen, tradesmen? What an accession of strength should we throw into the hands of our enemies, if we drive all our seamen to them!

Lee. Is it proper the non-exportation agreement should continue? For the interest of Americans to open our ports to foreign nations, that they should become our carriers, and protect their own vessels.

Johnson never had an idea that we should shut our export agreement closer than it is at present. If we leave it as it is, we shall get powder by way of New York, the lower counties, and North Carolina. In winter, our merchants will venture out to foreign nations. If Parliament should order our ships to be seized, we may begin a force in part to protect our own vessels, and invite foreigners to come here and protect their own trade.

J. Rutledge. We ought to postpone it, rather than not come to a decisive resolution.

Lee. We shall be prevented from exporting, if British power can do it. We ought to stop our own exports, and invite foreign nations to come and export our goods for us. I am for opening our exportations, to foreigners, further than we have.

Willing. The gentleman's favorite plan is to induce foreigners to come here. Shall we act like the dog in the manger, not suffer New York and the lower counties and North Carolina to export, because we can't? We may get salt and ammunition by those ports. Can't be for inviting foreigners to become our carriers; carriage is an amazing revenue. Holland and England have derived their maritime power from their carriage. The circulation of our paper will stop, and lose its credit, without trade. Seven millions of dollars have been struck by the continent and by the separate Colonies. *Lee.* The end of administration will be answered by the gentleman's plan; jealousies and dissensions will arise, and disunion and division. We shall become a rope of sand. *Zubly.* The question should be, whether the export should be kept or not.

Chase. I am for adhering to the association, and think that we ought not to determine these questions this day. Differ from R. Livingston that our exports are to be relaxed, except as to tobacco and lumber. This will produce a disunion of the Colonies. The advantage of cultivating tobacco is very great; the planters would complain; their negro females would be useless without raising tobacco; the country must grow rich that exports more than they import. There ought not to be a partial export to Great Britain. We affect the revenue and the remittance by stopping our exports; we have given a deadly blow to Britain and Ireland by our non-export; their people must murmur, must starve. The nation must have become bankrupt before this day if we had ceased exports at first. I look upon Britain, Ireland, and West Indies, as our enemies, and would not trade with them while at war. We can't support the war and our taxes without trade. Emissions of paper cannot continue. I dread an emission for another campaign. We can't stand it without trade.

I can't agree that New York, the lower counties, and North Carolina, should carry on trade; upon giving a bond, and making oath, they may export. I am against these Colonies trading according to the restraining act. It will produce division. A few weeks will put us all on a footing; New York, &c. are now all in rebellion, as the ministry call it, as much as Massachusetts Bay.

We must trade with foreign nations, at the risk indeed, but we may export our tobacco to France, Spain, or any other foreign nation. If we treat with foreign nations, we should send to them as well as they to us. What nation or countries shall we trade with? Shall we go to their ports and pay duties, and let them come here and pay none? To say you will trade with all the world deserves consideration.

I have not absolutely discarded every glimpse of a hope of a reconciliation; our prospect is gloomy. I can't agree that we shall not export our own produce. We must treat with foreign nations upon trade. They must protect and support us with their fleets. When you once offer your trade to foreign nations, away with all hopes of reconciliation.

E. Rutledge differs with all who think the non-exportation should be broke, or that any trade at all should be carried on. When a commodity is out of port, the master may carry it where he pleases. My Colony will receive your determination upon a general non-exportation; the people will not be restless. Proposes a general non-exportation until next Congress. Our people will go into manufactures, which is a source of riches to a country. We can take our men from agriculture and employ them in manufactures. Agriculture and manufactures cannot be lost; trade is precarious.

R. R. Livingston not convinced by any argument; thinks the exception of tobacco and lumber would not produce disunion. The Colonies affected can see the principles, and their virtue is such that they would not be disunited. The Americans are their own carriers now, chiefly; a few British ships will be out of employ. I am against exporting lumber. I grant that if we trade with other nations, some of our vessels will be seized, and some taken. Carolina is cultivated by rich planters; not so in the northern Colonies; the planters can bear a loss, and see the reason of it; the northern Colonies can't bear it. Not in our power to draw people from the plough to manufactures. We can't make contracts for powder without opening our ports. I am for exporting where Britain will allow us, to Britain itself. If we shut up our ports, we drive our sailors to Britain; the army will be supplied, in all events. *Lee* makes a motion for two resolutions. The trade of Virginia and Maryland may be stopped by a very small naval force. North Carolina is badly off. The northern Colonies are more fortunate. The force of Great Britain on the water being exceedingly great, that of America almost nothing, they may prevent almost all our trade in our own bottoms. Great Britain may exert every nerve next year to send fifteen, twenty, or even thirty thousand men to come here. The provisions of America are become necessary to several nations. France is in distress for them.— Tumults and attempts to destroy the grain in the ear. England has turned arable into grass; France into vines. Grain cannot be be got from Poland, nor across the Mediterranean. The dissensions in Poland continue. Spain is at war with the Algerines, and must have provisions; it would be much safer for them to carry our provisions than for us. We shall get necessary manufactures, and money, and powder. This is only a temporary expedient, at the present time and for a short duration, to end when the war ends. I agree we must sell our produce; foreigners must come in three or four months; the risk we must pay in the price of our produce. The insurance must be deducted. Insurance would not be high to foreigners on account of the novelty; it is no new thing; the British cruisers will be the danger.

The Same Debate Continued.

October 5. Thursday. *Gadsden.* I wish we may confine ourselves to one point. Let the point be, whether we shall shut up all our ports, and be all on a footing. The ministry will answer their end, if we let the custom-houses be open in New York, North Carolina, and the lower counties, and Georgia; they will divide us. One Colony will envy another, and be jealous. Mankind act by their feelings. Rice sold for three pounds; it wont sell now for thirty shillings. We have rich and poor there as well as in other Colonies; we know that the excepted Colonies don't want to take advantage of the others.

Zubly. Q. Whether the custom-houses be stopped, and the trade opened to all the world? The object is so great, that I would not discuss it, on horseback, riding post haste; it requires the debate of a week. We are lifting up a rod; if you don't repeal the acts, we will open our ports. Nations, as well as individuals, are sometimes intoxicated. It is fair to give them notice. If we give them warning, they will take warning; they will send ships out. Whether they can stop our trade, is the question. New England, I leave out of the question; New York is stopped by one ship; Philadelphia says her trade is in the power of the fleet; Virginia and Maryland are within the capes of Virginia; North Carolina is accessible; only one good harbor, Cape Fear. In Georgia, we have several harbors; but a small naval force may oppose or destroy all the naval force of Georgia. The navy can stop our harbors and distress our trade; therefore it is impracticable to open our ports. The question is, whether we must have trade or not. We can't do without trade; we must have trade; it is prudent not to put virtue to too serious a test. I would use American virtue as sparingly as possible, lest we wear it out. Are we sure one canoe will come to trade? Has any merchant received a letter from abroad that they will come? Very doubtful and precarious whether any French or Spanish vessel would be cleared out to America; it is a breach of the Treaty of Peace. The Spaniards may be too lazy to come to America; they may be supplied from Sicily. It is precarious and dilatory; extremely dangerous and pernicious. I am clearly against any proposition to open our ports to all the world; it is not prudent to threaten; the people of England will take it we design to break off, to separate. We have friends, in England, who have taken this up, upon virtuous principles.

Lee. I will follow Mr. Gadsden, and simplify the proposition, and confine it to the question, whether the custom-houses shall be shut. If they are open, the excepted Colonies may trade, others not, which will be unequal; the consequence, jealousy, division, and ruin. I would have all suffer equally. But we should have some offices set up, where bonds should be given that supplies shall not go to our enemies.

Extract from the Journals.

Friday, October 6th.

"*Resolved*, That it be recommended to the several Provincial Assemblies or Conventions, and Councils or Committees of Safety, to arrest and secure every person in their respective Colonies, whose going at large may, in their opinion, endanger the safety of the Colony, or the liberties of America."

Chase. I don't think the resolution goes far enough. Lord Dunmore has been many months committing hostilities against Virginia, and has extended his piracies to Maryland. I wish he had been seized by the Colony months ago. They would have received the thanks of all North America. Is it practicable now? Have the Committee any naval force? This order will be a mere piece of paper. Is there a power in the Committee to raise and pay a naval force? Is it to be done at the expense of the Continent? Have they ships or men?

Lee. I wish Congress would advise Virginia and Maryland to raise a force by sea to destroy Lord Dunmore's power. He is fond of his bottle, and may be taken by land, but ought to be taken at all events.

Zubly. I am sorry to see the very threatening condition that Virginia is likely to be in. I look on the plan we heard of yesterday, to be vile, abominable, and infernal; but I am afraid it is practicable.[1] Will these mischiefs be prevented by seizing Dunmore? Seizing the King's representatives will make a great impression in England, and probably things will be carried on afterwards with greater rage. I came here with two views; one, to secure the rights of America; second, a reconciliation with Great Britain.

Dyer. They can't be more irritated at home than they are; they are bent upon our destruction; therefore, that is no argument against seizing them. Dunmore can do no mischief in Virginia; his connections in England are such that he may be exchanged to advantage. Wentworth is gone to Boston; Franklin is not dangerous, Penn is not, Eden is not.

[1] Lord Dunmore had sworn "by the living God, that if any injury or insult was offered to himself, he would declare freedom to the slaves." At this time he went to Norfolk, threatening to execute his pledge. Tucker's *Life of Jefferson*, vol. i. pp. 74–76. His proclamation, fulfilling it, is dated a month later. Howison's *History of Virginia*, vol. ii. p. 99.

Johnson. Dunmore a very bad man. A defensive conduct was determined on in the Convention of Virginia. I am for leaving it to Virginia. We ought not to lay down a rule in a passion. I see less and less prospect of a reconciliation every day; but I would not render it impossible; if we should render it impossible, our Colony would take it into their own hands, and make concessions inconsistent with the rights of America. North Carolina, Virginia, Pennsylvania, New York, at least, have strong parties in each of them of that mind. This would make a disunion. Five or six weeks will give us the final determination of the people of Great Britain. Not a Governor on the Continent has the real power, but some have the shadow of it. A renunciation of all connection with Great Britain will be understood by a step of this kind. Thirteen Colonies connected with Great Britain in sixteen months have been brought to an armed opposition to the claims of Great Britain. The line we have pursued has been the line we ought to have pursued; if what we have done had been proposed two years ago, four Colonies would not have been for it. Suppose we had a dozen Crown officers in our possession, have we determined what to do with them? shall we hang them?

Lee. Those who apply general reasons to this particular case will draw improper conclusions. Those Crown officers who have advised his Lordship against his violent measures, have been quarrelled with by him. Virginia is pierced in all parts with navigable waters. His Lordship knows all these waters, and the plantations on them. Shuldham is coming to assist him in destroying these plantations. We see his influence with an abandoned administration is sufficient to obtain what he pleases. If six weeks may furnish decisive information, the same time may produce decisive destruction to Maryland and Virginia. Did we go fast enough when we suffered the troops at Boston to fortify?

Zubly. This is a sudden motion; the motion was yesterday to apprehend Governor Tryon. We have not yet conquered the army or navy of Great Britain; a navy, consisting of a cutter, rides triumphant in Virginia. There are persons in America who wish to break off with Great Britain; a proposal has been made to apply to France and Spain; before I agree to it, I will inform my constituents. I apprehend the man who should propose it would be torn to pieces like De Witt.

Wythe. It was from a reverence for this Congress that the Convention of Virginia neglected to arrest Lord Dunmore; it was not intended suddenly to form a precedent for Governor Tryon. If Maryland have a desire to have a share in the glory of seizing this nobleman, let them have it. The first objection is the impracticability of it. I don't say that it is practicable; but the attempt can do no harm. From seizing clothing in Delaware, seizing the transports, &c., the Battles of Lexington, Charlestown, &c., every man in Great Britain will be convinced by ministry and Parliament, that we are aiming at an independency on Great Britain; therefore, we need not fear from this step disaffecting our friends in England. As to a defection in the Colonies, I can't answer for Maryland, Pennsylvania, &c.; but I can for Virginia.

Johnson. I am not against allowing liberty to arrest Lord Dunmore; there is evidence that the scheme he is executing was recommended by himself. Maryland does not regard the connection with Great Britain as the first good.

Stone. If we signify to Virginia that it will not be disagreeable to us if they secure Lord Dunmore, that will be sufficient.

Lewis moves an amendment, that it be recommended to the Council of Virginia, that they take such measures to secure themselves from the practices of Lord Dunmore, either by seizing his person, or otherwise, as they think proper.

Hall. A material distinction between a peremptory order to the Council of Virginia, to seize his Lordship, and a recommendation to take such measures as they shall judge necessary to defend themselves against his measures.

Extract from the Journals.

"*Resolved,* That the Committee appointed for the importation of powder, be directed to export, agreeable to the Continental Association, as much provisions or other produce of these Colonies, as they shall judge expedient for the purchase of arms and ammunition."

Motion to Export Produce for Powder.

Sherman. I think we must have powder, and we may send out produce for powder. But upon some gentlemen's principles we must have a general exportation.

Paine. From the observations some gentlemen have made, I think this proposition of more importance than it appeared at first. In theory, I could carry it further, even to exportation and importation to Great Britain. A large continent can't act upon speculative principles, but must be governed by rules. Medicines we must have, some clothing, &c. I wish we could enter upon the question at large, and agree upon some system.

Chase. By that resolution we may send to Great Britain, Ireland, and West Indies.

Lee. Suppose provisions should be sold in Spain for money, and cash sent to England for powder.

Duane. We must have powder; I would send for powder to London or anywhere. We are undone if we have not powder.

Deane. I hope the words, "agreeable to the Association" will be inserted, but I would import from Great Britain powder.

R. R. Livingston. We are between hawk and buzzard; we puzzle ourselves between the commercial and warlike opposition.

Rutledge. If ammunition was to be had from England only, there would be weight in the gentleman's argument. The Captain, Reed, told us yesterday that he might have brought one thousand barrels of powder. Why? because he was not searched. But if he had attempted to bring powder, he would have been searched. I would let the Association stand as it is, and order the Committee to export our provisions consistent with it.

Lee. When a vessel comes to England against our Association, she must be observed and watched; they would keep the provisions, but not let us have the powder.

Deane. I have not the most distant idea of infringing the Association.

Duane. The resolution with the amendment amounts to nothing. The Committee may import now consistent with the Association. I apprehend that, by breaking the Association, we may import powder; without it, not. We must have powder. We must fight our battles, in two or three months, in every Colony.

J. Rutledge. They may export to any other place, and thence send money to England.

Extract from the Journals.

"The Congress, taking into consideration the letter from New York, respecting the fortifications ordered to be erected on Hudson's River,—

"*Resolved*, That a Committee of three be appointed to report to-morrow morning, an answer to the Convention of New York.

"The following members were chosen by ballot, namely, Mr. Morton, Mr. Deane, and Mr. R. Livingston."

New York Letter concerning a fortification on the Highlands considered.

Dyer. Can't say how far it would have been proper to have gone upon Romain's plan in the Spring, but thinks it too late now. There are places upon that river that might be thrown up in a few days, that would do. We must go upon some plan that will be expeditious.

Lee. Romain says a less or more imperfect plan would only be beginning a strong-hold for an enemy.

Deane. An order went to New York; they have employed an engineer. The people and he agree in the spot and the plan. Unless we rescind the whole we should go on; it ought to be done.

Saturday, October 7.

No trace of the next debate appears upon the Journals as originally printed, but much light is shed upon it in the extract from the Autobiography, which follows these reports.

On the third of October is this entry on the Journals: "One of the delegates for Rhode Island laid before the Congress a part of the instructions given them by their two Houses of Legislature, August 26, 1775.

"*Resolved*, That the Congress will, on Friday next, take *the above* into consideration."

From these words it is clear that the instructions were themselves to be inserted as a part of the record, which they are not. But in the republication by Mr. Force in the American Archives, 4th series, vol. iv. c. 1888–9, they are found in full. The purport of them was to recommend to the Congress the building a fleet at the Continental expense.

In the Journals as originally printed, it would appear as if, when the subject came up on the appointed day, Friday, the consideration of it had been put off until Monday the 16th, which would make this debate seem entirely out of place.

Mr. Force has here again rectified the first edition of the Journals by showing that the vote on Friday was to postpone to Saturday; so that it then came up the first thing in the order of business, and was again postponed until Monday the 16th.

From the report of the debate it would seem as if, notwithstanding this reference, a motion was then made to refer the matter to a Committee.

Chase. It is the maddest idea in the world to think of building an American fleet; its latitude is wonderful; we should mortgage the whole Continent. Recollect the intelligence on your table — defend New York — fortify upon Hudson's River. We should provide, for gaining intelligence, two swift sailing vessels.

Dyer. The affair of powder from New York should be referred to the Committee.

Hopkins. No objection to putting off the instruction from Rhode Island, provided it is to a future day.

Paine. Seconds Chase's motion that it be put off to a future day, *sine die.*

Chase. The gentleman from Maryland never made such a motion. I never used the copulative; the gentleman is very sarcastic, and thinks himself very sensible.

Zubly. If the plans of some gentlemen are to take place, an American fleet must be a part of it, extravagant as it is.

Randolph moves that all the orders of the day should be read every morning.

Deane. I wish it may be seriously debated. I don't think it romantic at all.

J. Rutledge moves that some gentlemen be appointed to prepare a plan and estimate of an American fleet. *Zubly* seconds the motion.

Gadsden. I am against the extensiveness of the Rhode Island plan; but it is absolutely necessary that some plan of defence, by sea, should be adopted.

J. Rutledge. I shall not form a conclusive opinion, till I hear the arguments. I want to know how many ships are to be built, and what they will cost.

S. Adams. The committee can't make an estimate, until they know how many ships are to be built.

Zubly. Rhode Island has taken the lead. I move that the delegates of Rhode Island prepare a plan; give us their opinion.

J. Adams. The motion is entirely out of order. The subject is put off for a week, and now a motion is to appoint a committee to consider the whole subject.

Zubly, *Rutledge*, *Paine*, *Gadsden*,—lightly skirmishing.

Deane. It is like the man that was appointed to tell the dream and the interpretation of it. The expense is to be estimated, without knowing what fleet there shall be, or whether any at all.

Gadsden. The design is, to throw it into ridicule. It should be considered, out of respect to the Colony of Rhode Island, who desired it.

Determined, against the appointment of a committee.

Report of the Committee, for fortifying upon Hudson's River, considered.[1]

J. Rutledge. I think we should add to the report, that they take the most effectual measures to obstruct the navigation of Hudson's River, by booms, or otherwise. *Gadsden* seconds the motion. *Deane* doubts the practicability of obstructing it with booms, it is so wide. The committee said, four or five booms chained together, and ready to be drawn across, would stop the passage.

The Congress of New York is to consult the Assembly of Connecticut, and the Congress of New Jersey, on the best method of taking posts, and making signals, and assembling forces for the defence of the river.

Gadsden moves that all the letters laid before us, from England, should be sent to the Convention of New York. Tryon is a dangerous man, and the Convention of that Colony should be upon their guard. *Lee*. I think the letters should, by all means, be sent. *Rutledge*. Dr. Franklin desired they might not be printed. Moves that General Wooster, with his troops, may be ordered down to New York. *Duane* moves that Wooster's men may be employed in building the fortifications. *Dyer* seconds the motion, allowing the men what is usual.

Sherman would have the order conditional, if Schuyler don't want them; understands that New York has the best militia upon the continent.

R. Livingston. They will be necessary at the Highlands. *Dyer* thinks they ought to have the usual allowance for work.

[1] This Report will be found at large in the printed Journals of this date.

S. Adams understands that the works at Cambridge were done without any allowance, but that General Washington has ordered, that, for future works, they be allowed half a pistareen a day.

Langdon would not have the order to Wooster,[1] but to Schuyler; for he would not run any risk of the northern expedition.

Rutledge thinks Schuyler can't want them; he waited only for boats to send five hundred men more. *Sherman.* Would it not be well to inform Schuyler of our endeavors to take the transports, and desire him to acquaint Colonel Arnold of it?

Rutledge. He may coöperate with Arnold in taking the transports. I hope he is in possession of Montreal before now.

Deane. I wish that whatever money is collected, may be sent along to Schuyler.

E. Rutledge. We have been represented as beggarly fellows, and the first impressions are the strongest. If we eat their provisions, and don't pay, it will make a bad impression.

Ross produces a Resolve of the Assembly of Pennsylvania, that their delegates lay the Connecticut Intrusion[2] before Congress, that something may be done to quiet the minds.

J. Rutledge moves that the papers be referred to the delegates of the two Colonies.

Willing thinks them parties, and that they must have an umpire. *Sherman* thinks they may agree on a temporary line.

Debate on the Report for fortifying upon Hudson's River, resumed.

Lee[3] moves that parliamentary or ministerial posts may be

[1] The following resolution made a part of the report under consideration: —
"*Resolved*, That orders be sent to General Wooster, in case he has no orders to the contrary from General Schuyler, that he immediately return to the batteries erecting in the Highlands, and there leave as many of his troops as the conductors of the work shall think necessary for completing them, and that he repair with the remainder to New York."

[2] A brief, but clear, account of the controversy between Connecticut and Pennsylvania, respecting the lands at Wyoming, is found in the life of Roger Sherman, in Sanderson's Biography of the Signers, &c. It was finally decided, in 1782, in favor of Pennsylvania. Reed's *Life of Reed*, vol. ii. p. 388.

[3] One part of the report was in these words: —
"That it be recommended to said Convention, to establish, at proper distances, posts to be ready to give intelligence to the country, in case of any invasion, or,

stopped, as a constitutional post is now established from New Hampshire to Georgia. *Langdon* seconds the motion.

Willing thinks it is interfering with that line of conduct which we have hitherto prescribed to ourselves; it is going back beyond the year 1763.

Lee. When the Ministry are mutilating our correspondence in England, and our enemies here are corresponding for our ruin, shall we not stop the ministerial post?

Willing looks upon this to be one of the offensive measures which are improper at this time. It will be time enough to throw this aside, when the time comes that we shall throw every thing aside; at present, we don't know but there may be a negotiation.

Dyer. We have already superseded the Act of Parliament effectually.

Deane is for a recommendation to the people to write by the constitutional post; not forbid a man to ride.

S. Adams thinks it a defensive measure; and advising people not to write by it, looks too cunning for me. I am for stopping the correspondence of our enemies.

Langdon. Administration are taking every method to come at our intentions. Why should not we prevent it? *Duane.* I shall vote against it. It may be true that we are come to the time when we are to lay aside all. I think there should be a full representation of the Colonies. North Carolina should be here. *Deane* seconds the motion for postponing it.

Zubly. The necessity of this measure does not appear to me. If we have gone beyond the line of 1763 and of defence, without apparent necessity, it was wrong; if with necessity, right. I look upon the invasion of Canada as a very different thing; I have a right to defend myself against persons who come against me, let them come from whence they will. We, in Georgia, have gained intelligence, by the King's Post, that we could not have got any other way. Some gentlemen think all merit lies in violent and unnecessary measures.

S. Adams. The gentleman's argument would prove that we

by signals, to give alarms in case of danger; and that they confer with the Assembly of Connecticut, and Convention of New Jersey, on the speediest manner of conveying intelligence in such cases, and receiving assistance when necessary."

should let the post go into Boston. *Morton.* Would not this stop the packet? Would it not be ordered to Boston? Does the packet bring any intelligence to us that is of use?

Lee. No intelligence comes to us, but constant intelligence to our enemies. *Stone* thinks it an innocent motion, but is for postponing it, because he is not at present clear. He thinks that the setting up a new post has already put down the old one.

Paine. My opinion was, that the ministerial post will die a natural death; it has been under a languishment a great while; it would be cowardice to issue a decree to kill that which is dying; it brought but one letter last time, and was obliged to retail newspapers to bear its expenses. I am very loth to say that this post shall not pass.

Lee. Is there not a Doctor, Lord North, who can keep this creature alive?

R. R. Livingston. I don't think that Tory letters are sent by the royal post. I consider it rather as a convenience than otherwise; we hear five times a week from New York. The letters, upon our table, advise us to adopt every conciliatory measure, that we may secure the affections of the people of England.

October 10. On the preceding day, the Congress had adopted a resolution, in the following words:—

"That it be recommended to the Convention of New Jersey, that they immediately raise, at the expense of the continent, two battalions, consisting of eight companies each, and each company of sixty-eight privates, officered with one captain, one lieutenant, one ensign, four sergeants, and four corporals."

Who shall have the appointment of the officers, in the two battalions to be raised in New Jersey?

Sherman. Best to leave it to the Provincial Conventions. *Ward* seconds the motion.

Chase. This is persisting in error, in spite of experience; we nave found, by experience, that giving the choice of officers to the people is attended with bad consequences. The French officers are allowed to exceed any in Europe, because a gentleman is hardly entitled to the smiles of the ladies, without serving a campaign. In my Province, we want officers. Gentlemen have recommended persons, from personal friendships, who were not suitable; such friendships will have more weight in the

Colonies. *Dyer.* We must derive all our knowledge from the delegates of that Colony. The representatives at large are as good judges, and would give more satisfaction. You can't raise an army, if you put officers over the men, whom they don't know. It requires time to bring people off from ancient usage. *E. Rutledge.* We don't mean to break in upon what has been done. In our Province we have raised our complement of men in the neighboring Colonies. I am for it, that we may have power to reward merit.

Ward. The motion is intended for a precedent. In the expedition to Carthagena and Canada, the Crown only appointed a lieutenant in my Colony; the men will not enlist. When the Militia Bill was before us, I was against giving the choice to the men. I don't know any man in the Jerseys. *Duane.* A subject of importance; a matter of delicacy; we ought to be all upon a footing; we are to form the grand outlines of an American army; a general regulation. Will such a regulation be salutary? The public good alone will govern me. If we were to set out anew, would the same plan be pursued? It has not been unprecedented in this Congress. Mr. Campbell, Allen, Warner, were promoted here. We ought to insist upon it; we shall be able to regulate an army better. Schuyler and Montgomery would govern my judgment. I would rather take the opinion of General Washington than of any convention. We can turn out the unworthy, and reward merit; the usage is for it. Governors used to make officers, except in Connecticut and Rhode Island. But we can't raise an army! We are then in a deplorable condition indeed. We pay!—can't we appoint, with the advice of our Generals?

Langdon looks upon this as a very extraordinary motion, and big with many mischiefs. *Deane.* It is the people's money, not ours; it will be fatal. We can't set up a sale for offices, like Lord Barrington. *E. Rutledge.* The appointment, hitherto, has been as if the money belonged to particular Provinces, not to the Continent. We can't reward merit; the Governor appointed officers with us.

Ross. My sentiments coincide with those of the gentlemen from New York and Carolina, and would go further and appoint every officer, even an ensign. We have no command of the army. They have different rules and articles. *Jay.* Am of opinion with the gentleman who spoke last. The Union depends much upon breaking down Provincial Conventions; the whole army refused to be mustered by your Muster-Master.

Debate on the State of Trade, continued from Page 457.

October 12. *Report, on Trade*, considered in a committee of the whole.

Lee. It has been moved to bring the debate to one point by putting the question, whether the custom-houses shall be shut up, and the officers discharged from their several functions. This would put New York, North Carolina, the lower Counties, and Georgia, upon the same footing with the other Colonies. I, therefore, move you, that the custom-houses be shut, and the officers discharged; this will remove jealousies and divisions.

Zubly. The measure we are now to consider is extremely interesting. I shall offer my thoughts. If we decide properly, I hope we shall establish our cause; if improperly, we shall overthrow it altogether.

1st Proposition. Trade is important. 2. We must have a reconciliation with Great Britain, or the means of carrying on the war; an unhappy day when we shall . . . A republican government is little better than government of devils. I have been acquainted with it from six years old. We must regulate our trade, so as that a reconciliation be obtained, or we enabled to carry on the war. Can't say, but I do hope for a reconciliation, and that this winter may bring it. I may enjoy my hopes for reconciliation; others may enjoy theirs, that none will take place. A vessel will not go without sails or oars. Wisdom is better than weapons of war. We don't mean to oppose Great Britain, merely for diversion; if it is necessary, that we make war, and that we have the means of it. This Continent ought to know what it is about; the nation don't. We ought to know what they mean to be about; we ought to have intelligence of the designs. King of Prussia and Count Daun marched and countermarched, until they could not impose upon each other any more. Every thing we want for the war is powder and shot. Second thing necessary, that we have arms and ammunition. Third, we must have money; the continental credit must be supported; we must keep up a notion that this paper is good for something; it has not yet a general circulation. The Mississippi scheme, in France, and the South Sea scheme, in England, were written for our learning; a hundred millions fell in one day. Twenty men-of-war may block up the harbor of New York, Delaware River, Chesapeake Bay, the Carolinas, and Georgia. Whether we can raise a navy, is an important question. We may have a navy, and, to carry on the war, we must have a navy. Can we do this without trade? Can we gain intelligence without trade? Can we get powder without trade? Every vessel you send out is thrown away. New England, where the war is, may live without trade; the money circulates there; they may live. Without trade our people must starve; we cannot live; we cannot feed or clothe our people. My resolution was, that I would do and suffer any thing, rather than not be free; but I am resolved not to do impossible things; if we must trade, we must trade with somebody, and with somebody that will trade with us; either with foreigners or Great Britain; if with foreigners, we must either go to them or they must come to us; we can't go to them, if our harbors are shut up. I look upon the trade with foreigners as impracticable. St. Lawrence being open is a supposition. New England people, last war, went to Cape François. Spaniards are too lazy to come to us. If we can't trade with foreigners, we must trade with Great Britain. Is it practicable? will it quit cost? will it do more hurt than good? This is breaking our association. Our people will think we are giving way, and giving all up; they will say, one mischievous man has overset the whole navigation. I speak from principle; it has been said here that the association was made *in terrorem*.

Gadsden seconds Lee's motion, and affirms that we can carry on trade from one end of the continent to the other.

Deane. Custom-house officers discharged! Were they ever in our pay, in our service? Let them stand where they are; let this Congress establish what offices they please; let the others die. I think that all the Colonies ought to be upon a footing; we must have trade. I think we ought to apply abroad; we must have powder and goods; we can't keep our people easy without.

Lee. The gentleman agrees that all ought to be upon a footing. Let him show how this can be done without shutting the custom-houses.

Jay. This should be the last business we undertake. It is like cutting the foot to the shoe, not making a shoe for the foot. Let us establish a system first.

I think we ought to consider the whole, before we come to any resolutions. Now gentlemen have their doubts whether the non-exportation was a good measure. I was, last year, clear against it. Because the enemy have burned Charlestown, would gentlemen have us burn New York? Let us lay every burden as equal on all the shoulders as we can. If Providence or Ministry inflict misfortunes on one, shall we inflict the same on all? I have one arm sore, why should not the other arm be made sore too? But jealousies will arise; are these reasonable? is it politic? We are to consult the general good of all America. Are we to do hurt, to remove unreasonable jealousies? Because Ministry have imposed hardships on one, shall we impose the same on all? It is not from affection to New York that I speak. If a man has lost his teeth, on one side of his jaws, shall he pull out the teeth from the other, that both sides may be upon a footing? Is it not realizing the quarrel of the belly and the members? The other Colonies may avail themselves of the custom-houses in the exempted Colonies.

Lee. All must bear a proportional share of the Continental expense. Will the exempted Colonies take upon themselves the whole expense? Virginia pays a sixth part, the lower Counties an eightieth; yet the lower counties may trade, Virginia not. The gentleman exercised an abundance of wit to show the unreasonableness of jealousies. If this ministerial bait is swallowed by America, another will be thrown out.

Jay. Why should not New York make money, and New Jersey not? One Colony can clothe them.

McKean. I have four reasons for putting the favored Colonies upon a footing with the rest. 1. To disappoint the ministry; their design was insidious. 2. I would not have it believed by ministry, or other Colonies, that those Colonies had less virtue than others. 3. I have a reconciliation in view; it would be in the power of those Colonies, it might become their interest, to prolong the war. 4. I believe Parliament has done, or will do it for us, that is, put us on the same footing. I would choose that the exempted Colonies should have the honor of it; not clear that this is the best way of putting them upon a footing.

If we should be successful in Canada, I would be for opening our trade to some places in Great Britain, Jamaica, &c.

J. Rutledge wonders that a subject so clear has taken up so much time. I was for a general non-exportation. Is it not surprising that there should so soon be a motion for breaking the Association? We have been reproached for our breach of faith in breaking the non-importation. I have the best authority to say that if we had abided by a former non-importation we should have had redress. We may be obliged hereafter to break the Association; but why should we break it before we feel it? I expected the delegates from the exempted Colonies would have moved to be put upon the same footing. Don't like shutting the custom-houses and discharging the officers, but moves that the resolve be, that people in New York, North Carolina, and lower Counties don't apply to the custom-house.

Zubly. Georgia is settled along Savannah River, two hundred miles in extent, and one hundred miles the other way. I look upon it, the Association altogether will be the ruin of the cause. We have ten thousand fighting Indians near us. Carolina has already smuggled goods from Georgia.

Chase. I will undertake to prove that if the reverend gentleman's positions are true, and his advice followed, we shall all be made slaves. If he speaks the opinion of Georgia, I sincerely lament that they ever appeared in Congress. They cannot, they will not comply! Why did they come here? Sir, we are deceived! Sir, we are abused! Why do they come here? I want to know why their Provincial Congress came to such resolutions. Did they come here to ruin America? The gentleman's advice will bring destruction upon all North America. I am for the resolution upon the table. There will be jealousies, if New York and the other exempted Colonies are not put upon a footing. It is not any great advantage to the exempted Colonies. What can they export, that will not be serviceable to Great Britain and the West Indies? The exports of North Carolina are of vast importance to Great Britain. If these Colonies are in rebellion, will not their effects be confiscated and seized even upon the ocean? Arms and ammunition must be obtained by what is called smuggling. I doubt not we shall have the supply. Leaving open New York &c. will prevent our getting arms and ammunition.

Houston. Where the protection of this room did not extend, I would not sit very tamely. *Chase.* I think the gentleman ought not to take offence at his brother delegate.

Wythe agrees with the gentleman from New York that we don't proceed regularly. The safety of America depends essentially on a union of the people in it. Can we think that union will be preserved if four Colonies are exempted? When New York Assembly did not approve the proceedings of the Congress, it was not only murmured at, but lamented as a defection from the public cause. When Attica was invaded by the Lacedemonians, Pericles ordered an estate to be ravaged and laid waste, because he thought it would be exempted by the Spartan King. Nothing was ever more unhappily applied than the fable of the stomach and the limbs.

Sherman. Another argument for putting . . .

On Trade, continued.

October 13. *R. Livingston* hopes the whole matter will be put off. Is willing, as it seems the general sense, that all should be put upon a footing.

Gadsden hopes it will not be put off. South Carolina will be in the utmost confusion if this matter is not decided. Let the Continent determine.

Stone can see no particular inconvenience to Carolina; seconds the motion of Mr. Livingston, for postponing the question, and gives his reasons. The Powder Committee must take clearances. If they are allowed to take clearances, and no other, then whenever they take a clearance, it will be known that it is for powder, and the vessel will be watched.

Lee. I see very clearly that the best time for putting a question is when it is best understood. That time is the present. As to powder, time may be allowed for the Committee to clear vessels.

J. Rutledge thinks this motion extraordinary; this subject has been under consideration three weeks. It is really trifling. The Committee may have time allowed to clear vessels for powder; but I had rather the Continent should run the risk of sending vessels without clearances. What confusion would ensue, if Congress should break up without any resolution of this sort! The motion seems intended to defeat the resolution entirely. Those who are against it are for postponing.

Jay. We have complied with the restraining act. The question is, whether we shall have trade or not? and this is to introduce a most destructive scheme, a scheme which will drive away all your sailors, and lay up all your ships to rot at the wharves.

Debate continued.

October 20. *Deane.* Their plunder only afforded one meal of fresh meat for the privates; all the rest was reserved for the officers, and their friends among the inhabitants. I would have traders prohibited from importing unnecessary articles, and from exporting live stock, except horses.

Gadsden. If we give one leave, when there are one hundred who have an equal right, it will occasion jealousy. Let each Colony export to the amount of so many thousand pounds, and no more.

Chase. We have letters from Guadaloupe, Martinique, and the Havana, that they will supply us with powder for tobacco.

Gadsden. France and Spain would be glad to see Great Britain despotic in America. Our being in a better state than their Colonies occasions complaints among them, insurrections and rebellions. But these powers would be glad we were an independent State.

Chase. The proposition is for exporting for a special purpose, — importing powder. I would not permit our cash to go for rum. Live stock is an inconsiderable part of our cargoes. I don't wish to intermix any thing in this debate. I would restrain the merchant from importing any thing but powder, &c. Molasses was an article of importance in the trade of the Northern Colonies. But now they can't carry on the African trade, and the rum is pernicious. If you give a latitude for any thing but arms and ammunition, we shan't agree what articles are necessary and what unnecessary. Each Colony should carry on this trade, not individuals. I would not limit the quantity of ammunition to be imported by each Colony. A hundred tons a Colony would supply the West Indies, mediately all the army and navy. Twenty tons would be a considerable adventure for a Colony. Debts are due from the British West India Islands to the inhabitants of these Colonies. I am not for permitting vessels to go in ballast and fetch cash; I wish to import cash from every place as much as possible.

Deane. It cannot be done with secrecy or despatch. I rather think it would be as well to leave it to traders.

Zubly. It is of great weight that there be no favorites.

Dyer. There will be such continual applications to the Assemblies by their friends among the traders, it will open a complete exportation; it would completely supply the West Indies.

Jay. We have more to expect from the enterprise, activity and industry of private adventurers, than from the lukewarmness of assemblies. We want French woollens, Dutch worsteds, duck for tents, German steel, &c. Public virtue is not so active as private love of gain. Shall we shut the door against private enterprise?

Lee. The gentleman may move for those things as exceptions to the general rule.

Randolph. We are making laws contradictory in terms. We say nobody shall export, and yet somebody shall. Against all rule.

Lee. It is a common rule in making laws, to make a rule and then make a proviso for special cases.

Dyer. The rule and the proviso are passed at once in the same act, though. If I give my voice for an unconditional proposition, what security have I that the condition or proviso will be added afterwards? The greatest impropriety in the world.

Chase. Both sides are right; and it arises from this, that one proposition is to be made public, and the other kept secret. We have very little confidence in each other.

Zubly. If half the law is to be public and the other half secret, will not half the people be governed by one half and the other half by the other? Will they not clash?

Jay. Lest your produce fall into the hands of your enemies, you publish a law that none go from the Continent; yet to get powder, we keep a secret law that produce may be exported. Then come the wrangles among the people. A vessel is seen loading, — a fellow runs to the committee.

Lee. The inconvenience may arise in some measure; but will not the people be quieted by the authority of the Conventions? If we give public notice, our enemies will be more active to intercept us. On the contrary, the people may be quieted by the committees of safety.

Wythe. The only persons who can be affected by this resolution, are those, who, on the other side of the water, will be called smugglers. Consider the danger these smugglers will run; liable to seizure by custom-house officers, by men of war at sea, and by custom-house officers in the port they go to. What can they bring? Cash, powder, or foreign manufactures? Can't see the least reason for restraining our trade, as little can be carried on. My opinion is, we had better open our trade altogether. It has long been my opinion, and I have heard no arguments against it.

Zubly. We can't do without trade. To be or not to be is too trifling a question for many gentlemen. All that wise men can do among many difficulties, is to choose the least.

Stone. Cannot agree to the propositions made by the gentleman from Maryland, — not for binding the people closer than they are bound already, — the proposition is the same with that which was made, that our vessels should be stopped, and foreigners invited to come here for our produce and protect their own trade. This appears to be a destructive system. It was a laborious task to get America into a general non-exportation to Great Britain, Ireland, and West Indies, — shall we now combine with Britain to distress our people in their trade, more than by the Association? People have looked up to this, and are unwilling to go further. The restraining bill, a most cruel, unjust, unconstitutional act; yet we are going to greater cruelties than they. We are all to be in the same circumstances of poverty and distress. Will the West Indies be supplied by a circuitous trade? I think not. How can the West Indies get supplies from Holland, France, or Spain? The whole produce will not be carried; it is said the men of war will take their produce; this argument will operate against exporting for powder. The army will be supplied; it is impossible to prevent their getting supplies, at least of bread. It appears to me this is not a temporary expedient, but will have a perpetual influence. It is a destructive, ruinous expedient, and our people never will bear it. Under the faith that your ports would be kept open to foreigners, people have made contracts with foreigners. You are giving a sanction to the Act of Parliament, and going further. Under such a regulation we never can exist. I would export produce to foreign West Indies, or anywhere for powder; but the mode of doing it will defeat it. The Assemblies never will turn merchants successfully. I would have private adventurers give bond to return powder, or the produce itself.

Chase. Differs from his colleague; a different proposition from that for restraining our people and inviting foreigners. This proposition invites your people. If you carry on your exports, without the protection of a foreign power you destroy America. If you stop provisions and not other produce, you create a jealousy. If you export provisions and not other produce, you create a jealousy. Don't think the risk will prevent supplies to the West India Islands.

We must prevent them lumber as well as provisions; great quantities will be exported, notwithstanding the risk. All the fleet of Britain cannot stop our trade; we can carry it all on. We must starve the West India Islands, and prevent them exporting their produce to Great Britain. There will be great quantities of provisions and lumber exported. It will enhance the expense, to carry them to Spain or France first, and thence to the West Indies; but the price will be such that the West Indies will get them. I hold it clearly, we can do without trade; this country produces all the necessaries, many of the conveniences, and some of the superfluities, of life. We can't grow rich; our provisions will be cheap; we can maintain our army and our poor. We shan't lose our sailors; the fishermen will serve in another capacity. We must defend the lakes and cities. Merchants will not grow rich; there is the rub. I have too good an opinion of the virtue of our people, to suppose they will grumble. If we drop our commercial system of opposition, we are undone; we must fail; we must give up the profits of trade, or lose our liberties. Let the door of reconciliation be once shut, I would trade with foreign powers, and apply to them for protection. Leave your ports open, and every man that can, will adventure; the risk will not prevent it.

It was strongly contended, at the first Congress, that trade should be stopped to all the world; that all remittances should cease. You would have saved a civil war, if you had; but it could not be carried; the gentlemen from South Carolina could not prevail to stop our exports to Britain, Ireland, and West Indies. Our vessels will all be liable to seizure; our trade must be a smuggling trade. Yet we can trade considerably, and many vessels will escape. No vessel can take a clearance. Many vessels will go out, unless you restrain them; all America is in suspense; the common sense of the people has pointed out this measure; they have stopped their vessels.

Lee. We possess a fine climate and a fertile soil; wood, iron, sheep, &c. We make eleven or twelve hundred thousand pounds' worth of provisions more than is necessary for our own consumption. Don't think it necessary to combat the opinion of some gentlemen, that we cannot live without trade. Money has debauched States, as well as individuals, but I hope its influence will not prevail over America against her rights and dearest interests. We shall distress the West Indies, so as immediately to quit coin for corn. Four millions go yearly from the West Indies to Britain, and a million at least returns. If our provisions go from these shores, then they will go where the best price is to be had. West Indies and our enemies will get them. If it was not proper a year ago, it may be now; this proposition is not perpetual. When we get powder, we may make ourselves strong by sea, and carry on trade.

J. Rutledge. A question of the greatest magnitude that has come before this Congress. If it is necessary to do without trade, our constituents will submit to it. The army will be supplied with flour from England, where it is now cheaper than here; but they would be supplied here, if they were to demand it upon pain of destroying our towns. West Indies are supplied, and have laid up stores, and some of them have been raising provisions on their own lands. It will bear hard upon the farmer, as well as the merchant. Don't think the reasons the same now as last year; it would then have destroyed the linen manufactory and the West Indies; but now they have had notice of it, they are prepared against it.

Same Subject continued.

October 21. *Zubly.* We can't do without powder, intelligence, drugs. Georgia must have an Indian war, if they can't supply the Indians. The Creeks and Cherokees are in our Province; we must have Indian trade. Four millions have been spent in six months. We have been successful, but we have gained little; all the power of Great Britain, it is true, has gained very little. New England has been at great expense, so has New York; Pennsylvania has spent a hundred thousand pounds of their money, to fortify their river; Virginia as much; North Carolina a great deal; South Carolina have issued a million. Eighteen millions of dollars is an enormous sum of money; whenever your money fails, you fail too. We are to pay six millions now, twelve millions more presently, and have no trade. I would bear the character of a madman, or that of an emissary of Lord North, rather than believe it possible to pay eighteen millions of dollars without trade. Can we make bricks without straw? We can live upon acorns; but will we?

Wythe. The rule, that the question should be put upon the last motion that is made and seconded, is productive of great confusion in our debates; six or seven motions at once. Commerce, whether we consider it in an economical, a moral, or political light, appears to be a great good; civility and charity, as well as knowledge, are promoted by it. The *auri sacra fames* is a fine subject for philosophers and orators to display themselves upon; but the abuse of a thing is not an argument against it. If the gentleman was possessed of the philosopher's stone, or Fortunatus's cap, would he not oblige the continent with the use of it? Why should not America have a navy? No maritime power near the sea-coast can be safe without it. It is no chimera. The Romans suddenly built one in their Carthaginian war. Why may not we lay a foundation for it? We abound with firs, iron ore, tar, pitch, turpentine; we have all the materials for construction of a navy. No country exceeds us in felicity of climate or fertility of soil. America is one of the wings upon which the British eagle has soared to the skies. I am sanguine and enthusiastical enough to wish and to hope that it will be sung, that America *inter nubila condit.*

British navy will never be able to effect our destruction. Before the days of Minos, nations round the Archipelago carried on piratical wars The Moors carry on such wars now, but the pillars of Hercules are their *ne plus ultra*. We are too far off for Britain to carry on a piratical war. We shall, sometime or other, rise superior to all the difficulties they may throw in our way. I wont say, there is none that doeth good in Britain, no, not one; but I will say, she has not righteous persons enough to save their State. They hold those things honorable which please them, and those for just which profit them. I know of no instance where a Colony has revolted, and a foreign nation has interposed to subdue them; but many of the contrary. If France and Spain should furnish ships and soldiers, England must pay them. Where are her finances? Why should we divert our people from commerce, and banish our seamen? Our petition may be declared to be received graciously, and promised to be laid before Parliament, but we can expect no success from it. Have they ever condescended to take notice of you? Rapine, depopulation, burning, murder. Turn your eyes to Concord, Lexington, Charlestown, Bristol, New York; there you see the character of Ministry and Parliament. We shall distress our enemies by stopping trade; granted. But how will the small quantities we shall be able to export supply our enemies? Tricks may be practised. If desire of gain prevails with merchants, so does caution against risks.

Gadsden. I wish we could keep to a point. I have heard the two gentlemen with a great deal of pleasure. I have argued for opening our ports, but am for shutting them until we hear the event of our petition to the King, and longer until the Congress shall determine otherwise. I am for a navy, too, and I think that shutting our ports for a time will help us to a navy. If we leave our ports open, warm men will have their ships seized, and moderate ones will be favored.

Lee. When you hoist out a glimmering of hope that the people are to be furnished from abroad, you give a check to our own manufactures. People are now everywhere attending to corn and sheep and cotton and linen.

Chase. A glove has been offered by the gentleman from Georgia, and I beg leave to discharge my promise to that gentleman, to answer his arguments. My position was this; that the gentleman's system would end in the total destruction of American liberty. I never shall dispute self-evident propositions.

The present state of things requires reconciliation or means to carry on war. Intelligence we must have; we must have powder and shot; we must support the credit of our money. You must have a navy to carry on the war. You can't have a navy says the gentleman. What is the consequence? I say, that we must submit. Great Britain, with twenty ships, can destroy all our trade, and ravage our sea-coast; can block up all your harbors, prevent your getting powder. What is the consequence? That we should submit. You can't trade with nobody; you must trade with somebody; you can't trade with anybody but Great Britain, therefore, I say, we must submit. We can't trade with foreigners, the gentleman said. The whole train of his reasoning proved that we must break our whole association, as to exports and imports. If we trade with Great Britain, will she furnish us with powder and arms? Our exports are about three millions; would Britain permit us to export to her, and receive cash in return? It would impoverish and ruin Great Britain. They will never permit a trade on our side, without a trade on theirs. Gentlemen from New York would not permit tobacco and naval stores to be sent to Great Britain; nothing that will support their naval power or revenue. But will not this break the Union? Would three Colonies stop their staple when the other Colonies exported theirs? Fifteen hundred seamen are employed by the tobacco Colonies — one hundred and twenty-five sail of British ships; but you may drop your staple, your tobacco; but it is difficult to alter old habits. We have a great number of female slaves that are best employed about tobacco. North Carolina cannot, will not, give up their staple. The gentleman from Georgia was for trading with Great Britain and all the world. He says we can't trade with any nation but Britain, therefore we must trade with Britain alone. What trade shall we have, if we exclude Britain, Ireland, West Indies, British and foreign? Eastern Provinces might carry it on with a small fleet, if their harbors were fortified. Southern Colonies cannot. Eastern Colonies can't carry on their trade to that extent, without a naval power to protect them, not only on the coast, but on the ocean, and to the port of their destination.

The same force that would assist the Eastern Colonies, would be of little service to us in summer time; it must be a small, narrow, and limited trade.

The best instrument we have, is our opposition by commerce. If we take into consideration Great Britain in all her glory; Commons voted eighteen, twenty millions last war; eighty thousand seamen, from her trade alone; her strength is all artificial, from her trade alone. Imports from Great Britain to the United Colonies are three millions per annum; fifteen millions to all the world; one fifth; three quarters is British manufactures. A thousand British vessels are employed in American trade; twelve thousand sailors; all out of employ. What a stroke! I don't take into view Ireland or West Indies. Colonies generally indebted about one year's importation; the revenue of tobacco alone half a million, if paid. North Britain enter less than the quantity, and don't pay what they ought; it employs a great number of manufacturers; reëxported abroad, is a million; it is more. Eighty thousand hogsheads are reëxported, and it pays British debts. The reëxport employs ships, sailors, freight, commissions, insurance.

Ireland; the flax seed, forty thousand pounds sterling. Linen brought, two million one hundred and fifty thousand pounds from Ireland to England; yards, two hundred thousand. Ireland can raise some flax seed, but not much.

West Indies. Glover, Burke, and other authors. They depend for Indian corn and provisions and lumber, and they depend upon us for a great part of the consumption of their produce. Indian corn and fish are not to be had, but from the Colonies, except pilchards and herrings. Jamaica can best provide for her wants, but not entirely. Ireland can send them beef and butter, but no grain. Britain can send them wheat, oats; not corn, without which they cannot do.

Stop rum and sugar, how do you affect the revenue and the trade?

They must relax the Navigation Act, to enable foreign nations to supply the West Indies. This is dangerous, as it would force open a trade between foreigners and them.

Britain can never support a war with us, at the loss of such a valuable trade. African trade dependent upon the West India trade; seven hundred thousand pounds.

Twenty-five thousand hogsheads of sugar are imported directly into these Colonies, and as much more, from Britain, manufactured. Jamaica alone takes one hundred and fifty thousand pounds sterling of our produce.

National debt, one hundred and forty millions; ten millions, the peace establishment; twenty millions, the whole current cash of the nation. Blackstone. I never read anybody that better understood the subject. For the state of the revenue he calculates the taxes of Ireland and England; taxes of Britain, perpetual and annual; funds, three, the aggregate, general, and South Sea; taxes, upon every article of luxuries and necessaries. These funds are mortgaged, for the civil list, eight hundred thousand pounds, as well as the interest of the debt.

Debate continued.

October 27. *R. R. Livingston.* Clothing will rise, though provisions will fall; laborers will be discharged; one quarter part of Rhode Island, New York, and Pennsylvania, depend upon trade, as merchants, shopkeepers, shipwrights, blockmakers, riggers, smiths, &c. &c.: the six northern Colonies must raise nine millions of dollars to support the poor. This vote will stop our trade for fourteen months, although it professes to do it only to the 20th of March; for the winter, when the men of war cannot cruise upon the coast, is the only time that we can trade. Wealthy merchants and moneyed men cannot get the interest of money. More virtue is expected from our people, than any people ever had. The low countries did not reason as we do about speculative opinions, but they felt the oppression for a long course of years, rich and poor.

Zubly. Concludes that the sense and bent of the people are against stopping trade, by the eagerness with which they exported before the 10th of September. We can't get intelligence without trade. All that are supported by trade, must be out of business. Every argument which shews that our association will materially affect the trade of Great Britain, will shew that we must be affected too, by a stoppage of our trade. Great Britain has many resources. I have bought two barrels of rice in Carolina for fifteen shillings, and negro cloth was three shillings instead of eighteen pence.

The West Indies will get supplies to keep soul and body together; the ingenious Dutchmen will smuggle some Indian corn from America. Is it right to starve one man because I have quarrelled with another? I have a great scruple whether it is just or prudent. In December, 1776, we shall owe between twenty and thirty millions of money.

J. Rutledge. Am for adhering to the Association, and going no further; the non export *in terrorem*, and generally agreed; the consequences will be dreadful if we ruin the merchants. Will not the army be supplied if vessels go from one Province to another? We may pass a resolution that no live stock shall be exported.

October 30. Monday. *Ross.*[1] We can't get seamen to man four vessels. We could not get seamen to man our boats, our galleys. *Wythe, Nelson, and Lee*, for fitting out four ships.

[1] *Extract from the Journals:* —

"The Committee appointed to prepare an estimate, and to fit out the vessels, brought in their report, which being taken into consideration, &c.

"*Resolved*, That two more vessels be fitted out with all expedition, &c."

Extract from the Journals.

1776. February 16. Friday.

"Agreeable to the order of the day, the Congress resolved itself into a committee of the whole, to take into consideration the propriety of opening the ports, and the restrictions and regulations of the trade of these Colonies after the first of March next."

(This discussion was continued from time to time until the sixth of April, when the Congress came in to sundry resolutions taking off the restrictions on trade.)

In Committee of the Whole.

Can't we oblige Britain to keep a navy on foot, the expense of which will be double to what they will take from us? I have heard of bullion Spanish flotas being stopped, lest they should be taken, but perishable commodities never were stopped. Open your ports to foreigners; your trade will become of so much consequence that foreigners will protect you.

Wilson. A gentleman from Massachusetts thinks that a middle way should be taken; that trade should be opened for some articles, and to some places, but not for all things and to all places. I think the merchants ought to judge for themselves of the danger and risk. We should be blamed if we did not leave it to them. I differ from the gentleman of Massachusetts. Trade ought in war to be carried on with greater vigor. By what means did Britain carry on their triumphs last war? the United Provinces their war against Spain? If we determine that our ports shall not be opened, our vessels abroad will not return. Our seamen are all abroad; will not return unless we open our trade. I am afraid it will be necessary to invite foreigners to trade with us, although we lose a great advantage, that of trading in our own bottoms.

Sherman. I fear we shall maintain the armies of our enemies at our own expense with provisions. We can't carry on a beneficial trade, as our enemies will take our ships. A treaty with a foreign power is necessary, before we open our trade, to protect it.

Harrison. We have hobbled on under a fatal attachment to Great Britain. I felt it as much as any man, but I feel a stronger to my country.

Wythe. The ports will be open the 1st March. The question is whether we shall shut them up. *Fæce Romuli non Republicâ Platonis.* Americans will hardly live without trade. It is said our trade will be of no advantage to us, because our vessels will be taken, our enemies will be supplied, the West Indies will be supplied at our expense. This is too true, unless we can provide a remedy. Our Virginia Convention have resolved, that our ports be opened to all nations that will trade with us, except Great Britain, Ireland, and West Indies. If the inclination of the people should become universal to trade, we must open our ports. Merchants will not export our produce, unless they get a profit.

We might get some of our produce to market, by authorizing adventurers to arm themselves, and giving letters of marque, make reprisals. 2d. By inviting foreign powers to make treaties of commerce with us.

But other things are to be considered, before such a measure is adopted; in what character shall we treat? — as subjects of Great Britain, — as rebels? Why should we be so fond of calling ourselves dutiful subjects? If we should offer our trade to the Court of France, would they take notice of it any more than if Bristol or Liverpool should offer theirs, while we profess to be subjects? No. Wc must declare ourselves a free people. If we were to tell them, that after a season, we would return to our subjection to Great Britain, would not a foreign Court wish to have something permanent? We should encourage our fleet. I am convinced that our fleet may become as formidable as we wish to make it. Moves a resolution.

Resolved, That the Committee of Secret Correspondence be directed to lay their letters before this Congress.

Resolved, That be a committee to prepare a draught of firm confederation, to be reported as soon as may be to this Congress, to be considered and digested and recommended to the several Assemblies and Conventions of these United Colonies, to be by them adopted, ratified, and confirmed.

Resolved, That it be recommended to the several Assemblies, Conventions, Councils of Safety, and Committees of Correspondence and Inspection, that they use their utmost endeavors, by all reasonable means, to promote the culture of flax, hemp, and cotton, and the growth of wool, in these United Colonies.[1]

Resolved, That it be recommended to the Assemblies, Conventions, and Councils of Safety, that they take the earliest measures for erecting, in each and every Colony, a society for the encouragement of agriculture, arts, manufactures, and commerce; and that a correspondence be maintained between such societies, that the numerous natural advantages of this country, for supporting its inhabitants, may not be neglected.

Resolved, That it be recommended to the said Assemblies, Conventions, and Councils of Safety, that they consider of ways and means of introducing the manufactures of duck and sailcloth[2] into such Colonies where they are not now understood, and of increasing and promoting them where they are.

Resolved, That   be a committee to receive all plans and proposals for encouraging and improving the agriculture, arts, manufactures, and commerce, both foreign and domestic, of America, to correspond with the several Assemblies, Conventions, Councils, and Committees of Safety, Committees of Correspondence and of Observation, in these United Colonies, upon these interesting subjects.

That these be published.

1776. March 1.[3] How is the interest of France and Spain affected, by the dispute between Britain and the Colonies?

[1] The first three of these resolutions are found, with only verbal amendments, in the Journals of the 21st of March. They were drawn, presented, and carried through by Mr. Adams, as may be seen in the Extract from the Autobiography, that follows these debates.

[2] In the resolutions, as adopted, the words "and steel," are here inserted.

[3] The three entries, which follow, seem to be notes of speeches made by the writer, at this period, in Congress, although it is not easy to decide precisely upon the form of the question proposed.

Is it the interest of France to stand neuter, to join with Britain, or to join with the Colonies? Is it not her interest to dismember the British empire? Will her dominions be safe, if Britain and America remain connected? Can she preserve her possessions in the West Indies? She has, in the West Indies, Martinico, Guadaloupe, and one half of Hispaniola. In case a reconciliation should take place between Britain and America, and a war should break out between Britain and France, would not all her islands be taken from her in six months? The Colonies are now much more warlike and powerful than they were during the last war. A martial spirit has seized all the Colonies. They are much improved in skill and discipline; they have now a large standing army; they have many good officers; they abound in provisions; they are in the neighborhood of the West Indies. A British fleet and army, united with an American fleet and army, and supplied with provisions and other necessaries from America, might conquer all the French Islands in the West Indies in six months, and a little more time than that would be required to destroy all their marine and commerce.

4. Monday. Resentment is a passion implanted by nature for the preservation of the individual. Injury is the object which excites it. Injustice, wrong, injury, excite the feeling of resentment as naturally and necessarily as frost and ice excite the feeling of cold, as fire excites heat, and as both excite pain. A man may have the faculty of concealing his resentment, or suppressing it, but he must and ought to feel it; nay, he ought to indulge it, to cultivate it; it is a duty. His person, his property, his liberty, his reputation, are not safe without it. He ought, for his own security and honor, and for the public good, to punish those who injure him, unless they repent, and then he should forgive, having satisfaction and compensation. Revenge is unlawful. It is the same with communities; they ought to resent and to punish.

Is any assistance attainable from France?

What connection may we safely form with her?

1. No political connection. Submit to none of her authority; receive no governors or officers from her. 2. No military connection. Receive no troops from her. 3. Only a commercial connection; that is, make a treaty to receive her ships into our

ports; let her engage to receive our ships into her ports; furnish us with arms, cannon, saltpetre, powder, duck, steel.

Whereas the present state of America, and the cruel efforts of our enemies, render the most perfect and cordial union of the Colonies, and the utmost exertions of their strength, necessary for the preservation and establishment of their liberties, therefore,

Resolved, That it be recommended to the several Assemblies and Conventions of these United Colonies, who have limited the powers of their delegates in this Congress, by any express instructions, that they repeal or suspend those instructions for a certain time, that this Congress may have power, without any unnecessary obstruction or embarrassment, to concert, direct, and order such further measures as may seem to them necessary for the defence and preservation, support and establishment of right and liberty in these Colonies.[1]

Extract from the Journals of Congress, for Friday, 10 *May,* 1776.

Congress resumed the consideration of the resolution reported from the Committee of the Whole, and the same was agreed to, as follows: —

"*Resolved*, That it be recommended to the respective Assemblies and Conventions of the United Colonies, where no government sufficient to the exigencies of their affairs hath been hitherto established, to adopt such government as shall, in the opinion of the representatives of the people, best conduce to the happiness and safety of their constituents in particular, and America in general.

"*Resolved*, That a committee of three be appointed to prepare a preamble to the foregoing resolution.

"The members chosen, Mr. J. Adams, Mr. Rutledge, and Mr. R. H. Lee."

A significant form of preamble was accordingly reported on Wednesday, the 15th of May, debated, and adopted. The following remarks were made in the course of the discussion: —

Mr. Duane moves that the delegation from New York might be read.

When we were invited by Massachusetts Bay to the first Congress, an objection was made to binding ourselves by votes of Congress. Congress ought not to determine a point of this

[1] This is perhaps the first draught of the well known motion made in Committee of the Whole, on the sixth of May, which was reported to the House, on the tenth, in the shape in which it appears extracted from the Journal of that day.

sort about instituting government. What is it to Congress how justice is administered? You have no right to pass the resolution, any more than Parliament has. How does it appear that no favorable answer is likely to be given to our petitions? Every account of foreign aid is accompanied with an account of commissioners. Why all this haste? why this urging? why this driving? Disputes about independence are in all the Colonies. What is this owing to but our indiscretion? I shall take the liberty of informing my constituents that I have not been guilty of a breach of trust. I do protest against this piece of mechanism, this preamble. If the facts in this preamble should prove to be true, there will not be one voice against independence. I suppose the votes have been numbered, and there is to be a majority.

McKean construes the instructions from New York as Mr. Sherman does, and thinks this measure the best to procure harmony with Great Britain. There are now two governments in direct opposition to each other. Don't doubt that foreign mercenaries are coming to destroy us. I do think we shall lose our liberties, properties, and lives too, if we do not take this step.

S. Adams. We have been favored with a reading of the instructions from New York; I am glad of it. The first object of that Colony is no doubt the establishment of their rights. Our petitions have not been heard, yet answered with fleets and armies, and are to be answered with myrmidons from abroad. The gentleman from New York, Mr. Duane, has not objected to the preamble, but this, that he has not a right to vote for it. We cannot go upon stronger reasons than that the King has thrown us out of his protection. Why should we support governments under his authority? I wonder that people have conducted so well as they have.

Mr. Wilson. Was not present in Congress when the resolution passed, to which this preamble is proposed. I was present, and one of the committee who reported the advice to Massachusetts Bay. New Hampshire, Carolina, and Virginia, had the same advice, and with my hearty concurrence.

The claim of Parliament will meet with resistance to the last extremity. Those Colonies were royal governments; they could not subsist without some government. A maxim, that all government originates from the people. We are the servants of the people, sent here to act under a delegated authority. If we exceed it, voluntarily, we deserve neither excuse nor justification. Some have been put under restraints by their constituents; they cannot vote without transgressing this line. Suppose they should hereafter be called to an account for it. This Province has not, by any public act, authorized us to vote upon this question; this Province has done much and asked little from this Congress; the Assembly, largely increased, will (not) meet till next Monday. Will the cause suffer much, if this preamble is not published at this time? if the resolve is published without the preamble? The preamble contains a reflection upon the conduct of some people in America. It was equally irreconcilable to good conscience, nine months ago, to take the oaths of allegiance, as it is now. Two respectable members, last February, took the oath of allegiance in our Assembly. Why should we expose any gentlemen to such an invidious reflection? In Magna Charta there is a clause which authorizes the people to seize the King's castles and oppose his arms when he exceeds his duty.

In this Province, if that preamble passes, there will be an immediate dissolution of every kind of authority; the people will be instantly in a state of nature. Why then precipitate this measure? Before we are prepared to build the new house, why should we pull down the old one, and expose ourselves to all the inclemencies of the season?

R. H. Lee. Most of the arguments apply to the resolve, not to the preamble.

CONFEDERATION.

On the eleventh of June, 1776, Congress voted that a committee should be appointed to prepare and report a plan of confederation for the Colonies. The next day, it was decided that the committee should consist of one member from each Colony. The following persons were appointed: — Mr. Bartlett, Mr. S. Adams, Mr. Hopkins, Mr. Sherman, Mr. R. R. Livingston, Mr. Dickinson, Mr. McKean, Mr. Stone, Mr. Nelson, Mr. Hewes, Mr. E. Rutledge and Mr. Gwinnett.

To whom Mr. Hopkinson was added on the 28th.

This committee reported on Friday the 12th of July, a draught, consisting of twenty articles. On Monday, the 22d, the Congress resolved itself into a committee of the whole to take the report into consideration, which continued from day to day to debate it until Tuesday the 20th of August, when the amended form was reported back to the House. It was laid aside until the 8th of April, 1777, when the articles were again taken up, and discussed until the 15th of November, at which time, having been reduced to thirteen, they were finally adopted.

The following discussions all took place in committee of the whole, upon the original draught of twenty articles. They embrace the main points upon which there was a marked difference of opinion: the western territories, the Indians, representation, and taxation.

In Committee of the Whole.

1776. July 25. Article 14 of the confederation.[1] Terms in this Article equivocal and indefinite.

Jefferson. The limits of the Southern Colonies are fixed. Moves an amendment, that all purchases of lands, not within the boundaries of any Colony, shall be made by Congress of the Indians in a great Council.

Sherman seconds the motion.

[1] This, in the first draught, reads as follows: "No purchases of lands, hereafter to be made of the Indians, by Colonies or private persons, before the limits of the Colonies are ascertained, to be valid. All purchases of lands not included within those limits, where ascertained, to be made by contracts between the United States assembled, or by persons for that purpose authorized by them and the great councils of the Indians, for the general benefit of all the United Colonies."

Chase. The intention of this Article is very obvious and plain. The Article appears to me to be right, and the amendment wrong. It is the intention of some gentlemen to limit the boundaries of particular States. No Colony has a right to go to the South Sea; they never had; they can't have. It would not be safe to the rest. It would be destructive to her sisters and to herself.[1]

Article 15.[2] *Jefferson.* What are reasonable limits? What security have we, that the Congress will not curtail the present settlements of the States? I have no doubt that the Colonies will limit themselves.

Wilson. Every gentleman has heard much of claims to the South Sea. They are extravagant. The grants were made upon mistakes. They were ignorant of the Geography. They thought the South Sea within one hundred miles of the Atlantic Ocean. It was not conceived that they extended three thousand miles. Lord Camden considers the claims to the South Sea, as what never can be reduced to practice. Pennsylvania has no right to interfere in those claims, but she has a right to say, that she will not confederate unless those claims are cut off. I wish the Colonies themselves would cut off those claims.[3]

Article 16.[4] *Chase* moves for the word *deputies*, instead of *delegates*, because the members of the Maryland Convention are called delegates, and he would have a distinction. *Answer.* In other Colonies the reverse is true. The members of the House are called deputies.[5]

1 This article was stricken out.

2 "When the boundaries of any Colony shall be ascertained by agreement, or in the manner hereinafter directed, all the other Colonies shall guarantee to such Colony the full and peaceable possession of, and the free and entire jurisdiction in, and over the territory included within such boundaries."

3 The article was stricken out.

4 "For the more convenient management of the general interests of the United States, delegates should be annually appointed in such manner as the Legislature of each Colony shall direct, to meet at the city of Philadelphia, in the Colony of Pennsylvania, until otherwise ordered by the United States assembled; which meeting shall be on the first Monday of November in every year, with a power reserved to those who appointed the said delegates, respectively, to re-call them, or any of them, at any time within the year, and to send new delegates in their stead for the remainder of the year. Each Colony shall support its own delegates in a meeting of the States, and while they act as members of the council of State, hereinafter mentioned."

5 This motion did not succeed.

Jefferson. Objects to the first of November. *Dr. Hall* moves for May, for the time to meet. *Jefferson* thinks that Congress will have a short meeting in the Fall, and another in the Spring. *Heyward.* Thinks the Spring the best time. *Wilson.* Thinks the Fall, and November better than October; because September is a busy month everywhere. *Dr. Hall.* September and October the most sickly and mortal months in the year. The season is more forward in Georgia in April, than here in May.[1]

Hopkinson moves that the power of recalling delegates be reserved to the State, not to the Assembly, because that may be changed.[2]

Article 17. "Each Colony shall have one vote."[3]

July 26.[4] *Rutledge* and *Lynch* oppose giving the power of regulating the trade and managing all affairs of the Indians to Congress. The trade is profitable, they say. *Gwinnett* is in favor of Congress having such power. *Braxton* is for excepting such Indians as are tributary to any State. Several nations are tributary to Virginia. *Jefferson* explains it to mean the Indians who live in the Colony. These are subject to the laws in some degree.

Wilson. We have no right over the Indians, whether within or without the real or pretended limits of any Colony. They will not allow themselves to be classed according to the bounds of Colonies. Grants made three thousand miles to the eastward, have no validity with the Indians. The trade of Pennsylvania has been more considerable with the Indians than that of the neighboring Colonies.

Walton. The Indian trade is of no essential service to any Colony. It must be a monopoly. If it is free, it produces jealousies and animosities and wars. Carolina, very passion-

1 The motion did not succeed.

2 This amendment prevailed in committee. The words "those who appointed the said delegates respectively," were stricken out and the words "each State" inserted. The word "Colony" was also stricken out where it occurs, and "State" inserted. It should be recollected that the first draught was reported by John Dickinson. The article was again amended in the House by cutting off the last clause, and striking out the city of Philadelphia as the place of meeting. In this last shape, it was transferred to, and made the first part of, the fifth article, where it stands in the paper as finally adopted.

3 Probably passed over for the moment.

4 The eighteenth article of the first draught enumerates the rights and powers of the United States. Among these is that of "regulating the trade, and managing all affairs with the Indians."

ately, considers this trade as contributing to her grandeur and dignity. Deerskins are a great part of the trade. A great difference between South Carolina and Georgia. Carolina is in no danger from the Indians at present. Georgia is a frontier and barrier to Carolina. Georgia must be overrun and extirpated before Carolina can be hurt. Georgia is not equal to the expense of giving the donations to the Indians, which will be necessary to keep them at peace. The emoluments of the trade are not a compensation for the expense of donations.

Rutledge differs from Walton in a variety of points. We must look forward with extensive views. Carolina has been run to an amazing expense to defend themselves against Indians; in 1760, &c., fifty thousand guineas were spent. We have now as many men on the frontiers, as in Charleston. We have forts in the Indian countries. We are connected with them by treaties.

Lynch. Congress may regulate the trade, if they will indemnify Carolina against the expense of keeping peace with the Indians, or defending us against them.

Witherspoon. Here are two adjacent provinces, situated alike with respect to the Indians, differing totally in their sentiments of their interests.

Chase. South Carolina claims to the South Sea; so does North, Virginia and Massachusetts Bay. South Carolina says they have a right to regulate the trade with the Indians; if so, four Colonies have all the power of regulating trade with the Indians. South Carolina could not stand alone against the Indian nations.

Sherman moves that Congress may have a superintending power, to prevent injustice to the Indians or Colonies.

Wilson. No lasting peace will be with the Indians, unless made by some one body. No such language as this ought to be held to the Indians. "We are stronger, we are better, we treat you better than another Colony." No power ought to treat with the Indians, but the United States. Indians know the striking benefits of confederation; they have an example of it in the union of the Six Nations. The idea of the union of the Colonies struck them forcibly last year. None should trade with Indians without a license from Congress. A perpetual war would be unavoidable, if everybody was allowed to trade with them.

Stone. This expedient is worse than either of the alternatives. What is the meaning of this superintendency? Colonies will claim the right first. Congress can't interpose until the evil has happened. Disputes will arise when Congress shall interpose.[1]

July 30. Article 17. "In determining questions, each Colony shall have one vote."

Dr. Franklin. Let the smaller Colonies give equal money and men, and then have an equal vote. But if they have an equal vote without bearing equal burthens, a confederation upon such iniquitous principles will never last long.

Dr. Witherspoon. We all agree that there must and shall be a confederation, for this war. It will diminish the glory of our object, and depreciate our hope; it will damp the ardor of the people. The greatest danger we have, is of disunion among ourselves. Is it not plausible that the small States will be oppressed by the great ones? The Spartans and Helotes. The Romans and their dependents. Every Colony is a distinct person. States of Holland.

Clark. We must apply for pardons if we don't confederate.

Wilson. We should settle upon some plan of representation.[2]

Chase.[3] Moves that the word "white," should be inserted in the eleventh Article. The negroes are wealth. Numbers are not a certain rule of wealth. It is the best rule we can lay down. Negroes a species of property, personal estate. If negroes are taken into the computation of numbers to ascertain wealth, they ought to be, in settling the representation.

[1] The clause was retained in committee, with the addition of the following words, "not members of any of the States," and makes a part of the ninth article as adopted.

[2] Probably passed over for the moment.

[3] The original draught of the eleventh article of the confederation, upon which this debate took place, was in these words:

"All charges of wars, and all other expenses that shall be incurred for the common defence, or general welfare, and allowed by the United States assembled, shall be defrayed out of a common treasury, which shall be supplied by the several Colonies in proportion to the number of inhabitants of every age, sex, and quality, except Indians not paying taxes, in each Colony, a true account of which, distinguishing the white inhabitants, shall be triennially taken and transmitted to the Assembly of the United States. Taxes for paying that proportion shall be laid and levied by the authority and directions of the legislature of the several Colonies within the time agreed upon by the United States assembled."

The Massachusetts fisheries, and navigation, ought to be taken into consideration. The young and old negroes are a burthen to their owners. The eastern Colonies have a great advantage in trade. This will give them a superiority. We shall be governed by our interests, and ought to be. If I am satisfied in the rule of levying and appropriating money, I am willing the small Colonies should have a vote.[1]

Wilson. If the war continues two years, each soul will have forty dollars to pay of the public debt. It will be the greatest

[1] Notes of this speech of Mr. Chase, and of a portion of the debate, were also taken by Mr. Jefferson, and they are found in the first volume of his papers published by his grandson, Mr. Randolph. A comparison of the two reports, as far as they go, shows a substantial agreement between them. But Mr. Jefferson's contains an abstract of two speeches by Mr. Adams, which are not found elsewhere. The first of them is inserted, as having been made immediately after that of Mr. Chase.

"Mr. John Adams observed, that the numbers of people were taken by this article, as an index of the wealth of the State, and not as subjects of taxation; that, as to this matter, it was of no consequence by what name you called your people, whether by that of freemen or slaves; that in some countries the laboring poor were called freemen, in others they were called slaves; but that the difference as to the State was imaginary only. What matters it whether a landlord employing ten laborers on his farm, gives them annually as much money as will buy them the necessaries of life, or gives them such necessaries at short hand? The ten laborers add as much wealth annually to the State, increase its exports as much, in the one case as the other. Certainly five hundred freemen produce no more profits, no greater surplus for the payment of taxes, than five hundred slaves. Therefore the State in which the laborers are called freemen, should be taxed no more than that in which are those called slaves. Suppose, by an extraordinary operation of nature or of law, one half the laborers of a State could in the course of one night be transformed into slaves. Would the State be made the poorer or the less able to pay taxes? That the condition of the laboring poor in most countries, that of the fishermen particularly, of the northern States, is as abject as that of slaves. It is the number of laborers which produces the surplus for taxation, and numbers, therefore, indiscriminately, are the fair index of wealth; that it is the use of the word 'property' here, and its application to some of the people of the State, which produces the fallacy. How does the southern farmer procure slaves? Either by importation, or by purchase from his neighbor. If he imports a slave, he adds one to the number of laborers in his country, and, proportionably, to its profits and ability to pay taxes; if he buys from his neighbor, it is only a transfer of a laborer from one farm to another, which does not change the annual produce of the State, and therefore should not change its tax; that if a northern farmer works ten laborers on his farm, he can, it is true, invest the surplus of ten men's labor in cattle; but so may the southern farmer, working ten slaves; that a State of one hundred thousand freemen can maintain no more cattle, than one of one hundred thousand slaves. Therefore, they have no more of that kind of property; that a slave may indeed, from the custom of speech, be more properly called the wealth of his master, than the free laborer might be called the wealth of his employer; but as to the State, both were equally its wealth, and should therefore equally add to the quota of its tax."

encouragement to continue slave-keeping, and to increase it, that can be, to exempt them from the numbers which are to vote and pay. Slaves are taxables in the Southern Colonies. It will be partial and unequal. Some Colonies have as many black as white; these will not pay more than half what they ought. Slaves prevent freemen from cultivating a country. It is attended with many inconveniences.

Lynch. If it is debated, whether their slaves are their property, there is an end of the confederation. Our slaves being our property, why should they be taxed more than the land, sheep, cattle, horses, &c.?

Freemen cannot be got to work in our Colonies; it is not in the ability or inclination of freemen to do the work that the negroes do. Carolina has taxed their negroes; so have other Colonies their lands.

Dr. Franklin. Slaves rather weaken than strengthen the State, and there is therefore some difference between them and sheep; sheep will never make any insurrections.

Rutledge. I shall be happy to get rid of the idea of slavery. The slaves do not signify property; the old and young cannot work. The property of some Colonies is to be taxed, in others, not. The Eastern Colonies will become the carriers for the Southern; they will obtain wealth for which they will not be taxed.

August 1. *Hooper.* North Carolina is a striking exception to the general rule that was laid down yesterday, that the riches of a country are in proportion to the numbers of inhabitants. A gentleman of three or four hundred negroes don't raise more corn than feeds them. A laborer can't be hired for less than twenty-four pounds a year in Massachusetts Bay. The net profit of a negro is not more than five or six pounds per annum. I wish to see the day that slaves are not necessary. Whites and negroes cannot work together. Negroes are goods and chattels, are property. A negro works under the impulse of fear, has no care of his master's interest.[1]

[1] Mr. Chase's amendment was lost. Seven States, New Hampshire, Massachusetts, Rhode Island, Connecticut, New York, New Jersey, and Pennsylvania, voting against it. Delaware, Maryland, Virginia, North and South Carolina, voting for it. Georgia divided.

The article, amended only by substituting the word "States," for "Colonies," was reported to the House as the ninth of the new draught.

The Consideration of the Seventeenth Article, resumed.[1]

Article 17. *Dr. Franklin* moves that votes should be in proportion to numbers. *Mr. Middleton* moves that the vote should be according to what they pay.

Sherman thinks we ought not to vote according to numbers. We are representatives of States, not individuals. States of Holland. The consent of every one is necessary. Three Colonies would govern the whole, but would not have a majority of strength to carry those votes into execution. The vote should be taken two ways; call the Colonies, and call the individuals, and have a majority of both.

Dr. Rush.[2] Abbé Raynal has attributed the ruin of the United Provinces to three causes. The principal one is, that the consent of every State is necessary; the other, that the members are obliged to consult their constituents upon all occasions. We lose an equal representation; we represent the people. It will tend to keep up colonial distinctions. We are now a new nation.

It was again taken up on the 9th of October, 1777, and discussed until the 14th, when the following important amendment was adopted: —

New Hampshire, Massachusetts, Rhode Island, Connecticut, voting unanimously in the negative.

New Jersey, Maryland, Virginia, North and South Carolina, unanimously in the affirmative.

New York and Pennsylvania equally divided.

"That the proportion of the public expense, incurred by the United States for their common defence and general welfare, to be paid by each State into the Treasury, be ascertained by the value of all land within each State granted to or surveyed for any person, as such land, the buildings and improvements thereon, shall be estimated according to such mode as Congress shall, from time to time, direct or appoint."

On the 22d, 23d, 24th, and 25th of June, 1778, the various States proposed, by their delegates, amendments. Maryland, Massachusetts, Rhode Island, Connecticut, New Jersey, and South Carolina, each offered some form of modification of this article, but they were all rejected. See the *History of the Confederation*, at the end of the first volume of the *Secret Journals*, vol. i. pp. 368–385.

1 From page 494.

2 The order of the speakers, in this debate, does not correspond with the report made by Mr. Jefferson. But, immediately before this speech of Dr. Rush, there is inserted, by him, a speech of Mr. Adams, which may properly find its place in this note.

"*John Adams* advocated the voting in proportion to numbers. He said that we stand here as the representatives of the people; that in some States the people are many, in others they are few; that, therefore, their vote here should be proportioned to the numbers from which it comes. Reason, justice, and equity, never had weight enough on the face of the earth, to govern the councils

Our trade, language, customs, manners, don't differ more than they do in Great Britain. The more a man aims at serving America, the more he serves his Colony. It will promote factions in Congress and in the States; it will prevent the growth of freedom in America; we shall be loth to admit new Colonies into the confederation. If we vote by numbers, liberty will be always safe. Massachusetts is contiguous to two small Colonies, Rhode Island and New Hampshire; Pennsylvania is near New Jersey and Delaware; Virginia is between Maryland and North Carolina. We have been too free with the word independence; we are dependent on each other, not totally independent States. Montesquieu pronounces the confederation of Lycia, the best that ever was made; the cities had different weights in the scale. China is not larger than one of our Colonies; how populous! It is said that the small Colonies deposit their all; this is deceiving us with a word. I would not have it understood that I am pleading the cause of Pennsylvania; when I entered that door, I considered myself a citizen of America.

Dr. Witherspoon.. Representation in England is unequal. Must I have three votes in a county, because I have three

of men. It is interest alone which does it, and it is interest alone which can be trusted; that, therefore, the interests, within doors, should be the mathematical representations of the interests without doors; that the individuality of the Colonies is a mere sound. Does the individuality of a Colony increase its wealth or numbers? If it does, pay equally. If it does not add weight in the scale of the confederacy, it cannot add to their rights, nor weigh in argument. A has fifty pounds; B five hundred pounds; C one thousand pounds, in partnership. Is it just they should equally dispose of the moneys of the partnership? It has been said, we are independent individuals making a bargain together. The question is not what we are now, but what we ought to be when our bargain shall be made. The confederacy is to make us one individual only; it is to form us, like separate parcels of metal, into one common mass. We shall no longer retain our separate individuality, but become a single individual as to all questions submitted to the confederacy. Therefore all those reasons which prove the justice and expediency of equal representation in other Assemblies, hold good here.

"It has been objected that a proportional vote will endanger the smaller States. We answer that an equal vote will endanger the larger. Virginia, Pennsylvania, and Massachusetts, are the three greater Colonies. Consider their distance, their difference of produce, of interests, and of manners, and it is apparent they can never have an interest or inclination to combine for the oppression of the smaller; that the smaller will naturally divide on all questions with the larger. Rhode Island, from its relation, similarity, and intercourse, will generally pursue the same objects with Massachusetts; Jersey, Delaware, and Maryland, with Pennsylvania."

times as much money as my neighbor? Congress are to determine the limits of Colonies.

G. Hopkins. A momentous question; many difficulties on each side; four larger, five lesser, four stand indifferent. Virginia, Massachusetts, Pennsylvania, Maryland, make more than half the people.

Connecticut, New York, two Carolinas, not concerned at all. The disinterested coolness of these Colonies ought to determine. I can easily feel the reasoning of the larger Colonies; pleasing theories always gave way to the prejudices, passions, and interests of mankind. The Germanic Confederation. The King of Prussia has an equal vote. The Helvetic confederacy. It can't be expected that nine Colonies will give way to be governed by four. The safety of the whole depends upon the distinctions of Colonies.

Dr. Franklin. I hear many ingenious arguments to persuade us that an unequal representation is a very good thing. If we had been born and bred under an unequal representation, we might bear it; but to set out with an unequal representation, is unreasonable. It is said the great Colonies will swallow up the less. Scotland said the same thing at the union.

Dr. Witherspoon rises to explain a few circumstances relating to Scotland; that was an incorporating union, not a federal; the nobility and gentry resort to England.

In determining all questions, each State shall have a weight, in proportion to what it contributes to the public expenses of the United States.[1]

August 2.[2] "Limiting the bounds of States, which by charter, &c. extend to the South Sea."

Sherman thinks the bounds ought to be settled. A majority of States have no claim to the South Sea. Moves this amend-

1 The seventeenth article was reported to the House, with only the change of the word "Colony" for "State," as article thirteen of the new draught. The struggle was renewed on the 7th of October, but without effect. Mr. Adams's vote stands recorded alone, north of Virginia, in favor of an amendment, basing representation upon population, every State to have one delegate for every thirty thousand of its inhabitants, and every delegate to have one vote. The vote by States was finally incorporated into the fifth article as at last adopted.

2 This makes, in the first draught, a part of the eighteenth article, defining the rights and power of the United States;

"Limiting the bounds of those Colonies which, by charter or proclamation, or under any pretence, are said to extend to the South Sea."

ment to be substituted in place of this clause, and also instead of the fifteenth article; — "No lands to be separated from any State, which are already settled, or become private property."

Chase denies that any Colony has a right to go to the South Sea.

Harrison. How came Maryland by its land, but by its charter? By its charter, Virginia owns to the South Sea. Gentlemen shall not pare away the Colony of Virginia. Rhode Island has more generosity than to wish the Massachusetts pared away. Delaware does not wish to pare away Pennsylvania.

Huntington. Admit there is danger from Virginia, does it follow that Congress has a right to limit her bounds? The consequence is, not to enter into confederation. But as to the question of right, we all unite against mutilating charters. I can't agree to the principle. We are a spectacle to all Europe. I am not so much alarmed at the danger from Virginia as some are; my fears are not alarmed; they have acted as noble a part as any. I doubt not the wisdom of Virginia will limit themselves. A man's right does not cease to be a right, because it is large; the question of right must be determined by the principles of the common law.

Stone. This argument is taken up upon very wrong ground. It is considered as if we were voting away the territory of particular Colonies, and gentlemen work themselves up into warmth upon that supposition. Suppose Virginia should. The small Colonies have a right to happiness and security; they would have no safety if the great Colonies were not limited. We shall grant lands, in small quantities, without rent or tribute or purchase-money. It is said that Virginia is attacked on every side. Is it meant that Virginia shall sell the lands for their own emolument? All the Colonies have defended these lands against the King of Britain, and at the expense of all. Does Virginia intend to establish quit rents? I don't mean that the United States shall sell them, to get money by them.

Jefferson. I protest against the right of Congress to decide upon the right of Virginia. Virginia has released all claims to the land settled by Maryland, &c.[1]

[1] This clause was stricken out in committee. The subsequent history of the struggle is well known, terminating in the acts of cession of claims to the Western territory.

AUTOBIOGRAPHY.

1775. September. [At the appointed time, we returned to Philadelphia, and Congress were reassembled. Mr. Richard Penn had sailed for England, and carried the petition, from which Mr. Dickinson and his party expected relief. I expected none, and was wholly occupied in measures to support the army and the expedition into Canada. Every important step was opposed, and carried by bare majorities, which obliged me to be almost constantly engaged in debate; but I was not content with all that was done, and almost every day I had something to say about advising the States to institute governments, to express my total despair of any good from the petition or any of those things which were called conciliatory measures. I constantly insisted that all such measures, instead of having any tendency to produce a reconciliation, would only be considered as proofs of our timidity and want of confidence in the ground we stood on, and would only encourage our enemies to greater exertions against us; that we should be driven to the necessity of declaring ourselves independent States, and that we ought now to be employed in preparing a plan of confederation for the Colonies, and treaties to be proposed to foreign powers, particularly to France and Spain; that all these measures ought to be maturely considered and carefully prepared, together with a declaration of independence; that these three measures, independence, confederation, and negotiations with foreign powers, particularly France, ought to go hand in hand, and be adopted all together; that foreign powers could not be expected to acknowledge us till we had acknowledged ourselves, and taken our station among them as a sovereign power and independent nation;[1] that now

[1] The following memorandum gives in brief the system probably dilated upon in the speeches of the writer at this time:—

Mem. The confederation to be taken up in paragraphs. An alliance to be formed with France and Spain. Ambassadors to be sent to both courts. Gov-

we were distressed for want of artillery, arms, ammunition, clothing, and even for flints; that the people had no markets for their produce, wanted clothing and many other things, which foreign commerce alone could fully supply, and we could not expect commerce till we were independent; that the people were wonderfully well united, and extremely ardent. There was no danger of our wanting support from them, if we did not discourage them by checking and quenching their zeal; that there was no doubt of our ability to defend the country, to support the war, and maintain our independence. We had men enough, our people were brave, and every day improving in all the exercises and discipline of war; that we ought immediately to give permission to our merchants to fit out privateers and make reprisals on the enemy; that Congress ought to arm ships, and commission officers, and lay the foundation of a navy; that immense advantages might be derived from this resource; that not only West India articles, in great abundance, and British manufactures, of all kinds, might be obtained, but artillery ammunitions and all kinds of supplies for the army; that a system of measures, taken with unanimity and pursued with resolution, would insure us the friendship and assistance of France.

Some gentlemen doubted of the sentiments of France; thought she would frown upon us as rebels, and be afraid to countenance the example. I replied to those gentlemen, that I apprehended they had not attended to the relative situation of France and England; that it was the unquestionable interest of France that the British Continental Colonies should be independent; that Britain, by the conquest of Canada and her naval triumphs during the last war, and by her vast possessions in America and the East Indies, was exalted to a height of power and preëminence that France must envy and could not endure. But there was much more than pride and jealousy in the case. Her rank,

ernment to be assumed in every Colony. Coin and currencies to be regulated. Forces to be raised and maintained in Canada and New York. St. Lawrence and Hudson Rivers to be secured. Hemp to be encouraged, and the manufacture of duck. Powder-mills to be built in every Colony, and fresh efforts to make saltpetre. An address to the inhabitants of the Colonies. The committee for lead and salt to be filled up, and sulphur added to their commission. Money to be sent to the paymaster, to pay our debts and fulfil our engagements. Taxes to be laid and levied. Funds established. New notes to be given on interest for bills borrowed. Treaties of commerce with France, Spain, Holland, Denmark, &c.

her consideration in Europe, and even her safety and independence, were at stake. The navy of Great Britain was now mistress of the seas, all over the globe. The navy of France almost annihilated. Its inferiority was so great and obvious, that all the dominions of France, in the West Indies and in the East Indies, lay at the mercy of Great Britain, and must remain so as long as North America belonged to Great Britain, and afforded them so many harbors abounding with naval stores and resources of all kinds, and so many men and seamen ready to assist them and man their ships; that interest could not lie; that the interest of France was so obvious, and her motives so cogent, that nothing but a judicial infatuation of her councils could restrain her from embracing us; that our negotiations with France ought, however, to be conducted with great caution, and with all the foresight we could possibly obtain; that we ought not to enter into any alliance with her, which should entangle us in any future wars in Europe; that we ought to lay it down, as a first principle and a maxim never to be forgotten, to maintain an entire neutrality in all future European wars; that it never could be our interest to unite with France in the destruction of England, or in any measures to break her spirit, or reduce her to a situation in which she could not support her independence. On the other hand, it could never be our duty to unite with Britain in too great a humiliation of France; that our real, if not our nominal, independence, would consist in our neutrality. If we united with either nation, in any future war, we must become too subordinate and dependent on that nation, and should be involved in all European wars, as we had been hitherto; that foreign powers would find means to corrupt our people, to influence our councils, and, in fine, we should be little better than puppets, danced on the wires of the cabinets of Europe. We should be the sport of European intrigues and politics; that, therefore, in preparing treaties to be proposed to foreign powers, and in the instructions to be given to our ministers, we ought to confine ourselves strictly to a treaty of commerce; that such a treaty would be an ample compensation to France for all the aid we should want from her. The opening of American trade to her, would be a vast resource for her commerce and naval power, and a great assistance to her in protecting her East and West India possessions, as well as her fisheries; but that the bare dismemberment of the British empire would be to her an incalculable security and benefit, worth more than all the exertions we should require of her, even if it should draw her into another eight or ten years' war.

When I first made these observations in Congress, I never saw a greater impression made upon that assembly or any other. Attention and approbation were marked upon every countenance. Several gentlemen came to me afterwards, to thank me for that speech, particularly Mr. Cæsar Rodney, of Delaware, and Mr. Duane, of New York. I remember these two gentlemen in particular, because both of them said that I had considered the subject of foreign connections more maturely than any man they had ever heard in America; that I had perfectly digested the subject, and had removed, Mr. Rodney said, all, and Mr. Duane said, the greatest part of his objections to foreign negotiations. Even Mr. Dickinson said, to gentlemen out of doors, that I had thrown great light on the subject.

These and such as these, were my constant and daily topics, sometimes of reasoning and no doubt often of declamation, from the meeting of Congress in the autumn of 1775, through the whole winter and spring of 1776.

Many motions were made, and after tedious discussions, lost. I received little assistance from my colleagues in all these contests; three of them were either inclined to lean towards Mr. Dickinson's system, or at least chose to be silent, and the fourth spoke but rarely in Congress, and never entered into any extensive arguments, though, when he did speak, his sentiments were clear and pertinent and neatly expressed. Mr. Richard Henry Lee, of Virginia, Mr. Sherman, of Connecticut, and Mr. Gadsden, of South Carolina, were always on my side, and Mr. Chase, of Maryland, when he did speak at all, was always powerful, and generally with us. Mr. Johnson, of Maryland, was the most frequent speaker from that State, and, while he remained with us, was inclined to Mr. Dickinson for some time, but ere long he and all his State came cordially into our system. In the fall of 1776, his State appointed him General of militia, and he marched to the relief of General Washington in the Jerseys. He was afterwards chosen Governor of Maryland, and he came no more to Congress.

In the course of this winter appeared a phenomenon in Philadelphia, a disastrous meteor, I mean Thomas Paine. He came from England, and got into such company as would converse with him, and ran about picking up what information he could concerning our affairs, and finding the great question was concerning independence, he gleaned from those he saw the common-place arguments, such as the necessity of independence at some time or other; the peculiar fitness at this time; the justice of it; the provocation to it; our ability to maintain it, &c. &c. Dr. Rush put him upon writing on the subject, furnished him with the arguments which had been urged in Congress a hundred times, and gave him his title of "Common Sense." In the latter part of winter, or early in the spring, he came out with his pamphlet. The arguments in favor of independence I liked very well; but one third part of the book was filled with arguments, from the Old Testament, to prove the unlawfulness of monarchy, and another third, in planning a form of government for the separate States, in one assembly, and for the United States, in a Congress. His arguments from the Old Testament were ridiculous, but whether they proceeded from honest ignorance or foolish superstition on one hand, or from wilful sophistry and knavish hypocrisy on the other, I know not. The other third part, relative to a form of government, I considered as flowing from simple ignorance, and a mere desire to please the democratic party in Philadelphia, at whose head were Mr. Matlack, Mr. Cannon, and Dr. Young. I regretted, however, to see so foolish a plan recommended to the people of the United States, who were all waiting only for the countenance of Congress to institute their State governments. I dreaded the effect so popular a pamphlet might have among the people, and determined to do all in my power to counteract the effect of it. My continual occupations in Congress allowed me no time to write any thing of any length; but I found moments to write a small pamphlet, which Mr. Richard Henry Lee, to whom I showed it, liked so well, that he insisted on my permitting him to publish it. He accordingly got Mr. Dunlap to print it, under the title of "Thoughts on Government, in a letter from a gentleman to his friend." Common Sense was published without a name, and I thought it best to suppress my name too. But as Common Sense, when it first appeared, was generally by the public ascribed to me or Mr. Samuel Adams, I soon regretted that my name did not appear. Afterwards I had a new edition of it printed, with my name and the name of Mr. Wythe, of Virginia, to whom the letter was at first intended to be addressed.[1] The gentlemen of New York availed themselves of the ideas in this morsel, in the formation of the constitution of that State. And Mr. Lee sent it to the convention of Virginia, when they met to form their government, and it went to North Carolina, New Jersey, and other States. Matlack, Cannon, Young, and Paine, had influence enough, however, to get their plan adopted in substance in Georgia and Vermont, as well as Pennsylvania. These three States have since found them such systems of anarchy, if that expression is not a contradiction in terms, that they have altered them and made them more conformable to my plan.

Paine, soon after the appearance of my pamphlet, hurried away to my lodgings and spent an evening with me. His business was to reprehend me for publishing my pamphlet; said he was afraid it would do hurt, and that it was repugnant to the plan he had proposed in his Common Sense. I told him it was true it was repugnant, and for that reason I had written it and consented to the publication of it; for I was as much afraid of his work as he was of mine. His plan was so democratical,[2] without any restraints or even an attempt at any equilibrium or counterpoise, that it must produce confusion and every evil work. I told him further, that his reasoning from the Old Testament was ridiculous, and I could hardly think him sincere. At this he laughed, and said he had taken his ideas in that part from Milton; and then expressed a contempt of the Old Testament, and indeed of the Bible at large, which surprised me. He saw that I did not relish this, and soon checked himself with these words: "However, I have some thoughts of publishing my thoughts on religion, but I believe it will be best to postpone it to the latter part of life." This conversation passed in good humor, without any harshness on either side; but I perceived in him a conceit of himself and a daring impudence, which have been developed more and more to this day.

The third part of Common Sense, which relates wholly to the question of independence, was clearly written, and contained a

[1] This Essay will be found in another portion of this work.

[2] This was the very objection made in the State of Virginia to his own, as will appear hereafter in a remarkable letter of Patrick Henry to the author.

tolerable summary of the arguments which I had been repeating again and again in Congress for nine months. But I am bold to say there is not a fact nor a reason stated in it, which had not been frequently urged in Congress. The temper and wishes of the people supplied every thing at that time; and the phrases, suitable for an emigrant from Newgate, or one who had chiefly associated with such company, such as, "The Royal Brute of England," "The blood upon his soul," and a few others of equal delicacy, had as much weight with the people as his arguments. It has been a general opinion that this pamphlet was of great importance in the Revolution. I doubted it at the time, and have doubted it to this day. It probably converted some to the doctrine of independence, and gave others an excuse for declaring in favor of it. But these would all have followed Congress with zeal; and on the other hand it excited many writers against it, particularly "Plain Truth," who contributed very largely to fortify and inflame the party against independence, and finally lost us the Allens, Penns, and many other persons of weight in the community.

Notwithstanding these doubts, I felt myself obliged to Paine for the pains he had taken, and for his good intentions to serve us, which I then had no doubt of. I saw he had a capacity and a ready pen; and, understanding he was poor and destitute, I thought we might put him into some employment where he might be useful and earn a living. Congress appointed a Committee of Foreign Affairs, not long after, and they wanted a clerk. I nominated Thomas Paine, supposing him a ready writer and an industrious man. Dr. Witherspoon, the President of New Jersey College, and then a delegate from that State, rose and objected to it with an earnestness that surprised me. The Doctor said he would give his reasons; he knew the man and his communication; when he first came over, he was on the other side, and had written pieces against the American cause; that he had afterwards been employed by his friend, Robert Aitkin, and finding the tide of popularity run rapidly, he had turned about; that he was very intemperate, and could not write until he had quickened his thoughts with large draughts of rum and water; that he was, in short, a bad character, and not fit to be placed in such a situation. General Roberdeau spoke in his favor; no one confirmed Witherspoon's account, though the truth of it has since been sufficiently established. Congress appointed him; but he was soon obnoxious by his manners, and dismissed.

There was one circumstance in his conversation with me about the pamphlets, which I could not account for. He was extremely earnest to convince me that "Common Sense" was his first born; declared again and again that he had never written a line nor a word that had been printed, before "Common Sense." I cared nothing for this, and said nothing; but Dr. Witherspoon's account of his writing against us, brought doubts into my mind of his veracity, which the subsequent histories of his writings and publications in England, when he was in the custom-house, did not remove. At this day it would be ridiculous to ask any questions about Tom Paine's veracity, integrity, or any other virtue.

I was incessantly employed through the whole fall, winter, and spring of 1775 and 1776, in Congress during their sittings, and on committees on mornings and evenings, and unquestionably did more business than any other member of that house. In the beginning of May, I procured the appointment of a committee, to prepare a resolution recommending to the people of the States to institute governments. The committee, of whom I was one, requested me to draught a resolve, which I did, and by their direction reported it.[1] Opposition was made to it, and Mr. Duane called it a machine to fabricate independence, but on the 15th of May, 1776, it passed. It was indeed, on all hands, considered by men of understanding as equivalent to a declaration of independence, though a formal declaration of it was still opposed by Mr. Dickinson and his party.

Not long after this, the three greatest measures of all were carried. Three committees were appointed, one for preparing a declaration of independence, another for reporting a plan of a treaty to be proposed to France, and a third to digest a system of articles of confederation to be proposed to the States. I was appointed on the committee of independence, and on that for preparing the form of a treaty with France. On the committee of confederation Mr. Samuel Adams was appointed. The committee of independence were Thomas Jefferson, John

[1] See page 489.

Adams, Benjamin Franklin, Roger Sherman, and Robert R. Livingston. Mr. Jefferson had been now about a year a member of Congress, but had attended his duty in the house a very small part of the time, and, when there, had never spoken in public. During the whole time I sat with him in Congress, I never heard him utter three sentences together. It will naturally be inquired how it happened that he was appointed on a committee of such importance. There were more reasons than one. Mr. Jefferson had the reputation of a masterly pen; he had been chosen a delegate in Virginia, in consequence of a very handsome public paper which he had written for the House of Burgesses, which had given him the character of a fine writer.[1] Another reason was, that Mr. Richard Henry Lee was not beloved by the most of his colleagues from Virginia, and Mr. Jefferson was set up to rival and supplant him. This could be done only by the pen, for Mr. Jefferson could stand no competition with him or any one else in elocution and public debate.

Here I will interrupt the narration for a moment to observe, that, from all I have read of the history of Greece and Rome, England and France, and all I have observed at home and abroad, eloquence in public assemblies is not the surest road to fame or preferment, at least, unless it be used with caution, very rarely, and with great reserve. The examples of Washington, Franklin, and Jefferson, are enough to show that silence and reserve in public, are more efficacious than argumentation or oratory. A public speaker who inserts himself, or is urged by others, into the conduct of affairs, by daily exertions to justify his measures, and answer the objections of opponents, makes himself too familiar with the public, and unavoidably makes himself enemies. Few persons can bear to be outdone in reasoning or declamation or wit or sarcasm or repartee or satire, and all these things are very apt to grow out of public debate. In this way, in a course of years, a nation becomes full of a man's enemies, or at least, of such as have been galled in some controversy, and take a secret pleasure in assisting to humble and mortify him. So much for this digression. We will now return to our memoirs.

[1] Afterwards published in Great Britain under the title of "A summary View of the Rights of British America." Mr. Jefferson's account of it is given in the first volume of his grandson's publication of his papers, p. 7

The committee had several meetings, in which were proposed the articles of which the declaration was to consist, and minutes made of them. The committee then appointed Mr. Jefferson and me to draw them up in form, and clothe them in a proper dress.[1] The sub-committee met, and considered the min-

[1] It is due to Mr. Jefferson here to say that his recollection of the event here described, materially differs from this account. In the month of August, 1822, Colonel Timothy Pickering addressed to Mr. Adams a letter of inquiry, respecting the origin of the Declaration of Independence. His reply contains so many other interesting particulars, besides those which relate to the single purpose of the letter, that it appears peculiarly suitable for insertion in this place in full.

TO TIMOTHY PICKERING.

6 August, 1822.

SIR: — Your favor of the 2d instant has prescribed a dismal plan, which I was never very well calculated to execute; but I am now utterly incapable. I can write nothing which will not be suspected of personal vanity, local prejudice, or Provincial and State partiality. However, as I hold myself responsible at this age, to one only tribunal in the universe, I will give you a few hints at all hazards.

As Mr. Hancock was sick and confined, Mr. Bowdoin was chosen at the head of the Massachusetts delegation to Congress. His relations thought his great fortune ought not to be hazarded. Cushing, two Adamses, and Paine, all destitute of fortune, four poor pilgrims, proceeded in one coach, were escorted through Massachusetts, Connecticut, New York, and New Jersey, into Pennsylvania. We were met at Frankfort by Dr. Rush, Mr. Mifflin, Mr. Bayard, and several other of the most active sons of liberty in Philadelphia, who desired a conference with us. We invited them to take tea with us in a private apartment. They asked leave to give us some information and advice, which we thankfully granted. They represented to us that the friends of government in Boston and in the Eastern States, in their correspondence with their friends in Pennsylvania and all the Southern States, had represented us as four desperate adventurers. "Mr. Cushing was a harmless kind of man, but poor, and wholly dependent on his popularity for his subsistence. Mr. Samuel Adams was a very artful, designing man, but desperately poor, and wholly dependent on his popularity with the lowest vulgar for his living. John Adams and Mr. Paine were two young lawyers, of no great talents, reputation, or weight, who had no other means of raising themselves into consequence, than by courting popularity." * We were all suspected of having independence in view. Now, said they, you must not utter the word independence, nor give the least hint or insinuation of the idea, either in Congress or any private conversation; if you do, you are undone; for the idea of independence is as unpopular in Pennsylvania, and in all the Middle and Southern States, as the Stamp Act itself. No man dares to speak of it. Moreover, you are the representatives of the suffering State. Boston and Massachusetts are under a rod of iron. British fleets and armies are tyrannizing over you; you yourselves are personally obnoxious to them and all the friends of government; you have been long persecuted by them all; your feelings have been hurt, your passions excited; you are thought to be too warm, too zealous, too sanguine. You must be, therefore, very cautious; you must not come forward with any bold measures, you must not pretend to take the lead. You

* Compare this with the language of the Rev. Jacob Duché, in his letter to General Washington: "Bankrupts, attorneys, and men of desperate fortunes, are the colleagues of Mr. Hancock." *Graydon's Memoirs of his own Time*, Littell's edition, Appendix, p. 432.

utes, making such observations on them as then occurred, when Mr. Jefferson desired me to take them to my lodgings, and

know Virginia is the most populous State in the Union. They are very proud of their ancient dominion, as they call it; they think they have a right to take the lead, and the Southern States, and Middle States too, are too much disposed to yield it to them."

This was plain dealing, Mr. Pickering; and I must confess that there appeared so much wisdom and good sense in it, that it made a deep impression on my mind, and it had an equal effect on all my colleagues.

This conversation, and the principles, facts, and motives, suggested in it, have given a color, complexion, and character, to the whole policy of the United States, from that day to this. Without it, Mr. Washington would never have commanded our armies; nor Mr. Jefferson have been the author of the Declaration of Independence; nor Mr. Richard Henry Lee the mover of it; nor Mr. Chase the mover of foreign connections. If I have ever had cause to repent of any part of this policy, that repentance ever has been, and ever will be, unavailing. I had forgot to say, nor had Mr. Johnson ever been the nominator of Washington for General.

Although this advice dwelt on my mind, I had not, in my nature, prudence and caution enough always to observe it. When I found the members of Congress, Virginians and all, so perfectly convinced that they should be able to persuade or terrify Great Britain into a relinquishment of her policy, and a restoration of us to the state of 1763, I was astonished, and could not help muttering, in Congress, and sometimes out of doors, that they would find, the proud, domineering spirit of Britain, their vain conceit of their own omnipotence, their total contempt of us, and the incessant representation of their friends and instruments in America, would drive us to extremities, and finally conquer us, transport us to England for trial, there to be hanged, drawn and quartered for treason, or to the necessity of declaring independence, however hazardous and uncertain such a measure might be.

It soon became rumored about the city that John Adams was for independence. The Quakers and proprietary gentlemen took the alarm; represented me as the worst of men; the true-blue sons of liberty pitied me; all put me under a kind of coventry. I was avoided, like a man infected with the leprosy. I walked the streets of Philadelphia in solitude, borne down by the weight of care and unpopularity.* But every ship, for the ensuing year, brought us fresh proof of the truth of my prophecies, and one after another became convinced of the necessity of independence. I did not sink under my discouragements. I had before experienced enough of the wantonness of popularity, in the trial of Preston and the soldiers, in Boston.

You inquire why so young a man as Mr. Jefferson was placed at the head of the Committee for preparing a Declaration of Independence? I answer; It was the Frankfort advice, to place Virginia at the head of every thing. Mr. Richard Henry Lee might be gone to Virginia, to his sick family, for aught I know, but that was not the reason of Mr. Jefferson's appointment. There were three committees appointed at the same time. One for the Declaration of Independence, another for preparing articles of Confederation, and another for preparing a treaty to be proposed to France. Mr. Lee was chosen for the Committee of Confederation, and it was not thought convenient that the same person should be upon both. Mr. Jefferson came into Congress, in June, 1775, and brought with him a reputation for literature, science, and a happy talent of

* Dr. Benjamin Rush says of the Author, in a manuscript in the Editor's hands, — "I saw this gentleman walk the streets of Philadelphia alone, after the publication of his intercepted letter in our newspapers, in 1775, an object of nearly universal scorn and detestation."

make the draught. This I declined, and gave several reasons for declining. 1. That he was a Virginian, and I a Massachu-

composition. Writings of his were handed about, remarkable for the peculiar felicity of expression. Though a silent member in Congress, he was so prompt, frank, explicit, and decisive upon committees and in conversation, not even Samuel Adams was more so, that he soon seized upon my heart; and upon this occasion I gave him my vote, and did all in my power to procure the votes of others. I think he had one more vote than any other, and that placed him at the head of the committee. I had the next highest number, and that placed me the second. The committee met, discussed the subject, and then appointed Mr. Jefferson and me to make the draught, I suppose because we were the two first on the list.

The sub-committee met. Jefferson proposed to me to make the draught. I said, "I will not." "You should do it." "Oh! no." "Why will you not? You ought to do it." "I will not." "Why?" "Reasons enough." "What can be your reasons?" "Reason first—You are a Virginian, and a Virginian ought to appear at the head of this business. Reason second—I am obnoxious, suspected, and unpopular. You are very much otherwise. Reason third—You can write ten times better than I can." "Well," said Jefferson, "if you are decided, I will do as well as I can." "Very well. When you have drawn it up, we will have a meeting."

A meeting we accordingly had, and conned the paper over. I was delighted with its high tone and the flights of oratory with which it abounded, especially that concerning negro slavery, which, though I knew his Southern brethren would never suffer to pass in Congress, I certainly never would oppose. There were other expressions which I would not have inserted, if I had drawn it up, particularly that which called the King tyrant. I thought this too personal; for I never believed George to be a tyrant in disposition and in nature; I always believed him to be deceived by his courtiers on both sides of the Atlantic, and in his official capacity only, cruel. I thought the expression too passionate, and too much like scolding, for so grave and solemn a document; but as Franklin and Sherman were to inspect it afterwards, I thought it would not become me to strike it out. I consented to report it, and do not now remember that I made or suggested a single alteration.

We reported it to the committee of five. It was read, and I do not remember that Franklin or Sherman criticized any thing. We were all in haste. Congress was impatient, and the instrument was reported, as I believe, in Jefferson's handwriting, as he first drew it. Congress cut off about a quarter of it, as I expected they would; but they obliterated some of the best of it, and left all that was exceptionable, if any thing in it was. I have long wondered that the original draught has not been published. I suppose the reason is, the vehement philippic against negro slavery.

As you justly observe, there is not an idea in it but what had been hackneyed in Congress for two years before. The substance of it is contained in the declaration of rights and the violation of those rights, in the Journals of Congress, in 1774. Indeed, the essence of it is contained in a pamphlet, voted and printed by the town of Boston, before the first Congress met, composed by James Otis, as I suppose, in one of his lucid intervals, and pruned and polished by Samuel Adams. Your friend and humble servant.

On the national anniversary succeeding the date of this letter, Colonel Pickering quoted the latter part of it, in the course of some remarks made by him at a celebration of the day in Salem. This drew forth a letter, from Mr. Jefferson to Mr. Madison, denying its accuracy, particularly in the matter of the sub-com-

settensian. 2. That he was a southern man, and I a northern one. 3. That I had been so obnoxious for my early and constant zeal in promoting the measure, that any draught of mine would undergo a more severe scrutiny and criticism in Congress, than one of his composition. 4. and lastly, and that would be reason enough if there were no other, I had a great opinion of the elegance of his pen, and none at all of my own. I therefore insisted that no hesitation should be made on his part. He accordingly took the minutes, and in a day or two produced to me his draught. Whether I made or suggested any correction, I remember not. The report was made to the committee of five, by them examined, but whether altered or corrected in any thing, I cannot recollect. But, in substance at least, it was reported to Congress, where, after a severe criticism, and striking out several of the most oratorical paragraphs, it was adopted on the fourth of July, 1776, and published to the world.

mittee, and attributing the error to the failing memory of eighty-eight, the assumed age of Mr. Adams at the time.* Mr. Jefferson did not then know, what the present publication of the Autobiography shows, not to speak of Mr. Pickering's letter of inquiry, that almost the identical statement had been made, not only in conversation long before, but also in this record, by Mr. Adams, nearly twenty years earlier, so that, if it be an error, it cannot be attributed merely to age.

Perceiving also the awkward nature of the charge made by one — himself — having, at the moment, nearly attained fourscore, Mr. Jefferson disclaims all reliance upon his recollection, and appeals to the unequivocal authority of his notes, made at the time. This seemed conclusive testimony, sufficient to set the matter at rest forever. But if by those notes is to be understood no more than what has since been published under that name, in the first volume of his correspondence, it is clear, on examination, that they present no evidence, excepting that which may be implied by their affirming nothing in corroboration. The question, in itself, does not rise beyond the character of a curiosity of literature, as the substantial facts in both accounts are the same. The case having been stated, the reader must be left to form his opinions from the materials before him.

Among the papers left by Mr. Adams, is a transcript, by his own hand, of the Declaration of Independence, very nearly as it appears in Mr. Jefferson's first draught. This must have been made by him before the paper had been subjected to any change in committee, as none of the alterations which appear on the original, as made at the instance of Dr. Franklin, and but one of the two suggested by himself, are found there. Several variations occur, however, in the phraseology, and one or two passages are wholly omitted. The most natural inference is, that he had modified it to suit his own notions of excellence, without deeming the alterations worth pressing in committee. As Mr. Jefferson says that his draught was submitted separately, first to Mr. Adams, and afterwards to Dr. Franklin, the presence of this copy does not affect the question of the correctness of either version of the proceedings.

* Jefferson's *Memoir and Correspondence*, vol. iv. p. 375.

The committee for preparing the model of a treaty to be proposed to France, consisted of Mr. Dickinson, Mr. Franklin, Mr. John Adams, Mr. Harrison, and Mr. Robert Morris. When we met to deliberate on the subject, I contended for the same principles which I had before avowed and defended in Congress, namely, that we should avoid all alliance which might embarrass us in after times, and involve us in future European wars; that a treaty of commerce which would operate as a repeal of the British acts of navigation so far as respected us, and admit France into an equal participation of the benefits of our commerce, would encourage her manufactures, increase her exports of the produce of her soil and agriculture, extend her navigation and trade, augment her resources of naval power, raise her from her present deep humiliation, distress, and decay, and place her on a more equal footing with England, for the protection of her foreign possessions; and maintaining her independence at sea, would be an ample compensation to France for acknowledging our independence, and for furnishing us, for our money, or upon credit for a time, with such supplies of necessaries as we should want, even if this conduct should involve her in a war; if a war should ensue, which did not necessarily follow, for a bare acknowledgment of our independence, after we had asserted it, was not by the law of nations an act of hostility, which would be a legitimate cause of war. Franklin, although he was commonly as silent on committees as in Congress, upon this occasion, ventured so far as to intimate his concurrence with me in these sentiments; though, as will be seen hereafter, he shifted them as easily as the wind ever shifted, and assumed a dogmatical tone in favor of an opposite system. The committee, after as much deliberation upon the subject as they chose to employ, appointed me to draw up a plan and report. Franklin had made some marks with a pencil against some articles in a printed volume of treaties, which he put into my hand. Some of these were judiciously selected, and I took them, with others which I found necessary, into the draught, and made my report to the committee at large, who, after a reasonable examination of it, agreed to report it. When it came before Congress, it occupied the attention of that body for several days. Many motions were made to insert in it articles of entangling alliance, of exclusive privileges, and of warranties of possessions; and it was argued that the present plan reported by the committee held out no sufficient temptation to France, who would despise it and refuse to receive our Ambassador. It was chiefly left to me to defend my report, though I had some able assistance, and we did defend it with so much success that the treaty passed without one particle of alliance, exclusive privilege, or warranty.[1]

[1] This plan of a treaty is found in the second volume of the Secret Journals of Congress, pp. 7 – 30.

APPENDIX

APPENDIX.

A.

The following abstract of the argument in the cause of writs of assistants or assistance is the one alluded to in the note to page 125 of this volume.

Gridley. The Constables distraining for rates, more inconsistent with English rights and liberties than Writs of Assistance; and necessity authorizes both.

Thacher. I have searched in all the ancient repertories of precedents, in Fitzherbert's Natura Brevium, and in the register (*Q.* What the register is) and have found no such writ of assistance as this petition prays. I have found two writs of assistance in the register, but they are very different from the writ prayed for. In a book, intituled the Modern Practice of the Court of Exchequer, there is indeed one such writ, and but one.

By the Act of Parliament, any other private person may, as well as a custom-house officer, take an officer, a sheriff or constable, &c., and go into any shop, store, &c., and seize; any person authorized by such a writ, under the seal of the Court of Exchequer, may; not custom-house officers only. *Strange.*

Only a temporary thing.

The most material question is, whether the practice of the Exchequer will warrant this Court in granting the same. The act empowers all the officers of the revenue to enter and seize in the plantations as well as in England. 7 & 8 William III. c. 22, s. 6, gives the same as 13 & 14 Charles II. gives in England. The ground of Mr. Gridley's argument is this, that this Court has the power of the Court of Exchequer. But this Court has renounced the Chancery Jurisdiction, which the Exchequer has, in cases where either party is the King's debtor. (*Q.* into that case.)

In England all informations of uncustomed or prohibited importations are in the Exchequer. So that the custom-house officers are the officers of that Court, under the eye and direction of the Barons.

The writ of assistance is not returnable. If such seizure were brought before your honors, you would often find a wanton exercise of their power. At home, the officers seize at their peril, even with probable cause.

Otis. This writ is against the fundamental principles of law. The privilege of House. A man who is quiet, is as secure in his house, as a prince in his castle — notwithstanding all his debts and civil processes of any kind. But —

For flagrant crimes and in cases of great public necessity, the privilege may be infringed on. For felonies an officer may break, upon process and oath, that is, by a special warrant to search such a house, sworn to be suspected, and good grounds of suspicion appearing.

Make oath *coram* Lord Treasurer, or Exchequer in England, or a magistrate here, and get a special warrant for the public good, to infringe the privilege of house.

General warrant to search for felonies. Hawkins, Pleas of the Crown. Every petty officer, from the highest to the lowest; and if some of them are common, others are uncommon.

Government justices used to issue such perpetual edicts. (*Q.* with what particular reference.) But one precedent, and that in the reign of Charles II., when star chamber powers, and all powers but lawful and useful powers, were pushed to extremity.

The authority of this modern practice of the Court of Exchequer. It has an Imprimatur. But what may not have? It may be owing to some ignorant Clerk of the Exchequer. But all precedents, and this among the rest, are under the control of the principles of law. Lord Talbot. Better to observe the known principles of law than any one precedent, though in the House of Lords.

As to Acts of Parliament. An act against the Constitution is void; an act against natural equity is void; and if an act of Parliament should be made, in the very words of this petition, it would be void. The executive Courts must pass such acts into disuse.

8 Rep. 118 from Viner Reason of the common law to control an act of Parliament. Iron manufacture. Noble Lord's proposal, that we should send our horses to England to be shod. If an officer will justify under a writ, he must return it. 12 Mod. 396, perpetual writ. Statute Charles II. We have all as good right to inform as custom-house officers, and every man may have a general irreturnable commission to break houses.

By 12 of Charles, on oath before Lord Treasurer, Barons of Exchequer, or Chief Magistrate, to break, with an officer. 14 C. to issue a warrant requiring sheriffs, &c., to assist the officers to search for goods not entered or prohibited. 7 & 8. W. & M. gives officers in plantations same powers with officers in England.

Continuance of writs and processes proves no more, nor so much, as I grant a special writ of assistance on special oath for special purpose.

Pew indorsed warrant to Ware. Justice Walley searched House. Province Law, p. 114.

Bill in chancery. This Court confined their chancery power to revenue, &c.

Gridley. By the 7 & 8 Wm. c. 22, s. 6, this authority of breaking and entering ships, warehouses, cellars, &c. given to the custom-house officers in England. By the statutes of the 12 & 14 of Charles II. it is extended to the custom-house officers in the plantations; and by the statute of 6 Anne, writs of assistance are continued, in company with all other legal processes used, for six months after the demise of the Crown. Now, what this writ of assistance is, we can know only by books of precedents. And we have produced, in a book intituled the Modern Practice of the Court of Exchequer, a form of such a writ of assistance to the officers of the customs. The book has the imprimatur of Wright C. J. of the K. B., which is as great a sanction as any books of precedents ever have, although books of reports are usually approved by all the

Judges, and I take Brown, the author of this book, to have been a very good collector of precedents. I have two volumes of precedents, of his collection, which I look upon as good as any, except Coke and Rastall.

And the power given in this writ, is no greater infringement of our liberty than the method of collecting taxes in this Province.

Everybody knows that the subject has the privilege of house only against his fellow subjects, not versus the King either in matters of crime or fine.[1]

The report of a part of Mr. Otis's speech as given in Minot's History, must have been written out by Mr. Adams, at a later moment. In his own copy of that work, he has underlined the passages in it, which he says were interpolated by the person who furnished it for publication. It is no more than just to all parties, the speaker as well as the reporter, that the correct version should be given, —

"MAY IT PLEASE YOUR HONORS,

"I was desired by one of the Court to look into the books, and consider the question now before them concerning writs of assistance. I have accordingly considered it, and now appear, not only in obedience to your order, but likewise in behalf of the inhabitants of this town, who have presented another petition, and out of regard to the liberties of the subject. And I take this opportunity to declare, that whether under a fee or not (for in such a cause as this I despise a fee) I will to my dying day oppose with all the powers and faculties God has given me, all such instruments of slavery on the one hand, and villany on the other, as this writ of assistance is.

It appears to me the worst instrument of arbitrary power, the most destructive of English liberty and the fundamental principles of law, that ever was found in an English law-book. I must, therefore, beg your Honors' patience and attention to the whole range of an argument, that may perhaps appear uncommon in many things, as well as to points of learning that are more remote and unusual; that the whole tendency of my design may the more easily be perceived, the conclusions better discerned, and the force of them be better felt. I shall not think much of my pains in this cause, as I engaged in it from principle. I was solicited to argue this cause as Advocate-General; and because I would not, I have been charged with desertion from my office. To this charge I can give a very sufficient answer. I renounced that office, and I argue this cause, from the same principle; and I argue it with the greater pleasure, as it is in favor of British liberty, at a time when we hear the greatest monarch upon earth declaring from his throne that he glories in the name of Briton, and that the privileges of his people are dearer to him than the most valuable prerogatives of his crown; and as it is in opposition to a kind of power, the exercise of which, in former periods of English history, cost one King of England his head, and another his throne. I have taken more pains in this cause, than I ever will take again, although my engaging in this and another popular cause has raised much resentment. But I think I can sincerely declare, that I cheerfully submit myself to every odious name for conscience' sake; and from my soul I despise all those, whose guilt, malice, or folly has made them

1 Here follow extracts from the Acts of Parliament and the Province Law, together with the forms of the petition and writ used

my foes. Let the consequences be what they will, I am determined to proceed. The only principles of public conduct, that are worthy of a gentleman or a man, are to sacrifice estate, ease, health, and applause, and even life, to the sacred calls of his country. These manly sentiments, in private life, make the good citizen; in public life, the patriot and the hero. I do not say, that when brought to the test, I shall be invincible. I pray God I may never be brought to the melancholy trial; but if ever I should, it will be then known how far I can reduce to practice principles, which I know to be founded in truth. In the mean time I will proceed to the subject of this writ.

"In the first place, may it please your Honors, I will admit that writs of one kind may be legal; that is, special writs, directed to special officers, and to search certain houses, &c. specially set forth in the writ, may be granted by the Court of Exchequer at home, upon oath made before the Lord Treasurer by the person who asks it, that he suspects such goods to be concealed in those very places he desires to search. The act of 14 Charles II. which Mr. Gridley mentions, proves this. And in this light the writ appears like a warrant from a Justice of the Peace to search for stolen goods. Your Honors will find in the old books concerning the office of a Justice of the Peace, precedents of general warrants to search suspected houses. But in more modern books you will find only special warrants to search such and such houses specially named, in which the complainant has before sworn that he suspects his goods are concealed; and you will find it adjudged that special warrants only are legal. In the same manner I rely on it, that the writ prayed for in this petition, being general, is illegal. It is a power, that places the liberty of every man in the hands of every petty officer. I say I admit that special writs of assistance, to search special places, may be granted to certain persons on oath; but I deny that the writ now prayed for can be granted, for I beg leave to make some observations on the writ itself, before I proceed to other acts of Parliament. In the first place, the writ is universal, being directed 'to all and singular Justices, Sheriffs, Constables, and all other officers and subjects;' so, that, in short, it is directed to every subject in the King's dominions. Every one with this writ may be a tyrant; if this commission be legal, a tyrant in a legal manner also may control, imprison, or murder any one within the realm. In the next place, it is perpetual; there is no return. A man is accountable to no person for his doings. Every man may reign secure in his petty tyranny, and spread terror and desolation around him. In the third place, a person with this writ, in the daytime, may enter all houses, shops, &c. at will, and command all to assist him. Fourthly, by this writ not only deputies, &c., but even their menial servants, are allowed to lord it over us. Now one of the most essential branches of English liberty is the freedom of one's house. A man's house is his castle; and whilst he is quiet, he is as well guarded as a prince in his castle. This writ, if it should be declared legal, would totally annihilate this privilege. Custom-house officers may enter our houses, when they please; we are commanded to permit their entry. Their menial servants may enter, may break locks, bars, and every thing in their way; and whether they break through malice or revenge, no man, no court, can inquire. Bare suspicion without oath is sufficient. This wanton exercise of this power is not a chimerical suggestion of a heated brain. I will mention some facts. Mr. Pew had one of these writs, and when Mr. Ware succeeded him, he endorsed this writ over to Mr. Ware; so that these writs are negotiable from one officer to another; and so your Honors have no opportunity of judging the persons to whom this vast power is delegated. Another instance is this: Mr. Justice Walley had called this same Mr. Ware before him, by a constable, to answer for a breach of Sabbath-day acts, or that of profane swearing. As soon as he had finished, Mr. Ware asked him if he had done. He replied, Yes. Well then, said Mr. Ware, I will show you a little of my power. I command you to permit me to search your house for uncustomed goods. And went on to search his house from the garret to the cellar; and then served the constable in the same manner. But to show another absurdity in this writ; if it should be established, I insist upon it, every person by the 14 Charles II. has this power as well as custom-house officers. The words are, 'It shall be lawful for any person or persons authorized,' &c. What a scene does this open! Every man, prompted by revenge, ill humor, or wantonness, to inspect the inside of his neighbor's house, may get a writ of assistance. Others will ask it from self-defence; one arbitrary exertion will provoke another, until society be involved in tumult and in blood.

"Again, these writs are not returned. Writs in their nature are temporary things. When the purposes for which they are issued are answered, they exist no more; but these live forever; no one can be called to account. Thus reason and the constitution are both against this writ. Let us see what authority there is for it. Not more than one instance can be found of it in all our law-books; and that was in the zenith of arbitrary power, namely, in the reign of Charles II., when star-chamber powers were pushed to extremity by some ignorant clerk of the exchequer. But had this writ been in any book whatever, it would have been illegal. All precedents are under the control of the principles of law. Lord Talbot says it is better to observe these than any precedents, though in the House of Lords, the last resort of the subject. No Acts of Parliament can establish such a writ; though it should be made in the very words of the petition, it would be void. An act against the constitution is void. (vid. Viner.) But these prove no more than what I before observed, that special writs may be granted *on oath and probable suspicion*. The act of 7 & 8 William III. that the officers of the plantations shall have the same powers, &c. is confined to this sense; that an officer should show probable ground; should take his oath of it; should do this before a magistrate; and that such magistrate, if he think proper, should issue a special warrant to a constable to search the places. That of 6 Anne can prove no more."

B.

(page 226.)

The following abstract, taken from one of Mr. Adams's note books, in addition to the interest attaching to the cause itself, may serve as a specimen of his manner of getting up his cases for argument: —

Case of Michael Corbet and others, charged with the murder of Lieutenant Panton, on the high seas.

28 Hen. VIII. c. 15. "FOR PIRATES." "Where *traitors, pirates, thieves, robbers, murderers* and *confederates* upon the sea, many times escaped unpunished, because the trial of their offences hath heretofore been ordered, judged, and determined before the *Admiral*, or his *Lieutenant* or *Commissary*, after the course of the civil laws, the nature whereof is, that before any judgment of death can be given against the offenders, either they must plainly confess their offences, (which they will never do without torture or pains,) or else their offences be so plainly and directly proved by witness indifferent, such as saw their offences committed, &c. for reformation whereof, be it enacted, That all *treasons, felonies, robberies, murders* and *confederacies* hereafter to be committed *in or upon the sea*, or in any other *haven, river, creek*, or *place*, where the Admiral or Admirals have or pretend to have the jurisdiction, authority, or power, shall be *inquired, tried, heard, determined*, and *judged*, in such shires and places in the realm as shall be limited by the King's commission, &c., as if the offence had been done upon the land, &c. after the common course of the laws of this realm."

"Sect. 2. To inquire by the oaths of twelve good and lawful men, &c. in the shire limited in the commission."

11 & 12 William III. c. 7. AN ACT for the more effectual suppression of piracy.

"All piracies, felonies, and robberies, committed in or upon the sea, or in any haven, river, creek, or place, where the Admiral or Admirals have power, authority, or jurisdiction, may be examined, inquired of, tried, heard, determined, and adjudged, in any place at sea, or upon the land, in any of his Majesty's Islands, Plantations, Colonies, dominions, forts, or factories, to be appointed for that purpose by the King's commission, &c. under the great seal of England, or the seal of the Admiralty of England, directed to all or any of the Admirals, Vice-Admirals, Rear-Admirals, Judges of Vice-Admiralties, or commanders of any of his Majesty's ships of war, and also to all or any such person or persons as his majesty shall please to appoint, &c. which said commissioners shall have full power, jointly or severally, by warrant under the hand and seal of them, or any one of them, to commit to safe custody any person, &c. against whom information of piracy, robbery, or felony, upon the sea, shall be given upon oath, &c. and to call and assemble a Court of Admiralty, on shipboard, or upon the land, &c. and such persons so assembled shall have full authority, *according to the course of the admiralty*, to issue warrants for bringing any persons accused of piracy or robbery, before them to be tried, &c. to summon and examine witnesses, &c. and to do all things necessary for the hearing and final determination of any case of piracy, robbery, and felony; and to give sentence and judgment of death, and to award execution, *according to the civil law* and the *methods and rules of the admiralty*."

This statute is the foundation of the special commission, and of the present proceedings, and upon it a question has been made by Mr. Otis, whether the prisoners have not a right to a jury? He says that Magna Charta, in a case of life at least, must be expressly repealed, not by implication or construction only; and that in England a jury is summoned every day for the trial of such offences committed at sea. But I think that the statute of 28 Henry VIII. before cited, explains this difficulty; and this case seems to be but one instance among many others of the partial distinctions made between British subjects at home and abroad. The *civil law*, the *course of the admiralty*, and the *methods and rules of the admiralty*, will be construed, to take away the benefit of a jury.

[[1] Mr. Otis, from his first retainer in the cause, has been very sanguine to move for a jury. He has mentioned his resolution in all companies, and last week, at Plymouth, he mentioned it to the Lieutenant-Governor, and the rest of the judges. Mr. Fitch, happening to hear of our design to move for a jury, went to rummaging up Acts of Parliament, to satisfy himself, and found the 4 of George, c. 11: An act for the further preventing of robbery, &c. and for declaring the law upon some points relating to pirates. In the seventh section of this statute, "It is hereby *declared*, that all and every person and persons, who have committed or shall commit any offence or offences, for which they ought to be adjudged, deemed, and taken to be *pirates*, *felons*, or *robbers*, by an act made in the Parliament holden in the 11 & 12 years of William III. intituled 'An Act for the more effectual suppression of piracy,' may be tried and judged for every such offence, *in such manner and form* as in and by an act 28 Henry VIII. is directed and appointed for the trial of pirates." This statute, Fitch discovered to Sewall, and Sewall showed it to the Governor and Lieutenant-Governor and the rest of the court, the first morning of the court's sitting, in the council chamber. They were all struck and surprized, and the Lieutenant-Governor observed that this statute cleared up what had always to him appeared a mystery. In the State trials, vol. 6, 156, the trial of *Stede Bonnet*, before Judge Trott, at Carolina, 1718, 5 George I., it being the next year after the statute, Bonnet had a grand and petit jury.

In the council chamber, the court, however, agreed that they would go into the Court House, and take the oaths, &c. and then the court would publicly propose a jury. This was done, and the Statutes 28 Henry VIII. 11 & 12 William III. and 4 George I. were read, and then the commission, &c.; and then the Governor proposed to adjourn the court to Thursday, and to hear counsel this afternoon, in the council chamber, upon the subject of a jury.

In the afternoon we accordingly attended, and a difficulty was started by the Lieutenant-Governor about the venires, whether they should be directed to the sheriff, to summon a jury, as in England, or whether the venires should issue in any manner analogous to the laws of this Province relative to this subject? In

[1] This portion of narrative, marked in brackets seems to have been afterwards appended, by way of note to the proceedings in the case.

the afternoon we had the argument, and the whole court seemed convinced that a jury must be had. The Governor, indeed, talked that they might be sent to England for trial, &c.

But the next morning, when Mr. Otis was to have prepared and produced a *venire facias* to the sheriff to return a jury, we found *all aback*. The whole court, advocate-general Mr. Sewall, and Mr. Fitch, all of opinion that we had been all wrong, and that a jury could not be had. The Lieutenant-Governor had, in the course of his lucubrations, discovered this great secret, that, by law, two ways of trial are pointed out and provided, one by 28 Henry VIII., the other by 11 & 12 of William III., and that his Majesty may grant a commission in pursuance of either. That this commission was expressly limited to 11 & 12 William III., and therefore could not proceed according to 28 Henry VIII.]

But the first question that is to be made, according to my opinion, is, whether impresses in any cases are legal? For if impresses are always illegal, and Lieutenant Panton acted as an impress officer, Michael Corbet and his associates had a right to resist him, and, if they could not otherwise preserve their liberty, to take away his life. His blood must lie at his own door, and they be held guiltless. Nay, I think that impresses may be allowed to be legal, and yet Corbet might have a right to resist. To be more particular, when I say impresses may be legal, I mean that the Lieutenant or other officer who impresses, may not be liable to any action of false imprisonment, at the suit of the party, or to any indictment, at the suit of the Crown, for an assault or riot; the custom may be admitted to extend so far, and yet it will not follow that the seaman has not a right to resist, and keep himself out of the officer's power, if he can. And whatever may be said of the antiquity of the custom, &c. it is very remarkable that no statute has ever been made to establish or even to approve it, and no single judgment of any court of law can be found in favor of it. It is found in the commissions of the admiralty, and in warrants from the admiralty, but nowhere else. However the general question concerning the legality of impresses may be determined, I humbly conceive it clear that in America they are illegal, and that by a particular statute. I mean 6 Anne, c. 37, s. 9. "No mariner or other person, who shall serve on board, or be retained to serve on board any privateer or *trading ship* or *vessel*, that shall be employed in *any part of America*, nor any mariner or other person being on shore in any part thereof, shall be *liable* to be *impressed or taken away*, or shall be impressed or taken away, by any *officer* or *officers*, of or belonging to any of *her* Majesty's ships of war, empowered by the Lord-High-Admiral, or any other person whatsoever, unless such mariner shall have deserted, &c. upon pain that any *officer* or *officers* so impressing or taking away, or causing to be impressed or taken away, any mariner or other person, contrary to the tenor and true meaning of this act, shall forfeit, to the master or owner or owners, of any such ship or vessel, twenty pounds for every man he or they shall so impress or take, to be recovered, with full costs of suit, in any court within any part of her Majesty's dominions."

This statute is clear and decisive, and if it is now in force, it places the illegality of all impresses in America beyond controversy. *No mariner, on board any trading vessel, in any part of America, shall be liable to be impressed, or shall be impressed, by any officer, empowered by the Lord-Admiral or any other person.* If, therefore, this statute is now in force, all that Lieutenant Panton did on board the vessel was tortious and illegal; he was a trespasser from the beginning; a trespasser in coming on board, and in every act that he did, until he received the mortal, fatal wound. He was a trespasser in going down below, but especially in firing a pistol among the men in the fore peak. It is said that the Lieutenant with his own hand discharged this pistol directly at Michael Corbet, but the ball missed him, and wounded the man, who was next him, in the arm. This, therefore, was a direct commencement of hostilities; it was an open act of piracy, and Corbet and his associates had a right, and it was their duty, to defend themselves. It was a direct attempt upon their lives, and surely these unhappy persons had a right to defend their lives. No custom-house officer, no impress-officer, has a right to attempt life. But it seems that a second pistol was discharged, and wounded Corbet in his cheek, with powder, before the fatal blow was struck. What could Corbet expect? Should he stand still and be shot, or should he have surrendered to a pirate? Should he have surrendered to the impress?

But it has been made a question, whether this statute of 6 Anne is now in force? It has been reported, as the opinion of Sir Dudley Rider and Sir John Strange, that this statute expired with the war of Queen Anne. These are venerable names; but their opinions are opinions only of private men, and there has been no judicial decision to this purpose in any court of law, and I trust never will be. Their opinions were expressed so very concisely, that there is great room to question whether they were given upon the whole act, or only on some particular clause in it. Supposing these opinions to extend to the whole act, I have taken pains to discover what reasons can be produced in support of them, and I confess I can think of none. There is not the least color for such an opinion. On the contrary, there is every argument for supposing the act perpetual.

1. It is a good rule to consider the title of an act, in order to ascertain its construction and operation in all respects. The title of this is, "An act for the encouragement of the trade to America." Encouragement of the trade to America, is the professed object, end, and design of this law. Is this trade only valuable in time of war? If the trade to America existed and was carried on only in time of war, the act made for the encouragement of it must expire when the trade expired, at the end of the war. But the trade did not expire with the war, but continued after it, and therefore the encouragement given it by this act continued and survived too. This is of equal importance in peace as in war, and there is stronger reason why it should be encouraged, by exempting seamen from impresses, in peace than in war, because there is not the same necessity for impressing seamen in peace as there is in war.

2. The preamble furnishes another argument to prove the act perpetual. "For *advancement* of the trade of her Majesty's kingdom of Great Britain, to and in the several parts of America." This is one end of this law. Is not this end as beneficial and important in peace as in war? Has there been a year, a day, an hour, since 1707, when this act was made, when the trade of Great Britain to and in the several parts of America was of less consequence to the nation than it was at that time? Surely the advancement of the British American trade is a perpetual object. It is no temporary object or expedient; it has lasted these sixty years, and I hope will last a thousand longer.

3. For the increase of shipping and of seamen, for the purposes mentioned

before in the preamble, is another end of this law. Now shipping and seamen are useful and necessary to a commercial nation, in times of peace as well as war.

4. Some clauses in this statute are in their nature temporary, and limited to the duration of the war. Sections 2, 3, 4, 5, 6, 7, 8, &c.; others are expressly limited to the continuance of war, as s. 14, "during the continuance of the present war," and s. 19, "during the continuance thereof," and s. 21. But s. 9 and s. 20 are not, by the nature of them, limited to war; they are not expressly and in terms limited to years or to war.

5. If it be not now in force, why is it bound up in the statute book, and why was not the whole act limited to years or to war?

If it be once established as a fact that Lieutenant Panton acted in the character of an impress-officer, not in that of an officer of the customs; and if it be also established as law, that no officer has a legal right to impress a seaman, our next inquiry must be, what the rules of the civil law are relative to homicide in cases of self-defence. Self-preservation is the first law of nature. Self-love is the strongest principle in our breasts, and self-preservation not only our inalienable right, but our clearest duty, by the law of nature. This right and duty are both confirmed by the municipal laws of every civilized society.

2 Domat, 638, s. 6. "He who is attacked by *robbers*, or by *other persons*, that are *armed in such a manner* as to put him in *danger of his life*, in case he does not defend himself, may kill the robber or the aggressor, without any fear of being punished as a murderer."

Wood's Inst. civil law, 270. "Necessary homicide is when one, for the defence of his own life, kills the aggressor. This may be done without expecting the first blow, for that may make him incapable to defend himself at all. But this ought not to exceed the bounds of self-defence. The manner of self-defence directs that you should not kill, if you can by any means escape, &c."

Cod. lib. 9, tit. 16. "2. *De eo, qui salutem suam defendit.* Is qui aggressorem vel quemcunque alium in dubio vitæ discrimine constitutus occiderit, nullam ob id factum calumniam metuere debet. 3. Si quis percussorem ad se venientem, *gladio repulerit;* non ut homicida tenetur: quia defensor propriæ salutis in nullo peccasse videtur. 4. Si (ut allegas) latrocinantem peremisti: dubium non est, eum, qui inferendæ cædis voluntate præcesserat, jure cæsum videri."

"Liceat cuilibet aggressorem nocturnum in agris, vel obsidentem vias, atque insidiantem prætereuntibus, impunè occidere, etiam si miles sit: melius namque est his occurrere et mederi, quàm injuriâ receptâ vindictam perquirere."

Note 4C. "Homicida non est, qui aggressorem in vitæ discrimine constitutus interficit, nec primum ictum quis expectare debet, quia irreparabilis esse potest."

Gaill. page 509. Pœna homicidii corporalis nunquam habet locum, nisi in homicidio voluntario, quando homicidium, ex proposito, destinata voluntate, et quidem *dolo malo* commissum est. Debet enim verus et expressus intervenire dolus, etc.; et hoc usque adeo verum est, ut etiam lata culpa non æquiparetur dolo, etc. Dolus autem non præsumitur regulariter, etc.;—quapropter dolum allegans, eum probare debet, etc. Natura enim bona est a suis principiis, etc. Ex hac principali regulâ, quod videlicet pœna ordinaria in homicidio requirat dolum, multa singularia et quotidie usu venientia inferri possunt. Et primo, quod homicidium, cum moderamine inculpatæ tutelæ commissum, non sit punibile:

puta, si quis provocatus se cum moderamine inculpatæ tutelæ defendat, et aggressorem occidat; talis enim homicida non puniri, sed plene absolvi debet, idque triplici ratione confirmatur. Primo, quod defensio sit juris naturalis, ab omni jure permissa, etc. Deinde, quod aggressor, sive provocans, non ab alio, sed a se ipso occidi videatur et per consequens, quod provocatus non censeatur esse in dolo. Tertio, quia occidens ad sui defensionem, non committit maleficium, cum vim vi repellere liceat, et ubi non est delictum, ibi pœna abesse debet.

Et regulariter ex communi opinione, aggressus præsumitur omnia facere ad sui defensionem, non autem ad vindictam. Necessitas doli præsumptionem excludit, etc. etc. Ratio, quia *necessaria defensio* omni jure, etiam divino permissa, et sine peccato est. Defensio autem moderata, sive cum moderamine inculpatæ tutelæ dicitur, quando quis non potuit aliter se ab offensione tueri, etc.

Præsumitur autem in discrimine vitæ quis constitutus, eo ipso quod ab alio, armata manu, et gladio evaginato aggreditur, *terror ille armorum* aliquem in vitæ discrimen adducit, etc.

Sed quid si provocatus *modum inculpatæ tutelæ excedat, et aggressorem in fugâ occidat*, an pœnâ ordinariâ legis Corneliæ, etc., plectendus sit? Minime, sed extra ordinem, judicis arbitrio, ratione excessus puniri debet, etc. Ratio, quia, ut paulo ante dictum, in provocato non præsumitur dolus, et animus occidendi, aut vindictæ studium, sed potius defensionis necessitas. Nec etiam fugere tenetur, si fuga ei periculum vitæ adferret; provocatus enim tanquam intenso dolore commotus, non est in plenitudine intellectus: metus improvisus instantis periculi tollit rectum judicium et consilium deliberandi, et ideo dicunt DD. quod provocatus non habeat stateram in manu, ut possit dare ictus et vulnera ad mensuram, etc. Puniendus igitur provocatus pro isto excessu, non ut dolosus, quia provocatio præcedens a dolo excusat; sed ut culpabilis, etc.

Adeo autem defensio favorabilis est, ut etiam tertius, puta amicus provocati, si intercedendo aggressorem occidat, excusetur a pœnâ ordinariâ.

Page 515. Sexto infertur, quod homicidium calore iracundiæ perpetratum non puniatur pœnâ ordinariâ: quod est intelligendum de iracundiâ lacessitâ, quando quis ab alio verbis injuriosis ad iram provocatur; nam eo casu ira excusat a pœna ordinaria, etc. Quo pertinet, quod supra dictum est, hominem intenso dolore permotum, non esse in plenitudine intellectus, etc.

Maranta, page 49, pars 4, dist. 1, 77. Hoc patet; quia homicidium commissum per culpam, dicitur crimen extraordinarium, et punitur pœnâ arbitraria, etc. Ubi si maritus occidit uxorem deprehensam in adulterio, non punitur pœnâ mortis sed alia pœnâ corporali mitiori; et ratio est; quia tale homicidium dicitur culposum, et non dolosum; ex quo difficile fuit temperare justum dolorem: cum ergo ex prædictis appareat, quod homicidium culpa commissum puniatur pœnâ arbitraria et extraordinaria, sequitur de necessitate, quod non potest judex imponere pœnam mortis, quæ est pœna ordinaria, etc.

So much for the distinction between homicide with deliberation and without deliberation, according to the civil law, which is analogous to that of the common law, between murder and manslaughter. But the case of these prisoners does not require this distinction. I am not contending for the sentence of manslaughter against my clients; I think they are entitled to an honorable acquittal. They have committed no crime whatever, but they have behaved with all that prudence and moderation, and at the same time with that fortitude and firmness, that the law requires and approves.

Mr. Panton and his associates and attendants had no authority for what they did. They were trespassers and rioters. The evidence must be carefully recapitulated; their arms, swords, pistols, &c.; their threats and menaces. Panton's orders for more men, his orders to break down the bulkhead, their execution of these orders, their fetching the adze and the crow, but above all their discharge of a pistol right in the face of Corbet, which, though loaded only with powder, wounded him so badly in his lip — these circumstances are abundantly sufficient to show who was the first aggressor, and to show that the lives of the present prisoners were in danger. What could Corbet think, when a pistol had been presented at his mouth, and discharged, loaded, he knew not with what? It had wounded him, he knew not how badly. He saw a desperate gang of armed sailors before him, other pistols cocked and presented at him and his companions, their heads and breasts, drawn swords in the hands of some, continued threats to blow their brains out; could he expect any thing but death? In these circumstances, what could he do but defend himself as he did? In these circumstances, what was his duty? He had an undoubted right, not merely to make a push at Lieutenant Panton, but to have darted an harpoon, a dagger, through the heart of every man in the whole gang.

If Mr. Panton came as a custom-house officer, and it may be true that he came in part to search the ship for uncustomed goods, he had a fair opportunity to do it. He asked and was told that the hatchways were open; he ordered the lazaretto open, and it was done, and after this, instead of searching for uncustomed goods, he proceeds directly to search for seamen.

The killing of Lieutenant Panton was justifiable homicide; homicide *se defendendo*.

1 Hawkins, 71, s. 4, middle. "The killing of dangerous rioters by any private persons, who cannot otherwise suppress them or defend themselves from them, inasmuch as every private person seems to be authorized by the law to arm himself for the purposes aforesaid."

Same page, s. 21. A woman kills one who attempts to ravish her, may be justified. Page 72, s. 23. towards the end. "It seems that a private person, and *a fortiori*, an officer of justice, who happens unavoidably to kill another in endeavoring to defend himself from, or to suppress dangerous rioters, may justify the fact, inasmuch as he only does his duty in aid of the public justice." s. 24. "I can see no reason why a person, who, without provocation, is assaulted by another in any place whatever, in such a manner as plainly shows an intent to murder him, as by discharging a pistol, or pushing at him with a drawn sword, may not justify killing such an assailant." Page 75, s. 14. "Not only he who on an assault retreats to a wall or some such strait, beyond which he can go no further, before he kills the other, is judged by the law to act upon unavoidable necessity; but also he who being assaulted in such a manner and such a place, that he cannot go back without manifestly endangering his life, kills the other without retreating at all."

Kelyng, page 128, bottom. "It is not reasonable for any man that is dangerously assaulted, and when he perceives his life in danger from his adversary, but to have liberty for the security of his own life, to pursue him who maliciously assaulted him; for he that hath manifested that he hath malice against another, is not fit to be trusted with a dangerous weapon in his hand."

Kelyng, page 136, top. Buckner's case. Imprisoned injuriously, without process of law, &c. Page 136, bottom. "3. If a man perceives another by force to be injuriously treated, pressed, and restrained of his liberty, though the person abused doth not complain, &c. &c., others, out of compassion, shall come to his rescue, and kill any of those that shall so restrain him, that is manslaughter."

Kelyng, 59. Hopkin Hugget's case, who killed a man in attempting to rescue a seaman impressed without warrant.

2 Ld. Raym., Queen *vs.* Tooley, & als. The case of the reforming constables. Holt, 484, 485. Mawgridge's case.

Foster, 312, 316. Vid. Foster, 292. The smart, &c. for manslaughter. Also 296.

A question has been started by Sir Francis Barnard, whether, (as there is no distinction between murder and manslaughter, in the civil law,) the court can allow clergy, if they find the prisoners guilty of manslaughter; that is, whether the court can do any thing but pass sentence of death, and respite execution, and recommend them to mercy? He said he had formerly attended at the admiralty sessions in England, and had heard it said, by the court, that clergy was expressly taken away by these statutes from manslaughter, and the court could not grant it. But see a paragraph in Foster to the contrary, 288.

In this case I shall not make a question whether Corbet and others are guilty of murder or of manslaughter. I am clear they are guilty of neither. All that they did was justifiable self-defence, or to use the expressions of most writers upon Crown law, it was justifiable and necessary homicide, *se defendendo.* This will be fully shown by a particular examination of the law and of the evidence.

But it may not be amiss to consider the observation of Sir Francis, in order to remove the clouds from his brain. 1. It is total ignorance to say there is no distinction between murder and manslaughter in civil law, as appears abundantly already.[1] 2. I say that clergy is not expressly taken away by the statutes from manslaughter; by the 28 Henry VIII., all felonies are to be tried according to the common course of the laws of this land. What is the common course of the laws of the land, relative to manslaughter, which is a felony? It has its clergy. It is true the word manslaughter is once mentioned in the statutes of Henry VIII. c. 15, s. 2. "Every indictment found, &c. of treasons, felonies, robberies, murders, *manslaughters*, or such other offences, &c. that then such order, &c. judgment and execution shall be had, as against such offences upon land." What is the judgment versus manslaughter upon land? They have their clergy. s. 3. For treasons, robberies, felonies, murders and confederacies done at sea, the offenders shall not have clergy. Here manslaughter is dropped, so that clergy is not taken from manslaughter by this act.

By 11 & 12 William III. Piracies, felonies, and robberies, are mentioned, but manslaughter is not. The word is not in the whole statute. It was needful to mention it in that of Henry VIII., because the trial was to be by the law of the land, and it clearly has its clergy. But, by this statute, the trial and judgment and sentence were to be all by the civil law, where the offence that is called

[1] Sed vid. Ld. Raymond, 1496. And especially Barrington's Observations on the Statutes, p. 54, bottom, note. "By the law of Scotland, there is no such thing as manslaughter, nor by the civil law; and then a criminal indicted for murder, under the statute of Henry VIII., when the Judges proceed by the rules of the civil law, must either be found guilty of the murder or acquitted"

manslaughter by the common law is never punished with death. But it is observable that clergy is not taken away by this statute from any crime.

By 4 George, c. 11, s. 7. Any pirate, felon or robber, within the 11 & 12 William, may be tried in the manner and form of 28 Henry VIII., and shall be excluded clergy. We see that whenever the trial is to be by a jury and the common law, clergy is excluded from such crimes as were not entitled to it upon land; and the reason was, because it is a known rule of law, that when the legislature creates any new felony, it shall be entitled to clergy, if not expressly taken away. Doubts might arise, whether making crimes at sea felonies, was not creating new felonies, and so they would be entitled to clergy. To avoid this, the clause was inserted.

Lord Raymond, 1496. "From these cases it appears, that, though the law of England is so far peculiarly favorable (I use the word peculiarly, because I know no other law that makes such a distinction between murder and manslaughter) as to permit the excess of anger and passion, (which a man ought to keep under and govern,) in some instances to extenuate the greatest of private injuries, as the taking away a man's life is; yet, in those cases, it must be such a passion, as for the time deprived him of his reasoning faculties."

Foster, 288. If taking general verdicts of acquittal in plain cases of death *per infortunium*, &c. deserveth the name of a deviation, it is far short of what is constantly practised at an admiralty sessions, under 28 Henry VIII., with regard to offences not ousted of clergy by particular statutes, which, had they been committed at land, would have been entitled to clergy. In these cases the jury is constantly directed to acquit the prisoner; because the marine law doth not allow of clergy in any case. And therefore in an indictment for murder on the high seas, if the fact cometh out, upon evidence, to be no more than manslaughter, supposing it to have been committed at land, the prisoner is constantly acquitted."

Observations on the statutes 422, note (z.) "I have before observed that by the civil law, as well as the law of Scotland, there is no such offence as what is with us termed manslaughter. The Scots, therefore, might have apprehended, that if not convicted of murder they should have been acquitted."

C.

Page 377.

The following is the draught of the articles referred to in connection with the declaration of rights and grievances made by the Congress of 1774, one of the most important papers of the revolutionary history. In order to facilitate the comparison of the two, they are here placed in parallel columns. The verbal alterations are marked in italics.

Heads of Grievances and Rights.

DRAUGHT.	DECLARATION AS ADOPTED.
Whereas, since the accession of the present King, Parliament has claimed a power of right to bind the people of the Colonies in North America by statutes in all cases whatsoever; and for carrying the said power into execution, has, by some statutes, expressly taxed the people of the said Colonies, and by divers other statutes under various pretences, but in fact for the purpose of raising a revenue, has imposed "rates and duties," payable in the said Colonies, established a Board of Commissioners, and extended the jurisdiction of Courts of Admiralty therein, for the collection of such "rates and duties."	"Whereas, since the *close of the last war, the British* Parliament, claiming a power, of right, to bind the people of America by statutes in all cases whatsoever, hath in some acts expressly *imposed* taxes on them, and in others, under various pretences, but in fact for the purpose of raising a revenue, hath imposed rates and duties payable in these Colonies, established a Board of Commissioners, *with unconstitutional powers*, and extended the jurisdiction of Courts of Admiralty, not only for collecting the said duties, *but for the trial of causes merely arising within the body of a county.*"
And whereas some of the said statutes are also intended to render all Judges in the said Colonies dependent upon the Crown only.	And whereas *in consequence of other* statutes, judges, *who before held only estates at will in their offices*, have been made dependent on the Crown alone *for their salaries, and standing armies kept in times of peace.*
And whereas since the said accession, statutes have been made for quartering and supplying troops to be kept in the said Colonies.	
And whereas since the conclusion of the last war, orders have been issued by the King, that the authority of the commander-in-chief, and under him, of the Brigadier-General in the Northern and Southern departments, in all military affairs shall be supreme, and must	

DRAUGHT.

be obeyed by the troops as such, in all the civil governments in America.

And whereas a statute was made in the seventh year of this reign "for suspending the proceedings of the Assembly of New York, &c." and Assemblies in these Colonies have of late years been very frequently dissolved.

And whereas, during the present reign, dutiful and reasonable petitions to the Crown, from the representatives of the people in these Colonies, have been repeatedly treated with contempt.

And whereas, it has been lately resolved in Parliament, that, by force of a statute made in the thirty-fifth year of Henry VIII., Colonists may be carried to England, and tried there, on accusations for offences committed in those Colonies. And by a statute made in the twelfth year of this reign such trials are directed in the cases therein mentioned.

And whereas in the last session of Parliament three statutes were made and declared to have force within the Province of Massachusetts Bay, one of them "for discontinuing, &c. the landing, &c. goods, wares, and merchandises, at the town and within the harbor of Boston," &c.; another, "for the better regulating the government, &c.;" and the third, "for the impartial administration of justice," &c.*

And whereas, in the same session, another statute was made, "for making more effectual provision for the government of the Province of Quebec," &c.

DECLARATION AS ADOPTED.

And whereas it has lately been resolved in Parliament, that, by force of a statute made in the thirty-fifth year of the reign of King Henry VIII. colonists may be *transported* to England, and tried there upon accusations for *treasons and misprisions, or concealment of treasons*, committed in the Colonies, and by a late statute, such trials have been directed in cases therein mentioned.

And whereas in the last session of Parliament three statutes were made; one entitled "An act to discontinue, in such manner and for such time as are therein mentioned, the landing and discharging, lading or shipping of goods, wares, and merchandise, at the town, and within the harbor of Boston, in the Province of Massachusetts Bay in North America;" another entitled "An act for the better regulating the government of the Province of Massachusetts Bay in New England;" and another entitled "An act for the impartial administration of justice, in the cases of persons questioned for any act done by them in the execution of the law, or for the suppression of riots and tumults in the Province of the Massachusetts Bay in New England;" and

* Note in the margin. Q. Which of these two last Statutes was first in time?

DRAUGHT.

And whereas the good people of these Colonies, justly alarmed by the proceedings of Parliament and Administration, have duly appointed and directed delegates to meet and sit in General Congress at Philadelphia, in this month of September, 1774, in order to such establishment as that their religion, laws, and liberties, may not be subverted; upon which appointment and direction, the said delegates being now assembled in a full and free representative * of these Colonies, taking into their most serious consideration the best means for attaining the ends aforesaid, do, in the first place, (as their ancestors in like case have usually done,) for vindicating and asserting their rights and liberties, declare —

DECLARATION AS ADOPTED.

another statute was then made, "for making more effectual provision for the government of the Province of Quebec," &c. All which statutes are impolitic, unjust, and cruel, as well as unconstitutional, and most dangerous and destructive of American rights.

And whereas Assemblies have been frequently dissolved, *contrary to the rights of the people, when they attempted to deliberate on grievances; and their dutiful, humble, loyal, and reasonable petitions to the Crown, for redress, have been repeatedly treated with contempt by his Majesty's Ministers of State.*

The good people of the several Colonies of New Hampshire, Massachusetts Bay, Rhode Island and Providence Plantations, Connecticut, New York, New Jersey, Pennsylvania, Newcastle Kent and Sussex on Delaware, Maryland, Virginia, North Carolina, and South Carolina, justly alarmed at these *arbitrary* proceedings of Parliament and Administration, have *severally elected, constituted*, and appointed *deputies*, to meet and sit in General Congress, in the city of Philadelphia, in order to *obtain* such establishment, as that their religion, laws, and liberties, may not be subverted. Whereupon the deputies so appointed, being now assembled, in a full and free representation of these Colonies, taking into their most serious consideration the best means of attaining the ends aforesaid, do in the first place, as *Englishmen*, their ancestors, in like cases have usually done, for asserting and vindicating their rights and liberties, DECLARE, —

That the inhabitants of the English Colonies in North America, by the immutable laws of nature, the principles of the English Constitution, and the several charters or compacts, have the following RIGHTS: —

* Note in the margin. Q. If the Colonies should not be named?

DRAUGHT.

1. That the power of making laws for ordering or regulating the internal polity of these Colonies, is, within the limits of each Colony, respectively and exclusively vested in the Provincial Legislature of such Colony; and that all statutes for ordering or regulating the internal polity of the said Colonies, or any of them, in any manner or in any case whatsoever, are illegal and void.

2. That all statutes, for taxing the people of the said Colonies, are illegal and void.

3. That all the statutes before mentioned, for the purpose of raising a revenue, by imposing "rates and duties" payable in these Colonies, establishing a Board of Commissioners, and extending the jurisdiction of Courts of Admiralty, for the collection of such "rates and duties," are illegal and void.

4. That Judges, within these Colonies, ought not to be dependent on the Crown only; and that their commissions ought to be during good behavior.

DECLARATION AS ADOPTED.

Resolved, N. C. D. 1. That they are entitled to life, liberty, and property, and they have never ceded to any sovereign power whatever a right to dispose of either, without their consent.

2. That our ancestors, who first settled these Colonies, were, at the time of their emigration from the mother country, entitled to all the rights, liberties, and immunities of free and natural born subjects, within the realm of England.

3. That by such emigration they by no means forfeited, surrendered, or lost any of those rights, but that they were, and their descendants now are, entitled to the exercise and enjoyment of all such of them, as their local and other circumstances enable them to exercise and enjoy.

4. That the foundation of English liberty, and of all free government, is a right in the people to participate in their legislative council; and as the English colonists are not represented, and from their local and other circumstances cannot be properly represented in the British Parliament, they are entitled to a free and exclusive power of legislation in their several Provincial Legislatures, where their right of representation can alone be preserved, in all cases of taxation and internal polity, subject only to the negative of their sovereign, in such manner as has been heretofore used and accustomed. But, from the necessity of the case, and a regard to the mutual interest of both countries, we cheerfully consent to the operation of such acts of the British

DRAUGHT.

5. That the raising or keeping a standing army within these Colonies in time of peace, unless it be with the consent of the Provincial Legislatures, is illegal, pernicious, and dangerous; and that every statute for quartering or supplying troops within the said Colonies is illegal and void.

6. That the orders aforesaid for rendering the authority of the Commander-in-chief, and under him, of the Brigadiers-General, supreme, are illegal and void.

7. That for redress of all grievances, and for the amending, strengthening, and preserving of the laws, Assemblies ought to be held in each of these Colonies frequently, and at least once in every year; that such Assemblies ought not to be prorogued or dissolved, before they have had sufficient time to deliberate, determine, and bring to conclusion their counsels on public affairs; that any statute for suspending the proceedings of any such Assembly, is illegal and void; and that every dissolution of an Assembly within these Colonies, during the present reign, on pretence of misbehavior in the representatives of the people, has been arbitrary and oppressive.

8. That it is the right of the subjects to petition the King; and that a contemptuous treatment of such petitions has a most pernicious tendency.

DECLARATION AS ADOPTED.

Parliament as are, *bonâ fide*, restrained to the regulation of our external commerce, for the purpose of securing the commercial advantages of the whole empire to the mother country, and the commercial benefits of its respective members; excluding every idea of taxation, internal or external, for raising a revenue on the subjects in America, without their consent.

5. That the respective Colonies are entitled to the common law of England, and more especially to the great and inestimable privilege of being tried by their peers of the vicinage, according to the course of that law.

6. That they are entitled to the benefit of such of the English statutes as existed at the time of their colonization, and which they have, by experience, respectively found to be applicable to their several local and other circumstances.

7. That these, his Majesty's Colonies, are likewise entitled to all the immunities and privileges granted and confirmed to them by royal charters, or secured by their several codes of provincial laws.

8. That they have a right peaceably to assemble, consider of their grievances, and petition the King; and that all prosecutions, prohibitory proclama

DRAUGHT.

9. That the resolution in Parliament on the statute made in the thirty-fifth year of Henry VIII., was arbitrary and erroneous; and that any statute directing the trials of Colonists to be had in England or elsewhere, on accusation for offences committed in the Colonies, is illegal and void.

10. That the three statutes made in the last session of Parliament, and declared to have force within the Province of Massachusetts Bay, are oppressive to the people of that Province, dangerous to the liberties of these Colonies, illegal and void.

11. That the statute made in the same session, "for making more effectual provision for the government of the Province of Quebec," &c. is not only unjust to the people in that Province, but dangerous to the interests of the Protestant religion and of these Colonies, and ought to be repealed.

12. And they do claim, demand, and insist, on all and singular the rights and liberties before mentioned as indubitably belonging to them; and no declarations, judgments, doings, proceedings, or statutes, to the prejudice of the people in any of the premises, ought in any wise to be drawn hereafter into consequence or example; and these, their undoubted rights and liberties, with the blessing of Divine Providence, which they humbly and ardently implore in favor of their just exertions to preserve the freedom of rendering to their Creator the worship they judge most acceptable to him,

DECLARATION AS ADOPTED.

tions, and commitments for the same, are illegal.

9. That the keeping a standing army in these Colonies, in times of peace, without the consent of the Legislature of that Colony in which such army is kept, is against law.

10. It is indispensably necessary to good government, and rendered essential by the English Constitution, that the constituent branches of the Legislature be independent of each other; that therefore the exercise of legislative power in several Colonies, by a Council appointed during pleasure by the Crown, is unconstitutional, dangerous, and destructive to the freedom of American legislation.

All and each of which the aforesaid deputies, in behalf of themselves and their constituents, do claim, demand, and insist on, as their indubitable rights and liberties; which cannot be legally taken from them, altered or abridged, by any power whatever, without their own consent, by their representatives in their several Provincial Legislatures.

In the course of our inquiry, we find many infringements and violations of the foregoing rights, which, from an ardent desire that harmony and mutual intercourse of affection and interest may be restored, we pass over for the present, and proceed to state such acts and measures as have been adopted since the last war, which demonstrate a system formed to enslave America.

Resolved, N. C. D. That the following Acts of Parliament are infringements and violations of the rights of the Colonists; and that the repeal of them is essentially necessary, in order to restore harmony between Great

DRAUGHT.

and of promoting the happiness of his creatures, they are resolved, to the utmost of their power, to maintain and defend.

DECLARATION AS ADOPTED.

Britain and the American Colonies, namely, —

The several acts of 4 George III. c. 15 and c. 34; 5 George III. c. 25; 6 George III. c. 52; 7 George III. c. 41 and c. 46; 8 George III. c. 22, which impose duties for the purpose of raising a revenue in America, extend the power of the Admiralty courts beyond their ancient limits, deprive the American subject of trial by jury, authorize the Judge's certificate to indemnify the prosecutor from damages that he might otherwise be liable to, requiring oppressive security from a claimant of ships and goods seized, before he shall be allowed to defend his property, and are subversive of American rights.

Also 12 George III. c. 24, intituled "An act for the better securing His Majesty's dock-yards, magazines, ships, ammunition and stores," which declares a new offence in America, and deprives the American subject of a constitutional trial by jury of the vicinage, by authorizing the trial of any person charged with the committing any offence described in the said act, out of the realm, to be indicted and tried for the same in any shire or county within the realm.

Also the three acts passed in the last session of Parliament, for stopping the port and blocking up the harbor of Boston, for altering the charter and government of Massachusetts Bay, and that which is intituled "An act for the better administration of justice," &c.

Also the act passed in the same session, for establishing the Roman Catholic religion in the Province of Quebec, abolishing the equitable system of English laws, and erecting a tyranny there, to the great danger, (from so total a dissimilarity of religion, law, and government) of the neighboring British Colonies, by the assistance of whose

DECLARATION AS ADOPTED.

blood and treasure the said country was conquered from France.

Also the act passed in the same session for the better providing suitable quarters for officers and soldiers in his Majesty's service in North America.

Also, that the keeping a standing army in several of these Colonies, in time of peace, without the consent of the Legislature of that Colony in which such army is kept, is against law.

To these grievous acts and measures Americans cannot submit; but in hopes their fellow subjects in Great Britain will, on a revision of them, restore us to that state in which both countries found happiness and prosperity, we have, for the present, only resolved to pursue the following peaceable measures.

1. To enter into a non-importation, non-consumption, and non-exportation agreement or association.

2. To prepare an address to the people of Great Britain, and a memorial to the inhabitants of British America; and

3. To prepare a loyal address to his Majesty, agreeable to resolutions already entered into.

END OF VOLUME II.